THE CAMBRIDG

BERTRANᴜ ᴋUSSELL

Each volume in this series of companions to major philosophers contains specially commissioned essays by an international team of scholars, together with a substantial bibliography, and will serve as a reference work for students and non-specialists. One aim of the series is to dispel the intimidation such readers often feel when faced with the work of a difficult and challenging thinker.

Bertrand Russell ranks as one of the giants of twentieth-century philosophy. Through his books, journalism, correspondence, and political activity he exerted a profound influence on modern thought. This companion centers on Russell's contributions to modern philosophy and, therefore, concentrates on the early part of his career. There are chapters on Russell's contributions to the foundations of mathematics and on his development of new logical methods in philosophy and their application to such fields as epistemology, metaphysics, and the philosophy of language. The intellectual background to his work is covered, as is his engagement with such contemporaries as Frege and G. E. Moore. The final chapter considers Russell as a moral philosopher.

New readers will find this the most convenient and accessible guide to Russell available. Advanced students and specialists will find a conspectus of recent developments in the interpretation of Russell.

Nicholas Griffin is Canada Research Chair in Philosophy and Director of the Bertrand Russell Research Centre, McMaster University.

OTHER VOLUMES IN THE SERIES OF CAMBRIDGE COMPANIONS:

AQUINAS *Edited by* NORMAN KRETZMANN *and* ELEONORE STUMP
HANNAH ARENDT *Edited by* DANA VILLA
ARISTOTLE *Edited by* JONATHAN BARNES
AUGUSTINE *Edited by* ELEONORE STUMP *and* NORMAN KRETZMANN
BACON *Edited by* MARKKU PELTONEN
DESCARTES *Edited by* JOHN COTTINGHAM
DUNS SCOTUS *Edited by* THOMAS WILLIAMS
EARLY GREEK PHILOSOPHY *Edited by* A. A. LONG
FEMINISM IN PHILOSOPHY *Edited by* MIRANDA FRICKER *and* JENNIFER HORNSBY
FOUCAULT *Edited by* GARY GUTTING
FREUD *Edited by* JEROME NEU
GADAMER *Edited by* ROBERT DOSTAL
GALILEO *Edited by* PETER MACHAMER
GERMAN IDEALISM *Edited by* KARL AMERIKS
HABERMAS *Edited by* STEPHEN K. WHITE
HEGEL *Edited by* FREDERICK BEISER
HEIDEGGER *Edited by* CHARLES GUIGNON
HOBBES *Edited by* TOM SORELL
HUME *Edited by* DAVID FATE NORTON
HUSSERL *Edited by* BARRY SMITH *and* DAVID WOODRUFF SMITH
WILLIAM JAMES *Edited by* RUTH ANNA PUTNAM
KANT *Edited by* PAUL GUYER
KIERKEGAARD *Edited by* ALASTAIR HANNAY *and* GORDON MARINO
LEIBNIZ *Edited by* NICHOLAS JOLLEY
LOCKE *Edited by* VERE CHAPPELL
MALEBRANCHE *Edited by* STEPHEN NADLER
MARX *Edited by* TERRELL CARVER
MILL *Edited by* JOHN SKORUPSKI
NEWTON *Edited by* I. BERNARD COHEN *and* GEORGE E. SMITH
NIETZSCHE *Edited by* BERND MAGNUS *and* KATHLEEN HIGGINS
OCKHAM *Edited by* PAUL VINCENT SPADE
PLATO *Edited by* RICHARD KRAUT
PLOTINUS *Edited by* LLOYD P. GERSON
RAWLS *Edited by* SAMUEL FREEMAN
ROUSSEAU *Edited by* PATRICK RILEY
SARTRE *Edited by* CHRISTINA HOWELLS
SCHOPENHAUER *Edited by* CHRISTOPHER JANAWAY
SPINOZA *Edited by* DON GARRETT
THE STOICS *Edited by* BRAD INWOOD
WITTGENSTEIN *Edited by* HANS SLUGA *and* DAVID STERN

The Cambridge Companion to
BERTRAND RUSSELL

Edited by

Nicholas Griffin
McMaster University

CAMBRIDGE
UNIVERSITY PRESS

PUBLISHED BY THE PRESS SYNDICATE OF THE UNIVERSITY OF CAMBRIDGE
The Pitt Building, Trumpington Street, Cambridge, United Kingdom

CAMBRIDGE UNIVERSITY PRESS
The Edinburgh Building, Cambridge CB2 2RU, UK
40 West 20th Street, New York, NY 10011-4211, USA
477 Williamstown Road, Port Melbourne, VIC 3207, Australia
Ruiz de Alarcón 13, 28014 Madrid, Spain
Dock House, The Waterfront, Cape Town 8001, South Africa

http://www.cambridge.org

© Cambridge University Press 2003

This book is in copyright. Subject to statutory exception
and to the provisions of relevant collective licensing agreements,
no reproduction of any part may take place without
the written permission of Cambridge University Press.

First published 2003

Printed in the United States of America

Typeface Trump Medieval 10/13 pt.   *System* LaTeX 2$_\varepsilon$ [TB]

A catalog record for this book is available from the British Library.

Library of Congress Cataloging in Publication Data
The Cambridge companion to Bertrand Russell / edited by Nicholas Griffin.
     p.   cm. – (Cambridge companions to philosophy)
     Includes bibliographical references and index.
     ISBN 0-521-63178-5 (hbk) – ISBN 0-521-63634-5 (pbk.)
     1. Russell, Bertrand, 1872–1970. I. Griffin, Nicholas. II. Series.
     B1649 .R94 C36   2003
     192 – dc21   2002031367

ISBN 0 521 63178 5 hardback
ISBN 0 521 63634 5 paperback

CONTENTS

Acknowledgments   *page* ix

List of Abbreviations Used in Citations   xi

List of Contributors   xv

Introduction   1
NICHOLAS GRIFFIN

1   Mathematics in and behind Russell's Logicism,
    and Its Reception   51
    I. GRATTAN-GUINNESS

2   Russell's Philosophical Background   84
    NICHOLAS GRIFFIN

3   Russell and Moore, 1898–1905   108
    RICHARD L. CARTWRIGHT

4   Russell and Frege   128
    MICHAEL BEANEY

5   Bertrand Russell's Logicism   171
    MARTIN GODWYN AND ANDREW D. IRVINE

6   The Theory of Descriptions   202
    PETER HYLTON

7   Russell's Substitutional Theory   241
    GREGORY LANDINI

8   The Theory of Types   286
    ALASDAIR URQUHART

vii

9   Russell's Method of Analysis   310
    PAUL HAGER

10 Russell's Neutral Monism   332
    R.E. TULLY

11 The Metaphysics of Logical Atomism   371
    BERNARD LINSKY

12 Russell's Structuralism and the Absolute
    Description of the World   392
    WILLIAM DEMOPOULOS

13 From Knowledge by Acquaintance to
    Knowledge by Causation   420
    THOMAS BALDWIN

14 Russell, Experience, and the Roots of Science   449
    A.C. GRAYLING

15 Bertrand Russell: Moral Philosopher or
    Unphilosophical Moralist?   475
    CHARLES R. PIGDEN

    Selective Bibliography   507
    Index   541

ACKNOWLEDGMENTS

I am very grateful to my contributors and their patience in what proved to be a much more time-consuming exercise than any of us anticipated. I benefited from discussing many of the papers in the volume with David Godden. For help with the references and bibliography I am grateful to Alison Roberts Miculan, Elizabeth Skakoon, Michael Potter, and Sarah Shulist. Financial support for my research was provided by the Social Sciences and Humanities Research Council of Canada.

LIST OF ABBREVIATIONS USED
IN CITATIONS

In this book, like many others on Russell, abbreviations have been used to identify his most frequently cited works. The list below identifies not only the work but also the edition cited in this volume (in the case of books, generally the first British edition). In the case of *The Problems of Philosophy*, however, there are a number of printings with different paginations, and references here are given to both the first British edition and to a widely available reprint, the pagination of which is shared by a number of other reprints. *Principia Mathematica* poses different problems: a new introduction and several new appendices, representing a different philosophical point of view, were added for the second edition of 1925–7. These major changes did not affect the pagination of the original. Nonetheless, pagination was altered as a result of the first two volumes being reset. The first edition is extremely rare and the second is, in any case, preferable since the resetting allowed misprints to be corrected. Accordingly, whenever *Principia* is cited, the reference is to the second edition; but when material is referred to which is only to be found in the second edition, the citation is to '*PM2*' rather than to '*PM*'.

The use of acronyms is much more selective in the case of Russell's articles. Wherever possible, the definitive version of the text as established in *The Collected Papers of Bertrand Russell* is cited. Some contributors to the volume cited other widely used editions. In such cases, the original citations have been kept and citations to the *Collected Papers* added. The volumes of the *Collected Papers* cited in this book are as follows:

Papers 1: *Cambridge Essays: 1888–99.* Edited by Kenneth Blackwell, Andrew Brink, Nicholas Griffin, Richard A. Rempel, and John G. Slater. London: Allen and Unwin, 1983.

Papers 2: *Philosophical Papers: 1896–99.* Edited by Nicholas Griffin and Albert C. Lewis. London: Unwin Hyman, 1990.

Papers 3: *Towards the 'Principles of Mathematics', 1900–2.* Edited by Gregory H. Moore. London: Routledge, 1993.

Papers 4: *Foundations of Logic, 1903–5.* Edited by Alasdair Urquhart. London: Routledge, 1994.

Papers 6: *Logical and Philosophical Papers, 1909–13.* Edited by John G. Slater. London: Routledge, 1992.

Papers 7: *Theory of Knowledge: The 1913 Manuscript.* Edited by Elizabeth Ramsden Eames and Kenneth Blackwell. London: Allen and Unwin, 1984.

Papers 8: *The Philosophy of Logical Atomism and Other Essays: 1914–19.* Edited by John G. Slater. London: Allen and Unwin, 1986.

Papers 9: *Essays on Language, Mind, and Matter: 1919–26.* Edited by John G. Slater. London: Unwin Hyman, 1988.

Papers 10: *A Fresh Look at Empiricism: 1927–42.* Edited by John G. Slater. London: Routledge, 1996.

Papers 11: *Last Philosophical Testament: 1943–68.* Edited by John G. Slater. London: Routledge, 1997.

Papers 28: *Man's Peril 1954–5.* Edited by Andrew G. Bone. London: Routledge, 2003.

Other works by Russell are cited as follows:

Auto   *The Autobiography of Bertrand Russell* 3 vols. (London: Allen and Unwin, 1967–9).

AMa   *The Analysis of Matter* (London: Kegan Paul, 1927).

AMi   *The Analysis of Mind* (London: Allen and Unwin, 1921).

AMR   'An Analysis of Mathematical Reasoning' (1898), in *Papers* 2, pp. 154–242.

EA   *Essays in Analysis.* Edited by Douglas Lackey (London: Allen and Unwin, 1974).

EFG   *An Essay on the Foundations of Geometry* (Cambridge: Cambridge University Press, 1897; New York: Dover, 1956).

HK   *Human Knowledge: Its Scope and Limits* (London: Allen and Unwin, 1984).

HWP   *History of Western Philosophy* (London: Allen and Unwin, 1946).

HSEP   *Human Society in Ethics and Politics* (London: Allen and Unwin, 1954).

IMP   *Introduction to Mathematical Philosophy* (London: Allen and Unwin, 1919).

IMT   *Inquiry into Meaning and Truth* (London: Allen and Unwin, 1940).

KAKD   'Knowledge by Acquaintance and Knowledge by Description' (1911), in *Papers* 6, pp. 147–61.

LA   'Logical Atomism' (1924), in *Papers* 9, pp. 160–79; and *LK*, pp. 323–43.

LK   *Logic and Knowledge.* Edited by R.C. Marsh (London: Allen and Unwin, 1956).

ML   *Mysticism and Logic and Other Essays* (London: Longmans Green, 1918).

MLT   'Mathematical Logic as based on the Theory of Types', *American Journal of Mathematics*, 30 (1908), pp. 222–62; reprinted in *LK*, pp. 59–102.

MPD   *My Philosophical Development* (London: Allen and Unwin, 1959).

MTCA   'Meinong's Theory of Complexes and Assumptions' (1904), in *Papers* 4, pp. 431–74; and *EA*, pp. 21–76.

OD   'On Denoting' (1905), in *Papers* 4, pp. 414–27; *LK*, pp. 41–56; *EA*, pp. 103–19.

OI   'On "Insolubilia" and their Solution by Symbolic Logic' in *EA*, pp. 190–214. (Originally published under the title 'Les Paradoxes de Logique' in the *Revue de métaphysique et de morale* 14 (1906), pp. 627–50.)

OKEW   *Our Knowledge of the External World* (London: Allen and Unwin, 1926; first edition, 1914).

OOP   *Outline of Philosophy* (London: Allen and Unwin, 1927).

OP   'On Propositions: What They Are and How They Mean' (1919), in *Papers* 8, pp. 276–306; *LK*, pp. 285–320.

PLA   'The Philosophy of Logical Atomism' (1918), in *Papers* 8, pp. 157–244; *LK*, pp. 177–281.

PM   *Principia Mathematica* (with A.N. Whitehead), 3 vols. (Cambridge: Cambridge University Press, 1925–7; first edition, 1910–13).

PM2   'Introduction to Second Edition' in *PM* vol. 1, pp. i–xlvi and Appendices A, B, C, in *PM* vol. 1, pp. 635–66.

POM   *The Principles of Mathematics* (London: Allen and Unwin, 1964; first edition, 1903).

POP   *The Problems of Philosophy* (London: Williams and Norgate, 1912).

POP2   *The Problems of Philosophy* (Oxford: Oxford University Press, 1959).

PSR   *Principles of Social Reconstruction* (London: Allen and Unwin, 1916).

RMDP   'The Regressive Method of Discovering the Premisses of Mathematics,' in *EA*, pp. 272–83.

ROE   *Russell on Ethics*. Edited by C. Pigden (London: Routledge, 1999).

RS   *Religion and Science* (London: Thornton Butterworth, 1935).

RSDP   'The Relation of Sense-Data to Physics' (1914), in *Papers* 8, pp. 3–26.

RTC   'Reply to Criticisms' (1944), in *Papers* 11, pp. 18–66.

SMP   'On Scientific Method in Philosophy' in *Papers* 8, pp. 55–73.

TK   *Theory of Knowledge. The 1913 Manuscript* = *Papers* 7.

CONTRIBUTORS

THOMAS BALDWIN is Professor of Philosophy at the University of York. He is the author of *G.E. Moore* and editor of Moore's *Selected Writings* and of the revised edition of *Principia Ethica*. He has contributed introductions to the new editions of *The Analysis of Mind*, *My Philosophical Development*, and *An Inquiry into Meaning and Truth*.

MICHAEL BEANEY is Lecturer in Philosophy at the Open University, Milton Keynes, England. He is author of *Frege: Making Sense* (Duckworth, 1996), *Analysis* (Acumen, forthcoming), and editor of *The Frege Reader* (Blackwell, 1997).

RICHARD L. CARTWRIGHT is Emeritus Professor of Philosophy at the Massachusetts Institute of Technology. Before joining the MIT faculty, he taught at the University of Michigan and Wayne State University. He has published articles on a variety of subjects in philosophy, some of which are included in his *Philosophical Essays* (1987).

WILLIAM DEMOPOULOS is Professor of Philosophy and a founding member of the Centre for Cognitive Science at The University of Western Ontario. He is the editor of *Frege's Philosophy of Mathematics* (Harvard University Press, 1995) and the author of numerous articles in the philosophy of logic and mathematics, the philosophy of science, and the history of analytic philosophy.

Born in London, MARTIN GODWYN is a graduate of the University of Southampton and Jesus College, Cambridge. He is presently engaged in research in the areas of philosophy of mind and language at University of British Columbia, Vancouver.

xv

A.C. GRAYLING is Reader in Philosophy at Birkbeck College, University of London. He is the author of *An Introduction to Philosophical Logic; Berkeley: The Central Arguments; The Refutation of Scepticism;* the Oxford University Press's "Past Masters" on Russell and Wittgenstein; and editor of *Philosophy 1: A Guide Through the Subject* and *Philosophy 2: Further Through the Subject.* He has also contributed to the *Cambridge Companion to Berkeley.*

I. GRATTAN-GUINNESS is Professor of the History of Mathematics and Logic at Middlesex University, England. He was editor of the history of science journal *Annals of Science* from 1974 to 1981. In 1979, he founded the journal *History and Philosophy of Logic*, editing it until 1992. He edited a substantial *Companion Encyclopedia of the History and Philosophy of the Mathematical Sciences* (two volumes, London: Routledge, 1994) and published *The Norton History of the Mathematical Sciences. The Rainbow of Mathematics* (New York: Norton, 1998). His book *The Search for Mathematical Roots, 1870–1940*, appeared in 2000 with Princeton University Press.

NICHOLAS GRIFFIN is Director of the Bertrand Russell Research Centre at McMaster University, Hamilton, Ontario, where he holds a Canada Research Chair in Philosophy. He has written widely on Russell and is the author of *Russell's Idealist Apprenticeship*, the editor of two volumes of Russell's *Selected Letters*, and a co-editor of two volumes of *The Collected Papers of Bertrand Russell.*

PAUL HAGER is Professor of Education of the University of Technology, Sydney. His varied research and writing interests include critical thinking, informal learning at work, and Bertrand Russell's philosophy. He is the author of *Continuity and Change in the Development of Russell's Philosophy* (Dordrecht Kluwer Academic Publishers, 1994), the entry on Russell in W. Newton-Smith (ed.) *A Companion to the Philosophy of Science* (Oxford Blackwell, 2000), and of various journal articles on Russell.

PETER HYLTON is Distinguished Professor at the University of Illinois, Chicago. He is the author of *Russell, Idealism, and the Emergence of Analytic Philosophy*, as well as of numerous essays on the history and development of analytic philosophy. Besides his essay in this volume, he also has essays in the Cambridge Companions to Hegel, Quine, and Frege (forthcoming).

ANDREW D. IRVINE is a graduate of the University of Saskatch-
ewan, the University of Western Ontario, and Sydney University. He
is now Professor of Philosophy at the University of British Columbia.
He has either held academic posts or been a visiting scholar at the
University of Toronto, Simon Fraser University, the University of
Pittsburgh, and Stanford University.

GREGORY LANDINI is a Professor of Philosophy at the University
of Iowa. He is the author of *Russell's Hidden Substitutional Theory*
(Oxford, 1998) and has published articles in the philosophy of logic
and metaphysics. His teaching and research interests include modal
logic, the foundations of mathematics, philosophy of mind, philosophy of language, and the history of analytic philosophy.

BERNARD LINSKY is Professor of Philosophy at the University of
Alberta. He is the author of *Russell's Metaphysical Logic* (CSLI, 1999)
and of articles on Russell, metaphysics, and philosophy of language.

CHARLES R. PIGDEN is Senior Lecturer in Philosophy at the University at Otago, Dunedin, New Zealand. He is the editor of *Russell
on Ethics* and the author of several articles on metaethics and related
topics.

R. E. TULLY is a Professor of Philosophy at the University of
Toronto. He is the author of numerous articles on Russell, Wittgen-
stein, and early analytic philosophy and coauthor (with F.D.
Portoraro) of *Logic with Symlog* (Prentice Hall).

ALASDAIR URQUHART teaches in the Department of Philosophy at
the University of Toronto. He is the editor of *The Collected Papers
of Bertrand Russell, Volume 4: Foundations of Logic, 1903–5*. He
works in the areas of mathematical logic, complexity theory, and
the history of logic.

Introduction

It is difficult to over-estimate the extent to which Russell's thought dominated twentieth century analytic philosophy: virtually every strand in its development either originated with him or was transformed by being transmitted through him. Analytic philosophy itself owes its existence more to Russell than to any other philosopher. He was not, of course, its only originator (Frege and Moore, must be acknowledged as well), but he contributed more across its central areas (logic, philosophy of language, epistemology, and metaphysics) than any other single philosopher, and he was certainly its most energetic propagandist. Moreover, as Pigden forcefully argues in his essay in this volume, even in areas such as ethics, where Russell's work has often been thought to be shallow and derivative, Russell has been the source of a number of innovations which might have made the reputation of a lesser philosopher. With Frege and Peano, Russell created modern formal logic and, much more than they, was responsible for bringing it to the attention of philosophers and demonstrating its usefulness in philosophical applications. His work had a profound influence on Carnap and the logical positivists, on Quine, on A.J. Ayer, and in diverse ways on Wittgenstein. Wittgenstein's *Tractatus Logico-Philosophicus* [1922] was an attempt (ultimately unsustainable) to push to the limit an approach to language which had been suggested, though not actually embraced, by Russell. Wittgenstein's later philosophy was an attempt to make good the defects of the *Tractatus* by pushing equally far in the opposite direction. The ordinary language philosophers of the middle of the century also reacted strongly against Russell; by the same token, their work would have been inconceivable without him. In fact, for much of the twentieth century those philosophers who were not pursuing the projects

I

Russell proposed, or using the methods he advocated, were usually pursuing projects conceived in and shaped by opposition to him and casting about for methods other than his. His influence was thus pervasive, even among the philosophers who disagreed with him.

Quite apart from his work in philosophy, Russell was one of the twentieth century's most colourful and controversial intellectuals. Throughout a very long life he took up a great many causes, most of them unpopular. He was certainly never afraid to take a stand, and some of those he took got him into quite spectacular amounts of trouble. Few philosophers have led as adventurous a life as Russell, and none have engaged with the world in so many different ways. In one way or another he involved himself with most of the important political and intellectual concerns of the twentieth century.

Although this book is exclusively concerned with Russell's contributions to philosophy, the first part of this *Introduction* is devoted to a brief survey of his life. The second part deals with the development of his philosophy, linking together some of the themes that are treated in much more detail in the individual essays in the volume.

I. LIFE[1]

Russell was born in 1872 into the upper echelons of the Whig aristocracy and inherited many of the values of its most radical wing. The first Earl Russell, Bertrand's grandfather, had twice been prime minister, though his greatest achievements had come earlier, in the 1830s, as one of the most radical members of Lord Grey's Cabinet. He is now best remembered as the architect of the electoral reform bill of 1832, the first and most difficult step on the long road to universal adult suffrage. Russell's parents were free-thinking, mid-Victorian radicals, advocating such unpopular causes as women's rights and birth control. Both his parents died before he was four and, although they had left provision for him to be brought up by freethinkers, his paternal grandparents had the will overturned and took charge of the two surviving children.

Russell's grandfather died in 1878, so Russell was brought up primarily by his grandmother, who was determined to protect him from

---

[1] This account of Russell's life is based on his *Autobiography* and documents in the Bertrand Russell Archives, McMaster University. For more detail see Clark [1975], Monk [1996] and [2000], and Russell [1991], [2001]. For more on Russell's political work, see Ryan [1988].

the world and equally from the influence of his parents. She had him educated at home by a succession of tutors, indoctrinating him with Victorian virtues and grooming him for a future political career. George Santayana, a close friend of Russell's brother, was convinced she was training Bertie to become prime minister – a not implausible ambition. Since he hardly remembered his parents, she had a clear field. He was told little about his parents' beliefs and discovered with amazement as an adult how closely they resembled his own.

As a child, Bertie adored his grandmother and he absorbed many of her values. As a result he became, in his brother's description, 'an unendurable little prig' (Frank Russell [1923], p. 38). In adolescence, however, he began to rebel. In this, he was helped by discovering the works of John Stuart Mill.[2] He read almost all of them at this time, and generally accepted Mill's views – except (significantly enough) his empiricist philosophy of mathematics. His grandmother was not impressed. She ridiculed him hurtfully about utilitarianism and after that he kept his opinions to himself, writing them down in a note-book using Greek letters and phonetic spelling for concealment (see *Papers* 1, pp. 5–21). The notebook charts Russell's gradual loss of religious faith and tends to confirm Nietzsche's dictum that the English paid penance for every emancipation from theology by showing what moral fanatics they were. It was Mill's *Autobiography* that turned Russell into an agnostic, by supplying a refutation of the argument from design.

Russell had shown an early aptitude for mathematics and in 1890 he went up to Trinity College, Cambridge, to study for Part I of the Mathematical Tripos. Since mathematics at Cambridge was generally accepted as a suitable preparation for a wide range of careers, this in itself did not conflict with granny's political hopes for him. But Russell was not interested in mathematics as training for a career; he studied it in pursuit of philosophical interests which had already clearly emerged. 'My original interest in philosophy had two sources,' he wrote some seventy years after the event.

On the one hand, I was anxious to discover whether philosophy would provide any defence for anything that could be called religious belief, however vague; on the other hand, I wished to persuade myself that something could

---

[2] Mill had been a close friend of Russell's parents and had agreed to be the secular equivalent of a godfather for Russell. His death, a year after Russell's birth, prevented him from having any influence on the way Russell was brought up.

be known, in pure mathematics if not elsewhere. I thought about both these problems during adolescence, in solitude and with little help from books. As regards religion, I came to disbelieve first in free will, then in immortality, and finally in God. As regards the foundations of mathematics, I got nowhere. (*MPD*, p. 11)

The mathematical training he got at Cambridge, however, did little to satisfy his quest for mathematical certainty: 'the "proofs" which were offered of mathematical theorems were an insult to the logical intelligence', he complained (*MPD*, p. 38).[3] Nonetheless, he got a first in the Mathematical Tripos of 1893 and then turned to philosophy for his fourth year, the only formal philosophical training he ever had.

At Cambridge, however, his intelligence was recognized early on and he began to come out of his shell. He lost his excruciating shyness and some of his priggishness. In large measure, this was due to his admission to the Cambridge Apostles, the well-known secret discussion society. In the 1890s its discussions tended to be philosophical and were dominated by the ideas of the Cambridge idealist philosopher, J.M.E. McTaggart. Russell's contemporaries in the Society became his lifelong friends. In this sheltered, but high-powered and exuberant setting, he began to develop his considerable aptitude for talking.[4]

After completing his undergraduate work in philosophy, the next step was to write a fellowship dissertation. Russell chose the philosophy of geometry for his topic – a revised version of his successful thesis was published as *An Essay on the Foundations of Geometry* (1897). For a time he considered writing a second dissertation in economics, a plan which owed much to the influence of Alys Pearsall Smith, with whom he had fallen in love. He had met her in 1889 and was immediately attracted, but realizing that his grandmother would oppose the match, he gave no indication of his interest until 1893 when he turned 21. At that age he could not only marry without his grandmother's consent, but also inherited enough from his father's estate for a couple with modest needs to live on.

Granny indeed opposed the marriage by every means at her disposal – most unscrupulously by inculcating fears of hereditary insanity. Bertie and Alys were not deterred; they married in December

---

[3] For further information about Russell's mathematical education see Lewis and Griffin [1990], and Griffin [1991] pp. 16–25.

[4] For the Cambridge Apostles in Russell's day, see Levy [1979]. For Russell's contributions to its debates, see *Papers* 1, pp. 76–116.

1894, but they decided not to have children and the fear of insanity cast a long pall.[5] In his *Autobiography* (vol. 1, p. 86), Russell said that on account of it he tried to avoid strong emotions and live 'a life of intellect tempered by flippancy', though this decision may also have been due to Alys's finding his emotions a little too strong to be comfortable.

Alys was an American Quaker, five years older than Russell, very high-minded and serious, and deeply involved in good causes. She hoped that she and Bertie would form a partnership devoted to political and social reform. Her model for this was the marriage of Sydney and Beatrice Webb, with whom the Russells were close friends. Alys anticipated that while she did the actual campaigning, Bertie would handle the more theoretical aspects of the work – hence his plans for a thesis in economics. Russell took the idea of collaboration seriously enough to attend economics lectures at the University of Berlin in January 1895, immediately after their honeymoon.

In Berlin they became interested in the German Social Democratic Party, then the largest Marxist party in the world. From this visit, and another one later in the year, Russell's first book, *German Social Democracy* [1896], emerged. Alys contributed an appendix on feminist issues. Though he found much to admire in the party's policies, especially its advanced feminism, Russell sharply criticized its Marxist philosophy, particularly dialectical materialism and the theory of surplus value, as well as its tactics, especially that of class confrontation. This was his first critique of Marxism and he never repented of it. It is not in the least surprising that he was critical, but it is surprising that he should have studied the German Social Democrats in the first place. They were at the time the most radical and revolutionary of all major leftwing parties in Europe and most British liberals would have regarded them as much too scary for close contact. Sir Edward Malet, the British ambassador in Berlin at the time, was a relative of Russell's but he made it clear that Bertie and Alys were not welcome at the embassy once it was known that they were consorting with Social Democrats.

This was as far as Bertie and Alys went towards the marriage of joint political work that Alys had hoped for. For the next fifteen years, until *Principia Mathematica* was complete, Russell devoted

---

[5] Though not, I think, so devastating a one as Monk [1996], [2000] suggests. Monk holds that the fear of insanity was one of the central themes of Russell's life – a considerable overstatement.

himself more or less single-mindedly to the philosophy of mathematics. This did not prevent occasional forays into politics, however. In 1904, when tariff reform was in the air, Russell took up the cause of free trade – for which, incidentally, his grandfather had fought in the days before the repeal of the Corn Laws. In 1906–10 he was active in the campaign for women's suffrage, serving on the executive of the National Union of Women's Suffrage Societies and standing for election on a women's suffrage ticket in a safely unwinnable Tory seat.

Despite that fact that Alys's hopes for a political collaboration never materialized, their marriage was a happy one for several years, with Alys working hard at her causes and Bertie at his philosophy. The life of intellect tempered by flippancy seemed to suit them both. Beatrice Webb, ever a perceptive observer, thought they were a model couple. Then, in 1901, Russell had a kind of crisis, occasioned by Evelyn Whitehead (the wife of his former teacher, A.N. Whitehead, with whom he was then beginning the collaboration that led to *Principia Mathematica* ten years later) having an apparent heart attack. Russell wrote eloquently of the experience in his *Autobiography*:

Ever since my marriage, my emotional life had been calm and superficial. I had forgotten all the deeper issues, and had been content with flippant cleverness. Suddenly the ground seemed to give way beneath me, and I found myself in quite another region. Within five minutes I went through some such reflections as the following: the loneliness of the human soul is unendurable; nothing can penetrate it except the highest intensity of the sort of love that religious teachers have preached; whatever does not spring from this motive is harmful, or at best useless ... in human relations one should penetrate to the core of loneliness in each person and speak to that. (*Auto.* 1, p. 146)

This sudden realization had a lasting effect on his emotional life, and even, by his own account, on his politics: he became at that point, he said, a pacifist.[6]

The flippant cleverness, on which his marriage had hitherto been based, was gone. In its place he tried, with grim determination, to put the deeper emotional concerns he had just discovered. Alys was not at all happy with this change and, after a year of trying, their

---

[6] The actual story of his conversion to pacifism is rather more complicated; see Blitz [1999] and Rempel [1979]. Russell's mystical experience has been widely discussed: see Clark [1975], pp. 84–6; Monk [1996], pp. 134–9 and Griffin [1984].

marriage fell apart. They did not, however, divorce – Alys threatened to kill herself if Bertie left her – but the foundation on which their life together was based had been destroyed. Ironically, Russell, by his efforts to speak to the 'core of loneliness' in each person, had plunged them both into a worse loneliness than they could well have imagined. Thus, during the years in which he did his greatest work in philosophy, Russell's personal life was unrelievedly bleak and grim. In the end, he escaped the emotional prison he had created – Alys never did, she remained devoted to him until her death.

During these years Russell supported himself from his inheritance, lecturing only occasionally at Cambridge: in 1899 when he lectured on Leibniz[7] and in 1901–2 when he lectured on mathematical logic. The six-year Fellowship at Trinity he won in 1895 carried a small stipend, but Russell gave it away. He was, in general, against inherited wealth, though he thought it could be justified when used for a good purpose, such as the encouragement of art and learning.[8] He and Alys lived frugally rather than modestly, and they gave a great deal of money away. By 1910, when *Principia* was complete, his capital was depleted. Moreover, he felt he no longer had a moral justification for living on unearned income, so he took up a five-year lectureship in logic and the principles of mathematics at Trinity.

The outbreak of World War I in 1914 brought politics to the forefront of his life. 'I never had a moment's doubt as to what I must do', he wrote. 'I have at times been paralyzed by scepticism, at times I have been cynical, at other times indifferent, but when the War came I felt as if I had heard the voice of God. I knew it was my business to protest, however futile protest might be' (*Auto.* 2, pp. 17–18). He protested in every way open to him. He was already too old to be conscripted but he threw his lot in with young, radical conscientious objectors, and worked to the point of exhaustion for their organization, The No-Conscription Fellowship (see Vellacott [1980]). He lobbied the government on behalf of COs, helped them face the Tribunals which heard their cases, visited them in prison, and wrote and spoke endlessly in their defence and against the war. The government fined him, took away his passport, restricted his

---

[7] An enduring classic, *A Critical Exposition of the Philosophy of Leibniz* [1900], resulted from this, and his study of Leibniz no doubt inclined him toward logicism. See the paper by Godwyn and Irvine in this volume.
[8] See his paper 'The Uses of Luxury' [1896], *Papers* 1, pp. 320–3.

freedom of movement, and eventually jailed him. He lost most of his old liberal friends, and switched allegiance from the Liberal to the Labour Party. He spent the last half of the war with no job, no money, and no fixed address.

Most hurtful of all, in 1916 he was dismissed from his lectureship at Trinity. Ever since leaving Pembroke Lodge, he had looked on Cambridge as his real home, and he had entertained hopes that reason and tolerance would prevail there if nowhere else. It took him a long time to forgive Trinity for the high opinion he had had of it, and the episode left him permanently suspicious of academia. After 1916 he had only relatively short periods of academic employment and was therefore dependent upon writing to make his living – a fact which only partially explains his huge subsequent output.

He was supported in his opposition to the war by Lady Ottoline Morrell, the famous Bloomsbury hostess. He fell in love with her in 1911 and the ensuing affair was the most passionate of his life. They were rarely together for long and filled their absences with a passionate correspondence, occasionally writing three times in one day. The affair with Ottoline finally led to his leaving Alys (though they did not divorce until 1921); it also brought him into closer contact with members of the Bloomsbury Group, many of whom were also opposed to the war. Despite many tempestuous estrangements, the affair lasted until 1916, when Russell took up with Lady Constance Malleson, a young actress (usually known by her stage name, Colette O'Niel) who worked for the No-Conscription Fellowship and was as passionately opposed to the war as he.

In 1917 Russell greeted the Russian revolution with unrestrained delight. He saw it as a blow against tyranny, and a giant step towards peace and social justice. In 1920 he visited Russia expecting to admire the new Bolshevik government. Instead he came away horrified by its cruelty and ruthlessness and wrote *The Practice and Theory of Bolshevism* [1920] about his experiences. It was the first book from the left to warn of the dangers of dictatorship under communism. The book, as he knew it would be, was hailed by his enemies and hated by his friends. Churchill greeted it enthusiastically; Sydney and Beatrice Webb thought he had finally shown himself up to be unreconstructed aristocrat.

After Russia he spent a year in China teaching philosophy at the University of Peking. His companion in China was Dora Black, a former Girton student with interests in leftwing politics and eighteenth-century French literature. They got married quickly upon their return to England, just in time to legitimize their son; a daughter was born in 1923.

During the 1920s Russell had to write fast and frequently to support his family. None of his books proved to be the sort of best-seller that establishes an author's fortune for life, so he was obliged to turn out one or more books a year throughout the decade. Just before the war, he had become very interested in the new developments in physics and had planned to write a technical work on the philosophy of physics. After Einstein's general theory of relativity was spectacularly confirmed in 1919, there was a huge wave of popular interest in the new physics, and Russell was able to cash in on it with two books, *The ABC of Atoms* [1923] and *The ABC of Relativity* [1925], and a great deal of commissioned journalism. His own technical work on the topic had to wait until *The Analysis of Matter* [1927].

Russell's political involvements were less during the interwar years than one might have expected. Reluctantly, he stood as a Labour candidate in the safe Tory seat of Chelsea in 1922 and 1923. (Dora stood, with a good deal more enthusiasm, in 1924.) The first Labour Government appointed him to the Boxer Indemnity Commission, but this proved short-lived: he was dismissed as soon as the Tories regained power. And he continued to speak and write about various political issues. But no campaign or programme seems to have aroused any great enthusiasm in him: he did what he could or what he was called upon to do by the various groups he supported, but he did not exhibit a great deal of political initiative between the wars.

This was largely due to his experience in Russia. It was not just that he found the Soviet government bad – he did not think it worse than the Tsarist regime it replaced. It was rather that his experience of Bolshevism brought home to him a sort of paradox in radical politics. On the one hand, his experiences in World War I had convinced him that radical changes were necessary. On the other, his experience in Russia suggested that only people as ruthless as the Bolsheviks would be able to effect such changes, but that their very ruthlessness would ensure that the system they created would be as bad as the one they replaced. 'I realized', he wrote to Colette O'Niel shortly after his return, 'that any attempt to improve the world politically rouses fierce opposition, and that only people with all the Bolshevik defects can hope to combat the opposition successfully, while only people utterly unlike the Bolsheviks could make good use of victory' (Russell [2001], p. 209; letter of 24 July 1920).

Through the 1920s and 1930s Russell tried to come to terms with this problem. Political developments between the wars did not do much to help him. Russia fell firmly under Stalinism, Italy under fascism, and Germany under Nazism. By contrast, Britain's first labour government lasted less than a year, and its second ended in utter defeat. If anything Russell's pessimistic diagnosis seemed to be confirmed: power ended up in the hands of the most ruthless, while the good were condemned to utter futility.

The only way out of this impasse seemed to be through a change in human nature. Russell was not optimistic, but any hope was better than none. He was inclined to think that psychology had reached (or at least would soon do so) the point where it might be able to effect such a change,[9] though he was often sceptical about the political will to effect the sort of changes that were desirable rather than those which were not.[10] The same motivation can be found in some of his writing on sexual morality: sexual repression, he thought, made people cruel (contra Freud, who thought it made them civilized). It helps, too, to explain why he took up campaigning against organized religion in the 1920s. Although Russell acquired a substantial reputation as a public critic of religion, he did little to earn it before the 1920s. Thereafter, his attacks on religion were notable for their claims that, contrary to general opinion, religion was not only false, but harmful.

However, of all the means by which he hoped human nature might be changed, none held out more hope to him during the 1920s than education. It was primarily to education that he looked for a way of producing people who could be resolute without being ruthless. He thought that the development of psychology had made it possible to educate children in a new way, replacing the superstition and moralizing that lingered on from the days when education was under

---

[9] He emphasized both psychoanalytic and behaviouristic methods and had hopes down the road for developments in psychopharmacology. Sometimes he maintained that a generation would be sufficient to effect the transformation (by which he meant a generation after the techniques were generally adopted, not a generation from the time of writing, as Monk [2000], p. 57 seems to think).

[10] He was most pessimistic in *Icarus* [1924] and *The Scientific Outlook* [1931], and most optimistic in *On Education* [1926].

religious control. With new educational methods he hoped to produce children who were courageous, tolerant, intellectually independent, and socially responsible.

In 1927 in collaboration with Dora he set up his own experimental school, Beacon Hill. This was partly an opportunity to put his ideas into practice, but it was also driven by the educational needs of his own children. He did not like the schools then available to them – even the progressive schools failed to satisfy him because he thought they did not adequately emphasize intellectual development. Yet he did not want to educate his children at home because, remembering the loneliness of his own childhood, he felt they needed the companionship of other children.

The school was not, in Russell's eyes, a success.[11] Not surprisingly it attracted a large number of 'problem children'. Rather than finding that the school was a way to create a new world, he came to the conclusion that '[a] school is like the world: only government can prevent brutal violence'. 'To let the children go free was to establish a reign of terror, in which the strong kept the weak trembling and miserable' (*Auto.* 2, p. 154).[12] More hurtful than this was the disastrous effect the school had on his own two children; his son John, in particular, was mercilessly bullied.[13] The school, moreover, was very expensive to run, requiring that Russell undertake regular lecture tours in the United States to raise money. His involvement with it ended, along with his marriage, in 1932, although Dora continued to run it on her own until 1943.

Freed from the burden of earning money to pay for the school, Russell in the 1930s turned to larger, more important, but less lucrative writing projects. He wrote a substantial work tracing conflicting themes in nineteenth-century history, *Freedom and Organization, 1814–1914* [1934], and a book on *Power* [1938], in which, against both communism and capitalism, he argued for democratic socialism with strong limits on the powers of state officials.[14] Perhaps the

---

[11] Dora was more sanguine. See her autobiography, *The Tamarisk Tree*, especially vol. 2 [1981].

[12] Significantly, in the aftermath of this debacle, Russell turned his attention to a general consideration of power. The result was *Power: A New Social Analysis* [1938], one of the most important of his later books on political and social issues.

[13] See his daughter's account, Tait [1975].

[14] The problem of balancing the claims of social organization and individual liberty was a constant theme in Russell's political writings. See Greenspan [1978].

least expected of these longer works was a two-volume compilation of his parents' papers, *The Amberley Papers* (1937).

Such works as these, however, took a long time to write (even for Russell) and earned less money than he expected on account of the Depression. Moreover, by the mid-1930s, Russell needed to support two families. He married Patricia Spence (usually known by her nickname of 'Peter') in 1936 and a third child was born in 1937. He was also paying alimony to Dora, support for the two children he had had with her, and, by some strange legal quirk, £400 alimony a year to his brother's second wife.[15] If Russell was to continue writing serious books, it was clear he needed some regular source of income. Accordingly, he made efforts to return to academic life. This was not easy; positions were scarce and Russell was a controversial figure, but in 1938 he gave a course of lectures on philosophy of language at Oxford. This was followed by a visiting appointment at the University of Chicago. So in the autumn of 1938, under the shadow of Munich, Russell, Peter, and their son set sail for America.

Russell had watched the rise of Nazi Germany with alarm. Its brutality and warlike intentions strained his pacifist principles. Nonetheless, in 1936 he wrote a book, *Which Way to Peace?*, which reaffirmed them, albeit with palpably lukewarm conviction. He welcomed the Munich agreement, though he did not think it would secure peace for long. When war broke out he very reluctantly abandoned his pacifism. It was, he said, 'the last stage in the slow abandonment of many of the beliefs' that he had acquired as a result of his mystical experience in 1901. Pacifism was right 'only when the holders of power were not ruthless beyond a point, and clearly the Nazis went beyond that point' (*Auto.* 2, pp. 191–2). Even so, his support of the war was not wholehearted:

Although my reason was wholly convinced, my emotions followed with reluctance. My whole nature had been involved in my opposition to the First War, whereas it was a divided self that favoured the Second. I have never since 1940 recovered the same degree of unity between opinion and emotion as I had possessed from 1914 to 1918. (*Auto.*, 2, p. 191)

In the summer of 1939, Russell's two older children joined him and Peter in America for a holiday, but before they could return war broke

---

[15] Frank died unexpectedly in 1931. By this time Frank was essentially bankrupt and Russell inherited little beside the earldom and the second wife's alimony. (It is worth noting that Alys refused alimony on feminist grounds.)

out and they had to stay. By this time, Russell's Chicago job had come to an end and he had another visiting appointment at UCLA. In 1940 he was to give the William James lectures at Harvard – they became his book *An Inquiry into Meaning and Truth* [1940] – but beyond that his prospects seemed bleak. At last, he was offered a permanent position at City College, New York, and it seemed as if his troubles were over. In fact, they were only just beginning. His appointment to CCNY provoked opposition from New York's Catholic community and the appointment was overturned in a celebrated court case in which Russell was declared morally unfit to teach (see Weidlich [2000]).

In 1940, therefore, Russell found himself, with three children and a wife to support, unemployed and marooned in America by the war. Wartime currency restrictions prevented his getting money from Britain, and the scandal surrounding the City College case made editors unwilling to publish him. At this point, the eccentric and irascible millionaire Albert Barnes came to his rescue with a five-year appointment to lecture on the history of philosophy at the Barnes Foundation in Philadelphia. Barnes had devoted his considerable fortune to amassing one of the world's finest privately-owned art collections. At the Barnes Foundation, surrounded by this truly extraordinary collection, he and a carefully selected staff taught art appreciation to equally carefully selected students, according to principles set down in minute detail by Barnes himself. The very features that in 1940 made Russell unwelcome to university administrators across the United States made him especially attractive to Barnes, who relished controversy and especially enjoyed thumbing his nose at the academic establishment.

After 1940, when Russell spoke of the importance of maintaining some private education to prevent the imposition of a uniform orthodoxy, he was speaking from experience. But private patronage had its drawbacks too and they became apparent when Barnes took a strong dislike to Peter and fired Russell. At the end of 1942, therefore, Russell once more found himself out of a job, but his situation was nowhere near so serious as it had been in 1940. He was virtually certain to win a breach of contract case against Barnes, so the emergency would only be temporary. Moreover, the scandal that made him unemployable in 1940 was now, like most press excitements, long passed, so he was able to support his family by journalism and lecturing. In 1943 he lectured on scientific inference at Bryn Mawr,

Wellesley College, and Princeton. Indeed, Barnes permanently solved Russell's financial problems, for not only did Russell eventually collect a sizeable sum for breach of contract but also the lectures he gave for Barnes became the basis for his enormously successful *History of Western Philosophy* [1945].

Russell returned to England in 1944 to take up a fellowship at Trinity College where he completed his last great philosophical work, *Human Knowledge* [1948]. He taught at Trinity until 1949 when he was given a fellowship for life. His return marked not only a mending of his relations with the College but also with the British establishment as a whole. In part, the establishment had now caught up with him. His pacifism during World War I was no longer generally regarded as treasonable folly but as humane wisdom. The election of a strongly reforming and genuinely socialist Labour government in 1945 meant that the country's policies were now much closer to what he would desire, and also, of course, that many of his political allies from before the war were now in positions of power. Even his unconventional views on sexual morality were now tolerated – the exigencies of war had done much to liberate sexual behaviour.[16]

But what chiefly made him respectable was his hatred of Russia. Events since 1920, when he wrote *The Practice and Theory of Bolshevism*, had exceeded his worst forebodings, though the full horror of Stalinism only became apparent once Stalin had ceased to be an ally. 'Ever since the end of the war', Russell told Colette O'Niel in February 1947, 'I have been as anti-Russian as one can be without being thought mad'. Rather unexpectedly, he had become a cold warrior. Russell's leftwing credentials made him useful to the British government, especially in the battle to keep left-leaning groups free from communist influence. From the government's point of view his opinions were ideally suited to the beginning of the cold war and it made many opportunities for him to spread his views, including a number of semi-official lecture trips to Europe. He continued to write prolifically, including a philosophical autobiography *My Philosophical Development* [1959] and several collections of essays.

In return, official honours poured in. He was awarded the Order of Merit, Britain's highest civilian honour, in 1949 and the Nobel

---

[16] In 1949 his marriage to Peter had ended and in 1952 he married Edith Finch, an American writer, his fourth and last wife. For the last two decades of his life, Edith was his constant companion and shared with him most of his political battles.

Prize for Literature in 1950. He broadcast frequently for the BBC. He gave the first series of BBC Reith Lectures, *Authority and the Individual* [1949], and became a regular contributor to the popular *Brains Trust* programme. All this introduced him to a much wider audience than he previously had and he began to acquire a degree of popular fame that philosophers hardly ever achieve: his face and voice (both very distinctive) became almost universally recognized. He became a fixture of the postwar British cultural scene.

All this was more respectability than a dedicated iconoclast could feel comfortable with, but it did not last long. He had been worried by nuclear weapons from the very beginning: he was writing his first article on the A-bomb when the second one was exploded over Nagasaki. To begin with, he thought that the period when America had a monopoly of nuclear weapons afforded an opportunity to bring them under international control. He realized that this period would be brief (indeed he seemed less surprised than most in the west when Russia exploded her first A-bomb in 1949), and that it was necessary to make the most of it. Accordingly, he welcomed the Baruch proposals when they were made, but, much more controversially, thought that Russia should, if necessary, be coerced into accepting them by threat of atomic war. This proposal caused him a good deal of embarrassment later on.[17] It did not embarrass the western governments: they told him it would be better to wait a few years until they had built more bombs.

Even Russia's acquisition of atomic weapons did not cause Russell immediately to change his stance. The development of the vastly more powerful hydrogen bomb did: when both sides had this weapon (America in 1952 and Russia in 1955), and the means to deliver it, the hope that either side would be able to coerce the other disappeared. At the same time, Russell became more optimistic about developments in Russia after Stalin's death in 1953. Despite initial scepticism he welcomed Khrushchev's reforms and eventually developed a rapport with the Soviet leader. This began in 1957 when Russell wrote an open letter to Eisenhower and Khrushchev urging them to peaceful coexistence, and Khrushchev, to everyone's surprise, replied. Thereafter, Russell exchanged many letters with him – most famously

---

[17] The actual details of what he said (and didn't say) and what he subsequently denied (and didn't deny) is too complex to enter into here. Perkins [1994] gives an admirably exact account.

during the Cuban Missile Crisis – and Khrushchev seems to have used Russell as an important back channel in communicating with the west.

The overwhelming danger of nuclear weapons concentrated Russell's efforts in a way few things had done since he worked on mathematical logic fifty years before. Apart from direct appeals to the superpower leaders, he appealed also to public opinion – most strikingly in his broadcast 'Man's Peril' (*Papers* 28, pp. 82–9) aired by the BBC just before Christmas 1954. For a time in the 1950s he had hopes of persuading the nonaligned nations, led by India, to help mediate great power rivalries. He was especially concerned that the public be made aware of the extraordinary destructive power of the hydrogen bomb. To this end he organized a statement to be signed by both communist and non-communist scientists warning of its dangers. This was the Russell–Einstein Manifesto of 1955 (*Papers* 28, pp. 304–33); it led soon after to the first contacts between western and Soviet scientists and to the creation of the Pugwash movement.

The pathetically slow progress of superpower disarmament discussions led Russell to think that a large-scale public campaign was needed to push the diplomats forward. In 1958, therefore, he helped found the Campaign for Nuclear Disarmament, which organized the largest demonstrations Britain had ever seen in support of its policy of British unilateral nuclear disarmament. When CND's demonstrations appeared to be running out of steam, he founded the more militant Committee of 100, dedicated to increasing the pressure for the CND's policy by means of direct action and civil disobedience. Thus, in 1961 Russell was jailed once more, this time for inciting demonstrators to civil disobedience.

In regard to nuclear confrontation, some hopeful signs appeared in the early 1960s. The mere fact that the nuclear powers did not go to war over Cuba in 1962 suggested that they were, in fact, more aware of the dangers of nuclear brinkmanship than they pretended – although the latest revelations about what happened suggest that the preservation of peace was more-or-less accidental. That this lesson had been learnt seemed further confirmed by the signing of the partial nuclear test ban treaty in 1963, to the success of which the Pugwash scientists had contributed a good deal behind the scenes. Russell quickly recognized that the days of nuclear brinkmanship were over and that superpower rivalry would now be conducted by means of proxy wars fought by and large in the third world and often by incredibly brutal means. In the 1960s the most bloody and barbaric of these wars was the American war against Vietnam. In his last five years, Russell lost no opportunity to oppose America in this conflict. His most ambitious undertaking was to set up the International War Crimes Tribunal (1967) which investigated American conduct in Vietnam and produced the first clear evidence available in the west of American atrocities there.

Russell was widely criticized for his anti-American position on both Vietnam and Cuba. In America the right had regarded him as anti-American since the mid-1950s, when he had savagely criticized McCarthyism. Those who criticized him for being anti-American often assumed that he was pro-Communist, but this was a complete mistake. He remained as critical of communism as ever – he kept *The Practice and Theory of Bolshevism* in print and allowed the re-printing of *German Social Democracy*. He was especially critical of civil rights abuses in communist countries and spent a great deal of time taking up general issues and particular cases with the authorities. During the Khrushchev years, however, he thought that Russia was slowly getting better in these respects, while America was slowly getting worse. After the mid-1950s, and especially after the Cuban crisis, he became convinced that Russia was less dangerous to world peace than America. The war in Vietnam confirmed his view. But when Russia invaded Czechoslovakia in 1968, he condemned the invasion on the same grounds as he condemned the American invasion of Vietnam – though he realized that the Czechs were being treated far less brutally than the Vietnamese.

The 1960s were a time of hectic political work for Russell. He became involved in many causes, from political prisoners in Iran to the British Who Killed Kennedy? Committee. He was involved in a quite serious way in efforts to broker a settlement of the Sino-Indian border dispute, corresponding with the heads of state involved, meeting their diplomatic representatives in London, and even sending emissaries to carry messages between New Delhi and Beijing. His last political statement, on the Middle East, was written on 31 January 1970, two days before his death.

II. PHILOSOPHY

Russell's philosophy has to be considered developmentally. He changed his position, even on fundamental matters, several times over a long career, prompting his former student, C.D. Broad, to remark that he produced a new system of philosophy every few years (Broad [1924], p. 79). This, of course, is an exaggeration, but like every good exaggeration it contains a element of truth. What it ignores is the extent to which the various phases of Russell's philosophy develop out of each other as different attempts to carry forward a single philosophical project.

Like many of the great philosophers of the past – including two of his special heroes, Leibniz and Spinoza – Russell hoped to produce a system of the world. Unlike his rationalist predecessors, however, who started with grand metaphysical principles and worked downwards, and unlike his empiricist predecessors, who started with the deliverances of sense experience and worked up, Russell began his investigations in the middle – with the sciences. The sciences, he reasonably maintained, are the most reliable bodies of systematized belief that we have access to. On the one hand, they are more reliable guides to truth than a priori metaphysical speculation. On the other hand, they are not only much more comprehensive and better organized than individual sense experience but also more likely to be true than the body of interpersonal belief that constitutes common sense. 'Science', Russell wrote, 'is at no moment quite right, but it is seldom quite wrong, and has, as a rule, a better chance of being right than the theories of the unscientific. It is, therefore, rational to accept it hypothetically' (*MPD*, p. 17). Accordingly, one main task of philosophy, in Russell's view, was to provide a comprehensive account of the world consistent with the best scientific knowledge of the day. This remained a constant in his philosophical career. As an undergraduate he wrote that the aim of epistemology was 'to make a self-consistent whole of the various Sciences' (*Papers* 1, p. 121), and at the end of his career, he described his final philosophical position as a 'synthesis of four ... sciences – namely, physics, physiology, psychology and mathematical logic' (*MPD*, p. 16). This suggests a considerable consistency of purpose underlying a wide diversity of approaches.

It also suggests that the line between science and philosophy was not, for Russell, a sharp one. He took very seriously the historical process by which the sciences had emerged from philosophical speculation. Psychology was emerging as an independent science at the beginning of his philosophical career, and he regarded his own work and Frege's as having achieved the same independence for mathematical logic. The criterion for demarcation – though rough and ready and capable of endless dispute – was that a discipline became science when it achieves sufficient definiteness that its hypotheses can be refuted or confirmed. 'Science', Russell was fond of saying, 'is what we know, and philosophy is what we don't know' (*Papers* 11, p. 378).[18] A significant part of the huge chasm that divides Russell's philosophy from that of the later (and even the earlier) Wittgenstein lies in differences in their attitudes to science and its relation to philosophy.

Russell's respect for science no doubt helped foster the view (quite widely held, especially by his critics) that he was a positivist. This was never the case. Although an inspiration to the logical positivists and sympathetic to many of their concerns, Russell never shared their hostility to metaphysics nor their verificationist view of meaning. The positivists themselves, though they greatly admired his work, especially in mathematical logic, never made the mistake of supposing he was one of them.

When Russell began his work in philosophy, the subject was dominated in Britain by the neo-Hegelians. It is not surprising, therefore, that his earliest work was done in that idiom.[19] It is more surprising that, even then, he started work, as no other neo-Hegelian did, with the sciences. His initial efforts were designed to separate the apriori from the aposteriori elements within each science, establishing the former as those principles which were necessary both for the science and for our experience of the subject matter with which the science dealt. By 1899, however, Russell had come to reject this essentially Kantian methodology, largely because he felt it could not be fully freed from psychologism. The method held that certain claims had to be accepted about space, for example, if our spatial experience was to be possible. But it could never be established that such claims were genuine geometrical truths about space rather than psychological truths about our experience. Unless the latter could be excluded,

---

[18] It will perhaps be thought insulting to the reader's intelligence to point out that this remark is intended tongue in cheek, but recent commentators have remained so blind to Russell's frequent use of irony and exaggeration that, alas, it is probably necessary.

[19] It is studied in detail in Griffin [1991] and, more briefly, in my paper in this volume.

space would be subjective and geometry subordinated to psychology. In developing this critique of idealism, he was certainly influenced by G.E. Moore, whose own criticisms of idealism along these lines were more forthright than Russell's.[20]

In place of idealism Russell and Moore developed an especially radical form of realism – called 'absolute realism' by Nelson ([1967], p. 373) – which received its main statement from Russell in *The Principles of Mathematics* (1903) and from Moore in *Principia Ethica* (1903).[21] Russell subsequently described this as the one genuine revolution in his thought – a change so great 'as to make my previous work, except such as was purely mathematical, irrelevant to everything that I did later' – all subsequent changes, he said, 'have been of the nature of an evolution' (*MPD*, p. 11). The realism that Russell adopted in the *Principles* was based on the assumption that (almost) every word occurring in a sentence has a meaning and what it means is a term (*POM*, p. 43). Terms are neither linguistic nor psychological, but objective constituents of the world. Concepts, universals, complexes, concrete and abstract particulars, physical objects, and mental states are all terms. Indeed, anything that can be counted as one or made the subject of a proposition is a term. Sentences express propositions which are complexes of terms related together. All complex unities are propositions (*POM*, pp. 139, 442),[22] and all propositions are complex terms. Not all terms exist but all have some kind of ontological standing, which Russell called *being*.

Russell's break from neo-Hegelianism was signalled by the title of an unpublished work he wrote in 1899: 'The Fundamental Ideas and Axioms of Mathematics' (*Papers* 2, pp. 265–305). For the first time, instead of employing transcendental arguments which sought the a priori principles which make mathematics possible as a science, he embraced the method he described as analysis which sought the primitive concepts in terms of which all mathematical concepts could be defined and the primitive propositions from which all mathematical theorems could be derived. This was exactly the project on which he and Whitehead collaborated in *Principia Mathematica*

---

[20] See Moore [1898] and [1899] and, somewhat later but more directly, [1903a].

[21] See Cartwright's paper in this volume.

[22] There are some complexes which do not form unities (e.g., classes as many) and which, therefore, are not propositions. Similarly, there may be unities which are not propositions because they are simple and have no parts. In all complex unities, there is a relation which gives the complex its unity by relating the other terms.

[1910–13], but Russell's progress with it was slow to begin with. As the surviving text of 'Fundamental Ideas' makes clear, he floundered in his attempts to base mathematics on the part–whole relation.

It was only when Russell discovered Peano's symbolic logic at the International Congress of Philosophy in Paris in 1900 that he was able to find a way forward. From that point on, however, progress was quick. He very quickly formulated and adopted the philosophy of mathematics known as logicism – according to which all mathematical concepts can be defined in purely logical terms and all mathematical theorems proven from purely logical axioms. There was no hint in 'Fundamental Ideas' that the fundamental ideas and axioms in question would *all* be logical ones. There was, however, the view, which he arrived at from a consideration of projective geometry, that one of the fundamental ideas of mathematics was the concept of order and that this, in turn, depended upon transitive, asymmetrical relations. Immediately after his discovery of Peano, in a very important paper, 'The Logic of Relations' [1901] (*Papers* 3, pp. 314–49), Russell developed a formal theory of relations in Peano's notation, which he immediately applied to the theory of series. He was also able in that paper to define the cardinal number of a class u as the class of all classes that could be put in 1–1 correlation with u. He was unaware that this definition had already been proposed by Frege [1884].[23] With these definitions, Russell felt able to show that the whole of arithmetic could be derived from purely logical principles using only concepts that were definable in logical terms. In this, also, he had been anticipated by Frege [1884] and [1893]. But Russell went further and claimed that the whole of *mathematics* could be thus derived from logic. In this, he was no doubt influenced by his own earlier work on projective geometry (cf. *Papers* 2, pp. 362–89) as well as by a good deal of work by other mathematicians on the arithmetization of mathematics (see Grattan-Guinness below). By early 1902 he had a set of twenty-two logical axioms from which, he thought, the whole of pure mathematics could be derived.[24]

Not all went well with this project, however. In May or June 1901 Russell discovered that the system of logic he was working with

[23] It was not until 1902, after *POM* had gone to press, that Russell discovered Frege's work. See Beaney's paper in this collection for this and their subsequent relationship.

[24] Cf. Russell [1992], p. 227. For these and subsequent developments see Grattan-Guinness's paper in this volume.

gave rise to the paradox, which now bears his name. The paradox is stated in the *Principles of Mathematics* (ch. x) as an unsolved problem and Russell devotes an appendix to dealing with it by means of an early version of his theory of types. This simple form of type theory proved ineffective and Russell eventually produced a much more complex version of the theory, the ramified theory of types, for inclusion in *Principia Mathematica*.[25] In between, he spent a great deal of time and ingenuity trying to solve the paradoxes without invoking a theory of types.[26]

The reason for Russell's reluctance to embrace the theory of types was, at least in part, due to his desire to keep his variables unrestricted. In *The Principles of Mathematics*, variables ranged unrestrictedly over terms. This gave a simple and attractive account of what was special about logic. The propositions of logic (and thus, via logicism, the propositions of mathematics) are unique in that they remain true when any of their terms (apart from logical constants) are replaced by *any* other term whatsoever. Type theory destroys this special feature by restricting the range of each variable to terms of a certain type and order.

The nature of propositions in *The Principles of Mathematics* is easily misunderstood. They are neither linguistic nor psychological items, but complexes in the world which actually contain the objects they are about. Thus, the proposition that Russell met Quine contains both Russell and Quine. But what about general propositions, such as the proposition that all men are mortal or that every number is either odd or even? It might seem that these contain every man or every number, respectively. But this makes the propositions much more complex than they seem to be, even infinitely complex in the case of the second proposition. Understanding such propositions would become an impossible task, in particular, because Russell demanded, in his famous 'principle of acquaintance', that in order to understand a proposition it is necessary to be acquainted with all its constituents.[27] If the principle of acquaintance is upheld, it would be impossible, on this analysis, to understand general propositions.

---

[25] See Urquhart's paper for details of both versions.

[26] For an account of the most elaborate of Russell's efforts along these lines, the substitutional theory of classes and relations, see Landini's paper and his [1998].

[27] This view is best known from somewhat later writings (e.g., OD and KAKD), but it appears as early as 1903 (cf. *Papers* 4, p. 307). Russell's views as to what were the constituents of propositions changed in the meantime, as we shall see shortly.

Russell circumvents this difficulty in the *Principles* by introducing the notion of a denoting concept. In the proposition that every number is odd or even, a denoting concept, expressed by the phrase 'every number', occurs in place of all the numbers. This concept denotes a complex comprised of all the numbers.[28] But to understand the proposition in which it occurs, it is necessary to be acquainted only with the denoting concept, rather than with the complex it denotes. None the less, the proposition is about all the numbers, not about the denoting concept which occurs within it, for it is not the concept *every number* that is odd or even. It is of the essence of Russell's notion of denoting, as introduced in the *Principles*, that when a proposition contains a denoting concept the proposition is about what the denoting concept denotes and not the denoting concept itself. The denoting concept in some way, which Russell never managed to explain, as it were transfers the 'aboutness' of the proposition from the concept to its denotation.

Denoting concepts are signalled in English by the words 'all', 'every', 'any', 'some', 'a', and 'the'. It will be noted that many such locutions are readily handled by the quantification theory that Frege had developed in the *Begriffsschrift* in 1879 and of which Russell was still unaware. The one case for which Frege provided no account was that of denoting concepts expressed by definite descriptions, phrases beginning with the word 'the': these Frege treated as proper names. Russell adopted Frege's treatment for all the other cases as soon as he learned of it. This eliminated all denoting concepts except those expressed by definite descriptions. It might be thought easy to eliminate this last category as well, for in this case there is just a single term denoted and it might seem as if this term could occur as a constituent of a proposition without incurring any of the problems caused by 'any man' and 'any number'. In other words, it would seem plausible at first sight to treat definite descriptions, like Frege did, as proper names which, on Russell's theory, signal the presence of the term they name in the proposition expressed by the sentence in which the name occurs.

Russell retained denoting concepts in this last case even after he had discovered Frege's quantification theory for two good reasons. First, it is obvious that the proposition expressed by 'Russell met

---

[28] These complexes are not propositional, their constituents are not related together and do not form a unity.

Quine' is a different proposition from the proposition expressed by 'Russell met the author of *Quiddities*', even though Quine is the author of *Quiddities*. Russell's theory in the *Principles* captures this, since the first sentence expresses a proposition containing Quine himself, while the second expresses a proposition containing the denoting concept expressed by the phrase 'the author of *Quiddities*'. The distinction between the two propositions is lost if we replace the denoting concept by its denotation.[29] Second, we have to be able to handle cases in which the denoting concept does not denote anything. In the proposition expressed by 'The present king of France is bald', we lack a term which could replace the denoting concept. Opinions differ on this point. Most authors deny that Russell countenances such cases in the *Principles*. They hold that, on Russell's absolute realism, every singular denoting concept denotes a term, resulting in a theory rather similar to Meinong's theory of objects. This leaves the theory of denoting concepts hanging by the first reason alone once Russell adopted Fregean quantification theory in 1903. It seems to me, however, that this was not, in fact, Russell's position in the *Principles*. It seems, rather, than he always held that some denoting concepts did not denote, and thus that the need to deal with definite descriptions where there was no denotation was always part of Russell's case for denoting concepts.[30]

Russell's account of denoting concepts, if it is to be statable, requires that there must be some way in which we can denote a denoting concept itself, rather than merely its denotation. After much effort, Russell concluded that there was not – he presents his case in an argument of baffling obscurity in 'On Denoting' (*Papers* 4, pp. 421–3). As best one can make out, the argument seems to run like this. The task is to find a sentence which will express a proposition which is about a certain denoting concept, D. It will not do to introduce a name for D in the sentence, because that will express a proposition in which D itself (as the referent of the name) occurs, and that proposition will not be about D but about what D denotes (since a proposition which contains a denoting concept is about what the concept denotes). Nor will it be possible systematically to find a

---

[29] The case of denoting concepts is the one point at which Russell's POM theory has something analogous to Frege's distinction between sense and reference. See Beaney's paper in this volume.

[30] For a defence of this interpretation, see Griffin [1996]. See also Cartwright below.

phrase which expresses another denoting concept, D^*, which denotes D, for D^* will be a function of D, and this makes D a constituent of D^*. Once again, it will be the denotation of D that determines the reference of D^*. For example, if 'D^*' is 'the F of D', then D^* will denote the F of the denotation of D. The root of the problem seems to be that stating the theory of denoting concepts requires that denoting concepts be nested, but the nature of the denoting relation ensures that the outer denoting concept is a function not of the inner denoting concept but of its denotation – and, as Russell notes (OD, *Papers* 4, p. 422), there is no backwards route from denotation to denoting concept, for every term is denoted by infinitely many denoting concepts. (See Makin [2000] for an important and detailed discussion of this argument and many other issues concerning Russell's theories of denoting.)

Whether or not this argument is a success, it led Russell to the conclusion that the notion of a denoting concept was incoherent. In 'On Denoting', Russell shows how denoting concepts can be dispensed with entirely, by means of his theory of definite descriptions, which treats definite descriptions entirely by means of quantification theory (see Hylton's paper).

Three general points about the theory of descriptions are worth emphasizing. The first is that it substantially refined the concept of analysis that was taken to be central to analytic philosophy. In the *Principles*, analysis was to be understood in a fairly literal way, as the breaking down of complex unities (i.e., propositions) into their parts (*POM*, p. 466).[31] With 'On Denoting', analysis became more sophisticated and more linguistic. On the new pattern of analysis, items of a certain kind, F, are held to have been analyzed into (or reduced to) items of a second kind, G, when all sentences apparently referring to Fs can be translated into ('reparsed as' is the phrase often used here) sentences which refer only to Gs. It is not that an ontological reduction is thereby performed by linguistic means, though much casual talk about the process gives this impression. It is rather that a linguistic criterion is provided for the possibility of an ontological reduction. As Russell frequently pointed out, a successful analysis does

---

[31] As early as 1900, in his *Leibniz* (p. 8) Russell had said that the analysis of propositions was the prime task of philosophy. The analogy with chemical analysis is quite close: W.E. Johnson had earlier spoken of analysis as the task of logic and made the analogy explicit (Johnson [1892], p. 6).

not prove that Fs do not exist, merely that there is no need to suppose that they do. Once the reparsing was accomplished, every theoretical purpose for which Fs were apparently required could be achieved without them, by means of Gs alone. Expressions which could, like definite descriptions, be eliminated through analysis Russell referred to as 'incomplete symbols' – though he often also used the phrase for the items to which the incomplete symbols apparently refer.

The second point to be noted is that the form of the sentences which are analysed is generally quite different from the form of the sentences which replace them. In the case of the theory of descriptions, as Hylton explains in his paper, the apparently simple subject–predicate form of 'The author of *Quiddities* is bald' is changed under analysis into a much more complicated quantificational statement. This was taken to show that the logical form of such statements was quite different from their grammatical form. Thus, although the methods of analysis were now much more linguistic than they had been in *The Principles of Mathematics*, explicit grammar is a much less direct guide to analysis than it had been in the days when Russell held that every word had a meaning and that the correctness of one's analysis of a proposition was to be checked by 'assigning the meaning of each word in the sentence expressing the proposition' (*POM*, p. 42).

The third point is that the new theory puts quite a different complexion on the principle of acquaintance. The statement of the principle remains unchanged, but what now counts as the constituent of a proposition has changed radically. On the earlier theory, acquaintance with denoting complexes was required. On the new theory, acquaintance was required only with those constituents of the proposition *after* analysis. This ran to acquaintance with universals – about which Russell remained a realist – and with certain kinds of particulars according to epistemological preference. It is notable that Russell's commitment to universals was much more unwavering than his commitment to particulars of any given type or even, in the end, to particulars of any type at all.

The theory of descriptions set in train a positive mania for analyzing away problematic items, and even items that did not seem problematic at all, in a search for minimum vocabularies[32] and minimal ontological commitments. Numerals had already been treated

---

[32] Russell seems to have introduced this term, but not apparently until Russell [1944].

as incomplete symbols via the Frege–Russell definition of numbers, which analysed them in terms of classes. Classes, in turn, were eliminated both in the substitutional theory (as described in Landini's paper) and in *Principia Mathematica*, where they are replaced by propositional functions.

After definite descriptions, the next type of expression that Russell treated as incomplete symbols were the 'that–' clauses which introduce propositions, for example in belief statements. Propositions were certainly problematic in their *Principles* form. They came in two varieties, true and false, and both alike were equally real. It is possible to make too much of the oddness of Russell's claim that the world is made up of propositions: propositions, after all, were just complex, unified terms. But, by the same token, on this account it is hard to make sense of the claim that there are both true and false ones and to give some appropriate account of the distinction between them. Yet false propositions, as well as true, were needed as the objects of belief.[33] In particular, the theory makes it hard to understand why we should prefer to believe only the true ones. One might be tempted to suggest that the actual world is made up of true ones, while the false ones occur in some non-actual (though, since necessary falsehoods may be believed, not always possible) world, but there is no hint of this account in Russell. Instead, he suggested at one point that we might have a fundamental moral obligation to believe only true ones, pointing out, with too much cleverness for his own good, that while we might hope that this principle was true, if it was not, there was no ground for thinking we did harm in believing it (MTCA, *Papers* 4, p. 474). Evidently, this state of affairs could not remain satisfying for long.

Russell attempted, by means of his multiple relation theory of judgment, to eliminate propositions in favour of their constituents in conjunction with relations such as belief or understanding, for which he introduced the now standard term 'propositional attitude'. As before, the test for the theory's success was a linguistic one, namely to show that all sentences in which propositions seem to be referred to could be replaced by sentences in which the apparent reference is

---

[33] On this account, since propositions are the objects of belief, the item believed is identical to the item which makes the belief true. This theory is a version of what is now called 'the identity theory of truth'. Cf Baldwin [1991].

eliminated. The targets for the analysis, therefore, are sentences in which the chief verb expresses a propositional attitude, such as 'Othello believes that Desdemona loves Cassio' (to use Russell's favourite example), where 'that Desdemona loves Cassio' seems to refer to a proposition. Russell's new analysis treats belief in this case as a four-place relation holding between Othello, Desdemona, love, and Cassio. The apparent reference to a proposition is thus eliminated, and only references to its constituents remain. This account of belief yields a correspondence theory of truth (replacing the earlier identity theory): the belief is true just in case there exists in the world a complex (or fact) consisting of Desdemona's loving Cassio.

Russell held this theory from 1910 to 1913, revising it several times in that short period to cope with difficulties.[34] The theory was never worked out in all requisite details: in *PM* Russell sketches a way in which higher order judgments involving quantifiers are to be based on elementary, atomic judgments, but no account of molecular judgments was ever suggested. The theory was abandoned in 1913 in the face of criticism from Wittgenstein, who was then Russell's student at Cambridge.

The exact nature of Wittgenstein's criticism is a matter of dispute. One interpretation[35] is that Wittgenstein pointed out that Russell's multiple relation was at odds with his theory of types. It is clear that, if the multiple relation theory is to provide a satisfactory account of propositions, the account provided must subject propositions (or whatever replaces them) to the restraints of ramified type theory. It is difficult to see how Russell's theory could do this because, in order for Othello to make the elementary judgement that Desdemona loves Cassio, it would be necessary for him to judge in advance that Desdemona, Cassio, and *loves* are of the right types and orders to form a proposition (or proposition-surrogate). But these judgments are necessarily higher-order judgments which cannot be presupposed by elementary ones – the Russellian theory of types and orders has to be built up from the bottom, not imposed from the top.

The theory of judgement as adumbrated in *Theory of Knowledge* [1913] was to be part of a much larger epistemological project. While

---

[34] It appears (in different forms) in POP, KAKD, *PM*, and *TK*. See Griffin [1985] for its evolution.

[35] See Sommerville [1981], and Griffin [1985]. For an alternative account, see Landini [1991].

working on the philosophy of mathematics, Russell had had little to say about epistemological matters. But the theory of descriptions made an important difference to the consequences that could be drawn from the principle of acquaintance, and once *Principia Mathematica* was finished Russell began to examine them. His first steps were taken in *Problems of Philosophy* [1912], a popular but in several respects important book,[36] and in 'Knowledge by Acquaintance and Knowledge by Description', which makes an important, and characteristically Russellian, distinction resulting from the theory of descriptions.

Theory of Knowledge was intended to be a large work in two parts. The first part would begin with the theory of acquaintance, on the basis of which the multiple relation theory of atomic judgements would be constructed. The multiple relation theory was required to observe the requirements of the principle of acquaintance, since all the terms of a multiple relation had to be items with which the believer was acquainted. The multiple relation theory would, in effect, give the theory of atomic propositions. The first part of the book would then conclude with an account of inference and molecular judgement. Of these three sections, only the first two were written and only the first of these was published in Russell's lifetime. They would, however, have formed only part of Russell's plan for the book. They were to be followed by a second part in which knowledge of the physical world, including the knowledge provided by physics, would be constructed on the basis of the epistemological doctrines of Part I.

By any standards, this was an ambitious project, but in 1913 and in Russell's hands, it was even more ambitious than might otherwise appear. Physics at that time was in a profound state of flux: Einstein was midway between the special and the general theories of relativity, quantum theory was yet in its infancy, and in 1913 itself Niels Bohr propounded an entirely new model of the atom. A science in such a state was too unstable a target for the sort of reconstruction Russell had in mind. But worse than this, Russell had become convinced (largely as a result of epistemological considerations such

---

[36] Not least because it anticipated by fifty years almost everything Gettier had to say about the definition of 'knowledge'. See Gettier [1963]. Russell came to think as a result that the concept of knowledge had been over-emphasized in philosophy – a conclusion to which many philosophers have now been driven by decades of doubtful success in solving the (misnamed) Gettier problem.

as the argument from illusion and its analogues) that we did not have acquaintance with material objects, but only with sense-data. In *Problems of Philosophy*, he had contented himself with establishing the existence of material objects by means of an argument to the best explanation, but he soon became disenchanted with this[37] and sought to demonstrate the existence of material objects by constructing them logically from sense-data.

It is important to realize that, for Russell, sense-data were physical objects (since they existed in physical space) but not material ones. His construction of material objects was therefore not, as many have supposed, a form of phenomenalism. Nor was it, since physical objects were *constructed* from sense-data, a form of representational realism. Moreover, because sense-data were physical, there were more of them than were actually given in acquaintance. (In fact Russell used 'sensibile' as the inclusive term, and 'sense-data' for those sensibilia with which someone was acquainted.) Admitting unsensed sensibilia certainly proved useful in the construction of enduring material objects, for it supplied the resources needed for their existence when no one was looking. None the less, there were many difficulties with the project; for example, difficulties about individuating sense-data, and about determining, in some non-question begging way, which sense-data belonged to which material object.

The most fundamental objections, however, are ones that are often overlooked. One of these is the argument by Dawes Hicks [1913] discussed in Demopoulos's paper in this volume. Another is set forth by Roderick Firth [1950], without particular reference to Russell. Since the construction of material objects was supposed to be logical, it required setting up a system of deductive arguments the premisses of which would be a set of statements about objects of acquaintance (sense-data) and the conclusion of which would be a statement that a material object had some property P. As Firth points out, no set of statements about sense-data could entail any such conclusion, because any such set would be logically consistent with the addition of further statements which would falsify the conclusion. It was impossible to specify in advance all such falsifying conditions and it

---

[37] Wittgenstein was an important, but often unacknowledged, influence here. See Miah [1987]. Here (and elsewhere), Wittgenstein's early deductivism was surely a mistake; Russell's initial philosophical instincts were better than those of his student.

was certainly impossible to exclude them all by appeal to further statements about sense data. To take a simple example, a set S of statements about red sense-data does not entail that some material object is red, simply because we could consistently add to S some statement about, say, abnormal lighting conditions which would be compatible with the object's not being red. Whatever inferential relation there may be between sense-datum statements and material object statements, it is not a deductive one, for deductive inferences are monotonic while the inference in this case is plainly not; that is, (using '$\rightarrow$' to represent the type of inference in question) $(S \,\&\, P) \rightarrow M$ may be a clearly unacceptable inference, even though $S \rightarrow M$ is clearly acceptable.

Wittgenstein's criticisms of the theory of judgement caused Russell to abandon *Theory of Knowledge*. He none the less preserved the material on acquaintance[38] in a series of papers in *The Monist*, and went on to sketch the construction of the external world in the Lowell Lectures delivered in Boston in 1914 and published as *Our Knowledge of the External World*.[39] He never published the chapters he had written on atomic judgements, and he never wrote the material he had planned on molecular judgement and inference.

Russell did not himself pursue the construction of the external world any further, though the project he outlined in *OKEW* inspired some of Carnap's early work (see Carnap [1928]). The outbreak of war put all of Russell's philosophical plans on hold. When he returned to philosophy in 1918, it was to give a series of popular lectures, 'The Philosophy of Logical Atomism', summarizing his position and outlining the problems it still faced. The problem of giving a satisfactory analysis of belief was foremost among them, but it was not until Russell was in jail that he had a chance to turn his attention to it.

In prison he completely revised his account of propositions, publishing his new theory shortly after his release in a major paper, 'On Propositions: What they are and how they Mean' (*Papers* 8,

---

[38] Apart, that is, from the chapter on acquaintance with logical items. Wittgenstein had convinced him that the logical constants were not constituents of propositions, which left him without a clear account of logical knowledge and thus of molecular judgment.

[39] At around the same time he published a very useful summary of his position, 'The Relation of Sense-Data to Physics' (*Papers* 8, pp. 5–26).

pp. 278–306). On the new theory, there are two types of propositions – word propositions and image propositions, of which the latter are the more fundamental – both alike are actual complex facts which have 'a certain analogy of structure ... with the fact which makes [them] true or false' (p. 297). The fact which makes one proposition true will make another, the negation of the first, false. A belief consists of a propositional content, consisting of words and/or images, accompanied by one of an appropriate range of 'feelings', e.g., memory, expectation, what Russell calls 'bare non-temporal assent', and possibly others (pp. 298–9).[40] 'On Propositions' marks a sharp turn towards naturalism in Russell's philosophy (see Grayling and Baldwin in this volume). It was driven, to some extent, by Russell's sympathy towards behaviourist methodology in psychology, though Russell's adherence to behaviourism was far from complete, as the central role the theory gives to images makes clear.

Underlying the new theory is a new philosophy of mind, neutral monism. Hitherto Russell had had little to say about the philosophy of mind, but up to this point he had been explicitly a dualist, maintaining that minds were simple ('pinpoint'), non-physical entities. But if minds were to contain complex image propositions and belief feelings, they could not be simple and so must be 'constructions'. They were not, however, constructed out of mental elements distinct from those from which material objects were constructed. Both minds and material objects were constructed out of some more fundamental 'neutral stuff' (see Tully in this volume). The theory was developed in *The Analysis of Mind* [1921], where the neutral elements were (rather misleadingly) called 'sensations' and in *The Analysis of Matter* [1927], where they were called 'events'.

Before he wrote 'On Propositions', Russell had always been reluctant to admit such items as propositional contents on the grounds that they would interpose a veil of representations between the mind and the external world, which would make knowledge of the latter

---

[40] The fullest account of belief on the new theory is given in Appendix C of *PM2*, where it can be seen as part of Russell's thoroughgoing efforts to extensionalize the work in its second edition. (See Linsky's paper in this volume.) This was part of the early Wittgenstein's legacy to Russell. The results were less than satisfying: large parts of arithmetic were lost to logicism. The theory of belief in Appendix C is an attempt to work out a theory along the lines hinted at in Wittgenstein [1922], 5.542; the theory of propositions in OP can be seen as an independent variant of Wittgenstein's picture theory.

impossible.[41] Before 1919, therefore, he had been a direct realist, maintaining that acquaintance gives us direct access to external objects (even if only to sensibilia, among particulars). His commitment to direct realism ended in 1919, but not his fears that scepticism might be the result. He ends 'On Propositions' with the following remark:

The further inquiry whether, if our definition of truth is correct, there is anything that can be known, is one that I cannot now undertake; but if the result of such an inquiry should prove adverse, I should not regard that as affording any theoretical objection to the proposed definition. (*Papers* 8, p. 306)

Russell says little about scepticism in *The Analysis of Mind*, though he did invent a new argument for it, from the possibility that the world sprang into existence five minutes ago with 'a population that "remembered" a wholly unreal past' (*AMi*, p. 159). This simple, by Russell's standards rather banal idea has achieved some currency.[42] Much more important, however, were the remarks on the subject in *The Analysis of Matter*, and these (predictably) have been largely ignored. In that book Russell explicitly breaks the traditional dependence of scepticism about the external world on a sharp distinction between a mental inner realm and an external physical one, by reconstruing scepticism as a boundary problem. An observer entirely confined in region *A* can only gain knowledge of events in a wholly distinct region *B* by means of the transmission of information (i.e., energy) across the boundary between *A* and *B*. Any two accounts of states of affairs in *B* which agree on all boundary conditions will be empirically indistinguishable to observers in *A*. Identifying the boundary with the surface of the observer's body then yields the traditional problem of scepticism about the external world, without the usual distinction between minds (which may be known) and bodies (which may not) (*AMa*, pp. 27–9).

Faced with this, Russell utilized an assumption of separable causal lines to link events in the two regions. On the assumption that

---

[41] See his famous remark in a letter to Frege that, unless Mont Blanc itself occurs in the proposition that Mont Blanc was more than 4,000 metres high, 'we get the conclusion that we know nothing at all about Mont Blanc' (letter of 12 December, 1904; published in Frege [1980], p. 169).

[42] Wittgenstein alludes to it in the *Philosophical Investigations* (Wittgenstein [1958], p. 221), though, of course, he does not mention where he got it from.

different effects have different causes, information could be obtained about what lay beyond the boundary. But this information was severely limited. In the case where the boundary is the surface of the observer's body, some events occurring within it are percepts. These are the only events to which we have direct cognitive access, and the only events of whose intrinsic properties we could have knowledge. Knowledge of events in the outside world has to be inferred by means of the different-effects-have-different-causes principle and is restricted to structural knowledge of their relations: from differences among our percepts we can infer differences in the external events causing them, but we can infer nothing as to the intrinsic nature of the external events.

This position – sometimes known as 'structural realism' – was the central doctrine of *The Analysis of Matter*. As soon as it was published, however, it came under devastating criticism from the mathematician M.H.A. Newman (Newman [1927]), who showed – in an argument that bears comparison to Hilary Putnam's much later model-theoretic argument (Putnam [1981]) – that percepts could be mapped onto any structure among purely physical events, provided there were enough of the latter (see Demopoulos, this volume). The collapse of structural realism left him with few defences against scepticism, but this was not his main problem, as Grayling points out below. He continued to believe that scepticism was a perfectly coherent position, but since it was one that no one actually held he did not think its refutation was the important task. As throughout his career, he continued to think that science yielded the best account of the external world that was available. The refutation of structural realism, however, left no possibility of connecting scientific results about the external world with empirical data by means of deductive logic alone.

Russell himself had partially anticipated Putnam's argument in his 1923 paper 'Vagueness' (*Papers* 9, pp. 147–54), where he argues that meaning is a one–many relation,[43] and that in consequence all language is vague. With the exception of his work on definite

---

43 This is Russell's way of putting it, though it is clear from context that what he means is what most contemporary philosophers would express by saying that *reference* is a one–many relation. Russell's paper was not widely discussed for many years after its publication but for the last twenty years it has been a standard point of departure for a rapidly expanding literature on the subject. Russell's central argument has been reinvented by Unger [1980] as 'The Problem of the Many', though without explicit acknowledgement to Russell.

descriptions, Russell had paid little attention to philosophical issues concerning language and, in particular, had tended to dismiss problems about meaning as of psychological rather than philosophical interest. This changed around 1918. Wittgenstein's influence is often held to be responsible for the change, but the real impetus came from Russell's new interest in psychology and the new account of propositions which arose from it. None the less, although Russell's interest in vagueness preceded his reading of Wittgenstein's *Tractatus*, his paper can be seen as an attack upon Tractarian aspirations to a logically perfect language.[44]

On linguistic matters in 'On Propositions' and even in *The Analysis of Mind*, there is much that looks back to the old empiricist tradition, rather than to behaviourism. The meaning of a word, for example, is mediated by an image that is causally associated with it; thus word propositions depend ultimately on image propositions. The image is an image of something, and what it is an image of is the meaning of the word (OP, *Papers* 8, pp. 290–2; *AMi*, pp. 191, 204–7). With sufficient flexibility in the application of 'image', this account might be salvageable, but Russell puts it beyond redemption by going on to claim that images resemble that of which they are the image (*Papers* 8, p. 292; *AMi*, p. 80). Such an account *might* work for medium-sized physical objects, but would seem to be wholly inapplicable to anything more abstract.

None the less, Russell's account does not succumb to the objection most commonly raised against it: that it confuses meaning with reference. Russell merely uses the word 'meaning', as was still quite common at the time he wrote, for what came to be called 'reference'. Contrary to widespread opinion, Russell does not identify understanding a word with knowing what it means (i.e., with knowing what is nowadays called its reference). On the contrary, he holds that one understands a word when one knows how to use it correctly (OP, *Papers* 8, p. 291; *AMi*, pp. 197–8).[45] The essential point is repeated

---

[44] Russell was no doubt aware of the aspirations before their attempted realization in the *Tractatus* and was rightly anticipating difficulties.

[45] It seems quite possible that *The Analysis of Mind* was the original source of Wittgenstein's view that meaning is use (Wittgenstein [1958], §43). Wittgenstein makes enough critical remarks about doctrines in *AMi* to establish that he read the book quite carefully. Curiously, Garth Hallett, in his otherwise apparently exhaustive survey of Wittgenstein's allusions to *AMi* in the *Philosophical Investigations* (Hallett, [1977]), fails to identify this one.

in *Inquiry into Meaning and Truth* (p. 26), but not elaborated on for largely methodological reasons: Russell held that in what he described as 'fundamental discussions of language' the social aspects of language should be ignored (*IMT*, p. 186). He was, as always, much more interested in a word's reference than in its correct use – the latter, he thought, had little to do with anything of philosophical substance.

The 'fundamental discussions' that Russell undertakes in *Inquiry* are largely epistemological in nature. He sets up a hierarchy of languages, at the bottom of which is what he calls the primary or object language, which consists entirely of words having, as Russell puts it, 'meaning in isolation' (*IMT*, p. 65). The meanings of such words are objects with which they have a learnt association, a relation of which Russell gives an essentially behaviourist account. One feature of such object words that Russell stresses repeatedly is that it is logically possible to learn them without presupposing that other words are already known. The primary language is thus restricted to expressing elementary states of affairs: logical constants, quantifiers, and semantic and syntactic expressions of all kinds all belong to higher levels of the language hierarchy.

Russell's language hierarchy is thus quite different from the much better known one developed by Tarski in order to avoid the semantic paradoxes, by ensuring that semantic predicates (such as the truth–predicate) for a language L were defined only in a language of higher order than L.[46] Long before Tarski, Russell had proposed a hierarchy of languages (*Papers* 9, pp. 111–12) as a means of avoiding Wittgenstein's doctrine of showing, according to which the syntax and semantics of a language (along with much else) could only be shown and not said. The hierarchy Russell sets out in the *Inquiry* is clearly designed to meet Wittgenstein's broad concerns rather than only Tarski's narrower ones. This is not to say, however, that Russell's primary language is identical (or intended to be identical) to the logically perfect language Wittgenstein gestures towards in the *Tractatus*: the two differ syntactically and semantically.

The most remarkable feature of the *Inquiry* is one that is hardly ever commented on, namely that it anticipates by a quarter of a

---

[46] Russell cites the need to avoid the semantic paradoxes as providing an 'overwhelming' reason for adopting a hierarchy of languages–though not necessarily exactly Tarski's hierarchy (*IMT*, p. 62).

century or more the idea, put into wide circulation by Michael Dummett (cf. especially Dummett [1978]), that the key difference between realists and anti-realists is that the former accept, while the latter do not, the law of excluded middle (*IMT*, chs. 20, 21). In this, of course, Russell takes his cue from the debate between Platonists and intuitionists in the philosophy of mathematics, but it was he, and not Dummett, who first had the idea of extending the debate about the consequences of accepting or rejecting the law of excluded middle beyond the philosophy of mathematics and applying it to contingent matters. Like Dummett, he considered as one of his examples propositions about the past for which no evidence whatsoever existed. Not surprisingly, however, he differed from Dummett in the conclusion he came to on these matters. Whereas Dummett was inclined to regard such propositions as lacking a truth-value, Russell maintained (though with a rather surprising tentativeness) that the law of excluded middle applied to them. This, he held, was due to 'our obstinate belief in a "real" world independent of our observation' (*IMT*, p. 277).

Two further points are worth noting in comparing Russell's version of the realism/anti-realism debate with the one started by Dummett. The first is that Russell's realist account is fully capable of meeting the so-called 'manifestation' constraint that Dummett imposes on meaning: namely, that the meaning of a sentence must be capable of being fully manifested by the observable use a speaker who grasps that meaning makes of the sentence. Dummett holds that unless this condition is met the meaning of sentences could never be taught or learnt, nor could the sentence be used for communication (cf., e.g., Dummett [1978], p. 216). Dummett's verificationism results from his imposing this requirement on whole sentences. Russell, however, avoids verificationism and meets the manifestation requirement at the level of words, relying upon the compositionality of meaning to ensure that syntactically correct sentences composed of meaningful words are significant. Despite Russell's references to images, he does give a fully manifestable account of word-meaning - for the meaning of a word is the object the word is used to refer to, not the image associated with it, and the correlation of word and object is a causal matter and thus, in principle, fully observable. (As far as words in the primary language are concerned their meanings are all learnable by ostension.) At the same time, as we have seen, a speaker's correct understanding of the word is manifested by his or her correct use of it.

Secondly, like most contemporary anti-realists, Russell distinguishes between a logical conception of truth, on which the law of excluded middle holds and which contemporary anti-realists hold to be incoherent, and an epistemological conception, on which it does not. Unlike the anti-realists, however, Russell treats both conceptions as versions of the correspondence theory of truth: in the epistemological conception, true propositions correspond to experiences; in the logical conception, they correspond to facts (*IMT*, pp. 289–90). Many contemporary anti-realists see their position as going hand-in-hand with a rejection of the correspondence theory of truth and cite the supposed difficulties of the correspondence theory in support of their anti-realism. Russell's position, unless it can be shown to be incoherent, suggests that the conventional alignment of anti-realists against the correspondence theory of truth needs to be reconsidered. The question of whether an anti-realist conception of truth escapes the difficulties (or can embrace the advantages) of the correspondence theory of truth is worth more serious consideration than it has been given.

Russell ends his discussion of realism and the law of excluded middle with the remark that 'empiricism, though not logically refutable, is in fact believed by no one' (*IMT*, p. 304). Russell had already come to exactly this conclusion in regard to solipsism and scepticism – remarks which are well-known and frequently quoted. But the same conclusion concerning empiricism is very largely ignored and comes as a surprise, since Russell is widely regarded as the last of the great British empiricists, fitting smoothly into, and continuing, the tradition of Locke, Berkeley, Hume, and Mill. Significantly, the first widely read English-language monograph on Russell was D.F. Pears's *Bertrand Russell and the British Tradition in Philosophy* (1967).[47] Pears certainly deserved credit for producing a seriously researched

---

[47] The lack of monographs on Russell's philosophy during his life is so extraordinary as to be worth commenting on. It is the more extraordinary because of the general view that Russell's useful contributions to philosophy had been made before 1920. By 1967, one could well conclude, an appraisal was long over-due. To my knowledge, there were before Pears only three English-language monographs on Russell's philosophy published after World War II: Fritz [1952], Gotlind [1952], and Aiken [1963], none of which achieved much currency. (Pre-war material is not significantly more extensive.)

book on Russell and thereby starting to fill an astonishingly large gap in the literature. None the less, his emphasis on 'the British tradition', though an accurate description of the book's content, is a serious distortion of Russell's thought.[48] Of all the major philosophers who had an important influence on Russell – Bradley, Kant, Leibniz, Plato, Spinoza, Frege, Wittgenstein – not one is an empiricist (and only one is British).[49] The formative influences on Russell's philosophy were outside the British tradition altogether. It is not helpful, therefore, that Pears (after a preliminary chapter on the concept of existence) starts his book with a chapter on Hume, and in the introduction had this to say about the relation of the two philosophers:

> What [Russell] did was to take over and strengthen the type of empiricism whose most distinguished exponent had been David Hume. The framework of Hume's system was psychological: the framework which Russell substituted for it was logical. (Pears [1967], p. 11)

Now certainly, of all the empiricists, it was Hume who Russell most admired (*HWP*, p. 685), but this was because Hume had followed the consequences of his empiricism wherever they led. As Russell goes on to say, in making empiricism consistent Hume had made it 'incredible'. He concluded that Hume 'represents ... a dead end: in his direction, it is impossible to go further' (*ibid.*).[50] Given this

---

[48] Some perceptive reviewers, such as Maurice Cranston in *The Sunday Times* (2 April 1967), pointed this out. See also Stuart Hampshire's comment to Brian Magee (Magee [1971], p. 46).

[49] British empiricists hardly fare better in the list of less important philosophical influences: McTaggart, James Ward, Peano, and Meinong. And when empiricists do begin to appear on the list, the most important were not British: Mach and James.

[50] It should be noted that Russell always saw Hume as a sceptic, an interpretation he absorbed from late nineteenth-century idealism, especially Green and Grose's edition of Hume's works (Hume [1874]) with its immensely long and highly critical introductions. The 'realist' interpretation of Hume, which began in the early twentieth century with Kemp Smith's [1905] articles in *Mind*, and achieved dominance in the latter part of the century with works such as Stroud [1977], was not taken seriously by Russell and might have caused his admiration to abate. Russell himself did not study Hume seriously until about 1911–12. Hume, following Green and Grose's devastating dismissal of him, did not figure significantly on the Cambridge Moral Sciences curriculum in Russell's day. One of Russell's first serious discussions of Hume was an attack on his view of universals ('On the Relations of Universals and Particulars' [1912] *Papers* 6, pp. 167–82). In *POP*, however, Russell takes a broadly Humean view of induction, though, significantly, in 'On the Notion of Cause' (*Papers* 6, pp. 193–210) Hume is not mentioned.

judgement, it would be natural to suppose that Russell was not tempted to try.

Pears' book was extremely influential, and its empiricist interpretation of Russell was enhanced by the books which immediately followed: Eames [1969] and Ayer [1971], both of which presented him firmly as an empiricist. Ayer wrote extensively (and sympathetically) about Russell through the 1970s and produced what is probably still the best short introduction to Russell's philosophy as a whole (Ayer [1972]).[51] Moreover, Ayer was himself an empiricist and was often thought, not least by Ayer himself, to have inherited Russell's mantle.

Eames, by contrast, is more a disinterested and not unsympathetic expositor of Russell's philosophy. None the less at the start of a chapter entitled 'Russell's Empiricism', she states that from *Problems of Philosophy* to *My Philosophical Development*, 'Russell maintains that all knowledge of what exists must come directly or indirectly from experience' (Eames, [1969], p. 90). For this judgment she cites (but does not quote) the following passage from *MPD* p. 132: 'I think that all knowledge as to what there is in the world, if it does not directly report facts known through perception or memory, must be inferred from premisses of which one, at least, in known by perception or memory'. If this makes a philosopher an empiricist, then only those who believe in the validity of an ontological argument of some kind would fail to qualify.

There was indeed a rather short time – around 1912 to 1914 – when Russell can be regarded as a fairly strict empiricist. This was the period, after writing *Problems of Philosophy*, when he thought he had not been sceptical enough in that work and desired to write a paper that his 'enemies would call "the bankruptcy of realism"'.[52] This was followed by the attempt to construct material objects out of sensibilia using deductive logic – an effort which his enemies might have called 'the overweening ambition of deductivism'. Even during this period, however, Russell should be regarded as an empiricist

---

[51] This is a slightly revised version of the Russell half of Ayer [1971]. A very different, and in my view rather better, short book on Russell which appeared at the about the same time was Watling [1970]. Watling's book deals with Russell's philosophy only up to 1914 and remains for that period the best short introduction available. Unfortunately, it never achieved the currency it deserved.

[52] Letter to Ottoline Morrell, 24 April 1912.

only in the qualified sense that Grayling explains in his paper in this volume. For example, even during this period most of the sensibilia out of which Russell proposed to construct material objects were not given in experience. Moreover, Russell continued to believe in universals as well as particulars – contrary to the usual empiricist view. Indeed, after he had presented his 1911 paper 'On the Relations of Universals and Particulars' to the Aristotelian Society, Bergson, who was present in the audience, remarked with surprise that Russell seemed to think it was the existence of particulars, rather than that of universals, that needed proving (*MPD*, p. 161). Indeed, by the time he wrote the *Inquiry*, Russell had come to think that particulars could be dispensed with. In that work he treated them as bundles of universals. Moreover, even in 1912–13, he admitted non-perceptual sources of synthetic knowledge (*POP*, ch. viii; *Papers* 7, pp. 97–101).

Russell remained, if not a card-carrying empiricist, at least a fellow-traveller through the 1920s. His inclination to behaviourism, though never unqualified, was often tempered, as we have seen, by elements drawn from a more traditional empiricism. During the same period, his pessimism grew about the possibility of showing how science could be established on the (augmented) empiricism he had hitherto been using. It was after the speedy collapse of his structural realism that he explicitly abandoned empiricism, in an important paper of 1936, 'The Limits of Empiricism' (*Papers* 10, pp. 314–28). In that paper, he clearly recognizes that empirical data together with the principles of deductive logic will be insufficient to produce any important knowledge of the external world and certainly insufficient to produce the kind of knowledge that science lays claim to. Chomsky [1971] is one of the few to recognize the importance of this project.

The task was thus to find what further principles – principles of non-demonstrative inference, as Russell came to call them – were required, in addition to those of deductive logic, in order to make scientific knowledge possible. This project lies in the background through much of the *Inquiry*, but it finally reaches centre stage in Russell's last great philosophical book, *Human Knowledge: Its Scope and Limits* (1948). In a valid deductive or demonstrative inference it is impossible for the premises to be true and the conclusion false. It follows that adding premises to a deductive inference will not affect the truth of the conclusion. Things are different in the case of non-deductive inferences: since the premises do not guarantee the conclusion, it is always possible that the addition of further premisses may show the conclusion to be false. This is evident in the case of inductive inferences where the premisses assert observed instances of a co-occurrence of two properties and the conclusion asserts that the two properties always occur together: the additional observation of a single case in which the properties do not co-occur is sufficient to refute the conclusion. None the less, the initial inference may have been perfectly good as an inductive inference: in the sense that the premisses gave good (but not conclusive) support to the conclusion.

Reasoning based on inferences of this non-demonstrative kind – known as defeasible reasoning to epistemologists and as non-monotonic reasoning to computer scientists – is now recognized to be an essential component in our ability to reason about empirical matters. Attempts to develop non-monotonic logics have been particularly important for scientists working in the area of artificial intelligence, where there is a need to make the rules of such a logic explicit in order to be able to program machines to reach conclusions about empirical data in something approximating the way humans do. Russell was not the first philosopher to suggest that inductive reasoning was not the only sort of non-demonstrative reasoning; he was, however, the first to suggest that simple enumerative inductive reasoning was not in fact a very good form of non-demonstrative reasoning, since it would lead from true premisses to false conclusions far more often than to true ones (*HK*, pp. 429–30). Seven years later, Nelson Goodman invented a cute example to illustrate the way in which bad inductive inferences could be endlessly generated from the same premisses as good ones and launched it as 'the new riddle of induction' (later generally known as 'Goodman's new riddle of induction') (cf. Goodman [1954]).[53]

None the less, the five postulates of non-demonstrative inference with which Russell ends *Human Knowledge* are not the sort of principles that would commend themselves to a contemporary logician

[53] Ironically, just as Russell came to this conclusion, Paul Edwards, normally a very sympathetic commentator on Russell, published his attack on Russell's 1912 view that induction stood in need of justification (Edwards [1949]). The fame of Edwards' article, which fitted neatly into an entire genre of ordinary language defences of induction of which Strawson [1952] is the *locus classicus*, entirely eclipsed Russell's new views on induction. Wesley Salmon [1974], [1975], seems to have been the first to recognize Russell's anticipation of Goodman. Johnsen [1979] gives a full account.

working on non-monotonic logic. It is not necessary to examine all five of them in detail, but a couple will illustrate their nature. The first two are as follows:

The postulate of quasi-permanence. Given any event *A*, it happens very frequently that, at any neighbouring time, there is at some neighbouring place an event very similar to *A*.

The postulate of separable causal lines. It is frequently possible to form a series of events such that, from one or two members of the series, something can be inferred as to all the other members. (*HK*, pp. 506–8)

These, of course, are not principles of inference at all, but statements about the world. There is a reason for this, and Russell might have served his cause better if he had been more explicit about it. His concern is not to establish transformation rules in a formal system, but to try to establish the conditions under which non-demonstrative inferences will be truth-conducive (rather than truth-preserving, as is the case with demonstrative inferences). Accordingly, what he gives as postulates of non-demonstrative inference are assumptions about what the world must be like if inductions satisfying certain conditions are to yield conclusions with a high degree of probability. Russell intends these postulates to be the minimum assumptions that are necessary if laws are to be inferred from collections of data. The postulates cannot be justified empirically, but have to be assumed prior to experience. None the less, they should not be thought of as having the status of a priori necessities. Russell approached them in the same manner in which he approached the choice of axioms for mathematical logic (cf Godwin and Irvine in this volume): they were to be justified in so far as they yield the right results. Their number, he thought, could well be reduced, and he did not insist on the exact form in which he stated them; the one firm claim he made on their behalf was that they were sufficient for both common sense and scientific knowledge of the external world. Like Russell, I should not want to defend the postulates in the exact form in which he gave them, any more than I should want to defend all his axioms in *Principia Mathematica*. But I do think that this, his last major philosophical project, like logicism, is one of enormous importance and that its neglect has been a misfortune in philosophy.

   Inevitably, the reputation of any writer as prolific as Russell is going to depend upon a good deal of canon-building, or more accurately, canon-pruning: there is just too much material for even the main works all to become canonical. Moreover, Russell's work did not progress towards some grand final system, which would have permitted a relatively comprehensive Whiggish distillation: there were just too many loose ends and false starts. Russell himself, of course, was outside the philosophy profession for most of his career and had little opportunity for building his own canon. In Russell's case an extraordinarily narrow canon was created. Chronologically it stretched from 'On Denoting' in 1905 to 'The Philosophy of Logical Atomism' in 1918 – thirteen years out of a career of more than five decades. But even within that limited period, not all works were included, indeed, the most important works were left out: *Principia* was widely referred to, but not much studied beyond the Introduction; *Theory of Knowledge* [1913], of course, remained completely unknown until shortly before its publication in 1983. In addition, most of the logic papers from the period, except to some degree 'Mathematical Logic as based on the Theory of Types' [1908], were also ignored, including even non-technical papers such as 'Analytic Realism' [1911] and 'The Philosophical Importance of Mathematical Logic' [1911]. The canonical emphasis was heavily on popular writings: *Problems of Philosophy* [1912] and 'Philosophy of Logic Atomism', a series of lectures delivered extempore before a largely non-philosophical audience in an attempt to alleviate Russell's financial difficulties during the war.[54] The lectures are an admirable summary of Russell's position at the time, and the outstanding problems it faced, but they hardly give a satisfactory idea of the depth and subtlety of his work. Among his papers 'On Denoting' and 'Knowledge by Acquaintance and Knowledge by Description' [1911] were given pride of place, the latter as a convenient bridge between Russell's philosophy of language and his epistemology. *Our Knowledge of the External World*, another series of lectures that Russell regarded as popular, was also included mainly so that its program of constructing material objects

---

[54] These lectures, although published in *The Monist* for 1918–19, were not very well known until the late 1940s when the University of Minnesota produced a mimeographed version of them. They entered the canon definitely in 1956 when Robert C. Marsh included them in *Logic and Knowledge*. Misfortune was compounded by the fact that they entered the canon long after Wittgenstein's version of logical atomism in the *Tractatus* had become well known. Philosophers ever since have had difficulty keeping the two doctrines distinct. Usually, some of Wittgenstein's views are attributed to Russell, who is then accused of inconsistency.

out of sense data could stand as a horrible example of the folly of attempting to construct what was not in need of construction.[55] The handful of works (and parts of works) just mentioned, might be called 'the narrow canon'. I should be surprised if they accounted for less than 70% of all citations of Russell's philosophical works by professional philosophers between 1945 and 1970.

The narrow canon can no doubt be justified by the demands of pedagogy: if Russell was to be taught at all, it could only be by means of a very restricted subset of his works. The narrow canon is, in fact, not a bad choice: it contains enough elementary material for an undergraduate course, with bits of tougher material for those going on to graduate school. Really difficult material was by and large excluded and claimed to be of mainly technical interest in logic. 'Mathematical Logic as Based on the Theory of Types' was not an invariable part of the canon, though its occasional inclusion did ensure that *some* material got covered that was both difficult and of more than purely logical interest. The only other really difficult matter that occurred as a central part of the narrow canon was the Gray's *Elegy* argument in 'On Denoting', and this was for a long time dismissed as based on a simple misuse of quotation marks. By such means, the narrow canon could be made safe for everyone. The trouble with the narrow canon was not so much what it included or excluded (about which there could be endless debates), but that it was adopted everywhere and material falling outside it became known by title only. Russell, whose contributions ranged far and wide and who after 1913 rarely had time for the systematic elaboration of philosophical theories, was especially ill-served by this combination of an extremely narrow canon almost universally adopted.

Since Russell's death, and the almost simultaneous opening of his Archives, the Russellian canon has begun to expand and diversify. This is especially true of his work, before 1914, where the publication of a great deal of previously unknown material has opened up entirely new areas for investigation (such as the substitutional theory) as well as leading philosophers to a reconsideration of some already very familiar works, such as *The Principles of Mathematics* and 'On

---

[55] This enterprise became so well-established a part of the canon that it became the subject of a joke in *Beyond the Fringe*. Significantly the three (out of eight) chapters of *OKEW* devoted to philosophical problems connected with the infinite were rarely referred to outside the specialist literature.

Denoting'. None the less, for the period after 1914, the lingering effects of the narrow canon are still felt. They can be readily observed in this volume in the relatively sketchy treatment of his later work, despite the best efforts of its editor! A great deal of Russell's work remains relatively unknown and is worthy of serious study. It may well turn out to contain significant contributions to contemporary debates. It would surely be easier to steal them from Russell than to reinvent them all over again.

REFERENCES

Aiken, Lillian W. [1963], *Bertrand Russell's Philosophy of Morals* (New York: Humanities Press).
Ayer, A.J. [1971], *Russell and Moore: The Analytical Heritage* (London: Macmillan).
Ayer, A.J. [1972], *Russell* (London: Fontana).
Baldwin, Thomas [1991], 'The Identity Theory of Truth', *Mind*, n.s. 100, pp. 35–52.
Blitz, David [1999], 'Russell and the Boer War: from Imperialist to Anti-imperialist', *Russell: The Journal of The Bertrand Russell Archives*, NS 19, pp. 117–42.
Broad, C.D. [1924], 'Critical and Speculative Philosophy', J.H. Muirhead (ed.), *Contemporary British Philosophy*, 2nd ser. (New York: Macmillan), pp. 77–100.
Carnap, Rudolf [1928], *The Logical Structure of the World*, transl. by Rolf George (London: Routledge and Kegan Paul, 1967).
Chomsky, Noam [1971], *Problems of Knowledge and Freedom* (London: Fontana).
Clark, Ronald William [1975], *The Life of Bertrand Russell* (London: Cape).
Dummett, Michael [1978], *Truth and Other Enigmas* (London: Duckworth).
Eames, Elizabeth Ramsden [1969] *Bertrand Russell's Theory of Knowledge*, (London: Allen and Unwin).
Eames, Elizabeth Ramsden [1989], *Bertrand Russell's Dialogue with his Contemporaries* (Carbondale: Southern Illinois University Press).
Edwards, Paul [1949], 'Russell's Doubts about Induction', *Mind*, 58. pp. 141–63.
Firth, Roderick [1950], 'Radical Empiricism and Perceptual Relativity', *The Philosophical Review*, 59, pp. 164–83, 319–31.
Frege, Gottlob [1879], *Begriffsschrift*, transl. by S. Bauer-Mengelberg, in J. van Heijenoort (ed.), *From Frege to Gödel. A Source Book in Mathematical Logic* (Cambridge, MA: Harvard University Press, 1967).

Frege, Gottlob [1884], *The Foundations of Arithmetic*, transl. by J.L. Austin (Oxford: Blackwell, 1959).

Frege, Gottlob [1892], 'On Sense and Reference' in Geach and Black.

Frege, Gottlob [1893], *Grundgesetze der Arithmetik*, 2 vols. (Jena: Pohle, 1893–1903).

Frege, Gottlob [1980], *Philosophical and Mathematical Correspondence*, ed. G. Gabriel *et al.* (Chicago: University of Chicago Press).

Fritz, Charles A. [1952], *Bertrand Russell's Construction of the External World* (London: Routledge and Kegan Paul).

Gettier, E.L. [1963], 'Is Justified True Belief Knowledge?', *Analysis*, 23, pp. 121–3.

Goodman, Nelson [1954], *Fact, Fiction and Forecast* (London: Athlone Press).

Gotlind, Erik J.A. [1962], *Bertrand Russell's Theories of Causation* (Uppsala: Almquist and Wiksell).

Greenspan, Louis [1978], *The Incompatible Prophecies: An Essay on Science and Liberty in the Political Writings of Bertrand Russell* (Oakville, Ont.: Mosaic).

Griffin, Nicholas [1984], 'Bertrand Russell's Crisis of Faith', in M. Moran and C. Spadoni, *Intellect and Social Conscience. Essays on Bertrand Russell's Early Work* (Hamilton, Ont.: McMaster University Library Press), pp. 101–22.

Griffin, Nicholas [1985], 'Russell's Multiple Relation Theory of Judgment', *Philosophical Studies*, 47, pp. 213–47.

Griffin, Nicholas [1991], *Russell's Idealist Apprenticeship* (Oxford: Clarendon Press).

Griffin, Nicholas [1996], 'Denoting Concepts in *The Principles of Mathematics*', Ray Monk and Anthony Palmer (eds.), *Bertrand Russell and the Origins of Analytical Philosophy* (Bristol: Thoemmes), pp. 23–64.

Hallett, Garth [1977], *A Companion to Wittgenstein's "Philosophical Investigations"* (Ithaca and London: Cornell University Press).

Hicks, G. Dawes [1913], 'Appearance and Real Existence', *Proceedings of the Aristotelian Society*, 14, pp. 1–48.

Hume, David [1874], *Hume's Philosophical Works*, ed. T.H. Green and T.H. Grose, 4 vols. (London: Longmans Green).

Jager, Ronald [1972], *The Development of Bertrand Russell's Philosophy* (London: Allen and Unwin).

Johnsen, Bredo [1979], 'Russell's New Riddle of Induction', *Philosophy*, 54, pp. 87–97.

Johnson, W.E. [1892], 'The Logical Calculus. I. General Principles', *Mind*, n.s. 1, pp. 3–30.

Kemp Smith, Norman [1905], 'The Naturalism of Hume', *Mind*, n.s. 14, pp. 149–73, 335–47.

Landini, Gregory [1991], 'A New Interpretation of Russell's Multiple Relation Theory of Judgment', *History and Philosophy of Logic*, 12, pp. 37–69.

Landini, Gregory [1998], *Russell's Hidden Substitutional Theory* (Oxford: Oxford University Press).

Levy, Paul [1979], *Moore: G.E. Moore and The Cambridge Apostles* (London: Weidenfeld and Nicolson).

Lewis, Albert and Nicholas Griffin [1990], 'Bertrand Russell's Mathematical Education', *Notes and Records of the Royal Society*, 44, pp. 51–71.

Magee, Brian [1971], *Modern British Philosophy* (Oxford: Oxford University Press, 1986).

Makin, Gideon [2000], *The Metaphysicians of Meaning. Russell and Frege on Sense and Denotation* (London: Routledge).

Miah, Sajahan [1987], 'The Emergence of Russell's Logical Construction of Physical Objects', *Russell*, 7, pp. 11–24.

Monk, Ray [1996], *Bertrand Russell: The Spirit of Solitude* (London: Cape).

Monk, Ray [2000], *Bertrand Russell: The Ghost of Madness* (London: Cape).

Moore, G.E. [1898], 'The Metaphysical Basis of Ethics', fellowship dissertation, (Moore Papers, Cambridge University Library, Add. Mss. A247).

Moore, G.E. [1899], 'The Nature of Judgment', *Mind*, n.s. 8, pp. 176–93; reprinted in Moore [1986], pp. 59–80.

Moore, G.E. [1903], *Principia Ethica*, rev. ed. by Thomas Baldwin (Cambridge: Cambridge University Press, 1993).

Moore, G.E. [1903a], 'Kant's Idealism', *Proceedings of the Aristotelian Society*, n.s. 4 (1903–04), pp. 127–40; reprinted in Moore [1986], pp. 233–246.

Moore, G.E. [1986], *G.E. Moore. The Early Essays*, ed. Tom Regan (Philadelphia: Temple University Press).

Nelson, J.O. [1967], 'Moore, George Edward', Paul Edwards (ed.), *The Encyclopedia of Philosophy* (New York: Macmillan, 1967), vol. 5, pp. 372–81.

Newman, M.H.A. [1928], 'Mr. Russell's "Causal Theory of Perception"', *Mind*, 37, pp. 137–48.

Pears, D.F. [1967], *Bertrand Russell and The British Tradition in Philosophy* (London: Collins).

Perkins, Ray [1994], 'Bertrand Russell and Preventative War', *Russell: The Journal of The Bertrand Russell Archives*, 14, pp. 135–53.

Putnam, Hilary [1981], *Reason, Truth and History* (Cambridge: Cambridge University Press).

Rempel, Richard A. [1979], 'From Imperialism to Free Trade: Couturat, Halévy and Russell's First Crusade', *Journal of the History of Ideas*, 39, pp. 423–43.

Russell, Bertrand [1896], *German Social Democracy* (London: Longmans, Green).

―――― [1911], 'The Philosophical Importance of Mathematical Logic', *Papers* 4, pp. 33–40.

―――― [1900], *A Critical Exposition of the Philosophy of Leibniz* (Cambridge: Cambridge University Press).

―――― [1911a], 'Analytic Realism', *Papers* 4, pp. 133–46.

―――― [1920], *The Practice and Theory of Bolshevism* (London: Allen and Unwin).

―――― [1923], *The ABC of Atoms* (London: Kegan Paul, Trench, Trubner).

―――― [1924], *Icarus, or the Future of Science* (London: Kegan Paul, Trench, Trubner).

―――― [1925], *The ABC of Relativity* (London: Kegan Paul, Trench, Trubner).

―――― [1926], *On Education* (London: Allen and Unwin).

―――― [1931], *The Scientific Outlook* (London: Allen and Unwin).

―――― [1934], *Freedom and Organization, 1814–1914* (London: Allen and Unwin).

―――― [1934], *The Scientific Outlook* (London: George Allen and Unwin).

―――― [1936], *Which Way to Peace?* (London: Michael Joseph).

―――― [1937], (ed. with Patricia Russell) *The Amberley Papers*, 2 vols. (London: Hogarth Press).

―――― [1938], *Power: A New Social Analysis* (London: George Allen and Unwin).

―――― [1944], 'My Mental Development', P.A. Schilpp (ed.), *The Philosophy of Bertrand Russell*, 2 vols. (New York: Harper and Row, 1963), vol. i, pp. 3–20.

―――― [1949], *Authority and the Individual* (London: George Allen and Unwin).

―――― [1992], *The Selected Letters of Bertrand Russell*, vol. 1, *The Private Years*, ed. Nicholas Griffin (London: Allen Lane).

―――― [2001], *The Selected Letters of Bertrand Russell*, vol. 2, *The Public Years*, ed. Nicholas Griffin with A.R. Miculan (London: Routledge).

Russell, Dora [1977–85], *The Tamarisk Tree*, 3 vols. (London: Virago).

Russell, Frank [1923], *My Life and Adventures* (London: Cassell).

Ryan, Alan [1988], *Bertrand Russell: A Political Life* (New York: Hill and Wang).

Salmon, Wesley C. [1974], 'Russell on Scientific Inference or Will the Real Deductivist Please Stand Up?', G. Nakhnikian (ed.), *Bertrand Russell's Philosophy* (London: Duckworth).

Salmon, Wesley C. [1975], 'Note on Russell's Anticipations', *Russell: The Journal of the Bertrand Russell Archives*, no. 17, p. 29.

Strawson, P.F. [1952], *An Introduction to Logical Theory* (London: Methuen).

Stroud, Barry [1977], *Hume* (London: Routledge and Kegan Paul).

Sommerville, Stephen [1981], 'Wittgenstein to Russell (July, 1913): "I am very sorry to hear that my objection paralyses you"', *Language, Logic and Philosophy: Proceedings of the 4th International Wittgenstein Symposium* (Vienna: Holder-Pichler-Tempsky), pp. 182–8.

Tait, Katherine [1975], *My Father Bertrand Russell* (London: Gollancz).

Unger, Peter [1980], 'The Problem of the Many', *Midwest Studies in Philosophy*, vol. 5, *Studies in Epistemology*, ed. by P.A. French *et al.* (Minneapolis: University of Minnesota Press), pp. 411–67.

Vellacott, Jo [1980], *Bertrand Russell and the Pacifists in the First World War* (New York: St. Martin's Press).

Watling, John [1970], *Bertrand Russell* (Edinburgh: Oliver and Boyd).

Weidlich, Thom [2000], *Appointment Denied* (Amherst: Prometheus Books).

Wittgenstein, Ludwig [1922], *Tractatus Logico-Philosophicus*, transl. by C.K. Ogden (London: Routledge and Kegan Paul).

Wittgenstein, Ludwig [1958], *Philosophical Investigations*, transl. by G.E.M. Anscombe (Oxford: Blackwell).

1 Mathematics in and behind Russell's Logicism, and Its Reception

Most of the interest in Russell's work in logic has lain in its philosophical consequences; however, the main thrust came from a mathematical aim, which is the concern of this article. Russell took over a logic of propositional and predicate calculi, added to it a logic of relations (predicates of more than one variable), and thought that "all" mathematics could be delivered from such resources, not merely the methods of reasoning required but also the objects. What is the prehistory of this 'logicism', as it has become known?[1] How much mathematics was captured by it? Which techniques were used to effect the construction? How was it received? Figure 1 gives a flow chart of the story.

I. THE FOUNDATIONS OF MATHEMATICAL ANALYSIS: CANTOR AND PEANO

The parent branch of mathematics was mathematical analysis, created by A.L. Cauchy (1789–1857) from the 1820s. The theory of limits was the underlying doctrine, upon which were constructed the theory of functions, the convergence of infinite series, and the differential and integral calculus. A main feature was to display proofs in full detail. The presence of logic was also raised, in that he considered

---

[1] Russell gave his position no particular name, but 'logistic' was used from 1904 to refer both to it and to the different one (explained below) held by Peano and his followers. 'Logicism' is due to Carnap 1929, 2–3, a book noted in §10; it also appeared, perhaps independently, in Fraenkel 1928 (title of the section on p. 244, explanation on p. 263). The word had taken a different meaning earlier, especially with Wilhelm Wundt, in the general context of phenomenology.

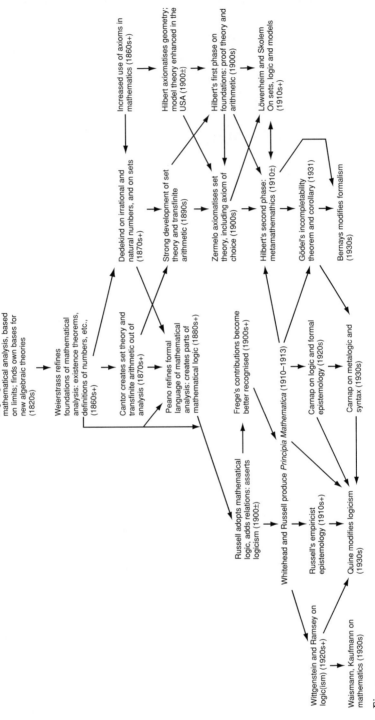

Cauchy reacts against Lagrange; created mathematical analysis, based on limits; finds own bases for new algebraic theories (1820s)

Weierstrass refines foundations of mathematical analysis: existence theorems, definitions of numbers, etc., (1860s+)

Cantor creates set theory and transfinite arithmetic out of analysis (1870s+)

Peano refines formal language of mathematical analysis: creates parts of mathematical logic (1880s+)

Frege's contributions become better recognised (1900s+)

Russell adopts mathematical logic, adds relations: asserts logicism (1900±)

Whitehead and Russell produce *Principia Mathematica* (1910–1913)

Russell's empiricist epistemology (1910s+)

Quine modifies logicism (1930s)

Wittgenstein and Ramsey on logic(ism) (1920s+)

Waismann, Kaufmann on mathematics (1930s)

Increased use of axioms in mathematics (1860s+)

Hilbert axiomatises geometry; model theory enhanced in the USA (1900±)

Hilbert's first phase on foundations: proof theory and arithmetic (1900s)

Löwenheim and Skolem On sets, logic and models (1910s+)

Dedekind on irrational and natural numbers, and on sets (1870s+)

Strong development of set theory and transfinite arithmetic (1890s)

Zermelo axiomatises set theory, including axiom of choice (1900s)

Hilbert's second phase: metamathemathics (1910±)

Gödel's incompletability theorem and corollary (1931)

Bernays modifies formalism (1930s)

Carnap on logic and formal epistemology (1920s)

Carnap on metalogic and syntax (1930s)

Fig. 1.

52

systematically the necessary and/or sufficient conditions for the truth of theorems; however, he did not treat logic explicitly.[2]

Gradually, this approach gained favour among those concerned with rigour in the subject, especially Karl Weierstrass (1815–1897) with his teaching from the late 1850s at Berlin University. He and his many followers prosecuted the same methodology and added further refinements to Cauchy's basic definitions (Dugac 1973). Another main imperative was to reduce the indefinables in the subject to the cardinal numbers, by introducing definitions of rational and especially irrational numbers: Weierstrass proffered one, but the best known theory was the 'cut' method (1872) of Richard Dedekind (1831–1916), in which real numbers were divided by a (arbitrary) cut C through their continuum at value V, and if there was neither a maximum rational value less than V nor a minimum one greater than V, then C was taken to define V as an irrational number.

Two further features formed the major influences upon Russell. One was the development of set theory by Georg Cantor (1845–1918) from the early 1870s, soon after he graduated from Berlin University. (To conform to Russell's usage, I shall speak of 'class' rather than 'set'; however, 'set theory' is now too durable to alter.) Inspired by a technical problem in mathematical analysis, Cantor offered a definition of irrational numbers and also developed the topology of classes of points. Distinguishing membership of an element to a class from the (im)proper inclusion of sub-classes, he worked out from the notion of the limit point of members of a class and the 'derived' set of such limit points and then considered its own derived class, and so on – transfinitely indeed, for it was in considering the infinitieth derived class and its own derived class(es) that he stumbled into the actual infinite in the first place. Then he defined various kinds of class in terms of relationships to its derived classes (closed, dense-itself, perfect, and so on). He secured the interest of Dedekind, who contributed some details.

Over the years, broader ambitions for mathematics emerged, with which Russell was to be more concerned. Cantor published details on the following features, especially in a long paper in two parts of 1895 and 1897 in *Mathematische Annalen* (Dauben 1979, esp.

---

[2] There are various studies of these developments; see especially Bottazzini 1986, Grattan-Guinness 1980, chs. 3–5; and 2000, chs. 2–5. On Cauchy's phase and its own background, see also Grattan-Guinness 1990, esp. chs. 3–4, 10–11.

Chapters 8–11):

1) the theory of transfinitely large ordinals and cardinals, which revolutionised understanding of the actual infinite;

2) different types of order of classes; the 'well order' of the positive cardinals was the premier form, but other important kinds included those of the negative cardinals, rational numbers, and real numbers, with the latter bearing upon the notion of continuity;

3) set theory as the basis of mathematics, starting out from the process of taking any class and abstracting from it the nature of its members to leave its 'order-type' and abstracting that to lay bare its cardinal;

4) methods of forming classes from given ones, especially 'covering', where the class of all sub-classes of any class S was formed and shown to have a cardinality greater than that of S.

The second main influence upon Russell came from Giuseppe Peano (1858–1932). Although not a student of Weierstrass, he was much impressed by the aspirations for rigour: one of his first publications was a collection of notes to a textbook on mathematical analysis of 1884 by his former teacher Angelo Genocchi, where he exposed various pertinent subtleties (counter-examples to apparently true theorems, and so on). By the end of the decade he was applying the method of axiomatisation to various branches of mathematics. He started in 1888 with the algebraic methods of the German mathematician Hermann Grassmann, in effect axiomatising the notion of a finite vector space. Then he switched next year to arithmetic, where he reduced the integers to three indefinables: initial ordinal, the successor operation, and proof by mathematical induction. (The year before Dedekind had offered a similar version, with a deeper understanding of induction.) Peano also soon treated geometry, where he found some of the axioms that Euclid had taken for granted; and in 1890 he tackled in *Mathematische Annalen* a problem concerning differential equations by means which used symbols as much as possible and reduced words to a remarkable minimum.

This procedure was to become Peano's principal contribution to raising the level of rigour in mathematics. Aware of the fine distinctions made by the Weierstrassians, he decided that ordinary language could be fatally ambiguous in such contexts; so he symbolised not only the mathematics involved but also the 'mathematical logic' (his name in this sense) and the attendant set theory, which he associated with predicates, or 'propositional functions'.

In the 1890s Peano formed a 'society of mathematicians' to help him develop this programme (Cassina 1961a, 1961b). A journal began in 1891; initially called *Rivista di matematica*, it was also known as *Revue des mathématiques* from its fifth volume (1895) and ended three volumes later in 1906. In 1895 he also began to edit a primer of logico-mathematical theories, called *Formulaire de mathématiques* in the first edition and continued in further and larger editions of 1897–9, 1901, 1902–3, and finally 1905–8. Dozens of colleagues and students contributed to these projects over the years; the three most prominent 'Peanists' (as they became known) were Cesari Burali-Forti (1861–1931), Mario Pieri (1860–1913), and Alessandro Padoa (1868–1937), who also published various papers of their own in other journals (Rodriguez-Consuegra 1991, Chapter 3). Burali-Forti also put out the first textbook on *Logica matematica* in 1894.

II. RUSSELL'S WAY INTO THE FOUNDATIONS OF MATHEMATICS

Also in 1894 Russell was studying philosophy at Cambridge having recently taken Part 1 of the mathematical Tripos. While the latter occupied a prominent place in the university, it was being roundly criticised as providing only a bunch of skills; for example, none of the developments described above were handled. Thus, young Russell's reaction in switching to philosophy for his Part 2 is symptomatic.

After graduation, Russell merged these two trainings in a search for a foundation of mathematics, starting with a Trinity College Fellowship dissertation in 1895, which he revised into the book *An Essay on the Foundations of Geometry* (1897). The philosophy brought to bear was the neo-Hegelian tradition, then dominant at Cambridge, which he used to combat empiricism. Dividing geometry into its 'projective' and 'metrical' parts by the criterion that the former involved only order but the latter also 'introduces the new idea of motion' in order to effect measurement, he construed each geometry as a construction made by us given space and time as an 'externality'. While exercised with skill, this philosophical basis did not yield results satisfactory for mathematics. It also brought him a rather bruising first contact with Henri Poincaré in the *Revue de méta-physique et de morale*; however, he also gained the support and friendship of Louis Couturat, who helped him over the editing of a French translation of the book, which appeared in 1901.

Couturat had become Cantor's main philosophical supporter in France (where the point set topology was already well received); the book *De l'infini mathématique* (1896) recounted in great detail all aspects of set theory. Russell had reviewed it for *Mind* in the following year (*Papers* 2, 59–67) and used some of its features in his next foundational studies. Cantor's emphasis on order-types was especially attractive, as he could connect them to different kinds of relation, which he had already deployed in his own book on geometry as a means of handling order and recognised as an important philosophical category.

The next major influences came from two Cambridge colleagues. Firstly, Russell's former tutor, Alfred North Whitehead (1861–1947), was working in applied mathematics, including Grassmann's methods, which he deployed in *A Treatise on Universal Algebra, with Applications* (1898). The title was unfortunate, for no unifying algebra was presented; various different ones were treated, including George Boole's algebra of logic. Following Grassmann, Whitehead called collections 'manifolds' and handled them in traditional terms of part–whole theory, not with Cantorian distinctions. Secondly, Russell's slightly younger colleague G.E. Moore (1873–1958) revolted against the neo-Hegelian tradition in 1899 and put forward a strongly realist alternative, which Russell soon adopted.

Armed with these new tools, between 1898 and 1900 Russell tried out books on the foundations of mathematics (Griffin 1991, esp. Chapter 7). Using methods of reasoning and proof including Boole's and Grassmann's algebras, he explored 'the fundamental conceptions, and the necessary postulates of mathematics', including Whitehead's treatment of finite cardinals as extensional manifolds (*Papers* 3, 155–305). These efforts were soon followed by a much longer account of arithmetic, continuous quantities, and aspects of mechanics, with order and series given great prominence and relations in close attendance (*Papers* 3, 9–180). Whitehead remained significant; and Cantor was much more evident than before, not only for order but also on continuity and the transfinite numbers. However, Peano was not yet in sight.

Then Russell and Whitehead went to Paris late in July 1900 for the International Congress of Philosophy. The visit turned out to be a crucial experience for both men.

III. FRIDAY 3 AUGUST 1900, AND RUSSELL'S CONCEPTION OF LOGICISM

The decisive event was a morning given over to the main Peanist quartet; Peano and Padoa were present in person, while organiser Couturat read contributions from Burali-Forti and Pieri. The magic moment came perhaps around 10.00. Peano had spoken about correct means of forming definitions in mathematical theories, and had emphasised the need for individuating the notion of 'the' when defining 'the class such that ...'. In the audience was the algebraic logician Ernst Schröder, who rejected the need for such fuss; in his post-Boolean theory classes were definable from nouns and adjectives alone, and treated part-whole style. However, Peano held his ground, and the young Russell must have realised that subtleties were involved, which he needed to learn.

In his autobiography, Russell tells us what happened next: he received all of Peano's publications at once in Paris 'and immediately read them all', and then wrote a book during the rest of the year [*Auto* 1, 145; also in *MPD*, 72–3]. Luckily, he kept its manuscript, so that we can see that the story is absurdly wrong; the writing and re-writing lasted until 1902 (Grattan-Guinness 1997). Firstly, he did not receive most of the Peanist writings for a month, during which time he proofread his book on Leibniz. When he read them he learned mathematical logic; but he also noted that the Peanists had not extended their logic to relations, so he produced the necessary theory and published it as a paper in 1901 in Peano's *Rivista* [*Papers* 3, 310–49, 618–27]. He used the main techniques, especially set theory rather than part-whole collections, to revise his treatment of continuous quantities (where he defined irrational numbers as classes of rational numbers less than some given one and without upper or lower limit), various aspects of set theory, order and relations, the differential and integral calculus, and metrical, descriptive, and projective geometry (with a quite different flavour from the earlier book). Four large Parts of a new book were produced; however, the foundations, especially the place of logic with relations and definitions of integers, were not formed.

The foundations came early in 1901. With his axiom system for arithmetic, Peano had reduced the foundations of the Weierstrassian edifice to three indefinables for the integers; Russell now proposed to define them nominally in terms of classes of similar classes, imitating Cantor's process of double abstraction but without its idealist character. Thus, 0 was the class containing the empty class, 1 the class of classes similar to that containing 0, 2 the class of classes similar to that containing 0 and 1, and so on, up to and including Cantor's transfinite numbers. A valuable feature was his clear distinction of 0, the empty class and literally nothing (*POM*, 75), a tri-distinction which had plagued mathematicians and philosophers for centuries, even Dedekind and Cantor. Ordinals were defined analogously as classes of well-ordered classes.

This use of set theory led Russell to reject the Peanist strategy of dividing logical notions from mathematical ones. Since set theoretical ones could appear under either heading, there was *no* dividing line: mathematical logic (with relations) alone could *subsume* all mathematical notions, objects as well as methods of reasoning. This was his logicism, which he articulated in the opening two parts of the new book during 1901 and 1902. More precisely, as he put it in the opening section there (*POM*, 3),

1. Pure Mathematics is the class of all propositions of the form '*p* implies *q*', where *p* and *q* are propositions each containing at least one or more variables, the same in the two propositions, and neither *p* nor *q* contains any constants except logical constants. And logical constants are all notions definable in terms of the following: Implication, the relation of a term to a class of which it is a member, the notion of *such that*, the notion of relation, and such further notions as may be involved in the general notion of propositions of the above form. In addition to these, mathematics *uses* a notion which is not a constituent of the propositions which it considers, namely the notion of truth.

The implicational form was crucial to his position; it may have come to him from noting the importance of necessary and sufficient conditions for the truth of theorems as assumed by and after Cauchy, and especially from considering his material already written on the hypothetical character of geometries given the legitimacy of non-Euclidean versions (p. 430). In addition, his policy of not restricting the range over which variables could range required that antecedent conditions be imposed on each occasion ('*p*' over propositions, '*x*' over real numbers, or whatever). The alliance with 'pure' mathematics was a non-standard use of the adjective.

IV. THE PRINCIPLES OF MATHEMATICS NEWLY FORMED

The first part of the new book began with the definition of logicism quoted above and continued with a detailed though largely non-symbolic account of mathematical logic including relations, classes and the mysteriousness of nothing, and quantification. The latter led Russell to focus on notions denoted by little words, especially the sextet '*all, every, any, a, some* and *the*' (*POM*, 72–3). Words such as 'proposition', 'propositional function', 'variable', 'term', 'entity' and 'concept' denoted *extra*-linguistic notions, while pieces of language indicating them included 'letter', 'symbol', 'sentence' and 'proper name' (Vuillemin 1968). A word 'indicated' a concept which (might) 'denote' a term (Richards 1980).

A related problem was denoting phrases (see Hylton in this volume). Mathematics motivated the need, for logicism required the expression of mathematical functions such as x^2, which Russell called 'denoting functions', in terms of propositional functions. It had been decreed by Cauchy and accepted by his successors that in mathematical analysis and connected topics functions should be single-valued so as to allow, for example, unique specification of the derivative (if it existed); hence Russell was concerned primarily with 'definite descriptions' (to use his own later name) rather than indefinite ones. However, he found no satisfactory theory to present in his book.

Still more serious was another matter. While developing set theory, Russell applied Cantor's power-class construction to the class of "all" classes and deployed identity as the attempted isomorphism. Thus, he came to consider the class C of all classes which do not belong to themselves, and Cantor's proof of the greater cardinality of the power-class now came out as the logical disaster that C belonged to itself *if and only if* it did not do so. This was a *double* contradiction, not just the single contradiction as used in, for example, proof by reduction to the absurd. He described 'the contradiction' in the new book (*POM*, Chapter 10); later he added an appendix proposing a solution, but he soon saw that it did not work.

The seventh and last part of the book was put together last, largely out of the manuscript finished shortly before Paris. Treating some aspects of dynamics, Russell drew upon the continuity of space as established in the treatment of irrational numbers, with geometry providing the environment; then within it 'rational Dynamics' was laid out as 'a branch of pure mathematics' in his implicational sense of the adjective, 'which introduces its subject-matter by definition, not by observation of the actual world' (p. 467). He then tried to lay out causal chains as implications, but assumed that 'from a sufficient [finite] number of events at a sufficient number of moments, one or more events at one or more moments can be inferred' (p. 478). One would have thought that an assiduous student of the finite and infinite would not commit such an elementary blunder. In any case, the link to logicism seems rather tenuous, especially to so-called 'pure' mathematics; for example, why dynamics but no statics, or mathematical physics?

In May 1902, Russell sent off his manuscript to Cambridge University Press for printing, under the title *The Principles of Mathematics*. In those happy days of book production he *then* (re-)read much of the pertinent literature, changing the text in places and adding most of the many footnotes. His reading included the main books of Gottlob Frege (1848–1925), from which he found that he had been anticipated in both his logicistic thesis (though asserted by Frege only of arithmetic and some mathematical analysis) and certain features of mathematical logic. So in June he wrote to Frege and told him of the paradox, which seemed to affect both of their systems. In reply Frege agreed, and attempted a repair which, like Russell's, failed. In later letters (published in Frege 1976, 217–51), they also discussed various features of logic, denoting and other topics, and Russell also revised on proof a few passages in his text. For example, a weak discussion of the little words 'a' and 'one' in arts. 128 and 132 was replaced by a warning that the distinction between '*one* involved in *one term* or *a class*' should not be confused with the cardinal number one.

Frege also sent to Russell several papers and booklets, and Russell wrote another appendix to his book in the autumn of 1902 reviewing Frege's achievements in some detail. However, as he stated very clearly and honestly in the preface to his book, 'If I should have become acquainted sooner with the work of Professor Frege, I should have owed a great deal to him, but as it is I arrived independently at many results which he had already established' (*POM*, xviii).

Table 1. Summary by Parts of Russell's *The principles of mathematics* (1903). The first column indicates the numbers of chapters and pages.

Part	Summary of main contents
1: 'The indefinables of mathematics'; 10, 105	'Definition of pure mathematics'; 'Symbolic logic', 'Implication and formal implication'; 'Proper names, adjectives and verbs', 'Denoting'; 'Classes', 'Propositional functions', 'The variable', 'Relations'; 'The contradiction'
2: 'Number'; 8, 43	Cardinals, definition and operations; 'Finite and infinite'; Peano axioms; Numbers as classes; 'Whole and part', 'Infinite wholes'; 'Ratios and fractions'
3: 'Quantity'; 5, 40	'The meaning of magnitude'; 'The range of quantity', numbers and measurement; 'Zero'; 'Infinite, the infinitesimal, and continuity'
4: 'Order'; 8, 58	Series, open and closed; 'Meaning of order', 'Asymmetrical relations', 'Difference of sense and of sign'; 'Progressions and ordinal numbers', 'Dedekind's theory of number'; 'Distance'
5: 'Infinity and continuity'; 12, 110	'Correlation of series'; real and irrational numbers, limits; continuity, Cantor's and ordinal; transfinite cardinals and ordinals; calculus; infinitesimals, infinite and the continuum
6: 'Space'; 9, 91	'Complex numbers'; geometries, projective, descriptive, metrical; Definitions of spaces; continuity, Kant; Philosophy of points
7: 'Matter and motion'; 7, 34	'Matter'; 'Motion', definition, absolute and relative, Newton's laws; 'Causality', 'Definition of dynamical world', 'Hertz's dynamics'
Appendix A: 23	Frege on logic and arithmetic
Appendix B: 6	'The doctrine of types'

Nevertheless, some commentators grossly exaggerate the extent of Frege's influence on Russell, both then and later.

The book finally appeared in May 1903. Table 1 summarises its main mathematical contents by part.

V. COLLABORATION BUT INDECISION

Russell had publicised his new interest with a lecture course at Trinity College in the winter of 1901–2. One of his select audience was Whitehead, who had begun to rework parts of Cantor's theory of infinitely large numbers in algebraic form. He published four papers in the *American Journal of Mathematics*, just over 100 pages in total length. He chose this venue because the editor of the journal was Frank Morley, a former fellow student at Trinity in the mid 1880s and by then professor at the Johns Hopkins University. Whitehead also found Russell's logicism a more clearly focused programme than his own investigations, and gradually their conversations turned into a formal collaboration to write a successor volume to *The Principles* (Lowe 1985). He gave courses himself at Cambridge on occasion; one is noted in §5. They were not often together, for he was living at Grantchester near Cambridge while in 1905 Russell built himself a house at Bagley Wood near Oxford.

Another student of his course, and undergraduate at the time, was Philip Jourdain (1879–1919). After graduation he worked on set theory and logic and launched an extensive correspondence with Russell (Grattan-Guinness 1977). In addition, the mathematician G.H. Hardy (1877–1947) was just starting his career with some papers in set theory and kept in quite close touch with Russell (Grattan-Guinness 1992); for example, he reviewed *The principles* perceptively, including pointing out the blunder in mechanics mentioned above (Hardy 1903). Finally, Moore was sympathetic to the enterprise; he moved to Edinburgh in 1904 for five years. Apart from Jourdain, all these associates were Apostles, like Russell himself.

As regards the technical work required, Russell gave much attention to the paradox, which he realised was very serious. He collected other paradoxes, or at least gave paradoxical status to certain results known previously (Garciadiego 1992). Two important ones concerned the largest possible infinite cardinal and ordinal numbers (N, say); assumption of either of their existences led to contradictions such as $N = N$ and $N > N$. Cantor had known both paradoxes but published neither; he told Jourdain that N belonged to the absolute infinite, *beyond* the actual infinite, and not a place for mankind to tread (Grattan-Guinness 1971, 115–16). Russell named the ordinal paradox after Burali-Forti, a name which has endured even though (Burali-Forti 1897) had not made such a claim but instead had exhibited an order-type for which trichotomy between ordinals did not apply. Curiously, around the same time, the American mathematician E.H. Moore (1862–1932), a close spectator of foundational studies, also found the result and took it to *be* a paradox; but he communicated it only in lectures at his University in Chicago and in a letter to Cantor (Garciadiego 1992, 205–6).

Russell also threw in the classical Greek paradox 'this proposition is false'; and new paradoxes of naming, such as 'the smallest number which cannot be defined in a finite number of syllables' and yet has just been done so. This kind, and also the visiting card paradox (a variant on the liar), were due to G.G. Berry (1867–1928), a junior librarian at the Bodleian Library and in Russell's opinion 'a man of very considerable ability in mathematical logic'. In France, Jules Richard also found a naming paradox.

Russell collected all these paradoxes partly to detect all leaks and also to help him find a solution for them, not just a means of avoiding them. From 1903 to 1907 he tried sorts of solutions which yet preserved the edifice of mathematics built upon his logic. He focused upon his own paradox, because it used only the notions of class and membership whereas the others required also other notions, such as arithmetic or naming. One main target was Cantor's power-class construction, since it led to perfectly legitimate theorems and yet could also be tweaked into generating his paradox. However, nothing worked to his satisfaction; some solutions let in paradoxes by another route, while others also excluded legitimate parts of mathematics and set theory.

Russell also worked on other mathematical aspects of logicism. An important issue arose in June 1904, from reading a draft of a treatment of arithmetic by Whitehead. Since cardinals were defined as classes of similar classes, then an infinite product of them was the cardinality of the class of all classes that could be formed by taking one member from each of the parent classes. However, what was the justification for forming classes in this way? Russell realised that it did not come proven from set theory, and so it had to be taken as an axiom. Because of the context in which it had arisen, he called it the 'multiplicative axiom'.

Soon afterwards in 1904 the German mathematician Ernst Zermelo, with Erhard Schmidt, saw that this kind of axiom was needed to prove Cantor's assertion that every class could be cast into good order, and published it in *Mathematische Annalen*; in a subsequent paper, he called it 'the axiom of choice'. A severe controversy rapidly developed among mathematicians and philosophers,

discussing the legitimacy of these axioms, seeking alternative equivalent forms (Russell's was one), detecting the theorems in which
they were used, and wondering if reproofs were possible without
their use (Moore 1982, Medvedev 1982). For Russell there was
an additional difficulty: mathematical logic worked with *finitely*
long propositions, whereas these axioms allowed an infinitude
of independent choices of members to be made from the given
classes.

Another possible and then actual axiom arose in 1904 when the
American mathematician and Christian believer Cassius J. Keyser
(1862–1947) argued that alleged proofs of the existence of an infinite
begged the issue at hand and that an axiom of infinity was needed.
Keyser had good mathematical points to make; but he also regarded
the actual infinite as beyond the grasp of humankind and in God's
realm, publishing one of his papers (1904) in *The Hibbert journal*, a
'quarterly review of religion, theology and philosophy'. In reply there
(Russell 1904) argued that no axiom was needed because proofs of
infinitude were available from mathematical induction. Keyser held
his ground in (1905); and by 1906 Russell agreed, although as a fervent
atheist he ignored the theological overlay but accepted that relying
upon mathematical induction begged the question.

This discussion overlapped with a second dispute with himself
and Couturat against Poincaré in 1905 and 1906 in the *Revue*. This
time *le maître* did not shine too strongly, construing a propositional
function as sometimes true and sometimes false. As well as the *état
primitif* of mathematical induction, the fruitfulness or *stérilité* of
mathematical logic was discussed and solutions to the paradoxes.

The search for a satisfactory theory of denoting functions continued, and in 1905 Russell laid down in *Mind* conditions for the
(non-)existence of definite descriptions in propositions such as 'the
present King of France is bald':[3] there should be one and only one
entity involved, and it should indeed have the property required;
otherwise the proposition was false, as in this example (OD). These
criteria were exactly those assumed by Cauchy and his successors
for a mathematical function to be single-valued; indeed, Peano had

---

[3] This Royal example was presumably not Russell's invention; he will have taken it
from a famous logic text of the 19th century (Whately 1829, and later editions).

stated them explicitly in that context in a survey (1897) of mathematical logic in the second edition of the *Formulaire*. This was one of the materials sent to Russell by Peano in 1900; presumably Russell had forgotten it when proposing his own criterion (in a more general setting, of course). His theory also exhibited parsimony: a denoting function was used in the *context* of a proposition asserting some property (such as baldness), not in isolation.

This theory helped Russell to formulate a new logical system, which he thought for much of 1905 and 1906 was the solution sought for the paradoxes. Abandoning variables completely, he worked just with individuals and propositions and truth-values of the latter. The main operation was 'substitution', in which given a proposition such as 'Socrates is a man' he substituted 'Plato' for 'Socrates' to obtain the (in the sense of a definite description) proposition 'Plato is a man'. With this machinery he laid out some basic axioms and was able to define numbers, even the initial transfinite ones, and solve paradoxes. He developed the theory far enough to submit a manuscript to the London Mathematical Society in April 1906, which was accepted for publication; however, he became dissatisfied with the theory and withdrew it. The difficulties included having enough equipment on board to furnish *all* the mathematics desired by logicism; offence to his realism by assuming 'objective falsehoods' to which false propositions corresponded; and above all susceptibility to a paradox, akin in structure to his own. However, the notion of substitution left important traces in his logic (see Landini in this volume).

Meanwhile, in addition to working on portions of Russell's second volume, Whitehead was thinking about geometry and space. In 1905 he published a long paper with the Royal Society on 'the material world' composed of points of space, instants of time, and particles of matter: using mathematical logic, especially of relations, he presented constructions, such as points being at a given location at different instants (Grattan-Guinness 2002). He also wrote two volumes on projective geometry (1906) and descriptive geometry (1907) for the new series of Cambridge Mathematical Tracts. Not for the first time, he also gave a lecture course on foundations at Cambridge in the spring of 1907; after the basic tools of mathematical logic, he treated the theory of definite descriptions, then the definitions of finite and transfinite numbers, and some material from the tracts and the recent paper. A more elaborate version of the latter was on his mind for the second volume, which now took on its definitive form.

VI. THE WRITING AND STRUCTURE OF
PRINCIPIA MATHEMATICA

During 1906 Russell abandoned the substitutional theory and went back to variables and propositional functions; soon he and Whitehead had a clear plan of the logical system to be used. The second volume of *The Principles* had been elevated to a separate book, called *Principia Mathematica*; a certain volume by their Trinity predecessor Isaac Newton may have suggested the title, and doubtless also Moore's *Principia Ethica* (1903). Russell placed a lengthy paper in the *American Journal of Mathematics*, summarising the system (MLT).

From early in 1907 until late in 1909, the two men worked out the contents. As with earlier drafts, one of them took initial responsibility for a Section or Part, and his material was read by the other. In the end, Russell actually wrote out the entire text, which was divided into three volumes. Several portions were read by another former student of Russell's course of 1901–2 (and an Apostle), Ralph Hawtrey (1879–1974), who had just begun a career in economics. In the end, the third volume was split into two, with Whitehead to write alone a fourth one on geometry.

They already had the agreement of Cambridge University Press to publish the book; but the printing costs simulated the infinite. So they applied for £300 from the Royal Society to help cover these costs and obtained £200 (Grattan-Guinness 1975b). The book appeared as three volumes in 1910 (750 copies, £1. 5s.), 1912, and 1913 (500 copies each, £1. 10s. and £1. 1s., respectively). The authors traversed their fiftieth and fortieth birthdays during this period.

Table 2 shows the content of *PM* by section. The text began with an account of the calculi of propositions and propositional functions with set theory, including the theory of definite descriptions and the definability of mathematical functions. Then they laid out in great detail the theory of both finite and transfinite numbers and their

Table 2. Summary by Sections of *Principia mathematica* (1910–1913). The numbers of pages are from the first edition. Volume 2 started at Section IIIA, volume 3 at Section VD. The titles of the Parts, and numbers of pages (omitting the short introductions) were: I. 'Mathematical logic' (251); II. 'Prolegomena to cardinal arithmetic' (322); III. 'Cardinal arithmetic' (296); IV. 'Relation-arithmatic' (210); V. 'Series, (490); VI. 'Quantity' (259).

Section; pages	(Short) 'Title' or Description: Other included topics
IA: *1–*5; 41	'Theory of deduction': Propositional calculus, axioms
IB: *9–*14; 65	'Theory of apparent variables': Predicate calculus, types, identity, definite descriptions
IC: *20–*25; 48	'Classes and relations': Basic calculi: empty, non-empty and universal
ID: *30–*38; 73	'Logic of relations': Referents and relata, Converse(s)
IE: *40–*43: 26	'Products of sums of classes': Relative product
IIA: *50–*56; 57	'Unit classes and couples': Diversity; cardinal 1 and ordinal 2
IIB: *60–*65; 33	'Sub-classes' and 'sub-relations': Membership, marking types
IIC: *70–*73; 63	'One-many, many-one, many-many relations': Similarity of classes
IID: *80–*88; 69	'Selections': Multiplicative axiom, existence of its class
IIE: *90–*97; 98	'Inductive relations': Ancestral, fields, 'posterity of a term'
IIIA: *100–*106; 63	'Definitions of cardinal numbers': Finite arithmetic, assignment to types
IIIB: *110–*117; 121	'Addition, multiplication and exponentiation' of finite cardinals: inequalities
IIIC: *118–*126; 112	'Finite and infinite': Inductive and reflexive cardinals, $\aleph_0$, axiom of infinity
IVA: *150–*155; 46	'Ordinal similarity': Small 'relation-numbers' assigned to types
IVB: *160–*166; 56	'Addition' and 'product' of relations: Adding a term to a relation, likeness
IVC: *170–*177; 71	'Multiplication and exponentiation of relations': Relations between sub-classes, laws of relation-arithmetic
IVD: *180–*186; 38	'Arithmetic of relation-numbers': Addition, products and powers

(*Cont.*)

Table 2. Continued

Section; pages	(Short) 'Title' or Description: Other included topics
VA: *200–*208; 99	'General theory of series': Generating relations, 'correlation of series'
VB: *210–*217; 103	'Sections, segments, stretches': Derived series, Dedekind continuity
VC: *230–*234; 58	'Convergence' and 'limits of functions': Continuity, oscillation
VD: *250–*259; 107	'Well-ordered series': Ordinals', their inequalities, well-ordering theorem
VE: *260–*265; 71	'Finite and infinite series and ordinals': 'Progressions', 'series of alpehs'
VF: *270–*276; 52	'Compact, rational and continuous series: Properties of sub-series
VIA: *300–*314; 105	'Generalisation of number': Negative integers, ratios, real numbers
IVB: *330–*337; 68	'Vector-families': 'Open families', vectors as directed magnitudes
IVC: *350–*359; 50	'Measurement': Coordinates, real numbers as measures
IVD: *370–*375; 35	'Cyclic families': Non-open families, such as angles

arithmetics, starting out from Russell's definitions of cardinals and ordinals, and went into continuity, real numbers and some point set topology.

VII. ON THE SCOPE AND AXIOMS OF
PRINCIPIA MATHEMATICA

The book started poorly, with a short introduction in which the authors failed to state logicism explicitly, though two pages on mathematical logic followed by two pages on mathematics conveys the purpose. More seriously, the form of logicism was unclear. It seems that an inferential version was intended, that from an asserted premise an asserted conclusion follows, in contrast to the implicational version of *The Principles* (§4); however, the first clear statement occurred at the start of the detailed presentation of the logic, where the propositional calculus was heralded as 'the first stage of the deduction of pure mathematics from its logical foundations' (*PM* vol. 1, 90) – 1903 all over again, with its non-standard use of the phrase 'pure mathematics'....

The scope of mathematics to be logicised was also not discussed. While they presented Cantorian mathematics in superb detail and laid the groundwork for several aspects of mathematical analysis and geometry, they made no effort to cover the rest of *The Principles*, never mind any mathematics beyond that – no calculus, no mechanics, and no explanation.

In the list of paradoxes they omitted that of the greatest cardinal (not for the first time); and also one due to the German philosopher Kurt Grelling, which had recently been published (Grelling and Nelson 1908). It concerned heterologicality, the property of a word that it does not possess the property which it expresses (for example, 'long' or 'French'); for 'heterological' itself scores if and only if it does not. The silence was curious, since this paradox is not obviously reducible to one on naming, and before *PM* appeared Grelling corresponded with Russell about translating *The Principles* into German (in the end not done) and about type theory.

The solution of the paradoxes was the theory of types, which is extraordinarily difficult to describe precisely (see Urquhart in this volume); for example, the versions in the 1908 paper and in *PM* do not quite coincide. It was based upon an assumption which had arisen during the recent dispute with Poincaré (§5), and called by Russell the 'vicious circle principle': that 'All that contains an apparent variable must not be one of possible values of that variable'. Upon this stricture, propositions were stratified by their truth level, so that, for example, the falsehood of 'all propositions are true' was located at the next level; hence, the liar and naming paradoxes were also evaded. Then propositional functions and relations were classified into 'orders' by the quantified variables which they contained, and then and within each order the remaining free variables specified a 'type'.[4] In terms of the associated classes (which were defined in terms of propositional functions, and also contextually, in line with parsimony), the initial type was the class of individuals; then came the types of classes of them, classes of classes of them, and so on infinitely (but not transfinitely) up. Similar stratifications were applied

---

[4] Most accounts of the theory lay orders within types; I take the reverse position since the vicious circle principle is a rule about the consequences of quantification, which determines orders. The difference is not major.

to ordered pairs, triples, ... of individuals. Any object in this hierarchy could only belong to an object in the immediately superior level; thus (non-)self membership was forbidden, and so Russell's and other paradoxes were avoided.

However, one of the few clarities of the theory were the sad effects upon mathematics. In particular, the stratification into types meant that integers, rational numbers, and irrational numbers were located in different types, and numbers defined by further processes such as iterated exponentiation were found still elsewhere. Thus, arithmetic was rendered impossible. So the authors proposed an 'axiom of reducibility', which asserted that to each propositional function in any type there corresponded a logically equivalent one free of quantifiers. This move allowed arithmetic and thereby more mathematics to be constructed in all types; however, they had no philosophical basis as support and knew it (*PM* vol. 1, 55–60, *12). Further, the restriction to indefinitely many types and orders meant that not only were the paradoxes of the greatest cardinal and ordinal avoided, their construction could not even advance as far as $\aleph_\omega$ or ω_ω (*PM* vol. 2, 183–4; vol. 3, 170, 173).

In addition (as it were), in order to meet mathematical needs, especially Cantor's theory of transfinite numbers, the axiom of infinity required an infinitude of *individuals* in the bottom type. Russell's realism now posed difficulties: individuals are hardly logical objects, but they could not be abstract structureless ones (Prior 1965). Thus, they had to be physical objects, thus making this axiom and thereby logicism *a posteriori* (Russell 1911, 23). To minimise damage he imposed a rule that whenever possible only one individual should be assumed (*PM* vol. 1, 325, *22·351), forming its own unit class '1 (Indiv)' (*PM* vol. 1, 345); but Whitehead had forgotten it when developing the theory of cardinals, and Russell had failed to notice. The error was spotted only when the second volume was in proof, and several months were lost while Whitehead effected a repair, adding a long 'Prefatory statement of symbolic conventions', which was intended to ensure that types sufficiently distant from the lonely type of one individual were always used in a given mathematical context (*PM* vol. 2, esp. pp. vii–xxxi: the means by which this security is achieved have always escaped me, I fear). This caused the two-year delay in appearance between the first two volumes.

The final troublesome axiom was that of choice. The authors did not explain their special difficulty over infinitary language as clearly as they might have done (*PM*, *88); on the other hand, they gave a fine account of current knowledge of the known forms and places of need.

VIII. THE (DE)(CON)STRUCTION OF SET THEORY, MATHEMATICAL ANALYSIS, AND GEOMETRY

The development of mathematics occupied the latter two volumes of *PM* (and the fourth, had it been finished). Volume two was divided into two Parts, starting with 'Cardinal arithmetic', including White-head's blunder just discussed but also many nice things. Two kinds of integer were defined: cardinal, where the classes similar to a given class α were chosen from all types; and 'homogeneous cardinal' (*PM*, *103), where the classes were restricted to that of α. Whitehead also devised a way of defining mutually disjoint classes in the same type from any two classes (*111), so that arithmetic could be developed with full generality.

The other part presented 'relation-arithmetic', a generalisation of Cantorian ordinals to relation-numbers, defined as the class of classes ordered by some particular order-type (*151–2). Conceived by Russell early in his Peanist phase and constituting his finest mathematical contribution to *PM*, it also drew on important contributions made by Hausdorff (Hausdorff 1906, 1907). The ordinals themselves were handled by means of Frege's ancestral relation (*90); transfinite cardinals and ordinals followed Cantor in the version using classes and relations elaborated in *The Principles* (*122, *263–5).

However, the low ordinals caused difficulties. o was the class containing the non-entity relation, and 2 that of ordered pairs (*56·03·02); but since apparently 'series must have more than one member if they have any members' (*PM* vol. 1, 375), the identity relation was symmetrical and so not serial, and therefore the relation-number 1 was not an ordinal. Instead, as 'the nearest possible approach' they offered '1_s' ('s' for 'series'?) as the class of symmetric relations (*153·01). They also defined '$\dot{2}$', the class of relations constituted by a single ordered pair (*56·01); and also a certain '$\dot{1}$', not defined formally but satisfying the property that $\dot{1} + \dot{1} = 2_r$ (where '+' denoted addition of ordinals) in order 'to minimize exceptions to the associative law of addition' (*PM* vol. 2, 467).

Continuity was presented in the Part on 'Series', spread between the second and third volumes. Series of terms were generated from ancestral and other relations, including a version of Dedekind's theory of irrational numbers and Cantor's theory of the principal order-types and also his theory of derived classes as the means to handle limiting points. Transfinite induction was also covered by means of 'the transfinite ancestral relation' (*257), where the 'transfinite posterity' of a relation was generated by a method imitating Cantor's principles (§1).

The Part on 'Quantity', mostly worked out by Whitehead, 'embraces the whole theory of ordinary [real-variable] mathematical analysis', as he told Russell on 12 October 1909. 'The comforting thing is that our previous ideas and notations are exactly adapted for the exposition', except for typing conventions and his restrictions imposed by the use of only one individual. It included a new theory of integers based upon counting members generated by a relation (*300). Rational numbers μ/ν were defined for co-prime cardinals μ and ν by the property that their corresponding relations R and S possessed at least one common pair of terms x and y such that $xR^\nu y . xS^\mu y$ (*303·01), where the superscripts indicated compounding a relation some cardinally finite number of times, a notion due to Russell (*301). 'The series of real numbers, positive and negative' was defined by specifying an 'irrational number' via a Dedekindian condition that a class of ratios had neither a maximum nor a minimum point with respect to the 'less than' relation (*310); the treatment of the arithmetic, however, was rather brief (*311–14). Negative numbers were furnished by relations converse to those for positive ones (*312·02·021), perhaps echoing Frege's strategy in his theory of real numbers (on which see Simons 1987).

A final Section on 'cyclic families' offered a treatment of vectors that could have more than one multiple: for example, angles between two straight lines, for which the ratio α/β could also be $(\alpha + 2N\pi)/\beta$ for any cardinal N. The theory was similar to defining complex numbers as ordered pairs, although they did not make the point. As for rigour, 'we have given proofs rather shortly in this Section', since many were 'perfectly straightforward, but tedious if written out at length' (PM vol. 3, 461) – a surprising statement in this of all works. Perhaps Whitehead was getting tired.

Then the third volume ended, rather jaggedly since many of the details were in place for the treatment of geometry on which Whitehead made much progress but never finished. However, its content can be inferred from various sources (Harrell 1988). The application to the Royal Society (§6) shows that four Sections were planned: projective and descriptive geometry, presumably drawing upon his two tracts of the mid 1900s; then metrical geometry, where much of the material on quantity and measurement was in place; and 'Constructions of space', probably following the scheme of his paper of 1905 (§5). The logic of relations was very prominent, using them up to six variables. But several branches of geometry were missing; in particular, since for some reason the differential and integral calculus had been omitted, there was no differential geometry.

IX. THE RECEPTION OF LOGIC(ISM) AND
EPISTEMOLOGY IN THE 1910S

In 1910 Whitehead moved to London; obtaining in 1912 a readership in applied mathematics at University College London, he moved two years later to a chair at Imperial College. His surviving letters to Russell up to 1914 suggest that he was making considerable progress in the fourth volume of PM; but during the Great War he abandoned it, seemingly in reaction to the loss of a son in 1918, and none of the manuscript survives. He had also worked much on mathematics education and relativity theory. In 1924 he removed to Harvard University, where he devoted himself to philosophy of a non-logicistic kind (Lowe 1990); however, he sketched out an alternative foundation for mathematical logic in a difficult paper in *Mind* (Whitehead 1934).

Russell was elected in 1910 to a lectureship at Trinity, in effect to replace Whitehead in the foundations of mathematics. He was visited in 1913 by Norbert Wiener (1894–1964), already a Ph.D. from Harvard University with a comparison between the logic of relations in *PM* with that of Schröder. Wiener showed that great similarity of structure held between the two theories; however, he was less sharp on some foundational issues, such as set theory with Russell and part-whole theory in Schröder, and Russell criticised him very severely. As a result Wiener never published a line of his thesis – a pity, as it is still the best study of its topic (Grattan-Guinness 1975a).

But he wrote some papers on set theory and logic in the 1910s, which were accepted via Hardy by the Cambridge Philosophical Society. The best known one, inspired by the axiom of reducibility, showed that ordered pairs, triples, ... could be defined in terms of classes alone (Wiener 1914).

Another foreigner arrived, from Manchester University: the Austrian engineer Ludwig Wittgenstein (1889–1951). His impact was quick and substantial. He and Russell created between them the truth-table method of representing the truth-values of propositions linked by logical connectives, and Russell used it in his Harvard course (Shosky 1997). Wittgenstein also criticised an epistemological book that Russell was preparing very seriously, so that Russell abandoned it. A little later, a French student arrived: Jean Nicod (1893–1924), who reduced the propositional calculus to axioms using a single axiom (Nicod 1917).

By contrast with Whitehead, Russell was drawing heavily on his logic (especially that of relations) and Moorean realism to develop an epistemology of the same reductionist style. The first detailed version was published in the book *Our Knowledge of the External World as a Field for Scientific Method in Philosophy* (1914), to quote for once its highly instructive full title; as with *The Principles*, the account given in his autobiography of dictating it in one go (*Auto* 1, 210; also Russell 1956, 195–6) is absurdly mistaken. This book was based on a course delivered in the spring of 1914 at Harvard University, where he also gave one on *PM*. On the staff there was Henry Maurice Sheffer (1882–1964), who had recently published a short paper (1913) on 'Boolean algebras' (the origin of this phrase), in which he showed that they could be defined solely from the operation 'not-and-not' (soon to be called the 'Sheffer stroke') and four laws, assuming two elements in the algebra.

Russell's Harvard courses excited interest in the United States, especially among former students of courses in logic taught by Josiah Royce around 1910. Wiener and Sheffer were among them; and so was C.I. Lewis. Understandably perturbed by the conflation of implication, inference, consequence, and entailment in *PM*, Lewis individuated the notion of 'strict implication' and hence gave the main impulse to the introduction of modal logics. A string of papers from the early 1910s led to a *Survey of Symbolic Logic* (1918), which is notable not only for the new logic but also for its detailed treatment of algebraic logic.[5]

In Britain, Jourdain gave Russell considerable publicity, including seven reviews of the volumes of *PM* in various places. In addition, he wrote several articles on Russell's logic and epistemology, especially in the American journal *The monist*. Most notable was a pair on 'The philosophy of Mr. B*rtr*nd R*ss*ll' (1911, 1916) in which he wrote very wittily on many aspects of Russell's concerns, such as denoting, identity, implication, and infinity, and showed how Lewis Carroll had anticipated many of them in the *Alice* books and elsewhere. Russell contributed some sections and recommended a book version to his new publisher, Allen and Unwin, which appeared in 1918. As European editor of *The monist*, Jourdain also placed there as articles some chapters from Russell's abandoned book; *Our knowledge* was the replacement volume, and it appeared in the United States with the publisher, Open Court.

Jourdain had also become deeply interested in the history of set theory and symbolic logic and published a series of lengthy articles on them in mathematical journals in the 1910s; Russell read drafts of the logic series.[6] But opinions on one aspect of the theory split them: Jourdain was obsessed with trying to prove the axiom of choice, and Russell was one of those who became tired of pointing out his mistakes.

Both Russell and Jourdain were pacifists, Russell aggressively so; as a result he spent four and a half months late in the War as a guest of His Majesty. This gave him leisure to write a popular *Introduction to mathematical philosophy*, which appeared in 1919 from Allen and Unwin. In prosodic vein he surveyed all the main features of the published *PM*: integers and mathematical induction, order relations, and ordinals, transfinite arithmetic, limits and continuity, and the axioms of choice and of infinity (with type theory and the paradoxes). But the treatment of logic was surprisingly modest; for example, the propositional calculus appeared only in Chapter 14. He introduced a 'non-formal principle of inference' to sanction substitution,

[5] Lewis tended to demote the significance of his partial anticipation by Hugh MacColl in the 1900s, when he had corresponded at length with Russell (Parry 1968). On MacColl's work and also his life, see Astroh (1999).

[6] A recent edition of Jourdain's articles and of the book version of R*ss*ll's philosophy may be found in Jourdain (1991).

regretting its absence from *PM* (*IMP*, 151). Some of the materials used by the prisoner were brought to him by Dorothy Wrinch (1894–1976), who also developed certain aspects of the arithmetic in *PM*, and of Russell's epistemology (Abir-Am 1987).

X. THE RECEPTION OF LOGIC(ISM) AND EPISTEMOLOGY IN THE 1920S

During the 1920s, Russellian logic, logicism, and epistemology became well known and received (not necessarily positively) by portions of the philosophical and mathematical communities. However, *PM* suffered the fate of being too close to each discipline to be properly understood by members of the other one. The story of the reception is far too complicated to be summarised here, *much richer* than the received wisdom of being just in competition with David Hilbert's formalism (so-called, but not by him...) and L.E.J. Brouwer's intuitionism. The full kaleidoscope is surveyed in some detail in Grattan-Guinness (2000), Chapters 8–9 and 11. Here are some general features; a few stray into the 1930s.

Interest was quite strong in German-speaking countries. Translations were made of the popular *Introduction* (1923), *The problems* (1926), *Our Knowledge* (1926), and the opening material of *PM* (1932). *PM* was quite widely used, especially for its logic but also for the logicism (especially the three dubious axioms) by various neo-Kantian mathematicians and philosophers (Ernst Cassirer and Otto Hölder stand out here) and by phenomenologists (especially Gerhard Stammler and Wilhelm Burkamp, both too little appreciated). When Polish logic began to emerge from the late 1910s, Russell's paradox was a central problem for Stanisław Leśniewski (1886–1939) and *PM* significant for Jan Łukasiewicz (1878–1956) (Wolenski 1989). In addition, Leon Chwistek (1884–1944) worked over *PM* in detail in the 1920s. The French set aside Poincaresque sneers: the *Introduction* was translated in 1928, and commentary came from neo-conventionalists of whom Emile Meyerson is the best known of that time and Albert Spaier also worth noting. The United States maintained an interest in *PM*, partly through the influence of Royce's students, and also of E.H. Moore and the strong development in the country of model theory: logicians of note from the late 1920s included Alonzo Church; and then W.V. Quine, the main follower of Russell's logic from his first book *A System of Logistic* (1934).[7]

Closer to Russell, a major event was the publication of Wittgenstein's *Tractatus* (1922), arranged by Wrinch and accepted on the guarantee that Russell agreed to write an introduction (§10). The second publication of the work was in a new book series in philosophy and psychology put out by Kegan, Paul, and edited by C.K. Ogden (1889–1957), another member of Russell's circle (Gordon 1990). It included an English translation which he and Wittgenstein had prepared out of a draft dictated to a stenographer in ten and a half hours by Frank Ramsey (1903–30) (Grattan-Guinness 1998).

Ramsey also helped Russell proof-read a second edition of *PM* (1925–7, for some reason the first two volumes re-set), and then he formulated his own version of logicism. Partly influenced by Wittgenstein (who rejected the position), Russell partly and Ramsey comprehensively gave logic and mathematics an extensional cast. Ramsey also divided the paradoxes into 'mathematical' ones such as Russell's own and those caused by too large numbers, and 'semantic' ones like the liar and naming. A distinction more or less made already by Chwistek, it has become standard, with the conclusion that semantic ones need not concern logicism.

Apart from the students mentioned in §9, and interested spectators such as Moore and Hardy, Cambridge did not encourage mathematical logic or logicism. But John Maynard Keynes was influenced by its reductionist character when he wrote his *A Treatise on Probability* (1921), and in the 1920s the young topologist Max Newman (1897–1984) examined some epistemological issues (see Demopoulos in this volume). Finally, W.W. Greg (1875–1959), who had been librarian at Trinity College when Russell and Whitehead were there, made an unusual application of the logic of relations in *The Calculus of Variants* (1927) to represent symbolically the relationships between an original text and later versions, thus helping to establish the notion of the copy-text.

During the 1930s Russell's main supporter in Britain was the philosopher Susan Stebbing (1885–1943) at the University of London; she publicised mathematical logic, especially in her *A Modern*

---

[7] The initial contact between Russell and Quine following this book is transcribed in Grattan-Guinness (2000), 586–92.

Introduction to Logic (1930, 1933). She was also a strong supporter of the Vienna Circle of philosophers,[8] upon several of whom Russell was already a major influence (Stadler 1997). Their leader, Moritz Schlick, admired the epistemology; Hans Hahn (1879–1934) drew upon Russell as a support for reductionism; Rudolf Carnap (1891–1970) followed the logic in detail in his *Abriss der Logistik* (1929), and many features of the epistemology in *Der logische Aufbau der Welt* (1928); and associated positivists such as Heinrich Behmann and Walter Dubislav discussed and popularised logicism.

Above all in the Circle, Kurt Gödel (1906–78) showed in a famous theorem of 1931 that in consistent logico-mathematical systems like that of *PM* true propositions could be stated but not proved, and in a corollary that consistency itself could be established only within a logically richer system (Gödel 1931). Thus, the desire of Whitehead and Russell that their system should 'embrace among its deductions all those propositions which we believe to be true and capable of deduction from logical premises alone' was untenable, and that it should 'lead to no contradiction' (*PM* vol. 1, 12–13) needed more demonstration than they had imagined.

XI. GÖDEL'S THEOREM AND COROLLARY, AND THE UNIVERSALITY OF RUSSELL'S LOGIC

Gödel's theorem and corollary were not the only consequences for logicism of his paper; he also showed that it was *centrally* important, and also very tricky, to distinguish logic from its metalogic. A great historical irony attends this feature.

In his *Tractatus*, Wittgenstein adopted a metaphysical monism, believing all physical and mental entities to be unified: 'There is no thinking, representing subject' (5.631) with his own private mental products (Cornish 1998, Chapter 5). Thus, 'What can be shown cannot be said', (the strangely minor clause 4.1212); for example, 'Every tautology itself shows that it is a tautology' (6.127). More generally,

---

[8] Another enthusiast for both logic and the Vienna Circle was the biologist J.H. Woodger (1894–1981), also in the University of London. In *The Axiomatic Method in Biology* (1937) he adapted *PM* to axiomatise biological theories such as gender and embryology. He had secured the interest of Carnap and also of Alfred Tarski, who contributed to the book a survey of properties of part–whole theory suitable for his purposes.

'The limits of my language marks the limits of my world' (5.6); thus 'The world and life are one' (5.621), so that 'Whereof one cannot speak, thereof must one be silent' (the famous closing clause 7, which followed a Viennese philosophical tradition).

Although Russell was a logical monist, taking bivalent logic as the only legitimate form, he reacted in his introduction against Wittgenstein's restrictions thus: 'every language has, as Mr. Wittgenstein says, a structure concerning which, *in the language*, nothing can be said, but that there may be another language dealing with the structure of the first language, and having itself a new structure, and that to this hierarchy of languages there may be no limit' (1922, xxii; *Papers* 9, 111–12). This was gold in his hands, but he never encashed it. For example, when he prepared the new material for the second edition of *PM*, only two and three years later, he made no use of it at all. When he arranged for a reprint of *The Principles* with Allen and Unwin in 1937, he wrote a long new introduction but ignored Gödel's theorem entirely.[9] Gödel's own contribution (1944) to the Schilpp volume on his philosophy came in too late for him to respond; but he may have been creating an opportunity for silence, since the article had politely exposed the importance of distinguishing logic from metalogic.

However, aware that colleagues were impressed by Gödel's theorem, Russell continued to try to understand its significance. In his philosophical autobiography, he even recalled his hierarchy of languages and claimed that it 'disposes of Wittgenstein's mysticism and, I think, also of the newer puzzles [*sic*] presented by Gödel' (*MPD*, 114), whereas of course the hierarchy is essential for *stating* the theorem in the first place. In 1963, his ninety-second year, he wrote to Leon Henkin that when *PM* was prepared 'we were indifferent to attempts to prove that our axioms could not lead to contradictions. In this, Gödel showed that we had been mistaken' (Grattan-Guinness 2000, 592–3; compare *Auto.* 3, p. 174). Two years later he prepared an addendum to his replies in the Schilpp volume, where he construed the theorem as asserting that 'in any [*sic*] symbolic logical language, there are propositions that can be stated, but cannot be either proved or disproved' (1971, xviii). Much sincere effort, but without success;

---

[9] Russell also misstated the logicist thesis here as 'mathematics and logic were identical' (*POM*, v), an error to be found also in *IMP*, 194 – and also in much Russell commentary.

the all-embracing conception of logic that he had learnt from his hero Peano stayed with him for ever.

BIBLIOGRAPHY

Abir-Am, P. 1987. 'Synergy or clash [...] the career of mathematical biologist Dorothy Wrinch', in Abir-Am and D. Outram (eds.), *Uneasy Careers and Intimate Lives*, New Brunswick and London (Rutgers UP), 239–80, 342–54.

Astroh, M. 1999. (Ed.), Special number on Hugh MacColl, *Nordic Journal of Philosophical Logic* 2, no. 4.

Bottazzini, U. 1986. *The Higher Calculus*, New York (Springer).

Burali-Forti, C. 1897. 'Una questione sui numeri transfiniti', *Rend. Circolo Mat. Palermo*, 11, 154–64. [English trans.: (van Heijenoort 1967), 104–111.]

Carnap, R. 1929. *Abriss der Logistik, mit besondere Berücksichtigung der Relationstheorie und ihre Anwendungen*, Vienna (Springer).

Cassina, U. 1961a. *Critica dei principî della matematica e questione di logica*, Rome (Cremonese).

Cassina, U. 1961b. *Dalle geometria egiziana all matematica moderna*, Rome (Cremonese).

Cornish, K. 1998. *The Jew of Linz*, London (Century).

Dauben, J.W. 1979. *Georg Cantor*, Cambridge, Mass. and London (Harvard University Press). [Repr. 1990, Princeton (Princeton University Press).]

Dugac, P. 1973. 'Eléments d'analyse de Karl Weierstrass', *Archive for history of exact sciences*, 10, 41–176.

Fraenkel, A. 1928. *Einleitung in der Mengenlehre* third edition, Berlin (Springer).

Frege, G. 1976. (Eds. H. Hermes and others), *Wissenschaftlicher Briefwechsel*, 1976, Hamburg (Meiner).

Garciadiego, A. 1992. *Bertrand Russell and the Origins of the Set-Theoretic 'Paradoxes'*, Basel (Birkhäuser).

Gödel, K. 1931. 'Über formal unentscheidbare Sätze der *Principia Mathematica* und verwandter Systeme', *Monats. Math. Physik* 38, 173–198. [English trans.: (van Heijenoort 1967), 596–616. Other transs. and reprs.]

Gödel, K. 1944. 'Russell's mathematical logic', in Schilpp 1944, 123–53. [Various reprs.]

Gordon, W.T. 1990. *C.K. Ogden: a Bio-Bibliographical Study*, Metuchen, New Jersey and London (Scarecrow).

Grattan-Guinness, I. 1971. 'The correspondence between Georg Cantor and Philip Jourdain', *Jhrb. Dtsch. Math.-Ver.*, 73, pt. 1, 111–30.

Grattan-Guinness, I. 1975a. 'Wiener on the logics of Russell and Schröder. An account of his doctoral thesis, and of his subsequent discussion of it with Russell', *Ann. of Sci.*, 32, 103–32.

Grattan-Guinness, I. 1975b. 'The Royal Society's financial support of the publication of *PM*', *Notes Rec. Roy. Soc. London* 30, 89–104.

Grattan-Guinness, I. 1977. *Dear Russell – Dear Jourdain. A Commentary on Russell's Logic, Based on His Correspondence with Philip Jourdain*, London (Duckworth) and New York (Columbia University Press).

Grattan-Guinness, I. 1980. (Ed.), *From the Calculus to Set Theory, 1630–1910: An Introductory History*, London (Duckworth).

Grattan-Guinness, I. 1990. *Convolutions in French Mathematics, 1800–1840. From the Calculus and Mechanics to Mathematical Analysis and Mathematical Physics*, 3 vols., Basel (Birkhäuser) and Berlin (Deutscher Verlag der Wissenschaften).

Grattan-Guinness, I. 1992. 'Russell and G.H. Hardy: a study of their relationship', *Russell*, n.s., 11, 165–79.

Grattan-Guinness, I. 1997. 'How did Russell write *The principles of mathematics* (1903)?', *Russell*, n.s. 16, 101–27.

Grattan-Guinness, I. 1998. 'New archival source on the publications of Wittgenstein's *Tractatus*', *Axiomathes*, 3 (1996), 435–6.

Grattan-Guinness, I. 2000. *The Search for Mathematical Roots, 1870–1940. Logics, Set Theories and the Foundations of Mathematics from Cantor through Russell to Gödel*, Princeton (Princeton University Press).

Grattan-Guinness, I. 2002. 'Algebras, projective geometry, mathematical logic, and constructing the world: intersections in the philosophy of mathematics of A.N. Whitehead', *Historia Mathematica*, 29, 427–462.

Grelling, K. and Nelson, L. 1908. 'Bemerkungen zu den Paradoxien von Russell und Burali-Forti' and three appendices, *Abh. Fries'schen Schule*, (2)2, 301–34. [Repr. in Nelson, *Beiträge zur Philosophie der Logik und Mathematik*, Frankfurt (Öffentliches Leben), 55–86.]

Griffin, N. 1991. *Russell's Idealist Apprenticeship*, Oxford (Clarendon Press).

Hardy, G.H. 1903. Review of Russell *The Principles*, *Times literary suppl.*, 263. [Repr. in *Collected papers*, vol. 7, 851–4. Anonymous.]

Harrell, M. 1988. 'Extension to geometry of *PM* and related systems II', *Russell* n.s. 8, 140–60.

Hausdorff, F. 1906, 1907. 'Untersuchungen über Ordnungstypen', *Ber. Verh. Königl. Sächs. Akad. Wiss. Leipzig* 58, 106–69; 59, 84–159.

Jourdain, P.E.B. 1991. (ed. I. Grattan-Guinness), *Selected Essays on the History of Set Theory and Logics* (1906–1918), Bologna (CLUEB).

Keyser, C.J. 1904. 'The axiom of infinity: a new supposition of thought', *Hibbert j.* 2, 532–53. [Repr. in *The Human Worth of Rigorous Thinking*, 1916, New York (Columbia University Press), ch. 7.]

Keyser, C.J. 1905. 'The axiom of infinity', *Hibbert j.* 3, 380–3.

Lowe, V. 1985, 1990. *Alfred North Whitehead. The Man and His work*, 2 vols. (vol. 2 ed. J.B. Schneewind), Baltimore (Johns Hopkins University Press).

Medvedev, F.A. 1982. *Rannyaya istoriya aksiomi vibora*, Moscow (Nauka).

Moore, G.H. 1982. *Zermelo's Axiom of Choice*, New York (Springer).

Nicod, J. 1917. 'A reduction in the number of primitive propositions of logic', *Proc. Cambridge Phil. Soc.* 19, 32–41.

Parry, W.T. 1968. 'The logic of C.I. Lewis', in P.A. Schilpp (ed.), *The Philosophy of C.I. Lewis*, La Salle, Ill. (Open Court), 15–54.

Peano, G. 1897. 'Logique mathématique', in *Formulaire de mathématique*, no. 1, 63 pp. [Repr. in *Opere scelte*, vol. 2, 218–87.]

Prior, A.N. 1965. 'Existence in Lesniewski and Russell', in J.N. Crossley and M.E. Dummett (eds.), *Formal systems and recursive functions*, Amsterdam (North-Holland), 149–55.

Richards, J. 1980. 'Propositional functions and Russell's philosophy of language, 1903–14', *The phil. forum*, 11, 315–39.

Rodriguez-Consuegra, F.A. 1991. *The Mathematical Philosophy of Bertrand Russell: Origins and Development*, Basel (Birkhäuser).

Russell, B.A.W. 1904. 'The axiom of infinity', *Hibbert j.* 2, 809–12. [Repr. in *Papers* 4, 475–8.]

Russell, B.A.W. 1911. 'Sur les axiomes de l'infini et du transfini', *C.r. seances Soc. Math. France*, no. 2, 22–35. [Repr. in *Bull. Soc. Math. France 39* (1911), 1967 reprint, 488–501; also in *Papers* 6, 398–408. English trans.: (Grattan-Guinness, 1977), 162–74; *Papers* 6, 41–53.]

Russell, B.A.W. 1922. 'Introduction', in Wittgenstein *Tractatus*, London (Kegan, Paul), 7–23. [Repr. in *Papers* 9, 96–112.]

Russell, B.A.W. 1956. *Portraits from Memory and Other Essays*, London (Allen and Unwin).

Russell, B.A.W. 1971. 'Addendum to' replies, in Schilpp 1944 4th ed., xvii–xx. [Written in 1965. Repr. in *Papers* 11, pp. 64–6].

Schilpp, P.A. 1944. (Ed.) *The Philosophy of Bertrand Russell₁*, New York (Tudor).

Sheffer, H. 1913. 'A set of five independent postulates for Boolean algebras', *Trans. American Math. Soc.*, 14, 481–8.

Shosky, J. 1997. 'Russell's use of truth tables', *Russell* n.s. 17, 11–26.

Simons, P.M. 1987. 'Frege's theory of real numbers', *Hist. Phil. Logic*, 8, 25–44.

Stadler, F. 1997. *Studien zum Wiener Kreis. Ursprung, Entwicklung und Wirkung des Logischen Empirismus im Kontext.* Frankfurt/Main (Suhrkamp).

van Heijenoort, J. 1967. [Ed.] *From Frege to Gödel. A source book in mathematical logic,* Cambridge, Mass. (Harvard University Press).

Vuillemin, J. 1968. *Leçons sur la première philosophie de Russell,* Paris (Colin).

Whately, R. 1829. *Elements of logic* third edition, London (Fellowes).

Whitehead, A.N. 1934. 'Indication, classes, number, validation', *Mind* n.s. *43,* 281–97, 543 [corrigenda]. [Repr. in [ed. D. Runes], *Essays in science and philosophy,* 1948, New York (Philosophical Library), 227–40; 1948, London (Rider), 313–30.]

Wiener, N. 1914. 'A simplification of the logic of relations', *Proc. Cambridge Phil. Soc.* 17, 387–90. [Repr. in *Works,* vol. 1, 29–32; also in van Heijenoort 1967, 224–7.]

Wittgenstein, Ludwig. 1922. *Tractatus Logico-Philosophicus,* trans. D.F. Pears and B.F. McGuinness. London: Routledge and Kegan Paul.

Wolenski, J. 1989. *Logic and Philosophy in the Lvov-Warsaw School,* Dordrecht (Kluwer).

2 Russell's Philosophical Background[1]

Like many important philosophers around the turn of the last century, Russell came to philosophy from mathematics. From 1890 to 1893 he studied for Part I of the Cambridge Mathematical Tripos, as the Cambridge examination was called. That he started with mathematics was inevitable: all Cambridge students had to take either classics or mathematics for Part I of their degree, and Russell was neither good at, nor interested in, classics. Nonetheless, mathematics recommended itself to Russell for other reasons than necessity.

He went up to Cambridge with the hope of discovering what, if anything, could be known with certainty and with the conviction that, if anything could, it would be found in mathematics. These high hopes were rapidly dashed by the realities of the Tripos. The fact that so many students with differing interests had to take mathematics at Cambridge meant that the mathematics taught was relatively elementary and strongly oriented to physical application and geometrical intuition. Not that the Mathematical Tripos was easy; study for it was a relentless grind of practice in the solution of mathematically trivial, but fiendishly complicated, applications problems. The great developments of nineteenth-century mathematics, for example, in analysis and non-Euclidean geometry, and all the developments mentioned by Grattan-Guinness in his paper in this volume, were entirely ignored as unsuitable to the needs of most students. In particular, the nineteenth-century drive towards rigour and unification in mathematics was absent from Cambridge, which, despite its continuing high reputation in

---

[1] The main themes of this paper are dealt with in much greater detail in Griffin [1991].

84

the subject, had become a mathematical backwater by the end of the century.[2]

To someone who entered the subject with Russell's hopes, this was the exact opposite of what he wanted. He graduated in 1893 (well-placed in a highly competitive exam) with a knowledge of fundamental mathematical concepts which might have passed muster in 1793. Though the Tripos required huge amounts of work in doing calculus examples, only the most rudimentary, intuitive understanding of the concept of a limit was demanded. Three years after graduation, Russell came upon De Morgan's already-dated and none too rigorous definition as if it were a revelation.[3] He was still miles away from anything like the $\epsilon - \delta$ approach of Weierstrass and Dedekind, which set contemporary standards of rigour in the area. By and large, Russell learnt what he knew of contemporary mathematics after he had finished his mathematics education at Cambridge.

In 1893, therefore, he was happy to abandon mathematics and take the second part of his Tripos in Moral Sciences. This seems always to have been his intention. His philosophical interests had begun with his attempts to combat his grandmother's religious views, and he later said that one of his reasons for turning to philosophy was his desire to know whether any comparable religious belief could be rationally defended (MPD, p. 11).

Before going up to Cambridge he had read a good deal of J.S. Mill and was generally sympathetic to his philosophy except, significantly, for Mill's inductive philosophy of mathematics. At Cambridge, however, he quickly came to think Mill, and the empiricism he represented, crude and old-fashioned. He was influenced in this by the German, predominantly Hegelian, idealism, which dominated British philosophy at the end of the nineteenth century. It was, however, easier to persuade him of the inadequacy of British empiricism than of the correctness of the German alternative: he said that he resisted Hegelianism until almost the end of his Moral Sciences year (MPD, p. 38). Given that he hoped philosophy might provide him

---

[2] The system was finally reformed in 1907, largely through the efforts of Russell's friend G.H. Hardy. For a scathing account of the old Tripos system see Forsyth, 1935. For further details on Russell's mathematical education, see Lewis and Griffin, 1990. The development of nineteenth-century mathematics is briefly described by Grattan-Guinness in this volume and more fully in his 2000.

[3] De Morgan, 1842, p. 27. See Griffin, 1991, pp. 237–8, for this episode.

with a rational justification for something akin to religious belief, it is perhaps surprising that he resisted so long, for Hegelianism had some standing in late Victorian Britain as a surrogate religion. It provided a response to the Victorian crisis of faith that was thought to be both reassuring and intellectually respectable.

Russell's conversion was brought about primarily by the writings of the Oxford philosopher, F.H. Bradley, the most important and original of the British idealists. Russell read Bradley's *Principles of Logic* [1883] at the beginning of his Moral Sciences year. He found there a swingeing attack on the principles of associationist psychology which undergirded the logic and epistemology of the British empiricists, together with a somewhat disjointed and highly idiosyncratic adumbration of logical principles, much of which remained in the background of Russell's thinking until near the end of the century. In 1893 Bradley published his *magnum opus, Appearance and Reality*. Significantly, Russell did not read this until August the following year, after his conversion to Hegelianism, though he certainly learnt beforehand of many of its main features.[4]

As its title suggests, *Appearance and Reality* is a work in two parts. The first is purely negative and seeks to show that most of what is ordinarily taken to be real – space and time, the self, matter, motion, change, and causation – is mere appearance. Bradley seeks to establish these claims by a series of *reductio ad absurdum* arguments, designed to show that each of these concepts leads to inescapable contradictions. A good deal of his case, however, depends upon a series of prior and now famous arguments which purport to show that the fundamental concept of a relation is incoherent. This shortens all subsequent arguments considerably, for Bradley has little trouble in showing that the concepts under attack depend in various essential ways on relations and thus suffer all the incoherence of the latter.

The second part of the book is concerned with reality, or the Absolute. Despite the fact that it is much longer than the first, there is really much less to say. The Absolute, more or less, is whatever cannot be dismissed as mere appearance, and that is not a great deal. Any

---

[4] Most subsequent philosophers have read the books in the reverse order, and have tended to see the *Logic*, somewhat slightingly, as setting the stage for *Appearance and Reality* (for an important exception see Manser, 1983). Russell never did. As we shall see, he tended to keep his distance from Bradleian metaphysics, while learning thoroughly the lessons of Bradley's *Logic*.

attempt to articulate its nature ends inevitably in failure, for thought is inherently relational and relations belong entirely to appearance. Bradley attempts to prove the Absolute's existence by means of an ontological argument[5] and attempts to characterize it in negative terms. Every effort to specify its positive nature, however, results in distortion and falsification. No thought of the Absolute is simply and exactly true. Little wonder, then, that Bradley describes *Appearance and Reality* as 'a sceptical study of first principles' (Bradley, 1893, p. xii).

This, of course, was not good news to someone who, like Russell, came to philosophy in the hope of discovering certain knowledge and an intellectually defensible surrogate for religious belief. It was here that the Cambridge Hegelian, J.M.E. McTaggart came to his rescue. In the same year that *Appearance and Reality* was published, McTaggart privately printed a small pamphlet, *A Further Determination of the Absolute*. In it he outlined a three-part program for idealism. The first task was to refute empiricism, and the second was to establish the existence of a non-material Absolute. McTaggart maintained that both these tasks had been accomplished by Bradley. The third part of the program, however, remained – to determine the nature of the Absolute. McTaggart was optimistic that this could be done and, with rare singleness of purpose, devoted his entire career to the task – his *magnum opus, The Nature of Existence* [1921] remained incomplete at his death. The key to his optimism lay in his refusal to follow Bradley in rejecting relations and his consequent espousal of a brand of idealistic pluralism. Russell made this project his own, but he found ways of carrying it out that were quite different from McTaggart's.

Russell's approach was entirely idiosyncratic: like McTaggart he embraced pluralism, like Bradley he rejected relations. Pluralism, he held, was essential, not only for knowledge, but even for thought. If a thing is simple, Russell said, 'it is unthinkable, since every object of thought can only be thought by means of some complexity' (*Papers*

---

[5] In May 1894 Russell came to think this argument, which he got from his teacher G.F. Stout, sound and he dated his conversion to neo-Hegelianism from this event (see Spadoni, 1976). It is important to realize that it was the existence of the Absolute, not God, that was supposedly proved by this argument. For Bradley, God was part of appearance, not reality. Nonetheless, God is accorded a grudging respect in *Appearance and Reality*, rather as if, had he tried harder, he might have been the Absolute.

2, p. 564). This widely held doctrine – often expressed by the slogan that thought is discursive – connects thought to pluralism, since the complexity required for thought implies a plurality of parts in the object of thought. The penalties for rejecting pluralism, therefore, were extreme – certainly more extreme than Russell was prepared to embrace. At the same time, however, he followed Bradley in rejecting relations, maintaining that putatively relational propositions could be shown to be equivalent to propositions which asserted intrinsic properties either of the terms of the original proposition or of the whole of which those terms were composed (*Papers* 2, p. 224).

This combination of views would seem to be inconsistent, and indeed the later Russell on many occasions maintained that it was just that, maintaining that the issue of monism vs. pluralism hangs on whether relations are rejected or accepted (cf. *POM*, p. 226; *HWP* pp. 703–4). The argument is simple: if pluralism is true, there must be a plurality of diverse items. Diversity is a relation, so pluralism requires relations. As a neo-Hegelian, however, Russell did not believe that diversity was itself a relation. He thought that any genuine relation would involve unity-in-diversity and thus that unity and diversity themselves cannot be genuine relations (*EFG*, p. 198). Elsewhere, I have called them 'proto-relations', since they are presupposed in all relations (Griffin, 1991, p. 185). Thus, Russell espoused a relationless pluralism. Only so, he thought, could knowledge be rendered possible in the aftermath of Bradley.

Unlike McTaggart, however, Russell did not propose to tackle the Absolute head-on, starting with metaphysics and moving on, when metaphysical issues were settled, to establish the basic postulates of the various sciences in conformity with metaphysical principle. Nor did he begin where empiricists did, with a survey of supposedly hard empirical data; nor again with our ordinary, common-sense beliefs about the world. Instead, he began, as it were, in the middle, with particular scientific theories. The deliverances of the special sciences, Russell held, were the most reliable results available to us about the nature of the world. The empirical data on its own was too fragmentary to yield much information about the world. Metaphysical principle and, even worse, common sense (the metaphysics of the stone age, in Russell's view) were too remote from the empirical data and too dependent upon human prejudice to be reliable. As a neo-Hegelian, as throughout his career, Russell thought that science was more likely to be right about the world than either common sense or philosophy. To start from metaphysical first principles would likely yield a system, such as Hegel's, embarrassingly at variance with the known facts. To start with nothing more than hard data would result in the sterile scepticism which had engulfed empiricism. In choosing his starting place, Russell was probably influenced by another Cambridge philosopher, his teacher James Ward, another pluralist who chose to work towards a metaphysical synthesis from a scientific starting point.

Russell's plans were nothing if not ambitious. He intended to re-do Hegel's encyclopaedia, this time getting the science right. He planned to work his way through the special sciences, starting with geometry, the subject of his Trinity fellowship dissertation. The results there were published as *An Essay on the Foundations of Geometry* in 1897. In that year, he drew up plans for a book on physics organized along very similar lines: historical chapters on the development of physics and the philosophy of physics were to be followed by Russell's own reconstruction of the science (*Papers* 2, p. 84). Several preparatory notes for this work have survived, but it seems likely that much material has been lost. At this time, Russell also turned his attention to arithmetic and the concept of measurement – although, in that field, it was some while before a clear line of thought emerged. And there were hints, also, of a treatment of psychology that was yet to be embarked upon.

The extent to which any neo-Hegelian doctrine harks back to Hegel is always doubtful. Hegel was little studied by the British Hegelians, with the exception of McTaggart, whose views (so C.D. Broad famously said) made orthodox Hegelians blush all over. Russell himself did not actually read Hegel until towards the end of his idealist period. He did, however, read Kant who had an important and easily discernible effect upon his work. Like Kant, Russell held that each of the special sciences contained a priori as well as empirical elements. In each science, the a priori component was to be isolated by a means of a two-stroke transcendental argument, which Russell describes in general terms as follows:

We may start from the existence of our science as a fact, and analyse the reasoning employed with a view to discovering the fundamental postulate on which its logical possibility depends: in this case, the postulate, and all which follows from it alone, will be a priori. *Or* we may accept the existence of the subject-matter of our science as our basis of fact, and deduce dogmatically whatever principles we can from the essential nature of this subject matter. In this latter case, however, it is not the whole empirical nature of the subject-matter, as revealed by the subsequent researches of our science, which forms our ground; for if it were, the whole science would, of course, be a priori. Rather it is that element, in the subject matter, which makes *possible* the branch of experience dealt with by the science in question.[6]

This two-part Kantian treatment is the precursor of Russell's later method of analysis and synthesis, described by Hager later in this volume.

Like all transcendental arguments, Russell's were intended to establish the necessary conditions for the possibility of certain kinds of experience or cognitive activity. As we have seen, Russell believed that thought itself was only possible if there were a plurality of objects of thought. The special sciences, however, dealt with more restricted types of experience, each of which had certain a priori conditions. For example, Russell held that for a plurality of diverse objects of thought to be presented simultaneously to the mind a form of externality was necessary. He argued in *An Essay on the Foundations of Geometry* that this form of externality was the subject matter of projective geometry, which deals with those properties of geometrical objects that are invariant under projection. Quantitative properties are not thus invariant and form no part of projective geometry, which is a purely qualitative and, in Russell's view, wholly a priori science. Quantitative properties appear first in metrical geometry. Russell argued that measurement of any kind depended upon spatial measurement, and spatial measurement depended for its possibility upon the existence of a space of constant curvature. The study of such spaces was the task of what Russell called general metrical geometry. General metrical geometry is also wholly a priori, but in a weaker sense than projective geometry because the type of experience which depends upon its object of study is narrower: a projective space was necessary for the simultaneous apprehension of diverse

---

[6] *Papers* I, pp. 291–2. The passage was incorporated into *EFG*, §7. Russell attributes both methods to Kant: the former to the *Prolegomena*, and the latter to the *Critique of Pure Reason*. The former is known as the 'analytic' or 'regressive' method and the latter the 'synthetic' or 'progressive' method. See Kemp Smith, 1918, pp. 44–50, for further discussion.

objects, while a space of constant curvature was necessary only if such objects were to admit of measurement. Any particular such space had, of course, a particular degree of curvature, which might be negative, positive, or zero, and this would be subject to empirical determination. Thus, the particular metrical geometries (those of positive, negative, or zero curvature) would involve empirical elements in addition to the a priori component supplied for all of them by general metrical geometry. Empirical observation revealed that the curvature of actual physical space was close to zero, i.e., that physical space was approximately Euclidean. That it was exactly zero, however, could never be established owing to the limits of observational accuracy.

A simple, but natural, way of regarding Russell's early idealist work on geometry is to see it as an attempt to bring Kant up to date. Kant (notoriously) had argued for the synthetic apriority of Euclidean geometry at the very time that non-Euclidean metrical geometries were being shown to be possible. Russell allowed explicitly both for these new developments and for differing degrees of apriority. The result was both scientifically more sophisticated and epistemologically more nuanced than Kant. He also brought a much greater degree of rigour to the argument than Kant mustered, though still considerably less than was then available (as Poincaré 1899 and several subsequent writers have complained.)

It would be a mistake, however, to think of Russell's enterprise in the *Essay* as just an enormous elaboration of Kant's project. There was one vital respect in which Russell's transcendental arguments were different from Kant's. Kant's form of externality was supplied by the mind; Russell's was, he hoped, entirely independent of the minds to which external objects were presented. Although Russell was an idealist, he was in no way a subjective idealist and rejected entirely the subjectivity of space. For Russell, the form of externality was an abstract structure necessarily presupposed by our ability to experience a plurality of things simultaneously. If one imagines these things as items for sale in a store, then Russell's form of externality resembles the store's display rack rather than the shopper's visual field.

Russell applies the two parts of his transcendental argument together, so that the whole treatment is supposedly self-correcting. Thus, the analysis of experience reveals the necessity of the form of externality, while the analysis of projective geometry reveals that it studies a structure with the same properties as the form of externality. The procedure is best illustrated, however, by the example of metrical geometry, where Russell's use of the technique is clearer and the geometrical principles involved are better-known. In the first move, various metrical geometries are analysed to determine the basic postulates common to all of them. These, on Russell's account, are the axiom of free mobility or congruence (figures may be moved freely through space without deformation), the axiom of dimensions (space has a finite, integral number of dimensions), and the axiom of the straight line (two points uniquely determine a distance). These three axioms constitute general metrical geometry. This result is then confirmed by the second stage of the argument, a transcendental deduction which starts from the (experiential) subject matter of metrical geometry, namely the form of externality insofar as it admits of measurement, and ends with the necessary conditions for such a form. Obviously, both parts of the investigation, the analytic investigation from geometry to its axioms and the synthetic investigation from the form of externality to the postulates which make it possible, are supposed to end in the same place, namely with the three axioms of general metrical geometry.

Russell makes brave efforts to maintain that this is so, but this requires rather strong assumptions. It must be supposed, (1) that there is a postulate, P, which is necessary for any possible theory about the subject matter, S, and (2), that if S can be experienced, then there is some possible theory about it. (1) looks implausible given the radically different types of theory that might be constructed to handle any given subject matter. Moreover, it would seem impossible in principle to prove that P was necessary for *every possible* theory about the subject matter. (2) will hold if the possibility of experiencing S implies the possibility of articulating propositions (or making judgments) about it, *and* if every such set of propositions closed under implication constitutes a theory about S. The first of these conditions might be granted: it amounts to the claim that experience is not ineffable. But the second condition imposes such weak constraints on what counts as a theory that (1) can no longer be satisfied. For if any deductively closed set of propositions about S is to count as a theory about S, then there will in general be no postulate P

necessary for every such theory. In particular, there can be no such necessary postulate P wherever two deductively closed, disjoint sets of propositions about S are possible.

It may be, however, that Russell held, on holist grounds, that no two such sets were possible for any subject matter. Russell hardly presses this claim, but there was a widespread belief among neo-Hegelians that the world was a logically interconnected whole, such that, from a (wholly) true proposition about any part of it, all true propositions about any other part could be inferred. This would block a definite counterexample to (1), but it does little to support (1) itself. For we have no guarantee that there may not be two or more different, but equally comprehensive, theories for any given subject matter.[7]

Yet without (1) and (2), there seems no way in which Russell can show that what is a necessary condition for the science will be a necessary condition for the experience of its subject matter. For there would seem to be no a priori guarantee that what makes the subject matter capable of being experienced will be what makes the necessary postulates of the science true. Of course, that the subject matter can be experienced is a necessary condition of our knowing the science, so any necessary condition of experiencing the subject matter will be a necessary condition of knowing the science. But there is no guarantee that the conditions necessary for knowing the science will be the axioms upon which the science is based.[8] Knowing the axioms is sufficient (in principle) for knowing the theory, but not necessary for knowing it.

The defects of Russell's approach are those inherent in transcendental deductions of all kinds (see Körner 1967), but especially damaging to those transcendental deductions designed, as Russell's in part was, to counter scepticism. As far as the analytic part is concerned, it would seem possible to establish that the axioms chosen were *sufficient* for the science in question; but not that they were *necessary*, for the possibility of alternative sufficient axiomatizations cannot be ruled out. The problem is a real one for Russell,

---

[7] Russell later established this as one of the main arguments against coherence theories of truth (cf. Russell 1906, Pt. I).
[8] Later on Russell was much clearer about this, distinguishing the logical from the epistemological order of the science (cf. RMDP). See further Godwyn and Irvine's contribution to this volume.

for, as is well known, his three axioms of general metrical geometry are not necessary for every metrical geometry.[9] Similar problems occur in the synthetic part of the program, compounded there by the difficulty of knowing when the basic postulates are even sufficient because of the inherently greater vagueness of the subject matter. At least in the analytic deduction, one has an articulated theory to deal with, which is more than can be said in the synthetic deduction where one has to determine the essential properties of such vague items as a form of externality. In short, Russell makes three claims: (a) that some postulate is necessary for the science; (b) that some postulate is necessary for the experience of the subject matter; and (c) that these two postulates are the same. It would seem impossible to show that any of these three claims is correct.

Russell did not believe that the task of philosophy in dealing with the sciences was exhausted by the two-stroke transcendental argument. That was, in many ways, a mere preliminary. The true task of philosophy (in particular, of metaphysics) was to weld the individual sciences together into a single comprehensive system of the world (*Papers* 1, p. 121). In this, Russell was doing no more than following conventional wisdom. In the way in which he planned to carry the program out, however, he went a good deal further. The limits of the special sciences were imposed by their subject matter which was formed by abstracting from experience special features for attention. '[E]very Science', Russell said, 'may be regarded as an attempt to construct a universe out of none but its own ideas' (*Papers* 2, p. 5). The result, of course, was always failure and each science required the addition of new fundamental ideas, thereby creating a new and more inclusive science.

The need for a system of the sciences seems undeniable, since each science obviously leaves out all those features of the world that are treated by other sciences. 'Every Science', Russell wrote in one of his undergraduate papers, 'deals necessarily with abstractions: its results must therefore be partial and one-sided expressions of truth' (*Papers*

---

[9] Differential geometries, which study spaces of variable curvature, are possible and were known at the time. Russell dismissed them on a priori grounds, thinking that measuring operations could not be coherently described within such a space. Subsequently, with Einstein's general theory of relativity, such spaces were found to have physical application. This, Russell later said (*MPD*, p. 40), 'swept away anything resembling [his earlier] point of view'.

1, 121). The language is Bradley's, but the basic point is hard to deny. Russell explains his position with regard to geometry in some reflections written in preparation for his Fellowship dissertation.

[W]e abstract the spatial qualities of things, not only from all other qualities, but also from the things themselves, leaving, as the matter of our Science, a subject totally devoid of what may be called Thinghood . . . . So in Geometry: our study concerns itself with what fills or may fill Space from time to time. The set of relations among things, which in presentation are distinguished as spatial, are abstracted from the things and set in a continuum, called space, whose only function is to allow the creation, *ad lib.*, of these relations.[10]

Such abstraction, though legitimate, is ultimately falsifying:

Of course such an abstraction cannot give us metaphysical truth – we know, all the while, that space would be meaningless if there were not things from which to abstract it – still, as the subject of a special Science, the abstraction is as legitimate as any other . . . . (*ibid.*, p. 93)

To remove the falsification which is inherent in geometry, it is necessary to make a transition to physics, which reintroduces those 'things' from which spatial relations are abstracted. Russell also mentions the need for a subsequent transition from physics to psychology, for physics abstracts matter from perception, even though matter 'wholly apart from perception is an absurdity' (*ibid.*, p. 94) Only when metaphysics is reached does this process stop. Metaphysics alone constituted 'independent and self-subsistent knowledge' (*Papers* 2, p. 5).

None of this, however, makes it clear why Russell thought the transitions required should be *dialectical* ones. He held the view, not easy to justify, that abstraction led to contradiction in the special sciences. That it should lead to incompleteness is not in question, but there seems no reason why an incomplete science should be inconsistent; and even less to suppose that an inconsistent science might be rendered consistent by adding new concepts and postulates to it. Nonetheless, this was Russell's view. The purpose of the analysis

---

[10] Russell, 'Observations on Space and Geometry', unpublished ms, 1895, RA 210.006551, pp. 93–4) This has to be modified somewhat in the light of the foregoing. At the time he wrote his dissertation, Russell did not accord projective geometry much philosophical importance. As a result, at the time this passage was written, he did not make the fundamental philosophical distinction just discussed between projective and metrical spaces.

of each individual science is to reduce to a minimum the number of contradictions it contains. Having uncovered its basic postulates and concepts with this aim in view, the task is 'to supply, to these postulates or ideas, such supplement as will abolish the special contradictions of the science in question, and thus pass to a new science, which may then be similarly treated' (*Papers* 2, p. 5).

He said little in general terms about this, he was far more concerned with the actual contradictions he found in the special sciences. Some of these were quite familiar. For example, in geometry there was a batch of antinomies arising from the continuity of space whose antecedents dated back to Zeno. A typical example arises from the composition of space out of points. Since each point is of zero volume, no number of them could be taken to compose a finite volume. In his early work on the dialectic of the sciences, Russell was inclined to adopt the view that supposedly continuous quantities were composed of finite indivisibles – a consistent but distinctly retrograde move. He was led, by reading Couturat's *De l'Infini mathématique* (1896), to study Cantor (in particular, the articles published as Cantor 1883), but for some time he rejected Cantor's work (see *Papers* 2, pp. 463–81). Once he had come to accept it, however, it became the focus of a good deal of his subsequent work in the foundations of mathematics.[11]

Much more enigmatic, at first sight, is the simplest of the antinomies Russell found in geometry, 'the antinomy of the point': all points are identical, yet each is distinct. Geometry presupposed the existence of abstract points as the required relata of spatial relations. These points were all intrinsically exactly alike, yet each was distinct from all the others. To modern eyes, this does not look like much of a contradiction. It would be natural now to say that all this means is that each point is numerically distinct from, though exactly similar to, all the others; that they are differentiated by their differing relations. There are, in fact, reasons, deeply bound up with Russell's neo-Hegelianism, which prevented him from taking this easy way out, and I shall come back to them shortly.

A related antinomy – the antinomy of free mobility – arises in general metrical geometry as a result of Russell's efforts to establish the axiom of free mobility. If space is purely relational, spatial points

---

[11] Cf. Grattan-Guinness, this volume.

and spatial figures must be individuated by their relations to other spatial points and figures. But in this case it makes no sense to talk of moving them from one place to another, thus changing the relations by which they are individuated. Yet such mobility is supposed to be an a priori necessity for metrical geometry. Here, at least, the problem is familiar, and so, too, is the solution: We should talk, not of moving spatial figures, but of moving extended physical objects in space. Here the resources of Russell's dialectic come into play for the first time. Geometry itself cannot provide the movable matter necessary for its own possibility, so a dialectical transition to physics is called for.

Russell uses the same transition to deal with the antinomy of the point. Following Boscovich, he adopted a theory of unextended, kinematic point-atoms. With his ontology thus expanded, spatial points could then be individuated by reference to the atoms which occupied them. The trouble was that point-atoms merely reproduce the problems of geometrical points, with kinematic relations replacing spatial relations. There was nothing intrinsic to a point-atom, any more than to a spatial point, to distinguish it from any other. To resolve this problem Russell introduced forces as properties of point-atoms, thereby transiting from kinematics to dynamics. But, once more, the antinomy re-emerged through what he called the essential relativity of force. Dynamical atoms can be distinguished in principle by their causal powers, but these powers can be exhibited only by their effects, and their effects consist of the relative motions of matter. Matter was introduced in order to resolve the problems of the relativity of space. It seems now that absolute space is required in order to resolve the problems of the relativity of matter.

Similar problems began to emerge from Russell's work on arithmetic. His extant writings on arithmetic from this period are more extensive than his notes on physics. They are also the most Hegelian of his writings.[12] He conceived arithmetic, as was then common, as the science of continuous and discrete quantity. The theory of number that he propounded as a neo-Hegelian was designed to avoid a simple one–many problem which faces the apparently common-sense view that numbers are properties of classes: The number n cannot be a property of an n-membered class, for the class itself is

---

[12] See especially, Russell, 1896, 1897 (*Papers* pp. 46–58, 70–82).

one.[13] Equally, it cannot be a property of the members of the class, for each of these is also one. Russell concludes that n is not a property at all, but a relation. He argues that numbers are ratios: in the case of counting they give the ratio between a single element of the class and the class as a whole; in the case of measurement they give the ratio between an arbitrarily chosen unit and the quantity to be measured.

An analogue of the antinomy of the point arises in arithmetic because in counting the differences between the members of the class being counted are ignored – each element, arithmetically, is exactly like any other. Similarly with units in the case of measurement: Each unit-quantity differs from all others, but all are qualitatively exactly alike. Qua quantity, every pint of beer is exactly alike, yet each pint is distinct, otherwise one would never get drunk. Russell states the antinomy of quantity with a certain Hegelian panache: between two quantities there is a conception of difference, but no difference of conception (*Papers* 2, pp. 24, 81). What he means is that we have a conception of the difference between the two quantities, of their being distinct; but exactly the same conceptions apply to both, so there is no difference of conception. He soon realized that this formulation would encompass the various contradictions he thought he had uncovered in geometry (e.g., the antimony of the point and an antinomy in projective geometry between points and lines), the antinomy of absolute motion in dynamics, as well as the antinomy of quantity and a whole range of antinomies which he uncovered in mathematics in the course of his work in 1898. In 1898 he formulated a quite general version, which he called 'the contradiction of relativity'. In fact, he came to think the contradiction of relativity so persuasive in mathematics that he used it to provide a partial definition of the subject (AMR, *Papers* 2, p. 166).

Russell's general difficulty is not hard to appreciate. In case after case, he found that each of the special sciences was committed to a plurality of items of some kind, but that it lacked the resources to individuate these items by means of their intrinsic qualities. The qualities that might have made the individuation possible were those that

---

[13] This argument leaves traces in *The Principles of Mathematics*, where Russell avoids it by denying that classes (as many) are terms, and thus that they are one. This position emerges out of a distinction between collections and wholes that Russell developed in unpublished work around 1899.

had been abstracted away in order to produce the subject matter of the science in question. The solution, or so it appeared, was to move to a new science, one with more extensive conceptual resources that could handle more concrete subject matter. The dialectic of the sciences thus leads from the abstract to the concrete. Even so, as we have seen, Russell had been unable to provide a non-relational individuation for the basic items of any of the special sciences up to physics. To this point, however, he found no cause for alarm. He was, after all, an idealist and did not expect a purely material world to pass muster metaphysically.

Russell's solution to the problem of the relativity of force was to turn point-atoms into monads, thereby transiting from dynamics to psychology in the hope that the perceptions of monads might provide the grounding he required for the whole system. Here, however, he faced huge problems in trying to dig the necessary physics out of the psychology of monads. Moreover, he still had no real guarantee that the perceptions of monads would be any less relative than the forces of atoms. Indeed, there were serious grounds for thinking that they would not be. In order to escape from the contradiction of relativity, the fundamental laws of the science of the Absolute had to be couched in terms of the intrinsic states of whatever type of item turned out to be ultimately real. According to Russell's program, these states would have to be the psychological states of monads. No matter how much of the psychology of monads might be stated initially in relational terms, ultimately all such claims would have to be cashed out in favour of claims about their intrinsic (non-relational) states. At this point the needs of Russell's dialectic ran up against the resources of contemporary psychology. According to the act-object psychology, which was then prevalent, all mental states involved direction to an object. Accordingly, mental states were inherently relational.[14] At this point, Russell's hope of providing an account of the Absolute in accordance with the best scientific knowledge of the day became unrealizable and he left the field with only a few brief notes to indicate the lines along which he was thinking.

There was in fact only one way in which the dialectic of the sciences could be brought to a satisfactory conclusion and that was by

[14] Russell would have had this doctrine from his teachers James Ward and G.F. Stout, who were among its leading exponents in Britain. See Ward, 1886; and Stout, 1896. The doctrine, of course, comes originally from Brentano.

a return to Bradley's monism. The need was to find an item which could be individuated by means of its own intrinsic features alone, and thus did not depend for its identity on relations to other items, and Bradley's Absolute filled the bill admirably. The Absolute, if anything, could stand on its own feet as independently real, if only because there was nothing outside for it to depend on. The progress of Russell's dialectic had equipped the items under consideration with progressively richer sets of properties, in the vain hope of reaching what was independently real. Only one more step was needed to be sure of success: choose an item, like Bradley's Absolute, which exemplifies all properties; by Leibniz's law, there will be only one such item.[15] The contradiction of relativity is thus eliminated: there is no conception of difference. The trouble is, according to Russell, the conception of difference is essential for thought. Without it, thought is confined to the realm of appearance and contradiction and the Absolute remains unknowable. This, for Russell, was a completely unacceptable conclusion, but to avoid it would require a complete revolution in his philosophy.

At the end of his life, Russell would characterize his rejection of neo-Hegelianism as a 'Revolt into Pluralism' (*MPD* , p. 54). This is puzzling since Russell was a pluralist for most of his neo-Hegelian phase. The explanation seems to be that, in the end, he came to think that monism was the only way out for the dialectic and that his efforts to defend any kind of monadology were ultimately failures.

Such drastic conclusions might seem premature to say the least, for we have done nothing so far to show that the contradiction of relativity is a genuine contradiction. For it seems that Russell has simply overlooked the distinction between numerical and qualitative identity and that, once this distinction is drawn, the problem will be completely avoided. No such simple resolution, however, was available to Russell as a neo-Hegelian. The difficulty was the doctrine of internal relations which Russell took over unquestioningly from the neo-Hegelians. According to this doctrine, all relations had to be grounded in the intrinsic properties of their terms. Different relations had to be grounded in different intrinsic properties, and the intrinsic properties of a when it was before b had to be different from the intrinsic properties of b when it was after a. Once this doctrine is

---

[15] In effect, a Russellian monad is inflated into the Absolute.

accepted, the contradiction of relativity is seen to be a genuine contradiction. Points have to be distinguished by their relations, which have to be based upon differences in their intrinsic properties. But all points share the same intrinsic properties.

This problem, of course, does not affect symmetrical relations. There is no reason, from the point of view of the doctrine of internal relations, why, when a symmetrical relation holds between two terms, both should not share exactly the same intrinsic properties. This, however, does little to improve the situation. By 1898, Russell had come up with what is essentially the modern classification of relations as reflexive, symmetrical and transitive (*Papers* 2, pp. 26-7, 138-9). His study of the formal properties of relations had been motivated by an investigation into the concept of order, which had played an important role in his treatment of projective geometry. Generalizing from projective geometry, he had come to the conclusion that order was the central concept in the whole of pure mathematics.[16] Equally important, Russell had discovered that order depended upon transitive, asymmetrical relations – the very ones which produced the contradiction of relativity. It was this that led him to suppose that the contradiction of relativity in part determined the scope of pure mathematics.

Russell states this explicitly for the first time in an incomplete manuscript of 1898, 'An Analysis of Mathematical Reasoning' (AMR, *Papers* 2, pp. 225-6). This extremely interesting document was first conceived as an instalment of the dialectic of sciences, and yet it shows unmistakable signs of Russell's breaking away from neo-Hegelianism. Nothing indicates this more dramatically than the passage just referred to. Ironically, it survives only because Russell moved the pages on which it occurs from the typescript of 'An Analysis' into an early draft of *The Principles of Mathematics*, which Russell started in 1899 and subsequently preserved.[17] Now, in the 1899-1900 draft of *The Principles of Mathematics*, there is no trace of the contradiction of relativity or of the dialectic of the sciences.

[16] Order thus replaced quantity as the fundamental concept of arithmetic. This was an important step on the way towards logicism, since order could be defined in purely logical terms. Order plays a central role throughout *Principia Mathematica*.

[17] There are both manuscript and typescript fragments of AMR – most of both versions has been lost. The only parts of the typescript to have survived are those which were physically incorporated into the 1899-1900 draft of *The Principles of Mathematics*.

As one would expect from the published book, the 1899–1900 draft is a thoroughly, even aggressively, non-Hegelian work.

What happened was this: In the 'Analysis', Russell argued from his (still not explicitly stated) neo-Hegelian theory of relations to the claim that the contradiction of relativity holds throughout mathematics. For the draft of the *Principles*, he switches the argument from *modus ponens* to *modus tollens* and converts it into a *reductio* argument against the neo-Hegelian theory of relations. No doubt with well-justified pride in his own cleverness, he preserved the argument in tact through the transition, merely changing the opening and closing lines. In what amounts to a Gestalt shift, he saw that his previous problems depended upon his theory of relations, rejected this theory and with it the entire system of philosophy on which he had been working for the previous four years.

Russell's Gestalt shift on the contradiction of relativity, though striking, was only part of his reason for abandoning neo-Hegelianism. Another line of criticism came to a head more slowly, but at about the same time. Two strands of Russell's thinking as a neo-Hegelian were in tension. The first was the anti-psychologism he had originally derived from Bradley and which had been reinforced by almost every other influence on him during this period. The extrusion of psychology from philosophy was a major intellectual undertaking of the time, pursued quite independently by philosophers as diverse as Frege, Bradley, and Husserl. Early in his *Logic*, Bradley had drawn a sharp distinction between ideas considered as mental events and ideas considered as symbols which had an external reference to something other than themselves, a distinction which, he argued, the associationists had disastrously confounded. This was a lesson Russell had learnt at the beginning of his philosophical career and he was not about to abandon it. In fact, it took him a considerable time before the elements of naturalism, which were a feature of his later philosophy emerged.[18]

The contrary impulse in Russell's idealism came from his heavy use of transcendental arguments. Historically, and perhaps naturally, transcendental arguments had been taken to show that features of the world usually thought of as external were in fact supplied, at least in part, by the human mind. Geometry, for example, according to Kant

---

[18] See Baldwin's contribution to this volume.

is possible because space is given a priori by the mind. Transcendental arguments, therefore, seem naturally to involve some degree of psychologism, and it is questionable whether they can be wholly de-psychologized without turning them into deductive arguments. There is, of course, nothing wrong with deductive arguments (provided they are sound), but the point of transcendental arguments was to take us beyond the results that could be reached from true premisses by deductive means. Psychologism was one of the key points on which the British Hegelians had broken from Kant: they thought Kant had left all too much to be supplied by the mind, and has thereby missed the true, objective nature of the Absolute spirit which only Hegel had had the metaphysical fortitude to reveal. Russell, as we have seen, had tried to combine Kant's methods with Hegelian anti-psychologism, by insisting that his transcendental arguments were 'purely logical' and 'without any psychological implication' (*EFG*, p. 3). It is far from clear, however, that this was the case. Looking back on his transcendental arguments in the dialectic of the sciences, a number of them have a decidedly verificationist cast. He argues, for example, that force is inherently relative, but his argument for this is that force reveals itself only by its effects (i.e., by the relative motion of matter). Similarly in the antinomy of points, points are held to be purely relative, though the argument for this conclusion is that *we* need to consider their relations to other points in order to distinguish them. Russell's conclusions are invariably couched in absolute, metaphysical terms, his grounds for them, however, often depend upon the mind's cognitive abilities.

This line of criticism was brought home to him most forcefully by G.E. Moore who reviewed Russell's *Essay* very critically (Moore, 1899a). One of Moore's chief complaints was the residual psychologism he found in the book. In fact, Moore had found a residual psychologism even in Bradley, and this had been the starting point for his own break with neo-Hegelianism. In his Fellowship dissertation, written at the same time as (and to a surprising degree, independently of) Russell's 'Analysis of Mathematical Reasoning', Moore had started the chapter on reason with a characteristically minute consideration of the way Bradley had distinguished the two senses of 'idea' that the associationists had muddled. His conclusion was that Bradley himself had failed to draw the distinction sharply enough – an error which Moore sought to correct in the rest of the chapter.

Moore's Bradley exegesis, however, was just the starting point from which he launched out on a theory of his own. The ontology of concepts and propositions which he went on to sketch was similar to, though less elaborate than, the ontology of terms and propositions Russell published in *The Principles of Mathematics* and which appeared first in 'An Analysis of Mathematical Reasoning'.[19]

Moore published his account as 'The Nature of Judgment' (Moore, 1899), which Russell described as 'the first published account of the new philosophy' (*MPD*, p. 54). Russell said that, in the revolt against Kant and Hegel, Moore had led the way, but that he had followed closely. Moore, he said, was most interested in the rejection of idealism, while he was most interested in the rejection of monism (*ibid.*), though he was happy to reject idealism too. He described the new philosophy as 'a great liberation, as if I had escaped from a hot-house on to a wind-swept headland .... In the first exuberance of liberation, I became a naive realist and rejoiced in the thought that grass is really green, in spite of the adverse opinion of all philosophers from Locke onwards' (*MPD*, pp. 61–2). In one of the most radical purges of psychologism from logic to date, Russell and Moore came to regard logic as a completely general theory of objective, mind-independent terms (or in Moore's terminology, 'concepts'). Propositions were regarded as (special kinds of) complex terms; and propositional analysis (the true task of philosophy, according to Russell 1900, p. 8) was the process of enumerating the constituents of propositions and explicating the manner in which they were combined. The general point of view is familiar from *The Principles of Mathematics*, but it is to be found already in 'An analysis of Mathematical Reasoning', and in intervening works.

Russell says nothing about transcendental arguments in the 'Analysis', but nonetheless the early parts of the manuscript can be seen as an attempt to deduce the a priori conditions for the possibility of judgment. The following year, however, in his next extended attempt to write a book on the philosophy of mathematics, all trace of his earlier methodology is swept away. The change is revealed by the title he chose: 'The Fundamental Ideas and Axioms of Mathematics' (*Papers* 2, pp. 265–305). The philosopher's task was now two-fold: to identify the fundamental concepts in terms of which all the other

---

[19] See Cartwright's paper in this volume.

concepts employed in a theory could be defined, and to identify the fundamental principles of the theory from which all its other claims could be derived. Transcendental arguments were banished, never to return.

The task Russell outlined in 'Fundamental Ideas' is easily recognizable, in a way that his previous endeavors are not, as the same sort of task that resulted in *Principia Mathematica* ten years later. Nonetheless, much had still to be done before the later project could be undertaken. Russell did not embrace logicism – the characteristic doctrine of *Principia* and *The Principles of Mathematics*, that all the axioms and fundamental concepts of mathematics were logical in nature – until the second half of 1900. In 'Fundamental Ideas and Axioms of Mathematics' numbers were treated as unanalyzable, simple terms.[20] Hopes were expressed for the reduction of the whole of mathematics to arithmetic, but the further reduction to logic was not yet envisaged.

The most evident difference between 'Fundamental Ideas' and the later writings is the relatively naive view of analysis Russell held in 1899. Analysis was taken to be the breaking up of complex objects into simpler ones.[21] Definition was seen as the creation of complex terms out of simpler ones. Propositions, as complex terms, literally contained their constituents. Much of this survives even into *The Principles of Mathematics*. But in 'Fundamental Ideas' the part–whole relation has a role which is altogether lost in the later work.[22] Russell attempted to construe not only the relation between a proposition and its constituents in terms of it, but also the relations between propositions. Implication was taken to be a containment relation. In some sense, not very clearly specified, a proposition was taken to contain all its logical consequences. Not much can be made of Russell's complex reflections on these issues in 'Fundamental

[20] In Russell and Moore's very early work there is a pervasive haecceity about terms and concepts, nicely revealed in Moore's epigraph from Bishop Butler in *Principia Ethica*: 'Everything is what it is, and not another thing.' Russell came to the view reluctantly – cf. his 'On the Constituents of Space' [1898] (*Papers* 2, pp. 311–321).

[21] It is often supposed that Russell thought of analysis as analysis into simples, but this is a mistake. He left it as an open question whether there were simples and certainly never supposed that any actual analysis would have arrived at them if there were. (See Hager's paper in this volume.)

[22] Interestingly, Husserl, quite independently, gave it the same sort of primacy at about this time (Husserl, 1900).

Ideas'. The underlying philosophical idea had some degree of plausibility, but the task of creating a logic powerful enough for use in mathematics (let alone for logicism) on this mereological base proved at this stage impossible. In some areas, however, Russell was able to make progress. In 1898–9, for example, he returned to geometry armed with the new philosophy and made a much more successful (though still not wholly satisfactory) attempt at the axiomatization of projective geometry (Russell, 1899). But Russell's research program, which had leapt forward so dramatically in 1898, was essentially stalled through 1899 and remained so until the summer of 1900 when he discovered Peano's mathematical logic. It was only then that he was able to capitalize on the advances of 1898 and chart a new way forward.[23]

[23] Research supported by the Social Sciences and Humanities Research Council of Canada.

REFERENCES

Bradley, F.H. 1883, *The Principles of Logic*, 2 vols. Oxford: OUP; second edition, 1969.

Bradley, F.H. 1893, *Appearance and Reality*, Oxford: OUP; second edition, 1969.

Cantor, Georg. 1883, Special Issue of *Acta Mathematica*, 2, pp. 305–408 devoted to French translations of Cantor's work.

Couturat, Louis. 1896, *De l'Infini mathématique*, Paris: Alcan.

DeMorgan, Augustus. 1842, *The Differential and Integral Calculus*, London: Baldwin and Craddock.

Forsyth, A.R. 1935, 'Old Tripos Days at Cambridge', *The Mathematical Gazette*, 19, pp. 162–79.

Grattan-Guinness, Ivor 2000, *The Search for Mathematical Roots, 1870–1940. Logics, set theories and the foundations of mathematics from Cantor through Russell to Gödel*, Princeton: Princeton University Press.

Griffin, Nicholas. 1991, *Russell's Idealist Apprenticeship*, Oxford: Clarendon.

Husserl, Edmund. 1900, *Logical Investigations*. J.N. Findlay (trans.) London: Routledge & Kegan Paul.

Kant, Immanuel. 1781, *Critique of Pure Reason*, trans. N. Kemp Smith. London: Macmillan, 1929.

Kant, Immanuel. 1783, *Prolegomena to Any Future Metaphysics*, trans. P. Carus, Revised J. W. Ellington. Indianapolis: Hackett, 1977.

Kemp Smith, Norman 1918, *A Commentary on Kant's 'Critique of Pure Reason'*, Atlantic Highlands: Humanities Press, second edition 1962.

Körner, S. 1967, 'The Impossibility of Transcendental Deductions', *The Monist*, 51, pp. 317–31.

Lewis, A.C. and Griffin, N. 1990, 'Russell's Mathematical Education', *Notes and Records of the Royal Society*, 44, 1990, pp. 51–71.

McTaggart, J.M.E. 1893, 'A Further Determination of the Absolute', repr. in *Philosophical Studies*, ed. S.V. Keeling. Freeport, N.Y.: Books for Libraries, 1968.

———, 1921, *The Nature of Existence*, Cambridge: CUP, 1921–7, 2 vols.

Manser, Anthony, *Bradley's Logic*, Oxford: Blackwell.

Moore, G.E. 1899, 'The Nature of Judgment', *Mind*. n.s. 8, pp. 176–193.

Moore, G.E. 1899a, Review of Russell, *An Essay on the Foundations of Geometry*. *Mind*. n.s. 8, pp. 397–405.

Moore, G.E., 1903. *Principia Ethica*. Cambridge University Press.

Poincaré, Henri, 1899, 'Des fondements de la géométrie: A propos d'un livre de M. Russell', *Revue de métaphysique et de morale*, 7, pp. 251–79.

Russell, Bertrand, 1896, 'On Some Difficulties of Continuous Quantity' in *Papers* 2, pp. 46–58.

Russell, Bertrand, 1897, 'On the Relations of Number and Quantity' in *Papers* 2, pp. 70–80.

Russell, Bertrand, 1899, 'On the Axioms of Geometry' in *Papers* 2, pp. 394–415.

Russell, Bertrand, 1900, *A Critical Exposition of the Philosophy of Leibniz*. London: Allen and Unwin; second edition 1937.

Russell, Bertrand, 1906 'On the Nature of Truth', *Proceedings of the Aristotelian Society*, 7, pp. 28–49.

Spadoni, Carl, 1976, 'Great God in Boots! – The Ontological Argument is Sound', *Russell*, 23–4, pp. 37–41.

Stout, G.F. 1896, *Analytical Psychology*. London: Sonnenschein.

Ward, James. 1886, 'Psychology' in *Encyclopedia Britannica*, ninth edition, vol. 20, pp. 37–85.

3   Russell and Moore, 1898–1905

When Russell and Moore entered Trinity College, Cambridge (in 1890 and 1892, respectively), the prevailing philosophies there, and elsewhere in Britain, were forms of idealism: Kant and Hegel were the heroes of the past, and F. H. Bradley of the present. It was chiefly through association with J.M.E. McTaggart, as both a teacher and a friend, that Moore and Russell absorbed idealism and, as Moore was later to put it, became for a time "enthusiastic admirers" of Bradley.[1] But only for a time. It has been said[2] that the beginning of Russell's break with Idealism can be discerned in a paper read to the Apostles on 11 December 1897, in which he argued that "for all purposes which are not *purely* intellectual, the world of Appearance is the real world – agin McTaggart's notion of getting religion out of philosophy".[3] Russell himself describes the revolt this way:

It was towards the end of 1898 that Moore and I rebelled against both Kant and Hegel. Moore led the way, but I followed closely in his footsteps. I think that the first published account of the new philosophy was Moore's article in *Mind* on 'The Nature of Judgement'. Although neither he nor I would now adhere to all the doctrines in that article, I, and I think he, would still agree with its negative part – i.e. with the doctrine that fact is in general independent of experience (*MPD*, p. 42).

The opening sentence of Russell's three-part article on Meinong, written probably in the first half of 1903, contains a succinct statement of certain elements of the "new philosophy":

That every presentation and every belief must have an object other than itself and, except in certain cases where mental existents happen to be concerned, extramental; that what is commonly called perception has as its object an existential proposition, into which enters as a constituent that whose existence is concerned, and not the idea of this existent; that truth and falsehood apply not to beliefs, but to their objects; and that the object of a thought, even when this object does not exist, has a Being which is in no way dependent on its being an object of thought: all these are theses which, though generally rejected, can nevertheless be supported by arguments which deserve at least a refutation. (MTCA, *Papers* 4, p. 432)

And to this sentence Russell appended a footnote: "I have been led to accept these theses by Mr. G.E. Moore, to whom, throughout the following pages, I am deeply indebted." A similar acknowledgement occurs in the preface to *The Principles of Mathematics*: "On fundamental questions of philosophy, my position, in all its chief features, is derived from Mr. G.E. Moore." (*POM*, p. xviii) Russell mentions in particular "the pluralism which regards the world, both that of existents and that of entities, as composed of an infinite number of mutually independent entities, with relations which are ultimate, and not reducible to adjectives of their terms or of the whole which these compose".

It has been questioned whether Russell's indebtedness to Moore was quite as great as these passages make it out to have been.[4] This much may certainly be said: if indeed Moore led Russell to adopt the doctrines that constitute the "new philosophy", Russell developed them well beyond anything to be found in Moore's own writings – and perhaps in some cases beyond what Moore himself was prepared to accept. It must be borne in mind also that there was a good deal more fluidity in the early views of Moore and Russell than Russell's talk of a "new philosophy" might suggest; the views of each changed rapidly, and not always in concert, and at least by 1911 both had abandoned most of the doctrines which the "new philosophy" comprised. It should not be inferred, however, that those early views can simply be ignored. At least some of them, and I think especially those to be discussed here, form an important background not only for the more mature views of Russell and Moore but also for the development of analytic philosophy in Britain and America.

I

In 1898 Moore arrived at what he thought to be a solution to the philosophical problem of the nature of truth. This was taken up and defended by Russell. Though both philosophers were soon to find fault with the proposed solution, it is of some interest in itself and an exposition of it will take us a good way into what is sometimes called their early "realism".

In lectures eventually published under the title *Some Main Problems of Philosophy*[5] and delivered in 1910–11, after both he and Russell had abandoned it, Moore described the proposed solution this way:

> It is simply this. It adopts the supposition that in the case of every belief, true or false, there is a proposition which is what is believed, and which certainly is. But the difference between a true and a false belief, it says, consists simply in this, that where the belief is true the proposition, which is believed, besides the fact that it *is* or "has being" also has another simple unanalysable property which is possessed by some propositions and not by others. The propositions which don't possess it, and which therefore we call false, *are* or "have being" – just as much as those which *do;* only they just have *not* got this additional property of being "true". (p. 261)

Herbert, we may suppose, believes that the earth orbits the sun. Given the supposition, the theory requires that there be something, a certain "proposition", which Herbert believes and which "is" or "has being" whether or not the earth orbits the sun. After all, if Herbert believes the earth orbits the sun, he certainly believes *something;* it seems to follow that there *is* something he believes.[6] Now, the proposition that the earth orbits the sun must be distinguished from belief in it. Of course, in ordinary discourse a "belief" is often something believed – that is, a proposition. Thus, we often speak of *the* belief that the earth orbits the sun, meaning thereby simply the proposition that the earth orbits the sun. But we may also mean rather the more or less permanent state of believers like Herbert, the state manifested in spoken or unspoken acts of assent to what Moore here calls the proposition that the earth orbits the sun. In another place, Moore says that 'true' and 'false' are ambiguous according as they are applied, on the one hand, to propositions and, on the other hand, to the states, or their manifestations, of which propositions are the "objects".[7] Thus, Herbert's belief that the earth orbits the sun is true, in the sense that its object has the simple unanalysable property of being true. If Elizabeth believes that the sun orbits the earth, her belief is false in the sense that *its* object, the proposition that the sun orbits the earth, *lacks* that simple unanalysable property.

A natural response to the theory is based on the inclination we all have to say that whether or not it is true that the earth orbits the sun depends, not on the simple properties possessed or not possessed by the proposition that the earth orbits the sun, but on the relation of the proposition to reality: the proposition is true if and only if it "corresponds to fact" or "agrees with reality". The theory that truth is a simple unanalysable property seems simply to ignore an essential ingredient in the ordinary concept.

Moore and Russell were aware that the theory invites this sort of response. As Russell remarked, the theory "*seems* to leave our preference for truth a mere unaccountable prejudice, and in no way to answer to the feeling of truth and falsehood". (MTCA, *Papers* 4, p. 473) They advocated it nevertheless, because they thought that correspondence theories, though natural, cannot survive close scrutiny. Thus, in his article on truth in Baldwin's *Dictionary*, Moore wrote:

It is commonly supposed that the truth of a proposition consists in some relation which it bears to reality; and falsehood in the absence of this relation. The relation in question is generally called a "correspondence" or "agreement"; and it seems to be generally conceived as one of partial similarity to something else, and hence it is essential to the theory that a truth should differ in some specific way from the reality, in relation to which its truth is to consist .... *It is the impossibility of finding any such difference between a truth and the reality to which it is supposed to correspond which refutes the theory.*

He went on to suggest that those who think there is a difference are probably confusing the proposition either with belief in it or with some sentence used to express it. He concluded that "once it is definitely recognized that a proposition is ... not a belief or form of words, but an *object* of a belief, it seems plain that a truth differs in no respect from the reality to which it was supposed merely to correspond".[8] Russell agreed, and added that "as for the preference which most people – so long as they are not annoyed by instances – feel in favour of true propositions, this must be based, apparently, upon an ultimate ethical proposition: 'It is good to believe true propositions, and bad to believe false ones'" (MTCA, *Papers* 4, p. 474).

II

Truth and falsity, according to Moore, are so related that "every proposition must be either true or false, and ... to every true proposition there corresponds a false one, and to every false proposition a true one, differing from it only as being its negation".[9] Russell would have agreed, but seemingly not for Moore's reasons. Moore took falsity to be absence of truth, and thus every proposition must be true or false simply because every proposition must be either true or not true. But according to Russell *both* truth and falsity are unanalysable,[10] and hence other grounds must be given for the principle of bivalence. Russell is silent as to what these might be.

In the case of two other doctrines about truth, both Moore and Russell apparently thought it enough to rebut objections. There are no degrees of truth, they claimed; and to the objection that we may without impropriety say of some proposition p that, though not quite true, it is more true than a competitor q, they would have responded that such a remark means simply that p is close to the truth and closer to it than q. And they agreed that neither are there any changes in truth value. We may indeed say, for example, that although it is true that state sales taxes are not deductible on federal tax returns, that was not true fifteen years ago. But this does not imply that a certain proposition is true now but was not true fifteen years ago. To think otherwise is to overlook the fact that the proposition one would assert now by uttering the *sentence*, 'State sales taxes are not deductible on federal returns' is not the same as the proposition that one would have asserted by assertively uttering that same sentence fifteen years ago.

III

Propositions have been introduced as objects of belief, as *what* someone believes who believes that the earth orbits the sun, or that Detroit is north of Windsor, and so on. But it will not do to *define* a proposition as anything believed, for there are hosts of propositions which are not believed – some because they are universally disbelieved or doubted, others because they have not even been contemplated. But even if no one believes that, say, the sum of 5 and 7 is 11, it is *possible* that someone should. So perhaps we may say, by way of giving a definition, that a proposition is anything that *can* be believed. But neither Moore nor Russell found this acceptable. Moore said that the proposed definition "merely states that [propositions] may come into a relation with a thinker; and in order that they *may* do anything, they must already *be* something",[11] his point being apparently that the definition does not tell us *what* a proposition *is*. Russell rejected the proposal without giving reasons, but he suggested an alternative. In a lecture given at Oxford in 1905 (but unpublished during his lifetime), he said that he "should not *define* [propositions] as possible objects of belief, but as things having a particular kind of complexity".[12]

One looks forward to a specification of that particular kind of complexity. But in vain. Later in the same lecture, Russell said:

Propositions are complexes of a certain kind, for some complexes are not propositions – for example, "the cow with the crumpled horn" "Charles I's execution", etc. Propositions are distinguished, as a rule, in language, by the presence of a verb; and verbs seem to be used to express just that particular kind of complexity which propositions have and other complexes do not have. But I do not know how to describe this kind of complexity. (Papers 4, p. 503)

We are thus left without a definition. It is nonetheless of some importance to explore the rudiments of the idea that propositions are "complexes". Here it is necessary to rely almost entirely on Russell; for though Moore, too, held that propositions are complex entities, his writings contain little of the detail to be found in Russell's.[13]

The more philosophical parts of *POM* are occupied in good part with the "philosophical analysis" of this or that proposition: the determination of its "constituents" and their manner of "occurrence" in it. "Grammar" is supposed to be the guide:

The study of grammar, in my opinion, is capable of throwing far more light on philosophical questions than is commonly supposed by philosophers. Although a grammatical distinction cannot be uncritically assumed to correspond to a genuine philosophical difference, yet the one is *prima facie* evidence of the other, and may often be most usefully employed as a source of discovery. Moreover, it must be admitted, I think, that every word occurring in a sentence must have *some* meaning: a perfectly meaningless sound could not be employed in the more or less fixed way in which language employs words. The correctness of our philosophical analysis of a proposition may therefore be usefully checked by the exercise of assigning the meaning of each word in the sentence expressing the proposition. On the whole, grammar seems to me to bring us much nearer to a correct logic than the current opinions of philosophers; and in what follows, grammar, though not our master, will yet be taken as our guide. (*POM*, p. 42)

Words have meaning "in the simple sense that they are symbols which stand for something other than themselves" and "a proposition contains the entities indicated by words" (*POM*, p. 47). The suggestion thus seems to be that to each occurrence of a word in a sentence there corresponds in the proposition expressed an occurrence of that for which the word stands. But rigid adherence to the suggestion seems difficult, if not impossible. The difficulties can be seen even in relatively simple cases.

Consider, for example, the proposition

1) Plato admires Socrates.

Its constituents are said to be the entities for which the names 'Plato' and 'Socrates' and the verb 'admires' stand – that is, according to Russell, the men Plato and Socrates, and the relation *admires*. Note that it is the very persons Plato and Socrates, and the very relation *admires*, that are constituents of (1); and note also that in this case the constitution of the proposition mirrors that of the sentence here used to express it. But

2) Socrates is admired by Plato

would seem to be the very same proposition, and yet, if it is, we have a case in which propositional complexity and verbal complexity do not match. And if we try to preserve a match by counting 'is admired by' as a single "word", or if we give up the alleged agreement of sentential and propositional complexity, we lose the identity, for (1) and (2) will have different constituents. The relation for which 'is admired by' stands is obviously not identical with that for which 'admires' stands; otherwise admiration would always be mutual. Russell is forced to conclude that (1) and (2) imply each other and are thus "equivalent", but are not identical.

Russell contends, perhaps more plausibly, that (1) is distinct not only from (2) but also from:

3) Plato bears *admires* to Socrates.

Every constituent of (1) is a constituent of (3); but (3) is said to have a constituent answering to 'bears ... to', which (1) does not. But although *admires* is a constituent of both (1) and (3), its manner of occurrence is not the same in the two propositions: it is a "term of" (3) but not of (1). In general, the *terms of* a proposition are those of its constituents that the proposition is *about*. The terms of (1) are said to be Plato and Socrates; the terms of (3) are Plato, Socrates, and also *admires*. Russell says that it is "a characteristic of the terms of a proposition that any one of them may be replaced by any other entity without our ceasing to have a proposition" (*POM*, p. 45). Taking for granted the notion of propositional position, we can cash the metaphor as follows: *x* is a term of a proposition *p* iff *x* is a constituent of *p* and, for every *y*, there is a proposition *q* which is like *p* except for having *y* where *p* has *x*. Notice: "any other *entity*". So, to take an extreme case, the following is a (false) proposition:

4) *Admires* admires Socrates.

The relation *admires* is a term of (4), just as it is of (3); and it is that very relation which is a constituent, though not a term, of (1). If Russell is conservative about propositional identity, he is liberal when it comes to propositional subsistence.

Anything that is a term of at least one proposition Russell calls simply a *term*. Now there is nothing that is a term of no proposition, for the proposition with respect to *x* that it is a term of no proposition is itself a proposition of which *x* is a term. Thus, it is that 'term' is "the widest word in the philosophical vocabulary .... A man, a moment, a number, a class, a relation, a chimera, or anything else that can be mentioned is sure to be a term; and to deny that such and such a thing is a term must always be false." (*POM*, p. 43)

Terms divide into *things* and *concepts*. The former are terms of all propositions of which they are constituents; the latter occur in some propositions otherwise than as terms. We have in effect seen that *admires* is a concept: in (1) and (3) it exhibits "that curious twofold use" of which concepts, but not things, are capable. (*POM*, p. 45) Russell would take it to be obvious that Plato and Socrates are things.

Are there propositions that have only one term? It would seem that

5) Socrates is human

differs from

6) Humanity characterizes Socrates

in a way analogous to that in which (1) differs from (3). Just as *admires* is a term of (3) but not of (1), so it would seem that humanity is a term of (6) but not of (5); hence it would seem that (5) has just two constituents, Socrates being its only term and humanity its only concept – a position Russell takes in a draft of Part I of *POM* (*Papers* 3, p. 182). But the published version exhibits some uncertainty:

> It seems plain that, if we were right in holding that "Socrates is human" is a proposition having only one term, the *is* in this proposition cannot express a relation in the ordinary sense. In fact, subject-predicate propositions are distinguished by just this non-relational character. Nevertheless, a relation between Socrates and humanity is certainly *implied*, and it is very difficult to conceive the proposition as expressing no relation at all. (*POM*, p. 49)

This effort to have it both ways results in obscurity: (5) "expresses" a relation in some non-ordinary sense, but as to what that sense is we know only that it precludes the identity of (5) with (6).

We have seen that, according to Russell, the kind of unity that distinguishes propositions from other complexes cannot be defined. This view is connected with Russell's thesis that the unity of a proposition cannot survive analysis. By this he means, at least in part, that a proposition is not identical with the set of its constituents or with an ordered n-tuple of its constituents. The set of constituents of (1) is identical with the set of constituents of the distinct proposition that Socrates admires Plato. And it is useless to invoke order; for with which of the various orderings of its constituents is the proposition to be identified? But how then *are* the constituents of a proposition united? Russell's view, at least at the time of *POM*, is that the unity of a simple proposition such as (1) is provided by the concept that occurs in it.

> Consider the proposition "*A* differs from *B*." The constituents of this proposition, if we analyze it, appear to be only *A*, difference, *B*. Yet these constituents, thus placed side by side, do not reconstitute the proposition. The difference which occurs in the proposition actually relates *A* and *B*, whereas the difference after analysis is a notion which has no connection with *A* and *B*. (*POM*, p. 49)

It should be noticed here that the mere presence of a relation among the constituents of a proposition is not what accounts for the unity of the proposition. The relation *admires* does not provide the unity of (3), for it does not in that proposition "actually relate" Plato and Socrates; as Russell would also say, it does not there "occur as a relation". As to exactly what that means, Russell confesses himself unable to say. But then he is left with a problem. If to provide the unity of a simple relational proposition such as (1), the relation must actually relate the terms, it becomes impossible to see how the proposition can be false.

IV

Everything there is, Russell says, is a term of some proposition and hence a term *simpliciter*. But what is there?

The question appears to be answered in a famous passage in *POM*, which elaborates on one of the theses mentioned at the outset of the articles on Meinong:

Being is that which belongs to every conceivable term, to every possible object of thought – in short, to everything that can possibly occur in any proposition, true or false, and to all such propositions themselves. Being belongs to whatever can be counted. If A be any term that can be counted as one, it is plain that A is something, and therefore that A is. "A is not" must always be either false or meaningless. For if A were nothing, it could not be said not to be; "A is not" implies that there is a term A whose being is denied, and hence that A is. Thus unless "A is not" be an empty sound, it must be false – whatever A may be, it certainly is. Numbers, the Homeric gods, relations, chimeras and four-dimensional spaces all have being, for if they were not entities of a kind, we could make no propositions about them. Thus being is a general attribute of everything, and to mention anything is to show that it is. (p. 449)

This passage, among others, has led some commentators to describe the ontology of *POM* as "intolerably indiscriminate".

For, take impossible numbers: prime numbers divisible by 6. It must in some sense be false that there are such; and this must be false in some sense in which it is true that there are prime numbers. In this sense are there chimeras? Are chimeras then as firm as the good prime numbers and firmer than the prime numbers divisible by 6?[14]

But the passage quoted from *POM*, and others like it, leave uncertain which of two doctrines Russell means to assert. Some of what he says suggests

7) Any result of putting a proper name or singular definite description for 'A' in 'There is no such thing as A' expresses a false proposition.

But he can also he understood as asserting rather

    8) Anything that can be mentioned has being.

Now, (7) and (8) are very different doctrines. Whereas (7) runs afoul of such evident truths as the proposition that there is no such thing as the least prime number divisible by 6, (8) is not thus easily refutable: any effort to cite a counterexample could be written off as a failure to mention anything at all.

No doubt Russell subscribed to (8) (not only in *POM* but throughout his career). No doubt, too, he there took a liberal view of what can be mentioned: witness the Homeric gods. But what about (7)? What, in particular, about impossible objects such as the greatest prime number and the round square on the chalkboard? For that matter, what about the present king of France or the author of *Principia Mathematica*? There are no clear answers in *POM*. We are told that '*A* is not' always expresses a false proposition or nothing at all. But we are also told that there is no such thing as the null class (p. 75), no such thing as the class (as one) of those classes (as ones) that are not members of themselves (p. 102), no such thing as the immediate predecessor of the first limit ordinal (p. 361), and so on. And of course it is hardly surprising that a work on the principles of mathematics should contain *some* such denials of being: there is no such thing as the greatest prime number, else Euclid's argument contains a mistake; there is no such thing as the class of those classes that are not members of themselves, else Russell's own argument is fallacious.[15]

The Homeric gods seem to remain, though this must somehow be reconciled with the apparent extrusion of chimeras (pp. 73–4). As for the present king of France, no such case is explicitly discussed in *POM*. But it may be pointed out that although we have at least some inclination to say that Zeus and Apollo can be mentioned, we have none in the case of the present king of France.

No doubt every term has being, but *POM* thus leaves it uncertain what terms there are.[16] Nevertheless, the impression of a bloated ontology remains. Perhaps it will be suggested that some mitigation is to be found in a distinction Russell and Moore made between *being* and *existence*. Although every term has being, "except space and time themselves, only those [terms] exist which have to particular parts of space and time the special relation of *occupying* them" (MTCA, *Papers* 4, p. 438). So in holding that the Homeric gods have being, Russell is not committed to holding (and he surely would not have held) that one might find them on top of Mt. Olympus. But what then is the import of saying that nonetheless they *are*?

V

It was not long before retrenchment set in.

Before it did, Russell had seemed to argue as follows. Think of '*A*' as some proper name or singular definite description, and let *p* be the proposition that there is no such thing as *A*. Then

9) *A* is a constituent of *p*.

But

10) Every constituent of a proposition has being.

So

11) *A* has being.

Now there is no denying (10); for every constituent of a proposition is a term of *some* proposition, hence a term *simpliciter*, and therefore has being. So if it is to be denied that, for example, the present king of France has being, it must be denied that the present king of France is a constituent of the proposition that there is no such thing. That is the tack Russell took not long after the publication of *POM*. We need to look at some of the details.

In a paper probably written in the second half of 1903, unfinished and published only posthumously, Russell wrote:

> If we say . . . "Arthur Balfour advocates retaliation", that expresses a thought which has for its object a complex containing as a constituent the man himself; no one who does not know what is the designation of the name "Arthur Balfour" can understand what we *mean*: the object of our thought cannot, by our statement, be communicated to him. But when we say "The present Prime Minister of England believes in retaliation", it is possible for a person to understand completely what we mean without his knowing that Mr. Arthur Balfour is Prime Minister, and indeed without his even having ever heard of Mr. Arthur Balfour.[17]

Thus, despite appearances, the present (i.e., 1903) Prime Minister of England is not a constituent of the proposition expressed by the sentence 'The present Prime Minister of England advocates retaliation', the reason being that the descriptive phrase does not designate the present Prime Minister (i.e., Arthur Balfour). And so it is with descriptive phrases generally: what such a phrase designates (if designates at all) is not a constituent of propositions expressed by sentences in which it occurs.

Now, so much was already implied by the theory of "denoting concepts" set forth in Chapter V of *POM*. But there Russell seemed unaware of the possibility of its application in the case of (9): the proposition that there is no such thing as the present king of France does not contain among its constituents the present king of France, and hence the being of the proposition does not depend on there being such a thing as the present king of France. Of course, from the fact that the present king of France is not a constituent of the proposition that there is no such thing, it does not follow that there simply is no such thing. But the point is not to prove that there is no such thing as the present king of France, but to undermine the purported proof that there is. And at least by 1903 Russell was ready to extend the theory to "imaginary proper names" – that is, names like 'Zeus', 'Apollo', and 'Odysseus'; these, he says, are "substitutes for descriptions".[18]

Although Arthur Balfour is not a constituent of the proposition that the present Prime Minister of England advocates retaliation, the proposition is *about* him. Russell gives an argument: the proposition is surely about the present Prime Minister, and Arthur Balfour *is* the present Prime Minister. He confesses to some discomfort:

From this conclusion there is no escape. And yet it has the strange consequence that we may know a proposition about a man, without knowing that it is about him, and without even having heard of him. A person might suppose that Mr. Chamberlain was the present Prime Minister of England, and might judge that the present Prime Minister of England was in favour of retaliation. He would then be making a true judgment about Mr. Arthur Balfour, while believing it to be about Mr. Chamberlain, and possibly never having discovered the existence of Mr. Arthur Balfour.[19]

Yet he sticks to the conclusion: what a proposition is about may or may not be a constituent of the proposition.

Moore objected to the conclusion[20] and seems as a result to have been dissatisfied with the theory of denoting expounded in *POM*. But as far as one can tell neither he nor Russell was aware that it opens the door to another familiar argument for there being such a thing as the present king of France.[21] Presumably

12) Anything a proposition is about has being

is as firm as (8), for anything a proposition is about will surely be mentioned in an assertion of the proposition. But how now is it to be shown that the proposition that the present king of France does not have being is not about the present king of France? It will not suffice to invoke a theory according to which no such thing is a constituent of the proposition. Maybe there is no temptation to say that the proposition in question, or for that matter any proposition, *is* about the present king of France. But there is surely *some* temptation when it comes to, for instance, Zeus and Odysseus.

VI

The "new philosophy" was based in large part on certain doctrines which Russell and Moore held about relations and which, rightly or wrongly, they took to be at least implicitly denied by idealists. Four doctrines in particular were of great importance: that relations are real (i.e., have being); that they are "objective", not "the work of the mind"; that relations are "irreducible" to "adjectives"; and that some, if not all, relations are "external". As we shall shortly see, it is not always clear what the content of these doctrines was taken to be and how they were thought to bear on one another; but let us proceed as best we can.

That relations are real might seem to be a straightforward result of doctrines already expounded. It is true that the earth orbits the sun, and hence there is such a thing as the proposition that the earth orbits the sun. If the constitution of the proposition can be read off from that of the sentence just now used to express it, the relation *orbits* is one of its constituents. Now every constituent of a proposition is a term of some proposition, hence a term, and hence has being. Therefore, *orbits* has being.

Moore and Russell would have taken no exception to the argument, but in trying to establish the "reality" of relations, they typically seek to demonstrate that relations are objective and irreducible. Perhaps they thought that the argument as it stands comes uncomfortably close to begging the question, or perhaps they took the "reality" of relations to involve more than just their having being. One suspects that in Russell's case there was simply a desire to slay a dragon, namely, the doctrine that every proposition is ultimately either a subject – predicate proposition or a compound of such, a doctrine he thought to be a pervasive cause of philosophical error.

That some propositions *appear* to be relational is undeniable. Russell says that advocates of the pernicious doctrine have two ways of dealing with a proposition apparently of the form *aRb*, one "monadistic", the other "monistic". According to the former, the proposition is a conjunction of two propositions, one attributing a property to *a* and the other attributing a property to *b*. According to the latter, the proposition attributes a property to the "whole" composed of *a* and *b*. But what properties? Consider the proposition that Detroit is north of Windsor. The monadist can of course point out that this proposition is equivalent to the conjunction of the proposition that Detroit has the property of being north of Windsor with the proposition that Windsor has the property of being south of Detroit. (Indeed, it is equivalent to each conjunct.) But the properties here invoked are relational, and thus, without further analysis, presuppose the reality of relations. It may be suggested that the monadist can appeal to *positional* properties: the location of Detroit is *A*, that of Windsor is *B*. But even if it can be assumed that positional properties are non-relational, it will be necessary that *A* and *B* themselves be appropriately related: *A* must be north of *B*. The monistic theory fares no better. Let *DW* be the whole composed of Detroit and Windsor (whatever that may be). If the proposition that Detroit is north of Windsor is a proposition to the effect that *DW* has a certain property, then the proposition that Windsor is north of Detroit will attribute the same property to *WD*. But *DW* is identical with *WD*, and hence propositions which are obviously distinct will have the same constituents, arranged in the same way.

As for the view attributed to Kant, that relations are "the work of the mind", Russell argues that it has the consequence that all relational propositions are false.

For ... when we assert that Caesar crossed the Rubicon or that the earth goes round the sun, we do not assert a relation of our ideas, but a relation of things; and if what we assert is true, we must be *apprehending* a relation not imputed by our thinking. But if the Kantian doctrine is pressed, it leads us to ... the view that, though we have ideas of relations between things, things are incapable of having relations ....

It must therefore be admitted "that things may really have relations; that their relations are *facts*, and that these facts are the objects of our judgments when the objects of our judgments are *true*".[22]

In defending the "externality" of (some, if not all) relations, Moore and Russell set themselves in opposition to what Russell called the *axiom of internal relations*, the proposition that "every relation is grounded in the nature of the related terms". Thus formulated, it is pretty obscure what this proposition is supposed to be. Sometimes Russell equates it with the doctrine, already considered, that no proposition is irreducibly relational. On what appears to be another understanding, he and Moore take the axiom to imply or be equivalent to the proposition that the relational properties of a term are parts of its "nature". This latter interpretation merits independent discussion, and that is best undertaken in connection with Moore's and Russell's view that every term is immutable.

VII

With a note of acknowledgement to Moore, Russell says that "every term is immutable and indestructible. What a term is, it is, and no change can be conceived in it which would not destroy its identity and make it another term" (*POM*, p. 44). Now, if a term is immutable, it never changes. But how is this to be reconciled with the fact, which we have just seen Russell rely on, that the earth orbits the sun? Nothing orbits without moving, and nothing moves without changing its location. There is, in fact, no need to call on astronomy: isn't it *obvious* that things change?

There is indeed a sense in which, according to Russell, terms are truly said to change. "Change", in that sense, "is the difference, in respect of truth or falsehood, between a proposition concerning an entity and a time T and a proposition concerning the same entity and another time T', provided that the two propositions differ only by the fact that T occurs in the one where T' occurs in the other" (*POM*, p. 469). Thus, an object o changes if and only if there are a property P and times T and T', such that the proposition that o has P at T differs in truth value from the proposition that o has P at T'. A change in this sense has come to be called a "Cambridge change",[23] and it cannot be denied that an object changes only if it is a subject of a Cambridge change. Russell would add that there is no other sense in which an object does change. Of course, it has often been held that a Cambridge change need not be a *genuine* change. When Theaetetus becomes taller than Socrates, Socrates undergoes a Cambridge change; but his height can remain the same, and therefore there need be no genuine change in him, though there is in Theaetetus. When Copernicus comes to believe that the earth orbits the sun, the earth undergoes a Cambridge change; but only Copernicus is subject of a genuine change.

It is perhaps such allegedly genuine changes that Russell means to exclude when he says, "Change, in this metaphysical sense, I do not at all admit" (*POM*, p. 471). But one cannot say with confidence, given only what he there says about the "metaphysical" sense. He suggests that acceptance of change in this sense is connected with the supposition that "a thing could, in some way, be different and yet the same". Now, it is indeed true that "genuine" change in a thing would require that something be true of it at one time that is not true of it at another; but the same is true of any Cambridge change. It is also true that some who defend "genuine" change think that among the properties of a thing there is a "distinction of the essential and the accidental", but so do some who oppose it; and neither party is guilty of some blunder in reasoning.

Perhaps when Russell links acceptance of change in the "metaphysical" sense to the supposition that "a thing could, in some way, be different and yet the same", the supposition in question is rather that a thing could have lacked some of the properties which it in fact possesses, such properties not being part of its "nature" or "essence". Russell objects on the ground that, at bottom, the supposition rests on a bogus distinction between necessary and contingent truths. Whether a term could have lacked a certain property that it in fact has depends on whether the proposition, with respect to the term, that it has the property, is true necessarily or only contingently. But:

Everything is in a sense a mere fact. A proposition is said to be proved when it is deduced from premises; but the premises, ultimately, and the rule of inference, have to be simply assumed. Thus any ultimate premiss is, in a certain sense, a mere fact. On the other hand, there seems to be no true proposition of which there is any sense in saying that it might have been false. One might as well say that redness might have been a taste and not a colour. What is true, is true; what is false, is false; and concerning fundamentals, there is nothing more to be said. (*POM*, p. 454)

For a time Russell adopted a sanitized version of necessity, suggested by Moore, according to which propositions "are necessary when they are implied in a large number of other propositions".[24] The idea was that necessity comes in degrees, one proposition being more necessary than another just in case it is implied in a larger number of propositions. But Russell soon came to think that this provides no means for distinguishing among truths those which are necessary from those which are contingent: every true proposition is (materially) implied by every proposition, and hence all true propositions will have the maximal degree of necessity.[25]

As for indestructibility, it is enough to remark that it is the *being* of a term that cannot cease. *Existence* can begin and end, for beginning and ending are only Cambridge changes. And a term which ceases to exist "is still an entity, which can be counted as *one*, and concerning which some propositions are true and others false" (*POM*, p. 471).

VIII

Near the beginning of this essay I said that at least by 1911 Russell and Moore had abandoned most of the doctrines that constituted the "new philosophy". The date was chosen because it seems to have been during the academic year 1910–11 that Moore changed his mind about a doctrine central to the "new philosophy" – the doctrine, namely, that every belief has an object, a proposition, that *is* or *has being* whether the belief is true or false.[26] Russell had already reached the same conclusion.[27] His objection, like Moore's, was to the early analysis of belief. The "single-object" theory, as he called it, had the implausible consequence that there are "objective falsehoods", entities denoted by such phrases as 'that the sun orbits the earth'. Neither he nor Moore objected as such to what on the earlier theory had been true propositions, that is, facts; indeed, facts remained in their ontologies for many years to come. But parity of analysis required that they not be thought of as objects of belief.

Even more fundamental, I think, to the "new philosophy" is the view, espoused explicitly by Russell in *POM*, that "grammar" can be taken as a guide to philosophical analysis. That view, always somewhat creaky, definitely collapsed in June 1905, when Russell discovered his Theory of Descriptions.[28] That discovery constitutes the beginning of the end of the "new philosophy": henceforth, there was to be no expectation that "logical form" should reflect "grammatical form".

NOTES

1. "An Autobiography", in P.A. Schilpp, ed., *The Philosophy of G.E. Moore*, 2nd edition (New York: Tudor, 1952), pp. 3–39, at p. 22.
2. In, e.g., a headnote by the editors, in *Papers* 1, p. 105. See also R.W. Clark, *The Life of Bertrand Russell* (New York: Knopf, 1976) p. 68; and John Slater, "Russell's Conception of Philosophy", *Russell* n. s. 8 (1988): 163–178.
3. Letter to Moore, 7 December, 1897. Quoted in the headnote to "Seems, Madam? Nay It Is", *Papers* 1, at p. 105.
4. For a full and judicious discussion of the issue, see Nicholas Griffin, *Russell's Idealist Apprenticeship*, Oxford: Oxford University Press, 1991, Section 7.2.
5. London: Allen and Unwin, 1953.
6. Russell wrote: "If I believe that A is the father of B, I believe something; the subsistence of the something, if not directly obvious, seems to follow from the fact that, if it did not subsist, I should be believing nothing, and therefore not believing" (MTCA, *Papers* 4, p. 462).
7. "Truth and Falsity", in J.M. Baldwin, ed., *Dictionary of Philosophy and Psychology* (London: Macmillan, 1901–1902), vol. 2, pp. 716–718. Reprinted in Thomas Baldwin, ed., *G.E. Moore: Selected Writings* (London and New York: Routledge, 1993), pp. 20–2.
8. *Selected Writings*, p. 21. My emphasis.
9. *Selected Writings*, p. 20.
10. See MTCA, *Papers* 4, p. 474.
11. "The Nature of Judgment", *Mind* 8 (1899): 176–93. Reprinted in *Selected Writings*, in which the quotation occurs at p. 4.
12. "The Nature of Truth", *Papers*, p. 494.
13. In his fellowship dissertation of 1898, from which "The Nature of Judgment" was apparently extracted, Moore seems to have taken the position that all complexity is propositional, that "a proposition is nothing other than a complex concept" (*Selected Writings*, p. 5). This provoked Russell to say, in a letter to Moore: "I believe that propositions are distinguished from mere concepts, not by their complexity only, but by always containing one specific concept, i.e., the copula 'is ....' 'The wise man' is not a proposition, as Leibniz says." (Russell to Moore, 1 December 1898, in Nicholas Griffin, ed., *The Selected Letters of Bertrand Russell* (Boston/New York/ London: Houghton Mifflin, 1992), p. 191).
14. W.V. Quine, "Russell's Ontological Development", *Journal of Philosophy* 63 (1966): 657–67; reprinted in *Theories and Things* (Cambridge, Mass.: Harvard University Press, 1981, wherein the description occurs on p. 75. A similar assessment is to be found in e.g. J.O. Urmson,

Philosophical Analysis: Its Development between the Two World Wars
(Oxford: Clarendon Press, 1956), pp. 23–4.

15. For that argument see *POM*, Chapter X.

16. A similar comment can be made in Moore's case. In Baldwin's *Dictionary* he had stated that being is "an absolutely universal term", possessed by "propositions, whether true or false, and any terms that can be used in a proposition". But from this alone we cannot tell whether a purported term is a genuine one, which can be used in a proposition.

17. "On Meaning and Denotation", in *Papers* 4, pp. 315–16.

18. See "Points about Denoting", *Papers* 4, p. 285.

19. "On Meaning and Denotation", in *Papers* 4, p. 317.

20. In an unpublished review of *POM*.

21. It should be remarked, however, that there is reason to think Moore was unusually sensitive to the force of arguments, other than those explicitly considered by Russell, for the reality of "imaginary objects". Such arguments are a major concern of *Some Main Problems of Philosophy* and later writings.

22. "The Nature of Truth", *Papers* 4, p. 495.

23. A name introduced by P.T. Geach in his *God and the Soul*, New York: Schocken Books, 1969, pp. 71–2.

24. Moore, "Necessity", *Mind* 9 (1900): 289–304, at p. 303.

25. See "Necessity and Possibility", in *Papers* 4, p. 513. In that essay Russell suggested a meaning for 'necessary' considered as an adjective applicable to propositional functions – a propositional function being in the proposed sense necessary just in case it "holds of everything" (p. 518). Evidently this notion is of no use in the present connection.

26. Moore had maintained early on in *Some Main Problems* that "There certainly are in the Universe such things as propositions" (p. 56); but in a later passage, probably written in 1911, he says that "the theory as to the analysis of belief which I wish to recommend . . . may be expressed by saying that there simply are no such things as *propositions*". In a preface dated 1953, Moore says that there may be no inconsistency between the two passages; for in the later he was certainly expressing a view as to the correct *analysis* of belief, whereas it is possible that in the earlier he was not. Perhaps. But in *Some Main Problems* he refers to the theory he "formerly held" as a "theory as to the analysis of belief". See pp. 260–1.

27. See "On the Nature of Truth", *Proceedings of the Aristotelian Society* 7 (1907): 28–49; "On the Nature of Truth and Falsehood", in *Philosophical Essays*, London: Longmans, 1910, pp. 170–85.

28. The first published statement of the Theory of Descriptions occurs in OD. See Hylton's paper in this volume.

4   Russell and Frege

I. INTRODUCTION

Bertrand Russell and Gottlob Frege are the two giants on whose shoulders analytic philosophy rests. Whilst G. E. Moore and Ludwig Wittgenstein also played a significant role in the emergence of analytic philosophy, it was Russell's and Frege's work on the foundations of mathematics and their development of new techniques of logical analysis that set the agenda, and without both Russell and Frege, Wittgenstein's own philosophy would simply not have evolved.

There are many similarities between Russell and Frege. Both were trained as mathematicians, and although they also studied philosophy, were both drawn seriously into philosophy through concern with the foundations of mathematics. Both wrote early works on geometry, but became increasingly interested in the nature of number. In the works that represent the highpoint of their intellectual achievements, both set out to demonstrate that arithmetic was reducible to logic, a project that required the development of logical theory itself. Both exerted a powerful influence on the young Ludwig Wittgenstein, whose *Tractatus Logico-Philosophicus* ushered in the second phase of analytic philosophy when the so-called 'linguistic turn' was taken. But despite these fundamental similarities in their mathematical background, achievements, and influence, their personal lives, characters, and careers were very different. Frege spent his entire working career (from 1874 to 1918) lecturing in mathematics at the University of Jena, remained a relative recluse, and grew increasingly embittered as he failed to receive the recognition he deserved. Russell, by contrast, as a well-connected aristocrat of independent means, strode the world stage from the very beginning of his career, had a colourful private life and took an active role in public affairs. Unlike Frege, who published relatively little and almost exclusively in the area of logic and the philosophy of mathematics, Russell's prolific output spanned the whole range of philosophical and political thought, and he has probably been more widely read in his own lifetime than any other philosopher in history.

Yet the work on logic and the foundations of mathematics that Russell and Frege have in common is what remains of greatest philosophical significance, and it on this that I focus in the present essay. In Sections III and IV, I outline the key elements of Frege's work – his logical theory and analysis of number – and compare his achievements with those of Russell. In Section V, I consider Frege's reaction to Russell's paradox; and in the final section, I offer an account of their differing conceptions and practices of analysis. I begin, however, with Russell's claim that it was he who first drew attention to Frege's work.

II. RUSSELL'S 'DISCOVERY' OF FREGE

The three major works that Frege published in his lifetime were the *Begriffsschrift* (*Conceptual Notation*), published in 1879, *Die Grundlagen der Arithmetik* (*The Foundations of Arithmetic*), published in 1884, and the *Grundgesetze der Arithmetik* (*Basic Laws of Arithmetic*), the first volume of which was published in 1893 and the second volume in 1903. In commenting on the significance of the first two works in his *History of Western Philosophy*, Russell claimed that "in spite of the epoch-making nature of his discoveries, [Frege] remained wholly without recognition until I drew attention to him in 1903" (*HWP*, p. 784). What Russell was referring to here was Appendix A of his *Principles of Mathematics*, entitled 'The Logical and Arithmetical Doctrines of Frege', which did indeed provide the first account of Frege's philosophy to appear in print (other than book reviews and the occasional criticism).[1] But Russell is exaggerating in suggesting that Frege remained "wholly without recognition"

---

[1] Criticism had been made of Frege's *Grundlagen*, in particular, by Benno Kerry in two articles, which prompted Frege's reply in his 1892 paper 'On Concept and Object' (cf. *The Frege Reader*, p. 181), and by Edmund Husserl in his *Philosophie der Arithmetik*, a detailed review of which Frege published in 1894 (cf. *The Frege Reader*, p. 224).

before 1903. Russell had himself been inspired to read Frege by Peano, whom Russell had met in 1900,[2] and who had been in communication with Frege on matters of common interest since 1894.[3] Peano knew Frege's *Grundlagen* and published a review of the first volume of the *Grundgesetze* in *Rivista di matematica* in 1895. Frege published a reply in the same journal in 1896 and a further piece comparing Peano's notation with his own in 1897.[4] Given Peano's role in the development of mathematical logic, if anyone can claim to have 'drawn attention' to Frege, then it is Peano rather than Russell. At the very least, one should note that it was Peano who drew Russell's attention to Frege, even if it was Russell who was instrumental in introducing Frege's work to the English-speaking world.[5]

This was not Russell's only exaggeration as far as Frege was concerned. In his *Introduction to Mathematical Philosophy*, Russell claimed that he was the first person to ever read the *Begriffsschrift*.[6] In fact, the book received six reviews in the two years following its publication, and although this is not in itself proof that it had been read properly (three of the reviews were very short), one of them was a detailed review by Ernst Schröder, the leading German logician at the time, who had certainly read the book carefully.[7] Although Schröder nevertheless failed to appreciate its real significance, it is not true that Frege's work was not noticed at all, at least in continental Europe.

In his autobiography, Russell reports that after his election to a Fellowship (in October 1895), his tutor at Cambridge, James Ward, gave him a copy of Frege's *Begriffsschrift*. But Russell writes that "I possessed the book for years before I could make out what it meant.

[2] Russell and Peano met at the International Congress of Philosophy held in Paris in July of that year, a meeting that Russell himself referred to as a "turning point in my intellectual life" (*Auto.*, p. 147).

[3] For their correspondence, see Frege, 1980, pp. 108–29. Topics discussed included notation for generality, conditional definition, and identity.

[4] The former is reprinted in Frege, 1980, pp. 113–18, and the latter in Frege, 1984, pp. 234–48.

[5] For more on Peano's role in the development of mathematical logic, see Nidditch, 1962; Rodríguez-Consuegra, 1991, ch. 3.

[6] *IMP*, p. 25, fn. 2. Cf. *MPD*, p. 71: "This notion of the ancestral relation was first developed by Frege as long ago as [1879], but his work remained unnoticed until Whitehead and I developed it."

[7] All the reviews are reprinted in Frege, 1972, pp. 209–35. Schröder's review was 14 pages long, and he read the book thoroughly enough to spot the slip Frege made in §5. Cf. Frege, 1997, p. 58.

Indeed, I did not understand it until I had myself independently discovered most of what it contained" (*Auto.*, p. 65; cf. *POM*, p. xxiii).
Although Russell could read German, there is no reason to doubt his
sincerity here, since the book is full of Frege's new notation, which
one of the reviewers at the time dismissed as "cumbrous and incon-
venient" and which never did succeed in becoming adopted.[8] The
same excuse cannot be offered in the case of Frege's *Grundlagen*,
however, which is free from technical notation, and which is widely
recognized as a masterpiece of philosophical lucidity. But here too
Russell reports that he only read it some sixteen years after its publication, and a year or so after he had discovered for himself its central
definition of number (*IMP*, p. 11; *MPD*, p. 54).

So the position seems to be this. Russell did not properly read
Frege's work until after he had thought out its main ideas for himself,
utilizing the notation developed by Peano. If Frege did have any influence on Russell before 1902, it can only have been through Peano,
who was responsible for drawing Russell's attention to Frege. And
even this indirect influence cannot have been substantial. Nevertheless, it was Russell who first offered an account of Frege's views
as a whole, and who first appreciated their real philosophical significance. In the next two sections, I explain this significance, and
compare Frege's ideas with what Russell discovered for himself, before turning in Section V to the contradiction that Russell discovered in Frege's system in 1902, which was the trigger for their direct
communication.

III. LOGIC

Frege's first book takes its name from the logical symbolism or
'Begriffsschrift' (literally, 'concept-script') that he designed to represent the 'conceptual content' ('Begriffsinhalt') of propositions.[9] His
aim, in particular, was to represent the content of arithmetical propositions so that the source of their truth could be investigated, which

---

[8] The reviewer was John Venn, whose review in *Mind* in 1880 was less than a page
(the review is reprinted in Frege, 1972, pp. 234–5). Cf. Russell, *IMP*, p. 95: "Frege's
work ... remained almost unknown, probably in the main on account of the difficulty of his symbolism." The remark was first made in *POM*, p. xxi.
[9] In this essay, I use the term 'Begriffsschrift' in italics for the book itself and the term
in inverted commas for Frege's logical symbolism.

Frege hoped to show was purely logical. Compared to this underlying ambition, the development of a mere symbolism might seem a relatively modest aim; but in fact, what Frege initiated in this short book (of around 90 pages) was nothing less than a revolution in logic. Traditional (Aristotelian) logic had on the whole worked well in the limited area in which it applied, but had had great difficulty in analysing propositions of the more complex kind that are common in mathematics – in particular, propositions of *multiple generality* (containing more than one quantifier, i.e., a term such as 'every' or 'some') and *relational* propositions. 'Every natural number has a successor' and 'Between any two rational numbers there is another rational number' are just two examples of propositions that involve both relations and multiple generality. By extending the use of function-argument analysis in mathematics to logic, and providing a notation for quantification, however, Frege was able not only to represent such propositions but also to analyse the characteristic principles of reasoning in mathematics. In doing so, he took the first big step towards the goal of demonstrating what has become known as the thesis of *logicism* – that mathematics is reducible to logic. (Frege, in fact, was only a logicist about arithmetic; Russell held the stronger thesis.)

The *Begriffsschrift* is divided into three parts. The first part explains the logical symbolism, the second shows how to represent and derive certain propositions, and the third uses the symbolism to provide an analysis of mathematical induction. In the first part, as well as providing an axiomatization of propositional logic, Frege introduces his quantificational theory. His first move is to represent simple propositions such as 'Socrates is mortal' not in subject–predicate form ('*S* is *P*', i.e., analysing it into subject and predicate joined by the copula) but in function-argument form ('*Fx*') – taking 'Socrates' as the argument and '*x* is mortal' as the function, which yields the proposition as value when the argument place indicated by the variable '*x*' is filled by the name 'Socrates'.[10] A similar move

---

[10] I gloss over here the issue as to whether Frege understands functions and arguments as expressions or as what those expressions stand for, which he did not clearly distinguish at the time of *Begriffsschrift*, as well as the related issue as to what he regards as the *value* of a (propositional) function for a given argument, often taken as the 'conceptual content' of the proposition. Throughout this essay, I also use modern notation rather than Frege's own two-dimensional notation in discussing his ideas. App. 2 of *The Frege Reader* contains an explanation of Frege's symbolism.

is made in the case of relational propositions, which are construed as functions of more than one argument. '*a* stands in relation *R* to *b*' can thus be represented as '*Rab*' or '*aRb*'. (Cf. 1879, §§9–10.)

With function-argument analysis introduced, Frege is then in a position to represent the four types of propositions contained in the traditional Aristotelian square of opposition, i.e., propositions of the form 'All *A*'s are *B*', 'Some *A*'s are *B*', 'No *A*'s are *B*' and 'Some *A*'s are not *B*'. By interpreting 'All *A*'s are *B*' as 'If anything is an *A*, then it is a *B*', the first can be seen as constructed from two simpler parts (functions, or propositional functions, as Russell was to call them), '*x* is an *A*' and '*x* is a *B*', linked together by the propositional connective 'if . . . then' (the logical properties of which Frege has already explained). To complete the analysis, we then need to bind what we have here by the quantifier, and provide suitable notation, yielding 'For all *x*, if *x* is an *A*, then *x* is a *B*', or in (modern) symbols, '$(\forall x) (Ax \rightarrow Bx)$'. With negation, 'Some *A*'s are *B*' can be represented as '$\neg(\forall x) (Ax \rightarrow \neg Bx)$', which is equivalent to '$(\exists x) (Ax \,\&\, Bx)$', using the existential quantifier and conjunction, 'No *A*'s are *B*' as '$(\forall x) (Ax \rightarrow \neg Bx)$', and 'Some *A*'s are not *B*' as '$\neg(\forall x) (Ax \rightarrow Bx)$', which is equivalent to '$(\exists x) (Ax \,\&\, \neg Bx)$'.[11] (Cf. 1879, §12.) The account is both elegant and a good illustration of Frege's claim that he has provided a notation not just for facilitating (recognition of) logical inference but also for representing 'conceptual content', exhibiting the logical relations *within* propositions.[12]

With this notation, propositions of whatever degree of quantificational or relational complexity can be analyzed. 'Every natural number has a successor', for example, can be represented as follows, '*Nx*' symbolizing '*x* is a natural number' and '*Syx*' symbolizing '*y* is a successor of *x*':

(S) $(\forall x)(Nx \rightarrow (\exists y)(Ny \,\&\, Syx))$.

This can be read as 'For all *x*, if *x* is a natural number, then there is some natural number which is its successor'.

---

[11] Frege does not himself use a separate symbol for the existential quantifier, relying on the equivalence, as we now write it, of '$(\forall x)\ Fx$' and '$\neg(\exists x)\neg Fx$' (cf. 1879, §12), nor for conjunction, which he defines in terms of conditionality and negation (1879, §7).

[12] Cf. Frege, 1972, pp. 90–1. I discuss Frege's claim, his advance on traditional logic, and the important notion of 'conceptual content' in more detail in ch. 2 of *Frege: Making Sense* (1996).

How does this compare with Russell's early views on logic? Up to the point at which Russell met Peano in 1900, there is no sign in Russell's writings that he understood quantification. The work in which it would be most obvious to look for such an understanding is 'An Analysis of Mathematical Reasoning', written in the middle of 1898 but abandoned before the end of the year, though parts of it were reworked into drafts of The Principles of Mathematics.[13] Having just read Whitehead's Universal Algebra, Russell set out in this work to articulate the necessary presuppositions of pure mathematics, by using Whitehead's logic in much the same way that Kant had relied upon the Aristotelian forms of judgement in expounding what he took as our fundamental conceptual framework. But since Whitehead's logic was essentially Boolean algebra, there was no radical break with traditional methods of analysis. 'All humans are mortal', for example, was seen as analysable either intensionally, viz. as 'human implies mortal', or extensionally, viz. as 'The assemblage of humans is part of the assemblage of mortals' (cf. AMR, pp. 188–9). The intensional construal, understood as expressing a necessary connection between predicates (cf. AMR, pp. 172–3), suggests agreement with Frege that such propositions are about concepts rather than objects; but as Russell himself recognized, such a purely intensional analysis cannot be offered of propositions involving the quantifier 'some' rather than 'all' (cf. AMR, p. 189); and the difficulty of providing a satisfying uniform account is exacerbated in cases of multiple generality.[14]

By the time of The Principles of Mathematics, which was published in 1903, Russell had learnt from Peano the method and advantages of function-argument analysis, and had begun to apply it for himself in developing Peano's work. In the second chapter, Russell remarks that symbolic logic "achieved almost nothing of utility either to philosophy or to other branches of mathematics, until it was transformed by the new methods of Professor Peano" (POM, p. 10), and makes clear his own debt to Peano (POM, p. 10, fn.; p. 26; cf. p. xxiii). The remark also suggests, however, that he failed to recognize even then the advances that Frege had made more than two

---

[13] What remains of the work has now been published in Papers 2.
[14] For a detailed account of AMR, and the problems that Russell gets into, see Griffin, 1991, ch. 7. As Griffin remarks (p. 285), "Russell's thinking about quantification in 1898 was rudimentary in the extreme, and remained so for several years."

decades earlier. But the Fregean ('interpretive') analysis of 'Any a is a b' as 'x is an a implies x is a b', understood in Russell's terms as a 'formal' rather than 'material' implication, i.e., as holding for all values of x, is clearly set out in his chapter on 'The Variable' (*POM*, ch. 7). Here too, though, Russell failed to break entirely with traditional subject–predicate analysis. 'Any a is a b' and 'x is an a implies x is a b', he writes, "do not *mean* the same thing: for *any* a is a concept denoting only a's, whereas in the formal implication x need not be an a" (*POM*, p. 91). Analysing 'Any a is a b' *decompositionally*, in accord with grammar, suggests that 'any a' is the subject, and hence must represent what Russell calls a 'denoting concept', somehow 'denoting' indefinitely the objects that are said to be b's (cf. *POM*, ch. 5). Russell's theory of denoting concepts was not abandoned until 1905, when the theory of descriptions took its place, and it was only then that the idea that the logical form of a proposition may differ radically from its grammatical form was finally cemented. (I return to the issue of 'interpretive' versus 'decompositional' analysis in Section VI below.)

It was in developing the theory of relations, however, that Russell most rapidly went beyond Peano's work in the period immediately after their first meeting. His paper on 'The Logic of Relations' was written in September 1900, employing Peano's notation, and published in Peano's journal the following year.[15] Here too, as we have seen, Frege had already provided a notation by means of which relations, of whatever complexity, could be represented; but it was Russell who first appreciated the wider philosophical significance of this achievement. Indeed, it is no exaggeration to say that it was the problem of relations that had led Russell to abandon his youthful idealism, and the tremendous excitement he felt in discovering and applying the new symbolic logic lay precisely in the resolution of his earlier problems. Traditional logic had tended to regard all propositions as fundamentally of subject–predicate form, but (like statements of multiple generality) relational propositions had proved particularly resistant to reduction. Propositions involving equivalence relations, such as 'a is as red as b' might (arguably) be straightforwardly reduced

[15] 'The Logic of Relations' is published in *Papers* 2. Cf. Russell's *Autobiography*, where Russell reports that he spent August, 1900, familiarizing himself with Peano's work, and September extending it to the logic of relations, the latter month being "the highest point of my life" (*Auto.* 1, pp. 147–8).

to 'a is red' and 'b is red', but propositions involving *asymmetrical* relations, such as 'a is heavier than b', were more problematic. It might be suggested that 'a' represents the subject and 'is heavier than b' the predicate here, but the latter does not represent an *intrinsic* property of a, since it involves reference to b, and is thus implicitly relational.[16] We might suggest instead that the proposition be analysed into two simpler propositions assigning particular weights to a and b, but aside from the fact that the weights themselves would have to be compared (involving a higher order relational proposition), such assignments too are implicitly relational, since they depend on measurement against an agreed standard. So such propositions cannot be reduced to simple subject–predicate propositions, and the only conclusion would seem to be to treat them as fundamental, of the form 'aRb', which, for Russell, meant recognizing the reality of relations, as ineliminable components of propositions, and a repudiation of what he had taken as a central tenet of British idealism.

What the irreducibility of asymmetrical relations indicates is the importance of *order*. Two points on a geometrical line may be identical in all their 'intrinsic' properties, but still be distinguishable in virtue of their order on the line – an 'extrinsic' difference that cannot be explained simply by 'analysing' (in the sense of 'decomposing' into their qualities) the points themselves. What is needed is thus an 'analysis' (in a different sense) of *order in a series*, and it was Frege who first achieved this in the third part of his *Begriffsschrift*. Entitled 'Some Elements from a General Theory of Series', Frege here offers a logical analysis not only of *following in a series* but also of various other concepts fundamental to mathematics.

Frege starts by defining the notion of an *hereditary property*, which we can understand as a property that is passed down the members of a series generated by an appropriate asymmetrical relation. For example, if we take the series starting with a particular person and generated by the relation (i.e., function with two arguments) represented by 'y is a child of x', then the property of being a human being is hereditary in this series. Symbolizing 'y is R-related to x' as

---

[16] For definitions of 'intrinsic' and 'extrinsic' properties, and correspondingly of 'internal' and 'external' relations, and for a thorough account of the complex development of Russell's ideas on relations, see Griffin, 1991, ch. 8.

'Rxy', a property F is defined as *hereditary in the R-series* if it meets the following condition:

(HP) $(\forall x)(Fx \to (\forall y)(Rxy \to Fy))$; i.e., for all x, if x has the property F, then every y that is R-related to x has the property F. (Cf. 1879, §24, formula 69.)[17]

With the notion of an hereditary property, Frege then defines the concept of *following in a series*, or as it is now termed, the concept of the *proper ancestral* of a relation. In the case of the relation *is a child of*, we have the proper ancestral *is a descendant of* (and in the case of the relation *is a parent of*, we have the proper ancestral *is an ancestor of*, whence the term). To say that b is a descendant of a is to say that b comes after a in the series generated by the relation *is a child of*. Using '(HP)' to abbreviate the formula just given, 'b follows a in the R-series' is defined thus:

(PA) $(\forall F)(\{(HP) \;\&\; (\forall y)(Ray \to Fy)\} \to Fb)$; i.e., for any property F, if F is hereditary in the R-series and everything that is R-related to a has the property F, then b has the property F. (Cf. 1879, §26, formula 76.)

Using these two formulae, a further formula can then be written down:

(MI) $(Fa \;\&\; (HP) \;\&\; (PA)) \to Fb$; i.e., if a has a property F which is hereditary in the R-series, and if b follows a in the R-series, then b has the property F. (Cf. 1879, §27, formula 81.)

From Fa and (HP), $(\forall y)(Ray \to Fy)$ can be derived, from which, with (HP) again, by (PA), Fb results. What we have here is the key move in mathematical induction. For with the additional assumption that the first member of the R-series has the hereditary property F, we can then show that every member of the series has the property F. What Frege has thus provided is a purely logical analysis of mathematical induction, making feasible the logicist project.

Frege gives one final definition that is worth noting here – the definition of a *many-one relation*, which obtains if the following

---

[17] Once again, I use modern notation here rather than Frege's own 'Begriffsschrift'. A summary of Frege's analysis in Part III of *Begriffsschrift* is provided in *The Frege Reader*, pp. 75–8, on which I draw here.

condition is met:

(MO) $(\forall x)(\forall y)(Rxy \rightarrow (\forall z)(Rxz \rightarrow z = y))$; i.e., for all x, if anything is R-related to x, then there is only one such thing. (Cf. 1879, §31, formula 115.)

Although Frege does not do so himself in the *Begriffsschrift*, a corresponding definition can be given of a *one–many relation*, which can then be combined with (MO) to define a *one–one relation*:

(OO) $(\forall x)(\forall y)(Rxy \rightarrow \{(\forall z)(Rxz \rightarrow z = y) \, \& \, (\forall w)(Rwy \rightarrow w = x)\})$.

For example, the relation of parent to eldest child is many-one, the relation of father to child (where there is more than one child) is one-many, and the relation of father to eldest child is one–one. The definition of a one–one relation was to play a crucial role in Frege's analysis of number.

Frege's account in the *Begriffsschrift* is a model of clarity, economy, and elegance, achieved with none of the effort or tortured philosophical excursions that seemed to mark Russell's path to the same point. Although Frege was the same age when the *Begriffsschrift* was published as Russell was when *The Principles of Mathematics* was published, Part IV of which is devoted to the topic of order, Russell's corresponding account is considerably inferior. The (informal) definitions of many–one and one–one relations are merely given in passing,[18] and there is no logical analysis of mathematical induction at all. In the *Principles*, Russell is clearly working it all out laboriously for himself, and this often detracts from his genuine advances. A formal treatment, with informal clarifications, is provided in *Principia Mathematica*, but it was not until 1919, in his *Introduction to Mathematical Philosophy*,[19] that Russell finally attained the clarity and economy that Frege had achieved straight off, and by this time Russell had had the benefit of studying Frege's works in detail.

However, in the *Principles*, Russell does provide an extensive discussion of relations generally, and he is much more sensitive than Frege to the philosophical issues involved, which, as we have noted, were pivotal in his reaction against British idealism. Furthermore,

---

[18] Cf. Russell, *POM*, pp. 113, 130, 246, 305.
[19] Mathematical induction is explained in ch. 3, and the theory of relations in chs. 4 and 5.

we might suggest that it was just because Russell had worked his own way through the problems that he was able to recognize Frege's genius, and (given his generosity in acknowledging the work of others) do what he did in making Frege's writings better known. So although it does seem that Russell arrived at his logical results independently of Frege, Frege nevertheless played a role in sharpening their articulation. In turn, it was Russell's deeper involvement in the philosophical debates of the day that brought out the significance of Frege's work, and indeed, later prompted Frege himself to clarify his own philosophical ideas, as their correspondence from 1902, in particular, shows. As we shall see, this mutual influence was equally important in the case of the analysis of number.

IV. THE ANALYSIS OF NUMBER

In his preface to the *Begriffsschrift*, Frege remarked that he had sought to provide a logical analysis of following in a series in order then to advance to the concept of number. The natural numbers themselves, of course, form a series, generated by the successor relation, so the obvious task is to logically define the first member of this series and the successor relation, and then use what has already been shown to demonstrate the logical definability of all the members of the series. It was this task that Frege set out to accomplish in his second book, *The Foundations of Arithmetic*. In the first three parts of this work, Frege criticizes previous conceptions of number, attacking empiricist, psychologistic, and Kantian views and explains his central claim that a number statement contains an assertion about a concept; and in Part IV he develops his logical analysis. I shall briefly sketch his positive account here, before comparing it with Russell's treatment.

Consider the following example of a number statement:

(Ja)   Jupiter has four moons.

It is tempting to construe this as a subject–predicate proposition with Jupiter as the subject and *has four moons* as the predicate. But the latter clearly demands further analysis, and this suggests that we need to rephrase the proposition:

(Jb)   The moons of Jupiter are four.

Here the moons of Jupiter are now the subject and *are four* the predicate. But to what precisely are we predicating the number four? (Jb) looks analogous to the following proposition:

(Jβ)   The moons of Jupiter are large.

But if we give the four (Galilean) moons their names, (Jβ) can be further analysed as a conjunction of four simpler propositions:

(Jβ*)   Callisto is large and Europa is large and Ganymede is large and Io is large.

But the corresponding analysis of (Jb) is clearly illegitimate:

(Jb*)   Callisto is four and Europa is four and Ganymede is four and Io is four.

Four is not a predicate in the way that *large* is; it is not the individual moons to which *four* is being predicated, but rather, we might suggest, the *class* of moons:

(Jc)   The class of Jupiter's moons is four.

But this is not right either, since the class itself is one, not four; it is the *members* of the class that number four:

(Jd)   The class of Jupiter's moons has four members.

Since the class here is determined by the associated concept, we can also offer an intensional rather than extensional analysis of (Ja):

(Je)   The concept *moon of Jupiter* has four instances.

(Ja) is to be understood, then, as predicating something not of Jupiter or even of Jupiter's moons, but of the concept *moon of Jupiter*, or of the class determined by this concept. (Frege tends to favour the first, and Russell the second, but they are clearly equivalent, ontological issues aside.) Analysis is still required of what it is for a concept to have four instances or a class four members,[20] but we can appreciate Frege's central claim that a number statement contains

---

[20] Comparing (Je) with the original (Ja), it might be objected that we are no further forward, but the point is that 'has four instances' can be logically defined, as we shall see.

an assertion about a concept (cf. 1884, §46). The point is reinforced when we realize that one and the same thing can be assigned different numbers, depending on the *concept* by means of which we conceptualize it. As Frege notes, I can say "Here are four companies" or "Here are 500 men" (ibid.), "two boots" or "one pair of boots" (cf. 1884, §25).

The importance of this idea can also be brought out by considering existential statements. Take the following:

(0a)   Unicorns do not exist. [There are no unicorns.]

Such negative existentials have caused problems throughout the history of philosophy. What *are* these unicorns that are being attributed the property of non-existence? How do we manage to talk about what is *not*? On Frege's account, however, existential statements are just a type of number statement (involving the number 0). To deny that something exists is to say that the relevant *concept* has no instances: there is no mysterious invoking of any *objects*. (0a) is thus to be analysed as (0b), which can be readily formalized in Frege's new logic as (0c):

(0b)   The concept *unicorn* is not instantiated. [The class of unicorns is empty.]

(0c) $\neg(\exists x)\, Fx.$ $[(\forall x)\neg Fx.]$

Similarly, to say that God exists is simply to say that the concept *God* is instantiated, i.e., to deny that the concept has 0 instances. On this view, existence is no longer seen as a (first-level) predicate, but instead, existential statements are analysed in terms of the (second-level) predicate *is instantiated*, represented by the existential quantifier.[21] As Frege notes, such an account provides a neat diagnosis of what is wrong with the ontological argument, at least in its traditional form.[22]

With this understanding, logical characterizations of number statements of the form 'There are $n\,F$'s' or, as Frege puts it, 'The

[21] It is sometimes said, loosely, that existence (or number) is not a first-level but a second-level predicate. But strictly speaking, existence is not a predicate at all; what the second-level predicate is is *is instantiated*, a property of concepts.

[22] Frege, 1884, §53; cf. 1997, pp. 82, 103, 146.

number n belongs to the concept F' can be readily given (cf. 1884, §55):

(F_0) 'There are no F's' is defined as 'For all x, x is not F' [$'(\forall x)\neg Fx'$].

(F_1) 'There is just one F' is defined as 'It is not true that, for all x, x is not F; and, for all x and y, if x is F and y is F, then $x = y'$ [$'\neg(\forall x)\neg Fx \ \& \ (\forall x)(\forall y)(Fx \ \& \ Fy \to x = y)'$].

(F_{n+1}) 'There are $n + 1$ F's' is defined as 'There is some x, such that x is F, and n is the number that belongs to the concept *falling under F, but not x'* [$'(\exists x)(Fx \ \& \ (\exists_n y)(Fy \ \& \ x \neq y))'$].[23]

However, such characterizations only define the phrase 'the number n belongs to' (or 'is instantiated n-fold') rather than number terms themselves; they do not specify *which* objects the relevant numbers are. As Frege notoriously puts it, such definitions provide us with no criterion for determining whether Julius Caesar is a number or not (1884, §56).

To properly carry through the logicist project, we need to consider *equations* – statements of the form '$x = y$' that express the identity of x and y. In the present case, Frege says, we need to define the following proposition (cf. 1884, §62):

(Nb) The number of F's equals the number of G's. (The number that belongs to the concept F is the same as the number that belongs to the concept G.)

It is at this point that Frege makes his most significant move, appealing to his principle that "Only in the context of a proposition do words mean something" (ibid.). Introducing the notion of *equinumerosity* (*Gleichzahligkeit*), Frege suggests that (Nb) is equivalent to (Na), which can therefore be used to define (Nb) and hence its constituent number terms:

(Na) The concept F is equinumerous to the concept G. (There are as many objects falling under concept F as under concept G, i.e., there are just as many F's as G's.)

---

[23] In the formalization in modern notation given in square brackets here, use is made of the *numerical quantifier*, '$\exists_n x$' being read as 'there are n x's such that'. Cf. *The Frege Reader*, p. 105.

(That (Na) and (Nb) are equivalent has since become known as *Hume's Principle*, after the formulation of it that Frege attributes to Hume; 1884, §63.) The crucial point about (Na) is that it can be defined purely logically. For to say that two concepts are 'equinumerous' is to say that there is a one–one relation between them, and this, as we have seen, can be defined purely logically (cf. 1884, §72). So if (Na) can be defined purely logically, and (Na) is equivalent to (Nb), then we have thereby defined (Nb) purely logically. Furthermore, if (Na) has a sense, then (Nb) must have a sense, and this in turn, according to Frege, by the context principle, means that its logically significant parts must also have a sense. So we have guaranteed that 'the number of *F*'s' and 'the number of *G*'s' have a sense.[24]

However, Frege notes that this still does not help us solve the Julius Caesar problem. 'The number of *F*'s' may have a sense, but the definition does not guarantee that it has a unique sense. What the definition of (Nb) by means of (Na) exemplifies is *definition by abstraction*, and this has proved highly problematic (as we shall see in more detail in the next section). Peano used the method in his *Formulaire de Mathématiques*, and Russell objected to it in *The Principles of Mathematics* for precisely the reason Frege gave. Such a process, Russell writes, "suffers from an absolutely fatal formal defect: it does not show that only one object satisfies the definition" (p. 114). The point may be easier to see if we consider the analogous case that Frege himself discussed in the *Grundlagen*:

(Da)   Line *a* is parallel to line *b*.

(Db)   The direction of line *a* is equal to the direction of line *b*.

Here too we have an equivalence which might be used to define 'direction'. But whilst it is true that if two lines are parallel, then their directions are equal, what guarantee is there that this is the only property that they have in common when they are parallel? Two parallel lines are said to meet at infinity, so a point at infinity

---

[24] At this point in his work (1884), Frege does not draw the distinction between sense and *Bedeutung* (which first appeared in 1891), and takes it that if a proposition has a sense, then its logically significant parts have a *Bedeutung*, i.e., that 'the number of *F*'s' does indeed stand for an object. (For the reasons given in *The Frege Reader*, pp. 36–46, I leave the term '*Bedeutung*' untranslated.) I return to the issues involved here in Section VI below.

is something else that they have in common. Or consider any other line, say line c, perpendicular to lines a and b. Then lines a and b also have in common the property of being perpendicular to line c. There is clearly an infinite number of properties that they have in common in virtue of being parallel.

In the *Principles*, Russell suggests that the correct response, in the number case, is not to identify the number of a class with some property that we take equinumerous classes to have in common, but with the class of all such classes (*POM*, p. 115). This is essentially Frege's response. He notes that (Na) is equivalent to the following (cf. 1884, §§68–9):

(Nd)   The extension of the concept *equinumerous to the concept F* is equal to the extension of the concept *equinumerous to the concept G*.

Like (Nb), this is also an identity statement, and equating the left-hand sides of each, suggests the following explicit definition:

(Ne)   The number of F's (the number that belongs to the concept F) is the extension of the concept *equinumerous to the concept F*.

In its Russellian version (cf. *POM*, p. 115), we have:

(Ne')   The number of F's is the class of all classes equinumerous to the class of F's.

However, as both Frege and Russell note, such a definition seems, at first sight, hardly plausible. For are not numbers quite a different kind of thing from extensions of concepts or classes? Their answer is that, for mathematical purposes, such a definition achieves everything we want: it allows us to derive all of the well-known properties of numbers (cf. Frege, 1884, §70; Russell, *POM*, p. 116). And in answer to the Julius Caesar problem, we can rule out Julius Caesar being a number to the extent that we can rule him out being an extension of a concept (or class). Clearly, this assumes that we know what extensions of concepts are. As we shall see in the next section, this crucial assumption turned out to be far from unproblematic.

To complete the logicist account of the natural numbers, all that then remains is to find suitable concepts to substitute into the definition (Ne). In the case of the number 0, Frege suggests that we take the concept *not identical with itself*, which can be specified purely logically ($x \neq x$), yielding the following explicit definition:

(E0)   The number 0 is the extension of the concept *equinumerous to the concept 'not identical with itself'*.

With 0 defined, each subsequent number can then be defined in terms of its predecessor(s):

(E1)   The number 1 is the extension of the concept *equinumerous to the concept 'identical with 0'*.

(E2)   The number 2 is the extension of the concept *equinumerous to the concept 'identical with 0 or 1'*.

With the successor relation and mathematical induction having already been defined in the *Begriffsschrift*, it then becomes possible to derive all the well-known properties of the natural numbers to which Frege and Russell had referred. The full task, carried out formally, was what Frege set out to achieve in the *Grundgesetze*.

Russell's own informal account, in his later *Introduction to Mathematical Philosophy*, follows Frege's, the number 0 being defined as the class of classes that have the same number of members as the null class (i.e., the class whose only member is the null class), the number 1 as the class of all unit classes (i.e., the class of classes that have the same number of members as the class whose only member is the null class), and so on (*IMP*, chs. 2–3; cf. *PM*, *52). But at the time that the *Principles* was written, Russell had refused to admit the existence of the null class and had treated any unit class as identical with its sole member, which ruled out taking the Fregean line with the numbers 0 and 1. (If the null class does not exist, then its unit class, also being the null class, does not exist, and 1 would end up being defined as the same non-existent null class as 0. Indeed, all the natural numbers would end up collapsing into the same non-existent null class.) His reason was his extensional view of classes: "a class which has no terms fails to be anything at all" (*POM*, p. 74), and since a class is *constituted* by its members, if a class has just one member, then that member *is* the class (*POM*, p. 67). As we have seen, it is a strength of Frege's account that existential and number statements are analysed similarly (as involving the ascription of second-level predicates);[25] and Russell does seem to have tangled himself up in knots about nothing, in particular, in the chapter on 'Zero' in the *Principles* (ch. 22; cf. ch. 6, §73). However, having read Frege, after the main text was finished, Russell admits his error in the appendix on Frege's doctrines (p. 517) and in the preface (p. xxi).[26] Once again, then, we find Russell refining his account under the influence of Frege's work. Of course, by the time *Principia Mathematica* and the *Introduction to Mathematical Philosophy* were written, Russell believes that all classes are 'logical fictions', so that the null class has been returned to the realm of the non-existent. But the null class is at least treated as a legitimate class, although Russell does define a secondary sense in which classes can be said to 'exist', when they have at least one member (cf. *PM*, vol. i, pp. 29, 216). That classes are 'logical fictions' was Russell's response to the paradox that he discovered in Frege's system.

V. FREGE'S RESPONSE TO RUSSELL'S PARADOX

Frege's definitions of the natural numbers in terms of extensions of concepts, and his response to the Julius Caesar problem, as given in the *Grundlagen*, were based on the assumption that it was known what extensions of concepts are. At the time, Frege had thought that he could do without them, but he soon became convinced that he could not.[27] In the *Grundgesetze*, his appeal to them was legitimized

---

[25] The inability to account for 0 and 1 is an important element in Frege's critique of alternative theories of number; see e.g., 1884, §§7, 28, and in particular, 29–39, where he examines misconceptions about unity.

[26] Russell presents the argument against identifying a unit class with its sole member as follows: "Let u be a class having more than one term; let ιu be the class of classes whose only member is u. Then ιu has one member, u has many; hence u and ιu are not identical." And if we accept this argument, Russell goes on, "we may of course also admit a [class] in the case of a null propositional function." (*POM*, p. 517; cf. *PM*, vol. i, p. 340.) For Frege's argument, see, e.g., 1984, pp. 218–9.

[27] For Frege's view in *Grundlagen*, see §68, fn. (1997, p. 115) and §107 (1997, p. 128); cf. *The Freze Reader*, p. 6. The issue is discussed in detail by Burge, 1984. The three seminal essays that Frege published between the *Grundlagen* and *Grundgesetze*, i.e., 1891, 1892a, and 1892b, were essentially written to lay the philosophical ground for the appeal to extensions of concepts.

by laying down a new axiom – his notorious Axiom V. In the particular case of concepts, Axiom V can be seen as asserting the equivalence between the following two propositions:

(Ca) The concept F applies to the same objects as the concept G (i.e., whatever falls under concept F falls under concept G, and vice versa).

(Cb) The extension of the concept F is identical with the extension of the concept G.[28]

The relationship between (Ca) and (Cb) is analogous to that between (Na) and (Nb) discussed in the last section; and Frege's idea is the same. As long as every concept is defined for every object, then Axiom V ensures that every concept has an extension in just the same way as Hume's Principle was seen as guaranteeing a *Bedeutung* to number terms.

Nevertheless, in his preface to the *Grundgesetze*, Frege expressed some unease: "A dispute can break out here, so far as I can see, only with regard to my fundamental law concerning value-ranges (V), which has not yet perhaps been expressly formulated by logicians, although one has it in mind, for example, when speaking of extensions of concepts. I hold it to be purely logical" (1997, p. 195). As he later explained in Volume II, Frege saw himself as simply making explicit what logicians and mathematicians had always done – transforming talk of concepts into talk of their extensions:

Logicians have long since spoken of the extension of a concept, and mathematicians have used the terms set, class, manifold; what lies behind this is a similar transformation; for we may well suppose that what mathematicians call a set (etc.) is nothing other than an extension of a concept, even if they have not always been clearly aware of this.

What we are doing by means of our transformation is thus not really anything novel; but we do it with full awareness, appealing to a fundamental law of logic. And what we thus do is quite different from the lawless, arbitrary construction of numbers by many mathematicians.

---

[28] In its full generality, Axiom V asserts the equivalence between 'Two functions F and G always have the same value for the same argument' and 'The function F has the same *value-range* as the function G'. Cf. 1893, I, §3; 1997, pp. 213–14. Concepts are functions of one argument whose value is a truth-value, and extensions of concepts are one type of value-range.

If there are logical objects at all – and the objects of arithmetic are such objects – then there must also be a means of apprehending, of recognizing, them. This service is performed for us by the fundamental law of logic that permits the transformation of an equality holding generally into an equation. Without such a means a scientific foundation for arithmetic would be impossible. (1903, II, §147; 1997, pp. 278–9.)

Despite this outward confidence, Frege's underlying unease turned out to be justified. On 16 June 1902, whilst the second volume of the *Grundgesetze* was in press, Russell wrote his first letter to Frege. After expressing his agreement with Frege on all main issues, he goes on:

I have encountered a difficulty only on one point. You assert [1879, §9] that a function could also constitute the indefinite element. This is what I used to believe, but this view now seems to me dubious because of the following contradiction: Let *w* be the predicate of being a predicate which cannot be predicated of itself. Can *w* be predicated of itself? From either answer follows its contradictory. We must therefore conclude that *w* is not a predicate. Likewise, there is no class (as a whole) of those classes which, as wholes, are not members of themselves. From this I conclude that under certain circumstances a definable set does not form a whole. (Quoted in Frege, 1997, p. 252)

The minor difficulty that Russell humbly announced was to prove devastating. Frege wrote back just six days later:

Your discovery of the contradiction has surprised me beyond words and, I should almost like to say, left me thunderstruck, because it has rocked the ground on which I meant to build arithmetic. It seems accordingly that the transformation of the generality of an identity into an identity of value-ranges (§9 of my *Grundgesetze*) is not always permissible, that my law V (§20, p.36) is false, and that my explanations in §31 do not suffice to secure a *Bedeutung* for my combinations of signs in all cases. I must give some further thought to the matter. It is all the more serious as the collapse of my law V seems to undermine not only the foundations of my arithmetic but the only possible foundations of arithmetic as such. And yet, I should think, it must be possible to set up conditions for the transformation of the generality of an equality into an equality of value-ranges so as to retain the essentials of my proofs. Your discovery is at any rate a very remarkable one, and it may perhaps lead to a great advance in logic, undesirable as it may seem at first sight. (1997, p. 254)

Frege goes on to note the looseness of Russell's formulation of the contradiction, which does not affect Frege's system, since predicates are seen as 'unsaturated' and hence cannot be predicated of themselves. But he recognizes that allowing that a concept can be predicated of its own extension, as he does, generates a similar contradiction. The paradox, in Fregean terms, can be stated as follows. If every concept is defined for all objects, then every concept can be thought of as dividing all objects into those that do, and those that do not, fall under it. If extensions of concepts are objects, then extensions themselves can be divided into those that fall under the concept whose extension they are (e.g., the extension of the concept *is an extension*) and those that do not (e.g., the extension of the concept *is a horse*). But now consider the concept *is the extension of a concept under which it does not fall*. Does the extension of *this* concept fall under the concept or not? If it does, then it does not, and if it does not, then it does.

Consider now the case in which the concept F and the concept G are one and the same. Then they have the same extension, so that (Cb) is true. But if this concept is the concept *is the extension of a concept under which it does not fall*, then it is not the case that anything that falls under this concept (the concept F) falls under this concept (the concept G), as the counterexample of its own extension shows, so that (Ca) is false. Axiom V, which asserts the equivalence between (Ca) and (Cb), is therefore false. Frege records his reaction in the appendix he wrote to Volume II of the *Grundgesetze*:

Hardly anything more unfortunate can befall a scientific writer than to have one of the foundations of his edifice shaken after the work is finished.

This was the position I was placed in by a letter of Mr Bertrand Russell, just when the printing of this volume was nearing its completion. It is a matter of my Axiom (V). I have never disguised from myself its lack of the self-evidence that belongs to the other axioms and that must properly be demanded of a logical law. And so in fact I indicated this weak point in the Preface to Vol. I (p. VII). I should gladly have dispensed with this foundation if I had known of any substitute for it. And even now I do not see how arithmetic can be scientifically established; how numbers can be apprehended as logical objects, and brought under review; unless we are permitted – at least conditionally – to pass from a concept to its extension.

(1997, pp. 279–80)

What response should be made to the paradox? The issue is debated by Russell and Frege in the correspondence that ensued, and Frege presents his own view, in the time he had available whilst the second volume of the *Grundgesetze* was in press, in the appendix. Given that one of the assumptions generating the paradox is that extensions of concepts are objects, an obvious response is to abandon this assumption. But as the passages quoted above show, this would have been unacceptable to Frege. For if numbers, as objects, cannot be defined as extensions of concepts, then how else is logicism to be established? Frege does, however, consider the possibility that extensions are *improper objects*, objects to which the law of excluded middle does not apply. However, he rejects this on the grounds that the resulting system would be far too complex. For every first-level function, it would have to be specified whether proper objects, improper objects or both were admissible as either argument or value. There would thus be nine types (*Arten*) of first-level functions, to which there would correspond nine types of value-ranges (i.e., improper objects), requiring yet further distinctions. "We should thus get an incalculable multiplicity of types; and in general objects belonging to different types could not occur as arguments of the same function. But it appears extraordinarily difficult to set up a complete system of rules for deciding which objects are allowable arguments of which functions" (1997, p. 282). Such a theory of types was just what Russell was to develop, and not only did it indeed prove complex but it also required, for the demonstration of logicism, additional axioms whose status as logical truths was also problematic.[29]

A third possible response is also dismissed by Frege – that names for extensions of concepts are 'sham proper names', with no *Bedeutung* of their own, only the expressions of which they are part having a *Bedeutung* as a whole (cf. 1997, p. 282). Such a response might seem thoroughly in accord with the context principle that Frege had laid down in the *Grundlagen* precisely to underwrite such moves as that contained in Hume's Principle and Frege's later Axiom V: "Only in the context of a proposition do words mean something" (1884, §62). But Frege did not interpret this as allowing names to

---

[29] See Urquhart, in the present volume.

have no *Bedeutung* of their own at all, whilst still contributing to the *Bedeutung* of the whole. On the contrary, if the proposition as a whole has a *Bedeutung*, then its logically significant parts must also have a *Bedeutung*, according to Frege. As we shall see in the next section, it was not until Russell's theory of descriptions that the 'eliminativist' use of contextual definition was seriously pursued. Only then could classes be treated as 'logical fictions' in the way that Russell proposed as part of his response to the paradox.

Given that the contradiction arises from allowing concepts to apply to their own extensions, Frege's own response was simply to outlaw this. (Ca) can then be restricted as follows:

(Ca')   Whatever falls under concept F, except its own extension, falls under concept G, and vice versa. (Cf. 1997, p. 288)

Unfortunately, the resulting modification of Axiom V has also been found to generate a contradiction, in domains of more than one object;[30] and although it is unclear whether Frege ever realized this, it was not a modification that could really have satisfied him. For if we now have 'Two concepts have the same extension if and only if whatever falls under one, except its own extension, falls under the other', then in trying to offer a criterion of identity for extensions, we are presupposing on the right-hand side of the biconditional that we can already identify extensions. As Frege remarks, "Obviously this cannot be taken as *defining* the extension of a concept, but only as specifying the distinctive property of this second-level function" (1997, p. 288). But if this is so, then talk of Axiom V as allowing us to apprehend extensions of concepts no longer seems appropriate. In any case, we want to know *why* we should exclude extensions from falling under their own concepts. If we outlaw this simply to avoid the contradiction, then we have merely made an *ad hoc* move that throws no philosophical light on the problem. Russell's approach, by contrast, which treats the extension of a concept as on a higher ontological level than the objects that legitimately fall under the concept, offers a more satisfying response.

What is wrong in Frege's view can also be seen by recalling that what the transformation captured by Axiom V involves is what

---

[30] See Quine, 1955; Geach, 1956.

Peano and Russell termed 'definition by abstraction'. The phrase itself suggests a move in ontological level, and it is notable that Frege does not himself use the phrase.[31] For him, there was one universal homogeneous domain, containing all objects without divisions of category or hierarchies. But if 'definition by abstraction' involves 'constructing' objects not there in the original domain over which the equivalence relation is specified, then we have a diagnosis of Frege's error. Extensions of concepts cannot be taken as members of the domain over which the concepts themselves are defined. Whatever the details of Russell's theory of types, his central insight was right: there are more types of things than were dreamt of in Frege's philosophy.

In the end, then, the emergence of the contradiction revealed deep flaws in Frege's thought, which he was never able to remove; and the planned third volume of the *Grundgesetze* was abandoned. Frege continued to lecture and write, publishing trenchant critiques of the work of his contemporaries and clarifying and developing his views on what Russell was to call 'philosophical logic'. In 1911 Wittgenstein visited him, having read about his writings in Russell's *Principles*, and Frege advised him to go to Cambridge to study with Russell, clearly feeling that it was now Russell who was at the forefront of work on the foundations of mathematics. In a diary dating from the very end of his life, he wrote: "My efforts to become clear about what is meant by number have resulted in failure. We are only too easily misled by language and in this particular case the way we are misled is little short of disastrous" (1979, p. 263). He turned instead to geometry to provide a foundation for arithmetic; but he died before he was able to offer anything more than the briefest sketch of how this might be done.

VI. ANALYSIS

In their preface to *Principia Mathematica*, Russell and Whitehead write that "In all questions of logical analysis, our chief debt is to Frege" (p. viii). What they clearly had in mind was Frege's analysis of number, the main elements of which they took over, but which

---

[31] In his letter to Russell of 28 July 1902, Frege recognizes that Russell uses the phrase, but he does not do so himself (1980, p. 141).

they also developed, through the theory of types in particular, to avoid the contradiction that had undermined Frege's system. But the example that Frege had provided was also seen by Russell as having wider philosophical significance, and it was Russell who showed how the scope of logical analysis could be extended beyond the realm of mathematics. His most notable achievement here was the theory of descriptions, which Ramsey famously called a 'paradigm of philosophy'.[32] From the time of his first meeting with Peano, when he started to understand and apply Fregean analysis, Russell became the dedicated champion of analysis as the fundamental method of philosophy.[33] With Frege's example and Russell's advocacy, 'analytic' philosophy emerged as a distinctive and powerful new force in philosophy.

Despite Russell's and Frege's joint status as founders of analytic philosophy, however, there are important differences in both their conceptions and practices of analysis. There are also discrepancies between what they say about analysis and what they actually do. This is particularly true in the case of Russell, who in working his way out of British idealism, retained a conception of analysis that was at odds with the practice of analysis in the mathematical tradition in which the logicist project was rooted. Part of the problem in discussing analysis is that there are a number of different conceptions in play, which are not always adequately distinguished. Perhaps in its broadest sense, 'analysis' might be characterised as *disclosing what is more fundamental*, but there are clearly many different kinds of things that can be analysed, and even where the same thing is being analysed (e.g., a 'proposition'), there are many different kinds of things that can be regarded as more fundamental and many different forms that such a process of 'disclosing' can take. For

---

[32] Ramsey, 1931, p. 263. Moore (1944) begins his paper on Russell's theory of descriptions with this remark, and after fifty pages of painstaking discussion, concludes by concurring.

[33] *POM* opens with the claim that "Our method will...be one of analysis" (p. 3); *IMP* too begins by advocating analysis (pp. 1–2); and in *PLA* he states that "the chief thesis that I have to maintain is the legitimacy of analysis" (*Papers* 8, p. 169; *LK*, p. 189). The final chapter of *HWP* is entitled 'The Philosophy of Logical Analysis'; and in *MPD* he writes: "Ever since I abandoned the philosophy of Kant and Hegel, I have sought solutions of philosophical problems by means of analysis; and I remain firmly persuaded, in spite of some modern tendencies to the contrary, that only by analysing is progress possible" (p. 11).

present purposes, we may distinguish three core *modes* of analysis, which may be realized and combined in a variety of ways in constituting specific conceptions or projects of analysis.[34] I call these the *regressive* mode, concerned to identify the 'starting-points' (principles, premisses, causes, etc.) by means of which something can be 'explained' or 'generated', the *resolutive* mode, concerned to identify the elements of something and the way they interrelate, and the *interpretive* mode, concerned to 'translate' something into a particular framework. All three are exemplified in the work of Frege and Russell.

The regressive mode has its roots in ancient Greek geometry and has had a significant influence throughout the history of philosophy. The key idea here is that of disclosing or working back to first principles, by means of which to solve a given problem (e.g., construct a particular geometrical figure, derive a particular conclusion or explain a particular fact). This mode is illustrated in Russell's paper, 'The Regressive Method of Discovering the Premises of Mathematics', read before the Cambridge Mathematical Club in 1907. Russell talks of 'analysis' here, understood as the process of working back to 'ultimate logical premises', a process that is 'inductive' rather than 'deductive', aimed at finding the 'irreducible minimum of assumptions' by means of which the more 'obvious' truths from which we started can then be deduced (cf. *RMDP*, pp. 272–4, 282).[35] Taking the example of arithmetic, he suggests that the five axioms that Peano had formulated are not as 'ultimate' as the logical definitions that Frege had provided, in the sense that Peano's axioms can be derived from Frege's definitions (pp. 276–7). One of the main aims of such a method is the "organisation of our knowledge, making it more manageable and more interesting", and Russell also mentions the 'new results' that such a discovery of premises may yield, and the impact that it may have in philosophy (pp. 282–3).

However, it is not the regressive but the resolutive mode of analysis that has dominated conceptions of analysis in the modern period. I use the term 'resolutive analysis' to cover both whole–part and

---

[34] For fuller discussion of the various forms of analysis in the history of philosophy, see Beaney, 2002, 2003. Some of this story is told in Beaney, 2000, on which I partly draw in what follows.

[35] Cf. also *OKEW*, pp. 185–6, 211–2, 241; *IMP*, p. 1. For further discussion of regressive analysis, see Peckhaus, 2002.

function-argument analysis. Although the latter came of age (in philosophy) in Frege's work (in mathematics it goes back to Descartes, and was well-developed by the end of the nineteenth century), it is the former – which I shall call *decompositional* analysis – that constitutes the core of the conception of analysis that prevails today, and which was certainly central in Russell's thought. Analysis is seen here as involving the *decomposition* of something, and in particular, a concept or proposition, into its constituents, where this may also include its form or structure.[36] This mode came to prominence in early modern philosophy and played a key role in Locke's and Hume's theory of ideas; and it was this mode of analysis to which Bradley objected in his critique of empiricism – whilst not, it should be emphasized, offering any alternative form of analysis. Given Russell's initial preoccupation with Bradley, not to mention his roots in the British tradition of philosophy generally, it is not surprising that he should have taken over this conception. It underlays his theory of denoting concepts, and indeed, his entire discussion of wholes and parts, in the *Principles*, and was no less central in the heyday of his logical atomism, where 'analysis' was defined as "the discovery of the constituents and the manner of combination of a given complex", as he put it in the chapter on 'Analysis and Synthesis' in his 1913 manuscript, *Theory of Knowledge*.[37] But whilst the decompositional mode of analysis may have been dominant in his work, it was not the only mode, and Russell is surprisingly quiet on the various constituents of his own complex – and developing – conception of analysis.

The distinction between the regressive and resolutive modes of analysis has been widely (though by no means sufficiently) recognized by philosophers. But it is also important to recognize a third main mode, which emerges explicitly in the work of Frege and Russell, although it has always been around implicitly in conceptions and projects of analysis. *Any analysis presupposes a particular*

---

[36] To take just one example, here is Blackburn's definition of 'analysis' in his recent *Oxford Dictionary of Philosophy*: "the process of breaking a concept down into more simple parts, so that its logical structure is displayed".

[37] *TK*, p. 119. This was the manuscript that was abandoned as a result of Wittgenstein's criticisms; although the conception of analysis was one that Wittgenstein took over in the *Tractatus*. In *OKEW*, however, which was written just a few months later, and published in August 1914, Russell reverted to the older *regressive* conception of analysis (see the refs. cited in n. 35 above).

framework of interpretation, and work is done in *interpreting* what it is we are seeking to analyse – the *analysandum* – as part of the process of disclosing what is more fundamental. In the case of the 'logical analysis' of a proposition, what is required is some kind of 'regimentation' or 'translation' in order for the resources of the logical system to be utilized. We have already seen this illustrated by the 'interpretation' of 'All A's are B' as 'For all x, if x is an A, then x is a B' and by Frege's analyses of existential and number statements. In the 'paradigm' case of Russell's theory of descriptions, 'The present King of France is bald' is 'interpreted' as 'There is one and only one King of France, and whatever is King of France is bald', which can then be readily formalized into predicate logic. In the *Tractatus*, Wittgenstein commended Russell for having shown the need to distinguish between the grammatical form and the logical form of a proposition (cf. 4.0031); and clearly part of the work of analysis consists in rephrasing the proposition into its correct logical form.

What this suggests, then, is that a distinction should be drawn between analysis as *rephrasal*, which aims to avoid the problems generated by misleading surface grammatical form but which carries no positive metaphysical commitments of its own, and analysis as *reduction*, which goes a step further in aiming to reveal 'deep structure' and 'ultimate constituents'. Let us call the conceptions reflected here *paraphrastic* and *reductive* analysis, respectively. The use of the first term alludes to Bentham's conception of paraphrasis, which John Wisdom, in his first book, published in 1931, saw as anticipating Russell's method of analysis.[38] The use of the second term indicates that the aim is to uncover the logically or metaphysically more primitive elements of a given complex (e.g., proposition or fact). Paraphrastic analysis involves 'interpretation', whilst reductive analysis involves 'resolution'.

This distinction reflects the distinction that was indeed drawn in the 1930s, by members of the so-called 'Cambridge School of

---

[38] In his *Essay on Logic* (published posthumously, in 1843), Bentham writes: "By the word paraphrasis may be designated that sort of exposition which may be afforded by transmuting into a proposition, having for its subject some real entity, a proposition which has not for its subject any other than a fictitious entity" (1843, p. 246). Bentham applies the method in 'analysing away' talk of 'obligations' (cf. 1843, p. 247). Wisdom discusses the relationships between Bentham's 'fictitious entities' and Russell's 'logical constructions' in the second half of his *Interpretation and Analysis*.

Analysis', between what was called 'logical' or 'same-level' analysis and 'philosophical' or 'metaphysical' or 'reductive' or 'directional' or 'new-level' analysis.[39] The first translates the proposition to be analysed into better logical form, whilst the second exhibits its underlying metaphysical commitments. In Russell's example, having 'analysed away' the definite description, what is then shown is just what commitments remain – to logical constants and concepts (such as *King of France*), which may in turn require further analysis to 're-duce' them to things of our supposed immediate acquaintance. The importance of the distinction lies in the possibility it opens up of accepting logical or paraphrastic analysis whilst rejecting metaphysical or reductive analysis, precisely the move that was made by the second generation of analytic philosophers.[40]

A good example of the use of mere paraphrastic analysis would appear to be Frege's analysis of existential statements. To rephrase existential statements in terms of the second-level predicate *is instantiated* allows the problems that traditionally arose (such as those involved in the ontological argument) to just drop away. We do not, in other words, have to construe 'Unicorns do not exist' *decompositionally*, as according unicorns some sort of subsistence in order for them to be meaningfully attributed the property of nonexistence. Of course, we still need an account of concepts and quantifiers, but the essential move has been made without metaphysical mystery-mongering of any obvious kind.

Such paraphrastic analysis clearly opens up the possibility of an eliminativist project, pruning the extravagant ontology that Russell had been tempted to posit in his initial revolt into pluralism (cf. *MPD*, ch. 5). But what is intriguing about Frege's work is that he does not, at least explicitly, pursue this project. Consider his notorious problems with the so-called 'paradox of the concept *horse*'. On any natural view, the following proposition seems to be obviously true:

(Ha)   The concept *horse* is a concept.

Yet *analysing (Ha) decompositionally*, the logically significant parts, on Frege's view, are the proper name 'the concept *horse*' and the

---

[39] See esp. Stebbing, 1932, 1933, 1934, and Wisdom, 1934. Cf. Urmson, 1956, pp. 39ff.
[40] The later Wittgenstein, Carnap, Ryle, and Quine, for example, whatever the in-dividual differences in their approaches, shared an emphasis on paraphrastic and anti-metaphysical forms of analysis.

concept expression '( ) is a concept'. If the proposition as a whole has a *Bedeutung*, then each of these parts must also have a *Bedeutung*, according to Frege. Since proper names stand for objects and concept expressions stand for concepts, and there is an absolute distinction between (unsaturated) concepts and (saturated) objects, 'The concept *horse*' must stand for an object, so that (Ha), taken literally, is false, not true. Clearly, something has gone wrong, and Frege's only response, biting the bullet, is to admit that 'The concept *horse*' does indeed stand for an object, but one that goes proxy for the concept, a response that seems as ontologically inflationary and metaphysically mysterious as the views of Meinong and the early Russell. (Cf. Frege, 1892b, pp. 184–5.)

In the light of what was said above, however, there is clearly a better response available. *(Ha) needs to be analysed not decompositionally, but paraphrastically.* And this is indeed just the response that Dummett (1981a, pp. 216–17) later made on Frege's behalf. On the assumption that the concept *horse* is sharp (i.e., that it divides all objects into those that fall under it and those that do not), (Ha) is to be interpreted as (Hb), which like (ob) above, can be given a straightforward formalization in the predicate calculus, as (Hc):

(Hb)   Everything is either a horse or not a horse.

(Hc) $(\forall x)\,(Hx \vee \neg Hx)$.

Given that the general strategy of analysing by paraphrasing had been just what Frege had done in the *Grundlagen*, it may seem surprising that he failed to pursue that further in the case of the paradox of the concept *horse*, especially since the paradox seems to cry out for such treatment. But as the history of Russell's development between the *Principles* and 'On Denoting' shows, the possibility of using paraphrastic analysis to resolve ontological problems was a hard-won insight, and Frege, despite introducing and powerfully employing this form of analysis within his logicist project, did not appreciate its full potential. Even whilst offering paraphrastic analysis, Frege's ontological outlook was still unduly influenced by a decompositional conception of analysis.

Frege's failure to appreciate the distinction between paraphrastic and decompositional analysis was also responsible for his problems concerning the status of his *Grundlagen* contextual definitions and

Axiom V of the *Grundgesetze*. In the *Grundlagen*, Frege clearly regards both (Da) and (Db), and (Na) and (Nb), as given in §4 above,
as having the same 'content' ('Inhalt'), but in his later work he vac-
illates somewhat between saying that they merely have the same
Bedeutung and saying that they have both the same *Bedeutung*
and the same sense (*Sinn*).[41] But in both the *Grundlagen* and the
Grundgesetze, it is clear how his thinking goes. Taking the key case
of (Na) and (Nb), if (Na) is true, and (Na) and (Nb) are equivalent (all
that is required here is that they are logically equivalent), then (Nb)
is true, i.e., has a *Bedeutung*, on Frege's view (since the *Bedeutung*
of a proposition just is its truth-value). But if this is so, then, by the
principle of compositionality mentioned above, that the *Bedeutung*
of a whole is dependent on the *Bedeutung* of its parts, all the logically significant parts of (Nb) must also have a *Bedeutung*. So the
number terms, in particular, as proper names, must stand for independent objects. Frege is clearly not using the method of contextual
definition here as a method of *abstraction* – in the way that Russell
understood it – in the sense of moving *up* an ontological level. (Na)
and (Nb) are seen as on the same ontological level, an assumption, as
we suggested in the last section, that was responsible for the contradiction in Frege's system. In seeking to explain or derive (Nb)
from (Na), through paraphrastic analysis, and at the same time understanding (Nb) decompositionally, Frege is trying to both have his
cake and eat it. Insofar as (Nb) is genuinely equivalent to (Na), then
(Nb) cannot involve any other ontological commitments than are
already involved in (Na), so (Nb) cannot be regarded as making reference to numbers construed as 'independent' objects. Rabbits can
only be pulled out of hats if they are already there. So if the account
of (Nb) runs through (Na), it cannot also be analysed – ontologically –
decompositionally.[42]

Of course, paraphrastic and decompositional analysis are not in
themselves incompatible. Indeed, in reductive projects, paraphrastic analysis gives way to some form of resolutive analysis once the

[41] For detailed discussion and references, see Beaney, 1996, §§5.3 – 5.5, 8.1.
[42] This is not to say that decompositional analysis cannot be employed for linguistic
purposes, for example, in explaining how we understand the *linguistic meaning* of
(Nb). The point is that we must respect the differences between linguistic meaning,
sense and reference, and not automatically assume that the same form of analysis
will be appropriate for each in a given case. This will become clear in what follows.

problematic proposition has been rephrased into its correct logical form, where what counts as its correct logical form is constrained by the principles governing resolutive analysis. If the aim is just to remove some philosophical puzzle (e.g., concerning the reification of non-existent entities), then paraphrastic analysis may be enough. But this will be unsatisfying to those who want an account of just what metaphysical commitments a proposition has.[43] However, this still leaves open the precise form that resolutive analysis takes, and there is no reason to suppose that there must be one canonical form. Again, the work of Frege and Russell illustrates this. As mentioned at the beginning of this section, the most important difference is that while Russell understood 'resolution' in whole–part terms (i.e., decompositionally), for Frege, function-argument analysis took centre–stage, although this was often glossed in whole–part terms. As well as the differences between them, there were also significant changes in the development of their views.

To appreciate this, let us return to the case of relations discussed in Section III above, and consider the example that Frege gives in the *Begriffsschrift* (§9):

(HLC)   Hydrogen is lighter than carbon dioxide.

According to Frege, this can be analysed in either of two ways, depending on whether we take hydrogen as the argument and *is lighter than carbon dioxide* as the function, or carbon dioxide as the argument and *is heavier than hydrogen* as the function. If we respected subject–predicate position, we might wish to express the latter thus:

(CHH)   Carbon dioxide is heavier than hydrogen.

But on Frege's view, (HLC) and (CHH) have the same 'content' ('Inhalt'), each merely representing alternative ways of 'analysing' that content. However, in the light of what was said in Section III above,

---

[43] If the later Wittgenstein is an example of someone who offered paraphrastic rather than reductive analyses, then one can understand (though not justify) Russell's charge that "The later Wittgenstein . . . seems to have grown tired of serious thinking and to have invented a doctrine which would make such an activity unnecessary", a new philosophy "that seems to concern itself, not with the world and our relation to it, but only with the different ways in which silly people can say silly things" (*MPD*, pp. 161, 170). Significantly, these remarks occur in Russell's review of Urmson's book on philosophical analysis (1956), where the distinction between 'logical' and 'metaphysical' analysis is drawn.

we might feel that both these analyses presuppose a more 'ultimate' one, which identifies *two arguments*, hydrogen and carbon dioxide, and a *relation* (a function with two arguments). But which relation do we choose, *is lighter than* or *is heavier than*? Clearly they are not the same, since one is the converse of the other. So if we accept that (HLC) and (CHH) have the same 'content' – there is undoubtedly something that they have in common – then it seems that there can be alternative analyses even at the supposedly 'ultimate' level.[44]

According to Russell at the time of the *Principles*, however, (HLC) and (CHH) would be regarded as representing different propositions (in Frege's terminology, as having different 'contents'), precisely on the grounds that there are two different relations involved here: "if we are to hold that "*a* is greater than *b*" and "*b* is less than *a*" are the same proposition, we shall have to maintain that both *greater* and *less* enter into each of these propositions, which seems obviously false" (*POM*, p. 228). What is clearly driving this is the idea that a proposition is literally composed of what 'analysis' yields as its constituents, and there is no room, so to speak, for a relational proposition to contain both the relevant relation and its converse, given that they are on the same level. (The proposition can be thought of as containing more than one concept, but only because these result from a merely partial analysis.)

How are we to decide the issue between Frege and Russell? Clearly, 'analysis' is not as metaphysically neutral as the naïve idea of 'decomposition' might suggest; it is not just a matter of separating out all those constituents that are there already, waiting to be separated out, as a child might dismantle a house of toy bricks. There are constraints on the process – in Frege's case, our intuitions about sameness of 'content' (as involved in the equivalence between (HLC) and (CHH), for example), and in Russell's case, the assumption that any complex whole, such as a proposition, is literally composed of its constituents. What is remarkable is just how resilient these core

---

[44] In response to the problem of alternative 'analyses', Dummett (1981b, ch. 17) has suggested that we distinguish between 'analysis' and 'decomposition': there can be alternative 'decompositions' (into 'component' concepts) but only one 'analysis' (into unique 'constituents'); but for the reason just given, this cannot work in the case of propositions involving asymmetrical relations. (Cf. Beaney, 1996, pp. 238–9.) By 'analysis' here Dummett means what I have been calling 'decomposition' (which does seem to imply whole–part analysis), and by 'decomposition' Dummett means 'resolution' in function-argument terms.

constraints were. Frege never gave up the idea that two sentences could represent the same 'content', or express the same 'sense' or 'thought' as he later put it, even if they had different forms, as the case of (Na) and (Nb) discussed in Section IV above shows. Russell never gave up the idea that complexes are literally composed of their constituents, even when the pressures of maintaining this with regard to propositions led to his rejecting the very existence of propositions. Along the way to this negative conclusion, the idea motivated the theory of denoting concepts, which was precisely introduced to ensure that quantifier phrases such as 'all men' represented something (a denoting concept) that was a *constituent* of the relevant proposition, in the face of the obvious implausibility or impossibility (e.g., in infinite domains) of maintaining that what such phrases denote (e.g., each and every man) could be constituents of the proposition. It was the problems with this theory that led to the theory of descriptions, which was nevertheless again driven by Russell's core idea: how can propositions about nonexistent objects be meaningful when those objects cannot be *constituents* of the propositions? The answer was to find an 'analysis' ('paraphrasis' and then 'decomposition') in which parts were revealed that were legitimate constituents of the proposition.[45] Whilst for Frege, then, intuitions about equivalences underpinned his ideas about analysis, for Russell, it was his ideas about 'analysis' ('decomposition') that drove his views on equivalences, ideas that were themselves underpinned, though, by the doctrine that complexes are literally made up of their constituents.

The differences between Russell and Frege also emerge in considering the so-called 'problem of the unity of the proposition'. To take Frege's example again, what is it that makes 'hydrogen', 'carbon dioxide' and 'is lighter than' a meaningful sentence and not just a list

---

[45] For a detailed account of the development of Russell's views on propositions, in relation to the issue of analysis, see Hylton, 1996. Hylton discusses, in particular, the epistemic constraint imposed on analysis by Russell's principle of acquaintance, which increasingly dominates his thought, and mentions also the logical constraint imposed by being in accord with logical theory. I am in substantial agreement with Hylton's main thesis: "The idea of 'finding and analysing the proposition expressed' by a given sentence is one that makes sense only within a given philosophical context, which imposes constraints on the process; the philosophical context cannot itself, therefore, be based on a neutral or uncontroversial notion of analysis" (pp. 183–4; cf. p. 213). Russell's own development illustrates this, but the point is even clearer in considering the differences between Frege and Russell.

of expressions? If we have 'decomposed' the 'content' of (HLC) into two objects and a relation, what is it that welds them into a whole? A whole, it would seem, is more than the sum of its parts; and this suggests that 'analysis' – in the sense of 'decomposition' – *falsifies* when it simply breaks something down into its constituents. This was essentially Bradley's objection to 'analysis',[46] and one which Russell took seriously. Even when he had broken free of British idealism, he remained sensitive to the problem. Although he rejected the conclusion that Bradley drew – that the parts of a whole, and in particular, relations, are not *real* – he did accept that something more was needed to explain the 'unity' of a whole. In the *Principles*, he wrote: "though analysis gives us the truth, and nothing but the truth, yet it can never give us the whole truth. This is the only sense in which the doctrine [that analysis is falsification] is to be accepted. In any wider sense, it becomes merely a cloak for laziness, by giving an excuse to those who dislike the labour of analysis." (*POM*, p. 141)[47] In his later work, he emphasized the role that *form* plays in binding the constituents into a whole, so that 'analysis' becomes divided into 'formal' and 'material' analysis.[48] Once again, we can see how Russell's conception of analysis is shaped by his metaphysical concerns, in this case, by the perceived need to solve the problem of the unity of the proposition.[49]

Frege too recognized the problem, and his own response, though different, was no less a fundamental feature of his philosophy. According to Frege, objects are 'saturated' and functions (concepts or relations) are 'unsaturated', the two requiring each other to form a

---

[46] See e.g. Bradley, *Principles of Logic*, pp. 95, 562.
[47] Later in the *Principles*, Russell writes that "The only kind of unity to which I can attach any precise sense – apart from the unity of the absolutely simple – is that of a whole composed of parts", which clearly underpins his view that "In every case of analysis, there is a whole consisting of parts with relations". He again notes what he sees as the truth in the doctrine that analysis is falsification, that 'unity' is indeed destroyed by analysis, but goes on: "There is, it must be confessed, a grave logical difficulty in this fact, for it is difficult not to believe that a whole must be constituted by its constituents." (*POM*, pp. 466–7) For later references to the doctrine that analysis is falsification, which Russell never feels able to completely repudiate, cf. *OKEW*, pp. 150–1; *PLA*, pp. 178–80; *MPD*, p. 49.
[48] Cf. *TK*, p. 119. On the 'form' of a proposition, see e.g. *TK*, pp. 97–101, 129ff.; *OKEW*, pp. 42–3; *PLA*, *Papers* 8, pp. 208–9; *LK*, pp. 238–9; *IMP*, pp. 198–9.
[49] For detailed discussion of the development of Russell's responses to the problem of the unity of the proposition, see Griffin, 1993; Candlish, 1996.

'whole'. The doctrine of the 'unsaturatedness' of concepts first appears in a letter Frege wrote in 1882 explaining the ideas of his *Begriffsschrift*: "A concept is unsaturated in that it requires something to fall under it; hence it cannot exist on its own."[50] This already suggests a difference from the early Russell, who felt that both objects and concepts could be the logical subjects of propositions, both being 'terms', as he put it in the *Principles*.[51] That it is the problem of the unity of the proposition that drives Frege's doctrine is made clear in his later essay 'On Concept and Object': "For not all the parts of a thought can be complete: at least one must be unsaturated or predicative; otherwise they would not hold together."[52]

The doctrine of the 'unsaturatedness' of concepts *predates* Frege's distinction between *Sinn* and *Bedeutung*, which was first drawn in 1891; and although the doctrine survives afterwards, it is significant that Frege explains it in 'On Concept and Object' at the level of *Sinn* (sense) and not *Bedeutung*. Take the thought expressed by 'Socrates is mortal'. On Frege's account, it is the *sense* of 'is mortal' that is 'unsaturated' and that needs to be completed by the sense of 'Socrates' to form the complete thought. But what about at the level of *Bedeutung*? There is talk of unsaturatedness here too, objects as the *Bedeutungen* of names being 'saturated' and concepts as the *Bedeutungen* of concept expressions being 'unsaturated'. But according to Frege, the *Bedeutung* of a sentence is a truth-value, either the True or the False, both conceived as objects. So does Frege think that Socrates and the concept *is mortal* combine to form the True in the way that their corresponding senses combine to form the thought?[53] Frege admits that talk of 'unsaturatedness' is only a metaphor (cf. 1892b, p. 193), but the metaphor is certainly misleading at the level of *Bedeutung*. As Frege himself remarks, "Things are different in

[50] Frege, 'Letter to Marty, 29.8.1882', in Frege, 1997, p. 81.
[51] Cf. *POM*, p. 44. Frege's distinction between concept and object is one of the main targets of Russell's criticism in his Appendix on Frege's doctrines; see esp. pp. 505–10. Russell notes that "Frege recognizes the unity of a proposition" (p. 507), but remains insistent that concepts can be 'terms'.
[52] Frege, 1892b, p. 193. Cf. also Frege, pp. 139, 173–6, 211–12, 363–4.
[53] If he did, then it would be tempting to see an analogy here with the monism of Bradley, everything in some form being part of the one object, the True (though also in some form of the False). Frege talks too of our attempts to speak of concepts as 'almost falsifying' the relevant thoughts (cf. 1892b, p. 174), which would equally be grist to Bradley's mill. But in fact, Frege is as much a pluralist as Russell in ontology.

the realm of *Bedeutung*" (1997, p. 365). Here it is function-argument analysis rather than whole-part analysis to which we must look to explain it.

According to Frege, concepts – like functions generally – *map* objects onto other objects. More specifically, a concept is a function that takes an object as argument and yields a truth-value – either of the two objects, the True or the False – as value. A concept is not therefore a funny kind of object with a 'hole' in it suitable for an object proper, but ontologically quite different. Talk of 'whole' and 'part' is simply not applicable at the level of *Bedeutung*. To say that something is the value of a function for a given argument is not at all the same as to say that it is a whole composed of its parts. Objects and concepts are neither constituents of the *Bedeutung* of a proposition nor of its sense (i.e., of the thought expressed by it), although the thought itself is seen as composed of its constituent senses.[54] On Frege's view, there is a universal domain of objects, and functions (including concepts) are *mappings* of those objects onto one another: they cannot themselves be objects, but are more like *rules* for taking us around the domain. Since to conceive of concepts as objects would be to misunderstand the underlying model, it is not surprising that Frege was so insistent on the distinction. The distinction between concept and object is, as it were, ontologically built in to the whole system. Function-argument analysis, then, plays a much deeper role in Frege's philosophy than it does in Russell's philosophy, where whole–part analysis is dominant. For Russell, the idea that wholes are literally composed of their parts was fundamental, whereas Frege only helped himself to this idea in an attempt to explain his views at the level of sense.

Frege's employment of function-argument analysis and Russell's continued adherence to whole–part analysis is perhaps most

[54] Given Frege's conviction, as we have noted, that one and the same thought can be analysed in different ways, even at the most fundamental level, then this produces a tension in his philosophy, since a thought cannot then also be seen as literally composed of its parts. The tension is most manifest in 1979, pp. 201–2: "one and the same thought can be split up in different ways and so can be seen as put together out of parts in different ways." What we have here is a conflict between function-argument analysis, which allows alternative analyses, and whole–part analysis, which does not. The former may have been more fundamental in Frege's thought, but the latter also played a role, as the paradox of the concept *horse* and the problem of the unity of the proposition show.

strikingly illustrated in their approach to the problem of empty names (including definite descriptions).[55] Take Russell's example:

(K)   The present King of France is bald.

This is a problem for Russell because a proposition is seen as *composed* of its constituents, and here we seem to *lack* a constituent. His considered answer is the theory of descriptions, which rephrases the proposition to make clear its 'real' constituents:

(KR)   There is one and only one King of France, and whatever is King of France is bald.

Empty names are a problem for Frege because they violate his principle that the *Bedeutung* of a proposition is determined by (i.e., is a function of) the *Bedeutungen* of its parts. Frege's technical solution is to introduce a new function that *supplies* empty names with a *Bedeutung*.[56] This is Frege's description stroke, symbolized by '\', which maps any extension of a concept onto itself when either no object or more than one object falls under the relevant concept and

---

[55] In what follows, I draw on Appendix 2 of *The Frege Reader*, pp. 384–5, where full references to Frege's work can be found.

[56] I call this Frege's 'technical' solution to bypass the controversial question as to what his views are in the case of ordinary language. Some scholars (e.g., Thiel, 1968, ch. 6) have argued that there is an important difference between Russell and Frege here. According to Russell, (K) is false if there is no King of France; according to Frege, it is neither true nor false, since a constituent and hence (K) itself lacks a *Bedeutung*. But if it lacks a *Bedeutung*, and if sense is a 'mode of presentation' of a *Bedeutung*, then it also lacks a sense. But then what is it that lacks a truth-value? It cannot be the sentence *qua* linguistic expression, since in other contexts there may be a truth-value. Conversely, it has been argued that, on Frege's view, if (K) does express a sense, then it *presupposes* that there is a King of France. But then we need an account of what this relation of presupposition is, and we are still left with the problem of what is going on when someone utters (K) when there is no King of France. Are they just confused? In fact, Frege seems to allow that expressions (outside the realm of 'science') can have a sense without a *Bedeutung*, so what it is that lacks a truth-value, if there is no King of France, is the *thought* expressed by (K). But if sense and *Bedeutung* come apart in ordinary language, then we need a clearer account of their relationship than Frege provides. Frege talks of 'mock thoughts' ('Scheingedanke') here, but their status is notoriously problematic. Nevertheless, for 'scientific' purposes, according to Frege, expressions must have both a sense and a *Bedeutung*, so if propositions such as (K) are to be handled logically, some 'corresponding' proposition, which is guaranteed a truth-value, must be found. This is where Frege introduces his description stroke, as a technical device for generating such a proposition. (I am grateful to Christian Thiel for prompting me to clarify this point.)

onto the object that falls under the concept when there is only one such object. (K) is then 'interpreted' as follows:

(KF) \\(extension of the concept *present King of France*) is bald.

If there *were* a King of France (and only one), then the expression '\\(extension of the concept *present King of France*)' would refer to him. Since there is not, the expression refers to the null set. It is not true that the null set is bald, so (KF) and hence (K) itself comes out as false. The result is thus the same as in the case of Russell's analysis – propositions with empty names are meaningful but false.

Which is the 'correct' analysis? Both Frege and Russell offer a 'paraphrase' and then a 'resolution' of (K). But whilst Russell 'analyses away' the definite description, Frege provides a replacement for it, defining a new function to ensure it has a *Bedeutung*.[57] Does Frege's analysis capture what we ordinarily mean? This is the wrong question to ask, for it is not his aim to remain faithful to ordinary language, but to develop a logical language adequate for demonstrating, in particular, the logicist thesis. Frege states explicitly that logical analysis cannot be answerable to our ordinary understanding, for our ordinary understanding is often confused. The aim is to make precise what was not precise before, as a propaedeutic to the construction of a system.[58] To object, for example, that no one would naturally come up with the definition of 'the number 0' as 'the extension of the concept *equinumerous to the concept "not identical with itself"*' is to miss the point. In the case of arithmetic, Russell broadly agrees, although even here the doctrine that analysis is falsification continues to trouble him. In 'The Philosophy of Logical Atomism', for example, after mentioning this doctrine, he writes: "When you pass from the vague to the precise by the method of analysis and reflection that I am speaking of, you always run a certain risk of error. If I start with the statement that there are so and so many people in this room, and then set to work to make that statement precise, I shall run a great many risks and it will be extremely likely that any precise statement

---

[57] This is not to conjure something into existence that does not exist, but just to facilitate its incorporation into Frege's logical system (cf. the previous fn.) This illustrates very well the dangers involved in translating 'Bedeutung' as 'reference' or 'referent' (as opposed, say, to 'significance').

[58] See esp. 'Logic in Mathematics', in Frege, pp. 316–8. The issue is discussed in Beaney, 1996, §§5.5 and 8.5.

I make will be something not true at all." (*PLA, Papers* 8, p. 162; *LK*, p. 180) Russell no doubt had in mind here the failure of Frege's project. But the issue seems different when the project of 'analysis' is extended, as Russell attempted to do, to our knowledge of the external world. If we recognize the role that the principle of acquaintance plays in this – analysis must yield constituents with which we are directly acquainted – then it does seem that this is more constrained by our ordinary understanding than in the case of arithmetic.

Any project of analysis that involves paraphrasis is torn between remaining close to our ordinary understanding, which runs the risk of triviality, and developing a new account, which runs the risk of error. This is precisely the paradox of analysis. The tension not only runs deep in Frege's and Russell's work but it also provides the central dynamic of later analytic philosophy, Wittgenstein and the ordinary language tradition being pulled more in the first direction and Carnap and Quine in the second. If 'analysis' were simply a matter of 'decomposition', then it is hard to see how there could be so much disagreement. But if 'analysis' involves 'paraphrasis', and this is constrained by differing logical and metaphysical conceptions, as the cases of Frege and Russell show, then it is clear instead why analytic philosophy has become such a vibrant force. Analytic philosophy is now a very broad church indeed, and to say that it is held together by the practice of 'analysis' is to say virtually nothing. 'Analysis' in the regressive sense has been around ever since the ancient Greeks; so it cannot be this that characterizes analytic philosophy. And despite the widespread (and mistaken) assumption that 'analysis' just means 'decomposition', it is not this either, although this was undoubtedly prominent in Russell's thought. Frege's introduction of function-argument analysis as an alternative to traditional subject–predicate and whole–part analysis was certainly crucial in the emergence of analytic philosophy. But if there is one thing that does, I think, mark a genuine turning point in philosophy, it is the explicit use of paraphrastic analysis. Although subject to differing philosophical constraints, it is this form of analysis which Frege and Russell developed, and which lies at the heart of analytic philosophy.[59]

[59] This paper draws on research undertaken whilst a Research Fellow at the Institut für Philosophie of the University of Erlangen-Nürnberg, funded by the Alexander von Humboldt-Stiftung. I am grateful to both institutions for their generous support, and in particular, to Christian Thiel and Volker Peckhaus for many helpful discussions of Frege, Russell and analysis.

REFERENCES

Beaney, Michael (1996), *Frege: Making Sense* (Duckworth).

—— (2000), 'Conceptions of Analysis in Early Analytic Philosophy', *Acta Analytica* 25, pp. 97–115.

—— (2002), 'Decompositions and Transformations: Conceptions of Analysis in the Early Analytic and Phenomenological Traditions', *Southern Journal of Philosophy* 40, Supp. Vol., pp. 53–99.

—— (2003), 'Analysis', *Stanford Encyclopedia of Philosophy*. http://plato. stanford. edu

Bentham, Jeremy (1843), 'Essay on Logic', in *The Works of Jeremy Bentham*, ed. John Bowring (Edinburgh, 1843), Vol. 8, pp. 213–93.

Blackburn, Simon (1996), *The Oxford Dictionary of Philosophy* (OUP).

Bradley, F.H., (1883), *Principles of Logic* (Oxford; 2nd ed. 1922; corrected impression 1928).

Burge, Tyler (1984), 'Frege on Extensions of Concepts, from 1884 to 1903', *Phil. Rev.* 93, pp. 3–34.

Candlish, Stewart (1996), 'The Unity of the Proposition and Russell's Theories of Judgement', in Monk & Palmer (1996), pp. 103–35.

Dummett, Michael (1981a), *Frege: Philosophy of Language*, 2nd ed. (Duckworth; 1st ed. 1973).

—— (1981b), *The Interpretation of Frege's Philosophy* (Duckworth).

Frege, Gottlob, (1879), *Begriffsschrift, eine der arithmetischen nachgebildete Formelsprache des reinen Denkens* (Halle: L. Nebert), tr. in Frege, 1972, pp. 101–203; Preface and most of Part I (§§1–12) also tr. in Frege, 1997, pp. 47–78.

——, (1884), *Die Grundlagen der Arithmetik, eine logisch mathematische Untersuchung über den Begriff der Zahl* (Breslau: W. Koebner), selections tr. in Frege, 1997, pp. 84–129.

——, (1891), 'Function and Concept', Frege, 1997, pp. 130–48.

——, (1892a), 'On *Sinn* and *Bedeutung*', in Frege, 1997, pp. 151–71.

——, (1892b), 'On Concept and Object', in Frege, 1997, pp. 181–93.

——, (1893, 1903), *Grundgesetze der Arithmetik* (Jena: H. Pohle, Band I 1893, Band II 1903; repr. together, Hildesheim: Georg Olms, 1962), selections from both vols. tr. in Frege, 1997, pp. 194–223, 258–89.

——, (1972), *Conceptual Notation and related articles*, ed. & tr. with a biog. & introd. by T. W. Bynum (OUP).

——, (1979), *Posthumous Writings*, tr. P. Long & R. White (Blackwell).

——, (1980), *Philosophical and Mathematical Correspondence*, ed. B. McGuinness, tr. H. Kaal (Blackwell).

——, (1984), *Collected Papers on Mathematics, Logic, and Philosophy*, ed. B. McGuinness, tr. M. Black *et al.* (Blackwell).

——, (1979), *The Frege Reader*, ed. with an introd. by M. Beaney (Blackwell).

Geach, P.T. (1956), 'On Frege's Way Out', *Mind* 65, pp. 408–9.

Griffin, Nicholas (1991), *Russell's Idealist Apprenticeship* (OUP).

—— (1993), 'Terms, Relations, Complexes', in Irvine & Wedeking (1993), pp. 159–92.

Hylton, Peter (1996), 'Beginning with Analysis', in Monk & Palmer (1996), pp. 183–216.

Irvine, A.D. & Wedeking, G.A. (1993), eds., *Russell and Analytic Philosophy* (Univ. of Toronto Press).

Monk, Ray & Palmer, Anthony (1996), eds., *Bertrand Russell and the Origins of Analytical Philosophy* (Bristol: Thoemmes Press).

Moore, G.E. (1944), 'Russell's "Theory of Descriptions"', in Schilpp (1944), pp. 175–225.

Nidditch, P.H. (1962), *The Development of Mathematical Logic* (Routledge).

Peckhaus, Volker (2002), 'Regressive Analysis', *Logical Analysis and the History of Philosophy*, 4, pp. 97–110.

Quine, W.V.O. (1955), 'On Frege's Way Out', *Mind* 64, pp. 145–59.

Ramsey, Frank P. (1931), *The Foundations of Mathematics* (Routledge).

Rodríguez-Consuegra, Francisco A. (1991), *The Mathematical Philosophy of Bertrand Russell: Origins and Development* (Basel: Birkhäuser).

Russell, Bertrand, (1901), 'The Logic of Relations, with some applications to the theory of series', in *Papers* 3, pp. 314–49.

Schilpp, P.A. (1944), ed., *The Philosophy of Bertrand Russell* (Evanston and Chicago: Northwestern Univ.).

Stebbing, L.S. (1932), 'The Method of Analysis in Metaphysics', *Proc. Aris. Soc.* 33, pp. 65–94.

—— (1933), 'Logical Positivism and Analysis', *Proc. Brit. Acad.* 19, pp. 53–87.

—— (1934), 'Directional Analysis and Basic Facts', *Analysis* 2, pp. 33–6.

Thiel, Christian (1968), *Sense and Reference in Frege's Logic*, tr. T.J. Blakeley (D. Reidel; first publ. 1965).

Urmson, J.O. (1956), *Philosophical Analysis: Its Development between the Two World Wars* (OUP).

Wisdom, John (1931), *Interpretation and Analysis in Relation to Bentham's Theory of Definition* (London: Kegan Paul).

—— (1934), 'Is Analysis a Useful Method in Philosophy?', *Proc. Aris. Soc. Supp.* 13, pp. 65–89.

Wittgenstein, Ludwig, (1922), *Tractatus Logico-Philosophicus*, tr. D.F. Pears & B. McGuinness (RKP; 1961, 1974); orig. tr. C.K. Ogden (RKP, 1922).

5 Bertrand Russell's Logicism

Logicism is the view that (some or all branches of) mathematics can be reduced to logic. As a result, most versions of logicism involve two goals. The first is to show that (some or all) mathematical concepts can be derived from purely logical concepts via a series of explicit definitions. In other words, if logicism is correct, the vocabulary of (some or all branches of) mathematics will turn out to be a proper part of the vocabulary of logic. The second is to show that (some or all) mathematical theorems are capable of being deduced from purely logical axioms by means of familiar rules of deductive inference. In other words, if logicism is correct, the theorems of (some or all branches of) mathematics will turn out to be a proper subset of the theorems of logic. Russell favoured the more universal form of logicism. In his words, it is the logicist's goal "to show that all pure mathematics follows from purely logical premises and uses only concepts definable in logical terms".[1]

In order to understand the various motivations behind logicism, it is helpful to consider the simple case in which basic arithmetical sentences are replaced by purely logical ones. For example, the sentence "There are at least two things that are P" can be replaced by a sentence that contains neither numerals nor any other specifically mathematical vocabulary, namely,

$$(\forall x)(\exists y)(x \neq y \,\&\, Py).$$

Similarly,

$$(\exists x)(\exists y)(x \neq y \,\&\,(\forall z)(Pz \equiv (z = x \lor z = y)))$$

---

[1] Russell, *MPD*, p. 74.

states that there are exactly two things that are P;

$$(\forall x)(\forall y)(\exists z)((x \neq z \ \& \ y \neq z) \ \& \ Pz)$$

states that there are at least three things that are P;

$$(\exists x)(\exists y)(\exists z)(((x \neq y \ \& \ x \neq z) \ \& \ y \neq z) \ \& \ (\forall w)(Pw \equiv (w = x \ \lor \ w = y) \lor$$
$$w = z))$$

states that there are exactly three things that are P, and so on for other similar sentences. By introducing second-order quantifiers, together with a modified series of first-order quantifiers, $(\exists_1 x)$, $(\exists_2 x)$, $(\exists_3 x)$, ..., defined as follows,

$$(\exists_1 x)Px =_{df} (\exists x)(\forall y)(Py \equiv (y = x))$$
$$(\exists_2 x)Px =_{df} (\exists x)(\exists y)(x \neq y \ \& \ (\forall z)(Pz \equiv (z = x \ \lor \ z = y)))$$
$$(\exists_3 x)Px =_{df} (\exists x)(\exists y)(\exists z)(((x \neq y \ \& \ x \neq z) \ \& \ y \neq z) \ \&$$
$$(\forall w)(Pw \equiv (w = x \ \lor \ w = y) \ \lor \ w = z))$$
$$\vdots$$

it is also possible to express familiar arithmetical truths such as $2 + 3 = 5$, again without the introduction of any specifically mathematical vocabulary; for example,

$$(\forall X)(\forall Y)((((\exists_2 x)Xx \ \& \ (\exists_3 x)Yx) \ \& \ \sim(\exists x)(Xx \ \& \ Yx)) \supset (\exists_5 x)(Xx \ v \ Yx)).$$

It is thus regularly claimed that, if successful, logicism would show that mathematical truth is a species of logical truth. It is also regularly claimed both that mathematical ontology would be (at most) a subset of logical ontology, and that mathematical knowledge would be (at most) a subset of logical knowledge. In other words, it would be plausible to conclude that (at least some branches of) mathematics will have the same (limited) ontology as that of logic, and that knowledge of (at least some) mathematical truths will have the same high degree of certainty as that of logical truths. Given that logical truths are often claimed to be topic-neutral, and so to involve no ontology, and that they are among the most certain of all our knowledge claims, logicism would explain the high degree of certainty associated with mathematics. It would also help us avoid commitment to potentially mysterious, nonphysical mathematical entities.

However, whether logicism is successful depends, in large measure, on how logic itself is defined. Should it turn out that mathematics is reducible only to second-order logic, and that second-order logic, in turn, is equivalent to set theory, it would remain unclear just how helpful such a reduction would be, either ontologically or epistemologically. Other concerns also can be raised.

This chapter is divided into four sections. The first, "The Advent of Logicism", summarizes the work of early logicists such as Gottfried Leibniz and Gottlob Frege. The second, "Russell's Paradox and the New Logicism", discusses the advances made by Bertrand Russell and Alfred North Whitehead, and the challenge of carrying Frege's program forward given the discovery of Russell's Paradox. The third, "Ontological Logicism", considers Russell's views concerning the ontological consequences of logicism. Finally, the fourth section, "Epistemic Logicism", does the same for Russell's views about the epistemic consequences of logicism.

I. THE ADVENT OF LOGICISM

Gottfried Leibniz is today almost universally credited as being the first logicist. That he is seen as such is due, in no small measure, to Russell's own contribution in one of his earliest published works, *A Critical Exposition of the Philosophy of Leibniz*, published in 1900. In this landmark book Russell argues that many important and (until then) largely ignored portions of Leibniz's philosophy are not only coherent and logical, but also quite profound. Moreover, Russell argues that Leibniz's philosophy "follows almost entirely from a small number of premises",[2] chief among which is the claim that every true proposition consists of (and must, in principle, be analysable into) a *subject* and a *predicate*. In keeping with this principle Leibniz divides all truths into two categories: *primary* truths and *secondary* truths. The former he characterises as specifically logical truths, namely "those which either state a term of itself, or deny an opposite of its opposite"[3] (*i.e.*, are of the form "A is A" or "A is not not-A"). He goes

[2] Russell, *A Critical Exposition of the Philosophy of Leibniz*, London: Allen and Unwin, 1900 p. 3.
[3] Gottfried Leibniz, "Primary Truths," in *Leibniz: Philosophical Writings*, G.H.R. Parkinson (ed.), London: Everyman, 1973, p. 87.

on to argue that, "All other truths are reduced to primary truths by the aid of definitions – *i.e.*, by the analysis of notions."[4] It is an immediate consequence of this claim that the truths of mathematics must be reducible to such logical truths. Thus, what distinguishes Leibniz's logicism from that of many subsequent logicists is that it stands within this much broader metaphysical position, for he goes on to insist that this analysis into logical truths "is true of every affirmative truth, universal or particular, necessary or contingent".[5] The essential difference between contingent truths and necessary truths (such as those of mathematics), he believes, lies in the infinite analysis required of the former in order to reveal their logical constituents – an analysis beyond our finite abilities, but not beyond the abilities of God.

It is equally clear (at least initially) that Leibniz believed not only that it was a metaphysical fact that all truths are reducible to primary logical truths, but also that, given an appropriate formal language, all truths should be capable (if only upon infinite analysis, as in the case of contingent truths) of *a priori* proof. The means of carrying out such proofs was the subject of one of Leibniz's earliest works, his dissertation *De Arte Combinatoria (On the Art of Combinations)*, written in 1666 when he was scarcely twenty. In it Leibniz reveals his vision of a *Characteristica Universalis*, or universal characteristic,[6] that would operate as a formal logic through which all true propositions would be demonstrable, merely through adherence to syntactical rules:

If controversies were to arise, there would be no more need of disputation between two philosophers than between two accountants. For it would suffice to take their pencils in their hands, to sit down with their slates, and to say to each other ... Let us calculate.[7]

---

[4] *Ibid.*
[5] *Ibid.*, p. 88.
[6] Russell prefers to translate this as "universal mathematics". A more perspicuous interpretation might be "universal sign-system". Leibniz formulated many different versions of his sign-system, only some of which were specifically numerical or mathematical in style. For a review of these, see G.H.R. Parkinson's Introduction to *Leibniz: Logical Papers*, G.H.R. Parkinson (ed.), Oxford: Clarendon, 1966, pp. xxii ff.
[7] Gottfried Leibniz, quoted in Russell, *Leibniz*, p. 170.

However, after many incomplete attempts at developing his universal characteristic, Leibniz lost confidence in the human capacity to reduce arbitrarily given truths to the primitive truths required for complete *a priori* deductibility. By 1679, he was concluding that "An analysis of concepts by which we are enabled to arrive at primitive notions, *i.e.*, those which are conceived through themselves, does not seem to be within the power of man".[8] While this put a damper on the prospect of the *a priori* deductibility of all truths, there is every reason to believe that Leibniz still held out hope for the *a priori* deductibility of all necessary truths. As late as 1714 he was insisting that, given the appropriate opportunity and help, "I should still hope to create a kind of *spécieuse générale*, in which all truths of reason would be reduced to a kind of calculus".[9]

Leibniz never carried his universal characteristic to fruition, hampered as his logic was by a commitment to the Aristotelian syllogism (with some improvements) and the supposed subject–predicate form of all true propositions.[10] Although some advances were made by George Boole,[11] which led in turn to the development of the propositional calculus, it was not until Gottlob Frege, over two centuries after Leibniz originally formulated his idea, that Leibniz's logicist hopes began to look feasible. In 1879, Frege's *Begriffsschrift*[12] (or "Concept-script") provided a foundational step in the pursuit of something that he hoped would be very similar to what Leibniz envisaged, and through which he hoped to be able to capture the conceptual content of propositions. In it, Frege made the crucial step of introducing quantification into a logic of relations, thereby freeing logic from its syllogistic shackles. Central to Frege's project was the

---

[8] Gottfried Leibniz, "An Introduction to a Secret Encyclopaedia", in *Leibniz: Philosophical Writings*, G.H.R. Parkinson (ed.), London: Everyman, 1973, p. 8.

[9] Gottfried Leibniz's letter to Raymond (1714), quoted by D. Rutherford in "Philosophy and Language in Leibniz", in N. Jolley (ed.), *The Cambridge Companion to Leibniz*, Cambridge: Cambridge University Press, 1995, p. 239.

[10] At least this is Russell's, and the generally accepted, diagnosis. Hide Ishiguro has suggested that the failure of Leibniz's logic has more to do with problems common to logical atomism in general, of which Leibniz is also plausibly an early proponent. See H. Ishiguro, *Leibniz's Philosophy of Logic and Language*, 2nd ed., Cambridge: Cambridge University Press, 1990.

[11] George Boole, *An Investigation of the Laws of Thought*, London: Walton & Maberly, 1854.

[12] Translated in Michael Beaney (ed.), *The Frege Reader*, Oxford: Blackwell, 1997, pp. 47–78.

analysis of propositions into concept and object, which itself was modelled on an analysis of mathematical terms into *function* and *argument*.[13]

Although Frege recognized the general applicability and utility of his *Begriffsschrift*, from the very beginning he was especially concerned with its use in providing a purely logical foundation for arithmetic. The course he took to this end was "first to seek to reduce the concept of ordering in a series to that of *logical* consequence, in order then to progress to the concept of number. So that nothing intuitive could intrude here unnoticed, everything had to depend on the chain of inference being free of gaps".[14] It was out of this need to close all the inferential gaps that the idea of his *Begriffsschrift* had been born. Having established his logical apparatus, he began the task of deriving arithmetic from logical principles and explicit definitions alone. His preliminary results were published in a philosophically sophisticated but relatively informal form in his *Grundlagen der Arithmetik* in 1884.[15] In it, after rehearsing several arguments against alternative approaches, Frege argues that judgements about numbers are entirely analyzable into statements about concepts and their extensions. In general, therefore, a statement of number contains an assertion about a concept. The number of a concept, F, is the extension of the concept "equinumerous to the concept F". This is not (as might at first appear) circular, because we do not, for example, have to count the number of elements that fall under the concept "is a knife on the table" in order to establish that its number is equinumerous with, say, the extension of the concept "is a fork on the table." Instead we establish this fact by placing the objects into a one-to-one correspondence. This, one-to-one "pairing-off" (often called Hume's Principle, and relying only upon the logical notion of identity) thus serves as the logically prior basis of number.

With this principle in place, Frege defines 0 as "the number which belongs to the concept 'not identical with itself'".[16] Though "not

---

[13] Frege's subtitle for the *Begriffsschrift* is "a formula language of pure thought modelled on that of arithmetic."

[14] Gottlob Frege, *Begriffsschrift*, in M. Beaney (ed.), *The Frege Reader*, Oxford: Blackwell, 1997, p. 48.

[15] Translated as *The Foundations of Arithmetic*, J.L. Austin (trans.), Oxford: Blackwell, 1950.

[16] *Ibid.*, §74.

identical with itself" is plainly contradictory, this does not bother
Frege since all that he requires of a concept is that it should be de-
terminate whether any object falls under it or not. In this case it
is plain that nothing can be not-identical-with-itself and, thus, that
nothing falls under this concept. It therefore serves perfectly to pick
out the number zero. Most importantly for Frege, the concept "not
identical with itself" is a purely logical one.[17] Subsequent numbers
in the series of natural numbers are then defined by iterating this
definition: 1 is defined as the number that belongs to the concept
"identical with 0"; 2 is defined as the number that belongs to the
concept "identical with 0 or 1", and so on. The formal fulfillment
of Frege's project began with the first volume of his *Grundgesetze
der Arithmetik*, which appeared in 1893.[18] The second volume (of
a planned three) appeared in 1903, but by then Frege had been in-
formed by Russell of the paradox (see below) which, in Frege's words
"had rocked the ground on which I meant to build arithmetic".[19]

In considering Frege's logicism, it is important to realize that his
primary motivation was epistemological; he wanted to secure the *a
priori* certainty of arithmetic. As Frege wrote, "the firmest proof is
obviously the purely logical, which, prescinding from the particularity of things, is based solely on the laws on which all knowledge
rests".[20] His primary aim then, was to show that the truths of arithmetic were absolutely certain in virtue of being founded upon, and
derivable from, purely logical axioms and suitable definitions. Inex-
tricably linked to this goal was the eradication of all psychological
and, what amounted to much the same thing for Frege, subjective
elements from the notions of truth and proof. As Frege was quick
to point out, there is a dangerous ambiguity in the notion of a *law
of thought*. In one sense, a law of thought describes those inferences
that we take to be valid. In another sense, it prescribes how we ought
to think in order always to move from true premises to true conclusions. Although Frege seems willing to admit that "it is impossible

---

[17] Other concepts, such as "is a unicorn", could serve equally well to pick out the
number zero but are neither logical nor self-evidently true.
[18] Translated as *The Basic Laws of Arithmetic*, Montgomery Furth (trans.), Berkeley:
University of California Press, 1967.
[19] Gottlob Frege's letter to Russell (1902), in Michael Beaney (ed.), *The Frege Reader*,
Oxford: Blackwell, 1997, p. 254.
[20] Gottlob Frege, *Begriffsschrift*, in Michael Beaney (ed.), *The Frege Reader*, Oxford:
Blackwell, 1997, p. 48.

to effect any sharp separation of the two",[21] he insists that the former falls squarely within the realm of psychology and has little or nothing to do with logic as he understands it. Just as there is a world of difference between being held to be true and actually being true, so there is a world of difference between being held to be a valid inference and actually being a valid inference. It is the latter that Frege takes to be the domain of logic and the subject of his logicist program. For Frege, the laws of logic "only deserve the name 'law of thought' with more right if it should be meant by this that they are the most general laws, which prescribe universally how one should think if one is to think at all".[22] They are not psychological laws but, rather, are "boundary stones set in an eternal foundation which our thought can overflow but not dislodge."[23]

One prominent mathematician and logicist whom Frege clearly thought had failed to keep distinct these separate notions of a law was Richard Dedekind. As is clear in the preface of *Was Sind und was Sollen die Zahlen*[24] published in 1888, a year before he became aware of Frege's *Grundlagen*, Dedekind shared Frege's view that the theory of numbers is a proper part of logic. Says Dedekind: "In speaking of arithmetic ... as a part of logic I mean to imply that I consider the number concept entirely independent of the notions or intuitions of space and time, that I consider it an immediate result of the laws of thought".[25] This might indicate a large measure of agreement with Frege and, despite acknowledged differences, that is just how Dedekind chose to see it, commenting later that Frege "stands upon the same ground with me".[26] Frege, however, was less enthusiastic about Dedekind's views than *vice versa*. As Frege saw it, that Dedekind appears to intend something psychological by "laws of thought" is suggested by his definition of number in §73. Number for Dedekind – and, unlike Frege, he took ordinal rather than cardinal number to be the more basic notion – was created by us through a process of abstraction:

[21] Gottlob Frege, *The Foundations of Arithmetic*, J.L. Austin (trans.), Oxford: Blackwell, 1950, p. ix.
[22] Gottlob Frege, *The Basic Laws of Arithmetic*, Montgomery Furth (trans.), Berkeley: University of California Press, 1967, p. xv.
[23] *Ibid.*, p. xvi.
[24] Translated as "The Nature and Meaning of Numbers", in Dedekind's *Essays on the Theory of Numbers*, Wooster Woodruff Beman (trans.), La Salle Open Court, 1901.
[25] *Ibid.*, p. 31
[26] *Ibid.*, p. 43.

If in the consideration of a simply infinite system N set in order by a trans-formation ϕ we entirely neglect the special character of the elements; simply retaining their distinguishability and taking into account only the relations to one another in which they are placed by the order-setting transforma-tion ϕ, then are these elements called *natural numbers* or *ordinal numbers* or simply *numbers*, and the base-element 1 is called the *base-number* of the *number-series N*. With reference to this freeing the elements from every other content (abstraction) we are justified in calling numbers a free creation of the human mind.[27]

Frege's concern with this is that if numbers and the logical laws on which they stand were creations of the mind, then they would be psychological; and if they were psychological, then they would be subjective and therefore lacking the certainty requisite for the foundations of arithmetic. Even so, in an interesting letter to Dr. H. Keferstein (dated 1890),[28] Dedekind reveals something of the process through which his essay came to be written and suggests that he would reject any suggestion of subjectivity. In this letter he describes *Was Sind und was Sollen die Zahlen* as a synthesis "preceded by and based upon an analysis of the sequence of natural numbers, just as it presents itself, in practice so to speak, to the mind."[29] He intends by this synthesis to answer the question,

Which are the mutually fundamental properties of this sequence N, i.e., those principles which are not deducible from one another and from which all others follow? ... which are necessary for all thinking, but at the same time sufficient, to secure reliability and completeness for our proofs, and to permit the construction of consistent concepts and definitions.[30]

Talk of such principles as are *necessary* for all thinking (rather than, say, merely universal) suggests that while Dedekind indeed takes laws of thought to be psychological, in as much as he takes thought itself to be psychological, he does not, thereby, take them to be subjective, arbitrary, or contingent upon the workings of the mind. Rather, he appears to take them to be (to echo a phrase of Frege's) the way that we *must* think, if we are to think at all. In another letter that Dedekind wrote to Weber (dated 1888) he suggests that we are "a

[27] *Ibid.*, p. 68.
[28] Quoted in Hao Wang, "The Axiomatization of Arithmetic", *Journal of Symbolic Logic*, 22 (1957), p. 150.
[29] *Ibid.*
[30] *Ibid.*

god-like race [*göttlischen Geschlechtes*] and without doubt possess creative power not merely in material things [railways, telegraphs] but especially in intellectual ones".[31] There is no suggestion by this that what we can and do create in arithmetic and mathematics is any less bound by objective and fixed logical laws than our free creation of material artifacts is bound by the objective and fixed laws of physics.

Nevertheless, further significant differences remain. Of their shared view that number is a part of logic, Frege comments that Dedekind's work "hardly helps to confirm this opinion, since the expressions 'system' [set] and 'a thing belongs to a thing' [set-membership] are not usual in logic and are not reduced to what is recognised as logical".[32] As Phillip Kitcher comments, it is perhaps puzzling that one of the great reformers of logic should be critical of Dedekind on grounds of unconventionality.[33] Dedekind, of course, is approaching the matter very much from the perspective of a practising mathematician who adopts standards of rigour and inference that are quite acceptable within mathematical practice, including such notions as set and set-membership. Moreover, it is clear that he considers the basic terms of his analysis to be fundamental to the very possibility of thought. The significance of this difference will turn largely on the extent to which set-theoretic concepts, axioms, and modes of inference are considered legitimate elements of a logical foundation of arithmetic. This is a concern that only deepened with the discovery of Russell's paradox and the development of Russell's new logicism.

II. RUSSELL'S PARADOX AND THE NEW LOGICISM

Russell first expresses his commitment to logicism in print in 1901. In his essay "Recent Work on the Principles of Mathematics" he confidently comments:

---

[31] Richard Dedekind's letter to Weber (1888), *Gesamelte Mathematische Werke*, R. Fricke, E. Noether and O. Ore (eds.), Vol. 3, Berlin: Vieweg & Sohn, 1932, p. 489.

[32] Gottlob Frege, *The Basic Laws of Arithmetic*, Montgomery Furth (trans.), Berkeley: University of California Press, 1967, p. viii.

[33] Phillip Kitcher, "Frege, Dedekind, and the Philosophy of Mathematics", in L. Haaparanta and J. Hintikka (eds.), *Frege Synthesized*, Dordrecht: D. Reidel, 1986, p. 324.

Now the fact is that, though there are indefinables and indemonstrables in every branch of applied mathematics, there are none in pure mathematics except such as belong to general logic .... All pure mathematics – Arithmetic, Analysis, and Geometry – is built up by combinations of the primitive ideas of logic, and its propositions are deduced from the general axioms of logic ....[34]

This foreshadowed his more famous 1903 statement in the Introduction to his *Principles of Mathematics*, where he states that

all pure mathematics deals exclusively with concepts definable in terms of a very small number of fundamental logical concepts, and ... all its propositions are deducible from a very small number of fundamental logical principles ....[35]

However, it was not long before Russell recognized that the project of reducing all of mathematics to logic might be more difficult than he first imagined.

Russell had completed the first draft of his Principles, he tells us, "on the last day of the century", 31 December 1900.[36] Five months later, in May 1901, Russell discovered his now famous paradox. The paradox comes from considering the set of all sets that are not members of themselves. Since this set must be a member of itself if and only if it is not a member of itself, postulating it clearly involves one in a contradiction. As a result, Russell needed to find a principled way of denying its existence. Cesare Burali-Forti had discovered a similar antinomy in 1897 when he had observed that since the set of ordinals is well-ordered, it must have an ordinal. However, this ordinal must be both an element of the set of ordinals and yet greater than any ordinal in that set.[37] Given the intimate relation between set theory and logic, such paradoxes failed to bode well for logicism.

After worrying about his paradox for over a year, Russell wrote to Frege on June 16, 1902. The antinomy was a crucial one, since Frege claimed that an expression such as $f(a)$ could be considered to be both a function of the argument f and a function of the argument a.

---

[34] Bertrand Russell, "Recent Work on the Principles of Mathematics", *International Monthly*, 4 (1901), p. 84 (*Papers* 3, p. 367); repr. with revisions as "Mathematics and the Metaphysicians" in *ML*, pp. 74ff. (In the reprint, the original article is mis-cited as "Recent Work in the Philosophy of Mathematics".)

[35] Russell, *POM*, p. xv.

[36] Russell, *Auto*, Vol. 1, p. 219.

[37] Much the same difficulty is outlined by Cantor in a 1899 letter to Dedekind.

In effect, it was this ambiguity that allowed Russell to construct his paradox within Frege's logic. As Russell explains,

this view [that $f(a)$ may be viewed as a function of either f or of a] seems doubtful to me because of the following contradiction. Let w be the predicate: to be a predicate that cannot be predicated of itself. Can w be predicated of itself? From each answer its opposite follows. Therefore we must conclude that w is not a predicate. Likewise there is no class (as a totality) of those classes which, each taken as a totality, do not belong to themselves. From this I conclude that under certain circumstances a definable collection does not form a totality.[38]

Russell's letter to Frege, in effect telling him that his axioms were inconsistent, arrived just as the second volume of his *Grundgesetze* was in press. Immediately appreciating the difficulty, Frege attempted to revise his work, adding an appendix to the *Grundgesetze*, which discussed Russell's discovery. Nevertheless, he eventually felt forced to abandon his logicism. A projected third volume of the *Grundgesetze* which had been planned never appeared. Frege's later writings show that Russell's discovery had convinced him of the falsehood of logicism. Instead, he opted for the view that all of mathematics, including number theory and analysis, was reducible only to geometry.

In contrast to Frege, Russell's response to the paradox was to forge ahead and develop his aptly named *theory of types*. Russell's basic idea was that by ordering the sentences of a language or theory into a hierarchy (beginning with sentences about individuals at the lowest level, sentences about sets of individuals at the next lowest level, sentences about sets of sets of individuals at the next lowest level, etc.), one could avoid reference to sets such as the set of all sets, since there would be no level at which reference to such a set appears. It is then possible to refer to all things for which a given condition (or predicate) holds only if they are all at the same level or of the same "type".

The theory itself appeared in two versions. According to the simple theory of types, it is the universe of discourse (of the relevant language) that is to be viewed as forming a hierarchy. Within this hierarchy, individuals form the lowest type; sets of individuals form the next lowest type; sets of sets of individuals form the next lowest

---

[38] Russell's letter to Frege (1902), in Jean van Heijenoort (ed.), *From Frege to Gödel*, Cambridge, Mass.: Harvard University Press, 1967, p. 125.

type; and so on. Individual variables are then indexed (using subscripts) to indicate the type of object over which they range, and the language's formation rules are restricted to allow only sentences such as "$a_n \in b_m$" (where $m > n$) to be counted among the (well-formed) formulas of the language. Such restrictions mean that strings such as "$x_n \in x_n$" are ill-formed, thereby blocking Russell's paradox.

The ramified theory of types goes further than the simple theory. It does so by describing a hierarchy, not only of objects, but of closed and open sentences (propositions and propositional functions, respectively) as well. The theory then adds the condition that no proposition or propositional function may contain quantifiers ranging over propositions or propositional functions of any order except those lower than itself. Intuitively, this means that no proposition or propositional function can refer to, or be about, any member of the hierarchy other than those that are defined in a logically prior manner. Since, for Russell, sets are to be understood as logical constructs based upon propositional functions, it follows that the simple theory of types can be viewed as a special case of the ramified theory. In order to justify both his simple and ramified theories, Russell introduced the principle that "Whatever involves *all* of a collection must not [itself] be one of the collection".[39] Taking his lead from the mathematician Henri Poincaré, Russell called this principle the *vicious circle principle* (or *VCP*).

Although Russell first introduced his theory in 1903 in a hastily added Appendix to his *Principles of Mathematics*, he continued to work on other solutions. In 1905, he temporarily set aside the theory in order to consider three potential alternatives: *the zigzag theory*, in which only "simple" propositional functions determine sets; the *theory of limitation of size*, in which the purported set of all entities is disallowed; and the *no-classes theory*, in which sets are outlawed, being replaced instead by sentences of certain kinds. Nevertheless, by 1908 Russell abandoned all three of these suggestions in order to return to his theory of types, which he develops in detail in his article "Mathematical Logic as Based on the Theory of Types".

By this time Russell was also hard at work with his former teacher, Alfred North Whitehead, on their monumental work defending

---

[39] Or perhaps equivalently, that no collection can be definable only in terms of itself. See Russell, "Mathematical Logic as Based on the Theory of Types", in *LK*, p. 63.

logicism, *Principia Mathematica*. Both men had begun preparing second volumes to earlier books on related topics: Whitehead's *A Treatise on Universal Algebra*[40] and Russell's *Principles*. Since their research overlapped considerably, they began collaboration, hoping to achieve what Frege could not.

Principia Mathematica appeared in three volumes in 1910, 1912, and 1913. Almost immediately its main goal of proving the detailed reduction of mathematics to logic proved to be controversial. Primarily at issue were the various assumptions that Whitehead and Russell had used to complete their project.

During the critical movement initiated in the 1820s, Bernard Bolzano, Niels Abel, Louis Cauchy, and Karl Weierstrass had succeeded in eliminating much of the vagueness and many of the contradictions present in the mathematical theories of their day. By the late 1800s, William Hamilton had also introduced ordered couples of reals as the first step in supplying a logical basis for the complex numbers, and Weierstrass, Richard Dedekind, and Georg Cantor had all developed methods for founding the irrationals in terms of the rationals. Using work by H.G. Grassmann and Dedekind, Guiseppe Peano had also gone on to develop a theory of the rationals based on his now famous axioms for the natural numbers. Thus, by Frege's day it was generally recognized that a large portion of mathematics could be derived from a relatively small set of primitive notions. With the addition of Frege's logic, together with the new symbolism and theory of types added by Russell to combat inconsistency, the ground had been laid to try to complete the logicist project.

However, although *Principia* succeeded in providing detailed derivations of major theorems in set theory, finite and transfinite arithmetic, and elementary measure theory, two axioms in particular were arguably non-logical in character.[41] These were the axiom of infinity and the axiom of reducibility. The former of these two axioms in effect assumed that there exists an infinity of objects. Thus, it made the kind of assumption that is generally thought to be empirical rather than logical in nature. The latter arose as a

---

[40] Alfred North Whitehead, *A Treatise on Universal Algebra*, Cambridge: Cambridge University Press, 1898.
[41] A third axiom, the axiom of choice – or, as Russell calls it, the multiplicative axiom – was also controversial, but less for reasons of logic than simple incredulity on the part of its constructivist critics.

means of limiting the not completely satisfactory effects of the theory of types, the theory that Russell and Whitehead used to restrict the notion of a well-formed expression, and so to avoid the paradoxes. Although technically feasible, many critics claimed that this axiom was simply too *ad hoc* to be justified philosophically. As a result, the question of whether mathematics could be reduced to logic, or whether it could be reduced only to set theory, remained open.

This issue was complicated by Russell's ambiguous use of the term "propositional function". If ontological comfort is to be taken from the construction of mathematical entities out of other more manageable, and ontologically less problematic, entities it is important to know what these more basic entities are. By constructing classes out of propositional functions, Russell and Whitehead felt entitled to claim that "classes, so far as we introduce them, are merely symbolic or linguistic conveniences, not genuine objects ... ".[42] However, as Quine has pointed out, this phrase was sometimes used to mean an open sentence; at other times it was used to refer to attributes.[43] The moral Quine draws is that mathematics can therefore be reduced at most to set theory. This helps lessen our ontological commitment, but not to the same degree as hoped for by traditional logicists.

Despite these criticisms, *Principia Mathematica* proved to be remarkably influential in at least three other ways. First, it popularized modern mathematical logic to an extent undreamt of by its authors. By using a notation superior in many ways to that of Frege, Whitehead and Russell managed to convey the remarkable expressive power of modern logic in a way that previous writers had been unable to achieve. Second, by exhibiting so clearly the deductive power of the new logic, Whitehead and Russell were also able to show how powerful the modern idea of a formal system could be. Third, it introduced clear and interesting connections between logicism and two main branches of traditional philosophy: metaphysics (or at least its main component discipline, ontology) and epistemology.

---

[42] See Whitehead and Russell, *PM* Vol. 1, p. 72. Also compare Hans Hahn, "Superfluous Entities, or Occam's Razor", in *Empiricism, Logic, and Mathematics*, Brian McGuinness (ed.), Dordrecht: Reidel, 1980, especially pp. 14ff.

[43] See W.V. Quine, "Logic and the Reification of Universals", in *From a Logical Point of View*, 2nd ed., Cambridge, Mass.: Harvard University Press, 1961, pp. 122f.

Thus, not only did *Principia* introduce a wide range of philosophically rich notions (such as propositional function, logical construction, and type theory), it also set the stage for the discovery of classical metatheoretic results (such as those of Kurt Gödel and others) and initiated a tradition of technical work in fields as diverse as philosophy, mathematics, linguistics, economics, and computer science. It is to some of these consequences – specifically those dealing with ontology and epistemology – that we now turn.

III. ONTOLOGICAL LOGICISM

What ontological commitments (if any) arise from Russell's logicism? Russell's approach to ontological commitment with respect to logicism broadly parallels his approach to ontological commitment more generally. In his early work, he emphasises a direct and intimate connection between the appearance of a term in a proposition and a speaker's commitment to the existence (or at least the subsistence) of the apparent referent of that term. This is especially evident in his *Principles of Mathematics* where, having freed himself from the monistic ontology of neo-Hegelianism, and feeling considerable influence from G.E. Moore's account of propositional analysis,[44] he adopts an extreme and unfettered realism incorporating a decidedly profligate ontology. Beginning with the notion of a *term* as the basic constitutive element into which all propositions are to be exhaustively analysed, Russell goes on to define *being* as

that which belongs to every conceivable term, to every possible object of thought – in short to everything that can possibly occur in any proposition, true or false, and to all such propositions themselves .... Numbers, the Homeric gods, relations, chimeras and four-dimensional spaces all have being, for if they were not entities of a kind, we could make no propositions about them. Thus being is a general attribute of everything, and to mention anything is to show that it is.[45]

What is especially clear here is the way that Russell's ontology derives from essentially semantic considerations. As Russell later puts

---

[44] See especially G.E. Moore, "The Nature of Judgement", *Mind*, n.s. 8 (1899), 176–193. For Moore, a proposition is analysable into "concepts", something akin to a "possible object of thought", or what Russell would later call a "logical atom".

[45] Russell, *POM*, p. 449.

it, his ontology during these early days stems almost wholly from "the belief that, if a word means something, there must be some thing that it means".[46]

However, only two years later in "On Denoting" (1905), his theory of descriptions changes matters considerably. The most obvious change is that Russell no longer takes the propositions of ordinary language at face value. Instead, superficially referential propositions are to be paraphrased into propositions expressed in the language of predicate logic, whereupon their true underlying logical structure is revealed. By such means it can be shown that apparently referential expressions, such as the denoting phrase "the present King of France" in the context of the proposition "the present King of France is bald", make no ineliminable reference to such an entity; or, in other words, that the phrase does not contain an unanalysable term naming the present King of France. We can, for example, paraphrase "the present King of France is bald" into an existential claim involving a conjunction of three propositions: "there is a present King of France", "there is at most one such thing", and "that thing is bald".[47] This analysis contains only propositional functions (i.e., "x is a present King of France" and "x is bald") together with logical terms such as quantifiers and their bound variables. The former he explicitly denies have ontological significance, referring to them at various times as "nothing", "mere schema", and "mere ambiguity awaiting determination".[48] Since it happens that there is no present King of France, the first conjunct of the above proposition is always false, thereby demonstrating how it is that the expression as a whole, although perfectly meaningful, is likewise false.

It is important to note that the analysis of denoting phrases by means of the theory of descriptions does not necessarily reduce one's ontological commitments. Rather, it serves to lay bare precisely what the ontological commitment of a definite description amounts to, just in case the proposition is true. In other words, ontological commitment is not removed by analysis, but merely perspicuously displayed by it. If we hold the proposition in question to be false, all ontological commitment is avoided. "The present Queen of England

---

[46] Russell, *MPD*, p. 63.

[47] In logical notation: $(\exists x)[Kx \ \& \ (\forall y)((Ky \equiv y = x) \ \& \ Bx)]$.

[48] For example, see Russell, "The Theory of Logical Types", in *EA*, p. 230; *Papers 6*, p. 15.

is unmarried", since it is false, avoids ontological commitment; the resulting analysis reveals an expression that is, for any x, always false. By the same token, ontological commitment towards a true existential proposition is not removed by analysis into components, none of which are names; "The present Queen of England is married" retains ontological commitment to the individual whom the expression "the present Queen of England" serves to pick out, despite the subsequent analysis containing no term directly naming that individual.

Russell's theory of descriptions therefore provides the requisite means to avoid ontological commitment with respect to definite descriptions that superficially refer to nonexistent or self-contradictory entities such as chimera or round squares. But while this opens the way for him to pare down his ontology considerably, this is not itself Russell's only or even main motivation for ontological reduction, the sources of which lie elsewhere. In part, Russell's motivation derives from a commitment to realism that he describes as "that feeling for reality that ought to be preserved even in the most abstract studies. Logic, I should maintain, must no more admit a unicorn than zoology can; for logic is concerned with the real world just as truly as zoology".[49] But it also derives from a growing emphasis on a form of Occam's Razor that remains an important principle throughout the ensuing development of Russell's ontology. Writing in 1914, Russell states that, "The supreme maxim in scientific philosophising is this: *wherever possible, logical constructions are to be substituted for inferred entities*".[50] Elsewhere he writes, "*Entities are not to be multiplied without necessity*. In other words, in dealing with any subject matter, find out what entities are undeniably involved, and state everything in terms of these entities".[51]

Talk of finding, in any discipline, such entities as "are undeniably involved" suggests that Russell's ontological scruples are motivated at least partly, and perhaps mainly, by an epistemological concern, specifically that of avoiding commitment to the existence of logically dispensable and epistemically uncertain inferred entities. Within the domain of logic and pure mathematics, we find Russell interpreting Frege's and his own earlier definition of number

[49] Russell, *IMP*, p. 171.
[50] Russell, RSDP, in *ML*, p. 155; in *Papers* 8, p. 11.
[51] Russell, *OKEW*, p. 107.

as equivalence classes in the light of this principle. Considering any two equally numerous collections, he says,

so long as the cardinal number is inferred from the collections, not constructed in terms of them, its existence must remain in doubt, unless in virtue of a metaphysical postulate *ad hoc*. By defining the cardinal number of a given collection as the class of all equally numerous collections we avoid the necessity of this metaphysical postulate, and thereby remove a needless doubt from the philosophy of arithmetic.[52]

We can dispense with cardinal numbers precisely because we can get all their usual arithmetical properties out of classes: just as numbers must satisfy the formulae of arithmetic, "any indubitable set of objects fulfilling this requirement may be called numbers. So far, the simplest set known to fulfil this requirement is the set introduced by the above definition".[53]

But if numbers are logically and ontologically dispensable in favour of classes, what are we to say, in turn, about the ontological status of classes? Russell argues, at least when he admits his no class theory, that classes, too, are nothing more than "logical fictions". By a similar analysis to that used in eliminating such pseudo-referents as "the present King of France" – *i.e.*, by analysis into propositional functions[54] – he concludes that they are "nothing" (literally, no thing). For example,

We shall then be able to say that the symbols for classes are mere conveniences, not representing objects called "classes", and that classes are in fact, like descriptions, logical fictions or (as we say) "incomplete symbols".[55]

Elsewhere he makes much the same point:

Numbers are classes of classes, and classes are logical fictions, so that numbers are, as it were, fictions at two removes, fictions of fictions. Therefore, you do not have as ultimate constituents of your world, these queer things that you are inclined to call numbers.[56]

It is difficult to understand Russell's position without a closer examination of his understanding of "ultimate constituent of your

---

[52] Russell, RSDP, in *ML*, p. 156; in *Papers* 8, p. 11.
[53] Russell, *OKEW*, p. 205.
[54] Given formally in *PM* at *20.01.
[55] Russell, *IMP*, p. 182.
[56] Russell, PLA, in *LK*, p. 270; in *Papers* 8, p. 234.

world" and "logical fiction" or, as he sometimes puts it, "logical construction". His elucidation of the former is given in terms of the ineliminable terms appearing in propositions, *i.e.*, as symbols appearing in the propositions of a logically perfect and complete symbolic language. According to Russell, it is the undefined primitive symbols of such a language that would represent symbolically all and only the ultimate constituents of the world – namely, the individuals or particulars and properties and relations that make up the world. It may be because of the intimate relationship that he sees between the primitive symbols of such a language and the ultimate constituents of the world that Russell speaks, rather incautiously, both about things and the symbols for such things in the same breath.

Classes, however, cannot be such individuals. Russell's reasons for making this claim stem, in the first place, from his own class paradox and the resulting theory of types: he claims that "nothing that can be said significantly about a thing can be said significantly about a class of things, [from which] it follows that classes of things cannot have the same kind of reality as things have".[57] In the second place he cites Cantor's proof that the number of classes is greater than the number of individuals.[58] Any attempt to avoid this by identifying classes in a purely extensional way with their members is barred on the ground that there are no individuals in the null class and, furthermore, that we would deprive ourselves of any means with which to differentiate a class that has one member from that member. Russell allows a closer association between classes and propositional functions, for, subject to the restrictions imposed by his theory of types, he holds that every propositional function determines a class. But even here, a class cannot be identified with any one propositional function since "it can equally well be defined by any other which is true whenever the first is true and false whenever the first is false".[59] For example, the propositional function "x is a featherless biped" determines the same class of objects (the class of humans) as the intensionally quite different, though "formally equivalent", propositional function "x is a rational animal". Since Russell concludes that a class can be neither a thing nor some individual propositional function, he is drawn to the conclusion that it can be little more than a mere symbolic fiction.

[57] Russell, *OKEW*, p. 206.
[58] Russell, *IMP*, p. 183.
[59] *Ibid.*

Notwithstanding that classes are not particulars or individuals and, thus, not ultimate constituents of the world, there remains the matter of whether they (and other logical constructions) are constituents of the world in any sense. The reference to them as logical *fictions* suggests that they are not, while the occasional and apparently synonymous use of the term logical *construction* suggests something a little different. In the ordinary sense of the term, a "construction" is typically composed of parts arranged in certain relations, and is, one would think, at least as real as its parts. To take a very ordinary example, a table may be constructed from, and composed of, nothing more or less than its atoms,[60] but in a very important sense the table is something more than its atoms – namely, it is its atoms standing in some certain set of relations to one another. The very same atoms, scattered hither and thither, would not be a table precisely because they would not stand in the appropriate relations to each other, and for that reason we would typically say that we bring a new entity into being whenever we construct a table. Even so, the structures we might be said to create by way of a *logical* construction are not constructions in quite this sense. In the logical construction of material objects out of classes of series of sense data, the sense data and the relations in which they stand are given, not created. Similarly, in the construction of, say, some order or series out of the class of natural numbers,

We can no more "arrange" the natural numbers than we can the starry heavens; but just as we may notice among the fixed stars either their order of brightness or their distribution in the sky, so there are various relations among numbers which may be observed, and which give rise to various different orders among numbers, all equally legitimate.[61]

As a result, Russell does not appear to be concerned to deny the objective reality of complex structures. There *are* various objective relations holding between equivalence classes and, thus, there are, for example, various series of numbers awaiting our notice or discovery. The constituents of logical constructions and the relations in which they stand are objectively given, both in mathematics and

---

[60] Roughly speaking, Russell takes a table to be a logical construction of a series of classes of sense data, but the point remains essentially the same, namely that if sense data are real, then anything constituted by sense data is equally so.
[61] Russell, *IMP*, p. 30.

sensory experience, rather than created or brought about by human endeavour or cognition.[62]

Russell's central concern appears to be with avoiding ontological commitment to such things as tables or classes considered as entities *in addition* to their formally equivalent logical constructions, but not with denying the existence of the logical constructions themselves. Logical constructions add nothing to the furniture of the world in that both the particulars and the relations in which they stand are objective and real. What we do in creating a logical construction is "notice" or "pick out" some such class of particulars, together with the relations in which they stand, and speak of it, for the sake of convenience, as a single entity or thing. Thus, in the case of classes we find, not a denial of their reality, but a self-confessed agnosticism or ontological neutrality in which "we avoid the need of assuming that there are classes without being compelled to make the opposite assumption that there are no classes. We merely abstain from both assumptions".[63]

There is, however, a crucial difference between the logical construction of, say, material objects out of sense data and classes out of propositional functions, namely, that sense data are acknowledged by Russell to be things, but propositional functions are not. Thus, even if logical constructions are at least as real as their constituents and the relations in which they stand, since the constituents of classes are held to be nothing, classes are nothing. Even so, to say that a propositional function is nothing would not, just as with definite descriptions, appear to be sufficient to remove ontological commitment in cases where the propositional function forms a part of an existential claim held to be (sometimes or always) true. Unfortunately for Russell, the reduction of mathematics to logic appears to involve us in making just such claims.

Consider, for example, the apparently existential axiom of infinity, which, in the language of propositional functions, is the following: "The propositional function 'if n is an inductive [natural]

---

[62] There is some indication that Russell changed his view on this in his later years, at least with regard to mathematics. Writing in 1959 he says, "Mathematics has ceased to seem to me to be nonhuman in its subject matter. I have come to believe, though very reluctantly, that it consists of tautologies". See Russell, *MPD*, p. 157. See also Russell's 1951 paper, "Is Mathematics Purely Linguistic?", in *EA*, pp. 295–306 and *Papers* 11, pp. 353–362, to which he answers with a resounding yes.

[63] Russell, *IMP*, p. 184.

number, it is true for some value of a that a is a class of n individuals' is always true".[64] This might appear to commit Russell to the existence of a class of individuals for every natural number, and thus, to an infinite class. That it does so does not seem to bother Russell unduly, for he goes on to suggest that this axiom (along with the other contestable axioms of reducibility and choice) "could perfectly well be stated as an hypothesis whenever it is used, instead of being assumed to be actually true".[65] Moreover, the role of an existential hypothesis seems entirely intrinsic to the elimination of classes by way of propositional functions: "all statements nominally about a class can be reduced to statements about what follows from the hypothesis of anything's having the defining property of the class".[66] The propositions of mathematics, therefore, are properly constituted by what *follows from* certain hypotheses, without concern for the literal truth of the hypotheses themselves. Propositions about numbers and classes do not refer to things but have

only a certain logical form which is not a part of propositions having this form. This is in fact the case with all the apparent objects of logic and mathematics. Such words as *or, not, if, there is, identity, greater, plus, nothing, everything, function*, and so on, are not names of definite objects like "John" or "Jones", but are words which require a context in order to have meaning. All of them are *formal*, that is to say, their occurrence indicates a certain form of proposition, not a certain constituent.[67]

Nevertheless, together with Quine we may reasonably wonder whether such an apparently sanguine attitude to the apparent ontological commitments of our hypotheses can be squared with our and Russell's intuitions, both about truth in general and the supposed necessity of mathematical truth in particular.

IV. EPISTEMIC LOGICISM

Turning now to the question of mathematical knowledge, it is clear that most accounts of logicism include an epistemic component. The reduction of mathematics to logic, it is claimed, is not just of

[64] *Ibid.*, p. 160.
[65] *Ibid.*, p. 191.
[66] Russell, *OKEW*, p. 207.
[67] *Ibid.*, p. 208.

formal or ontological interest, but of epistemic importance as well. In fact, from the time of Leibniz, logicism has often been identified with the view that the reduction of mathematical knowledge to the more certain, and perhaps more easily justified, *a priori* principles of logic would provide a secure, otherwise unavailable, foundation for mathematical knowledge.

How was it that Russell's logicism would meet these epistemic goals? The received view is that, according to Russell, clear and immediate epistemic gains would result from the formal reduction of mathematics to logic. By reducing mathematics to logic, the problem of justifying mathematical belief would be reduced to the comparatively easier problem of justifying the self-evident principles of logic. Frege's idea had been that if the principles of logic are self-evident, and that if the laws of arithmetic can be shown to be derivable from them, arithmetic will have become epistemically justified. As he himself reports at the beginning of his *Grundgesetze*, "In my *Grundlagen der Arithmetic*, I sought to make it plausible that arithmetic is a branch of logic and *need not borrow any ground of proof whatever from either experience or intuition*. In the present book this shall now be confirmed ...."[68] On such an account, arithmetic would become just as certain as logic itself. In Russell's enlarged program, it was supposed that all of mathematics would acquire, in Haack's helpful phrase, this "innocence by association."[69]

[68] Gottlob Frege, *The Basic Laws of Arithmetic*, Montgomery Furth (trans.), Berkeley: University of California Press, 1967, p. 29, emphasis added. Also compare Frege's comments at the beginning of his *Grundlagen* in which he notes that a primary purpose of proof in arithmetic is to "place the truth of a proposition beyond all doubt" and in which he inquires after the "ultimate ground upon which rests the justification for holding" arithmetical propositions. (Gottlob Frege, *The Foundations of Arithmetic*, J.L. Austin (trans.), Oxford: Blackwell, 1950, pp. 2^{e}f.)

[69] Susan Haack, *Philosophy of Logics*, Cambridge: Cambridge University Press, 1978, p. 10. Also see Mark Steiner, *Mathematical Knowledge*, Ithaca, N.Y.: Cornell University Press, 1975, who comments: "It is certain that logicists attributed epistemological significance to their 'reduction.' The reduction was supposed to provide a foundation for mathematical knowledge, to the extent that Frege felt that arithmetic was 'tottering' when his logical system was proved inconsistent .... *Principia Mathematica* itself was supposed to supply such a justification ... " (pp. 17f); and again: "logicism, then, is intended by its proponents to explain mathematical knowledge ..." (p. 24).

However, this standard epistemic interpretation of Russell's logicism needs to be carefully appraised.[70] In and of itself, this account is susceptible to a number of well-known objections. According to both Poincaré[71] and Wittgenstein,[72] for example, it is unlikely that mathematics should gain its sole epistemic justification via logic, since parts of mathematics are themselves more certain than, and are often known independently of, the requisite body of logical belief.

In addition, and perhaps surprisingly, such an account is clearly inconsistent with Russell's explicitly stated views on the subject. After all, as Russell puts it,

> There is an apparent absurdity in proceeding, as one does in the logical theory of arithmetic, through many rather recondite propositions of symbolic logic, to the "proof" of such truisms as $2 + 2 = 4$: for it is plain that the conclusion is more certain than the premises, and the supposed proof therefore seems futile.[73]

For Russell, it is a simple Moorean fact that we are more certain of much of elementary mathematics than we are of many logical axioms and their derivative proofs. Despite his commitment to logicism, this observation alone is sufficient to vitiate Frege's *epistemic* version of logicism. Perhaps surprisingly, Russell even concludes that it is in part our knowledge of elementary mathematical propositions that eventually helps form the ground for our knowledge of many principles of logic, rather than vice-versa.

Because he recognizes that many propositions of elementary mathematics are more evident than those of logic, Russell sees two tasks as being of primary importance for the logicist. The first is the task of explaining in what sense "a comparatively obscure and difficult proposition may be said to be a premise for a comparatively

---

[70] The account that follows is developed in greater detail in A.D. Irvine, "Epistemic Logicism and Russell's Regressive Method", *Philosophical Studies*, 55 (1989), pp. 303–327 (© 1989 by Kluwer Academic Publishers). Our thanks go to Kluwer Academic Publishers for their kind permission to draw upon some sections of this paper in what follows.

[71] See Henri Poincaré, *Science and Hypothesis*, New York: Dover, 1952, pp. 3f.

[72] See Ludwig Wittgenstein, *Remarks on the Foundations of Mathematics*, G.E.M. Anscombe, R. Rhees and G.H. von Wright (eds.), Oxford: Blackwell, 1956, §65^{e}ff.

[73] Russell, RMDP, in *EA*, p. 272.

obvious proposition".[74] The second is the task of explaining how such comparatively obscure premises are ever discovered and then justified.

In response to the first of these two tasks, Russell distinguishes between two quite different types of premise. The first type is what he calls an *empirical premise*; a premise "from which we are actually led to believe the proposition in question".[75] An empirical premise is a premise which is of epistemic value in that from it, usually together with other relevant premises, less certain or less commonly known results follow. The second type of premise is what Russell calls a *logical premise*. A logical premise is a "logically simpler proposition [roughly speaking, a proposition with fewer logical constituents] ... from which, by a valid deduction, the proposition in question can be obtained".[76] Most often in mathematics the empirical and logical premises coincide. It is in exactly these cases that a mathematical proof is of direct epistemological value. However, as Russell points out, this is not always the case. It is simply not true that a logically simpler idea or proposition is always more readily accepted than a more complicated one. Just as is the case with our intuitions about the physical world, it is the mid-range concepts (concepts which are neither extremely fundamental nor extremely complex) that are commonly comprehended most readily. In some cases, despite their logical simplicity, such premises will have less epistemic simplicity (and less certainty) than the conclusion which follows from them. Hence, there exists the possibility of a "comparatively obscure and difficult proposition" acting as a (logical) premise for a "comparatively obvious proposition".

Russell goes on to note that in these cases it is not the purpose of a proof so much to *prove* the conclusion as it is to prove that the conclusion *follows from* those premises. What such proofs show is that from a particular set of logically simple (but sometimes epistemologically complex) premises, other (sometimes epistemologically

---

[74] *Ibid.*
[75] *Ibid.* Russell's use of the phrase "empirical premise" is somewhat misleading. Not all of his "empirical premises" need be observational, although some are. Nor need they be directly about the empirical world. Rather, what Russell means by an "empirical premise" is simply a premise which has epistemic value. A more suggestive name for such a premise would have been "epistemological premise".
[76] *Ibid.*, pp. 272f.

simple) conclusions follow deductively. This is important since such proofs help resolve the second of Russell's two tasks, that of explaining how it is that such "comparatively obscure and difficult propositions" can themselves ever be discovered and justified.

Russell's explanation is that in cases where previously accepted conclusions can be shown to follow from a particular logical premise (or set of premises) via a valid deduction, such a deduction tends to help justify, not the previously accepted conclusion, but rather the original premise (or set of premises) in question. This is as a result of what Russell calls the "regressive method". Russell contends that because of this "regressive" aspect of mathematics, the methodology of mathematics is closely related to that of the ordinary sciences of observation. In Russell's words,

We tend to believe the premises because we can see that their consequences are true, instead of believing the consequences because we know the premises to be true. But the inferring of premises from consequences is the essence of induction; thus the method in investigating the principles of mathematics is really an inductive method, and is substantially the same as the method of discovering general laws in any other science.[77]

Science begins with the ordinary facts of observation of which we are all quite certain. It then attempts to answer two resulting questions: First, what follows from these facts? Second, from what do these facts themselves follow? Answers to the second of these questions determine the general laws of the science, propositions which are logically simpler than the observation statements but which are often epistemologically more difficult to justify. When the initial facts are conjoined with these general laws, answers to the first question yield further observation statements and it is with these that science gains its predictive power.

According to Russell, mathematics is no exception to this general account. Epistemologically simple propositions, such as the most elementary propositions of arithmetic, are originally justified via inference from concrete, often physical, cases.[78] These observations form the basic facts within mathematics of which we are most certain. Statements describing these facts in turn follow from the logically simpler general laws which become as certain as our original

[77] Ibid., pp. 273f.
[78] Ibid., p. 272.

empirical premises only if one of the following two cases obtains: either it must be shown that no significantly different hypotheses or general laws could lead to the same empirical premises, or (what Russell says is often the case in logic and mathematics) the general laws, once discovered, turn out to be just as obvious as the original empirical premises. As an example of the latter, Russell cites the law of contradiction. This law, Russell feels, "must have been originally discovered by generalizing from instances, though, once discovered, it was found to be quite as indubitable as the instances. Thus it is both an empirical and a logical premise".[79] In the cases where the general laws cannot be shown to be the only ones possible, and are not themselves evident to the same extent as are empirical premises, they must remain merely probable, but often probable to a very high degree. Thus, it is by answering the question, "From what do empirical premises follow"? that Russell's second task (the task of explaining how even epistemologically complex logical premises are discovered and justified) is resolved.

As a result of the above observations, the following general reconstruction of Russell's account of mathematical knowledge can be given. According to Russell, mathematical knowledge begins in the first instance from particular observations, e.g., the observation that two objects together with two distinct objects are four objects. These observations form our first epistemologically relevant premises. From these empirical premises we obtain generalizations, e.g., that $2 + 2 = 4$. Such generalizations in turn are often recognized to be "sufficiently obvious to be themselves taken as empirical premises"[80] and so to have additional epistemic value.

Then, in addition to these initial empirical premises of which we are quite certain, there exist two other classes of mathematical knowledge. The first consists of the mathematical knowledge which follows from empirical premises (or from empirical premises together with other known premises) by means of deductive proof. The second consists of that "regressively" justified mathematical knowledge (which includes the general laws of logic and mathematics) from which the original empirical premises can be shown to follow. The first of these two types of mathematical knowledge is reasonably straightforward in terms of its justification. As Russell points out,

[79] *Ibid.*, p. 274.
[80] *Ibid.*, p. 275.

the expanded body of empirical premises "... when discovered, [is] pretty certain to lead to a number of new results which could not otherwise have been known: in the sciences, this is so obvious that it needs no illustration, and in mathematics it is no less true."[81]

In contrast, the second of these two additional classes of knowledge requires a somewhat more sophisticated account for its justification. Here the general laws of mathematics are discovered "regressively" when the mathematician inquires after the fewest and logically simplest premises from which all known empirical premises can themselves be deduced. Because of the inductive method which underlies it, such knowledge is sometimes less certain than the (deductively) proven parts of mathematics. As with fundamental laws in the physical sciences, those general laws of logic which do not appear to be as obvious as the original empirical premises will be justified only to the extent that they can be shown to be the most plausible source from which those original premises may be deduced. The result is that even the most fundamental of logical laws may remain merely probable. Russell himself is explicit on this inductivist point:

In induction, if p is our logical premise and q our empirical premise, we know that p implies q, and in a text-book we are apt to begin with p and deduce q. But p is only believed on account of q. Thus we require a greater or less probability that q implies p, or, what comes to the same thing, that not-p implies not-q. If we can *prove* that not-p implies not-q, i.e., that p is the only hypothesis consistent with the facts, that settles the question. But usually what we do is to test as many alternative hypotheses as we can think of. If they all fail, that makes it probable, more or less, that any hypothesis other than p will fail. But in this we are simply betting on our inventiveness: we think it unlikely that we should not have thought of a better hypothesis if there were one.[82]

This inductivist element of Russell's mathematical epistemology, articulated so clearly by the mature Russell in 1907 in the midst of his work on *Principia*, was held with remarkable consistency for the remainder of his life. For example, in the first volume of *Principia*, the position is again stated clearly as follows:

But in fact self-evidence is never more than a part of the reason for accepting an axiom, and is never indispensable. The reason for accepting an axiom, as for accepting any other proposition, is always largely inductive, namely that

[81] *Ibid.*, pp. 282f.
[82] *Ibid.*, pp. 274f.

many propositions which are nearly indubitable can be deduced from it, and that no equally plausible way is known by which these propositions could be true if the axiom were false, and nothing which is probably false can be deduced from it. If the axiom is apparently self-evident, that only means, practically, that it is nearly indubitable; for things have been thought to be self-evident and have yet turned out to be false. And if the axiom itself is nearly indubitable, that merely adds to the inductive evidence derived from the fact that its consequences are nearly indubitable: it does not provide new evidence of a radically different kind. Infallibility is never attainable, and therefore some element of doubt should always attach to every axiom and to all its consequences. In formal logic, the element of doubt is less than in most sciences, but it is not absent, as appears from the fact that the paradoxes followed from premises which were not previously known to require limitations.[83]

In the Introduction to the second edition in 1927, Russell's comments are to much the same effect when he mentions the "purely pragmatic justification" of the axiom of reducibility.[84]

Précis of this same position are given in several of Russell's other publications. In his *Introduction to Mathematical Philosophy*, for example, Russell observes that the propositions of simple arithmetic are more obvious than those of logic and that "The most obvious and easy things in mathematics are not those that come logically at the beginning; they are things that, from the point of view of logical deduction, come somewhere in the middle".[85] Later, in his 1924 essay "Logical Atomism", Russell again explains his position but in greater detail. His comments are worth quoting in their entirety because of their clarity:

When pure mathematics is organized as a deductive system ... it becomes obvious that, if we are to believe in the truth of pure mathematics, it cannot be solely because we believe in the truth of the set of premises. Some of the premises are much less obvious than some of their consequences, and are believed chiefly because of their consequences. This will be found to be al-

---

[83] Whitehead and Russell, *PM*, Vol. 1, p. 59.

[84] *Ibid.*, p. xiv. Despite such comments, Russell apparently never gave up the hope of deducing such axioms from other, more self-evident logical truths. For example, see the Introduction to the second edition of *Principia*, Vol. 1, p. xiv. Once it is admitted, as Russell does, that these axioms are in part empirical, such hope seems inexplicably misguided since if this is so it follows immediately that one would not expect them to be derivable from purely logical premises, whether self-evident or not.

[85] Russell, *IMP*, p. 2.

ways the case when a science is arranged as a deductive system. It is not the logically simplest propositions of the system that are the most obvious, or that provide the chief part of our reasons for believing in the system. With the empirical sciences this is evident. Electro-dynamics, for example, can be concentrated into Maxwell's equations, but these equations are believed because of the observed truth of certain of their logical consequences. Exactly the same thing happens in the pure realm of logic; the logically first principles of logic – at least some of them – are to be believed, not on their own account, but on account of their consequences. The epistemological question: "Why should I believe this set of propositions"? is quite different from the logical question: "What is the smallest and logically simplest group of propositions from which this set of propositions can be deduced"? Our reasons for believing logic and pure mathematics are, in part, only inductive and probable, in spite of the fact that, in their *logical* order, the propositions of logic and pure mathematics follow from the premises of logic by pure deduction. I think this point important, since errors are liable to arise from assimilating the logical to the epistemological order, and also, conversely, from assimilating the epistemological to the logical order.[86]

Just what lessons are to be learned from such comments? The major one is that Russell's regressive method, emphasizing as it does the distinction between logical and epistemological order, shows how closely Russell's mathematical epistemology was integrated within his general theory of knowledge. The second lesson concerns just how important Russell felt the analogy between epistemological concerns in mathematics and in the sciences to be. Given the number of times that Russell emphasizes this analogy, together with the fact that the stated purpose of his original paper on the regressive method was, in part, "to emphasize the close analogy between the methods of pure mathematics and the methods of the sciences of observation",[87] Russell's intention should be clear: only by emphasizing this analogy can a complete and accurate picture of the acquisition and nature of mathematical knowledge be obtained.

The ultimate moral is that, in the end, there may not turn out to be any clear or absolute demarcation between mathematical knowledge and scientific knowledge more generally. This is not a feature historically associated with logicism. Even so, it indicates, as much as anything, what a sophisticated and philosophically fruitful version of logicism Russell developed in the early part of the twentieth century.

---

[86] Russell, LA, in *LK*, pp. 325f; in *Papers* 9, pp. 163f.
[87] Russell, RMDP, in *EA*, p. 272.

6   The Theory of Descriptions

Russell's theory of descriptions was first published in his 1905 essay, "On Denoting", which is surely one of the two or three most famous articles in twentieth-century analytic philosophy.[1] It has been described as "a paradigm of philosophy",[2] and has been employed by many later analytic philosophers, such as Quine,[3] although disputed by others, perhaps most notably Strawson.[4] Writing in 1967, an astute commentator said: "In the forty-five years preceding the publication of Strawson's 'On Referring', Russell's theory was practically immune from criticism. There is not a similar phenomenon in contemporary analytic philosophy".[5]

What is the theory which has excited such interest and acclaim? To put it briefly and more or less neutrally, it is a method of analyzing *definite descriptions,* also called *singular descriptions,* i.e., phrases, in English typically beginning with the word "the", which pick out or purport to pick out a single ("definite") object – e.g., "the man who broke the bank at Monte Carlo", or "the first President of the USA". Many philosophers who have accepted the theory of definite descriptions, including Russell himself, have also treated some or all proper names in similar fashion. They are taken to be disguised definite descriptions,[6] and then subjected to the same analysis as overt definite descriptions. Definite descriptions may be contrasted with indefinite descriptions, which do not purport to pick out any particular number of objects – e.g., "any President of the USA". Note that while the two phrases "the even prime number" and "any even prime number" in fact direct our attention to the same object – the number two – the first is a definite description, while the second is an indefinite description. Either definite or indefinite descriptions may in fact fail to describe any object or objects; as we have said, the difference is that definite descriptions *purport* to pick out a single object.[7]

The theory of descriptions has appeared to some philosophers as a definite philosophical advance, a *result*, which is independent of disputed metaphysical assumptions, including Russell's. We need to pay some attention to the theory as it appears in this light. On the other hand, to understand the importance that it had for Russell we need to relate it to his more general views around 1905, and this is a more complicated matter. We also need to see, at least briefly, how the theory has been exploited or criticized by philosophers whose metaphysical assumptions are, in most cases, quite different from those of Russell. We shall therefore proceed as follows. The first section will state the method of analysis, as neutrally as possible, and will also briefly point out some of its putative advantages which do not depend on particular features of Russell's views in the early years of the twentieth century. The next five sections will be devoted to placing the theory in its Russellian context. We shall start, in Section II, by sketching the relevant parts of Russell's general views in the period leading up to 1905. Those views pose a problem for him, which will be the subject of Section III; in Section IV we shall see how he attempted to solve that problem in the period before he discovered the theory of descriptions. Then, in Section V, we shall discuss his reasons for adopting the theory of descriptions; the most important such reason, I shall claim, is that it enables him to give a more satisfactory solution to the problem discussed in sections III and IV. Section VI will discuss the general significance of the theory of descriptions in Russell's thought. Finally, in Section VII, we shall consider more or less recent reactions to the theory, especially criticisms of it.

I. OUTLINE OF THE THEORY

Modern logic – quantification theory with identity – provides the essential background to the idea of analysis that is in question when we speak of *analyzing* definite descriptions. It gives us both the method by which the analysis proceeds and part of the point of the enterprise. Analysis here is to provide a way of reading definite descriptions that enables them to be incorporated into a system of logic in a way that gives the correct account of their inferential powers.

Let us begin by seeing how this goes in the case of *indefinite* descriptions, for the treatment of definite descriptions is analogous, though in some ways more complicated. The application of quantification theory to sentences in English presupposes that a phrase of the form "any F" (for example "any prime number") is not to be treated as the name of one or more objects (very similar points apply to descriptive phrases of other forms, such as "Some Fs", "All Fs" or "No Fs"). A sentence in which it occurs, a sentence of the form "Any F is G" (for example "any prime number is odd") is, rather, equated with:

1) Take any object: if it is F then it is G.

This clumsy, though comprehensible, piece of English goes over into logical notation very smoothly, as:[8]

2) $(\forall x)(Fx \supset Gx)$

Now the machinery of first-order logic can be applied in familiar fashion. Note that one feature of this analysis is that there is no very obvious answer to the question: how is the phrase "any prime number" itself treated? What we are given is a method of analyzing complete sentences in which that phrase occurs. It might be said that the analysis provides no obvious account of the functioning of the phrase in isolation – but then it is far from clear what sense it makes to speak of that phrase as having a function in isolation at all. The most obvious sort of account of a phrase in isolation is perhaps an account of what the phrase names. One is not likely to think that an indefinite description names something; according to the above analysis it certainly does not.[9]

The analysis of definite descriptions is analogous, but more complex. A sentence of the form "The F is G" is treated as making three related claims:

 i) that there is something which is F,
 ii) that nothing other than that thing is F, and
 iii) that thing – the unique thing which is F – is also G.

(These claims are related because they are all talking about the same object, saying that *it* is F, that *it* is uniquely F, and that *it* is G.) More compactly, a sentence of that form is treated as saying:

3) there is one and only one object which is F, and it is G.

This can be put into logical notation as:

4) (∃x)[Fx & (∀y)(Fy ⊃ x=y) & Gx].

So a sentence such as "The even prime number is less than ten" becomes:

5) there is one and only one object which is an even prime number, and it is less than ten.

And this in turn goes into logical notation as:

6) (∃x)[x is an even prime & (∀y)(y is an even prime ⊃ x=y) & x is less than ten]

The predicate which we put in for "F" may itself be complex, as it is in this case and usually is where we have something that looks like a plausible definite description. So it may be broken down further, to give, in this example, this:

7) (∃x)[x is a prime number & x is even & (∀y)(y is a prime number & y is even ⊃ x=y) & x is less than ten]

When sentences involving definite descriptions are treated in this way, they fit smoothly into our system of logic, which can then handle them formally without any additional axioms or rules. Let us distinguish two aspects here. One is that definite descriptions have semantic structure and complexity. Unlike proper names, they are significant phrases which are made up of independently significant parts. (The name "Aristotle" contains the letters "i" and "s" in sequence, but it does not contain the English word "is"; those letters are not in that context independently significant. Contrast the word "even" in "the even prime number".) This complexity is exploited in the way we reason. It follows immediately from "The even prime number is less than ten" that there is at least one prime number less than ten. If we were to treat the definite description simply as a name, without semantically significant structure, then this inference would be quite opaque. Obviously, the definite description does have semantically significant structure, and obviously it is this that makes the inference a good one. But how can we understand the semantic structure of the phrase so as to make the correctness of the inference transparent to ourselves? How does the inference exploit the structure of the definite description? Russell's analysis of definite descriptions answers these questions. By treating the sentence in Russellian fashion the inference becomes a simple application of ordinary first-order logic.

The second aspect is a little less straightforward. It is very easy to construct definite descriptions which do not in fact describe anything: "the largest natural number" is an obvious example. If we simply treat definite descriptions as singular terms, we are then faced with a large class of such terms which are evidently meaningful, yet do not in fact refer to anything. The existence of such singular terms threatens standard logic. From "$(\forall x)$ Fx", "Fa" follows by the usual rules of logic, whatever predicate we may put for "F", and whatever singular term we may put for "a". Yet this inference fails if "a" does not in fact refer to anything. One response is to reconstruct logic so that it takes the possibility of empty singular terms into account; the result is so-called "free logic", logic adapted to the possibility that there may be singular terms which do not refer to anything.[10] There is, however, reason to avoid the complications of free logic, and to retain the simpler structure of classical first-order logic. The theory of descriptions, by eliminating definite descriptions from the category of singular terms, removes one obstacle to our doing so. There is, however, another possible obstacle. On most accounts it is not only definite descriptions but also ordinary names – terms without significant semantic structure – which can fail to refer. If we wish to retain the advantage of ordinary logic, we can do so by eliminating names as primitive terms of the language; such names as we want can be introduced by definition in terms of definite descriptions: a given name is introduced as short for a given definite description.

The mention of empty names suggests a further problem, independent of logic, to which such names are sometimes thought to give rise. How, it is asked, can a name be meaningful if it does not in fact name anything? And if a name which fails to name is not meaningful, then how can we ever sensibly deny that something exists – as we seem to be able to do? How can a sentence such as "Homer never existed" even be a candidate for discussion? Treating names as definite descriptions, and subjecting them to Russellian analysis, certainly avoids this problem. But this is not generally taken as a very powerful argument for Russellian analysis, because the problem is easily avoided by a wholly different method. We may claim, plausibly enough, that the sense or meaning of an ordinary name is quite distinct from its reference or denotation, i.e., the object it names.

Sense or meaning, here, is what the name must have to be understood, and to be used in a significant way; its reference or denotation is the actual object, if any, that it names.[11] Once the distinction is made, there is, on many views, no obvious reason to think that a name which lacks reference must on that account lack sense. Yet this is not to deny that philosophers have more or less explicitly made the assumption that a meaningful name must name an object, and been led into various kinds of excess by this assumption.

This issue will be of great relevance to our discussion, for Russell sought to deny the distinction between sense and reference. Indeed it might be said that part of the significance of the theory of descriptions for him was precisely that it made such a denial plausible (or at least less implausible).

II. RUSSELLIAN BACKGROUND

In this section we shall discuss relevant aspects of Russell's thought in the period leading up to and including his discovery of the theory of descriptions; a central text for these purposes is his 1903 book *Principles of Mathematics*.[12]

Until some time in the late 1890s, Russell had been an adherent of Absolute Idealism.[13] At some point in 1898 or 1899 he followed G.E. Moore in rejecting that doctrine and argued against it with the fervour of a convert. We can work our way into the views he held in the first few years of this century by seeing how they are directed against Idealism.[14] A central thought of Idealism is that our knowledge and understanding of the world are mediated by conceptual structures.[15] There are then questions as to where these structures come from, and whether their role is compatible with our having knowledge of an objective world. If the concepts through which I understand the world are purely subjective or arbitrary, just imposed by me with no particular reason, then my knowledge of the world – or what I claim as knowledge – will likewise be subjective or arbitrary. So it is natural to seek to deny that our conceptual structures are subjective. The claim that my conceptual structures are *objective*, that they correspond to the way the world really is, however, is a difficult one to sustain. For if *all* our knowledge of the world is mediated, then the knowledge that such-and-such a conceptual structure is objectively correct must in turn be mediated. So it might look as if we need some other conceptual structure, by means of which we come to know that our first conceptual structure corresponds to the world. But then our attention needs to be focused on the second conceptual structure: how do we know that the use of those concepts gives us objective knowledge, rather than a subjective pretense to knowledge? Clearly a regress would threaten.

The Idealists, of course, did not accept the view that what passes for knowledge is simply subjective; neither did they embark on the regress that I have sketched. On the contrary, they evolved extremely subtle and sophisticated ways of reconciling the idea that we have knowledge of a world that is, in some sense, independent of us with what I have taken as a central thought of Idealism.[16] The details of these attempts, however, do not concern us here. What is relevant is that they are all vulnerable to the charge that they do not give an account of knowledge which makes it objective, in a sufficiently strong sense of that word. In other words, if one reads "objective" and "independent of us" very strongly, then it may seem as if none of the Idealists succeed in giving an account of knowledge which makes it out to be objective. This was the position of Moore and Russell, after they rejected Idealism. They claimed that it is a result of that view that we cannot have knowledge of the world as it really is. If some form of Idealism were true, they claimed, then we would at best know the world as it is modified by our conceptual structure, which is not the same thing as really knowing the world. In this way, they argued, all judgments are, on the Idealist account, inevitably distorted or falsified. And this result they found to be unacceptable.

To deny the unacceptable results of Idealism, Moore and Russell denied the central thought that we began with. They cut through the idea that our knowledge of the world is mediated by postulating a direct and unmediated knowledge of reality. Thus it is that Moore speaks of a "direct cognitive relation" which the mind may have to things, both abstract and concrete (including, it would seem, to that very relation itself); in *Principia Ethica* he speaks freely, and not in any obvious way metaphorically, of our having a "direct perception" of this or that matter.[17] In the Preface to the *Principles of Mathematics*, Russell says that "the chief part of philosophical logic" is "the endeavour to see clearly, and to make others see clearly, the entities concerned, in order that the mind may have that kind of acquaintance with them which it has with redness or the taste of a

pineapple" (p. xv). As time went by, the notion of acquaintance occupied an increasingly prominent place in his thought. The importance
of acquaintance is that it is a relation between the mind and what is
outside the mind, a relation which is direct, immediate, and wholly
presuppositionless.

One way in which this notion is important for Russell's thought
is in his conception of a proposition – roughly, what is expressed by a
declarative sentence. He takes propositions to be non-linguistic and
non-mental, abstract entities existing independently of us. When we
make a judgment or assertion we are, in his view, directly and immediately related to such an entity. Propositions themselves, on his
account, are objects of acquaintance: understanding a proposition
involves being acquainted with it. More to the present point, however, are Russell's views on the constituents of propositions. One
might think that a proposition about Bill Clinton, say, would contain some element which represents that man – an idea or meaning
which stands in some representational relation to him. Such is not
Russell's view, however, at least for the propositions which he takes
as paradigmatic.[18] For him this would mean that our thought was
not really getting through to Clinton himself: while we wanted to
think about *him*, we would instead be confined to the idea of him;
our thought would never really get through to the man himself.[19] It
is, rather, Russell's view that in paradigmatic cases propositions actually *contain* the objects they are about (propositions, recall, are not
mental entities on Russell's account). He would thus take the proposition about Clinton to have that man as one of its constituents. For
Russell, then, a proposition (again, in paradigm cases) does not have
a representational element. It does not contain a constituent which
somehow *represents* the things it is about; rather, it contains those
very things. –In what follows I shall sometimes call this nexus of
views "direct realism", including under this head both Russell's in-
sistence on a direct and unmediated relation between the mind and
the known object and the idea that propositions paradigmatically
contain the entities they are about.

According to Russell's direct realism, when we understand a sentence about something we are directly acquainted both with the object we are talking about and with a proposition which contains it,
or has it as a constituent. This holds, at least, in the sorts of cases
that Russell takes as paradigmatic. We have seen that he rejects the
view that in making a judgment we are most directly related to *ideas*,

psychological entities in our own minds. It is not only the subjectivity of ideas to which he objects. It is also – and more importantly, for present purposes – their role as intermediaries between us and the things we are attempting to talk about. This shows up in his attitude towards Frege's distinction between the *Sinn* of an expression and its *Bedeutung*, between what the words say, their sense or meaning, and what they are about, their denotation or reference. I shall quote an extended passage from a letter of Russell's to Frege which makes this point.

The issue arose from a discussion of truth. In a letter dated November 13, 1904. Frege had said: "Truth is not a component part of a thought, just as Mont Blanc with its snowfields is not itself a component part of the thought that Mont Blanc is more than 4,000 metres high."[20] Russell's reply, dated December 12, ignored the issue about truth, which was the point of Frege's remark (and with which he agreed), and seized on the incidental illustration to articulate his objections to Frege's distinction between *Sinn* and *Bedeutung*[21]:

I believe that in spite of all its snowfields Mont Blanc itself is a component part of what is actually asserted in the *Satze* 'Mont Blanc is more than 4,000 metres high'. We do not assert the thought, for this is a private psychological matter: we assert the object of the thought, and this is, to my mind, a certain complex (an *objectiver Satz*, one might say) in which Mont Blanc is itself a component part. *If we do not admit this, then we get the conclusion that we know nothing at all about Mont Blanc* .... In the case of a simple proper name like 'Socrates', I cannot distinguish between *Sinn* and *Bedeutung*; I see only the idea, which is psychological, and the object. Or better: I do not admit the *Sinn* at all, but only the idea and the *Bedeutung*.[22]

The sentence I have emphasized in this passage reveals and illustrates the motivation we have been discussing: only if the object we are talking about – Mont Blanc, in this case – is actually a component part of the proposition which we grasp can our thought actually get through to that object; only so can we have knowledge which is really about it. I take this sentence, that is to say, as indicating that the danger is not that all of our beliefs about Mont Blanc are false, but rather that none of our beliefs are really *about* it at all. It is in response to the threat of this kind of difficulty that Russell holds the nexus of views which I have labeled "direct realism".

One consequence of Russell's direct realism, at least as we have so far articulated it, is that Russell is led to accept that there are certain entities which, on any ordinary account, do not really exist. The issue here is one that was briefly raised in the first section of this essay: how to deal with empty names, i.e., names (or definite descriptions) which do not in fact name (or uniquely describe) anything. The name "Vulcan" was at one point introduced to name a supposed tenth planet in our solar system. For one who is familiar with that usage, the sentence "Vulcan is between Mars and the Sun" presumably makes sense; it is even more plausible to say that the sentence "Vulcan does not exist" must make sense, since some people were (presumably) surprised to be told that Vulcan does not exist. If these sentences make sense, then according to Russell's account they express propositions. And what are the constituents of these propositions? In particular, what constituent of them corresponds to the word "Vulcan"? Russell's direct realism seems to imply that those propositions must contain Vulcan – that the (alleged) planet must therefore have some kind of ontological status. Since the planet does not really exist, there must be some other ontological status for it to have; Russell calls this status *subsistence*. All entities subsist, or have Being, as Russell also puts it. Some of them, those which are in space and time, have the interesting additional property of *existence*. So the non-existent objects, the merely subsistent objects, include both abstract objects such as numbers and classes, which are of course not in space and time, and also alleged concrete objects such as Vulcan which might exist but which merely happen not to, so to speak. (I shall speak of these latter as non-existent *concreta*.)

The fundamental line of thought here is what I shall call the Meinongian argument, after Alexius Meinong, who advanced a sophisticated theory on the basis of a version of the argument. Russell accepts the argument, and puts it like this:

Being is that which belongs to every conceivable term, to every possible object of thought... If *A* be any term that can be counted as one, it is plain that *A* is something, and therefore that *A* is. "*A* is not" must always be either false or meaningless. For if *A* were nothing, it could not be said to not be; "*A* is not" implies that there is a term *A* whose being is denied, and hence that *A* is. Thus unless "*A* is not" be an empty sound it must be false – whatever *A* be, it certainly is. Numbers, the Homeric gods, relations, chimeras and four-dimensional spaces all have being, for if they were not entities of a kind, we could make no propositions about them. (*POM* section 427)

The crux of the argument is that if a sentence containing a name is to make sense, then the name must in fact succeed in naming something – something that, in some sense at least, *is*. We shall return to this argument at the end of Section IV; as we shall see there, the views of *Principles* do not in fact commit Russell to accepting it, though clearly he does so at least at some points in that book.

III. DIFFICULTIES OF DIRECT REALISM

As we have said more than once, the idea that a proposition contains the object or objects it is about functions as a paradigm for Russell. It is, that is to say, a view which he finds natural and often takes for granted (as in the passage quoted above, from his December 1904 letter to Frege). But it is not a view that he can really hold without restriction, for in its unrestricted version it faces considerable difficulties. He attempted to resolve or to avoid those difficulties in one way in the period from 1900 or 1901 until June 1905; this way of resolving them I shall call "the theory of denoting concepts". In June 1905 he came across the fundamental idea of the theory of descriptions, which gave him quite a different way of resolving the same difficulties.[23]

Let us set out the relevant problems facing the underlying picture. One class of difficulty concerns the scope of acquaintance. Here direct realism generates conclusions which might seem to be quite implausible but which Russell was, at the time of *Principles*, simply willing to accept. (He later came to change his mind, even before "On Denoting".) There are various cases. One concerns distant or no-longer existing concrete objects. It is undeniable, one might suppose, that I understand propositions about Socrates, say, but it may appear as quite implausible that I stand in some direct epistemological relation to him, for he no longer exists. It might similarly be thought to be implausible that I stand in a direct epistemic relation to abstract objects. (In this case Russell continues to accept that we do stand in such relations; the most obvious sense in which Russell in 1914, say, is *not* an empiricist is that he holds that we have direct knowledge of abstract entities. This is knowledge which is not based on any of the five senses; it is altogether *sui generis*, though analogous to knowledge given by sensory perception, as Russell thinks of it.) The case of non-existent *concreta*, objects which might exist, so to speak, but in fact do not, such as Pegasus or the present King of France, might be thought to be even more troubling. In *Principles*, however, Russell has no scruples at all about accepting that such entities subsist and that we can be acquainted with them. So he was, for a time, willing to accept all these sorts of apparently implausible consequences of his direct realism.

There is another sort of difficulty, however, which he never accepted. Suppose I say, for example, "Every natural number is either odd or even". The underlying picture of direct realism might suggest that I am expressing (and grasping) a proposition which contains all of the infinitely many natural numbers. Russell was agnostic about whether there in fact *are* any such infinitely complex propositions. But he denied that we can grasp propositions that have this sort of infinite complexity (see *POM*, section 72). Even in the most extreme and unrestrained phase of his realism, the idea that we grasp infinitely complex propositions was too implausible for Russell to accept. So the issue of *generality* – how we can, for example, grasp a proposition about all the natural numbers – is one which does not fit neatly into his direct realism. The difficulty which this issue creates for direct realism forces upon Russell some modification of that doctrine.

It is worth emphasizing that the problem of giving an account of generality – of the variable, or of *any*, as he sometimes says – had central importance for Russell at this period. In the Preface to the *Principles of Mathematics* he speaks of his work on the philosophy of dynamics, and says: "I was led to a re-examination of the principles of Geometry, thence to the philosophy of continuity and infinity, and thence, with a view to discovering the meaning of the word *any*, to Symbolic Logic" (p. xvii). Why does he give such importance to this issue? Obviously, any account of mathematics must explain the use of variables. In the case of Russell's account this need is especially clear, since it is precisely the *generality* of mathematics that he emphasizes. His philosophical purposes also give him another reason for being concerned with generality. *Principles* was part of an argument against Idealism. Russell set out to show, in opposition to the Idealists, as he understood them, that mathematics gives genuine knowledge, something absolutely and unrestrictedly true. An obstacle to this task was the difficulty of understanding the infinite, which some had taken as showing that mathematics is inconsistent;

Russell held that an understanding of generality was one of the essential points in defeating this view. Thus he says:

Almost all mathematical idea present one great difficulty: the difficulty of infinity. This is usually regarded by philosophers as an antinomy.... From this received opinion I am compelled to dissent.... all apparent antinomies... are, in my opinion, reducible to the one difficulty of infinite number, yet this difficulty itself appears to be soluble by a correct philosophy of any... (POM, section 179, p. 188)

The need to arrive at some understanding of generality thus operates at the most fundamental level of Russell's metaphysics; and it is this need which, in the first instance, forces upon him a modification of his direct realism.

IV. THE THEORY OF DENOTING CONCEPTS

An unqualified version of direct realism serves as a paradigm for Russell. He relies on it and presupposes it at many points, and makes statements which seem to imply this unqualified view. But it is always a modified or qualified version which he explicitly advocates. He takes it that the most direct way in which a proposition can be about an object is simply by containing it; but he recognizes that we must have some way of making sense of cases in which a proposition is about an entity or entities which it does not contain – we might speak of a proposition's being indirectly about an entity.

From 1900 or 1901 until June 1905 the modification to the underlying picture, the way of accommodating indirect aboutness, is the theory of denoting concepts. This doctrine simply accepts that direct realism does not hold in all cases; it allows a large class of exceptions to the general rule that the entity which a proposition is about is contained in the proposition. The general rule functions as a paradigm in Russell's thought, but certain cases are allowed to violate it. For certain kinds of phrases Russell accepts a distinction in some ways analogous to Frege's distinction between Sinn and Bedeutung. The analogue of the Sinn of an expression is what Russell calls the denoting concept which it expresses, or as he later comes to say, its meaning; the analogue of the Bedeutung is denotation of the expression, or object it denotes, if in fact it denotes anything. (Russell explicitly accepts that it is possible that a proposition contain a denoting concept which does not in fact denote anything; see the end of this section.)

Russell's primary motive for introducing the distinction between denoting concept and denoted object[s] is to resolve the problem of generality which we emphasized above. (As we shall see, however, his attempted explanation does not succeed.) For this purpose, the crucial application of the theory is to indefinite descriptions, such as "any prime number" or, perhaps most important, to the wholly general phrase "any object". From the outset, however, he also applies it to definite descriptions such as "the President of the USA in 1999".[24]

The theory functions like this. Where a description, definite or indefinite, occurs in a sentence, that sentence is taken to express a proposition which contains not the corresponding object or objects but rather a concept which *denotes* that object or those objects; the proposition contains a denoting concept but is about – indirectly about – the denoted object or objects. In these cases there is what we might speak of as a *representational* element in the proposition. On the other hand, a paradigmatic subject–predicate proposition for Russell, one that does not contain a denoting concept, will, as we saw, contain the subject itself. It does not contain something which represents its subject. When we employ a description, however, we express a proposition which contains an element that does in this sense *represent* the subject; this element is of course the denoting concept corresponding to the description, for that denoting concept is not itself the subject of the proposition, not what the proposition is about.[25]

In the *Principles of Mathematics*, Russell devoted considerable time and ingenuity to attempts to work out the details of this theory. A few examples will give us the flavour, at least, of the sorts of questions that occupied him. In the propositions expressed by the sentences "All men are mortal" and "Every man is mortal", do we have the same object or objects denoted? And if the same objects are denoted, are they denoted in the same way, or in different ways? And what of "Any man is mortal"? Russell in fact concludes that there are differences among these cases: the denoting concept *all men* denotes all the men taken together; *every man* denotes men taken severally, not collectively; *any man* denotes an arbitrary man (see especially Section 60). Questions of this sort can be multiplied indefinitely, and there is bound to be an element of arbitrariness in the answers. With few evident constraints on the theory, except for the alleged deliverances of 'direct inspection', such questions threaten to become quite vacuous.

Our concern here, however, is not with the fine details of the theory of denoting concepts but with the basic structure of that view. In particular, the theory presupposes, as fundamental and unexplained, a relation between denoting concepts and the objects or combinations of objects which they denote. The effect of this relation is to allow that a proposition which *contains* one entity – a denoting concept – is *about* another entity or entities, the denoted object or objects. Thus, we have exactly that representational element which Russell's direct realism in general hoped to avoid. He has no account of how representation, in this sense, is possible. If we ask: how, in virtue of containing a denoting concept, is the proposition *about* an entity distinct from it? – then Russell has no answer: the relation of denoting is simply stipulated to have that effect.

The theory of denoting concepts affects the Meinongian argument, discussed at the end of Section II; in the context of our concern with the theory of descriptions, this is a crucial consequence of the theory. (I put the matter this way because there is no sign that consequence was Russell's motive for introducing the theory. It is only in retrospect that this appears as the crucial aspect.) An unqualified form of direct realism would commit Russell to accepting the Meinongian argument. He does not, however, hold direct realism in unqualified form, because he holds the theory of denoting concepts. That theory permits violations of direct realism; by so doing, it undermines the Meinongian argument. If we have a sentence containing the name or the definite description "*A*" then, as before, if the sentence is meaningful it must express a proposition. Given the theory of denoting concepts, however, this proposition need not contain the object *A* itself; it may, rather, contain a denoting concept which denotes *A* (or purports to do so). There being a proposition of that kind, however, does not require that there actually be such an object as *A* (or at least the requirement is by no means obvious). It now becomes possible for the sentence "*A* is not" to be both meaningful and true – i.e., to be meaningful even though there is no such thing as *A*. The difference is that now *A* need not be counted among the constituents of the proposition; instead of containing an object (*A*), the proposition is now said to contain a denoting concept which, as it happens, does not denote anything.

The theory of denoting concepts thus undercuts the force of the Meinongian argument. Clearly, Russell does not fully appreciate that fact in *Principles*, for otherwise he would not have endorsed the argument as we saw him do (see the end of Section II above). Yet even in that book he explicitly recognizes that a denoting concept may in fact fail to denote, because there is no such thing as the purported denotation: "A concept may denote although it does not denote anything" (Section 73, p. 73). In the period between the completion of *Principles* and his discovery of the theory of descriptions, Russell came to a clearer realization of the fact that his theory of denoting concepts blocks the Meinongian argument. He comes to see quite clearly that this makes it possible for there to be definite descriptions which describe nothing, and also names that name nothing. The crucial text in the regard is his essay, "The Existential Import of Propositions".[26] There he says quite explicitly[27]:

"The present king of England" is a denoting concept denoting an individual; "The present king of France" is a similar complex concept denoting nothing. The phrase intends to point out an individual, but fails to do so: it does not point out an unreal individual but no individual at all. The same explanation applies to mythical personages, Apollo, Priam, etc. These words all have a meaning, which can be found by looking them up in a classical dictionary; but they have not a *denotation*; there is no individual, real or imaginary, which they point out.

Russell's attitude towards the Meinongian argument at the time of *Principles* and in the period between that book and his discovery of the theory of descriptions is thus complicated. In *Principles* he advances a form of the argument as his own. Yet even in that book he explicitly accepts ideas which fairly obviously undercut it. Why does he do this? From a Russellian point of view, at least, the Meinongian argument stands or falls with the unqualified form of direct realism. As I have emphasized, this is a view which Russell often tends to assume, even though he does not actually hold it; it fits his metaphysical prejudices better than what he takes to be the alternatives. Certainly he is, in the early years after his rejection of Idealism, prejudiced in favour of an extreme form of realism. For most philosophers the Meinongian argument is something whose conclusion they would wish to avoid, if they can see a way. For Russell when he wrote *Principles*, I suspect, the conclusion was something that he welcomed, so he too easily allowed himself to avoid recognizing that his theory of denoting concepts blocks the argument. Over the subsequent few years his attitude began to shift. Even before he discovered the theory of descriptions he came to realize that he was not in fact committed to accepting the Meinongian argument, and he also started to think that there are reasons not to accept that argument.[28]

V. THE THEORY OF DESCRIPTIONS IN RUSSELLIAN CONTEXT

We now have in place the background we need to understand the change that took place when Russell abandoned the theory of denoting concepts, and adopted the theory of descriptions. One important point here is negative. It is – or at least was until quite recently – very widely believed that Russell adopted the theory of descriptions in order not to have to accept the present King of France, the golden mountain, and other nonexistent *concreta*; more generally, it was widely believed that he adopted the theory in order to avoid the conclusion of the Meinongian argument. This idea is, indeed, asserted by Russell himself, although writing over fifty years later. In *My Philosophical Development*[29] he says:

[Meinong] argued, if you say that the golden mountain does not exist, it is obvious that there is something that you are saying does not exist – namely the golden mountain; therefore the golden mountain must subsist in some shadowy Platonic realm of being, for otherwise your statement that the golden mountain does not exist would have no meaning. I confess that, until I hit upon the theory of descriptions, his argument seemed to me convincing.

This statement seems quite mistaken, for reasons that we emphasized at the end of the previous section. The view that Russell held in the years before he adopted the theory of descriptions also enabled him to avoid golden mountains in shadowy Platonic realms; his "Existential Import of Propositions" shows that he was aware of this fact. That a theory have this result may, by mid-1905, have become for him a criterion of adequacy, but it is a criterion that is equally met by the theory of denoting concepts. It cannot, therefore, be Russell's reason, or even one among a number of reasons he had, for discarding that theory and adopting the theory of descriptions.

We cannot then suppose that Russell adopted the theory of descriptions in order to avoid the Meinongian argument – in spite of his own later statements. What other reasons can we attribute to him? Let us distinguish four.

First, as we saw in section I, the theory of descriptions gives us an analysis of definite descriptions – and of names, if we treat them as disguised definite descriptions – which is well integrated with the needs of logic. Obviously correct inferences involving definite descriptions become a matter of ordinary logic, as antecedently understood. Failure of reference is treated without resort to truth-value gaps, which would complicate logic. No doubt these matters carried considerable weight with Russell, but I shall not discuss them further here.

Second, the theory of denoting concepts is subject to considerable internal difficulties. Some of these are simply about what denotes what – the sorts of questions indicated in Section III, above. Others concern threatened incoherences in the very idea of such a theory. In "On Denoting", Russell argues for the theory of descriptions by using difficulties of this sort as reasons to reject the theory of denoting concepts.[30] This passage of "On Denoting" is notoriously difficult, and commentators have not arrived at any agreed understanding of it. We can gain some inkling of the difficulties faced by the theory of denoting concepts by seeing that a proposition which is *about* a given denoting concept cannot contain that denoting concept, for then, of course, it would be about its denotation. There are no propositions which are about denoting concepts in what for Russell remains the paradigmatic way, i.e., directly about them, by containing them. A proposition which is about a denoting concept must be indirectly about it, by containing another denoting concept which denotes it. A consequence of this is that there must be an infinite hierarchy of denoting concepts, each one after the first denoting the previous member of the hierarchy. To investigate the details of the difficulties that Russell finds in that theory would occupy more space than we have to spare.[31]

Third, the theory of denoting concepts was simply not successful on Russell's own terms. Although he exploited it, more or less successfully, for various other purposes, it does not in fact succeed in performing the task for which he primarily introduced it. This task, as we saw, was to explain generality. The idea here was that one could explain the proposition expressed by "All prime numbers are odd" by saying that it contains the denoting concept, *all prime numbers* (or possibly that it should be understood as containing an unrestricted variable; in that case we explain the variable by means of the denoting concept *any term*, and we take the proposition as a whole to say of any term that if it is a prime number then it is odd). Given the mechanism of denoting, this explanation seems to work well for examples of this kind. As Russell himself came to see in *Principles*, however, the same sort of explanation cannot be extended to more complex cases, at least not without auxiliary assumptions which he was not prepared to make. In particular, suppose we have a sentence containing two or more variables (unrestricted variables, let's say). In that case we can hardly explain each variable by means of the denoting concept *any term*, for the distinctness of the variables is crucial. Yet, from within the theory of denoting concepts, no other means of explanation readily suggests itself. (See *POM*, Chapters VII and VIII, and especially Section 93, pp. 93–4, for these difficulties.)

Fourth, and I believe most fundamentally, is the fact that the theory of denoting concepts was an anomaly from the outset. It flatly contradicted the direct realism which issued from Russell's most general philosophical views; it simply stipulated a class of exceptions to direct realism, with no explanation of how exceptions are possible. I shall enlarge upon this point shortly.

There are important connections among these various reasons. First, the fact that the theory of denoting concepts cannot give a satisfactory explanation of generality makes it possible for Russell to adopt the theory of descriptions without loss. This latter theory begins by assuming generality as a primitive and unexplained idea. It does not attempt an explanation of generality, nor does it contain the materials from which an explanation of that sort might be constructed. If the theory of denoting concepts did in fact explain generality, then giving up that theory would be a considerable loss. As it does not, however, Russell is free to abandon the theory of denoting concepts as soon as he sees another way of dealing with the problems other than generality which had led him to that theory in the first place. Second, it is the general background of Russell's direct realism which lies behind the detailed arguments which Russell gives, in

"On Denoting" against the theory of denoting concepts. Only in the context of Russell's views in general can we hope to arrive at a satisfactory understanding of those arguments, which should therefore not be thought of as operating independently of those more general considerations. It is to those considerations (and hence to the fourth of the above reasons) that we now turn.

As a first step here we can say: the theory of descriptions avoids the representational element which plays the central role in the theory of denoting concepts. (Here and in what follows I ignore the complications arising from the fact that Russell now assumes generality as a primitive notion. It might be said that this fact means that he does not, after all, eliminate the representational element, but merely reduces it all to that one case.) At first sight, the claim that the theory of descriptions eliminates representation may seem odd, even paradoxical, for the theory of descriptions does not seem to eliminate what we called 'indirect aboutness'. When subject to the new method of analysis, the sentence "The President of the USA in 1999 is a Democrat" is still about Bill Clinton, and the proposition which it expresses still does not contain that man, so the sentence is still indirectly about him. And one might think that indirect aboutness invariably demands a representational element. But this is not so (unless, again, one takes the variable as such an element). The difference is that as analyzed by the theory of descriptions, the sentence is directly about its constituents, and is indirectly about Bill Clinton in virtue of being directly about those constituents. Most obviously: the sentence is directly about the property, *being President of the USA in 1999* (no doubt this property is complex, and must be subject to further analysis; but let us ignore that point). And it says of this property that one and only one thing satisfies it or falls under it (and that thing is a Democrat). That is how it gets to be (indirectly) about Bill Clinton: by being (directly) about a property which he and only he satisfies.

Contrast this with the way that sentence looks when analyzed according to the theory of denoting concepts. On that analysis the sentence is not directly about anything. It is not in any sense *about* the denoting concept *the President of the USA in 1999*. Rather it contains that concept without being about it. This is why the role of the denoting concept is a representational one: its only role is to point to another object, which the proposition is indirectly about.

This fact – that the proposition contains an entity which it is in no sense about – is, it seems to me, quite contrary to the spirit of Russell's direct realism. The 'pointing to' involved in the theory of denoting concepts, moreover, relies on the mysterious and *ad hoc* relation of denoting. In virtue of containing *this* entity (a denoting concept) the proposition is about *that* entity, with no story about how this is possible beyond the bare statement that the one entity denotes the other, i.e., stands towards it in a relation which just does have the desired effect. When the sentence is analyzed according to the theory of descriptions, by contrast, the crucial relation is that of an object's satisfying or falling under a property, and this is not in the same way mysterious or *ad hoc*.

In eliminating the representational element of the theory of denoting concepts, the theory of descriptions thus restores Russell's direct realism – it enables him to avoid a large class of exceptions to that paradigm. This is not to say that the triumph of direct realism is complete in Russell's view after the theory of descriptions. That theory, after all, begins by taking for granted the notion of generality, the very issue which first prompted him to make an exception to his paradigm by invoking the theory of denoting concepts. Generality continues not to fit the paradigm; Russell simply gives up the attempt to explain it. On the other hand, the theory of denoting concepts, as we briefly saw, also does not actually succeed in explaining generality either, so Russell certainly has every reason to prefer the theory of descriptions.

VI. THE SIGNIFICANCE OF THE THEORY IN RUSSELL'S PHILOSOPHY

What is the significance of the theory of descriptions for Russell's philosophy more generally? One major point here is summed up in the slogan: definite descriptions are incomplete symbols. What Russell means by an incomplete symbol is, he says, "a symbol which is not supposed to have any meaning in isolation, but is only defined in certain contexts" (*Principia Mathematica*, vol. 1, p. 66). Why should we think that, according to the theory of descriptions, a definite description has no meaning in isolation? Russell's fundamental idea of meaning is referential: a symbol has a meaning if it stands for something, and the thing for which it stands *is* its meaning. There is a certain sense in which a definite description may stand for something – "The President of the USA in 1999" we may say, stands for a certain man. But according to the theory of descriptions, a definite description does not function referentially. In a proposition expressed by a sentence using a definite description, that is to say, there is no entity for which the definite description stands. The proposition expressed by "The President of the USA in 1999" does not contain Bill Clinton. Nor does it contain a denoting concept which denotes him. There is no entity in that proposition for which the definite description stands. That is what Russell means by saying that definite descriptions have no meaning in isolation. Sentences in which definite descriptions occur, however, often succeed in expressing propositions: the sentences as wholes *are* meaningful. This is what Russell means by saying that definite descriptions, like other incomplete symbols, are "defined in certain contexts". An incomplete symbol makes a systematic contribution to a sentence in which it occurs, only it does not do so by indicating an entity which is contained in the proposition which the sentence expresses.

The idea of an incomplete symbol made an immense difference to Russell's thought. Before "On Denoting" he had generally taken the unit of analysis to be subsentential. A referring term, or a predicate, is analyzed to see exactly what entity it stands for. A paradigm here is the analysis of numbers in terms of classes: we understand a number-word by seeing that it should be taken as standing for a certain class. Another way of putting the same point is to say that analysis will, at least in general, leave unaltered the overall form of the sentence being analyzed. The constituents of the proposition may not be those suggested by the parts of the sentence, but each part of the sentence will generally stand for some constituent in the proposition, and the constituents will generally be arranged in the sort of way suggested by the arrangement of the parts of the sentence. Thus in *Principles of Mathematics* he says:

The correctness of our philosophical analysis of a proposition may . . . be usefully checked by the exercise of assigning the meaning of each word in the sentence expressing the proposition. On the whole, grammar seems to me to bring us much nearer to a correct logic than the current opinions of philosophers . . . (p. 42, section 46)

After "On Denoting", Russell's idea of analysis is quite different. He comes to assume that analysis of a sentence will generally reveal that it expresses a proposition of a quite different logical form. The unit of analysis becomes the sentence, and Russell's attention is focused on the logical forms of propositions. The analysis of sentences containing definite descriptions is a paradigm here: the sentence has subject–predicate form, but analysis in accordance with the theory of descriptions reveals that it expresses a proposition which is an existential quantification.

A consequence of Russell's new view is that he comes to take it for granted that our ordinary language is generally misleading.[32] In sharp contrast to his view in *Principles*, he holds that our sentences generally have forms quite different from the real forms of the propositions which they express. A primary task of philosophy thus becomes that of getting past the misleading surface structure of language to the underlying structure. Here we have a crucial contribution to an important theme in twentieth-century analytic philosophy quite generally: the idea that language is systematically misleading, in philosophically significant ways. We also have one of the points of origin for the more specific idea of a contrast between the surface structure of language and its deep structure, or between grammatical form and underlying logical form. Along with this, however, Russell is also forced to pay more attention to language (in the sense of surface structure) and symbolism. In *Principles* language, in this sense, was never at the centre of his attention; he treated it as a more or less transparent medium through which we can perceive the underlying reality which is our concern. Now, however, he has to be more self-conscious about symbolism, if only to avoid being misled by it. In a course of lectures given early in 1918, Russell said[33]:

There is a great deal of importance to philosophy in the theory of symbolism, a good deal more than at one time I thought. I think the importance is almost entirely negative, i.e., the importance lies in the fact that unless you are fairly self-conscious about symbols ... you will find yourself attributing to the thing properties which only belong to the symbol.

This shift of attention towards language – towards the actual words spoken or written – was to be of the greatest importance both for Russell's own thought and for that of philosophers who came after him.

A further aspect of the importance of the idea of an incomplete symbol in Russell's thought is simply that it goes along with the notion of contextual definition – that is, that in order to define a symbol it is sufficient to define the contribution that it makes to all the sentences in which it may occur. This was an idea that Russell exploited increasingly over the ensuring ten years, perhaps most notably with his definition of classes in terms of propositional functions. According to this definition, a subject-predicate sentence whose subject is a class-symbol is to be understood as an existential quantification, asserting the existence of a propositional function satisfying certain conditions.

Russell's idea of an incomplete symbol is clearly new with "On Denoting". According to the theory of denoting concepts definite descriptions *do* stand for constituents of propositions, namely denoting concepts; hence they are not incomplete symbols. In the case of other Russellian ideas which are also associated with the theory of descriptions, however, the contrast is less clear-cut. I have in mind here Russell's views having to do with names, acquaintance, and the elimination of non-existent *concreta*. These views could have been developed in the context of the theory of denoting concepts and to a limited extent were. But it was the theory of descriptions which provided the context within which the views were developed in detail. To some extent we may have here coincidences of timing: Russell's views on a number of related topics began to shift, or at least to become sharper, at around the same time that he developed the theory of descriptions or perhaps a little earlier. This may not entirely be a matter of coincidence, however. Russell's theory of denoting concepts was, as we have emphasized, in rather open conflict with his fundamental metaphysical tenets. Under these circumstances, one might expect him to shrink from taking steps which would require heavy use of that theory. The theory of descriptions (except for the worry about generality) was, by contrast, right in line with his basic views, and it is not surprising that he was ready to exploit it to the full.

Let us begin with the question of non-existent *concreta* – whether there *is*, in some sense, such a thing as the planet Vulcan or the present King of France. As we saw, the theory of denoting concepts in fact gives Russell the means to avoid accepting that there are any such things. He can say that whenever we appear to have a proposition containing a non-existent *concretum*, what we really have is a proposition containing a denoting concept which lacks a denotation. Russell, as we saw, came to appreciate this possibility before

"On Denoting" but, whether by coincidence of timing or not, he does not fully exploit it. Once the theory of descriptions is in place, by contrast, he has no hesitation in exploiting that theory to rid his ontology of non-existent *concreta*. What appears to be a definite description of such an object is, of course, analyzed to show that the proposition does not contain the alleged object, but only properties which are claimed to be uniquely satisfied. More strikingly, *names* which appear to name such objects must be treated in the same fashion. They are, on this view, not genuine proper names at all, but rather disguised definite descriptions. Understanding a sentence in which a (non-genuine) name of this sort appears does not involve simply fastening the name to an object with which one is acquainted. It involves, rather, having in mind (being acquainted with) a property (possibly quite complex), and asserting that it is uniquely satisfied.

How widely is this tactic to be applied? Obviously, it is to be applied whenever we have a sentence which appears or purports to be about a concrete object which in fact does not exist. What of sentences which appear to be about concrete objects which, as far as the speaker knows, may or may not exist? Russell seems to think that the analysis of a proposition should be available to one who understands it. But clearly he does not think that merely by analyzing propositions one can tell whether some supposed object in fact exists. So the general rule is: if there is a proposition apparently about a certain concrete object, but the existence of that object is at all open to doubt, then the proposition is to be analyzed in accordance with the theory of descriptions, i.e., as not really containing the object after all. So the presence of a name in a sentence does not indicate the presence of the named object in the corresponding proposition unless we have a guarantee that the object really exists. (Without such a guarantee the name is thus not, by Russell's standards a genuine proper name at all.)

What could give us such a guarantee? From within Russell's thought, the answer is easy: our being *acquainted* with an object of course guarantees that it is real (and hence, if it is a concrete object, that it exists). In a proposition which I can understand, all the constituents must be entities with which I am acquainted. At the end of "On Denoting" Russell claims that this principle – sometimes known as the Principle of Acquaintance – is a *result* of the theory of descriptions.[34] Superficially this claim is quite misleading. In one sense the Principle of Acquaintance is by no means new in Russell's thought with the theory of descriptions; it is implicit, at least, in *Principles*, and I think Russell would have accepted it at any time from 1900 onwards. But in a deeper sense there is something new. Russell's denial of non-existent *concreta* goes along with a difference in the role that acquaintance plays in his thought. (This new role, and the denial of non-existent *concreta*, perhaps could have been worked out in terms of the theory of denoting concepts, but in fact were not.)

In *Principles* Russell took a very lax attitude towards acquaintance: if the exigencies of his theorizing required that we be acquainted with objects of a certain kind, then he was willing to assert that we are in fact acquainted with objects of that kind. The notion of acquaintance, we might say, functioned to deflect epistemological worries but did not impose any constraints on Russell's thought. This changes from 1905 on; over the following decade the constraints imposed by the notion of acquaintance come to dominate his views. The denial of non-existent *concreta* is the first step in this process. We are not acquainted with the (alleged) planet Vulcan. By the argument which we indicated above, it seems that we cannot be acquainted with the (actual) planet Mars either, since we have no absolute epistemological guarantee of its existence. But then it is clearly an open question: with what (concrete) objects are we acquainted? Once Russell's attention is focused on this question he draws narrower and narrower limits to the scope of our acquaintance with concrete objects. (In the case of abstract objects, however, it is notable that Russell continues to think that acquaintance has a very wide scope; here, it seems, the notion continues to impose no independent constraints.)

Russell's thought after 1905 (at least up to and including his lectures on the "Philosophy of Logical Atomism", given in the first few months of 1918) thus makes heavy use of the theory of descriptions. He no longer took at face value most – or, as time went by almost all – words which appear to refer to concrete objects, the most familiar words there are. Instead of being thought of as names of the relevant objects, such words were treated as definite descriptions, and analyzed accordingly. He invoked the notion of a *sense-datum* in order to have appropriate objects for us to be acquainted with. When I look at and touch a familiar table, say, what I am actually acquainted with is not the table itself but certain immediate deliverances of the senses – a certain coloured shape and a certain sensation of hardness, perhaps. A sentence which is, as we ordinarily say, about the table, in fact expresses a proposition which does not contain the table itself but rather contains immediate deliverances of the senses – sense-data – and uses them to give a definite description of the table. Here we have a vivid illustration of the point made in connection with incomplete symbols: most sentences that we utter, perhaps in the end just about all of them, express propositions whose real constituents, and real structure, are quite different from what is suggested by the superficial structure of the sentence uttered. Language is systematically misleading.

VII. OBJECTIONS TO THE THEORY

The concern of this essay, as of this volume, is with Russell; to this point we have dealt primarily with Russell's reasons for adopting the theory of descriptions and with the significance of that theory in his thought. In this final section, however, we shall shift focus and consider objections made to Russell's theory since 1950.[35] The discussion will, necessarily, be very brief; the aim is merely to give some idea of the best-known objections to Russell's theory. These objections can be divided into two sorts: those that concern the analysis of definite descriptions and those that concern the idea that some or all proper names can be treated as if they were definite descriptions. It will be convenient to discuss these separately.

i) Objections to the theory as an analysis of definite descriptions

One objection of this sort is put forward by Strawson, who argued that Russell's theory is mistaken or misleading about what we ordinarily mean by sentences of the form "The F is G". Such a sentence, Strawson claims, does not *assert* that there is one and only thing which is F, rather it *presupposes* that fact. If someone said that "The King of France is wise", then we would not say that he had said something false (as we should, on Russell's view), nor, of course, would we say that he had said something true. Rather, we "would be inclined, with some hesitation" to say that "the question of whether his statement was true or false simply *did not arise*" (*Logico-Linguistic Papers*, p. 12).

It is hard to assess this objection. One fundamental point at stake is how we are to think of the relation between ordinary language and the notation of modern logic, and on this point we have a true missing of minds. The advantages of the sort of method of analysis that Russell adopts, it might be said, are precisely that they make explicit what is otherwise merely presupposed – that is, they replace presupposition with assertion. But this is the very thing to which Strawson objects. We can think of the advantages of the theory of descriptions as arising from the fact that it shows us how we can smoothly incorporate the idiom of definite descriptions into logic, with corresponding gains in clarity. Standard modern logic, the logic inherited from Frege and Russell, leaves no room for the category of the merely presupposed, as opposed to the asserted. Strawson rejects the theory of descriptions on the grounds that it does not do justice to the nuances of ordinary usage. Advocates of the theory, such as Quine, may insist upon the benefits of the theory in facilitating inference and may claim that Strawson's concern with ordinary usage is not to the point.[36] This may seem to leave matters at a complete impasse, but there is more that can be said on each side.

The Strawsonian side might emphasize that there are systems of logic which take some account of the idea of presupposition.[37] This fact holds out the prospect of the best of both worlds: enabling us to have the advantages of representing our ordinary discourse in logical terms without giving up on the idea of presupposition which is, presumably, part of that discourse. It may be doubted, however, whether any system of logic will really do what the Strawsonian wants. It may be doubted, that is to say, whether it is possible to do full justice to the nuance and subtlety of ordinary discourse while also imposing on that discourse the sort of clarity of form that would enable us to subject it to the mathematical treatment of modern (Russellian and post-Russellian) logic.

On the Russellian or Quinean side, it may be possible to undermine the idea that ordinary discourse is really committed to the notion of presupposition. Strawson bases his claim upon the fact that we do not actually say, of a sentence containing a definite description which we know to be empty, that it is *false*; we tend to use more complicated terms of criticism. For all that, it might be said, such sentences *are* false. The reason we do not call them false, according to this suggestion, is not that they are not false, or even that we do not hold them to be false. It is, rather, that calling them false is liable to be misleading, by suggesting that they are false in the most straightforward way (by there being a unique F which is not G). Our reluctance simply to say of such a sentence that it is false is, on this account, to be explained in terms of our wish to avoid misleading our audience – a reluctance which therefore does not suggest that the sentence is in fact anything other than false. This line of thought gets some encouragement and theoretical backing from ideas of Paul Grice's.[38] Grice emphasizes that the thought conveyed in a sentence is often not, or not only, what the sentence literally says. Thus, to adapt his famous (though by now anachronistic) example. Suppose I am asked to give my opinion of a student of mine who is being considered for a position teaching philosophy, and I say: "He has beautiful handwriting, and is always punctual". If that is all that I say, then the reader of my letter will quite rightly infer that I have a poor opinion of the student's ability. Yet that is certainly not what my letter literally says, as is shown by the fact that I could without contradiction add a paragraph saying how able the student is, what a good philosopher, and how well read. Similarly, it might be said, our reluctance to say of a sentence such as "The King of France is bald" that it is false, and nothing else, arises from the fact that we could reasonably expect our audience to infer, from our saying that, that there is a King of France (or at least that we think there is); we wish to prevent that inference. So our reluctance to *say* that the sentence is false, even when all the facts are before us, may be compatible with the sentence's in fact being false.

Another kind of criticism of the theory of descriptions arises from the fact that our definite descriptions are very often radically incomplete. Strawson gives as an example the sentence: "The table is covered with books" (*Logico-Linguistic Papers*, p. 14). Certainly there are contexts in which this sentence seems to express something true; yet there are, of course a large number of tables in the world, not only one. The response to this sort of case is that much of what we say is dependent upon the context in which we say it, and not only when we are using definite descriptions. (Russell was largely concerned with the context-independent propositions of mathematics, and so perhaps gave this point less weight than it should carry.) On the way to a party with a group of friends I may say "No one knows the street number"; once safely at the party I may say "There's no more wine". In each case, the remark may be perfectly appropriate, yet each is obviously false unless one supposes some tacit restriction – no one *in my group of friends* knows the street number; there is no more wine *at the party*. In the case of the table, if the remark is a sensible one then most likely we are in a room containing only one table, or one table in the room is more noticeable than any other. Yet perhaps there are cases where the room contains two tables, equally noticeable but for the fact that one of them is covered with books. In such a case "the table" is perhaps being used to mean "that table". Perhaps this usage can be dismissed as incorrect; if we accept it as correct, then we have here a limited class of exceptions to the theory of descriptions.

Another category of criticism of the theory of descriptions is associated with Keith Donnellan.[39] Suppose we are at a party, and I see a man, looking slightly inebriated, drinking a clear liquid from a martini glass. (Suppose further, if you like, that there are open bottles of gin and vermouth on the table beside him, and that everyone else in the room is, quite evidently, drinking red wine.) I know that he is a famous philosopher, and say to you: "The man drinking the martini is a famous philosopher". In fact, however, his glass contains water.

Building on this kind of example, Donnellan distinguishes two kinds of uses of definite descriptions: the *attributive* use, which is as the theory of descriptions claims, and the *referential* use, in which a definite description is used simply to refer to some person or thing, without regard for whether the descriptive predicate in fact holds uniquely, or holds at all, of the object being referred to. On Donnellan's account, the example of the previous paragraph is a referential use. I use the phrase to refer to the inebriated-looking man with the martini glass and go on to say something about him; since he in fact is a famous philosopher, my utterance is true. As interpreted by the theory of descriptions, by contrast, the utterance is false (since there is no man – within the relevant context – drinking a martini).

Donnellan appeals to the alleged fact that, in the above sort of example, the utterance clearly is a true one. But a number of philosophers who have discussed this sort of case dispute this claim. They appeal to the same Gricean distinction which we invoked above. Clearly, one of the things I mean when I make my remark, is that that man, the one we can both see, is a famous philosopher. Perhaps, in context, it is clear that this is the thing I mostly mean to convey.

Yet this fact is compatible with the idea that what I literally say is something else, something in accord with the way the sentence reads according to the theory of descriptions. Further plausibility accrues to this idea from the thought that what I say at the party has both something right about it and something wrong. The Russellian line, as supplemented by Grice, seems able to do justice to this: what I literally say is false, but what I clearly mean to convey is correct. Donnellan's line, however, seems harder pressed to explain why there is anything at all wrong with what I say.

Both Donnellan and his opponents here agree that there is such a thing as what I literally say in such a case. Perhaps it is fitting to close this section on a note of partial scepticism about this assumption. If we are to fit our language into the scheme of logic (of any logic), then we have to find a definite claim made by any given utterance. To think that Russell's theory gives us as good a way of doing this as any is compatible with acknowledging that any such schematization will distort our ordinary thought and language, if only because in casual contexts we are not as definite as logic requires.

ii) Objections to the theory as a way of treating ordinary proper names

Our concern here is with objections not to Russell's analysis of definite descriptions but rather to the idea that it can be extended to ordinary proper names, via the claim that names are 'disguised definite descriptions'. All the objections that I shall mention are to be found in Kripke's *Naming and Necessity*.[40]

One objection here concerns the behaviour of proper names and definite descriptions in counterfactual or modal contexts. Suppose I say, for example,

1) Alexander Fleming might have died in childhood

I am inviting my audience to imagine circumstances which (fortunately) did not actually occur. To whom, in those circumstances, does the name "Alexander Fleming" refer? To Alexander Fleming, the same person to whom it refers in fact, in the actual circumstances. But consider the description, "the inventor of penicillin", which is perhaps the most plausible description to use if we think of the name as a disguised definite description. To whom does that description refer in the imagined circumstances? *Not* to Alexander Fleming, for in those circumstances he would not have been the inventor of penicillin. Kripke puts the point by saying that proper names are "rigid designators", meaning that they designate the same thing in all possible circumstances; whereas a definite description is not, for it may designate various distinct objects in various counter-factual situations.[41] (Hence, he of course concludes, proper names cannot be satisfactorily analyzed as definite descriptions.)

Kripke claims that this distinction can make a difference. Contrast 1) with:

2) The inventor of penicillin might have died in childhood

1) seems to be straightforwardly true (at least as straightforwardly as claims about what might have been are). 2), however, is less clear. If it is making the claim that penicillin might have been discovered by a child genius who then died young we may be inclined to dismiss it as false; discovering penicillin in fact took more scientific sophistication, and more time, than any child could have had. Clearly, however, this is not the only or even the most natural way in which to construe 2). Perhaps because we tend to interpret what we are told charitably, we would be more likely to construe it as saying that the person who in fact (that is, in the actual circumstances, not in the counterfactual circumstances we are being asked to imagine) discovered penicillin might have died in childhood. This ambiguity can be captured by Russell's analysis. On the first reading, less plausible both as a reading and as a truth, we have:

3) It might have been the case that: $(\exists x)$ [x discovered penicillin & $(\forall y)(y$ discovered penicillin $\supset$ y=x) & x died in childhood]

On the second, more plausible, reading we have:

4) $(\exists x)$ [x discovered penicillin & $(\forall y)(y$ discovered penicillin $\supset$ y=x) & it might have been the case that: x died in childhood][42]

The difference is one of *scope*; in 3) the modal operator ("might have") has larger scope than the definite description; in 4) it is the other way around.

Note that 4) achieves the same effect as 1). This has led some to claim that there is nothing more to the distinction between rigid and non-rigid designators than that the former must always be read with largest scope.[43] On that view, Kripke's argument has little force against the view that names are disguised definite descriptions; it merely shows that they are disguised definite descriptions which must be read with largest scope. Kripke denies that his distinction amounts to no more than a distinction in scope, and he adduces various arguments to this effect. One is that the distinction applies when we have a simple sentence – one lacking modal operators, and to which no scope distinctions apply – which is evaluated for truth or falsehood in counterfactual circumstances. (You say: Alexander Fleming was a great scientist. I reply: Yes, but that would not have been true if he had died in childhood.)

Another ground on which Kripke objects to using Russell's theory to analyze names is that people often use names although they have in mind nothing like an identifying description of the thing or person they are talking about. Kripke's example is the physicist, Feynman. Non-specialists are unlikely to be able to produce a definite description of him. Nevertheless, Kripke says: "The man in the street ... may ... still use the name 'Feynman'. When asked he will say: well he's a physicist or something. He may not think that this picks our anyone uniquely. I still think he uses 'Feynman' as a name for Feynman". (p. 81). It is, however, unclear that Kripke's man in the street really does lack identifying knowledge of Feynman, because he knows enough to use his name. The description: "famous physicist called 'Feynman'" presumably applies uniquely to Feynman. Russell, indeed, seems to have anticipated this point. When we talk of Julius Caesar, he says: "We have in mind some *description* of Julius Caesar ... perhaps, merely 'the man whose name was *Julius Caesar'*".[44] Kripke objects to this idea on the grounds of circularity, but it not clear that his objections are conclusive. If they are not, then one might use Russell's theory to get a picture not unlike that which Kripke himself suggests: some people have identifying descriptions of (say) Feynman which are independent of uses of his name; others (most of us) do not, but refer to him as the person called 'Feynman', where what we mean is the person so-called by members of the first group.

The last objection I shall consider arises in a different way. Most people who have an identifying description of Gödel which is *not* dependent upon his being called "Gödel" probably identify him as the person who proved the incompleteness of any formalization of arithmetic, or the person who proved the completeness of first-order logic. But, Kripke asks, what if the man called "Kurt Gödel", who held a position at the Institute for Advanced Study in Princeton, did not in fact prove those results? What if he stole them from someone else, who died "under mysterious circumstances" (p. 84)? Nevertheless, Kripke maintains, our ordinary uses of the name "Gödel" would refer to the man who lived in Princeton, not the one who died in Vienna in the nineteen-thirties. Again, the example is compelling; again, however, it is not entirely clear that it shows as much as Kripke claims. For one thing, it may be that "the man who was called 'Gödel' " is a crucial part of the identifying description of Gödel for all of us who did not actually know that famous logician. For another, the non-expert would perhaps make no very clear distinction between identifying Gödel as "the man who proved such-and-such" and identifying him as "the man who is widely thought to have proved such-and-such". The experts to whom the second description implicitly defers would presumably have other ways of referring to Gödel, which would survive any discoveries about the true provenance of the theorems attributed to him.[45]

NOTES

1. "On Denoting", *Mind* n. s. 14 (1905), pp. 479–93; *Papers* 4, pp. 415–27; very widely reprinted.
2. The phrase "that paradigm of philosophy" was used by Ramsey to describe Russell's theory of descriptions, and endorsed by Moore. See Moore's essay "Russell's Theory of Descriptions" in ed. P.A. Schilpp, *The Philosophy of Bertrand Russell*, (Evanston, IL: The Library of Living Philosophers, 1946), pp. 175–225.
3. See for example *Word and Object* (Cambridge, MA: MIT Press, 1960), sections 37–8.
4. See especially "On Referring", *Mind*, n. s. 59 (1950), pp. 320–44, reprinted in P.F. Strawson, *Logico-Linguistic Papers* (London: Methuen, 1971), pp. 1–27.
5. Leonard Linsky, *Referring* (New York: Humanities Press, 1967), p. ix.
6. In KAKD, *Papers* 6, pp. 148–61, and in ML pp. 209–32, Russell says: "Common words, even proper names, are usually really descriptions." (*Papers* 6, p. 152); in Lecture V of his lectures on the "Philosophy of Logical Atomism" he says that the (apparent) name "Romulus" "is really a sort of truncated or telescoped description" (*Papers* 8, p. 213).
7. What does it mean to speak of a phrase "purporting" to pick out a single object? As Quine comments: "Such talk of purport is only a picturesque way of alluding to distinctive grammatical roles that singular and general terms play in sentences. It is by grammatical role that

general and singular terms are properly to be distinguished". (*Word and Object*, p. 96)

8. I use the upside-down "A", used before the variable in parentheses including both it and the variable, to represent the universal quantifier, which is sometimes represented simply by putting the variable by itself in parentheses ["(x)"]. I use the horseshoe, "⊃", to represent the truth-functional conditional, and the backwards "E" to represent the existential quantifier.

9. I leave out of account here the idea that a phrase such as "any prime number" might be treated as naming a higher-order property, or anything of that sort. For the purposes of the analogy with definite descriptions, the important point is that it does not name an object of the ordinary sort – in this case, that it does not name a prime number, or all the prime numbers, or any combination of them.

10. See for example Karel Lambert, "The Nature of Free Logic", in *Philosophical Applications of Free Logic*, ed., Karel Lambert, Oxford: Oxford University Press, 1991, and references given there.

11. Frege's distinction between the *Sinn* of a word and its *Bedeutung* is obviously an example of the sort of distinction that I have in mind here. See "Über Sinn und Bedeutung", *Zeitschrift für Philosophie und philosophische Kritik*, 100 (1892), pp. 25–50; translated in G. Frege, *Collected Papers on Mathematics, Logic and Philosophy*, Oxford: Basil Blackwell, 1984, under the title "On Sense and Meaning" and elsewhere (sometimes with the title differently translated). But Frege's distinction is only an example: the vaguer and more general idea of distinguishing intension from extension, or connotation from denotation, long antedates his work. (Note that Frege's word for what falls on the side of reference or denotation – for the actual object which the name names – is "*Bedeutung*". This is apt to be confusing, because that word is in most contexts naturally translated as "meaning", yet that English word is naturally used for the other side of the distinction. The confusions which threaten here are, I think, quite superficial.)

12. London: George Allen and Unwin, 1937; first edn. Cambridge: Cambridge University Press, 1903. Abbreviated as *POM*.

13. I have in mind primarily the work of Hegel and his followers, especially his British followers such as T.H. Green and F.H. Bradley. Russell, and a number of the Idealists, counted Kant as more or less a member of the Idealist camp. (From here on I shall speak of "Idealism", always meaning *Absolute* Idealism.)

14. For a far more detailed account, see the present author's *Russell, Idealism and the Emergence of Analytic Philosophy* (Oxford: Oxford University Press, 1990).

15. The application of this to Kant is problematic. He distinguished the conceptual from the intuitional and argued that Space and Time are matters of intuition, not of concepts. He accordingly held that our knowledge of the world is mediated by *a priori* forms of intuition (Space and Time), as well as by *a priori* concepts. For some purposes this distinction is crucial, but not for ours. I mean to be using the expression "conceptual structures" to include Kant's view about Space and Time, in spite of the violence that this does to Kantian usage.

16. It is crucial to remember here that one philosopher's sophistication and subtlety is another philosopher's sophistry and illusion.

17. See *Principia Ethica* (Cambridge: Cambridge University Press, 1903), e.g., p. 126. The notion of the good is of course one of the things of which we have this sort of direct perception, according to that book.

18. We shall see in the next section why this qualification is needed.

19. Thus Russell, speaking of "the theory that judgments consist of ideas" says: "in this view ideas become a veil between us and outside things – we never really, in knowledge, attain to the things we are supposed to be judging about, but only to the ideas of those things." KAKD, *Papers* 6, pp. 155–6.

20. *Nachgelassene Schriften und Wissenschaftliche Briefwechsel*, vol. 2, eds. G. Gabriel, *et al.* (Hamburg: Felix Meiner Verlag, 1976), p. 245; I rely on the English translation in *Philosophical and Mathematical Correspondence*, eds. G. Gabriel *et al*, trans. Hans Hermes *et al.* (Oxford: Basil Blackwell, 1979), p. 163.

21. Russell wrote to Frege in German, using Fregean terminology, presumably in (what he took to be) Frege's sense. I leave the terms *Sinn, Bedeutung, Satz*, and their cognates untranslated, so as to avoid confusion between Frege's terminology and Russell's.

22. *Nachgelassene Schriften und Wissenschaftliche Briefwechsel*, vol. 2, pp. 250–1; translation in *Philosophical and Mathematical Correspondence*, p. 169; emphasis added.

23. The first statement of the new view is in a manuscript entitled "On Fundamentals", published for the first time in *Papers 4*, pp. 360–413; the manuscript is dated "1905", and the words "begun June 7" are on the first folio.

24. As we shall see shortly, before he rejected the theory of denoting concepts he came to see that it could be extended to phrases other than descriptions, whether definite or indefinite – in particular, to proper names.

25. Of course there can be propositions which are about denoting concepts, but a proposition of that sort does not contain the denoting concept which it is about, but rather some other denoting concept which denotes that denoting concept. For every instance of denoting there thus

seems to be an infinite series of denoting concepts, each member past the first denoting the previous member. (See Russell, *Idealism, and the Emergence of Analytic Philosophy*, cited in fn. 14, above, Ch. 6, especially pp. 248 ff.)

26. *Mind* n. s. 14 (July 1905), pp. 398–401, reprinted in *Papers* 4, pp. 486–9. The question of timing is important here. The manuscript in which we see Russell first coming across the crucial idea of the theory of descriptions is dated 1905, and contains, on the first folio, the note "Begun 7 June". The essay "On the Existential Import of Propositions" was *published* in July 1905, and Russell's correspondence about it dates from April and May of that year. (For these points, see *Papers* 4, pp. 359, 480–1.) These facts, as well as internal evidence, make it clear that the essay was written while Russell still held the theory of denoting concepts.

27. The passage quoted is at p. 399 of *Mind* for 1905, and p. 487 of *Papers* 4.

28. Early in 1903 Russell studied Meinong's work closely, and wrote a long article on the subject (published in three parts in *Mind* n. s. 13 (1904), pp. 204–19, 336–54, and 509–24; reprinted in *Papers* 4, pp. 432–74). The article is generally very laudatory, and accepts Meinong's ontological views, which are similar to those which Russell held in *Principles*. Russell does, however, begin to find problems with those views. It is thus a reasonable speculation that it was his thinking through these issues in connection with Meinong which led to a shift in his own ontological views.

29. London: George Allen and Unwin, 1959. The passage quoted is on p. 84.

30. Russell's ostensible target here is Frege's distinction between the *Sinn* of an expression (its sense, more or less equivalent to its meaning, in Russell's sense) and its *Bedeutung* (the object to which it refers, more or less equivalent to its denotation in Russell's sense). His arguments, however, apply more clearly to his own distinction between denoting concept and denoted object than they do to its Fregean analogue.

31. For an attempt to come to terms with these arguments of "On Denoting" in detail see Michael Pakaluk "The interpretation of Russell's 'Gray's Elegy' Argument", in A.D. Irvine and G.A. Wedeking, eds., *Russell and Analytic Philosophy* (Toronto: University of Toronto Press, 1993), pp. 37–65. See also Harold Noonan "The 'Gray's *Elegy* Argument – and Others" in Ray Monk and Anthony Palmer (eds.), *Bertrand Russell and the origins of analytical philosophy* (Bristol: Thoemmes Press, 1996), and Michael Kremer, "The Argument of 'On Denoting'" in *The Philosophical Review*, vol. 103, number 2 (April 1994).

32. Thus, Wittgenstein in the *Tractatus* says that it is Russell's service to have shown that the apparent form of the sentence need not be its real

form: "Russells Verdienst ist es, gezeight zu haben, dass die scheinbare logische Form des Satzes nicht seine wirkliche sein muss". *Tractatus Logico-Philsophicus*, 4.0031.

33. PLA, *Papers* 8, p. 166.

34. The principle is reiterated in "Knowledge by Acquaintance and Knowledge by Description", without the claim that it follows from the theory of descriptions; see *Papers* 6, p. 154.

35. We should also point out that by no means all references to Russell's theory in the second half of the twentieth-century have been unfavourable. On the contrary, a number of authors adhere to the theory, and put it to their own uses. Perhaps most notable is Quine; see the references in fn. 3, above. Not surprisingly, various authors have put the theory to various philosophical uses. See the present author's "Analysis and Analytic Philosophy", *The Story of Analytic Philosophy*, eds. Anat Biletzki and Anat Matar, (London: Routledge, 1998), pp. 37–55.

   Russell's theory as an analysis of definite descriptions (though not of names) is the subject of a sustained defense in Stephen Neale, *Descriptions* (Cambridge, MA: MIT Press, 1990). I have to some extent drawn on that work in part i) of the present section, and on Mark Sainsbury's "Philosophical Logic", in *Philosophy: A Guide through the Subject*, ed., A.C. Grayling (Oxford: OUP, 1995), pp. 61–122, in both parts i) and ii).

36. Besides the section of *Word and Object* referred to in fn. 3, see also Quine's review of Strawson's *Introduction to Logical Theory* (London: Methuen, 1952), first published in *Mind* n. s. 62 (1953) and reprinted in Quine's *Ways of Paradox* (Cambridge, MA: Harvard University Press, 1966; revised edition 1976), pp. 137–157. Reacting to what he takes to be Strawson's general attitude, Quine says there: "even the humdrum spinning out of elementary logical principles in modern logic brings insights, concerning the general relation of premise to conclusion in actual science and common sense, which are denied to men who scruple to disturb a particle of natural language in its full philological correctness." (*Ways of Paradox*, revised ed., p. 149).

37. See, for example, Bas C. van Frassen, "Singular Terms, Truth-Value Gaps, and Free Logic", and "Presupposition, Implication, and Self-Reference", both in *Philosophical Applications of Free Logic* (see note 10, above), pp. 82–97 and 205–21, respectively.

38. See especially his "Logic and Conversation", in *Studies in the Ways of Words* (Cambridge, MA: Harvard University Press, 1989).

39. See his "Reference and Definite Descriptions", *Philosophical Review*, 77 (1966), pp. 203–15, from which the following example is adapted.

40. Saul A. Kripke, *Naming and Necessity*, (Cambridge MA: Harvard University Press, 1980). The text is based on lectures given in 1970; a slightly different version was published under the same title in *Semantics of*

Natural Language, eds. D. Davidson and G. Harman, (Dordrecht: D. Reidel, 1972).

41. In this explanation of the notion of a rigid designator I have attempted to avoid the technical, and philosophically disputed, interpretations of modality which are usually invoked in such explanations.

42. This sentence involves quantifying in to the intensional context created by the phrase, 'it might have been the case that', i.e., a quantifier outside the scope of that phrase binds a variable within its scope. The difficulties involved in such cases have been forcefully argued by Quine. See especially his "Quantifiers and Propositional Attitudes", *Journal of Philosophy*, 53 (1956), reprinted as essay 17 of his *Ways of Paradox* (Cambridge, MA: Harvard University Press, 1966 and 1967), and "Intensions Revisited", *Midwest Studies in Philosophy*, (1977), reprinted as Essay 13 of his *Theories and Things* (Cambridge, MA: Harvard University Press, 1981). It should be noted that Quine has little sympathy with the sorts of considerations that seem to give rise to a need for rigid designators, or for definite descriptions to be read in a way that involves quantifying in to intensional contexts.

43. See for example Michael Dummett, *Frege: Philosophy of Language* (London: Duckworth, 1973), especially pp. 113f.

44. *POP* pp. 91–2 [= *POP2*, P. 59]. cf. a similar passage in KAKD, *Papers 6*, p. 155.

45. For their comments on an earlier draft, I am indebted to Nicholas Griffin and to Thomas Ricketts.

7 Russell's Substitutional Theory

I. INTRODUCTION

In his 1893 *Grundgesetze der Arithmetik* Frege sought to demonstrate a thesis which has come to be called Logicism. Frege maintained that there are no uniquely arithmetic intuitions that ground mathematical induction and the foundational principles of arithmetic. Couched within a proper conceptual analysis of cardinal number, arithmetic truths will be seen to be truths of the science of logic. Frege set out a formal system – a *characteristica universalis* – after Leibniz, whose formation rules and transformation (inference) rules were explicit and, he thought, clearly within the domain of the science of logic. Confident that no nonlogical intuitions could seep into such a tightly articulated system, Frege endeavored to demonstrate logicism by deducing the principle of mathematical induction and foundational theorems for arithmetic.

In his 1903 *The Principles of Mathematics*, Russell set out a doctrine of Logicism according to which there are no special intuitions unique to the branches of non-applied mathematics. All the truths of non-applied mathematics are truths of the science of logic. Russell embraced this more encompassing form of logicism because, unlike Frege, he accepted the arithmetization of all of non-applied mathematics, including Geometry and Rational Dynamics.

Both Frege and Russell regarded logic as itself a science. Frege refrained from calling it a synthetic *a priori* science so as to mark his departure from the notion of pure empirical intuition (*anschauung*) set forth in Kant's 1781 *Critique of Pure Reason*. In Frege's view, Kant's transcendental argument for a form of pure empirical (aesthetic) intuition that grounds the synthetic *a priori* truths of arithmetic is unwarranted. Russell concurred, but spoke unabashedly of a purely logical intuition grounding our knowledge of logical truths. Russell wrote that Kant "never doubted for a moment that the propositions of logic are analytic, whereas he rightly perceived that those of mathematics are synthetic...It has since appeared that logic is just as synthetic..." (*POM*, p. 457). In *Principles*, Russell took logic to be the abstract science of structure (logical form) and reified structures as propositions – mind and language independent "states of affairs" (as it were) which may or may not obtain. Logic is to be an all-encompassing, wholly general, science of propositional structure. Accordingly, he held that a symbolic calculus for logic is a calculus of the science of propositions.

Russell adopted the fundamental principle "*quodlibet ens est unum*" from Leibniz. "Whatever is, is one." By this Russell meant that it is metaphysically essential that every entity occur as a constituent of a true proposition in which it exemplifies a property or stands in a relation (*POM*, p. 132). Russell called this sort of occurrence an "occurrence as logical subject," or "occurrence as term" and used the word "entity" synonymously with "logical subject," "one," "term," and "individual" (*POM*, p. 43). He took it that an entity has a property or stands in a relation only in virtue of such an occurrence in a true proposition predicating the property or relation. Properties and relations have what Russell calls an "indefinable twofold capacity," for they may also occur "as concept" in a proposition. For instance, the property *humanity* occurs "as concept" in the proposition *Socrates's being human*. It occurs "as logical subject," on the other hand, in the proposition *Humanity's belonging to Socrates*. Every entity, be it a property, a relation, or a concrete particular, is a logical subject. Thus, "logical subject," is the fundamental and only logical category.

With pure logic conceived of as a universal science applying to every entity *quā* logical subject, Russell held that any calculus for pure logic should embrace only one style of genuine variables – viz., logical subject (entity/individual) variables. In Russell's view, the calculus for pure logic should not adopt special predicate or function constants that pertain to any particular special science, nor indeed should it embrace special variables for certain kinds of entities particular to the branches of the special sciences. A many sorted language, with distinct sorts of variables for distinct types of entities, attributes, particulars, classes, or whatever, was antithetical to Russell's conception of a proper calculus for the science of logic. The calculus for pure logic must have only one style of variables; and it must be wholly type-free. This is Russell's "doctrine of the unrestricted variables of pure logic."[1]

Frege's calculus for logic, on the other hand, is two-sorted. Frege distinguished special "function" variables from "object" variables. Functions are not objects, and accordingly in a functional expression such as "fx" a function symbol cannot occupy the position of the argument "x." Frege introduced the use of variables into the calculus for pure logic by adopting the notion of mathematical functionality. Predication is transcribed into Frege's *Begriffsschrift* notation via special truth-functions. The value of such a function is not a complex composed of the function and its arguments. It is one of two exclusive values: 'the True' or 'the False.' Moreover, unlike Russell's attributes in intension, Frege maintained that functions are not themselves objects. He assumed, however, that they are correlated one-to-one with objects. The correlate of the function f is $źfz$. Frege took it as a logical truth that an object a belongs to the correlate $źfz$ if the value of the function f with a as its argument is 'the True;' and does not belong otherwise.

In 1901 Russell discovered his paradoxes of attributes and classes. Reformulating his contradiction of classes in terms of Frege's function-correlates, he wrote Frege of his discovery of the class of all classes not members of themselves. Frege's system was shattered, but Frege took solace in his feeling that "everyone [including Dedekind] who in his proofs has made use of extensions of concepts, classes, sets, is in the same position. It is not just a matter of my particular method of laying the foundations, but of whether a logical foundation for arithmetic is possible at all."[2] Not everyone, however, was advancing a form of logicism; and with the appearance of Zermelo's 1908 "*Untersuchungen über die Grundlagen der Mengenlehre: I*" it became clear that a theory capable of recovering mathematical uses

---

[1] Alas, ever since van Heijenoort's "Logic as Calculus and Logic as Language," *Synthese* 17, pp. 324–30, Russell's doctrine of the unrestricted variable has been conflated with a semantic doctrine that he did not hold – viz., that a calculus for logic, being that it codifies a universal science, must somehow include its own metatheory.

[2] See Appendix II of Frege's *Grundgesetze der Arithmetik*, vol. II, (Jena 1903).

of sets would be possible by postulating axioms none of which could be regarded as truths of logic.

For the logicist, membership in a class is not a primitive idea governed by special non-logical intuitions governing the existence of classes; it is but an extensional shadow of the fundamental logic of predication. Naively, every condition determines an attribute. Attributes, Russell thought, are surely entities of pure logic, and classes are but innocuous posits to capture the extensionality that attributes lack. (Coexemplifying attributes are not identical; classes with the same members are.) Indeed, as Russell came to realize, so long as attributes have both an individual and a predicable nature, the feature of extensionality, which is characteristic of classes, can be captured without any extra existential posit beyond the subsistence of the attributes themselves. In 1906 Russell discovered what would become part of *Principia Mathematica*'s contextual definitions for the introduction of class expressions:

*20.01 $[\hat{y}(Ay)]B\{\hat{y}(Ay)\} =$df $(\exists\varphi)(\varphi x \equiv_x Ax$.&. $B(\varphi\hat{y}))$.
*20.02 $x \in \varphi\hat{y} =$df φx

For classes of classes (of non-classes), Russell has:

*20.07 $(\alpha)B\alpha =$df $(\varphi)(B\{\hat{y}\varphi y\})$
*20.071 $(\exists\alpha)B\alpha =$df $(\exists\varphi)(B\{\hat{y}\varphi y\})$
*20.08 $[\alpha A\alpha]B\{\alpha A\alpha\} =$df $(\exists\varphi)(\varphi\alpha \equiv_\alpha A\alpha$.&. $B(\varphi\hat{\alpha}))$
*20.081 $\alpha \in \varphi\hat{\alpha} =$df $\varphi\alpha$

In a similar way, Russell introduces parallel definitions contextually defining expressions for relations-in-extension.[3] By means of the definitions, contexts B in which an apparent class term occurs are definitional abbreviations for contexts where attribute terms occur. Extensionality is a construct, for the following is provable from the contextual definition:

$$\hat{y}(Ay) = \hat{y}(By) .\equiv. (z)(z \in \hat{y}(Ay) .\equiv. z \in \hat{y}(By)).$$

Where attributes in intension are assumed, a separate assumption of an ontology of classes is therefore wholly unnecessary. Class terms

---

[3] Oddly, *20.01 and *20.02 are frequently cited as if they were the only contextual definitions for class symbols. Worse, *Principia*'s explicit comment that *21.02 is the analog of *20.02 for (dyadic) relations-in-extension (*PM*, 81, 201), has often been ignored and *21.02 has been misconstrued as a concretion principle for circumflex terms.

are *façons de parler*. From this perspective, the assumption of classes is not the source of the contradictions. Rather, it is the naïve assumption of attributes with both a predicable and individual nature that is questionable. Its apparent logical status notwithstanding, the unbridled assumption of attributes leads to contradiction. There would be the attribute an entity has just when it is an attribute that is not exemplified by itself. (This is the paradox of attributes, the extensional shadow of which is the class of all classes not members of themselves.) As Russell saw matters, "... the postulate of the existence of classes and relations is exposed to the same arguments, *pro* and *con*, as the existence of propositional functions as separable entities distinct from all their values" (1906, *EA*, 154n).

In the years between 1903 and 1905, Russell entertained many different avenues for skirting the paradoxes. One approach is his "zig-zag" theory which sets limits to the complexity of the formulas comprehending classes. The idea bears a resemblance to that of Quine's "New Foundations for Mathematical Logic," which adopts a type-free language but requires that any wff comprehending a class be type-stratifiable.[4] Cocchiarella employs a similar idea to form a type-free theory of attributes in intension. In Cocchiarella's system, any formula comprehending an attribute must be homogeneously type-stratifiable.[5] (Heterogeneous type stratification is allowed in Quine's system because he adopts the Wiener-Kuratowski construction of relations-in-extension.) There is a universal concept and a universal class V, and V ∈ V is a theorem of the system. Alternatively, Russell contemplated a "limitation of size" approach which stipulates rules to prevent certain classes from becoming too large. Roughly speaking, this is akin to the approach taken by Zermelo and von-Neumann-Bernays traditions in axiomatic set-theory, where there is no universal set V. But in the end, Russell's quest to establish logicism led him to reject both the "zig-zag" and "limitation of size" approaches because they relied upon stipulations as to what classes exist and such stipulations could not be regarded as truths of pure logic.

Russell concluded that attributes, classes, and relations-in-extension cannot be purely logical objects. There are no *logical truths* governing the subsistence of classes and the conditions for class

---

[4] Quine, W.V. O. "New Foundations for Mathematical Logic," *American Mathematical Monthly* 44, (1937): 70–80.

[5] Cocchiarella, Nino B. "Frege's Double Correlation Thesis and Quine's Set Theories NF and ML," *Journal of Philosophical Logic* 14, (1985): 1–39.

membership, or for the subsistence of attributes in intension and the conditions for exemplification of an attribute. Between 1903 and 1907, however, Russell held fast to the view that the paradoxes do not undermine his conception of logic as a genuine science of propositional structure, and remained committed to the subsistence of propositions as purely logical entities. Russell knew that type stratification of the language of attributes (or analogously the language of classes and relations-in-extension) would syntactically dodge the paradoxes. *Principles* set out a rudimentary sketch of such an approach. But as we noted, type stratification is the very antithesis of Russell's conception of logic as a universal science. Therefore, the task to which Russell set himself was to find a bridge between the science of propositions couched *within a calculus which adopts only one style of variables* and a type stratified language with predicate variables allowed in subject as well as predicate positions.

In 1903 and 1904, Russell worked on a philosophical explanation of the use of single letters as variables. Beginning from a formula of the form $A\mu$, it is not always legitimate to represent the logical form as φx, where "φ" is a predicate variable and "x" an individual variable. This sort of variation is what produces the paradox of predication, for one apparently has an attribute θ such that,

$$(x)(\theta x .\equiv. (\exists \varphi)(x = \varphi .\&. \sim\varphi x)).$$

Russell called formulas that involve variation of this sort "quadratic forms". In *Principles*, the use of a predicate variable was to be introduced via definition since only individual variables are adopted in the formal calculus. Russell hoped that the proper philosophical ground for the introduction of predicate variables would show what uses of quadratic forms are safe. Of course, the sweeping conclusion is that they are never safe. But this would destroy the constructions essential to much of mathematics.

The breakthrough came in 1905 with Russell's discovery of the theory of descriptions. This theory quickly unfolded into what Russell called his "no-classes" theory and later his "substitutional" theory. The plan of the substitutional technique is to *proxy* a type-stratified language that allows predicate variables in subject as well as predicate positions from within the type-free calculus for the logic of propositions. The substitutional theory offers a genuine *solution* of Russell's paradoxes of classes and attributes, and not the *ad hoc* dodges of the "zig-zag" and "limitation of size" approaches. Indeed, Russell had no small hopes for substitution. In 1905 he read a paper entitled "On Some Difficulties in the Theory of Transfinite Numbers and Order Types" to the London Mathematical Society. It compared his substitutional theory with his other attempts at solving the paradoxes. Later he added the following note: "From further investigation, I now feel hardly any doubt that the no-classes theory affords the complete solution of all the difficulties stated in the first section of this paper" (1906, *EA*, 164n). The same enthusiasm occurs in a paper entitled "On the Substitutional Theory of Classes and Relations," which Russell read to the London Mathematical Society in May of 1906. Russell wrote that the theory ". . . affords what at least seems to be a complete solution of all the hoary difficulties about the one and the many; for while allowing that there are many entities, it adheres with drastic pedantry to the old maxim that 'whatever is, is one'" (1906a, *EA*, p. 189).[6] Russell originally conceived of writing a second volume of his *Principles* that would offer a demonstration of logicism in formal symbols. The substitutional theory was to have been the centerpiece of this volume, showing how the new theory of logical form inaugurated by Russell's theory of definite descriptions salvages logicism from the grip of the contradictions of classes and attributes.

II. SUBSTITUTION (PHILOSOPHICAL ASPECTS)

The fundamental idea underlying the substitutional theory is analogous to that of eliminativistic approaches in the philosophy of science. For example, eighteenth- and nineteenth-century physics and chemistry offered a number of subtle fluid and aether theories that were highly successful at explaining a wide variety of phenomena. In the process of theory change, the research programs that gave rise to such theories were supplanted by atomistic physical theories couched within a new research program. Empirical and conceptual problems pertaining to the aether (such as its elasticity) were dropped, and an entirely new research program, with a new language and a new set of empirical and conceptual techniques was

---

[6] The paper was submitted for publication, but Russell withdrew it when he discovered that it was inconsistent. The contradiction formulable within it is called the p_0/a_0 paradox and will be discussed anon.

inaugurated. Many successes of the earlier aether theories were retained by the theories of the new research program. Retention, however, is only partial; the confirmed predictions of an earlier theory
in a rival research tradition do not always survive into the supplanting research tradition. Indeed, theoretical processes and mechanisms
of earlier theories are at times treated as flotsam.[7] The supplanting
tradition may come to regard the terms of the earlier theories as
non-referential, or regard them as idle wheels that serve no explana-
tory purpose even if referential.

Analogously, Russell's substitutional theory maintains that the
language of the type-stratified theory of attributes in intension (and
thereby a type-stratified theory of classes and relations-in-extension)
is to be supplanted by the language of the substitutional theory. It
explains in an entirely new way what the theory of classes was getting at and preserves, wherever possible, its mathematical successes.
At times, Russell spoke of this as the denial there are classes, but he
also put his position as a form of agnosticism about classes. From
the perspective of the supplanting research program, they are idle
wheels that play no role in mathematical constructions. The major
successes obtained by appeal to the existence of classes, the positive constructions of Cantor, Dedekind, and Weierstrass, are to be
retained within substitution. Russell explained that "... the principles of mathematics may be stated in conformity with the theory,"
and the theory "... avoids all known contradictions, while at the
same time preserves nearly the whole of Cantor's work on the infinite" (1906e, 231). The substitutional theory involves, as Russell put
it, "an elaborate restatement of logical principles." The results obtained by appeal to the existence of classes are conceptualized in an
entirely new way within the research program of the substitutional
theory. There will be some loss – some flotsam – such as Cantor's
transfinite ordinal number ω_ω, the usual generative process for the
series of ordinals, and the class of all ordinals. But this loss is to
be measured against the successes of the new program. Indeed, had
the program yielded the conceptual successes that Russell had anticipated, one might venture to say that present mathematics would
regard the notion of a class as present science regards phlogiston,
caloric fluid, the aether, and other relics of the past.

---

[7] See Laudan, Larry. *Progress and its Problems* (Berkeley: University of California
Press, 1977).

Unfortunately, the formal calculus of propositions underlying the substitutional theory has not been well understood. As Quine characterized it, the central idea of the theory was that "instead of speaking of the class of all the objects that fulfill some given sentence, one might speak of the sentence itself and of substitutions within it. Now discourse about specified classes lends itself well enough to paraphrase in terms thus of sentences and substitution, but when we talk rather of classes in general, as values of quantifiable variables, it is not evident how to continue such paraphrase."[8] Quine's difficulty in understanding how to continue the paraphrase lies in his failure to appreciate that the substitutional theory is couched within Russell's calculus for the logic of propositions. The notion that a given entity is *in* (a constituent of) a proposition is quite different than the notion of a singular term occurring in a sentence.

In a modern predicate calculus, the logical particle "→" is a statement connective; it is flanked by well-formed formulas (wffs) A and B of the language of the calculus to form a formula A → B. Similarly, the modern logical particle "¬" is a statement connective; it is flanked by a wff A to form a wff ¬A. In reconstructing Russell's theory of propositions, Church adopts the usual logical particles as statement connectives and then introduces special "propositional" variables "P," "Q," "R," etc., and a quadruple bar sign for propositional identity so that wffs can flank an identity sign.[9] This approach is out of sorts with Russell's conviction that a proper calculus for the science for logic should adopt only individual variables. In the language of substitution, the only variables are individual variables. Russell's logical particle "⊃" is a *dyadic predicate expression* for the relation of 'implication.' It is flanked by terms to form a formula. Accordingly, where α and β are any terms, $\alpha \supset \beta$ is a wff. (I use lowercase Greek for any singular term of the language of substitution.) The positions of "x" and "y" in the formula "$x \supset y$" are subject positions, and the individual (entity) variables "x" and "y" here are bindable, so that, "$(x)(y)(x \supset y)$" is a formula of the language. (It says that for all x and y, x implies y.) Moreover, in Russell's view, any

[8] Quine, W.V.O. Introduction to Russell's "Mathematical Logic as Based on the Theory of Types," in ed., J. van Heijenoort, *From Frege to Gödel: A Source Book in Mathematical Logic 1879–1931* (Harvard, University Press, 1967), pp 150–2.

[9] Church, Alonzo. "Russell's Theory of the Identity of Propositions," *Philosophia Naturalis* 21 (1984): 513–22.

wff of the formal language can be nominalized to generate a genuine singular term. It is useful to use nominalizing braces "{" and "}" for this purpose. Thus, where "x" and "y" are individual variables, "$\{x \supset y\}$" is a term. The distinction between terms and formulas is respected by Russell. The expression, "$x \supset \{x \supset y\}$" is a formula. But since subject position is sufficient by itself to indicate a nominalizing transformation has taken place, we can drop the brackets in this formula and use dots for punctuation. Thus, instead of writing "$x \supset \{x \supset y\}$" we can write "$x \mathbin{.\supset.} x \supset y$" as our formula.[10]

To be sure, it may appear odd for entities such as people, rocks, and trees, to be said to stand in, or even fail to stand in, a relation of implication. Perhaps a relation $a|b$ of a's being noncopresent with b (adapted from the Peirce/Sheffer stroke)[11] is better suited for the role. In any event, it is essential to a proper understanding of the substitutional theory *not* to identify its sign "$\supset$" with the modern statement connective "$\rightarrow$."

Of course, a deductive system that allows individual variables to flank the implication sign would be incoherent if an individual variable could appear isolated on a line of proof. This problem, no doubt, explains the motivation of so many interpreters to identify Russell's sign "$\supset$" with the statement connective "$\rightarrow$" and to adopt special "propositional" variables which can occur isolated on a line of proof. But in Russell's system the inference rule *Modus Ponens*, is not the incoherent:

> From α and $\alpha \supset \beta$, infer β.

It is rather the following:

> From A and $\{A\} \supset \{B\}$, infer B.

Similarly, it is very important to resist the temptation to read Russell's "$x \mathbin{\&} y$" as if it were "x is true and y is true." The conjunction and negation signs are defined as follows:

$$\alpha \mathbin{\&} \beta = \text{df } (x)(\alpha \mathbin{.\supset.} \beta \supset x \mathbin{:\supset:} x)$$
$$\sim\alpha = \text{df } (x)(\alpha \supset x)$$

---

[10] Russell himself took subject position to be sufficient to mark the nominalizing transformation and so did not employ brackets as we have above. In what follows I shall used dots symmetrically for punctuation.

[11] Of course, the Peirce/Sheffer stroke A|B for alternative denial and A↓B for joint denial are statement connectives.

Thus, "x & y" says that every entity is such that it is implied by x's implying y's implying it.[12] Alternatively, one could put:

$$\alpha \,\&\, \beta =\mathrm{df}\ \alpha \,.\supset.\ \beta \supset f :\supset: f$$
$$\sim\!\alpha =\mathrm{df}\ \alpha \supset f$$
$$f =\mathrm{df}\ (x)(y)(x \supset y)$$

On this formulation, "x & y" says that x's implying y's implying f implies f. The derived rule of *Simplification* is formulated as follows:

From {A} & α, infer A.

One shall never arrive at an individual variable isolated on a line of proof.

As we see, the assumption of Russellian propositions is the center-piece of the substitutional theory. But interpretative disagreements about the nature of Russellian propositions have been a continued source of controversy, and unfortunately they have lent themselves to obfuscations of the theory.

In the substitutional theory, propositions are akin to what we now call "states of affairs." They are structures such as *the cat's being on the mat*, or *Mont Blanc's being snow covered*. Some obtain ("are true") and others do not obtain ("are false"). Russell put the point strikingly: "It may be said – and this is, I believe, the correct view – that there is no problem at all in truth and falsehood; that some propositions are true and some are false, just as some roses are red and some are white . . . " (*MTCA, EA* 75 and *Papers* 4, 473). The proposition *Socrates's being mortal*, contains Socrates with the property mortality occurring predicatively in it. The proposition *the cat's being on the mat*, is a structure containing the cat, the mat, and a spatial relation 'on' occurring predicatively. Understood in terms of

---

[12] This tracks the definition Russell gave in his 1905 paper "The Theory of Implication." In the *Principles*, Russell held that only propositions can stand in true implication relations, and that all implications (formal or material) are propositions. Accordingly, he had the definition:

x & y =df $(z)(z \supset z .\supset. (x .\supset. y \supset z :\supset: z))$.

That is, "x & y" says that for every proposition, x's implying y's implying it, implies it. In "The Theory of Implication," Russell decided that the antecedent clauses were cumbersome and unnecessary. Accordingly, he allows non-propositions to stand in true implications. Thus, for example, he takes $(x)(y)(x .\supset. y \supset x)$ as a truth of the calculus for the logic of propositions. All entities x and y are such that x implies y's implying x. In *Principles*, he had $(x)(y)(x \supset x :\supset: y \supset y .\supset. (x .\supset. y \supset x))$, which says that all propositions x and y are such that x implies y's implying x.

the modern notion of an obtaining or unobtaining state of affairs, Russell's propositions are fairly well-understood intensional entities. Nonetheless, Russellian propositions have remained creatures of darkness. It is worth pausing for an explanation.

Observe, firstly, that one names a proposition by nominalizing a formula. If we employ nominalizing brackets, we can transform a formula A into a genuine singular term {A}, which on the intended interpretation picks out a proposition. The device of brackets plays the formal role that is played in natural language when we move from the sentence "Socrates is mortal" to the term *"Socrates's being mortal."* "Socrates is mortal" is a formula, and in using it to make an assertion, we are not committed to the existence of a proposition. On the other hand, "{Socrates is mortal}" is a genuine singular term. It is in allowing such nominalizing transformations that we are committed to entities such as propositions. There are, of course, open singular terms as well. Just as "$x + 3$" is an open singular term for a number in a mathematical language, one can nominalize open wffs (containing free variables) to form genuine terms for propositions. Thus, "x is mortal" is a formula, and again its use in no way commits one to propositions. When this formula is nominalized, we get "{x is mortal}" or "x's being mortal." What proposition is picked out by "{x is mortal}" will depend upon the assignment to the variable in the meta-linguistic semantics for the theory – as occurs in the usual a Tarski-style semantic treatment of free variables. One must not be misled into thinking that since there are singular terms such as "{x is mortal}," there must be propositions "containing" variables – what ever that is to mean. Unfortunately, such views abound in interpretations of Russell.

Russellian propositions do not contain variables in an ontological sense. Nonetheless, Russell did hold (for a time) that some propositions are general propositions. The sentence "Every man is mortal" can be nominalized to form a term *"Every man's being mortal,"* and this term names a proposition in Russell's view. But what are the constituents of such general propositions? In *Principles*, Russell held that general propositions contain "denoting concepts." The constituents of the proposition *Every man's being mortal*, are the property *humanity* and the denoting concept *'every man.'* Of course, Russell must also offer an analysis of the constituents of the equivalent but quite different proposition $\{(x)(\text{Man}(x) \supset \text{Mortal}(x))\}$, i.e., the state of affairs, *Every thing's being such that its being a man implies its being mortal.* The expression of this proposition uses variables, and this poses serious questions as to the ontological constituents of the proposition. Though he never quite felt it to be satisfactory, Russell's explanation in *Principles* was that the proposition contains denoting concepts such as '*every entity*' among its constituents.

Another source of trouble for a proper understanding of the substitutional theory is that Russellian propositions have been interpreted as intentional entities. Until 1907, Russell regarded belief (and other intentional mental states) as having propositions as their objects. Continuing the above quote concerning the analogy between propositions, true or false, and red or white roses, we find Russell stating that "...belief is a certain attitude towards propositions, which is called knowledge when they are true, error when they are false." (MTCA, *Papers* 4, p. 473, *EA*, p. 75.) Conceived of as intentional objects, it seems as if propositions *must* be composed of mental entities, not cats, mats, mountains, and the like. Indeed, it is commonly thought that Frege got the better of Russell when he wrote that "...Mont Blanc with its snowfields is not itself a component part of the thought that Mont Blanc is more that 4000 meters high."[13] Heels dug in, Russell replied that "I believe that in spite of all its snowfields Mont Blanc itself is a component part of what is actually asserted in the proposition 'Mont Blanc is more than 4000 meters high.' We do not assert the thought, for this is a private psychological matter: we assert the object of the thought, and this is, to my mind, a certain complex (an objective proposition, one might say) in which Mont Blanc is itself a component part. If we do not admit this, then we get the conclusion that we know nothing at all about Mont Blanc."[14] At first blush, Russell's propositions seem obscure indeed. Russell seems to hold that mountains can be parts of the intentional objects of thought.

The proper explanation of Russell's position, however, is that propositions are intensional entities, *not* intentional entities. The apparent intentionality (aboutness) of Russell's propositions does not

---

[13] Frege, Gottlob. Letter to Russell (13 November 1904) in eds., G. Gabriel, H. Hermes, F. Kambartel, C. Thiel, A. Veraart, and trans. by Hans Kaal, *Gottlob Frege: Philosophical and Mathematical Correspondence* (Chicago: University of Chicago Press, 1980), pp. 160–6.

[14] Ibid., pp. 167–70.

reside in the proposition itself, it resides in the mental state, say, belief, which has the proposition as its object. That is, the intentionality resides in the proposition quā object of the mental state. This should be clear enough for a proposition such as *Mont Blanc's being over 4000 meters high*. This is a state of affairs, and viewing it as such, we can understand how it contains the mountain as its constituent. The difficult Russellian doctrine is not that of a proposition, but rather the direct realism about the objects of mental states.

The fact that propositions are not intentional entities is, however, obscured by Russell's characterizing them as having *aboutness*. In the *Principles*, he sometimes speaks of the proposition *Socrates's being mortal* as being *about* Socrates. And he takes it to be very important to his theory that a general proposition such as, *every whole number's being odd or even*, contains the denoting concept *'every whole number.'* For he exploits this feature to explain how it is that the proposition is *about* every whole number. If the proposition were an infinite conjunction of propositions each containing a number among its constituents, the general proposition could not be a direct object of any finite mind. As Russell put it, denoting concepts provide "the inmost secret of our power to deal with infinity," for denoting concepts point toward entities other than themselves (*POM*, 73). These passages suggest that Russell's propositions are intentional entities.

But Russell's language is far from clear. He clearly says that denoting is not a psychological or mental relationship, but a purely logical relationship (*POM*, 53). Properly speaking then, the proposition *every whole number's being odd or even* is not about anything; it is rather a state of the world. Though it contains a denoting concept, the proposition itself is not intentional. The intentionality resides in the mental state which has the proposition as its object. In any event, in the substitutional theory propositions are clearly intensional entities not intentional entities. The theory of denoting concepts of the 1903 *Principles* does not appear in the substitutional theory which began in December of 1905. By then Russell had abandoned denoting concepts altogether in favor of the theory of "incomplete symbols" he set forth in his October 1905 article "On Denoting."

A Russellian proposition is a state of affairs. This is quite important, for it reveals that, unlike the naïve assumption of attributes in intension (with both an individual and predicable nature) and the naïve assumption of classes, an ontology of (infinitely many) propositions as purely logical entities is not upturned by any known paradox. To be sure, in *Appendix B* of *Principles* Russell set out a paradox that may seem to jeopardize an ontological commitment to propositions. Correlate each class m with a unique proposition,

$$\{x \in m . \supset_x. x\}.$$

Then form the class of all propositions not members of the class to which they are correlated. That is, consider the following class:

$$\hat{y} \, (\exists m)(y = \{x \in m \supset_x x\} .\&. \, y \notin m).$$

Call this class w. It follows that

$$\{x \in w \supset_x x\} \in w .\equiv. \{x \in w \supset_x x\} \notin w.$$

Russell knew that the contradiction could be formulated by means of attributes rather than classes.[15] Correlate each attribute φ with a unique proposition,

$$\{\varphi x \supset_x x\}.$$

Then instead of the class w, we just consider the attribute θ which is such that:

$$(z)(\theta z .\equiv. (\exists \varphi)(z = \{\varphi x \supset_x x\} .\&. \sim \varphi z))$$

We then arrive at the contradiction:

$$\theta \{\theta x \supset_x x\} .\equiv. \sim \theta \{\theta x \supset_x x\}.[16]$$

But these paradoxes assume either the existence of classes or the existence of attributes. Therefore, they do not jeopardize the ontology of propositions.

Neither is the propositional paradox of the *Liar* germane to Russell's efforts to salvage logicism via the substitutional theory. The propositional *Liar* is a contingent paradox and can be expressed in substitution only in an applied form of the theory. To generate the *Liar*, one needs to introduce a new a predicate constant such as "$B^{st}y$" whose intended interpretation would be "s believes y at time t." Then, abbreviating with

$$\wp =df \{(p)(B^{st}p .\supset. \sim p)\},$$

---

[15] See Russell's 24 May 1903 letter to Frege (Frege, 1980, *op. cit.*).
[16] See Gregory Landini, "Russell to Frege 2 May 1904: 'I Believe I have Discovered that Classes are Entirely Superfluous,'" *Russell* 12 (1992), pp. 160–85.

one needs a contingent assumption such as the following:

$$(\exists x)(B^{xt}\wp .\&. (q)(B^{xt}q .\&. q \neq \wp :\supset: \sim q)).$$

A contradiction follows. The ingredients essential for the propositional *Liar* are not present in Russell's *pure* calculus for the logic of propositions. Indeed, there is nothing in the notion of a Russellian proposition that mandates that an applied logic of propositions construe belief as a relation between a mind and a proposition. Russell discussed the propositional *Liar* in his manuscript "On Fundamentals" dated June 1905. By December of that year he wrote "On Substitution," which advanced a thesis according to which the paradoxes (of classes and attributes) plaguing logicism are solved by means of his conception of logic as a theory of propositions. Accordingly, though Russell's manuscripts find him dallying with the propositional *Liar* early in 1905, we must understand that the *Liar* did not shake him of his conviction that logic is the science of propositions. The view that propositions are purely logical entities is not mired by the sort of paradoxes that confront the assumption that every condition comprehends an attribute (with both an individual and predicable nature) or the assumption that every condition determines a class of just those entities satisfying the condition.

It is instructive at this point to recall Quine's *dénouement* of the Russell paradoxes (of classes and attributes). Beginning from the logical truth,

$$(\forall x_1), \ldots (\forall x_n)(F(x_1, \ldots, x_n) \leftrightarrow F(x_1, \ldots, x_n)),$$

it seems possible to arrive at the comprehension principle,

$$(\exists \varphi)(\forall x_1), \ldots, (\forall x_n)(\varphi(x_1, \ldots, x_n) \leftrightarrow F(x_1, \ldots, x_n)),$$

by means of an application of the logically impeccable rule of existential generalization. Yet the comprehension principle yields a contradiction. In Quine's view, the innocent looking existential generalization slights the distinction between a schematic use of the predicate letter F and the use of bindable predicate variables.[17] Now Quine's characterization inappropriately dismisses a Fregean calculus for logic which permits bindable predicate variables in *predicate*

---

[17] Quine, W.V.O. *Set Theory and Its Logic* (Harvard: University Press, 1980), p. 258.

positions only.[18] But Quine shares with Russell the view that any calculus for logic must adopt only one style of variables – viz., individual variables. Accordingly, instead of comprehension such as,

(1) $(\exists\varphi)(\forall x)(\varphi(x) \leftrightarrow A(x))$,

where A is any formula of the formal language not containing φ free, Quine demands individual variables and comprehension such as:

(2) $(\exists z)$ (Attribute(z) .&. $(\forall x)(Rxz \leftrightarrow A(x))$,

where z is not free in A and R a primitive relation. In this way, Quine hopes to reveal the ontological breach between logic and the theory of classes. Clause (2) involves an explicitly new existential postulation. Indeed, the analog of (2), with membership replacing exemplification, and class replacing attribute, is just the naïve postulation of classes:

$(\exists z)$ (class(z) .&. $(\forall x)(x \in z \leftrightarrow A(x))$,

where z is not free in A. Following Quine, the lesson that many modern logicians have drawn from the paradoxes is that no ontological assumption of entities can be part of logic proper – a calculus for logic must be identified with what is now called the "first-order" calculus. Logical truth is then characterized as invariant truth in every domain (including even the empty domain) of every admissible interpretation of the non-logical particles of the language of this calculus.

Russell's account of the source of the paradox of attributes is not unlike Quine's. As Russell put it, φ must not be varied independently from x in φx. That is, it is not always possible to take a wff Au, and imagine it picking out a proposition which has a constituent which can be represented by a bindable variable x and a predicable constituent which can be represented by a bindable variable φ. But unlike Quine, Russell did not conclude that logic must be first-order, or that there is an important cleavage between logic and the theory of classes. Quine missed the possibility of Russell's substitutional theory. The lesson Russell drew is that since a calculus for logic must

---

[18] See Cocchiarella, Nino. "Conceptual Realism versus Quine on Classes and Higher-Order Logic," *Synthese* 90 (1992), pp. 179–201.

adopt only individual variables, one must follow an ontologically eliminivistic and structurally retentive treatment of the languages of classes (and languages allowing bindable predicate variables). Those languages (and their ontologies) are to be supplanted by the substitutional language. Within substitution, the type-stratified language of attributes (and thereby classes) is proxied within a wholly type free calculus for the logic of propositions.

III. THE FORMAL CALCULUS OF SUBSTITUTION

In an unpublished manuscript of 22 December 1905 entitled "On Substitution," Russell set out a formalization of the basic calculus for substitution (1905, 1–13). In the same year, he sent a paper to the *American Journal of Mathematics* entitled "The Theory of Implication." In this paper, Russell set out a quantificational calculus for the logic of propositions. Putting the two together, we can reconstruct the formal calculus for the substitutional theory that Russell had in mind.

The substitutional language takes the following as primitive signs: (,), {, }, ', /, !, and $\supset$. The individual variables of the substitutional language are x, followed by one or more occurrences of "'". Informally we shall use any lowercase letter of the English alphabet. The terms are given inductively as follows. (1) All individual variables are terms; (2) If A is a wff, then {A} is a term; (3) There are no other terms. The atomic wffs are of the form:

$$(x \supset y),$$
$$(p/a;x!q),$$

where x, y, p, a, q, are variables. The wffs are those of the smallest set K containing all atomic wffs and such that $(\alpha \supset \beta)$, $(\alpha/\beta;\mu!\delta)$, and $(x)C$, are in K just when $\alpha, \beta, \delta, \mu$, are any terms and C is any wff in K in which x occurs free.

The expression "$p/a;x!q$" says that q results from substituting x for every occurrence of a in p. The notion of *substitution* is primitive and it is Russell's means of getting at the notion of similarity of structure. Structurally the entity q is exactly like the entity p except that the entity x is *in* q at exactly those positions at which the entity a has *in* p. The notion of one entity being *in* another is the technical notion, originating in *Principles*, of an entity's "occurring as logical subject" (or "occurring as term"). Only entities occurring "as logical subject" may be substituted. Consider the nominalized formula $\{\sim y\}$. This nominalized formula names a proposition, though which one will be determined only in the semantics relative to a given Tarski-style assignment of objects to the free variables in the domain of the interpretation. Suppose we have an assignment to the free variables with y assigned to a proposition $\mathbf{p}$, and z assigned to a proposition $\mathbf{q}$. The proposition structurally identical to $\{\sim\mathbf{p}\}$ except containing $\mathbf{q}$ at every occurrence of $\mathbf{p}$ in $\{\sim\mathbf{p}\}$ is the proposition $\{\sim\mathbf{q}\}$. Accordingly,

$$\{\sim y\}/y;z!\{\sim z\}$$

is true under this assignment to the variables.

In the above case, the replacement of the variable y by the variable z tracks the substitution of the entities the semantics assigns to the variables. But the presence of free variables in substitution calls for careful attention. Russell must take special precautions to assure that the *replacement* of variables in formulas tracks the *substitution* of entities in propositions. Russell was well aware that it would be improper to adopt the following as an axiom schema:

$$\{Ay\}/y;z!\{Az|y\},$$

where z is free for y in A. Consider for instance, the nominalized formula $\{y = w\}$, and an assignment that assigns both y and w to Russell and z to Frege. Then the formula,

$$\{y = w\}/y;z!\{z = w\},$$

which replaces the variable y in $\{y = w\}$ with z, does not properly track the substitution of entities. Under the assignment, $\{z = w\}$ names the proposition {Frege = Russell}, but the proposition resulting from the substitution of Frege for Russell in the proposition {Russell = Russell} is {Frege = Frege}. As Russell expressed it, the problem shows that one must respect the difference between *determination* (i.e., the assignment of a variable) and *substitution* of entities (1906a, *EA* 168, 172). To deal with this problem, Russell has the following axiom schema:

$$(\exists u)(\alpha \ out \ \{Au|v\}) .\supset. (u)(\{A\alpha|v\}/\alpha;u!\{Au|v\}),$$

where α and u are free for v in A. Applying this schema to our above example, we have:

$$(\exists u)(y \ out \ \{u = w\}) \ .\supset. \ (u)(\{y = w\}/y;u!\{u = w\}).$$

Even though the variable y does not occur in the term $\{u = w\}$, the antecedent clause is false under an assignment to the variables that assigns both y and w to the same entity.[19]

The axiom schemata for the calculus for the substitutional logic of propositions may be stated as follows:

S1 $\alpha \ .\supset. \ \beta \supset \alpha$

S2 $\alpha \ .\supset. \ \beta \supset \delta \ :\supset: \ \beta.\supset. \ \alpha \supset \delta$

S3 $\alpha \supset \beta \ :\supset: \ \beta \supset \delta \ .\supset. \ \alpha \supset \delta$

S4 $\alpha \supset \beta \ .\supset. \ \alpha \ :\supset: \ \alpha$

S5 $(u)Au \supset A[\alpha|u]$, where α is free for u in A.

S6 $(u)(\alpha \supset Au) \ .\supset. \ \alpha \supset (u)Au$, where u is not free in α.

S7 $\alpha \ in \ \{A\alpha\}$

S8 $\alpha \ in \ \{A\beta_1, \ldots, \beta_n\} \ :\supset: \ \alpha = \{A\beta_1, \ldots, \beta_n\} \ .\lor. \ \alpha \ in \ \beta_1 \ .\lor., \ldots,.\lor.$ $\alpha \ in \ \beta_n$, where A is any wff all of whose distinct free terms are $\beta_1, \ldots, \beta_n$.

S9 $(x, y)(x \ in \ y \ .\&. \ y \ in \ x \ :\supset: \ x = y)$

S10 $(x, y, z)(x \ in \ y \ .\&. \ y \ in \ z \ :\supset: \ x \ in \ z)$

S11 $(p, a)(q)(x, y)(p/a;x!q \ .\&. \ p/a;y!q \ .\&. \ a \ in \ p \ :\supset: \ x = y)$

S12 $(p, a)(z)(q)(p/a;z!q \ .\&. \ a \ in \ p \ .\&. \ a \neq p \ :\supset: \ z \ in \ q \ .\&. \ z \neq q)$

S13 $(x, y)(x/x;y!y)$

S14 $(x, y)(x/y;y!x)$

S15 $(p, a)(x)(\exists q)(p/a;x!q \ .\&. \ (r)(p/a;x!r \ :\supset: \ q = r))$

S16 $(p)(\exists q)(q \ ex \ p)$

S17 $(\exists u)(\alpha \ out \ \{Au|v\}) \ .\supset. \ (u)(\{A\alpha|v\}/\alpha;u!\{Au|v\})$, where α and u are free for v in A.

S18 $(\exists u_1, \ldots, u_n)(\alpha \ out \ \{Au_1|v_1, \ldots, u_n|v_n\} \ :\&: \ \alpha \ \neq \{Au_1|v_1, \ldots, u_n|v_n\} \ .\&. \ \alpha \neq \beta_1.\&., \ldots, .\&. \ \alpha \neq \beta_n).:\supset:.$ $(x)(\exists u_1, \ldots, u_n)(\{A\sigma_1|v_1, \ldots, \sigma_n|v_n\}/\alpha;x!\{Au_1|v_1, \ldots, u_n|v_n\} :\&: \sigma_1/\alpha;x!u_1 \ .\&., \ldots, .\&. \ \sigma_n/\alpha;x!u_n)$, where each u_i and σ_i, $1 \leq i \leq N$, are free for their respective v_i in A, and $\beta_1, \ldots, \beta_n$ are all the terms occurring free in A.

S19 $\{(u)Au\} = \{(v)Av|u\}$, where v is free for u in A.

S20 $\{(u)Au\} = \{(u)Bu\} \ .\supset. \ (u)(\{Au\} = \{Bu\})$

S21 $\{(u)Au\} \neq \{\alpha \supset \beta\}$

---

[19] Russell's distinction between *determination* and *substitution* is evidence that he did not "ontologize" variables in the substitutional theory.

S22 α *in* $\{(u)Au\}$.&. $\alpha \neq \{(u)Au\}$:⊃: $(u)(\alpha$ *in* $\{Au\})$, where α is not the individual variable u, and u is not free in α.

S23 $\{\alpha \supset \beta\} \neq \supset$.&. $\{(u)Au\} \neq \supset$

The inference rules of the system are as follows:
Modus Ponens:

> From A and $\{A\} \supset \{B\}$, infer B.

Universal Generalization:

> From A infer $(u)A$,
>
> where u is an individual variable free in A.

Replacement of Defined Signs:

> Definiens and definiendum may replace one another in any context.

The following definitions are then introduced:

> df($\sim$) $\sim\alpha$ =df $(x)(\alpha \supset x)$
>
> df($\exists$) $(\exists x)A$ =df $\sim(x) \sim A$
>
> df(v) α v β =df $\sim\alpha \supset \beta$
>
> df(&) α & β =df $\sim(\alpha \supset \sim\beta)$
>
> df(=) $\alpha = \beta$ =df $(p)(a)(q)(r)(p/a;\alpha!q$.&. $p/a;\beta!r$:⊃: $q \supset r)$
>
> df(E) $(\exists x_1, \ldots, x_n)A$ =df $(\exists x_1), \ldots, (\exists x_n)A$
>
> df(A) $(x_1, \ldots, x_n)A$ =df $(x_1), \ldots, (x_n)A$
>
> df(out) α *out* β =df $(u)(\beta/\alpha;u!\beta)$.
>
> df(in) α *in* β =df $\sim (\alpha$ *out* $\beta)$.
>
> df(ind) α *ind* β =df α *out* β .&. β *out* α.
>
> df(ex) α *ex* β =df $\sim(\exists u)(u$ *in* α .&. u *in* $\beta)$.

With substitution as a primitive notion, Russell defines what it is for one entity to be *out* (not a constituent) of another. An entity a is *out* of b if and only if every substitution of an entity u for a *in* b does not alter b. Russell then defines the notion of an entity being *in* (a constituent of) another. On this definition, there is a trivial sense in which every entity is *in* itself. But given Russell axioms (S9) and (S10), it follows that no entity is *in* itself in a non-trivial sense. That is, no entity a is *in* an another entity, which is, in turn, *in* a. Russell also has df(ind), the definition of an entity being *independent* of another. An entity a is independent of b if and only if neither is a constituent of the other. More important is df(ex), Russell's definition of an entity's *excluding* another. An entity *a* excludes *b* if and only if no entity is a constituent of both *a* and *b*. This definition is important to axiom (S16), which is needed so that the antecedent clause of (S17) can be detached when needed. For if *a* excludes *b*, then since *a in a*, it follows that *a* is *out* of *b*. It also plays a role in Russell's definition of multiple or "simultaneous" substitution. (This is discussed anon.) This reconstructs (with a bit of updating)[20] the system for the substitutional calculus of logic that Russell set out late in 1905.

IV. TYPE-THEORY AS FORMAL GRAMMAR

To understand how the substitutional language proxies a type-stratified second-order calculus with nominalized predicates, let us begin with a formal characterization of such a calculus. The primitive symbols of the language are (,), o, ʹ, ∀, ¬, and →. A *type symbol* is any expression that satisfies the following recursive definition:

1) "o" is a type symbol.
2) If $t_1, \ldots, t_n$ are all type symbols, then the expression $(t_1, \ldots, t_n)$ is also a type symbol.
3) These are the only type symbols.

The variables are small letters x with any type symbol superscript and followed by any number of occurrences of the sign " ʹ ". Informally, we shall use x^t, y^t, z^t, where t is a type symbol. When the type symbol t is not "o" we shall use Greek letters φ^t, θ^t, ψ^t, and also these followed by one or more occurrences of " ʹ " for convenience. The terms of the language are just the variables; the individual variables are those variables with type index "o", and the predicate variables are just the variables whose type index is not "o". The atomic formulae of the language have the following form:

$$x^{(t_1, \ldots, t_n)}(y^{t_1}, \ldots, y^{t_n}).$$

The wffs of the language are those of the smallest set containing all atomic wffs and such that $(A \to B)$, $(\sim A)$, and $(\forall x^t)C$ are in K wherever

---

[20] The axiom schemata S19, S20 and S21 are adapted from Church. See Alonzo Church, "Russell's Theory of the Identity of Propositions," *Philosophia Naturalis* 21, (1984), pp. 513–22.

A, B, and C are wffs in K and x^t is a variable free in C. The axiom schemata for the type theory of attributes are then as follows.

A1 $A \rightarrow (B \rightarrow A)$

A2 $(A \rightarrow (B \rightarrow C)) \rightarrow ((A \rightarrow B) \rightarrow (A \rightarrow C))$

A3 $(\sim B \rightarrow \sim A) \rightarrow (A \rightarrow B)$

A4 $(\forall x^t)(A \rightarrow B) \rightarrow (A \rightarrow (\forall x^t)B)$,

    where x^t is not free in A.

A5 $(\forall x^t)A \rightarrow A[y^t|x^t]$,

    where y^t is free for x^t in A.

A6 $(\exists \varphi^{(t_1,\ldots,t_n)})(\forall x^{t_1}, \ldots, x^{t_n})(\varphi^{(t_1,\ldots,t_n)}(x^{t_1}, \ldots, x^{t_n}) .\leftrightarrow. A)$,

    where $\varphi^{(t_1,\ldots,t_n)}$ does not occur free in A.

Modus Ponens: From A and $A \rightarrow B$, infer B.
Universal Generalization: From A infer $(u^t)A$, where u^t is free in A.
Replacement of Defined Signs: Definiens and definiendum may replace one another.
Definitions then include:

$(\exists x^t)A =_{df} \neg(\forall x^t)\neg A$

$x^t = y^t =_{df} (\forall \varphi^{t+1})(\varphi^{t+1}(x^t) .\leftrightarrow. \varphi^{t+1}(y^t))$

$A \wedge B =_{df} \neg(A \rightarrow \neg B)$

$A \vee B =_{df} \neg A \rightarrow B$.

This completes the system.

Now to understand how the substitutional theory proxies a type-stratified theory of attributes, let us simply focus on the matter of comprehension principles. From (S17) and (S16) the following theorem schema is readily forthcoming:

$(CP_{sub})^1$ $(\exists p, a)(a \ in \ p .\&. (z)(p/a;z!\{A\})$,

where p and a are not free in the wff A. From this, we get the following comprehension theorem schema:

$(CP)^1$ $(\exists p, a)(z)(p/a;z .\equiv. \{A\})$,

where p and a are not free in the wff A. The expression "$p/a;z$" is but a notational convenience. It is a definite description of an entity q just like p except for containing z wherever p contains a. Russell puts (1905, p. 4):

$$p/a_;z =df (\iota q)(p/a_;z!q).$$

Russell calls α/β of a definite description $(\iota\delta)(\alpha/\beta_;\mu!\delta)$ its "matrix," and he speaks of the α (and albeit improper, the proposition it names) as the "prototype" of the matrix. Russell speaks of the matrix as an "incomplete symbol," which has no meaning in isolation. But the incomplete symbols to focus upon are the definite descriptions of the form $(\iota\delta)(\alpha/\beta_;\mu!\delta)$. The theory of definite descriptions is straightforwardly applied to these new definite descriptions of propositions. Where B(v) is a formula, we have:

$$[(\iota q)(p/a_;z!q)][B((\iota q)(p/a_;z!q)|v)] =df (\exists q)((r)(p/a_;z!r .\equiv. r = q) \& B(q|v)).$$

All the same scope distinctions of definite descriptions apply, including the conventions on omission of scope marker when narrowest possible scope is intended. It should be recalled that definite descriptions are not genuine terms of Russell's formal language. Accordingly, one cannot apply definitions which are framed in terms of genuine singular terms to definite descriptions. For example, in defining "&" Russell has

$$\alpha \& \beta =df \sim(\alpha \supset \sim\beta).$$

This cannot be applied to

$$p/a_;b \& s,$$

because α and β are expressions for genuine singular terms of the language. One must first eliminate the definite description, to yield

$$(\exists q)((r)(p/a_;b!r .\equiv. r = q) .\&. q \& s).$$

Then since q and s are variables one arrives at,

$$(\exists q)((r)(p/a_;b!r .\equiv. r = q) .\&. \sim(q \supset \sim s)),$$

by applying df(&) to the clause "$q \& s$."

Russell goes on to define what he calls "simultaneous dual substitutions," "simultaneous triple substitutions," and so on. These are just carefully crafted successions of single substitutions. The expression "$p/a,b_;x,y!q$" for instance, is for a dual substitution and says that q results from substituting x for a at every occurrence of a in p and simultaneously substituting y for b at every occurrence of b in p. One must take care in the definition so that q is the entity intended –

since, for example, the substitution of x for a may remove b from p. Russell's definitions are complicated and we shall avoid discussion of them here for there is a simpler approach. There is no need to define "simultaneous substitutions." We can simply put:

df(dual) $p/a,b;x,y!q$ =df $(\exists e, h, t)(p/a;e!h .\&. h/b;y!t .\&. t/e;x!q)$.

For any formula Auv, we can employ (S16) to find appropriate entities p, a, and b, so that

$(x, y)(p/a,b;x,y!$ {$Ax|v, y|v$}).

Accordingly, we arrive at the following theorem schema for dual substitutions:

$(CP_{sub})^2$ $(\exists p, a, b)(a \text{ in } p .\&. b \text{ in } p .\&. (x, y)(p/a,b;x,y .\equiv. \{A\}))$,

where p, a, b, do not occur free in A. This, in turn, yields the comprehension theorem schema:

$(CP)^2$ $(\exists p, a, b)(x, y)(p/a,b;x,y .\equiv. \{A\})$,

where p and a and b are not free in A. Here the expression "$p/a,b;x,y$" is a convenient way of writing the definite description, "$(\iota q)(p/a,b;x,y!q)$." In a similar way, we can go on to triple substitutions and the comprehension theorem schema:

$(CP)^3$ $(\exists j, k, u, v)(q, p, a)(j/k,u,v;q,p,a .\equiv. \{A\})$,

where j and k and u and v, are not free in the wff A. The process continues for any finite number of substitutions.

The comprehension theorem schemata above replace instances of the comprehension axiom schema (A6) of simple second-order type theory. Consider the following pairs:

#1 $(\exists\varphi^{(o)})(\forall x^o)(\varphi^{(o)}(x^o) .\leftrightarrow. x^o = x^o)$

#1s $(\exists p, a)(x)(p/a;x .\equiv. x = x)$

#2 $(\exists\varphi^{((o))})(\forall\psi^{(o)})(\varphi^{((o))}(\psi^{(o)}) .\leftrightarrow. (\forall x^o)\neg\psi^{(o)}(x^o))$

#2s $(\exists q, p, a)(r, c)(q/p,a;r,c .\equiv. (x) \sim (r/c;x))$

#3 $(\exists\varphi^{(o,o)})(\forall x^o)(\forall y^o)(\varphi^{(o,o)}(x^o, y^o) .\leftrightarrow. x^o = y^o)$

#3s $(\exists q, p, a)(r, c)(q/p,a;r,c .\equiv. r = c)$

The first of the pairs are instances of the comprehension axiom schema A6; the second are their translations into the language of the substitutional theory. The notion of type has been built into the logical grammar of substitution. It will be noted that #2s and #3s both employ dual substitutions, yet #2s replaces a type $((o))$ attribute (an attribute of attributes of individuals) and #3s replaces a type (o,o) relation between individuals. This shows that the notion of type does not correspond simply to the number of substitutions employed. The structure is central as well. But in every case, the expression "$\varphi(\varphi)$" cannot be expressed. It would require a sequence such as "$p/a;p/a!q$" and this, as well as its negation, is ungrammatical.

The substitutional theory is entirely type-free. It countenances no types of entities, and there is only one style of variables – individual variables. (Recall that every lowercase letter of the English alphabet is used as an individual variable for convenience. There are no special "propositional" variables in the theory.) At the same time, it should be clear enough from the above that any instance of the comprehension schema A6 in the primitive notation of second-order simple type-theory is translatable into the language of substitution. Indeed, any formula in primitive notation of simple type-theory can be translated into the language of substitution. Instances of the axiom schemata of the simple type theory become theorem schemata or instances of axiom schemata of substitution. Types become part of logical grammar.

V. CLASSES IN SUBSTITUTION

To introduce class symbols in the language of substitution, Russell originally thought of replacing a class symbol $\hat{y}^o(Ay^o)$ by using a matrix $\{Aa\}/a$. The idea was that

$$z \in \hat{y}^o(Ay^o)$$

would be supplanted by

$$z \in \{Aa\}/a$$

with the following supporting definition,

$$x \in p/a =\text{df} (\exists q)(p/a;x!q .\&. q).[21]$$

---

[21] In the manuscript "On Substitution" of September 1906, Russell put (1906b p. 117):
$x \in p/a =\text{df} p/a;x$.
This is a less convenient approach, however. Since $z^o\epsilon\hat{y}^o(Ay^o)$ is a formula of the ordinary theory of classes, substitution affords a better analog when $x \in \{Aa\}/a$ is construed as a formula.

Class abstraction for the lowest type,

$$z^o \in \hat{y}^o(Ay^o) \leftrightarrow Az^o$$

would then be supplanted by

$$z \in \{Aa\}/a .\equiv. Az.$$

In the next higher type, we have:

$$p/a \in s/t, w =\text{df} \; (\exists q)(s/t,w;p,a!q .\&. q).$$

Then class abstraction,

$$\hat{y}^o(Ay^o) \in \hat{y}^{(o)}(By^{(o)}) \leftrightarrow B(\hat{y}^o(Ay^o))$$

is supplanted by:

$$\{Aa\}/a \in \{B(t, w)\}/t, w .\equiv. B(\{Aa\}, a).$$

The process continues as one ascends types. On this approach, the extensionality of classes is treated by introducing definitions such as:

$$\text{Cls}^2(s, t, w) =\text{df} \, (p, a)(r, c)((x)(p/a;x .\equiv. r/c;x) :\supset: s/t,w;p,a .\equiv. s/t,w;r,c)$$
$$\text{Cls}^3(j, k, u, v) =\text{df} \, (p, a, b)(r, c, e)((x, y)(p/a,b;x, y .\equiv. r/c,e;x,y) :\supset:$$
$$j/k, u, v; p, a, b .\equiv. j/k, u, v;r, c, e)$$

To illustrate, the sentence,

$$\Lambda^{(o)} \in o^{((o))}$$

which says (for lowest type) that the empty class is in zero, is expressed by

$$\{a \neq a\}/a \in \{(x) \sim (r/c;x)\}/r, c.$$

Then to proxy,

$$(\exists z^{((o))})(\Lambda^{(o)} \in z^{((o))}),$$

which says (for lowest type) that the empty class is in some class, one writes:

$$(\exists s, t, w)(\mathrm{Cls}^2(s, t, w) .\&. \{a \neq a\}/a \in s/t, w).$$

In short, extensionality is captured by quantifying over those attributes (via substitution) that are extensional.

Russell came to rework this early approach to the development of class symbols in substitution, however. Consider attempting to recover:

$$(\forall z^{\circ})(z^{\circ} \in \hat{y}^{\circ}(y^{\circ} = z^{\circ})).$$

Russell's original approach was to put:

$$(z)(z \in \{a = z\}/a).$$

But this cannot work. Instantiating the universal quantifier to the entity $\{\sim a\}$ yields a falsehood. The outcome of the substitution would be,

$$\{\sim a\} = \{\sim\{\sim a\}\}.$$

The source of the problem is that in the class expression, $\hat{y}^{\circ}(Ay^{\circ})$, the variable "$y^{\circ}$" is bound. This feature must be captured in the substitutional proxy.

On Russell's revised view, the class symbol $\hat{y}^{\circ}(Ay^{\circ})$ is not replaced by use of a matrix $\{Aa\}/a$. Rather, it is replaced by use of $\iota(p/a)[p/a \approx_x Ax]$. The new expression is supported by definitions such as:

$$p/a \approx_x Ax =\text{df} \ (x)(p/a;x \equiv Ax)$$
$$z \in \iota(p/a)[p/a \approx_x Ax] =\text{df} \ (\exists p, a)(p/a;x \equiv_x Ax .\&. z \in p/a))$$
$$x \in p/a =\text{df} \ (\exists q)(p/a;x!q .\&. q).$$
$$\iota(p/a)[p/a \approx_x Ax] = \iota(p/a)[p/a \approx_x Bx] =\text{df}$$
$$\quad (\exists p, a)(p/a \approx_x Ax .\&. (\exists l, m)(l/m \approx_x Bx .\&. p/a = l/m))$$
$$p/a = l/m =\text{df} \ p = l .\&. a = m.$$

In this way, the use of bound variables in class abstract symbols is recovered. Returning to the problem Russell encountered in attempting to recover the theorem, $(\forall z^o)(z^o \epsilon \hat{y}^o(y^o = z^o))$. Russell can now put:

$$(z)(z \epsilon \iota(p/a)[p/a .\approx_x x = z]).$$

The difficulty is avoided. Similarly, in the next type, a class $\hat{y}^{(o)}(By^{(o)})$ of type $((o))$ is recovered by use of:

$$\iota(s/t, w)[s/t, w .\approx_{r,c}. B(r, c)].$$

The use of the new class symbols is supported by new definitions governing each context of their use. For instance, there are the following:

$$\iota(p/a)[p/a \approx_x Ax] \epsilon \iota(s/t, w)[s/t, w \approx_{r,c} B(r, c)] =df$$
$$(\exists s, t, w)(s/t, w \approx_{r,c} B(r, c) .\&. (\exists p, a)(p/a \approx_x Ax .\&. p/a \epsilon s/t, w))$$
$$s/t, w \approx_{r,c} B(r, c) =df (r, c)((\exists l, m)(l/m;x \equiv_x r/c; x .\&. l/m \epsilon s/t, w) \equiv$$
$$(\exists l, m)(l/m;x \equiv_x r/c;x .\&. B(l, m))).$$
$$\iota(s/t, w)[s/t, w \approx_{r,c} A(r, c)] = \iota(s/t, w)[s/t, w \approx_{r,c} B(r, c)] =df (\exists s/t, w)$$
$$(s/t, w \approx_{r,c} A(r, c) .\&. (\exists h, d, e)(h/d, e \approx_{r,c} B(r, c) .\&. s/t, w = h/d, e))$$
$$s/t, w = h/d, e =df s = h .\&. t = d .\&. w = e.$$

To illustrate, let us introduce the following abbreviations:

$$\Lambda(x) =df x \neq x$$
$$o(r, c) =df (z) \sim (z \epsilon \iota(l/m)[l/m;x \equiv_x r/c;x]).$$

Russell can now recover the theorem, $\Lambda^{(o)} \epsilon o^{((o))}$ with:

$$\iota(p/a)[p/a \approx_x \Lambda(x)] \epsilon \iota(s/t, w)[s/t, w \approx_{r,c} o(r, c)].$$

In a similar way, the usual Frege/Russell cardinals can be written and the theorem of mathematical induction proved. Indeed, the entire simple type-theory of classes can be captured in the substitutional system. To form the theorem schema of class abstraction

$$z^o \epsilon \hat{y}^o(Ay^o) \leftrightarrow Az^o$$

the substitutional theory has

$$z \epsilon \iota(p/a)[p/a \approx_x Ax] .\equiv. Az.$$

In the next type, class abstraction,

$$\hat{y}^{o}(Ay^{o}) \in \hat{y}^{(o)}(By^{(o)}) \leftrightarrow B(\hat{y}^{o}(Ay^{o}))$$

is replaced by

$$\iota(p/a)[p/a \approx_x Ax] \in \iota(s/t, w)[s/t, w \approx_{r,c} B(r, c)] .\equiv.$$
$$(\exists p, a)(p/a \approx_x Ax .\&. B(p, a)).$$

Working through the definitions, it is clear that class abstraction schemata for each type are forthcoming as theorem schemata. To take a simple illustration, the substitutional proxy of

$$\Lambda^{(o)} \in o^{((o))} \equiv (\forall z^{o}) \neg (z^{o} \in \Lambda^{(o)}),$$

is the following:

$$\iota(p/a)[p/a \approx_x \Lambda x] \in \iota(s/t, w)[s/t, w \approx_{r,c} o(r, c)] .\equiv.$$
$$(\exists p, a)(p/a \approx_x \Lambda x .\&. (z) \sim (z \in \iota(l/m)[l/m; x \equiv_x p/a; x])).$$

The theorem relies upon the existence theorems afforded by (CP)^{1} and (CP)^{2}.

It will be recalled that in the first edition of *Principia Mathematica*, Whitehead and Russell offered a contextual definition of class symbols. *Principia* advanced a *ramified* type theory, where predicate variables come with suppressed order/type indices. The contextual definitions, however, can be adapted to simple type theory – i.e., they can be reformulated within the type-regimented second-order language with nominalized predicates set out above. We saw that any statement in the *primitive notation* of simple type theory of attributes has a translation into the language of substitution. It is not possible, however, to introduce class symbols into the language of substitution in a way that exactly parallels their introduction into *Principia*. For the lowest type, one might imagine that since $\iota(p/a)[p/a; x \equiv_y Ay]$ is analogous to a class expression $\hat{y}^{o}(Ay^{o})$, we can parallel *20.01 and *20.02 with

$$[\iota(p/a)[p/a \approx_x Ax]][B(\iota(p/a)[p/a \approx_x Ax])] =df (\exists p, a)(p/a \approx_x Ax .\&. B(p/a))$$
$$x \in p/a =df (\exists q)(p/a; x!q .\&. q).$$

For example, consider

$$z \in \iota(p/a)[p/a \approx_x Ax].$$

By applying the contextual definition, one gets,

$(\exists p, a)(p/a \approx_x Ax\ .\&.\ z \in p/a)$.

Then finally one arrives at:

$(\exists p, a)(p/a \approx_x Ax\ .\&.\ (\exists q)(p/a;z!q\ .\&.\ q))$.

But the contextual definition is ill-formed. In the expression $B(\iota(p/a)[p/a \approx_x Ax])$ the context B appears to be a one-placed context. But if $B(p/a)$ is to be allowed, then the context B is not a one-placed context. It abbreviates the two-placed context $B(p,a)$. There is no singular term "p/a". This situation is quite unlike that of *Principia*, where predicate variables may occur in subject as well as predicate positions.

It was just this sort of notational inconvenience to which White-head strongly objected. Delighted by Russell's progress on the substitutional theory, Whitehead nonetheless cautioned him of the practical needs of class notation. On 30 April 1905 he wrote that Russell's extreme rigor must be tempered by practical considerations: "... our object is to systematize the reasoning concerning classes, even when it is a primitive which might be avoided."[22] In this respect, the type-stratified language of predicate variables (of simple type theory) is preferable to the substitutional language, though a translation from this language into substitution is always possible (MLT *LK*, p. 77). Inconvenience aside, however, the substitutional notation does allow for a proxy for the simple type-theory of classes. Indeed, instead of the language of the simple type theory of attributes, one may simply work within a language for the simple type-theory of classes, equipped with a manual for translation into the type-free language of substitution.

VI. THE DEMISE OF THE SUBSTITUTIONAL THEORY

Alas, the substitutional theory as sketched above is inconsistent. By April of 1906, Russell discovered a new paradox distinct from the propositional *liar*, the propositional paradox of Appendix B of

[22] See the manuscript "Miscellaneous notes on PM," #230.031230f1 in the Russell Archives, McMaster University, Hamilton, Ontario.

Principles, and distinct from his paradoxes of classes and attributes.[23] Its existence as a new paradox and its unique significance for the historical development of Russell's ramified type-theory were largely unknown until I unearthed it from the archival manuscripts.[24] I called it Russell's "p_0/a_0 paradox". Abbreviate by putting:

$$p_0 =\text{df} \, (p, a, r)(a_0 = \{p/a;b!q\} \,.\&.\, p/a;a_0!r :\supset: \sim r)).$$

Then observe that:

$$p_0/a_0; \{p_0/a_0;b!q\}!(p, a, r)(\{p_0/a_0;b!q\} = \{p/a;b!q\} \,.\&.\,$$
$$p/a; \{p_0/a_0;b!q\}!r :\supset: \sim r)\}$$

But given that,

$$(p, a)(r, c)(b, q)(\{p/a;b!q\} = \{r/c;b!q\} :\supset: p = r \,.\&.\, a = c),$$

one arrives at the following contradiction:

$$(p, a, r)(\{p_0/a_0;b!q\} = \{p/a;b!q\} \,.\&.\, p/a; \{p_0/a_0;b!q\}!r :\supset: \sim r) \equiv$$
$$\sim(p, a, r)(\{p_0/a_0;b!q\} = \{p/a;b!q\} \,.\&.\, p/a; \{p_0/a_0;b!q\}!r :\supset: \sim r).$$

The problematic axiom schema is (S17). Coupled with (S16) one arrives at the theorem schema $(\text{CP}_{sub})^1$. Russell's formulation is derived from the following instance:

$$(\exists t, w)(x)(t/w;x!(p, a, r)(x = \{p/a;b!q\} \,.\&.\, p/a;x!r :\supset: \sim r)).$$

But Russell was aware that there are even simpler variants of the paradox. The following is also an instance of $(\text{CP}_{sub})^1$:

$$(\exists t, w)(x)(t/w;x!(p, a, r)(x = \{p \supset a\} \,.\&.\, p/a;x!r :\supset: \sim r)).$$

By existential instantiation we arrive at:

$$(x)(t/w;x!(p, a, r)(x = \{p \supset a\} \,.\&.\, p/a;x!r :\supset: \sim r)$$

[23] The paradox is the central theme of a number of Russell's worknotes for 1906. See pp. 7, 57, 71 of "On Substitution" (April/May 1906), "Logic in Which Propositions are Not Entities," (p. 15f), and "The Paradox of the Liar," (p. 72ff), all catalogued in the Russell Archives (McMaster University, Hamilton, Ontario, Canada).

[24] Cocchiarella showed the way, proclaiming that Russell had blundered in thinking that substitution would be able to capture the Cantorian fact that there must be more classes of propositions than propositions. See Nino Cocchiarella, "The Development of the Theory of Logical Types and the Notion of a Logical Subject in Russell's Early Philosophy" *Synthese* 45 (1980), pp. 71–115.

Then by universal instantiation we have:

$$t/w_i \{t \supset w\}!(p, a, r)(\{t \supset w\} = \{p \supset a\} \;.\&.\; p/a_i \{t \supset w\}!r :\supset: \sim r)$$

Since it is provable in substitution that:

$$(p, a)(r, c)(\{p \supset a\} = \{r \supset c\} :\supset: p = r \;.\&.\; a = c).$$

We shall be able to deduce the following contradiction:

$$(p, a, r)(\{t \supset w\} = \{p \supset a\} \;.\&.\; p/a_i \{t \supset w\}!r :\supset: \sim r)$$
$$\equiv \sim (p, a, r)(\{t \supset w\} = \{p \supset a\} \;.\&.\; p/a_i \{t \supset w\}!r :\supset: \sim r).$$

The flaw in the substitutional system lies with schema (S17).

But what precisely is wrong with (S17)? Russell's assessment in May of 1906 was that his assumption of general propositions was the source of the contradiction. The abandonment of denoting concepts in 1905 left Russell with no theory of the constituents of general propositions. This had been something of an embarrassment, but now Russell was chagrined. It seemed to him high time to face the problem squarely, and in his article "On 'Insolubilia' and Their Solution by Symbolic Logic," he abandoned his ontological commitment to general propositions entirely.

The basic quantification theory for the calculus of the logic of propositions has to be modified to accommodate the abandonment of general propositions. Unlike the original theory, it is no longer possible to nominalize a wff $(x)A$, to form a term of the form $\{(x)A\}$. Only quantifier-free formulas can be nominalized. Russell's sign "$\supset$," is a dyadic predicate constant that must be flanked by terms, so an expression such as,

$$\{(x)(x = x)\} \supset \{x = x\}$$

is no longer well formed. This means as well that

$$\{(x)(x = x)\} \;.\supset.\; q \supset \{(x)(x = x)\}$$

is not a proper instance of axiom schema (S1). Russell therefore reformulates quantification theory by defining subordinate occurrences of quantified formulas in terms of an equivalent in prenex normal form.[25] Thus, for example,

$$(z)(z = z) \supset \{x = x\} = \text{df } (\exists z)(\{z \supset z\} \supset \{x = x\}).$$

$$(x)(x = x) .\supset. q \supset (x)(x = x) = \text{df } (x)(\exists z)(\{z = z\} .\supset. q \supset \{x = x\}).$$

The full revision of quantification theory is not set out in "On Insolubilia," but it does not impose insurmountable problems.

The basic system Russell had in mind for "On Insolubilia" is the following. The primitive signs for the substitutional language are: (,), $\prime$, {, }, /, !, $\supset$, $\mathbf{f}$, and $\exists$. The individual variables of the substitutional language are x, followed by one or more occurrences of $"\prime"$. Informally, we shall use any lowercase letter of the English alphabet. It is not essential to adopt $\mathbf{f}$ as a primitive sign. One could offer the definition,

$$\mathbf{f} = \text{df } \supset /\supset;\supset! \{\supset\supset\supset\}.$$

Alternatively, one could take the tilde sign as a primitive, introducing appropriate supporting axiom schemata.[26] The terms are given inductively as follows. (1) All individual variables are terms; (2) If A is a quantifier-free wff, then {A} is a term; (4) There are no other terms. The atomic wffs are: $\mathbf{f}$, $(x \supset y)$, and $(p/a; x!q)$, where x, y, p, a, and q are variables. The wffs are those of the smallest set K containing all atomic wff and such that $(\alpha \supset \beta)$, $(\alpha/\beta;\mu!\delta)$, $(x)C$ and $(\exists x)C$ are in K just when α, β, δ, μ, are any terms, and C is any wff in prenex-normal form in K in which x occurs free. The axiom schemata for the calculus as follows:

S1 $\alpha .\supset. \beta \supset \alpha$

S2 $\alpha .\supset. \beta \supset \delta :\supset: \alpha \supset \beta .\supset. \alpha \supset \delta$

S3 $\sim\sim\alpha \supset \alpha$

S4 $\alpha = \beta .\supset. A[\alpha|u] \supset A[\beta|u]$, where α, β are free for u in A.

S5 $A[\alpha|u] \supset (\exists u)Au$, where α is free for u in A.

S6 $A[\alpha|u] \vee A[\beta|u] .\supset. (\exists u)Au$, where α, β are free for u in A.

---

[25] In *Principia Mathematica*'s *9, we get a glimpse of how the calculus would be formulated. *Principia*, however, regards its logical particles as *statement* connectives because it explicitly abandons the ontology of propositions.

[26] This was Russell's preference. But in an ontology of propositions it seems appropriate to avoid taking tilde as a primitive.

S7 α *in* $\{A\alpha\}$, where A is quantifier-free

S8 α *in* $\{A\beta_1, \ldots, \beta_n\}$ $:\supset:$ $\alpha = \{A\beta_1, \ldots, \beta_n\}.\vee. \alpha$ *in* $\beta_1.\vee.,\ldots,.\vee. \alpha$ *in* β_n,

 where A is any quantifier-free wff all of whose distinct free terms

 are $\beta_1, \ldots, \beta_n$.

S9 $(x, y)(x$ *in* y .&. y *in* $x :\supset: x = y)$

S10 $(x, y, z)(x$ *in* y .&. y *in* $z :\supset: x$ *in* $z)$

S11 $(p, a)(q)(x, y)(p/a;x!q$.&. $p/a;y!q$.&. a *in* $p :\supset: x = y)$

S12 $(p, a)(z)(q)(p/a;z!q$.&. a *in* p .&. $a \neq p :\supset: z$ *in* q .&. $z \neq q)$

S13 $(x, y)(x/x;y!y)$

S14 $(x, y)(x/y;y!x)$

S15 $(p, a)(x)(\exists q)(p/a;x!q$.&. $(r)(p/a;x!r :\supset: q = r))$

S16 $(p)(\exists q)(q$ *ex* $p)$

S17 $(\exists u)(\alpha$ *out* $\{Au|v\})$.$\supset$. $(u)(\{A\alpha v\}/\alpha;u!\{Au|v\})$,

 where α and u are free for v in A, and A is quantifier-free.

S18 $(\exists u_1, \ldots, u_n)(\alpha$ *out* $\{Au_1|v_1, \ldots, u_n|v_n\})$ $:\&: \alpha \neq \{Au_1|v_1, \ldots, u_n|v_n\}$

 .&. $\alpha \neq \beta_1$.&., $\ldots$, .&. $\alpha \neq \beta_n$.$:\supset:$.

 $(x)(\exists u_1, \ldots, u_n)(\{A\sigma_1|v_1, \ldots, \sigma_n|v_n\}/\alpha; x!\{Au_1|v_1, \ldots, u_n|v_n\}$ $:\&:$

 $\sigma_1/\alpha;x!u_1$.&., $\ldots$, .&. $\sigma_n/\alpha;x!u_n)$,

 where each u_i and $\sigma_i, 1 \leq i \leq N$, are free for their respective v_i in A,

 and $\beta_1, \ldots, \beta_n$ are all the terms occurring free in A, and A is

 quantifier-free.

The inference rules of the system are as follows:

Modus Ponens$_1$:

 From A and $\{A\} \supset \{B\}$, infer B.

Modus Ponens$_2$

 From A and $A \supset B$, infer B.

Universal Generalization

 From A infer $(u)A$,

 where u is an individual variable free in A.

Switch

 From $B[(u)(\exists v)A]$, infer $B[(\exists v)(u)A]$,

 where all free occurrences of the variable u in A are on one side

 of a logical particle and all free occurrences of the variable v in A

 are on the other.

Replacement of Defined Signs:
Definiens and definiendum may replace one another in any context.

The following definitions are then introduced:

df(out) α *out* β =df $(u)(\beta/\alpha;u!\beta)$.

df(in) α *in* β =df $\sim(\alpha$ *out* $\beta)$.

df(ind) α *ind* β =df α *out* β .&. β *out* α.

df(ex) α *ex* β =df $\sim(\exists u)(u$ *in* α .&. u *in* $\beta)$.

df(=) $x = y$ =df $x/x;y!x$

df($\sim$)$_1$ $\sim\alpha$ =df $\alpha \supset \mathbf{f}$

dfs($\sim$)$_2$ $\sim(u)A$ =df $(\exists u) \sim A$

dfs($\sim$)$_3$ $\sim(\exists u)A$ =df $(u) \sim A$

df($\vee$)$_1$ $\alpha \vee \beta$ =df $\sim\alpha \supset \beta$

df($\vee$)$_2$ $A \vee B$ =df $\sim A \supset B$

df(&)$_1$ α & β =df $\sim(\alpha \supset \sim\beta)$

df(&)$_2$ A & B =df $\sim(A \supset \sim B)$

df($\equiv$)$_1$ $\alpha \equiv \beta$ =df $(\alpha \supset \beta)$ & $(\beta \supset \alpha)$

df($\equiv$)$_2$ $A \equiv B$ =df $(A \supset B)$ & $(B \supset A)$

Assuming that u and v are distinct and that u has no free occurrence in α or B and v has no free occurrence in A, the system has

dfs(P)$_1$ $(\exists u)Au \supset \alpha$ =df $(u)(Au \supset \alpha)$

dfs(P)$_2$ $\alpha \supset (u)Au$ =df $(u)(\alpha \supset Au)$

dfs(P)$_3$ $(u)Au \supset \alpha$ =df $(\exists u)(Au \supset \alpha)$

dfs(P)$_4$ $\alpha \supset (\exists u)Au$ =df $(\exists u)(\alpha \supset Au)$

dfs(X)$_1$ $(\exists u)Au \supset (\exists v)Bu$ =df $(u)(\exists v)(Au \supset Bv)$

dfs(X)$_2$ $(u)Au \supset (v)Bv$ =df $(v)(\exists u)((Au \supset Bv)$

dfs(X)$_3$ $(\exists u)Au \supset (v)Av$ =df $(u)(v)(Au \supset Bv)$

dfs(X)$_4$ $(u)Au \supset (\exists v)Bv$ =df $(\exists u)(\exists v)(Au \supset Bv)$.

This system is complete with respect to quantification theory.[27]

---

[27] See Gregory Landini, "Quantification Theory in *9 of *Principia Mathematica*," *History and Philosophy of Logic*, 21 (2000), pp. 57–78.

There was a major hurdle, however. Without general propositions, Russell cannot generate the existence theorems in substitution that are needed to generate arithmetic. Axiom schema (S17) is now such that its formulas A must be quantifier-free. Consider the following comprehension theorem schemata derived from (S17):

(CP)^1

$(\exists p, a)(x)(p/a; x \equiv \{A\})$,

where p and a are not free in A.

(CP)^2

$(\exists p, a, b)(x, y)(p/a,b; x,y \equiv \{A\})$,

where p, a and b are not free in A. These will be well-formed only if the formula A in them is quantifier-free. This is a severe limitation. For example, it will no longer be possible to generate the existence theorems needed for the theorem $\Lambda^{(o)} \in o^{((o))}$. One would need

$(\exists s, t, w)(s/t, w \approx_{r,c} \{o(r, c)\})$,

and this no longer follows from (CP)^2. The expression $\{o(r, c)\}$ is ill-formed because it is not possible in "On Insolubilia" to nominalize a general formula.

To mitigate the effect of the abandonment of general propositions, Russell offered what amounts to auxiliary axioms for comprehension. For example, he has:

1906(Aux)^1

$(\exists p, a)(x)(\exists q)(p/a; x!q .\&. q \equiv A)$,

where A is any wff (quantifier-free or otherwise) in which p, a are not free.

1906(Aux)^2

$(\exists s, t, w)(r, c)(\exists q)(s/t, w; r, c!q .\&. q \equiv A)$,

where A is any wff (quantifier-free or otherwise) in which s, t, w are not free. (It is in virtue of Russell's contextual definitions of quantified-formulas flanking logical particles that the formula A in these comprehension axiom schemata can contain quantifiers.) By means of these new comprehension principles, arithmetic can be recovered in the revised substitutional theory of "On Insolubilia."

Russell's additional comprehension principles are not "reducibility" principles of a system espousing a hierarchy of orders of propositions. In "On Insolubilia" there are no orders of propositions.[28] So the revised theory preserves Russell's doctrine that any proper calculus for the science of logic must have only one style of variables – viz., individual variables. Moreover, the new comprehension principles do not reintroduce a revised form of the paradox of propositions of *Appendix B* of *Principles*. To be sure, one can reformulate that paradox of propositions in the early substitutional theory.[29] The following is an instance of $(CP_{sub})^1$:

$$(\exists t, w)(x)(t/w;x!(p, a, r)(x = \{(z)(p/a; z \supset z)\} \mathbin{.\&.} p/a;x!r :\supset: \sim r)\}).$$

The contradiction will ensue given the theorem,

$$(p, a)(r, c)(\{(z)(p/a;z \supset z)\} = \{(z)(r/c;z \supset z)\} :\supset: p = r \mathbin{.\&.} a = c).$$

But in the theory of "On Insolubilia," this paradox is ill-formed. The paradox essentially involves identity with a general proposition, and in the substitutional theory of "On Insolubilia," general propositions are abandoned. Unfortunately, however, Russell overlooked the fact that the additional comprehension principles will resurrect the p_0/a_0 paradox! The following is an instance of $1906(Aux)^1$:

$$(\exists t, w)(x)(\exists s)(t/w;x!s \mathbin{.\&.} s \equiv (p, a, r)(x = \{p/a;b!q\} \mathbin{.\&.} p/a;x!r :\supset: \sim r)).$$

The paradox goes through. Russell had to admit that the system of "On Insolubilia," with its abandonment of general propositions, fails to be strong enough to recover arithmetic.

---

[28] Cocchiarella makes this point. See Nino Cocchiarella, "The Development of the Theory of Logical Types and the Notion of a Logical Subject in Russell's Early Philosophy," *Synthese* 45 (1980), p. 71–115. Hylton mistakenly attributes orders of propositions to the system of "On Insolubilia." See Peter Hylton, "Russell's Substitutional Theory," *Synthese* 45 (1980), pp. 1–31.

[29] Hylton (op. cit.) attempted to do this, but his rendition is flawed by employing "truth" as an object-language expression of the substitutional theory and his view that the paradox is semantic in nature.

VII. SUBSTITUTION AND THE HISTORICAL DEVELOPMENT OF RAMIFIED TYPE THEORY

In 1926 F. P. Ramsey argued for a systematic division of paradoxes into two distinct categories. The logical paradoxes, according to Ramsey, are those that involve only logical or mathematical terms such as "class" and "number." The other paradoxes (of which the paradox of the *liar* is paradigmatic) are "epistemic" (or semantic) insofar as they involve notions such as those of "designation," "reference," or "truth" and "falsehood."[30] It is often assumed that notions of "truth" and "falsehood," "designation" and "aboutness" are inseparable components of the notion of a Russellian proposition. This assumption has colored the interpretation of Russell's work for many years. Under the assumption, Russell's substitutional theory essentially involves semantic components, and the p_0/a_0 paradox is to be grouped (with the *Liar*) among semantic paradoxes.

The assumption is quite mistaken. To see beyond it required that we understand a number of points about Russell's philosophy of logic. It is essential to see that his logical particle "$\supset$" is a predicate sign (flanked by terms to make a formula) and not the conditional sign "$\rightarrow$" (if...then), which is a statement connective flanked by formulas to make a formula. Missing this, one will feel pressured into injecting the notion of "truth" and reading Russell's "$p \supset q$", as "If p is true then q is true." And the pressure seems especially acute to read "$p \,\&\, q$" as "p is true and q is true." We saw as well that semantic features such as "aboutness", "denoting", and "designation" are foisted upon Russell's notion of a proposition because he embraced general propositions and because he held that belief and judgment are relations between minds and propositions. But we found that Russell's propositions are not properly construed as intentional entities; they are rather akin to "states of affairs." Accordingly, the notion of a proposition that Russell espoused in the era of the substitutional theory involves no semantic elements. Realizing this, we see that the p_0/a_0 paradox is properly a logical paradox, not a semantic one.

Now this is of utmost importance, for in 1907 Russell entertained the possibility of "ramifying" the substitutional theory by

---

[30] Ramsey, Frank. "The Foundations of Mathematics," *Proceedings of the London Mathematical Society* 25 (1926), pp. 338–84.

introducing indexed variables in an effort to avoid the p_0/a_0 paradox (and its variants). Ramification is commonly thought to be the product of Russell's failure to see the distinction between semantic paradoxes such as the *liar* and the logical paradoxes. The 1910 *Principia Mathematica*, it will be recalled, espouses a ramified type-indexed language. In *Principia*, predicate variables adorned with order\type indices may occupy subject as well as predicate positions. Many have interpreted the order index of a predicate variable as reflecting the sort of generality "involved" in attributes. Where n is the highest order index of any variable in the formula A, an attribute comprehended by A has order index $n + 1$ if the variable is bound in A, and has order n if it is free. Quine[31] has steadfastly defended the position that the notion that there are orders of attributes (properties and relations in intension) can only be a product of a confusion of use and mention – a confusion of a predicate expression with the mind and language independent attribute comprehended by such an expression. Quine's argument is unassailable if attributes are conceived of in this way.

In the context of the substitutional theory, however, the matter of ramification fares differently. The abandonment of general propositions in "On Insolubilia" had not yielded a solution of the p_0/a_0 paradox which could recover arithmetic. So in 1907 Russell began to investigate what formal system would result if the substitutional theory were fitted with order indexed variables. On this view, general propositions would be assumed and propositions would be split into orders on the basis of the kind of generality they "involve" or "presuppose." Aspects of Russell's ideas surfaced in his paper "Mathematical Logic as Based on the Theory of Types" (*MLT*), which was written in 1907 and, after a long wait, came to publication in 1908. In manuscripts of 1907 Russell demurred about the nature of order 0 entities. Should they include non-general propositions and non-propositions (and thereby allow him to preserve an infinity theorem for order 0 entities), or should they be for non-propositions alone? In any event, order 1 included those general propositions involving ontological counterparts of bound order 0 variables and no higher; order 2 was for those general propositions involving ontological counterparts of bound order 1 variables and no higher; and so on. In nominalizing a formula A to make a term {A}, the order index of

[31] W.V.O. Quine, "Russell's ontological Development" in R. Schoenman (ed.) *Bertrand Russell: Philosopher of the Century* (London: Allen and Unwin, 1967).

the term was to be rendered as follows: If n is the highest index of any variable x_n in A, then if x_n occurs free in A, then the index of $\{A\}$ is n; and if it occurs bound, then the index of $\{A\}$ is $n + 1$. With substitution retrofitted with order indexed variables, axioms of reducibility of the orders of propositions can be added, which enable the theory to recover its constructions of arithmetic without reviving the p_0/a_0 paradox.

The notion of a general proposition (state of affairs) is indeed perplexing, for it is unclear what would be its constituents. The introduction of orders of general propositions based on the "kind" of generality they involve demands that Russell face the long neglected problem of explaining what the constituents of general propositions are. Russell had no explanation to give. But it is important to understand that the ramification of propositions came about because of the p_0/a_0 paradox, and not because of any semantic paradox. We saw that the pristine substitutional theory begun in 1905, proxies a simple type theory of attributes. When the substitutional theory is fitted with order indices, it will proxy a ramified type-theory of attributes, just as Russell intimates in his "Mathematical Logic" paper. Russell acknowledges that the language of predicate variables fitted with order/type indices is convenient because it supports the introduction of ordinary class symbols. But the underlying foundation of ramified types in "Mathematical Logic" lies in the substitutional theory.

"Mathematical Logic" took a long time at the press, and when it finally appeared in 1908, Russell thought differently. In a letter to Hawtrey of 1907, we find Russell explaining that the p_0/a_0 paradox had "pilled" the substitutional theory and that he was never satisfied with the patches he devised.[32] By 1908, the era of substitution was over. Its successor was the ramified type-theory of *Principia Mathematica*, and its formal system introduced predicate variables adorned with order\type indices. Because of its many-sorted variables, *Principia* has been interpreted as a ramified order\type theory of attributes ("propositional functions in intension"). On this interpretation, the system abandons the doctrine of the unrestricted variable set out in the 1903 *Principles of Mathematics* – a doctrine that had driven Russell's thinking for several years. This interpretation has left a significant gap in the understanding of both Russell's

---

[32] Russell, Bertrand. Letter to Hawtrey, dated 22 January 1907 (Russell Archives).

motives for the ramified type theory of *Principia* and his reasons for abandoning substitution. A hierarchy of types of attributes in intension becomes little more than an *ad hoc* dodge of the Russell paradox. Moreover, a type hierarchy of attributes would require the assumption of a contingent truth – an infinity of individuals at the lowest type – to recover proofs of the Peano/Dedekind Postulates for arithmetic. Worse, when conceived of as mind and language independent entities, the notion of orders of attributes seems wholly unmotivated. Attributes do not contain ontological counterparts of bound variables. There can be no viable distinction between attributes that are "simple" (atomic) and those that are "complex." These notions apply properly to the contingent matter of what expressions are available in a given language.

Philosophically, the substitutional theory with orders of propositions is vastly superior to an order\type hierarchy of attributes in intension with non-logical axioms of infinity and reducibility. If Russell abandons the doctrine of the unrestricted variable, he has every reason to prefer his version of substitutional theory modified by orders of propositions. The patch that Russell devised in "Mathematical Logic" is a ramified theory of propositions, and this is far less objectionable than a ramified order\type hierarchy of attributes ("propositional functions" in intension). It is far less objectionable because there is no type hierarchy and only an order hierarchy of entities. In fact, Russell knew that the order hierarchy of propositions, unlike a type hierarchy of attributes, could be made to preserve an infinity theorem (1907, 3). Russell even entertained the idea that the substitutional theory would be set out in an Appendix to *Principia*. The gap in understanding Russell's reasons for abandoning substitution is a necessary by-product of interpreting Russell as having abandoned the doctrine of the unrestricted variable in *Principia*. In truth, the reason Russell abandoned substitution was because he came to believe that the system of *Principia* could be interpreted as *preserving* the doctrine of the unrestricted variable.

The doctrine of the unrestricted variable – i.e., that any calculus for logic must adopt only one style of genuine variables, viz., individual (entity) variables – is realized syntactically in the substitutional theory. A type-indexed language of predicate variables is proxied by the logical syntax of the type-free language of substitution. In substitution, no predicate variables are allowed. In the *Principia*, the syntactic doctrine of the unrestricted variable gives way to the semantic doctrine of the "variable internally limited by its conditions of significance." Predicate variables with order\type indices are introduced in *Principia*, but they are semantically interpreted (nominalistically) so as not to be genuine. In *Principia*, the only genuine variables are the individual variables. All entities, universals, particulars, facts, and complexes are treated on a par as individuals. Russell is convinced that there are universals, and that universals have both a predicable and an individual nature. But he maintains that there are no purely logical axioms that determine what universals there are, or assure that there are infinitely many of them. Logic in the *Principia* endeavors to show how to proceed to mathematics without assuming logical axioms for the comprehension of propositional functions (attributes), universals, classes, or propositions. Instead of the syntactic approach of the substitutional theory, the *doctrine of the unrestricted variable* is preserved in *Principia* by the approach of a nominalistic *semantics* according to which internal limitations on predicate variables are built into their conditions of significance. Russell abandoned his ontology of propositions and his substitutional theory precisely because he had a new recursive theory of truth, which he thought would provide a philosophical explanation for the order part of the order\type indices on predicate variables. The new recursive theory was based on the multiple-relation theory of judgment that Russell developed in his 1907 paper "On the Nature of Truth." The order indices on the predicate variables of *Principia* track the truth-conditions of the formulas involved in the comprehension of principles of predicative type-theory.

The substitutional theory is the conceptual linchpin connecting Russell's 1903 *Principles of Mathematics* with the mature system of the 1910 *Principia Mathematica*. In being the immediate product of Russell's 1905 discovery of the theory of definite descriptions, the substitutional theory explains Russell's recollection that the theory of definite descriptions "... was the first step toward the solution of the contradiction that had baffled me for so long" (*Auto.* 1, 229). It reveals that the historical continuity of Russell's work toward solving the paradoxes plaguing logicism lies on his tireless efforts to build the structural distinctions of types (and then of orders) into logical form.

The system of *Principia* was philosophically unsuccessful, for it failed to establish logicism. It required reducibility principles, instances of which, Russell came to agree, could not be counted as truths of logic. As we saw, *Principia* requires an axiom of the infinity of individuals (entities of lowest type) if arithmetic is to be founded upon logical principles alone. Though Russell hoped to avoid infinity by appending a statement of infinity as an antecedent where needed, this comes well short of the logicist goal of a foundation of arithmetic in pure logic. The substitutional theory, on the other hand, has only recently begun to be explored. The theory offers a genuine *solution* to the paradoxes of classes and attributes plaguing logicism. It generates an infinity theorem for propositions and is as strong as simple type-theory. With logic construed as the science of propositional structure, a way may yet be found to *solve* the p_0/a_0 paradox. If so, the substitutional theory will recover logicism just as Russell had originally hoped.

FURTHER READING

Church, Alonzo. "Russell's Theory of the Identity of Propositions," *Philosophia Naturalis* 21 (1984), pp. 513–22.

Cocchiarella, Nino. "The Development of the Theory of Logical Types and the Notion of a Logical Subject in Russell's Early Philosophy," *Synthese* 45 (1980), pp. 71–115.

De Rouilhan, Philippe. *Russell et le cercle des paradoxes*, (Paris: Presses Universitaires de France, 1996).

Fitch, Frederick. "Propositions as the Only Realities," *American Philosophical Quarterly* 8 (1971), pp. 99–103.

Grattan-Guinness, Ivor. "The Russell Archives: Some New Light on Russell's Logicism," *Annals of Science* 31 (1974), pp. 387–406.

———. "Bertrand Russell's Manuscripts: An Apprehensive Brief," *History and Philosophy of Logic* 6 (1977), pp. 53–74.

———. *Dear Russell – Dear Jourdain* (London: Duckworth, 1977).

Hylton, Peter. "Russell's Substitutional Theory," *Synthese* 45 (1980), pp. 1–31.

Lackey, Douglas. "Russell's Unknown Theory of Classes: The Substitutional System of 1906," *Journal of the History of Philosophy* 14 (1976), pp. 69–78.

Landini, Gregory. "New Evidence Concerning Russell's Substitutional Theory of Classes," *Russell* 9, (1989), pp. 26–42.

———. "Russell to Frege, 2 May 1904: 'I Believe I have Discovered that Classes are Entirely Superfluous," *Russell* 12 (1992), pp. 160–185.

————. *Russell's Hidden Substitutional Theory* (New York: Oxford University Press, 1998).

Pelham, Judy. "A Reconstruction of Russell's Substitution Theory," in eds., M. Marion and R.S. Cohen, *Quebec Studies in the Philosophy of Logic I* (Kluwer Academic Publishers, 1995), pp. 123–133.

Pelham, Judy and Urquhart, Alasdair. "Russellian Propositions," in eds., D. Prawitz, B. Skyrms, and D. Westerståhl, *Logic, Methodology, and the Philosophy of Science* XI (1994), pp. 307–325.

WORKS BY RUSSELL:

(1905) "On Substitution," unpublished manuscript dated 22 December 1905. (Russell Archives, McMaster University, Hamilton, Ontario, Canada). Forthcoming in *Papers* 5.

(1906) "On Some Difficulties in the Theory of Transfinite Numbers and Order Types," *Proceedings of the London Mathematical Society* 4, pp. 29–53. The paper was read to the Society on 14 December 1905. Pagination is to the paper as reprinted in *EA*, pp. 135–64.

(1906a) "On the Substitutional Theory of Classes and Relations," in *EA*, pp. 165–89. Received by the London Mathematical Society on 24 April 1906, and read before the Society on 10 May 1906.

(1906b) "On Substitution," unpublished manuscript of April-May 1906 (Russell Archives). Forthcoming in *Papers* 5.

(1906c) "The Theory of Implication," *American Journal of Mathematics* 28 (1906), pp. 159–202.

(1906d) "Logic in which Propositions are Not Entities," unpublished manuscript of April 1906 (Russell Archives, McMaster University, Hamilton, Ontario, Canada). Forthcoming in *Papers* 5.

(1906e) "On 'Insolubilia' and their Solution by Symbolic Logic," in *EA*, pp. 190–214. First published as "Les Paradoxes de la Logique" in *Revue de Métaphysique et de Morale* 14 (1906), pp. 627–50.

(1906f) "The Paradox of the Liar," unpublished manuscript of September 1906 (Russell Archives, McMaster University, Hamilton, Ontario, Canada). Forthcoming in *Papers* 5.

(1907) "On the Nature of Truth," *Proceedings of the Aristotelian Society* 7 (1907), pp. 28–49.

(1907a) "On Types," unpublished manuscript of 1907 (Russell Archives, McMaster University, Hamilton, Ontario, Canada). Forthcoming in *Papers* 5.

8 The Theory of Types

I. INTRODUCTION

A surprising feature of Russell's work in logic is that he began and ended with a theory of types. This chapter begins with a summary of the 1903 theory of types and then proceeds to the much more complex ramified theory of types that emerged from Russell's intense work on the foundations of logic from 1903 to 1907. After discussing the problems connected with the Axiom of Reducibility, the chapter concludes with the simple theory of types, and the later history of type theory, after the demise of the logicist programme.

II. THE 1903 THEORY OF TYPES

Russell's early theory of types, presented in Appendix B to the *Principles of Mathematics*, already contains many of the basic features of the mature system given in his fundamental paper of 1908 and in *Principia Mathematica*. In 1901, Russell had begun writing out the derivation of mathematics from logic, employing the methods of Peano and his school. This led him to examine Cantor's proof that there is no greatest cardinal number. This result conflicted with his assumption that there is a universal class, having all objects as members, which ought to have the greatest cardinal number. Close analysis of the diagonal argument used in Cantor's proof led to the discovery of the paradox of the class of all classes that are not members of themselves, now called "Russell's paradox," but which Russell called "the Contradiction."

The logical paradoxes emerged at an awkward moment, when Russell had already written most of the penultimate draft of the *Principles*. Rather than hold up its publication indefinitely, he took the manuscript of his book to the printer in May 1902 before finding a solution. His initial reaction was that the Contradiction was of a somewhat trivial character, and that it could be avoided by a simple modification of the primitive propositions of logic. It appears from Russell's correspondence that he embarked on the publication of the *Principles* in the hope that he could dispose of the Contradiction in an appendix after the printing of the main text. On 8 August 1902, in a letter to Gottlob Frege [Frege 1980, 143–5], Russell sketched an idea for a theory of types, taking his inspiration from the hierarchy of functions that forms part of Frege's *Grundgesetze der Arithmetik* [Frege 1893]. Russell, however, abandons Frege's distinction between individuals, said to be "saturated" entities, and functions, which are "unsaturated" entities that need to be completed by an argument just as the argument places of a function need to be filled in Frege's logical formulas.

The theory, as presented in Appendix B to the *Principles*, starts from the assumption that every propositional function $\phi(x)$ has a range of significance, that is, a range within which x must lie if $\phi(x)$ is to be a proposition at all, whether true or false. These ranges of significance form *types*. The lowest type of object is that of *terms* or *individuals*. Somewhat surprisingly, this type contains certain classes, that form "classes as one" rather than "classes as many" such as persons (classes of psychical existents) and tables and chairs (classes of material points). The next type is that of classes of individuals, and Russell goes on to describe a hierarchy of classes of classes of individuals, relations of individuals, classes of relations of individuals, and so on. So far the theory is basically the same as the later simple theory of types.

Differences appear, though, in the case of numbers and propositions. Numbers form a range lying outside the simple type hierarchy just described. In this case, Russell argues as follows:

Since all ranges have numbers, ranges are a range; consequently $x \in x$ is sometimes significant, and in these cases its denial is also significant. Consequently there is a range w of ranges for which $x \in x$ is false: thus the Contradiction proves that this range w does not belong to the range of significance of $x \in x$. We may observe that $x \in x$ can only be significant when x is of a type of infinite order, since, in $x \in u$, u must always be of a type higher by one than x; but the range of all ranges is of course of a type of infinite order [*POM*, 525].

This view of the type of numbers is already a considerable departure from the familiar simple theory of types. The real difficulties,
though, begin with propositions. Propositions form a type because
of the fact (about which Russell expresses doubts) that only propositions can significantly be said to be true or false. But then, Russell
argues, "the number of propositions is as great as that of all objects
absolutely, since every object is identical with itself, and "x is identical with x" has a one-one relation to x" [POM, 526]. A problem
arises, though, from an application of Cantor's theorem that the cardinal number of a class is smaller than the cardinal number of the
class of all its subclasses (recall that it was an application of Cantor's
theorem to the supposed class of all entities that led to Russell's
paradox). It would seem, contrary to the argument above, that there
must be more ranges of propositions than there are propositions.

The contemporary reader, used to thinking about propositions in
linguistic terms, might wonder about Russell's assumption that for
every individual x there is a proposition $x = x$, in view of the fact that
there might be individuals with no names. However, Russell at the
time of writing the Principles, and for many years afterwards, held to
the view that propositions are complex abstract entities containing
as constituents the very objects about which they make assertions.
Russell maintained the view that the proposition 'Mont Blanc is over
4000 metres high" has Mont Blanc itself as a component part, in spite
of Frege's vehement opposition [Frege 1980, 169]. For more on this
topic, see Pelham and Urquhart [PelUrq 1994].

The difficulty arising from Cantor's theorem can be given a more
concrete form by examining the diagonal argument used to prove
Cantor's basic result. If m is a class of propositions, then the proposition $(p) (p \in m \supset p)$ asserts that all propositions in m are true.
This proposition itself can be either a member of the class m or not.
Let w be the class of all propositions of the above form that are not
members of the pertinent class m; that is,

$$w = \{q \mid (\exists m)[(q = (p)(p \in m \supset p) . q \notin m]\},$$

and let r be the proposition $(p)(p \in w \supset p)$. Then if $r \in w$, it satisfies
the defining condition; hence, there is a class of propositions m so
that r is identical with the proposition $q = (p)(p \in m \supset p)$. But since
r is identical with this proposition, it follows that the constituents
of r are identical with the corresponding constituents of q, so that

$m = w$. Hence, $r \notin w$. Conversely, if $r \notin w$, then by its definition, it satisfies the condition defining w, so that $r \in w$. Thus, we have derived a contradiction.

It is essential to the preceding proof that we have adopted Russell's view of the nature of propositions sketched above. A crucial step in this derivation is where we infer that the constituents m and w of two propositions are identical from the assumption that the propositions containing them are identical. Alonzo Church [Church 1984] has given a rigorous and detailed analysis of the assumptions about identity of propositions that are implicit in Russell's derivation of the propositional contradiction.

As a result of the propositional contradiction, Russell was forced to admit that his early attempt at a theory of types was a failure, as he explained to Frege in a letter of 29 September 1902 [Frege 1980, 147–8]. The verdict of Appendix B is essentially negative. Although the doctrine of types deals in a satisfactory way with the original Contradiction, Russell sees no obvious escape from the propositional contradiction. He briefly considers the idea that propositions themselves are of various types and that logical products must have propositions of only one type as factors, but rejects the suggestion as "harsh and highly artificial." He concludes:

The totality of all logical objects, or of all propositions, involves, it would seem, a fundamental logical difficulty. What the complete solution of the difficulty may be, I have not succeeded in discovering; but as it affects the very foundations of reasoning, I earnestly commend the study of it to the attention of all students of logic [*POM*, 528].

After abandoning his early version of the theory of types, Russell tried an extraordinary variety of schemes for the foundations of logic. Most of these can be considered as attempts to carry through modified versions of Frege's abortive attempt at patching his system after Russell had communicated to him in June 1902 the disastrous news that the system of his *Grundgesetze* was inconsistent. When he received Russell's letter of 16 June 1902 [Frege 1980, 130–1], the second volume of the *Grundgesetze* [Frege 1903] was already in press. Frege had time to add a hasty last-minute patch to the volume as an appendix. Unfortunately, the attempt failed, since a contradiction can be deduced in the amended system if we add to Frege's axiom system the assumption that at least two objects exist [Quine 1955].

Russell's attempts at logical foundations from the years 1903 to 1906 suffered from a similar fate as that of Frege's ill-starred appendix. Russell expressed cautious optimism about Frege's solution in the conclusion of Appendix A of the *Principles*, devoted to the doctrines of Frege, and remarks: "As it seems very likely that this is the true solution, the reader is strongly recommended to examine Frege's argument on this point" [*POM*, 522]. The foundational schemes that Russell tried in the years 1903 to 1905 have (in spite of their varied character) some clear common features. They all involve type-free theories of functions, in which the basic idea is to avoid the paradoxes by direct restrictions on the means for defining functions. The hope was to avoid the "bad" definitions leading to paradoxes; an analysis of the paradoxes themselves might reveal what the key features of these inadmissible definitions might be. At the same time, it was essential to retain a sufficiently large stock of functions to deduce the basic axioms of mathematics. However, Russell was never able to carry out this balancing act in a satisfactory way, and all his attempts along these lines (which he described later as the "zig-zag theory") led to abject failure. The manuscripts recording this discouraging period in Russell's logical career are reproduced in Volume 4 of the *Collected Papers* [*Papers* 4].

In 1905, new hope dawned for Russell with the discovery of the theory of descriptions. This led to an expectation that a final solution to the paradoxes might be in sight because of the reduction in the basic entities of logic that it made possible. The result was the substitutional theory, a theory of remarkable economy in which the basic notions (apart from the logical connectives) are those of proposition and the substitution of one entity for another. The reader is referred to the chapter by Landini for the details of this fascinating theory.

Unfortunately, in spite of Russell's high hopes, the substitutional theory was not the final answer to the paradoxes. Like the functional or "zig-zag" theories of 1903 to 1905, the substitutional theory is essentially type-free. This led to a paradox, expressed purely in terms of propositions and substitution that Russell was unable to avoid in spite of numerous attempts; the details are to be found in the chapter by Landini. Eventually, Russell was forced, in spite of his earlier reluctance, to classify propositions according to a hierarchy of types. The result was the ramified theory of types.

III. THE VICIOUS CIRCLE PRINCIPLE

Russell was always convinced that there should be a single, unified solution to the paradoxes of logic. This differs from the currently popular point of view, since most logicians follow Peano and Ramsey in making a distinction between set-theoretical and semantical paradoxes. Nevertheless, there is a good deal to be said for Russell's point of view. The paradoxes have a clear common structure; in particular, they all involve a diagonal construction. Thus there is no absurdity in looking for a common solution.

In his seminal paper, "Mathematical Logic as based on the Theory of Types," Russell begins by enumerating seven paradoxes, among them the original Contradiction, the Epimenides or "liar paradox," Berry's paradox, and the Burali-Forti paradox. His diagnosis of these contradictions is that they have in common "the assumption of a totality such that, if it were legitimate, it would at once be enlarged by new members defined in terms of itself" [MLT, 225; LK, 63]. Russell gives two other formulations of the principle:

This leads us to the rule: "Whatever involves *all* of a collection must not be one of the collection;" or, conversely: "If, provided a certain collection had a total, it would have members only definable in terms of that total, then the said collection has no total" [MLT, 225; LK, 63].

These formulations are certainly not completely clear, but we should bear in mind that we are dealing with a heuristic idea rather than a precise logical principle.

The idea of a system founded on the avoidance of vicious circles appears earlier in Russell's unpublished manuscripts from 1904 (see, for instance, [*Papers* 4, 88, 138–40]). However, a more immediate source for the idea of the vicious circle principle is the polemical interchange with Henri Poincaré in 1905–1906. Towards the end of his series of articles [Poincaré 1905–06] violently attacking the logicist school, Poincaré, taking his cue from some earlier remarks of Richard, stated that the "true solution" to the paradoxes lay in the avoidance of definitions containing a vicious circle [Ewald 1996, 1063]. In his reply to Poincaré [OI], Russell agreed that all of the paradoxes spring from some kind of vicious circle. He states the principle in the form: "Whatever involves an apparent variable must not be among the possible values of that variable" [EA, 198]. The reader is referred to Chihara's book [Chihara 1973] for a detailed discussion of the historical and philosophical background to the vicious circle principle.

Russell presupposes certain "collections" of which some are said to be "legitimate," or to "have a total," ideas that to some extent recall the earlier distinction of the *Principles* between classes as one and classes as many. The vicious circle principle rules out certain collections as totalities by the rule that if they were legitimate, then we could enlarge them by defining new members in terms of the whole collection. It is very significant here that Russell talks about "enlarging" a collection by adding a "new member." It shows that an underlying conception in the vicious circle principle is that of members of classes being created through the process of definition. The conception of a class here is not that of a static entity, but rather of a class that comes into being through the mathematical activity of definition. Thus, we may describe Russell's idea of mathematics at the stage of the 1908 paper as having a rather constructive slant, in contrast to the bold Platonism of his earlier, more realistic phase represented by the *Principles*.

The principle can be thought of as ruling out certain collections as totalities, but can also be considered as a prohibition on certain kinds of definition. A definition that picks out an object from a collection by quantifying over that collection is said to be *impredicative*. Here are some examples of such definitions:

1) The tallest woman in this room.
2) The smallest natural number.
3) The smallest real number r such that $r^2 \geq 2$.
4) The smallest set N containing 0 such that $(x)(x \in N \supset x + 1 \in N)$.

In each of these cases, an object is picked out from a totality to which it belongs. For example, in the first definition, the totality is that of people in the room, while in the last the totality is that of all sets containing the natural numbers. These examples also illustrate the fact that impredicative definitions are common in mathematics. For example, the third example exemplifies the principle that a non-empty set of numbers has a least upper bound, which is ubiquitous in calculus, while the fourth represents the definition of the set of natural numbers that is at the base of the Frege/Russell logicist reconstruction of mathematics. This highlights a serious difficulty for Russell. In ruling out impredicative definitions, it appears that he has ruled out a large part of classical mathematics, for which the logicist enterprise aimed to provide a logical foundation. We shall discuss this problem in detail in the section on the ramified theory of types and the Axiom of Reducibility.

IV. THE RAMIFIED THEORY OF TYPES

The formal presentation of the theory of types by Russell and Whitehead leaves a great deal to be desired from the present day point of view. As Gödel noted in his famous essay on Russell's mathematical logic, *Principia Mathematica* "is so greatly lacking in formal precision in the foundations... that it presents in this respect a considerable step backwards as compared with Frege" [Gödel 1944, 126]. In this section, we present a precise formal version of the ramified theory of types.

A *type* is introduced by Russell as the range of significance of a propositional function, "within which lie the arguments for which the function has values. Within this range of arguments, the function is true or false; outside this range, it is nonsense" [MLT, 234; LK, 73]. This leads to a restriction on quantification; a statement about all of a collection makes sense only when the collection forms part or the whole of the range of significance of some propositional function.

The ramified hierarchy of types arises from the vicious circle principle by giving it the following more precise form:

This principle, in our technical language, becomes: "Whatever contains an apparent variable must not be a possible value of that variable." Thus whatever contains an apparent variable must be of a different type from the possible values of that variable; we will say that it is of a *higher* type [MLT, 237; LK, 75].

The hierarchy of propositional functions arising from this idea is most fully described by Whitehead and Russell in the introduction to *Principia Mathematica* [PM, Vol. 1, 37–65].

The hierarchy begins at the lowest level with the type of individuals, described as objects that are neither propositions nor functions. The overall metaphysical picture is described as follows:

The universe consists of objects having various qualities and standing in various relations. Some of the objects which occur in the universe are complex.

When an object is complex, it consists of interrelated parts. Let us consider a complex object composed of two parts a and b standing to each other in the relation R. The complex object "a-in-the-relation-R-to-b" may be capable of being *perceived*; when perceived, it is perceived as one object.... When we judge "a has the relation R to b," our judgment is said to *true* when there is a complex "a-in-the-relation-R-to-b," and is said to be *false* when this is not the case. This is a definition of truth and falsehood in relation to judgments of this kind [*PM*, Vol. 1, 43].

Thus, at the most fundamental level, there are certain individuals and primitive, directly perceived relations between them. Whitehead and Russell leave unspecified the nature of these relations, and in fact, it would be a mistake to think of *Principia Mathematica* as a formal system in the modern sense, where all primitive concepts are spelled out in advance. Rather, the language of *Principia* is a universal language that is indefinitely extensible by adding primitive concepts on the lowest level and possibly higher type levels.

Whitehead and Russell describe the basic concept of propositional function as follows:

By a "propositional function" we mean something which contains a variable x, and expresses a *proposition* as soon as a value is assigned to x. That is to say, it differs from a proposition solely by the fact that it is ambiguous: it contains a variable of which the value is unassigned [*PM* Vol. 1, 38].

It may seem surprising to the modern reader that they describe a function as "containing a variable," since the current view of functions sees variables as part of syntactic apparatus used in defining functions, but not as part of the functions themselves.

The modern, extensional view of functions holds that they are simply sets F of ordered pairs, satisfying the property that

$$(x)(y)(z)[\langle x, y \rangle \in F . \langle x, z \rangle \in F . \supset . y = z].$$

That is to say, a function is completely determined by the description of its input/output behaviour. There is, however, an older concept of function with a pedigree extending back to Euler and beyond, according to which a function is a certain kind of *formula*. It is clear that the concept of function described by Whitehead and Russell, at least initially, is closer to the traditional Eulerian conception than the modern.

The next level in the hierarchy is constituted by first-order functions, defined by formulas of predicate logic, where the quantifiers range over individuals. For example, if $\phi(x, y, z)$ is a primitive relation between individuals, then $(x)(\exists y)\phi(x, y, z)$ defines a first-order function of one argument. We obtain in this way the totality of first-order functions, which in turn can form the domain of quantification used in defining second-order functions. From there, we can proceed to the definition of third-order functions and so forth.

At this point, it is better to abandon the original Whitehead–Russell presentation of the ramified theory of types and to follow a modern exposition. The original presentation in *Principia Mathematica* is both imprecise and notationally clumsy. Above all, the original formulation is unsatisfactory because there is no precise presentation of the syntax of the system. The version given here is based largely on that given by Church [Church 1976], though it also owes something to [Myhill 1979] and [Schütte 1960].

We begin by introducing a precise notation for types, which we may call *r-types* (short for "ramified types") to distinguish them from the notion of types familiar from the simple theory of types. We start with a r-type i to which the individual variables belong. If $\beta_1, \beta_2, \cdots, \beta_m$ are given r-types, $m \geq 0$, then there is an r-type $(\beta_1, \beta_2, \cdots, \beta_m)/n$ to which there belong m-place functional variables of level n, where $n \geq 1$. The r-type $(\alpha_1, \alpha_2, \cdots, \alpha_m)/k$ is said to be *directly lower* than the r-type $(\beta_1, \beta_2, \cdots, \beta_m)/n$ if $\alpha_1 = \beta_1, \alpha_2 = \beta_2, \cdots, \alpha_m = \beta_m$ and $k < n$.

The r-types are cumulative in the sense that the range of a variable of a given r-type includes the ranges of all variables of directly lower r-type. This convention is natural in view of the fact that we can always add dummy quantifiers to a formula to raise its order.

The *order* of an r-type is defined recursively as follows. The order of the r-type i of individuals is 0. The order of an r-type $(\beta_1, \beta_2, \cdots, \beta_m)/n$ is $N + n$, where N is the maximum of the orders of the r-types $\beta_1, \beta_2, \cdots, \beta_m$.

There is an infinite alphabet of variables for each r-type β, the r-type of a variable being indicated by a superscript on the letter. Thus, for example, $x^i, y^i, z^i, \cdots$ are individual variables, while $x^\beta, y^\beta, z^\beta, \cdots$, where $\beta = (i, i)/2$ are variables ranging over second-order relations between individuals. The *order* of a variable x^β is the same as the order of β. Thus a variable of r-type $(\beta_1, \beta_2, \cdots, \beta_m)/n$, ranges over m-place propositional functions with arguments of type $\beta_1, \beta_2, \cdots, \beta_m$, in which no quantification is involved over any r-types of level $\geq n$.

The notations for r-types are abbreviated by writing the numeral m to stand for $(i, i, \cdots, i)$, where there m occurrences of i between the parentheses. For example, $()/n$ is abbreviated $0/n$, $(i, i, i)/n$ is abbreviated $3/n$ and $((i)/2, ()/2)/1$ is abbreviated as $(1/2, 0/2)/1$. As a particular case of this notation, the type $0/n$ stands for propositions of type n.[1]

The formation rules provide that a propositional variable (that is, a variable of one of the r-types $0/n$) constitutes a well-formed formula when standing alone. If f is a variable or constant of type $(\beta_1, \beta_2, \cdots, \beta_m)/n$, and each of the variables x_i is of r-type β_i or of an r-type directly lower than β_i, then $f(x_1, x_2, \cdots, x_m)$ is a well-formed formula. If x^β and y^γ are variables of the same type, then $x^\beta = y^\gamma$ is well-formed. If the conditions on typing are not fulfilled, then neither $f(x_1, x_2, \cdots, x_m)$ nor $x^\beta = y^\gamma$ is well-formed. In addition to the infinite alphabet of variables for each r-type, and the notation for functional application (as above), the primitive symbols comprise an unspecified list of primitive constants, each of a definite r-type, and the usual notations for negation, disjunction, and the universal quantifier. Hence, the remaining formation rules provide that $\sim P$, $(P \vee Q)$ and $(v)P$ are well-formed formulas, when P and Q are well-formed formulas and v is a variable.

As axioms for the ramified theory of types, we suppose that we adopt a standard system of propositional calculus and quantification theory with identity (taking into account the many-sorted nature of our basic logic). To the logical axioms, we adjoin the comprehension axiom schemata:

$$(\exists p) \cdot p \equiv P,$$

where p is a propositional variable of r-type $0/n$, the bound variables of P are all of order less than n, and the free variables of P and the constants of P are all of order not greater than n;

$$(\exists f)(x_1) \ldots (x_m)[f(x_1, x_2, \cdots, x_m) \equiv P],$$

where f is a functional variable of r-type $(\beta_1, \beta_2, \cdots, \beta_m)/n$ and $x_1, x_2, \cdots, x_m$ are distinct variables of r-types $\beta_1, \beta_2, \cdots, \beta_m$, the bound variables of P are all of order less than the order of f, and the free variables of P (among which of course some or all of $x_1, x_2, \cdots, x_m$ may be included) and the constants occurring in P are all of order not greater than the order of f.

The reader who compares Church's formulation of ramified type theory as presented above with the original system of *Principia Mathematica* may feel somewhat confused, since the notational complications of Church's system do not appear to be present in the original version. Part of the contrast between the two lies in the fact that (as was mentioned above) Whitehead and Russell do not present the syntax in an explicit manner, but instead give an informal presentation of their hierarchy, leaving the syntax implicit. A further difference lies in the fact that they do not use explicit type indices, but rather employ the device of "typical ambiguity" in which the type of a variable is to be determined contextually. Whitehead and Russell indicate predicative variables by the notation $\phi!x$; that is to say, a variable that we might write as $\phi^{(\beta_1,\dots,\beta_m)/1}$ would be written in *Principia Mathematica* as $\phi!$, where the precise type of ϕ is to be determined by the context.

V. THE AXIOM OF REDUCIBILITY

Unfortunately, the ramified theory of types, as presented above, is completely inadequate for the derivation of the standard postulates of mathematics. The most obvious inadequacy is that we cannot prove that there are infinitely many objects of any r-type, since the axioms do not allow us to deduce that there is more than one individual (hence we cannot deduce that there are more than two predicates of individuals, and so on). Thus, it is impossible to deduce the existence of infinitely many natural numbers in the system (assuming the Frege–Russell definition of natural numbers as classes of classes of individuals). This problem, though, can be dealt with by the method of Whitehead and Russell, by explicitly prefixing the Axiom of Infinity (stating that there are infinitely many individuals) to mathematical theorems that require it. Thus, if P is a mathematical postulate (such as the existence of a non-zero successor for any natural number) that requires the assumption of infinitely many individuals, then the corresponding theorem of *Principia Mathematica* is [Infin Ax . ⊃ . P].

A much more fundamental problem is that even if we postulate the Axiom of Infinity outright, it is still not possible to define the class of natural numbers in such a way that we can prove that Peano's basic postulates hold. This can be seen in an informal way by examining the definition of the set of natural numbers given towards the end of Section III, namely: "The smallest set N containing o such that $(x)(x \in N \supset x + 1 \in N)$." If we spell out what is meant by the "smallest set" satisfying a certain property, it can be seen that this involves quantifying over the family of all sets satisfying this property. However, in the context of the ramified theory of types, this definition is illegitimate, since the set N itself belongs to this totality. Hence, this definition is not usable in the context of a ramified theory.

We might hope that the defects of the obvious definition could be avoided by a different method. Unfortunately, though, this is a vain hope. John Myhill [Myhill 1974] proved that it is in fact impossible to define the natural numbers in ramified type theory in such a way that all instances of the induction axiom are provable. To be more precise, let us suppose that we have defined the natural numbers as objects of a certain fixed type, say as classes of classes of individuals, following the Frege/Russell definition. In particular, let us suppose that we have defined o, the successor function $s(x) = x + 1$, and also a predicate N (of a certain fixed order) defining the set of all natural numbers for which we can demonstrate $N(o)$ and $(x)[N(x) \supset N(s(x))]$. Then the induction axiom is not provable, that is to say, the formula

$$B(o) \cdot (x)[B(u) \supset B(s(x))] \cdot \supset \cdot (y)[N(y) \supset B(y)]$$

is unprovable, where $B(x)$ is a predicate variable of appropriate type. This shows that Russell's attempt to derive the axioms of arithmetic without using the Axiom of Reducibility in Appendix B to the second edition of *Principia Mathematica* [PM, Vol. 1, 650–8] is definitely in error.

Further problems appear if we consider the real numbers as well as the natural numbers. Even if we postulate the Peano axioms for the natural numbers on the appropriate type level, it will still be impossible to derive the usual axioms that form the basis of the standard constructions of the calculus. If we define the real numbers in the usual way as certain sets of natural numbers, then every real number will have a certain order (given by the predicate defining it). But now consider the basic axiom of the theory of real numbers that states that each nonempty set S of real numbers that is bounded from above (that is, there is a real number r so that $(x)(x \in S \supset x < r)$), then S has a least upper bound. Any such set S must consist of a set of real numbers of a certain order. The least upper bound of the set S can be defined in ramified type theory, but unfortunately, it must be of an order higher than any of the members of S (since it is defined by quantifying over the members of S). It follows that even if we postulate the Peano axioms, we still cannot derive anything resembling standard mathematics in the context of ramified type theory.

In view of these failings of the ramified theory, Russell was driven to postulate the Axiom of Reducibility. Let us say that r-type $(\beta_1, \beta_2, \cdots, \beta_m)/n$ is *predicative* if $n = 1$. A propositional function is defined to be *predicative* if it is of a predicative type. Then the Axiom of Reducibility states that any propositional function is logically equivalent to a predicative propositional function (strictly speaking, the Axiom of Reducibility is an infinite collection of axioms, one for each finite sequence of r-types). In symbols, if $x_1, \ldots, x_m$ are variables of r-types $\beta_1, \beta_2, \cdots, \beta_m$, then for any function symbol F of r-type $(\beta_1, \beta_2, \cdots, \beta_m)/n$, the corresponding Axiom of Reducibility takes the form:

$$(F)(\exists G)(x_1, \ldots, x_m)[F(x_1, \ldots, x_m) \equiv G(x_1, \ldots, x_m)],$$

where G is a functional variable of r-type $(\beta_1, \beta_2, \cdots, \beta_m)/1$.

With the introduction of the Axiom of Reducibility, it is possible to give a contextual definition of classes so that the defined entities have the same properties as classes in the ramified theory of types. The fundamental idea is that two equivalent propositional functions determine the same class. Whitehead and Russell give the definition *20.01 as their basic principle for the contextual elimination of classes as incomplete symbols:

$$f\{\hat{z}(\psi z)\} = (\exists \phi)[(x)(\phi!x \equiv \psi x) . f\{\phi!\hat{z}\}] \quad \text{Df.}$$

This definition, read informally, says: in a context $f\{\}$, an assertion about the class $\hat{z}(\psi z)$ is to be interpreted as saying that there is a predicative function $\phi!x$ that is logically equivalent to ψ about which the corresponding assertion is made. The fact that the resulting theory of classes is essentially the same as the simple theory of types can be seen as follows. Consider an r-type that is built completely from predicative r-types (that is to say, the levels of the r-types are all equal to 1). Then if we erase all the level numerals, the result is a type belonging to the simple theory of types. For example, if we start with the type $(0/1, 2/1)/1$ and erase the level numerals, the result is the simple type $(0, 2)$, that is to say, the type of two-place relations between propositions and two-place relations of individuals.

It is important to note that the Axiom of Reducibility does not state that every propositional function is predicative, but rather it asserts the weaker statement that every propositional function is *logically equivalent* to a predicative function. Thus, in *Principia Mathematica*, we can still distinguish propositional functions on the basis of their order, even though they may be logically equivalent. Russell held that it was essential to retain these distinctions in the light of the paradoxes. However, it remains true that after the introduction of the Axiom of Reducibility, the formal development in *Principia Mathematica* takes place very much as in the simple theory of types. One might question, then, why the elaborate apparatus of the ramified theory was introduced in the first place, if the distinctions are almost immediately erased by the Axiom of Reducibility.

This criticism has been stated in sharper form in [Chwistek 1921], and also in [Ramsey 1925] [Copi 1950]. The point of view taken by these authors is that the ramified theory of types with the Axiom of Reducibility is either inconsistent or redundant (as the title of Copi's article explicitly says). In the last part of this section, we sketch Myhill's defence of the Axiom of Reducibility [Myhill 1979] against these attacks. This sketch also allows us to show the characteristic approach of the ramified theory of types to the paradoxes.

As a typical example of the semantical paradoxes, let us choose the Epimenides paradox. Russell presents the paradox in the following way:

Epimenides the Cretan said that all Cretans were liars, and all other statements made by Cretans were certainly lies. Was this a lie? The simplest form of this contradiction is afforded by the man who says "I am lying"; if he is lying, he is speaking the truth, and vice versa [MLT, 222; LK, 59].

Let us attempt to formalize this paradox in the simple theory of types. Let E be the set of all propositions asserted by Epimenides; to simplify the analysis, let us suppose that the paradox was the one and only proposition asserted by him. Then we have:

$$E(p) \equiv [p = (q)(E(q) \supset {\sim}q)].$$

Let us abbreviate $(q)(E(q) \supset {\sim}q)$ as $\mathcal{E}$. Then a simple argument (left to the reader) establishes the contradiction $\mathcal{E} \equiv {\sim}\mathcal{E}$. Let us examine how this paradox appears in the ramified theory of types. It is clear that we have to assign types to the variables p and q, and to the propositional function E. Let us suppose that the propositional variable p has type $0/m$. Then the order n of the propositional function E must be greater than m. Thus, the assumption leading to the Epimenides paradox can be written:

$$E^{(0/m)/n}(p^{0/m}) \equiv [p^{0/m} = (q)(E^{(0/m)/n}(q) \supset \sim q)].$$

It follows that the variable q must have order at most m. But then the identity statement on the right-hand side cannot be well formed, since it equates a proposition of order at most m with a universal proposition of an order greater than m. Thus, the assumption leading to the contradiction cannot even be formulated in the ramified theory of types, and even the Axiom of Reducibility fails to lead to a contradiction. As Russell puts it:

When a man says "I am lying," we must interpret him as meaning: "There is a proposition of order n which I affirm and which is false." This is a proposition of order $n + 1$; hence the man is not affirming any proposition of order n; hence his statement is false, and yet its falsehood does not imply, as that of "I am lying" appeared to do, that he is making a true statement. This solves the liar [MLT, 240; LK 79].

A similar analysis applies to the other semantic paradoxes, such as Berry's paradox and the Richard paradox.

We might try to reinstate the Epimenides paradox by replacing identity by logical equivalence in the assumption above. Thus, we consider the variant:

$$E^{(0/m)/n}(p^{0/m}) \equiv [p^{0/m} \equiv (q^{0/m})(E^{(0/m)/n}(q^{0/m}) \supset \sim q^{0/m})],$$

which is now a well-formed formula. In fact, this new assumption *does* lead to a contradiction, as the reader may easily verify – for details see [Myhill 1979]. However, an examination of the derivation of the contradiction shows that the Axiom of Reducibility is nowhere needed, so that the contradiction is already derivable in the pure ramified theory of types. The solution to this new formulation is simply to deny the existence of any such person as is asserted to exist in this formula, just as the pseudo-paradox of the barber who shaves all those in the town who do not shave themselves is solved by denying the existence of any such barber.

VI. THE SIMPLE THEORY OF TYPES

The basic logic of *Principia Mathematica*, even with the inclusion of the Axiom of Reducibility, is an intensional logic, in the sense that it allows the possibility of distinct but logically equivalent propositional functions. F.P. Ramsey, influenced strongly by Wittgenstein's *Tractatus Logico-Philosophicus*, advocated in Ramsey [1925] a completely extensional approach to the logicist foundations of mathematics.

Ramsey begins his reworking of the logicist project by introducing the Wittgensteinian notion of tautology, with the usual examples of truth-tables. His idea of truth-functions, though, is somewhat broader than his simple examples would suggest, since he permits truth-functions with infinitely many arguments. For example, he allows the disjunction of an infinite family of propositions. On this subject, he remarks:

Mr Wittgenstein has perceived that, if we accept this account of truth-functions as expressing agreement and disagreement with truth-possibilities, there is no reason why the arguments to a truth-function should not be infinite in number. As no previous writer has considered truth-functions as capable of more than a finite number of arguments, this is a most important innovation. Of course if the arguments are infinite in number they cannot all be enumerated and written down separately; but there is no need for us to enumerate them if we can determine them in any other way, as we can by using propositional functions [Ramsey 1978, 158–9].

Ramsey was well aware that he was making a radical departure from the *Principia Mathematica* view of propositional functions, in which the identity of a function is tightly bound to its logical expression. He remarks [Ramsey 1978, 174]: "The possibility of indefinable classes and relations in extension is an essential part of the extensional attitude of modern mathematics . . . , and that it is neglected in *Principia Mathematica* is the first of the three great defects in that work." On the subject of the vicious circle principle, he says:

To take a particularly simple case, $(\phi) \cdot \phi a$ is the logical product of the propositions ϕa, of which it is itself one; but this is no more remarkable and no more vicious than is the fact that $p \cdot q$ is the logical product of the set $p, q, p \cdot q$, of which it is itself a member [Ramsey 1978, 192].

Ramsey extends his extensional view of functions to form a hierarchy of functions of functions, and so on. The result is a system that is essentially equivalent to the simple theory of types, although his presentation leaves a lot to be desired by current standards of logical rigour. From the modern point of view, the first fully satisfactory presentation of the simple theory of types is to be found in [Gödel 1931] and [Tarski 1935].

Ramsey, of course, has to deal with the objection that in abandoning the ramified theory of types in favour of the simple theory, he is allowing the derivation of the paradoxes the original system was intended to avoid. He answers it by introducing the now familiar distinction between set-theoretical paradoxes, such as Russell's paradox, and the Burali-Forti paradox, and the semantic paradoxes, such as the Epimenides paradox and Richard's paradox. Ramsey draws the distinction between the two by claiming that those of the first group involve only logical or mathematical terms such as class and number, while the semantical paradoxes "all contain some reference to thought, language, or symbolism, which are not formal but empirical terms" [Ramsey 1978, 171]. Thus, the logical paradoxes are to be solved by the simple theory of types alone, while the ramification thought by Russell to be necessary to avoid the semantic paradoxes can be avoided. It may be remarked, though, that concepts such as truth and definability, in view of the later work of writers like Gödel, Tarski, and others, can be expressed in purely logical, mathematical terms, showing that the distinction between the two groups of paradoxes is perhaps not as clear-cut as Ramsey presented.

Ramsey's cavalier introduction of infinitary disjunctions and conjunctions certainly seems extremely bold, particularly from the quasi-constructive viewpoint adopted by Whitehead and Russell in the first edition of *Principia Mathematica*. The sarcastic remarks of Hermann Weyl (originally directed against the system of *Principia Mathematica* with the axiom of reducibility) seem apposite:

In the resulting system mathematics is no longer founded on logic, but on a sort of logician's paradise, a universe endowed with an "ultimate furniture" of rather complex structure and governed by quite a number of sweeping axioms of closure. The motives are clear, but belief in this transcendental world taxes the strength of our faith hardly less than the doctrines of the early Fathers of the Church or of the scholastic philosophers of the Middle Ages ([Weyl 1946, 6] and [Weyl 1968, 272]).

In the second edition of *Principia Mathematica*, Russell too (like Ramsey, strongly influenced by Wittgenstein's *Tractatus*) attempted a reworking of *PM* in extensional terms, though his approach is less radical than that of Ramsey. In the introduction to the second edition [*PM*, Vol. 1, xiii–xlvi], Russell gives a very sketchy account of this approach. The Axiom of Reducibility is dropped, and all functions are declared to be extensional. The only primitive propositional functions are atomic predicates of individuals (in contrast to the first edition approach, where the Axiom of Reducibility may be understood as postulating an infinite hierarchy of higher order primitive predicates). First-order quantification over individuals is introduced. Higher-order quantifiers, such as quantifiers ranging over first-order propositions, are explained in terms of infinite conjunctions and disjunctions of lower-order propositions. Russell points out, though, that such infinite conjunctions or disjunctions cannot be manipulated without *ad hoc* assumptions, in the absence of mathematical induction. He is therefore forced to adopt certain primitive propositions governing higher-order quantifiers.

Russell admits that the system of the second edition is inadequate to the theory of real numbers and well-ordered series, but attempts to show in a new Appendix B that the Peano postulates for the natural numbers, including the scheme of mathematical induction, can be derived in the absence of the Axiom of Reducibility. Unfortunately, his proof in the appendix is in error, as was first pointed out in [Gödel 1944]. In view of the result of [Myhill 1974] cited earlier, there appears to be no way to patch up Russell's attempted derivation. Thus, the system of the second edition can only be accounted a complete failure, considered as a foundation for mathematics.

VII. CONCLUSION

After the withdrawal of Russell and Whitehead from work in logic, and the tragically early death of F.P. Ramsey at the age of 25, the logicist programme in the foundations of mathematics gradually lost its impetus, as the initiative in logic passed to the Hilbert school in Germany and the Polish school of Łukasiewicz, Lindenbaum, Tarski, and others. The new emphasis was on proving general meta-theoretical results about logical systems, rather than developing mathematics within one single grand axiomatic framework. Quine in the United States continued the logicist approach in his own fashion, but the logical systems that he developed were tailored for maximum formal elegance, so that he avoided the notational complexities of type theory as far as possible. His system of "New Foundations" [Quine 1937], although taking its inspiration from Whitehead and Russell, manages to avoid the use of explicit type indices altogether.

The simple theory of types, when augmented by the axiom of infinity, is of course fully adequate for the derivation of all of standard mathematics, and is the basic system discussed in Gödel's great incompleteness paper [Gödel 1931]. Nevertheless, it was increasingly displaced by the rival foundational scheme of Zermelo's axiomatic set theory, of which the first version [Zermelo 1908] was published in the same year as Russell's fundamental paper on type theory.

Zermelo's system has the notational advantage of not containing any explicitly typed variables, although in fact it can be seen as having an implicit type structure built into it, at least if the axiom of regularity is included. The details of this implicit typing are spelled out in [Zermelo 1930], and again in a well-known article of George Boolos [Boolos 1971].

The ramified theory of types is in the main regarded today as a logical curiosity or relic, although it continues to interest philosophers of mathematics and logicians interested in predicative mathematics. Hermann Weyl accepted the philosophical criticism implicit in the vicious circle principle, and as a result rejected the Axiom of Reducibility, accepted for purely pragmatic reasons by Whitehead and Russell. As a result, he was forced to jettison a good deal of the conventional theory of real numbers and function theory. Nevertheless, he was able to show [Weyl 1918] that a surprisingly large part of the usual foundations of the infinitesimal calculus could be reconstructed in a predicative system based on the Peano axioms with set quantification restricted to first-order propositional functions. Thus, predicative mathematics (assuming we take the existence of the natural numbers for granted) is more extensive than we might at first think. Readers interested in the philosophy and practice of predicative mathematics are referred to the excellent survey article by Allen Hazen [Hazen 1983].

The ideas behind the ramified theory nevertheless played an important part in one of the most fundamental advances in the foundations of set theory. Gödel's proof of the relative consistency of the Axiom of Choice and the Generalized Continuum Hypothesis with the remaining axioms of Zermelo–Fraenkel set theory [Gödel 1938] was obtained by extending a version of the ramified hierarchy to transfinite type levels. Whitehead and Russell allow only finite type levels; Gödel's great insight was that if we allow a non-constructive extension of the ramified hierarchy to transfinite type levels, then we obtain a very well behaved structure in which not only can the Axiom of Choice be shown to hold, but in addition the Generalized Continuum Hypothesis can be seen to be true by a clever generalization of the Löwenheim–Skolem theorem. Paul Cohen's later result [Cohen 1963], [Cohen 1964] showing the independence of the Continuum Hypothesis from the axioms of set theory also uses an extension of Gödel's ramified hierarchy, although it was shortly afterwards simplified to a version using a simple, rather than a ramified concept of types.

Although the theory of types, whether in the ramified or simple version, is no longer the preferred vehicle for investigating the foundations of mathematics, having been largely displaced by Zermelo–Fraenkel set theory, type theory has recently experienced a significant revival in the foundations of programming languages. Explicit typing, a nuisance in most pure mathematical contexts, turns out to be very useful both in increasing the reliability of computer programmes and in proving them correct. Simple type-checking routines are often sufficient to catch many errors in programs, while elaborate systems of automated type theory have played a role in developing sophisticated algorithms and in proving their correctness. There is now a very large literature devoted to this topic; the reader is directed to the excellent survey by John C. Mitchell [Mitchell 1990] for an introduction to this area.

NOTE

1.   Although Whitehead and Russell explicitly claim that propositions can be eliminated by their device of incomplete symbols [PM, Vol. 1, 43–4], the details of the contextual definitions required are never fully supplied, and it is doubtful if the purported elimination is possible. In any case, the fact that propositions are values of the propositional variables seems clearly required by the motivation of Russell's logic, and furthermore is required in the analysis of paradoxes such as the Epimenides or liar.

REFERENCES

Boolos, George, 1971. "The iterative conception of set." *Journal of Philosophy* 68: 215–231. Reprinted in [Boolos 1998], 13–29.

Boolos, George, 1998. *Logic, Logic and Logic.* Cambridge, MA: Harvard University Press.

Chihara, Charles S., 1973. *Ontology and the Vicious-Circle Principle.* Ithaca, NY: Cornell University Press.

Church, Alonzo, 1976. "Comparison of Russell's resolution of the semantical antinomies with that of Tarski." *Journal of Symbolic Logic,* 41: 747–60.

Church, Alonzo, 1984. "Russell's Theory of Identity of Propositions." *Philosophia Naturalis,* 21: 513–22.

Cohen, Paul J., 1963. "The independence of the continuum hypothesis I." *Proceedings of the National Academy of Sciences, U.S.A.* 50: 1143–8.

Cohen, Paul J., 1964. "The independence of the continuum hypothesis II." *Proceedings of the National Academy of Sciences, U.S.A.* 51: 105–10.

Chwistek, Leon, 1921. "Antynomje logiki formalnej." *Przegląd Filozoficzny,* 24: 164–71. Translated in [McCall 1967], 338–45.

Copi, Irving M., 1950. "The Inconsistency or Redundancy of *Principia Mathematica.*" *Philosophy and Phenomenological Research,* 11: 190–99.

Ewald, W.B., Ed., 1996. *From Kant to Hilbert: A Source Book in the Foundations of Mathematics* Vol. 2. Oxford: Clarendon Press.

Frege, Gottlob, 1893. *Grundgesetze der Arithmetik, begriffschriftlich abgeleitet.* Vol. 1, Hermann Pohle, Jena.

Frege, Gottlob, 1903. *Grundgesetze der Arithmetik, begriffschriftlich abgeleitet.* Vol. 2, Hermann Pohle, Jena.

Frege, Gottlob, 1980. *Philosophical and Mathematical Correspondence.* Ed. Gottfried Gabriel, Hans Hermes, Friedrich Kambartel, Christian Thiel and Albert Veraart. Abridged from the German edition by Brian McGuinness. Trans. Hans Kaal. Chicago, IL: University of Chicago Press.

Handbook of Philosophical Logic Volume I. 1983. Ed. D. Gabbay and F. Guenthner. Dordrecht: Reidel.

Gödel, Kurt, 1931. "Über formal unentscheidbare Sätze der *Principia Mathematica* und verwandter Systeme I." *Monatshefte für Mathematik und Physik,* 38: 173–98. Reprinted with facing English trans. in [Gödel 1986, 144–95].

Gödel, Kurt, 1938. "The consistency of the axiom of choice and of the generalized continuum hypothesis." *Proceedings of the National Academy of Sciences, U.S.A.* 24: 556–7. Reprinted in [Gödel 1990], 26–7.

Gödel, Kurt, 1944. "Russell's mathematical logic" in [Schilpp 1944, 123–53].

Gödel, Kurt, 1986. *Collected Works, Volume I: Publications 1929–1936.* Ed. Solomon Feferman, John W. Dawson, Jr., Stephen C. Kleene, Gregory

H. Moore, Robert M. Solovay, and Jean van Heijenoort. Oxford, UK: Oxford University Press.

Gödel, Kurt, 1990. *Collected Works, Volume II: Publications 1938–1974*. Ed. Solomon Feferman, John W. Dawson, Jr., Stephen C. Kleene, Gregory H. Moore, Robert M. Solovay, and Jean van Heijenoort. Oxford, UK: Oxford University Press.

Hazen, Allen, 1983. "Predicative Logics" in [Handbook 1983, 331–407].

van Heijenoort, Jean, 1967. *From Frege to Gödel*. Cambridge, MA: Harvard University Press.

McCall, S., Ed., 1967. *Polish Logic 1920–1939*. Oxford, UK: Oxford University Press.

Mitchell, John C., 1990. "Type Systems for Programming Languages." In *Handbook of Theoretical Computer Science. Volume B: Formal Models and Semantics*, ed. J. van Leeuwen, 365–458. Cambridge, MA: MIT Press, and Amsterdam: Elsevier.

Myhill, John, 1974. "The Undefinability of the Set of Natural Numbers in the Ramified *Principia*" in: [Nakhnikian 1974, 19–27].

Myhill, John, 1979. "A refutation of an unjustified attack on the Axiom of Reducibility" in: [Roberts 1979, 81–90].

Nakhnikian, G., Ed. *Bertrand Russell's Philosophy*. London: Duckworth.

Pelham, Judy, and Urquhart, Alasdair, 1994. "Russellian Propositions" in: *Logic, Methodology and Philosophy of Science IX*, ed. Prawitz, Skyrms and Westerståhl. Amsterdam: North Holland, 307–26.

Poincaré, Henri, 1905–06, "Les mathématiques et la logique." *Revue de métaphysique et de morale* 13:815–35, 14:17–34, 14: 294–317. English trans. in [Ewald 1996, 1021–71].

Quine, W.V., 1937. "New Foundations for Mathematical Logic." *American Mathematical Monthly* 44: 70–80. Reprinted with additions in [Quine 1961].

Quine, W.V., 1955. "On Frege's Way Out." *Mind*, 64: 145–59. Partially reprinted in [Quine 1995].

Quine, W.V., 1961. *From a Logical Point of View*. Cambridge, MA: Harvard University Press. Second rev. ed.

Quine, W.V., 1995. *Selected Logic Papers*. Enlarged ed. Cambridge, MA: Harvard University Press.

Ramsey, Frank P., 1925. "The Foundations of Mathematics." *Proceedings of the London Mathematical Society*, Ser. 2, 25, 338–384. Reprinted in [Ramsey 1978], 152–212.

Ramsey, Frank P., 1978. *Foundations: Essays in Philosophy, Logic, Mathematics and Economics*, ed. D.H. Mellor. London: Routledge and Kegan Paul.

Roberts, George, Ed. 1979. *Bertrand Russell Memorial Volume*, London: Allen and Unwin.

Schilpp, Paul A., Ed. 1944. *The Philosophy of Bertrand Russell*, Library of living philosophers, Vol. 5. Evanston: Northwestern University Press.

Schütte, Kurt, 1960. *Beweistheorie*. Berlin: Springer.

Tarski, Alfred, 1935. "Der Wahrheitsbegriff in den formalisierten Sprachen." *Studia Philosophica*, 1: 261–405. English trans. in [Tarski 1956, 152–278].

Tarski, Alfred, 1956. *Logic, Semantics, Metamathematics: Papers from 1923 to 1938*. Trans. into English and ed. J.H. Woodger. Oxford: Clarendon Press.

Weyl, Hermann, 1918. *Das Kontinuum. Kritische Untersuchungen über die Grundlagen der Analysis*. Veit, Leipzig. English trans. [Weyl 1987].

Weyl, Hermann, 1946. "Mathematics and logic. A brief survey serving as a preface to a review of *The Philosophy of Bertrand Russell*." *American Mathematical Monthly*, 53: 2–13. Reprinted in [Weyl 1968], 268–79.

Weyl, Hermann, 1968. *Gesammelte Abhandlungen*. Vol. 4. Ed. K. Chandrasekharan. Berlin: Springer-Verlag.

Weyl, Hermann, 1987. *The Continuum: A Critical Examination of the Foundations of Analysis*. Kirksville, Missouri: Thomas Jefferson University Press. Corrected republication, New York: Dover, 1994.

Zermelo, Ernst, 1908. "Untersuchungen über die Grundlagen der Mengenlehre I." *Mathematische Annalen* 65: 261–81. English trans. in [van Heijenoort 1967].

Zermelo, Ernst, 1930. "Über Grenzzahlen und Mengenbereiche. Neue Untersuchungen über die Grundlagen der Mengenlehre." *Fundamenta Mathematicae* 16: 29–47. English trans. in [Ewald 1996], 1219–33.

9 Russell's Method of Analysis

A major component of Russell's philosophical work was the development of a distinctive method of philosophising, which, though he consistently applied it throughout his career, has been largely ignored. This lack of understanding of Russell's method has been a main cause of the still widespread perception that the progress of his philosophy is fragmented and erratic. This chapter will, firstly, outline key characteristics of Russell's method of philosophical analysis and show how this method underpins a number of his best known contributions to philosophy. Secondly, because his philosophical writings from the 1920s onwards have been rather neglected, some of his work of the late 1940s and early 1950s will be discussed to show that it exemplifies the same basic philosophical method. This will have the effect of emphasising the unity and continuity of Russell's philosophy. Finally, defective accounts of Russell's philosophy in some critical works are traced to misunderstanding of his method of analysis.

RUSSELL'S METHOD OF PHILOSOPHICAL ANALYSIS

Throughout his career Russell adhered to a characteristic view of the nature of philosophical analysis according to which it has two parts. Firstly, philosophical analysis proceeds backwards from a body of knowledge to its premises, and, secondly, it proceeds forwards from the premises to a reconstruction of the original body of knowledge. Russell often called the first stage of philosophical analysis simply "analysis", in contrast to the second stage which he called "synthesis" (or, sometimes, "construction"). While the first stage was seen as being the most philosophical, both stages were nonetheless essential to philosophical analysis. It is beyond the scope of this chapter to fully document the claim that Russell consistently adhered to this two-directional view of philosophical analysis throughout his career; however, a consideration of some representative writings of Russell will further clarify his view of philosophical analysis and its implications.[1]

Russell's initial major applications of his method of philosophical analysis were to mathematics in *Principles of Mathematics* and *Principia Mathematica*. So we find in his writings of this period a very clear account of philosophical analysis applied to mathematics (Hager 1994, Chapter 2). However, he held also that this mathematical work was, in principle, no different from work in the foundations of any science or discipline. Increasingly from the first decade of the twentieth century, Russell turned his method of analysis from mathematics and logic to other philosophical concerns such as epistemology, metaphysics, philosophy of language, and philosophy of science. In all cases, philosophical analysis was aimed at a non-empirical intellectual discovery of propositions and concepts from which could be fashioned premises for the basic data from which the analysis had begun.

Russell was very specific about the two-directional character of his philosophical method: "The business of philosophy, as I conceive it, is essentially that of logical analysis, followed by logical synthesis" (LA, p. 162). The first or backwards stage, logical analysis, was seen as general across all philosophy:

... every truly philosophical problem is a problem of analysis; and in problems of analysis the best method is that which sets out from results and arrives at the premises. (Russell 1911, *Papers* 6, p. 33)

The second or forwards stage, logical synthesis, was seen as following upon and mirroring imperfectly the earlier logical analysis stage:

When the philosopher's work has been perfectly accomplished, its results can be wholly embodied in premises from which deduction may proceed. (*POM*, p. 129)

The logical synthesis can only mirror imperfectly the logical analysis stage because it is capable of yielding more than the knowledge

---

[1] For detailed discussion see Hager (1994) for 1900 onwards, while Griffin (1991) details the period up to 1900. See also Irvine (1989), and Godwyn and Irvine in this volume.

(results or data) that was the starting point of the analysis. According to Russell (*IMP*, p. 2), we "shall find that by analysing our ordinary mathematical notions we acquire fresh insight, new powers, and the means of reaching whole new mathematical subjects by adopting fresh lines of advance after our backward journey." This capacity of the synthesis stage to expand knowledge needs emphasising since it has usually been overlooked. When "we have decided upon our premisses, we have to build up again as much as may seem necessary of the data previously analysed, and as many other consequences of our premisses as are of sufficient general interest to deserve a statement" (*PM*, vol 1, p. v).

Each of the quotations in the last few paragraphs has been taken from a context where Russell was asserting the general features of the method of philosophical analysis. Likewise, when summing up his career, Russell repeatedly stated that a *single* method was common to all of his philosophical ventures. (See, e.g., *HWP*, pp. 788–9 and *MPD*, pp. 98 and 162.) Given this definiteness on Russell's part, the relative lack of attention to his method of analysis is puzzling.

A careful consideration of the wide range of descriptions that Russell provides of his method of philosophical analysis points to some important characteristics that he repeatedly emphasises:

i)   Analysis is unlikely to be final.

This applies in several ways. Not only is analysis never final in the sense that new premisses may be discovered in relation to which existing premisses are results, but there also is the ever present possibility of alternative sets of premisses for the same results. In the former case, further stages of analysis in no way invalidate earlier ones. As Russell repeatedly emphasised, no error will flow from taking complex objects to be simple at one level of analysis, as long as it is not assumed that such objects are incapable of further analysis. Thus "... points may be defined as classes of events, but that does not falsify anything in traditional geometry, which treated points as simples" (*HK*, p. 269).[2] In the latter case, to ask what are the minimum premisses for a given set of results "is a technical question and it has no unique answer" (*MPD*, p. 162). Hence, one important task for philosophy is to devise alternative sets of premisses.

---

[2] See also *LA*, p. 158 and *MPD*, pp. 164–5.

However, Russell's use of the terms 'premisses' and 'results' in his discussions of analysis does require some comment. Strictly speaking, of course, premisses and results, being components of deductive arguments, can only be *propositions* or *statements*. However, analysis leads not only to propositions, but also to *concepts* or *ideas* which are *primitive* at one level of analysis and *defined* at the next level down. (See, e.g., *IMP*, pp. 3–4.) At the higher level these concepts or ideas are used in *definitions* that provide further premisses. When characterizing his method of analysis, Russell sometimes, for convenience, uses 'premisses' in a *wider sense* to refer to concepts or ideas, as well as propositions. Take, for instance, Peano's analysis of natural number theory via three primitive concepts and five primitive propositions. In Russell's wider sense, the three concepts and five propositions are the premisses, yet, strictly speaking, the only premisses are the five primitive propositions. However, including the concepts (o, number and successor) amongst the premisses is fairly innocuous since they are used in the statements of the propositional premisses as well as in the definition of further concepts used in subsequent results. In the next breakthrough in analysis, due to Frege, the concepts ceased to be primitive (e.g., he provided a definition of number). This wider sense of 'premisses' is typically employed in Russell's descriptions of philosophical analysis.

ii) Analysis enlarges the domains of particular subjects.

The current science or mathematics on which analysis is practised changes as the science itself evolves. What were formerly tentative premisses for science or mathematics later become a part of those disciplines. This view locates philosophy at the frontiers of the particular disciplines. As these frontiers are extended, territory that once belonged to philosophy becomes exact enough to be incorporated into those disciplines. Thus "every advance in knowledge robs philosophy of some problems which formerly it had . . . ." (PLA, p. 243). So for Russellian analysis, yesterday's premisses become tomorrow's results from which a new generation of philosophers will start the backwards journey of analysis. Thus, the philosophy/science distinction "is one, not in the subject matter, but in the state of mind of the investigator" (*IMP*, p. 1). It remains for philosophy to move to the new frontier. Hence, Russell's maxim that "science is what you more or less know and philosophy is what you do not know" (PLA, p. 243).

iii) Analysis leads to premisses that are decreasingly self-evident.

Russell made this point emphatically (LA, pp. 145–6) where he considers the case of pure mathematics organized as a deductive system in which all of its propositions are deducible from a particular set of premisses. Russell points out that

.... it becomes obvious that, if we are to believe in the truth of pure mathematics, it cannot be solely because we believe in the truth of the set of premisses. Some of the premisses are much less obvious than some of their consequences, and are believed chiefly because of their consequences.[3]

He argues that this is always so when a science is arranged as a deductive system. So the logically simplest propositions of the system are never the most obvious in physics either. For example, taking Maxwell's equations as the premisses of electrodynamics, these equations are far from obvious and "... are believed because of the observed truth of certain of their logical consequences" (LA, p. 146). Hence, in general, philosophical analysis gives us grounds "for believing the premisses because true consequences follow from them, than for believing the consequences because they follow from the premisses" (PM, vol 1, p. v). An example of the premisses being far from self-evident is provided by Russell's definition of number. A "number is anything which is the number of some class", where the "number of a class is the class of all those classes that are similar to it" (IMP, pp. 18–19) is clearly a less self-evident definition than "a number is any of 1,2,3,4....etc".

The decreasing self-evidence of the premisses has ontological implications. According to Russell the current premisses provide our best guide to the nature of the most fundamental entities, hence, e.g., his replacement of common sense physical objects by sense-data and events. The decreasing self-evidence of the premisses was also the basis of Russell's vintage statement that "the point of philosophy is

---

[3] This point appears to have made little impact on Russell commentators. An exception is Irvine (1989) and Godwyn and Irvine in this volume.

to start with something so simple as not to seem worth stating, and to end up with something so paradoxical that no one will believe it" (PLA, p. 172). This decreasing self-evidence of the premisses, coupled with the earlier claim that there may be alternative premisses from which the same given set of results is deducible, is the basis of Russell's characteristic open-mindedness about the finality or otherwise of his philosophical views at any given stage.

Since the decreasing self-evidence of the premisses is the feature of Russellian analysis that is most at odds with some common interpretations of Russell's work, it will pay us to consider it in more detail. The following table catalogues the multitude of ways that Russell describes the results and premisses in his accounts of analysis:

Characteristics of Russellian Results and Premisses[4]

Results (or Data)	Premisses
More complex	Simpler
Relatively concrete	Abstract
Common knowledge	[The outcome of special inquiry]
Vague	Precise
Logically interdependent	Logically independent
More obvious	Less obvious
Undeniable	[Disputable]
Inexact and approximate	Definite
Indubitable	Dubitable
Puzzling	[Explanatory]
Confused	Clear
Self-evident	[Requiring justification]
Ambiguous	[Unambiguous]
[Disorganised]	[Ordered]

At first sight it may appear puzzling that though the results (as compared with the premisses) are "self-evident", "undeniable", and

---

[4] The sources for these characteristics include *OKEW*, PLA, LA, RTC, *HWP*, and *MPD*. For full details of all of the sources and the relevant quotations that span fifty five years, see Hager (1994, Chapter 3). The characteristics shown in brackets are implied by what Russell says whereas the others are direct quotations.

"indubitable", they are also "inexact", "vague", and "confused". Russell produces some striking examples to show that there is no inconsistency here: the something approaching us through a thick fog is undeniably (indubitably) some object or other though we have only a vague (confused, inexact) idea of just *what* it is (*MPD*, pp. 98–99); likewise, the novice hearing a symphony might be impressed by the parts evidently (indubitably) forming a whole, yet be very vague (confused) about how the parts relate to one another to constitute the whole (*MPD*, pp. 169–70).

The characteristics of results and premises listed in the table clarify an ambiguity in Russell's use of 'simple'. The premises are *simple* in the primary sense that the results can be *compounded* from them. However, as the Oxford dictionary confirms, 'simple' also means 'easily understood', i.e., the *results* could also be seen as simple in that they are concrete, common knowledge, obvious, and indubitable. Russell appears to have been using the term in this second sense when he said that "the point of philosophy is to start with something so simple as not to seem worth stating, and to end up with something so paradoxical that no one will believe it" (PLA, p. 172).

However, there is an even more fundamental reason why there is confusion about simples in Russell's philosophy. It stems, I believe, from another ambiguity – this time in what Russell means by 'analysis'. It has been pointed out already that, on one understanding of the term, *analysis* refers only to the first, and more philosophical, stage of Russell's method. The second, more mathematical or logical, stage is, of course, synthesis. However, on the other understanding, *analysis* is the name of Russell's entire philosophical method. Let me call the former understanding the *narrow* interpretation of analysis, and the latter the *broad* interpretation. I suggest that the confusion resulting from these two meanings of 'analysis' has led people to concentrate on the first stage of Russell's philosophical method and treat that as all there is to it. What is left out makes all the difference about how one treats relations in Russell's philosophy (Hager 1994, Chs. 5–7).

Russell's work is, of course, replete with examples of philosophical analysis that exemplify the scheme that has been detailed so far in this chapter. These include the overall program of *Principia Mathematica* as well as the specific analyses that make up that program, such as the analyis of classes; points and instants analysed as events; everyday objects such as tables and chairs as logical constructions; the theory of definite descriptions, and many others.[5]

HUMAN KNOWLEDGE AS AN EXAMPLE OF RUSSELLIAN ANALYSIS

Judging by the frequency with which they are referred to and discussed, it appears that Russell's works prior to the 1920s, such as *Principles of Mathematics*, *Principia Mathematica*, 'Philosophy of Logical Atomism', the theory of descriptions, etc., have made the greatest impact on philosophers. By comparison, later works, though substantial, have been somewhat ignored. The general belief seems to be that Russell, having set much of the philosophical agenda up to 1920, was overtaken by events as philosophy moved on, leaving him in isolation to produce unpopular theories, such as his neutral monism, which were thought to have little connection with his earlier work. I have argued in detail that, on the contrary, all of Russell's work in philosophy displays striking continuity (Hager 1994). In this section, the 1948 *Human Knowledge* will be examined in some detail as an example of Russellian philosophical analysis. Other substantial later works such as *Analysis of Mind* (1921), *Analysis of Matter* (1927), and *An Inquiry into Meaning and Truth* (1940) could equally well have been considered.

In some ways *Human Knowledge* is a followup to *Analysis of Matter*, a book which set out a philosophical analysis of physics focused on ontology. It sought to answer the following questions:

What are the ultimate existents in terms of which physics is true (assuming that there are such)? And what is their general structure? And what are the relations of space-time, causality, and qualitative series respectively? (*AMa*, p. 9)

The outcome of this analysis was that an ontology of events and universals would suffice for physics (Hager 1994, pp. 59–60). However, in 1943, Russell noted that the

... canons of scientific inference have never yet been formulated; if I have leisure, I hope to try to formulate them myself. (RTC, p. 718)

---

[5] See Hager (1994) for detailed discussion and further examples.

This work became the 1948 *Human Knowledge* the "central purpose" of which "is to examine the relation between individual experience and the general body of scientific knowledge" (*HK*, p. 9). Russell assumes scientific knowledge to be broadly and most likely true, and he seeks to investigate what principles need to supplement our empirical experience if that assumption is valid. Hence, "one of the main purposes of this book" is to "discover the minimum principles required to justify scientific inferences" (*HK*, p. 11). Thus, Russell's prime target for philosophical analysis is the nature of scientific inference. I will describe Russell's procedure in *Human Knowledge* as an instance of his two-directional method of philosophical analysis.

As we have seen, Russellian philosophical analysis begins with the 'results' or 'data' which are 'vague', 'common knowledge', 'inexact and approximate', 'indubitable', and 'puzzling'. The 'result' to be analysed in *Human Knowledge* is the 'vague' claim that 'scientific knowledge is developed from observational data via inductive or probabilistic inference'. It is because of the vagueness and inexactness of the various terms in this claim that Russell spends a lot of space in *Human Knowledge* clarifying the 'results' or 'data' for the analysis. Thus, Part I (in a six part book) outlines the general body of scientific knowledge that he takes to be generally and most likely true. So Part I covers "what do we know?" (*HK*, p. 66). Part II, "still concerned with preliminaries" (*HK*, p. 11), clarifies meanings of central fundamental terms like 'fact' and 'truth' and examines the relation of sensible experience to empirical concepts. In brief, Part II deals with "how do we know it?" At last, in Part III, "we begin out main inquiry" but "are not yet concerned to justify inferences, or to investigate the principles according to which they are made" (*HK*, pp. 11–12). The main focus of Part III is 'how does what we know relate to our empirical data?' This is still part of the clarification of vague and inexact 'results'. After a detailed consideration of what can be counted as empirical data, Russell finds "that inferences (as opposed to logical constructions out of data) are necessary to science" (*HK*, p. 12). The conclusion to Part III is that

while mental events and their qualities can be known without inference, physical events are known only as regards their space-time structure. The qualities that compose such events are unknown – so completely unknown that we cannot say either that they are, or that they are not, different from the qualities that we know as belonging to mental events. (*HK*, p. 247)

Having clarified considerably in the first half of *Human Knowledge* the 'vague' claim that 'scientific knowledge is developed from observational data via inductive or probabilistic inference', Russell is ready in Part IV to conduct the backwards step in analysis to identify some premisses of scientific inference. Recall that as against the 'results', the 'premisses' are 'precise', 'logically independent', 'less obvious', 'definite', and 'dubitable'. In this case the premisses that he reaches in Part IV include fundamental concepts like 'causal line' (defined on p. 477), 'space-time structure' (defined on pp. 344ff), 'event' (defined on pp. 97–8), and other basic notions such as 'similarity' and 'series'. The first two of these are particularly central to the analysis:

Throughout [Part IV] the two concepts of space-time structure and causal chains (causal lines) assume a gradually increasing importance. (*HK*, p. 12)

Russell continues the backwards search for premisses in Part V. Because "scientific inferences, as a rule, only confer probability on their conclusions" (*HK*, p. 12), it is crucial to clarify the different types of probability and their roles in scientific inference. Russell distinguishes the mathematical theory of probability from the different notion of probability that he calls "degree of credibility". The latter is derived from Keynes' work on probability and refers to propositions that have a finite degree of probability, but not one that can be quantified. Finally, in Part VI, Russell is ready for the forwards (or synthesis) step in the analysis. From the concepts and principles arrived at in the previous two sections, he proceeds to deduce "five postulates" which are "required to validate scientific method" (*HK*, p. 506). These 'reconstructed results', which replace the earlier vague notion of 'inductive or probabilistic inference' are:

I) The postulate of quasi-permanence
II) The postulate of separable causal lines
III) The postulate of spatio-temporal continuity in causal lines
IV) The postulate of the common causal origin of similar structures ranged about a centre, or, more simply, the structural postulate
V) The postulate of analogy

None of these postulates is certain, but each has some significant degree of probability. As Russell sees it:

Given a number of propositions, each having a fairly high degree of intrinsic credibility, and given a system of inferences by virtue of which these various propositions increase each other's credibility, ... [we] arrive at a body of interconnected propositions having, as a whole, a very high degree of credibility. (HK, p. 413)

As usual, Russell recognises the non-finality of his analysis. Pointing out that it is "highly probable" that the number of postulates "can be further reduced", he adds that "I have not myself succeeded in doing so" (HK, p. 506). This characteristic recognition of the tentative findings of his philosophical analysis is reflected in a concluding comment:

Induction, we have seen, is not quite the universal proposition that we need to justify scientific inference. But we most certainly do need *some* universal proposition or propositions, whether the five canons ..... or something different. (HK, p. 524)

LATER WRITINGS ON ANALYSIS

When Russell published *Human Knowledge*, he was feeling increasingly isolated in the British philosophical world as the influence of the later Wittgenstein grew stronger. This led him to provide searching reviews and responses to the writings of a number of emerging philosophical opponents.[6] In this section I will discuss Russell's review of Urmson's book *Philosophical Analysis* (reprinted in *MPD*, it originally appeared in the *Hibbert Journal* in 1956), an article by McKinney in reply to Russell's review (which appeared in the succeeding volume of the *Hibbert Journal*), and a letter from Russell to McKinney commenting on his article in reply.[7] The reason for considering these three documents here is that, not only do they serve to show Russell's continuing commitment to the method of philosophical analysis outlined earlier in this chapter, but they also clarify a number of aspects of that method that have not been discussed so far.

---

[6] Four of these reviews/responses were later reprinted as Chapter 18 of *My Philosophical Development*.

[7] I am grateful to Nicholas Griffin for bringing this letter to my attention.

In his review Russell finds that some of Urmson's comments on philosophical analysis are due to misunderstandings and some to philosophical disagreements. In an attempt to clear away the former, Russell undertakes to "try to state as concisely as I can the purposes and methods which have guided my work in philosophy" (*MPD*, p. 161). To that end, Russell characterises his method of philosophical analysis (*MPD*, p. 162). Within the subsequent discussion, clear reference can be found to each of the three important features of analysis outlined earlier in this chapter:

(i) ANALYSIS IS UNLIKELY TO BE FINAL

Earlier, two senses in which analysis is never final were noted. Regarding the first of these, Russell responds to Urmson's criticism that "however far you may carry your analysis you will never reach simples" (*MPD*, p. 164). Russell replies that even when he and Wittgenstein spoke of 'atomic facts' as the final residue of analysis, it was "never an essential part of the analytic philosophy which Mr. Urmson is criticising to suppose that such facts were attainable" (*MPD*, p. 164). Russell's standard position has been that he can see no reason either to assert or deny that simples can be reached by analysis. He repeats verbatim some discussion from the 1918 lectures 'The Philosophy of Logical Atomism' to show his long commitment to this position, adding that since then he has become even more convinced that there is no reason to expect analysis to reach simples. Russell then uses the example of the human skeleton to illustrate the point that no error will flow from taking complex objects to be simple at one level of analysis, as long as it is not assumed that such objects are incapable of further analysis. The skeleton is composed of bones, cells, molecules, atoms, electrons, etc.

Bones, molecules, atoms, and electrons may each be treated, for certain purposes, as if they were unanalysable units devoid of structure, but at no stage is there any positive reason to suppose that this is in fact the case. The ultimate units so far reached may at any moment turn out to be capable of analysis. Whether there must be units incapable of analysis because they are destitute of parts, is a question which there seems no way of deciding. Nor is it important, since there is nothing erroneous in an account of structure which starts from units that are afterwards found to be themselves complex. (*MPD*, p. 165).

Regarding the second point, that alternative sets of premisses are always a possibility, Russell spells out reasons why it is important for philosophy to devise alternative sets of premisses.

Any reduction in the number of undefined terms and unproved premisses is an improvement since it diminishes the range of possible error and provides a smaller assemblage of hostages for the truth of the whole system. (*MPD*, p. 162)

The successive historical stages in the analysis of mathematics are then outlined by Russell to illustrate this point.

ii) Analysis enlarges the domains of particular subjects.

As discussed earlier, the current science or mathematics on which analysis is practised changes as the subject itself evolves. Formerly tentative premisses for science or mathematics later become a part of those disciplines. This aspect of analysis is raised indirectly in Urmson's objection to analysis that "the collection of statements that you reach by analysing is not equivalent to the original unanalysed statement" (*MPD*, p. 164) and in Russell's reply to this objection. Perhaps confusing Russell with a logical positivist, Urmson takes it as obvious that for analysis to be any good, the premisses reached by analysis must be logically equivalent to the results from which the analysis started. Thus, his criticism of analysis is that when a complex statement like "England declared war in 1939" is analysed into a series of simpler statements, the two will not be equivalent. Now the problem here is that Russell never maintained logical equivalence between results and premisses, only that what was well founded in the results can be deduced from the premisses; i.e., the synthesis step in philosophical analysis leads to a reconstructed version of the results. Thus, for example, replacing the desk of common sense by a complex structure of sense-data involves not only some continuity but also some novelty. No wonder, then, that Russell was unsure of what was Urmson's exact point here.

As noted earlier, for Russell this creation of new premisses that imply a reconstruction of the results is precisely the way that knowledge advances. Russell charges that had Urmson's approach to philosophy, rooted in ordinary language, flourished in the Greek world, science might still be at the stage of earth, air, fire, and water as the four 'elements' (*MPD*, p. 169).

iii) Analysis leads to premisses that are decreasingly self-evident.

In explaining his method of philosophical analysis in the Urmson review, Russell refers to the minimum of undefined terms and unproved premisses that is achieved by the analysis step. But he goes on to point out that "such a minimum, when arrived at, does not give the reasons for which we believe the system to be true" (MPD, p. 163). Generally, then, the premisses are less self-evident than the results. This point is connected by Russell with the "intolerable prolixity" of a perfect logical language (MPD, p. 166). Such languages, with their characteristics of simplicity and abstractness are useful in moving in the backwards direction of analysis. However, when moving the other way to synthesis, more everyday language is better suited to the task. Given Russell's account of the historical movement of analysis through successive generations of thinkers, it seems that he would need to argue that one generation's technical language will become a later generation's everyday language.

It is clear, then, that in his 1956 review of the Urmson book, Russell provided a detailed account of his method of philosophical analysis that in all key details was the same as the method he was developing and expounding in the first decade of the twentieth century. Russell's Urmson review stimulated a response from McKinney (1957) that sought to explicate further the nature of analysis. Its chief interest today is in its conflation of Russell's method of analysis with scientific method, an error that Russell focused on in his subsequent letter to McKinney (Russell 1958).

The McKinney article shows an awareness of the two-directional nature of Russellian analysis. But McKinney equates the first stage (analysis) with scientific hypothesis formation. He thinks of the second stage (synthesis) as akin to deduction from scientific laws and theories. Russell's 1958 letter bluntly rejects this interpretation by distinguishing sharply between "analysis" (logical analysis) and inference to things not perceived, i.e., scientific hypothesis, or nondeductive or nondemonstrative inference. He adds that this contrast between the methods of philosophy and of science should be clear from Human Knowledge. Russell expands on the difference in the letter by arguing that while in philosophical analysis the "whole is given", in scientific hypothesising the "whole is not given". Russell's aim in making this contrast is to emphasise that the data or results that are the starting point for philosophical analysis are very different from the data that play a central part in scientific method. By the "whole being given" in philosophical analysis, Russell means that there is no question of the data being expanded indefinitely, as happens in science, as further observations are made or experiments conducted. Since philosophical analysis is a conceptual activity, all that is needed is an understanding of the present state of the field being investigated. This special feature of the data for philosophical analysis, that it is already freely available, is reflected in some of the kinds of characteristics of 'results' or 'data' noted earlier in this chapter, i.e., 'relatively concrete', 'common knowledge', 'more obvious', 'undeniable', 'indubitable' and 'self-evident', while also 'inexact and approximate', 'confused' and 'ambiguous'. In contrast, Russell views scientific hypothesising as essentially dependent on testing by observational data, data that by its nature is always incomplete. In scientific hypothesising, the "whole is not given" because inference to unobserved instances is an unavoidable part of the enterprise.

Russell provides some illustrative examples of what he sees as the perennial incompleteness in the data in scientific hypothesising. An example discussed in both *Human Knowledge* and in the letter to McKinney is the inference to Kepler's laws from data consisting of a finite set of planetary positions. Clearly, the data here is less than the whole in that it consists of particular positions for particular planets at particular times, a subset of all of the positions of all of the planets at all times. In this case, there is the further complication that while two of the three positional coordinates come from measurements, the third cooordinate is a guess chosen to yield simple laws of planetary motion. Russell points out that it follows from scientific hypothesising being based on less than the whole data, that scientific hypotheses can never be *proved* true:

The hypothesis embodied in Kepler's laws is not *proved* by observation; what observation proves is that the facts are *compatible* with this hypothesis. (*HK*, p. 499)

Another example that Russell discussed in *Human Knowledge* is the law of falling bodies (p. 497). Based on a small number of rough measurements, Galileo hypothesised that the acceleration of vertically falling bodies is approximately constant. Further support for the hypothesis was added when the invention of the air pump enabled measurements in the absence of air resistance. However, later observations and theoretical developments suggested slight variations in acceleration with both latitude and altitude. Thus, Galileo's simple hypothesis was displaced successively by increasingly more complicated Newtonian and then Einsteinian laws.

Russell's view of the roles of observation and hypothesis in science, as illustrated in these examples, is well captured in the following quotation in which he offers a "model of the scientific method":

> Hypothesis and observation alternate; each new hypothesis calls for new observations, and, if it is to be accepted, must fit the facts better than any previous hypothesis. But it always remains possible, if not probable, that some further hypothesis may be called for to explain further observations. New hypotheses do not show old ones to have been false, but only to have been approximations.... (Russell 1974, pp. 21–2)

Readers will have noticed that Russell's characterisation of scientific method in the preceding paragraphs bears a strong resemblance to Popper's fallibilism.[8]

By now Russell's sharp contrast between his distinctive method of philosophical analysis and his view of the scientific method, with its alternations of hypothesising and observation, should be clear. However, it is unsurprising that McKinney and others might confuse the two for a number of reasons. Firstly, it was not unknown for Russell to refer to his method of philosophical analysis as a 'scientific method in philosophy' or as a 'method of scientific philosophising' (see, e.g., OKEW). Secondly, as was shown earlier in this chapter, Russell saw the frontiers between science and philosophy as somewhat blurred. This might have been taken to suggest that he viewed their methods as blurred as well, had not the discussion of the last few pages shown any such inference to be erroneous.

A third reason why Russell's method of philosophical analysis might be confused with scientific method is his frequent use of certain examples as illustrations of particular points about analysis. For instance, whenever he is discussing the non-finality of analysis, Russell often uses examples like water (e.g., MPD, pp. 169–70). His point is that when you learn that water is two parts hydrogen and one part oxygen, you do not cease thereby to know anything that you previously knew about water. While this type of example may be useful for making particular points about analysis, it should

---

[8] Russell's fallibilist understanding of science has not received much attention. For more on Russell's philosophy of science, see Hager (2000).

not be inferred that the analysis of water into hydrogen and oxygen was inspired by Russell's method of philosophical analysis. Rather, that feat was achieved by quite other means. Interestingly, while strongly influenced by G.E. Moore in the early years of his revolt against idealism, Russell had regarded analysis of propositions as akin to chemical decomposition. This line of thought can be found in W.E. Johnson, Husserl, Meinong, and other writers of that era. However, in Russell's case, rapid advances in his philosophical position, such as the theory of descriptions, quickly disposed of any lingering tendency to entertain a naive realist view of propositions.

McKinney based his paper on Russell's Urmson review and on *Human Knowledge*. It should be clear from the previous section of this chapter that *Human Knowledge* used Russellian philosophical analysis to propose tentatively five postulates of scientific method. That is, the premises of scientific method were the object of the analysis, but the analysis itself was very clearly not an instance of scientific method.

In the letter to McKinney, Russell also denied that his "construction of the external world" was an exercise in philosophical analysis. This might seem puzzling until we realise that in wanting to remove confusions between scientific and philosophical analysis, Russell would avoid a description that made it sound like philosophy alone did all of the work. Certainly that is the impression that "Russell's construction of the external world" conveys. In fact, Russell took science to be broadly correct in its account of the world and sought to reconcile the philosophy and psychology of perception with this. So his construction was a philosophical analysis heavily supplemented by the contributions of scientific method. Rather than developing a grand system of the world, his philosophical construction was somewhat more modest. A more accurate title would be something like "Russell's construction of a way of reconciling what we know of human perception with the external world portrayed by science".

THE ROLE OF LANGUAGE IN RUSSELLIAN ANALYSIS

Despite Russell's method of analysis, as set out above, being fairly explicit in his writings, it is still not well understood. Major critical works that have sought to engage significantly with Russell's philosophy (e.g., Jager 1972, Pears 1967, Eames 1969), have been limited by insufficient treatment of his refined philosophical method. This trend is continued in the first volume (1996a) of Monk's long-awaited biography of Russell. Though he covers the years up to 1921 Monk provides only cursory mentions of analysis, viewing it as an isolated philosophical conundrum about parts and wholes that engaged Russell in the early years of his revolt against idealism. Without more attention to the details of Russell's method of analysis and its central role in his work, no biography could hope to delve very deeply into his philosophy.

The main reason why Russell's philosophical method is absent from Monk's account is that he misunderstands the important role of language in Russell's work. As Russell's preferred terminology for describing analysis (such as 'premisses', 'conclusions' (or 'results') that are 'deducible' from the premisses, and so on) makes clear, propositions and their associated linguistic forms are important in analysis. However, this central role of language in Russellian analysis does not mean that philosophy ends at analysis of language. Thus, although analysis is primarily analysis of propositions (language), it is carried out for purposes other than the analysis of propositions.

This means that Russellian analysis is primarily analysis of propositions and only *indirectly* is it analysis of objects. So, in his famous analysis of the desk (PLA, p. 236ff), it is not the desk that is analysed, but rather propositions *about* the desk. This analysis of common sense propositions about the desk leads to a set of basic premisses from which is synthesised a set of propositions which captures the truths embodied in the initial common sense propositions, yet avoids their shortcomings such as vagueness, ambiguity, etc. These analysed results are substituted for the initial unanalysed results about the desk. This completes the primary part of the Russellian analysis of the desk, i.e., the analysis of propositions.

The sense in which the desk as an *ontological object* is analysed is quite different. Russell's view is emphatically *not* one that has the physical desk of the metaphysics of common sense analysed into smaller parts and then resynthesised (say) as a swarm of sub-atomic particles (PLA, p. 161). (Though, of course, Russell claims all along that his theories are compatible with those of physics as realistically understood.) Instead ontological analysis is an *indirect* outcome of the analysis of propositions. The desk of the metaphysics of common sense is inferred uncritically from the initial set of common sense propositions. Since, as we have seen, a set of analysed results is substituted for the common sense propositions, and since, in addition, the desk of common sense cannot be logically inferred from the refined, substitute set of propositions, it follows that the existence of the supposed desk of common sense cannot be established. Instead, the analysed results invite inference to a somewhat different ontological object – a complex structure of sensa or events.

Monk's work misses the centrality of analysis in Russell's philosophy because he misunderstands the important role of language in this philosophy. As Monk sees it, through

all the various transformations of Russell's philosophical doctrines, one thing remained quite constant, and that was the conviction that, whatever it is the philosopher is concerned with, it is precisely *not* language. (Monk 1996b, p. 4)[9]

As we have just seen, in an important sense, for Russell, philosophy *is* concerned with language. However, as we have also seen, this in no way signals that Russell thought that language was the prime object of study for philosophy. Rather, it recognises his important position that language is inescapably the medium through which philosophical analysis engages with matters that are nonlinguistic.[10]

A major contributing factor to Monk's overlooking these fundamental points about Russell's work is his fondness for stark opposites when characterising differences between philosophical positions. In critiquing Dummett's claim that what distinguishes analytical philosophy is its claim that "philosophy of language" is "the foundation

---

9 If Russell's philosophical concern really was "precisely *not* language", it would be surprising that "language" features so prominently in his works, e.g. Part II of *Human Knowledge* is titled "Language", key chapters in Part IV are "Minimum Vocabularies" and "Structure and Minimum Vocabularies". Similar examples can be found in other major works, such as *An Inquiry into Meaning and Truth*.

10 For a perceptive account of this point see Kung (1967). Monk mistakenly concludes from Russell's characterisation of *some* instances of the 'linguistic' as 'trivial' that he thereby regards all 'linguistic' items as "trivial and beneath consideration" (1996b, p. 6). In fact the instances that Monk mentions are ones where the terms which initially interested Russell, such as numbers, turned out to be be fully definable via other terms. Thus, he came to view propositions about numbers as mere verbal conveniences of no interest to philosophical analysis. However, Russell's philosophical analyses typically centre on more robust terms that appear not to be definable in this way. For Russell, such linguistic items are far from trivial. An example is the term 'similar' (see Hager 1994, pp. 116–7).

of all other philosophy", Monk rightly objects against Dummett that this excludes Russell. However, in seeking to rescue Russell's credentials as an analytical philosopher, Monk portrays him as taking a "precisely opposite" tack of excluding language from the philosophical agenda. Monk suggests that what really distinguishes analytical philosophy is analysis itself:

It is this notion of a complex – and the concomitant notion that to understand a complex is to analyse it, to break it down into the simples that compose it – that lies at the heart of analytical philosophy. (Monk 1996b, p. 12)

He has Russell committed to a non-linguistic interpretation of analysis in which it is applied to complex objects.[11] Thus, having rejected two earlier attempts to characterise 'analytical philosophy' in terms of its supposed opposite, 'analytical vs continental' and 'analytical vs phenomenological' (Dummett's position), Monk proposes that the correct opposition is 'analytical vs Wittgensteinian'. Monk then quotes with approval, and at length, Wittgenstein's attack on this conception of analysis with which Russell has been saddled by Monk. According to Monk, Wittgenstein's rejection of analysis centres on the claim that it would be odd to substitute "Bring me the broomstick and the brush which is fitted on to it" for "Bring me the broom". We can all agree with Wittgenstein's point here. But this has as little to do with Russell's conception of analysis as did Urmson's argument, discussed above, about "England declared war in 1939" not being equivalent to a series of simpler statements. Quite simply, Urmson's 1956 misunderstandings of Russellian analysis are repeated in 1996 by Monk.

On Monk's misunderstanding of Russellian analysis, Russell analyses the desk, for example, into legs, top, sides, etc. Rather, as already demonstrated, Russellian analysis is analysis of propositions about the desk and only indirectly is it analysis of the desk. The result is that, as shown above, rather than analysing the common sense physical desk into its parts, what Russellian analysis does is to suggest its replacement by a quite different ontological object. This is true of

---

[11] Perhaps Monk has fallen into the trap, discussed in the previous section, of taking too literally Russell's use of examples like the analysis of water into hydrogen and oxygen as examples of analysis. Such examples may be useful for making particular points about analysis, but should not be taken as examples of *philosophical* analysis.

all of the paradigmatic examples of Russellian analysis – the definition of number, definite descriptions, the analysis of classes, the analysis of cardinal numbers, etc. I am unaware of any instance of Russellian analysis that squares with Monk's account. No wonder that
Monk is dimly aware that his position might face some difficulties:

> ... Russell is sometimes regarded as having forgotten – or perhaps misun-
> derstood – the nature of his own philosophical achievements. For isn't his
> theory of descriptions, for example, a 'paradigm of philosophy' precisely
> because it demonstrates the value of linguistic analysis in philosophy, of
> demonstrating that philosophical clarity can be achieved through the analy-
> sis of sentences? It is true, of course, that this is how this theory – and much
> else in Russell's work – has been absorbed in 'the literature', but we should,
> I think, not lose sight of the fact that this is not, and never was, how Russell
> himself understood the matter. (Monk 1996b, pp. 4–5)

On the contrary, I take it that enough has been said in this chapter
to show that, *prima facie*, any misunderstandings on these matters
are entirely Monk's.

CONCLUSION

This chapter has sought to provide a brief account of Russell's crucial but little appreciated method of analysis. Major characteristics of
the method of philosophical analysis have been described. It has been
argued that this method underpins Russell's best known contributions to philosophy. Then, because his later work has been rather neglected, some of this work was discussed in detail to show that it exemplified the same overall philosophical method. This procedure has
had the effect of emphasising the unity and continuity of Russell's
philosophy, as well as clearing up a number of common misconceptions, in particular the relationship of philosophical analysis to
scientific method. However, as the discussion of Monk's erroneous
interpretation has shown, there is a long way to go before Russell's
distinctive contribution to philosophy will be properly appreciated.

REFERENCES

Eames E.R. (1969) *Bertrand Russell's Theory of Knowledge*. London: Allen
    and Unwin.
Griffin N. (1991) *Russell's Idealist Apprenticeship*. Oxford: Clarendon Press.

Hager P. (1994) *Continuity and Change in the Development of Russell's Philosophy.* Nijhoff International Philosophy Series. Dordrecht: Kluwer Academic Publishers.

Hager P. (2000) 'Russell' in W. H. Newton-Smith (ed.) *A Companion to the Philosophy of Science.* Oxford: Basil Blackwell, pp. 408–12.

Irvine A. D. (1989) 'Epistemic Logicism & Russell's Regressive Method', *Philosophical Studies*, Vol. 55, pp. 303–27.

Jager R. (1972)*The Development of Bertrand Russell's Philosophy.* London: Allen and Unwin.

Kung G. (1967) *Ontology and the Logistic Analysis of Language.* Synthese Library. Dordrecht: Reidel.

McKinney J. P. (1957) 'Philosophical Implications of Logical Analysis', *Hibbert Journal*, Vol. 55, 1956/1957, pp. 249–59.

Monk (1996a) *Bertrand Russell: The Spirit of Solitude.* London: Jonathan Cape.

Monk (1996b) 'What Is Analytical Philosophy?' in R. Monk and A. Palmer (eds.) *Bertrand Russell and the Origins of Analytical Philosophy.* Bristol: Thoemmes Press.

Pears D.F. (1967) *Bertrand Russell and the British Tradition in Philosophy.* London: Collins.

Russell B. (1911) 'The Philosophical Importance of Mathematical Logic' in *Papers 6*, pp. 33–40.

Russell B. (1956) 'Philosophical Analysis', *Hibbert Journal*, Vol. 54 1955/1956. (Page numbers in the chapter refer to the reprint in *MPD*).

Russell B. (1958) Letter to J. P. McKinney from Plas Penrhyn dated 18 July (Russell Archives).

Russell B. (1974) *The Art of Philosophizing and Other Essays.* Totowa, NJ: Littlefield, Adams and Co. (Essays originally published in the 1940s).

10 Russell's Neutral Monism

INTRODUCTION

The doctrine of Neutral Monism was an avowed part of Russell's metaphysics for only a relatively short period in his amazingly long philosophical career, although it remained an active ingredient for considerably longer. His acceptance of this doctrine was gradual. To a lecture audience in early 1918, when he was in his mid-forties, he declared: "I feel more and more inclined to think that [Neutral Monism] may be true. I feel more and more that the difficulties that occur in regard to it are all of the sort that may be solved by ingenuity" [PLA *Papers* 8, p. 242]. Shortly afterwards, Russell gave a partial endorsement of the doctrine and then, during the next decade, in major works like *The Analysis of Mind, An Outline of Philosophy* and *The Analysis of Matter*, he set about to deepen and refine that endorsement. For more than two decades thereafter, the metaphysical imprint of Neutral Monism remained evident in Russell's major philosophical writings (*An Inquiry into Meaning and Truth, Human Knowledge*), though he no longer marshalled his views explicitly under its banner. Neutral Monism constitutes, therefore, a major part of Russell's philosophy outside the area of formal logic. Indeed, the doctrine plays a kind of antipodal role in the whole development of his thought, for prior to taking the first steps towards accepting Neutral Monism, Russell had been its most severe critic.

FORMATIVE THEMES

To see why Russell regarded Neutral Monism as an important doctrine even when he was its staunch opponent, it is necessary to recall some of the ideals and values which shaped his philosophical outlook from nearly the start of his career and which continued to be active, though in different proportions and with changing interpretations, to the end. These foundational themes can be summarized under three related headings – Metaphysics, Science, and Language. Taken together, they display an underlying unity that is distinctive of Russell's philosophy. Russell drew heavily upon them, first in challenging Neutral Monism, later in coming to terms with the doctrine.

Metaphysics

Although one of the founders of the modern Analytic movement, Russell was heir to a long metaphysical tradition extending back through Kant, the British Empiricists, Leibniz, and Spinoza to Descartes, a tradition that (for all its internal differences) upheld the goal of tracing human knowledge to its roots in immediate or first-person experience, which comes to be known directly by means of introspection. Since a major portion of such knowledge happens to be studied and codified in the natural sciences, the tradition had a correlative goal of explaining the connections between the contents of immediate experience and the objective nature of things, or what there is in the world. Usually, this goal was realized by subordinating scientific truths to a more comprehensive, metaphysical framework that sets down the categories of what is ultimately real. For Russell, this metaphysical tradition was less important for its actual achievements than for the fact that it represented a legitimate way of doing philosophy. He seems never to have lost interest in the ideal of a grand synthesis of human knowledge or the hope of adding significantly to this tradition.

Science

By the time Russell took up philosophy in the 1890s, systematic philosophy (at least in England) had taken a turn down one road and the natural sciences were heading down another. In keeping with the tradition, however, Russell had many of the technical skills needed to appreciate developments in modern physics, for (like Descartes, Leibniz, Berkeley, and Kant) he was well trained in mathematics and geometry. Even before becoming a Neutral Monist, Russell set himself the challenge of making physics mesh with immediate experience and, accordingly, to metaphysical questions regarding what things are real he sought answers based on whatever certainty can be obtained from such experience. Adopting the scientific perspective, he classified his own metaphysical theories as "working hypotheses" rather than as definitive revelations of the nature of reality. This enabled him to avoid the charge of dogmatism as well as to condemn extreme philosophical skeptics for being dogmatic. Although the scientific outlook deeply affected his systematic thought, Russell was not a philosopher of science in today's sense and, apart from his reliance on mathematics and geometry, his approach to the natural sciences was limited to physics and some physiology. He did not try to accommodate chemistry or biology in the picture he wanted to give of experience, despite the significant role assigned to the human brain in his own version of Neutral Monism. But just as electromagnetic theory lay beyond Newton's horizon, so too did modern cognitive science and computer theory lie beyond Russell's. As for psychology, Russell's approach was decisively influenced by his metaphysical orientation, both before and after he adopted Neutral Monism.

Language

In keeping with the metaphysical tradition, Russell's approach to logic went well beyond merely providing the rigour and elegance demanded of a formal system. As a pioneer in the area of philosophical logic, he investigated the nature of relations, judgments and propositions, characteristically treating all of them not as mere abstractions but as things of which one can have direct experience. Furthermore, logic served Russell as a tool for analyzing natural language and for exposing what he confidently believed to be its true underlying structure. In this way, he thought it possible to eliminate mistakes and confusions about meaning that thrive on the surface of natural language. Russell believed that modern logic liberated philosophy from traditional metaphysical beliefs embedded in the grammatical forms of natural language, thus making it possible at last for metaphysical truths to be formulated in a way that more closely matched what there is in the world. His opinion was that natural language itself, like common sense beliefs about perception, was rife with archaic metaphysical assumptions and unworthy of philosophical credence.

Russell was, above all, a demanding Realist about names: he held that genuine names stand for objects which exist independent of experience and that such objects are the meanings of these names. An important job for philosophical logic was to show that many names found in ordinary language are not names in what he called a logically proper sense but should be interpreted as disguised descriptions; and an important job for metaphysics, therefore, guided by what he called an instinct for reality, was to locate the real objects that constitute the meanings of genuine names. In the course of his career, Russell changed his mind several times about just what those objects are and eventually altered even his views on logically proper names, without surrendering however his basic claim to be called a Realist.

OUTLINE OF NEUTRAL MONISM

In broad historical perspective, Neutral Monism is a metaphysical doctrine of the early twentieth century that was intended to supplant the two traditional and more familiar forms of monistic doctrine: Idealism, which prescribes a world consisting exclusively of minds and their contents, and Materialism, which sees the identity of everything (persons and minds included) to consist in configurations of material particles of some pre-defined type. Although the doctrine is often associated with Russell, its origin, as Russell himself attests, lies in the work of Ernst Mach (the nineteenth-century Austrian philosopher) and William James, as well as in the writings before World War I of a group of American philosophers who called themselves the New Realists. Russell's role, however, was not merely to be the chief promoter of Neutral Monism or to bring it to the attention of British philosophers, who might otherwise have little noticed it; he also gave the doctrine its most systematic and comprehensive shape. The Neutral Monists as a group contributed to the rise of twentieth-century analytic philosophy, specifically to that part of it which kept a close watch on science and adapted to its developments. In this respect and in numerous others, Russell and his predecessors had much in common. How much and in what areas his own version of the doctrine differs from theirs, however, are questions that must be put aside.

Neutral Monists sought to dissolve centuries-old disputes about the nature of mind and matter by denying ontological primacy to both of them. Reality, they claimed, is ultimately neither material in nature nor mental. These properties do not radically define the objective world, whose ultimate components are not atoms or particles any more than they are minds and ideas, but something more basic. Russell called this something "neutral-stuff" and once even characterized it as "more primitive" than mind and matter and lying "in a sense above them both, like a common ancestor" [*AMi*, 10–11; 25]. Such descriptions are picturesque but distorting because they misleadingly suggest that Neutral Monists thought they had stumbled upon an entity which had eluded other philosophers, something having special properties and capable of being isolated. Fortunately, Russell also used other comparisons which avoid the suggestion of a real but remote third kind of thing. He likened Neutral Monism's approach to the double sorting of names in the (old style) London postal directory, the same names being arranged alphabetically as well as being listed geographically by their street addresses. Another simile was that of columns and rows. The very same item can be located by either its vertical or its horizontal position. It falls within two different series of items to which it has definably different relations. Since the item is assumed to occur only within these two series, its identity is determined by these relations. This way of putting things helps to reduce the doctrine's mystery somewhat by placing the emphasis on "neutral" rather than on "stuff", even though it shares the defect which all similes have of deliberately aiming off-target. They describe only what a thing is like instead of what it is.

Russell's goal, like that of earlier Neutral Monists, was to analyze ontology rather than to increase its stock, and the framework for pursuing close analysis was that of modern science. This meant physics, dating from the late nineteenth century through the early twentieth, including, for Russell, Relativity Theory, and experimental psychology with a preference for the method of behaviourism. According to Neutral Monism, scientific accounts of mental and physical phenomena, while objective, are essentially theory-dependent. Concepts pertaining to mind and matter belong within physics and psychology, where they are defined and systematically developed with related concepts as part of the whole scientific enterprise. The conviction that inspired Neutral Monism, however, is that these concepts have a common ontological basis to which neither physics nor psychology can claim any absolute right. These two sciences borrow the same stuff but for different purposes. What constitutes a material thing, for example, is basic to physics but is not basic, without qualification, to everything. The concepts of mind and matter do not stand for anything which science can be said to discover in a world independent of itself. A corollary of the Neutral Monists' approach is that it is pointless to speak of *reducing* mental (or material) phenomena to material (or mental) phenomena or to try showing in a philosophically important sense that the one is *really nothing but* the other. A further corollary of their approach is that traditional monistic doctrines of Idealism and Materialism are to be cut loose from philosophy and left to fossilize. The world in itself does not conform to the metaphysical tenets of either Idealism or Materialism, and still less to the dualistic categories implicit in a common sense view of what there is.

Curiously, Neutral Monism presents to science an ontology and theory that are immune to its methods of verification. The doctrine thus seems afflicted with a vice found in the systems of traditional metaphysics which it wanted to supersede. Yet Neutral Monism was cast from the beginning as metaphysics synchronized with modern science and chiefly concerned with promoting its unification rather than with defending an obscure pseudo-science. The first Neutral Monists thus looked upon their doctrine as progressive and integrative, and Russell shared their viewpoint. Despite its vaulting metaphysical character – and despite the hubris of any project by metaphysicians to explain science to scientists – the early Neutral Monists regarded their doctrine as the right metaphysics for modern science. They also sought to correct traditional metaphysical assumptions and biases embedded in scientific practice, principally the belief held by some schools of psychology that mental phenomena differ essentially from physical ones and can only be accessed through introspection. All such phenomena are to be "constructed" out of the neutral stuff, and it is the business of Neutral Monism to show how this can be achieved. To this task, once he became a Neutral Monist, Russell would bring much ingenuity.

PROBLEMS OF REFERENCE AND TERMINOLOGY

The very character of Neutral Monism makes it difficult to take its measure, for if the neutrality of the "neutral-stuff" is to be preserved, then the stuff must be identified and described in terms which avoid portraying it as either physical or mental. Material objects are obviously not neutral in the required sense, neither are minds and ideas, as ordinarily understood. Unfortunately for the doctrine, most descriptions expressed in ordinary language are tied to one or both of these categories, and much the same applies to the more special- ized concepts used by philosophers for talking about ourselves and the world. The very meaning of the word "construct" for Neutral Monism is thus inevitably abstract, formal, and otherwise metaphor- ical. Neither do Russell's similes about neutral stuff provide any re- lief or insight. The analogy of the postal directory suggests that every name does in fact occur twice listed. In Neutral Monism, however, it is not logically necessary that every neutral item occur in this dual mode. A material object in physics would still consist of neu- tral items even if no one were on hand to perceive it, which is what any anti-Idealistic doctrine properly demands. Also, the basic ingre- dients in the two postal directories were people's names even before they came to be sorted, but there is no way of identifying neutral stuff outside of the context of the relations which such items bear to each other. As Russell's other simile makes clear, these items occur within the framework provided by horizontal and vertical columns.

The problem of identifying and describing neutral stuff would seem therefore to be awkward for Neutral Monism, possibly even grave. If neutral items do not comprise a separate class of things with their own properties, which is what the doctrine insists, then how are they to be picked out for the purpose of being constructed into mate- rial and mental things? If an item of neutral stuff, considered in itself, is neither mental nor physical, then what is it? An identity statement may assure us that the same thing constitutes part of what it is to be a physical object and part of what it is for someone to be aware of that object, but it does not begin to settle either question. And there are other difficult questions. If neutral items constitute both mental and material things, then why not simply eliminate the confusing talk of a "common denominator" and accept instead that mental things *are the same as* material things? What special contribution does the neutral stuff make to their separate identities? Since the doctrine it- self cannot be tested, the very conception of it as a working hypothe- sis (to use Russell's phrase) seems hollow. Challenges like these raise doubts about the tenets, goals, and method of Neutral Monism and thus threaten the connection it wanted to forge between physics and psychology. The doctrine seems to point towards something that it can never reach. Perhaps David Hume's famous remark about an old system of French metaphysics applies just as accurately to Neutral Monism: "Our line is too short to fathom such immense abysses" (*An Enquiry Concerning Human Understanding*, Sect. VII, Pt. I).

Philosophical conundrums about the identity of neutral stuff were not a preoccupation of the Neutral Monists, who always appeared optimistic about the fundamentals of their project. They never doubted that neutral things were within reach. There was no reason for doubt, because the steps needed for locating such things involved stipulation rather than discovery. Despite talk of constructing mental and material things out of neutral stuff, the process they followed began from the opposite direction, a process of paring down ordinary descriptions of things until a level was reached where the object referred to could be declared neither mental nor material and, hence, simply neutral. Lack of a properly 'neutral' vocabulary for this purpose does not seem to have been regarded by the early Neutral Monists as a serious drawback. The term "sense-datum", which had not yet come into wide use in philosophy, might have served their needs quite well if defined in a suitable way, although it would not have been Russell's way. Even so, they found the terminology they needed in psychology. William James spoke of "pure consciousness", and Mach of "sensations". When Russell first appropriated the doctrine he too identified the neutral things as sensations, despite the word's psychological connotation. Later on he chose "percepts" to stand for the neutral items. However, both the early Neutral Monists and Russell certainly wished to deny to such words a purely psychological sense. They held that calling any item a sensation (or a percept) does not exclude its classification as physical rather than mental. The technical terms they selected nevertheless tilt clearly towards the side of experience and away from the impersonal. The choice was deliberate and probably unavoidable.

What motivated their choice was the need to relate neutral stuff to perceptual observation. Since empirical claims are grounded in what is (or might be) directly observed, the Neutral Monists required a concept of observation that would not perpetuate the traditional divide between mind and matter, or between self and the external world. To be scientifically credible, empirical claims must be objective and confirmable. A person who observes the world must therefore have access to its contents directly, so far as possible, rather than through a subjective medium. What Neutral Monism called sensations (or percepts) are meant to be those contents. A sensation is the same thing, whether grouped with other sensations to form a public object, or considered merely as an ingredient of the observer's experience. It is, therefore, as much a proper object for physics as for psychology. For the Neutral Monist, the observed world consists of sensations; paradoxically, so also does the unobserved world – the vast system of things that might never be observed by anyone. This means that sensations are not logically tied to episodes of observation and that they can be actual or real even when they are only possible objects of observation. Consequently, the paradox flows not from the core of Neutral Monism itself but merely from its decision to call such things sensations. The doctrine's firm belief in the difference between a thing's being and its being observed clearly sets Neutral Monism apart from any form of Phenomenalism.

In the interest of weaning metaphysics from a subjective orientation, the early Neutral Monists favoured taking an external or public standpoint from which to characterize certain cognitive concepts that are closely associated with observation. This reflects the doctrine's scientific perspective. Chief among these were the concepts of perception and belief. Russell seems to have been instinctively hostile to the New Realists' approach to these concepts, a fact partly explained by his own early commitment to dualism. Yet, even after he had accepted the doctrine and reconciled himself to its behaviouristic leanings, Russell still fought to nurture an internal point of view – the viewpoint of the person who does the perceiving and who forms the beliefs – as an essential part of the total framework. His defense of this perspective was very much in character.

RUSSELLIAN DUALISM

Predictably, the views of the early Neutral Monists appealed to Russell. Not only did the doctrine create a strong metaphysical bond with modern science, it clearly preserved the commitment to Realism that Russell himself had made. By basing physics and psychology on a single kind of stuff, Neutral Monism even displayed a systematic elegance that Russell sincerely commended. He said that it exemplified the principle known as Occam's Razor, which stipulates that entities must not be multiplied beyond necessity, and confessed that he felt a similar reluctance to accept that "the things given in experience should be of two fundamentally different kinds, mental and physical" [Papers 7, p. 21]. If the theory, therefore, could manage on the basis of neutral stuff alone, then that was clearly a mark in its favour. But early Neutral Monism's chief drawback for Russell was that it was a thoroughgoing monism. Its proponents went beyond taking the objects of immediate experience as the common point of reference for physics and psychology. They also thought that such objects provide sufficient material to explain cognitive states like perceiving, remembering, and believing, which could be understood as complex responses that people make to changes in their surroundings. The Neutral Monists saw no need for either science or metaphysics to assume the existence of specifically mental relations. For his part, Russell considered that the experience of objects defines the fundamental structure of human knowledge and that mental relations cannot be adequately described in terms of how observers behave in a physical environment. It was in defense of this position that he took his stand against the early Neutral Monists.

Russell gave the name "acquaintance" to the simplest of these relations. He classified it in 1913 as "the most pervading aspect of experience", [*Papers* 7, p. 5] a mental relation through which a person is aware of an object. In fact, the concept of acquaintance had exercised Russell's thought for some time before this. He discussed it briefly in his famous essay, "On Denoting" (1905), where its particular role in obtaining knowledge is overshadowed by his analysis of an important linguistic concept called "description". As Russell distinguishes them, acquaintance deals with what might be called the inner circle of knowledge: it puts us in direct contact *with* objects, which we can pick out and name. Descriptions, on the other hand, express what we know *about* objects with which we may or may not have acquaintance. To use his example, the centre of mass of the solar system is something which we can know about, although no one has direct contact with it. All knowledge starts with objects of acquaintance, he claimed, but it succeeds in thinking about and describing many other things. Russell wanted to keep the linguistic functions of names and descriptions quite distinct. The rules of ordinary language, in contrast, are looser. Not only is "France" counted as a name, so also is a phrase like "the present king of France", a type of expression which Russell called a definite description. While meaningful, "the present King of France" does not designate any object of possible acquaintance (since France has no current monarch), and hence he thought that it should not be classified as a name. For logical and linguistic reasons, Russell argued, definite descriptions as a class of expression require a much more detailed account of what makes them meaningful and therefore very different from genuine names. He also showed that making the distinction readily solves philosophical puzzles traceable to the confusion of names with descriptions. (See Hylton in this volume.)

A later essay, "Knowledge by Acquaintance and Knowledge by Description" (1911), put this pair of concepts into a fuller epistemological context. On the side of acquaintance, however, Russell's focus was fixed on objects rather than on the mental relation itself. Among objects of acquaintance, he lists individual sense-data (such as particular instances of the colour yellow), complexes consisting of both sense-data and relations (such as one particular sound occurring before another), and even universals (such as yellowness). But this essay does give prominence to the overall relation between acquaintance and description, which was only sketched in "On Denoting". Russell advanced what he called a "fundamental epistemological principle": "*Every proposition which we can understand must be composed wholly of constituents with which we are acquainted*" (where by "proposition" he meant what is actually understood by the person, rather than a sentence) [*Papers* 6:154]. He extended and applied this principle in his popular short text, *The Problems of Philosophy* (1912), which brought together many strands of his thought that, until then, had stayed hidden in technical journals, but even in this new book Russell had little to say about the nature of acquaintance itself, other than to describe it as a relation involving a subject's direct awareness of objects, such as sense-data, "without the intermediary of any process of inference or any knowledge of truths" [*POP*, chap. V, p. 73].

In 1913, however, Russell began writing a major work, to be called *Theory of Knowledge*, that was intended not only to fill this gap but also to present to the philosophical world a systematic account of epistemology based on the relation of acquaintance. Russell envisioned a project of immense scope covering not only the immediate experience of objects but also knowledge of truths, logical inference and scientific reasoning, systematically related one to another and bonded to the relation of acquaintance. This project, of course, did not have the field all to itself. Facing it was a doctrine from across the Atlantic that claimed to analyze away the very concept that Russell took to be essential to his whole project. There was no choice but to deploy arguments in an effort to drive Neutral Monism from the field.

THE ASSAULT LAUNCHED

Theory of Knowledge begins with a general characterization of the relation of acquaintance and a renewal of Russell's commitment to Realism (as opposed to Idealism), right after which come two chapters of criticism aimed principally at the Neutral Monists and (to a much lesser extent) the Austrian philosopher, Meinong, who like Russell was a dualist. Among the former group, Russell directed his comments to the views of James and the New Realists rather than those of Mach. (The likely explanation is that Russell first published these chapters in an American journal just prior to his arrival as a visiting professor at Harvard, where one of the principal New Realists chaired the Department of Philosophy.) The criticisms fall into three main categories which concern the nature of belief, the problem of false propositions, and what might be called the intuited immediacy of experience. Although the early Neutral Monists' treatment of these topics was consistent with Realism, in Russell's eyes their position was seriously deficient and he thought it could be proven so, indeed even refuted.

In retrospect, Russell's moves seem more bold than decisive. His arguments have uneven force. Several of them show only that Neutral Monism is weak in certain areas (unrelated to the issue of dualism) where Russell's own position is strong. For instance, Russell had already devised a sophisticated account that avoided having to treat true propositions as a strange class of objects (and false ones as an even stranger class); but, he contends, Neutral Monists subscribe to the older view, which commits them to an overpopulated world. Also, they hold the simplistic view that beliefs are about objects (e.g., belief in God); whereas, Russell says, appealing to another of his analytical achievements, beliefs should be taken as propositional in nature (e.g., the belief that God exists), in which the names for anything not immediately present are to be replaced by definite descriptions. Even if both of Russell's views are more plausible than the Neutral Monists', however, it would not undermine their doctrine. There is, besides, an unwillingness to meet that doctrine on its own ground. James and the early Neutral Monists sought to interpret beliefs in general by reference to observed behaviour and to associate the holding of individual beliefs with particular patterns of action. This approach was closely related to the doctrine of Pragmatism and the so-called pragmatist theory of truth, both advocated by James, which Russell had already sharply criticized in his *Philosophical Essays* (1910). Instead of examining their overall approach, Russell all too quickly insists that beliefs have an essential cognitive component (such as the relations of acquaintance or memory), a response that might have struck his opponents as question-begging. They may have similarly reacted to his contention that "neutral monism cannot be true, for it is obliged to have recourse to extraneous considerations, such as the nervous system, in order to explain the difference between what I experience and what I do not experience" [*Papers* 7, p. 31]. Perhaps all that the Neutral Monists meant is that physiology provides a *better* explanation, in the sense of a scientifically more satisfactory one, than any which might be given by intuitive appeals to experience, for it is possible to be a monist without being a foundationalist. To the Neutral Monists, the Self becomes more fully known by understanding the nervous system and one's own nature as a complex organism that interacts with its environment. Unlike Russell, they were not disposed to rest the whole question of what makes a Self on discovering the "bond which unites the parts of this bundle" of immediate experiences [*Papers* 7, p. 29]. Russell's demand that they should find one, and his claim that they cannot, do not constitute an argument.

There is one argument, however, which Russell considered so powerful as to be "the most conclusive" refutation of Neutral Monism. This can be called the argument from emphatic particulars, after his declaration that "to me it seems obvious that such 'emphatic particulars' as 'this' and 'I' and 'now' would be impossible without the selectiveness of mind" [*Papers* 7, pp. 40-41]. Russell elsewhere calls such items egocentric particulars (the words are now more commonly known as indexical expressions). It is important to recognize that by "particulars" Russell means the objects which these words designate. His argument is that knowledge in its most elementary form depends not simply on the existence of particulars but on their presence to a subject, and that the presence of a particular involves the subject's concentrated attention on it – selectiveness – which is thus a form of acquaintance. Without such a relation to particulars, there could be no knowledge, Russell maintains. But

Neutral Monism does not accept this relation. Consequently, it is unable to account for knowledge in its most elementary form, nor (by implication) could it account for more complex forms.

At first glance, this argument seems another instance of begging the question against Neutral Monism. There might well be other ways of defining "the selectiveness of mind" without presupposing the relation of acquaintance, such as in terms of the observable behaviour and actions of a person (the *I*) in the presence of an object (*this*) during a brief period of time (*now*). Or perhaps a Neutral Monist might reply that, undoubtedly, when words like "this" and "I" and "now" are used together in the sort of cases described by Russell, some selectiveness of mind is likely to be occurring, since that is pretty much what selectiveness *means* in such cases. In other words, the Neutral Monist might grant the tautology but hardly feel threatened by it. But Russell's argument goes deeper and, if nothing else, seems to pose a serious challenge to Neutral Monism. Although his argument appears to be concerned with a psychological phenomenon, selective attention, its basis in fact is the theory of meaning which ties names to objects (in this case, simple objects). Russell's emphatic particulars are the various terms joined by the relation of acquaintance: a particular is present to a person and thereby becomes not only the focus of attention but also the very meaning of the word "this" on that occasion for that person. "'This' is the point from which the whole process starts," he writes, "and 'this' itself is not defined, but simply given" [*Papers* 7, p. 40]. It therefore counts as a logically proper name, a point of contact between language and the world. According to Russell's philosophical analysis of meaning, our language about objects works basically in this way. While definite descriptions refer to objects but may fail to be true, a logically proper name cannot fail to be meaningful, since the particular to which it refers on a given occasion is literally its meaning.

Thus, Russell's challenge employed a systematic account of language against opponents who had not yet acquired a serious alternative – in 1913, behaviouristic accounts of meaning were still under development – and this gave his argument a damaging advantage against early Neutral Monism. But a further consideration suggests why he may have been entitled to consider this argument a refutation of the doctrine. Both sides were committed to a class of particulars (*sensations* for the Neutral Monists, *sense-data* for Russell) which enter into both mental and physical states of affairs. However, so far as Russell could see, since the Neutral Monists had no means of explaining what experience is except by reference to physical things like the brain, they created a major gap. Their doctrine offered no way of showing how these (so-called) sensations, when joined together, constitute distinctly mental phenomena rather than merely more complicated physical ones. By invoking the relation of acquaintance, Russell was showing them how.

In defending the concept of acquaintance against the Neutral Monists, Russell was prepared to admit that the words "I" and "now", unlike "this", are not logically proper names of particulars. "I" is actually a disguised description, expressing something like "the subject attending to what 'this' names", while "now" indicates an experienced aspect of acquaintance itself. Russell was thus willing to narrow down the list of logically proper names to the single demonstrative, "this", when used to refer to an experienced sense-datum, but he was not about to relinquish the relation of acquaintance itself. It is hard to say which was the more powerful motivation for him, the indubitable character of immediate sense experience or his conviction that in the doctrine of logically proper names he had located the level where words touch things, exemplified in his specialized use of "this". The entrenchment of the concept of acquaintance in Russell's thinking is evident in his writings immediately following *Theory of Knowledge*, such as "The Relation of Sense-Data to Physics". He proffered a Neutral Monism-inspired account of sense-data for the purpose of describing a vast range of physical phenomena; yet, for all that, he remained the committed dualist, insisting that awareness is "merely" something added to sense-data in the constitution of mental phenomena [RSDP, *Papers* 8, p. 8].

During the course of the 1918 lectures on themes of logical atomism, Russell confessed to his audience that "some of the arguments" he had published against Neutral Monism were "not valid" [PLA, *Papers* 8, pp. 195–6]. While not reporting which ones, he exempted the argument based on "this" and the other emphatic (or egocentric) particulars. A few lectures later he returned to the topic. After mentioning his hopes concerning Neutral Monism, Russell was quick to point out two important problems standing in the way. One of these concerned the nature of belief, the other concerned emphatic particulars. As it happens, Russell would try to find a solution to the former problem long before he found a way of handling the difficulties represented by "this".

ATTACK FROM THE REAR

Although Russell kept a firm grip on the relation of acquaintance, it is a difficult concept to manipulate. For one thing, particulars like sense-data keep shifting for the person who has them; and for another (as Russell pointed out on several occasions), two different persons do not share the same sense-data because they occupy different standpoints. Accordingly, he took the privacy of sense-data for granted and regularly appealed to his readers to corroborate through their own individual experience of sense-data what he was claiming about his. The very same method, which Russell called introspection or inspection, was applied to the relation of acquaintance itself. In building his case against Neutral Monism, he delineated two different features of this relation in terms of what he called presence and awareness or attention. A later chapter of *Theory of Knowledge* deals with further aspects of acquaintance relating to memory, imagination, and sensation. In a phenomenological sense, therefore, acquaintance in Russell's dualism takes on the look of a finely faceted concept, or rather an array of concepts, each to be carefully noted and appreciated through introspection, each contributing to the structure of experience yet all the while remaining indefinable by means of other concepts. Russell did not seem worried that he might be asking too much of this fundamental doctrine.

The project of *Theory of Knowledge* included extending the doctrine of acquaintance beyond the immediate awareness of particulars like sense-data and into the sphere of what Russell called atomic and molecular propositional thought. An example of the former would be the judgment that Socrates preceded Plato; an example of the latter would be the judgment that if Socrates preceded Plato, then Plato did not precede Socrates. The 'atoms' and 'molecules' in question were called propositions. Like Meinong and others, Russell considered propositions to be intimately related to judgments or beliefs, which were in turn classified as mental acts performed by a person, often called the subject. From this standpoint, propositions have a dependent status in relation to the subject, being components of mental acts, and the semantical properties of truth and falsity belong primarily to the judgments or beliefs rather than to the propositions they contain. In the sentence, "Aristotle believed that Socrates preceded Plato", the phrase "that Socrates preceded Plato", which expresses the proposition, cannot stand on its own but must be attached to another phrase like "Aristotle believed" in order for all the words to make complete sense. Alluding to this grammatical model, Russell described propositions as "incomplete symbols". Strictly, however, the proposition is what is expressed by the symbolizing phrase. It literally forms part of someone's believing or judging, or a similar cognitive act. Russell's plan in *Theory of Knowledge* was to examine the structure of these cognitive acts and their propositional components, beginning with the atomic propositions.

The territory was not unfamiliar to Russell. Well before encountering the New Realists he had renounced the view (attributed to Meinong) that propositions are entities occupying an intermediate position between the mind and facts. Such a view had conflicted with Russell's sense of Realism, and in response he had formulated his so-called "multiple relation" theory of judgment which avoids treating propositions as objects in their own right separate from facts. Russell's ingenious move was to analyze propositions into all the separate components related to the subject or person making the judgment. Suppose, for instance, that Aristotle judges that Socrates preceded Plato. According to Russell's theory, this judgment itself counts as a cognitive fact or complex. It includes Aristotle, Socrates, and Plato, a subordinate relation (that of preceding), and finally the cognitive relation of judging which joins all of these other components into one fact. As the subject making this judgment, Aristotle is acquainted with each of the components expressed in the proposition that Socrates preceded Plato (hence, the judgment comprises multiple relations). In addition, the judging relation connects Aristotle with these components in a certain order, and it so happens that his judgment is true. But now suppose that Aristotle, suffering from premature memory lapses, judges instead that Plato preceded Socrates. Russell's analysis would follow the same routine: the same components would be related in this new proposition, only now Aristotle's judgment would be false. The difference would lie not with the components themselves, which are identical, but with their order, and history determines which of Aristotle's two judgments is true. In making his second judgment, Aristotle has put the components in the wrong order. According to Russell's theory, therefore, propositions are a function of judgments and, whether true or false, consist of objects (including relations) with which the person who forms the judgment is acquainted. Propositions have been dissolved into their components and what constitute true or false orderings of those components. To speak of a true ordering is to speak of the fact or complex which makes the proposition true – or, more exactly, which makes the judgment itself true. In the case of a false ordering, the objects which make up the proposition do not, independently of the subject's judgment, constitute a separate fact.

For all of its ingenuity, however, Russell's theory created the serious problem that, once a proposition is reduced to its components, it becomes difficult to reconstitute them from those components alone. Something essential seems to have been sacrificed in the analysis. The problem shows up in two different ways. According to Russell's account, the person making the judgment is acquainted with the components of the proposition individually as objects. In the example, these objects are *Socrates*, *Plato*, and *preceded*. What, then, makes *preceded* to be a relation between the other two objects? If just another object, then it would not relate them. Again, since two different orderings of Socrates and Plato are possible in a judgment, how does one decide which order is meant from the components alone? The fact that one of these orderings yields a false judgment would not determine that the other must be the one meant, for people do hold false beliefs and do make false judgments. Objections pointing out these two problems appear to have originated with Russell's student, Wittgenstein, who was working with him at the time *Theory of Knowledge* was being written. To meet them and to save the theory of judgment, Russell took several countermeasures in what amounted to a 'deluxe' version of his original theory. He declared that the objects making up the content of a proposition conform to different logical types. *Preceded* is given as a relation of two terms, and *Socrates* and *Plato* are given as the terms of that relation, a difference which Russell marked in judgments by what he called a "logical datum" or the "logical form" of a two-termed relation. As for the difficulty that a relation like *preceded* can order its terms in two different and incompatible ways, his solution involved a highly creative analysis of such relations and introduced a class of definite descriptions referring to what he called "associated complexes". Consistent with the original theory's basic requirement, Russell further maintained that these additional items – the logical datum and the definite description of the associated complex – were also components of the judgment.

How much more complicated this revised version of the theory would have become, had Russell taken up the topic of molecular propositional thought, is difficult to guess. He abandoned the project of *Theory of Knowledge* after completing the treatment of atomic propositional thought but seems to have lost confidence even before reaching that stage. No doubt Wittgenstein's criticisms contributed strongly to Russell's growing doubts about the route he had chosen. A proposition perhaps does not deserve the status of an incomplete symbol, of being no more than "a fictitious constituent of certain mental complexes" [*Papers* 7, p. 113]. He admits that his definition of a proposition may be inadequate and that "some non-psychological meaning" for it must be found [*Papers* 7, p. 134]. Wittgenstein was demanding an account of propositions that would serve the purposes of logic. In Russell's theory, propositions remained encumbered by a massive cognitive apparatus that for seemingly all purposes was irrelevant to logic. Even before the plateau of molecular propositional thought had been reached, the relation of acquaintance itself had become overburdened and was near the point of exhaustion.

RETRENCHMENT

Wittgenstein's attack was directed against Russell's theory of judgment, not his doctrine of acquaintance, and it is not surprising, therefore, that the theory was the first to go, despite the fact that Russell had no substitute at hand. Referring to Wittgenstein, he told the audience midway through his 1918 lectures that there remained a genuine unsolved problem about the correct analysis of belief, but then indicated in the final lecture that possibly the answer to this problem was to be found in a behaviouristic account of belief. In fact, Russell would remain wary of behaviourism as an acceptable method in epistemology for quite some time, while his attachment to the doctrine of acquaintance was so deep it remained entrenched in his epistemology even after he gave up writing *Theory of Knowledge*. Acquaintance's role is prominent in *Our Knowledge of the External World* as well as in essays from the same period. The concept also makes several appearances in the 1918 lectures.

Constructing things out of momentary particulars was a far more interesting topic to Russell during this period than portraying the fine-grained details of the relation of acquaintance. An overview of the topic occupies most of his concluding lecture. Construction was a job for symbolic logic and a worthwhile challenge besides, he thought, since the use of Occam's Razor to build physics on an adequate basis consisting of "the smallest number of simple undefined things...[and] of undemonstrated premises" would diminish the risk of error.

Desks and chairs, atoms and ions were all to be defined as logical fictions, more exactly, redefined as "systems, series of classes of particulars" [PLA, *Papers* 8, p. 238], by which he meant that the ordinary objects of daily life as well as the objects presupposed by physical theory, when identified from a metaphysical standpoint, are nothing but logical orderings of particulars. Only the particulars themselves are real, in Russell's view, whereas classes as such are not; and particulars become sense-data "when they happen to be given to you" [PLA, *Papers* 8, p. 238]. Sense-data, then, are particulars, "the real things" that happen to be presented to one in immediate experience, particulars which have become objects of acquaintance. Other things valued by traditional metaphysics, such as a continuing material substance or an immaterial ego, because no such entities are given in experience, are also cut away by the Razor. Russell is careful to insist that this only means that no provision is made to include them in the system's undefined basis. Rather than being declared outright not to exist, however, which the evidence would not justify, they are simply not assumed to exist. To compensate for any presumed loss, the system will contain 'analogues' of persons, atoms and chairs, that is, concepts constructed in terms of simpler things. Construction thus served Russell as much more than a formal technique – it was a metaphysical device by which ordinary objects are, as he put it, "extruded from the world of what there is" [PLA, *Papers* 8, p. 237]. Russell's concluding remarks in the lecture make it clear that, by relating all such concepts to a common basis of particulars alone, his metaphysical outlook had become the same in spirit as the Neutral Monists'. The relation of acquaintance itself was kept in the background.

But a few months later, without hesitation or ceremony, the relation of acquaintance was summoned and dismissed in his lengthy essay, "On Propositions" (1919), along with other mental acts such as judging. The episode takes place during Russell's discussion of belief and propositions, two concepts which he continued to see as closely connected. Given the importance of acquaintance to Russell's views on metaphysics and theory of knowledge over many years, what is perhaps more extraordinary than the brevity of the episode is the reason he gives for the dismissal. He now declares that such mental acts are "not empirically discoverable" [OP, *Papers* 8, p. 294] and must, therefore, like the extrudible objects of science and ordinary life, be constructed from simpler things. The existence of such acts, while not denied, will at least no longer be assumed. Russell thereby renounced his longstanding metaphysical commitment to the irreducibility of mental relations involving a subject's acquaintance with an object. The distinction "between sensation and sense-datum lapses, and it becomes impossible to regard a sensation as in any sense cognitive" [OP, *Papers* 8, p. 295]. The class of particulars no longer contains sense-data, apparently because the latter are understood to possess a relational character by virtue of being objects of acquaintance. Such particulars are rechristened "sensations". By definition, that any sensation is sensed becomes a contingent fact, though a very important one in Russell's metaphysical scheme, because a sensation is "equally part of the subject-matter of physics and of psychology" [OP, *Papers* 8, p. 295]. In making these new claims about sensations, Russell seems to have forgotten that he had assigned virtually the same dual role to sense-data in his writings immediately following the *Theory of Knowledge* project, such as "The Relation of Sense-Data to Physics". This makes it all the more regrettable that he did not pause to explain why he should now be "at a loss to discover any actual phenomenon which could be called an 'act' and could be regarded as a constituent of a presentation" [OP Papers 8, p. 294]. A few years earlier nothing was more obvious to Russell than that the relation of acquaintance pervades experience. How, then, can this relation have vanished? As things now stood, Russell wanted to redirect attention to the objects themselves, the sensations, which determine whatever relational structures are to be classified as mental, none of which is to possess an irreducibly mental character. In *Theory of Knowledge* he remarked that an act of acquaintance "which is acquainted with nothing is not an acquaintance, but a mere absurdity" [*Papers* 7, p. 48]. No longer, it seems, are there relations in search of objects. The Cheshire cat has disappeared, though perhaps not its smile.

Having abandoned dualism in the form defended against early Neutral Monism, Russell would seem ready to take the next step of accepting that doctrine in full. However, this is not the path that he chose to follow, either in "On Propositions" or in *The Analysis of Mind* (1921), the book in which he refined and considerably expanded the views presented in that essay. The reasons for his holding back are rather complicated and, depending on how his views are weighed, Russell appears to be either a reluctant monist or an unreconstructed dualist. In retrospect it seems clear that, even when he had finished *The Analysis of Mind*, Russell had not yet worked out a satisfactory analysis of belief, along with a closely related theory of propositions, that would clearly fit within the existing framework of Neutral Monism. Although "On Propositions" officially disowns his older multiple relation theory of judgment, according to which propositions are parts of actual judgments, the replacement theory he offered both there and in *The Analysis of Mind* seems bizarre, and in view of the constraints he was putting on himself, it probably was bound to be. He continued to hold that propositions are parts of larger complexes called judgments or beliefs and that the properties of truth and falsity belong, in the first instance, to such complexes. However, since he no longer assumed the existence of mental acts, his new theory could not assign the job of *uniting* the components of a complex to a mental relation like that of judging or believing, nor of course could it identify the components of the proposition within that complex as objects of acquaintance for the person who made the judgment. In short, Russell left himself most of the pieces of the multiple relation theory except for the relations that were meant to join them into a cognitive whole. To solve this problem, he added a new category of entity called "images" which (somewhat like Hume's "ideas") are reckoned to be copies of sensations. Individual images are the meanings of words (a vestige of Russell's earlier view that identifies the meaning of a name as an object of acquaintance). Structures of images attended by certain feelings are called "image-propositions" that, similarly, are the meanings of "word-propositions". Propositions of either sort depend for their truth on the existence of facts. Finally, in this new account of belief, images conform to causal laws that, at least in the understanding of current science, are fundamentally different from the physical laws that pertain to sensations.

According to Russell, the existence of images is established by the method of introspection: "On grounds of observation . . . it seems impossible to deny that such images [of sensations] occur" [OP, *Papers*

8, p. 286]. By appealing to this method he was taking a stand against classical behaviourism, whose practitioners had no use either for it or for images. Russell associated behaviourism with the version of Neutral Monism he had previously attacked and he believed that, in their approach to psychological phenomena, the behaviourists inclined too far towards Materialism. His defense of introspection, however, was not meant so much to disprove behaviourism as to supplement its results with a source of knowledge that was scientifically respectable, which is probably the main reason that *The Analysis of Mind* devotes several chapters to the empirical character of images, classified as "mnemic phenomena", and to the topic of "mnemic causation" between images and sensations. Nevertheless, it remains curious that, for Russell, images were observable whereas mental acts proved empirically undiscoverable, for it cannot be that he was using the wrong method to locate them. Russell was in any event careful not to declare that images are of a radically different nature from sensations. The differences between them, he thought, lie in two main areas: their different associations and the laws by which they are organized. Although images "may be in some sense exclusively psychological data, [they] can only be distinguished from sensations by their correlations, not by what they are in themselves" [*AMi*, 297]. Russell's treatment of these correlations shows more than faint traces of his earlier dualism. When an image clusters with other images and perhaps with sensations, beliefs are formed. Indeed, he claims, apart from a belief, "there cannot be a datum". A single sensation, he also points out, is not itself a datum: "it only becomes a datum when it is remembered" [*AMi*, 297]. Images, therefore, may not differ essentially from sensations but they do possess cognitive features that distinguish them from mere sensations. In addition, it should be recalled, images form structures that are the propositional components of beliefs. Besides these structures, beliefs consist of both a feeling of assent and a relation, "actually subsisting, between the assent and the proposition" [*AMi*, 251], whose role is to bind the two other components. Russell has managed, thus, to invest both images and beliefs with features closely resembling those that he had formerly found in mental acts and, as far as their constructional use is concerned, these features hardly appear to simplify what they were meant to replace.

Despite his professed enthusiasm for Neutral Monism in its trans-Atlantic form, Russell's own version during this period stops at the

level of sensations, the entities which succeed sense-data as the official neutral stuff. In their constructional role, however, sensations do
not appreciably differ from their predecessors and Russell continues
to describe them as particulars. Collected one way, sensations form
part of the biography of the person who would be said (in ordinary
usage) to 'have them'. Collected another way, they constitute part
of what would be identified (again, in ordinary usage) as a material
object. In Russell's illustration, a person's sensation 'of' a star is assigned by physics to two different places: an active place (where the
astronomical object is located) and a passive place, where the brain
of the perceiver happens to be at the moment the aspect of the star
(the sensation) is perceived. From the viewpoint of physics, therefore, sensations are locatable in physical space (just as Russell had
claimed for sense-data). The star would have causal connections to
the place where the perceiver is, even if the perceiver's brain were
replaced by a photographic plate. The operative difference between
them is that, where brains are involved, sensations give rise to mnemic phenomena such as images. Such phenomena, he says, are "what
transforms a biography ... into a life" [AMi, 129].

Along with sense-data, the acquaintance relation whereby such
objects are directly known has disappeared in Russell's first version
of Neutral Monism. At least officially. As a relation directed towards
a special class of objects (images), introspection shares a close family
resemblance with acquaintance. Thanks to the use of introspection,
images have acquired a leading role, at least in psychology. And, since
sensations become data and, therefore, parts of knowledge only when
images join with them, it appears that even sense-data have made a
comeback, though now under new management. These veteran products of Russell's former epistemology have been recycled in his first
attempt at becoming a Neutral Monist. Perhaps, then, it is preferable to see Russell's metaphysical doctrine during this transitional
period as one of revisionary dualism rather than unalloyed monism.
At most, in The Analysis of Mind, he has formed a federation with
the Neutral Monists, not a union.

THE MATURE DOCTRINE

In the Spring of 1913, with Principia Mathematica and a large
amount of other important work behind him, Russell began his
Theory of Knowledge project with optimism and vast ambition,

envisioning that in its later stages he would be able to provide an account of logical reasoning, the concepts of Space and Time, scientific inference involving probability theory, and the basic concepts of physics – all of them tied to experience, however indirectly. Although the project ended abruptly a few months later, Russell never lost the spirit that had enlivened it or the determination to reach these goals, despite the fact that it would henceforth take him 35 years, nearly the equivalent of a professional lifetime to get there. From 1914 until 1927 Russell was occupied, though not preoccupied, with what may be conveniently called the Neutral Monism project. This period begins with an overture made to the early Neutral Monists in "The Relation of Sense-Data to Physics", written during the first week of January 1914. Russell declares that while he does "not hold, with Mach and James and the 'new realists', that the difference between the mental and the physical is *merely* one of arrangement, yet what I have to say in the present paper is compatible with their doctrine and might have been reached from their standpoint" [RSDP, *Papers* 8, p. 8]. But the period consists mainly of two successive efforts to fashion a version of their doctrine that would meet his own philosophical standards and, perhaps more importantly, would also satisfy his deeper instincts about constructing the 'right' system of metaphysics. *The Analysis of Mind* marks the end of the first phase, an unsuccessful one, if Russell supposed that having rejected the acquaintance relation and mental acts, he had managed to establish how images and beliefs are constructible from the neutral stuff of sensations. During the second phase, Russell's treatment of cognitive concepts shows the widening influence on his thought of both behaviourism and theoretical physics. This stage culminated in two volumes intended to provide a comprehensive statement of his Neutral Monism, *An Outline of Philosophy* and *The Analysis of Matter*, both published in 1927. With them, Russell's Neutral Monism project reached a high plateau. Major publications during the following decades, such as *Human Knowledge* (1948), while bringing important refinements and extensions to the mature doctrine, should also be seen in the light of the sweeping goals Russell formulated years before when he began writing *Theory of Knowledge*.

Despite the prominence Russell gives to them, however, neither behaviourism nor theoretical physics were allowed to weaken the role and importance of first-person experience, a theme so evident in his earlier work. If Russell favoured psychology over physics in his

Neutral Monism project, it was a foundational bias that he regarded as intuitively justified. These two sciences are both anchored to neutral stuff, though at different distances. Matter, he had concluded in *The Analysis of Mind*, "is both inferred and constructed, never a datum. In this respect psychology is nearer to what actually exists" (*AMi*, 308). Evidently, however, there remained some difficulty about what to *call* what actually exists. "Sensations", the preferred designation in *The Analysis of Mind*, probably began to seem too mentalistic. That book, in any case, contained a regrettable mash of technical terms. Russell occasionally described material things as systems of momentary "aspects or appearances", but the obvious drawback is that the phrase suggests a *contrast* with what is real rather than a definition of it. On the other hand, because the concept of a datum had become considerably enriched, Russell recognized that it was awkward to speak of particulars and simples (see *AMi*, 193), even though this did not stop him from identifying the appearances of a material thing as particulars, but elsewhere in the book he calls them "happenings". This last word captures a dynamic quality that was attractive to Russell, since it indicated not only the transitory character of appearances but also their natural place within some sort of causal network. Russell later acknowledged the influence of Whitehead in making this choice (see *MPD*, p 10). In the new phase of his Neutral Monism project Russell would select the word "events" to convey this quality; it becomes his official designation for neutral stuff.

Although Russell had previously used the concept of an event to define geometrical points and instances, he began to apply it now to neutral stuff considered under the perspective of Relativity Theory. A neutral event is not only something real in itself but essentially part of a four-dimensional or spatio-temporal continuum in which events form systems of causal interconnections that are in turn parts of larger and still larger causal systems. Neutral stuff is thus categorized in a way that makes it a natural though primitive part of the framework of theoretical science. Russell makes spatio-temporal events the starting point for the physical description of what there is. It follows as a corollary that when science defines further properties for these events they cease to be neutral but become part of the content of physical theory. In this way, the 'primordial' events stipulated by Neutral Monism take on the material characteristics assigned to them by science and contribute to the causal explanation of both physical and mental phenomena.

At the end of his essay, "Logical Atomism" (1924), Russell outlined this new version, offering a "summary hypothesis" that correlates the neutral with the physical. (See LA, *Papers* 9, pp. 177–9.) While not neglecting cognitive concepts altogether, he deals with them solely from this perspective, to such an extent that these concepts are barely recognizable. In Russell's scheme, neutral events belong to compresent collections which he calls "minimal regions" of space-time. Such regions form a "four-dimensional manifold" from which "the manifold of space-time that physics requires" can be constructed. By comparing adjacent regions, science discovers physical laws regarding things like light and sound as well as various other properties associated with matter. The "history" of matter in four dimensions takes the form of what Russell calls "tracks or tubes" (an allusion to the Minkowski diagrams known as world-lines). Some tubes contain nervous tissue – a brain – which has the property of reacting to its environment in a manner that makes learning possible through the formation of habits, and on this basis Russell offers the following highly compact definition: "a mind is a track of sets of compresent events in a region of space-time where there is matter which is peculiarly liable to form habits." Since the "peculiarities of what we call 'mind'" can be constructed out of habits, just as the brain can be constructed from the properties of particular tracks, he contends that "a mind and a brain are not really distinct" [LA, *Papers* 9, p. 178]. The difference between them lies at another level. Descriptions of brains concern the overall shape of a tube (and its causal relations to other four-dimensional regions), while those relating to mind refer to the "events of which each cross-section" of the tube is composed. In this rarefied, somewhat cosmic portrayal of the physical and the mental, the compresent events composing each cross-section are "what would be called the contents of one man's mind at one time – i.e., all his sensations, images, memories, thoughts, etc., which can coexist temporally" [LA, *Papers*, 9, 177]. These appear to be none other than the mnemic phenomena that he had dealt with in *The Analysis of Mind*, but in the compressed treatment he gives this topic in "Logical Atomism", apart from mentioning habits as a basis for constructing minds, Russell provides no definition of mental phenomena in physical terms. Instead, he makes a clear effort to contrast compresent events of this special kind with others, distinguishing between the "external relations" which one tube can have to another and those relations *within* a single tube that comprise its individual "history". Although the formulations found in this essay are new and Russell's ideas merely sketched, the theme he meant them to express is not. It is the recurrent theme of the privacy of immediate experience that Russell had been expounding for years in numerous works, including *The Problems of Philosophy* and *The Philosophy of Logical Atomism*, when he was still a defender of dualism, a cherished theme that he was not about to surrender on becoming a Neutral Monist.

The recasting of neutral stuff as events within the framework of theoretical physics had several advantages for Russell. The first was that it conferred legitimacy on a metaphysical claim which could not otherwise be gained by appealing to experience alone, in particular to sensations. By concentrating on sensations, his first version of Neutral Monism appeared to tilt towards the subjective and thus created the risk of being misconstrued as a modern attempt to interpret science within the tradition of Idealism. While this was certainly contrary to Russell's intention, the approach to physics through sensations lacked what was needed for the sophisticated construction of physical concepts. Nor was the situation improved by the introduction of images, since these were tied to a special class of nonphysical laws. With events, however, Russell's new version of Neutral Monism starts in a sense at the opposite end of things: postulated as real, neutral events become a proper part of the working hypothesis. The second advantage was to enable Russell to show how, against the background of physical science, these events have epistemological importance. By definition, neutral events provide no content to physical theory beyond their being components of a spatio-temporal matrix. From the viewpoint of physics, their contribution to Realism is therefore schematic, somewhat like the things known in formal logic as real variables – mere place holders. But Russell wants to add something to this picture. More precisely, he wants to locate within this picture the qualitative features of experience (colours, sounds, and so on), which remain the basis of his theory of knowledge. His new version of Neutral Monism makes a radical connection between the properties of events described by physics and the intrinsic qualities that are directly experienced whenever perception takes place. Russell defines a subclass of events which are at once part of the causal network on which perception depends and is a directly experienced part of that network. These events he labels "percepts". From the physiological point of view, percepts are events that take place in the brain of the perceiver; from an epistemological one, they are the qualitative ingredients with which perceivers construct their knowledge of the world.

The functional role Russell gives to percepts is similar to that carried out in *The Analysis of Mind* by sensations. However, by bringing percepts into the new version's elaborate theoretical framework, Russell was able to revise his account of images. Like a percept, an image is the qualitative feature of a physiological event. The difference between them lies in the range of their causal connections. A percept (in physiological terms) is causally related to extra-cranial events arising in the perceiver's sense organs as well as in regions of space adjacent to the perceiver's body, whereas in the case of an image the causal connections are almost wholly contained within the brain of the perceiver. This approach enabled Russell to divest images of the mentalistic trappings of mnemic phenomena, which had led him earlier to isolate them from sensations and subject them to a different type of law. Moreover, by gathering percepts and images into the same physiological network, itself part of the grander scheme of things envisioned by theoretical physics, he also gained a tremendous strategic advantage in his new version of Neutral Monism. It provided a systematic defense against behaviourism, more effective than his earlier criticisms. Behaviourism's account of belief, he once contended, was a weak spot in the views of the early Neutral Monists. In *The Analysis of Mind*, he gave the job of defending his epistemology against behaviourism to images and the method of introspection. Russell's strategy in the new version of Neutral Monism was to maneuver around behaviourism by removing percepts from its definitional grasp and by treating the doctrine itself as a no more than an advanced form of common-sense Realism, which is finally eclipsed by theoretical science.

Looking back on this period many years later, Russell wrote that behaviourism held his interest as a "method", never as a philosophy, and that he had been determined to push this method "as far as possible while remaining persuaded that it had very definite limits" [*MPD*, 96]. Such a plan is very evident in *An Outline of Philosophy*. Russell's strategy was not to reject behaviourism but only to establish its philosophical limitations. In fact, the book proceeds quite far on behaviourist principles, devoting the earliest chapters to a detailed consideration of topics like habit formation in persons and animals, the acquisition of language, and the stimulus-response model applied to perceiving, remembering, and inferring. However, a major group of chapters widens the scientific picture to include physics, and before these have ended Russell issues a dilemma to "behaviourism as a metaphysic". Either physics is valid "in its main lines", he states, or it is not [*OOP*, 139]. Since behaviourism accepts the former, it must also accept that "what we know most indubitably through perception is not the movements of matter, but certain events in ourselves which are connected" with them [*OOP*, 140]. Therefore, he says, the behaviourist cannot claim to have knowledge of material objects by "direct observation". The starting point for the behaviourist is not the rat in a maze but events in the behaviourist's own brain, where "*something* is really happening, as to which, if we turn our attention to it, we can obtain knowledge that is not misleading" [*OOP*, 140]. These events are the percepts whose "interpretation as knowledge of this or that event in the physical world is liable to be mistaken, for reasons which physics and physiology can make fairly clear" [*OOP*, 140]. But if human knowledge is to be made as reliable as possible, "it must start from percepts" [*OOP*, 141]. This, then, is the charge that Russell makes against behaviourism. The limits of its self-contained methodology are easily reached. Information of the sort gained from rats has not been invalidated but has been found to need a scientific foundation deeper than what the methodology itself could ever provide. Russell's objection, made from the side of physics, is that behaviourism's handling of psychological concepts, especially those relating to the foundations of human knowledge, is scientifically incomplete and, therefore, philosophically inadequate. Far from being a support to Neutral Monism, the doctrine proves to be a shallow friend.

Russell's new version of Neutral Monism prescribes two routes for metaphysics to follow, one internal and the other external, which proceed from a common origin. He maintains that "the facts of physics, like those of psychology, are obtained by what is really self-observation, although common sense mistakenly supposes that it is observation of external objects" [*OOP*, 180]. In describing the difference between these two sciences, Russell modified his earlier simile of the London postal directory in a way that brings out their dynamic roles. Like the postman who knows "the movements of many letters", the physicist can track the movements of light and sound waves "that go about the world"; and just as the recipient (unlike the postman) knows the content of a letter, the delivery of those waves to a human being will "give psychological knowledge" [*OOP*, 300]. This form of knowledge is indispensable, Russell holds, for "our knowledge of the physical world is purely abstract: we know certain logical characteristics of its structure, but nothing of its intrinsic character", which may, for all we know, resemble that of "the mental world" [*OOP*, 306–7]. (See Demopoulos, this volume.) The remark echoes his claim in *The Analysis of Mind* about psychology being nearer to what "actually exists" [*AMi*, 308].

By assigning such considerable responsibility to percepts, Russell was attempting to fulfill the challenge posed by Neutral Monism that he had mentioned to his lecture audience in 1918, the challenge of substituting logical constructions for inferred entities. But his new version of the doctrine does not use Occam's Razor to cut away everything but percepts, making these the sole material for constructing everything else. The causal framework of events is also left intact and it helps define his allegiance to Realism. Even if it is not demonstrable, he maintained, the assumption that neutral events exist independently of experience was a reasonable and proper defense against the solipsistic view that the laws of physics can be "verified by me" only insofar as "they lead to predictions of *my* percepts" [*OOP*, 302]. Russell regarded solipsism as a form of scepticism wearing the disguise of "logical caution". Resistance to any virulent form of scepticism was a leitmotif throughout his thought. Like Hume, however, he could offer no refutation of extreme scepticism, only congenital disbelief.

In its broad sweep and personal touch, even to the extent of elaborating a philosophical attitude towards the universe, *An Outline of Philosophy* was as much a testament to Russell's monistic philosophy as the much earlier *Problems of Philosophy* had been to his dualism. In contrast, *The Analysis of Matter*, 'sequel' to *The Analysis of Mind*, was a rather more specialized work concentrating on physics just as its predecessor had on psychology. The doctrine of behaviourism is left to one side, as is the analysis of the concept of belief, and what is said about perception largely concerns the role of percepts within the framework of theoretical physics. When Russell mentions psychology in the non-behaviouristic sections of *An Outline of Philosophy* and in most of *The Analysis of Matter*, he seems to be thinking mainly of the qualitative or experiential side of percepts.

He recognizes no self-contained science of psychology. Its scientific data are physical, and the causal laws of mental phenomena, while not so well-ordered in the present state of science, are assumed to be ultimately quantitative in character and based on the discoverable or theorized structure of physical events. Accordingly, Russell often uses the term "psychological" in a mainly epistemological sense that points to the special status given to percepts by Neutral Monism.

With regard to physics, however, *The Analysis of Matter* has very much to say. Three years earlier, in "Logical Atomism", Russell had noted that his summary hypothesis would "need to be amplified and refined in many ways in order to fit in completely with scientific facts" [LA, *Papers* 9, 178]. Doubtless, *The Analysis of Matter* was intended to meet this requirement.

Drawing on the work of Whitehead, Eddington and others, Russell gives an account of electromagnetic theory, special and general theories of relativity, quantum theory, determinism and causal laws, the abstract concepts of points and intervals, Space and Time separately, and of course Space-Time. In fact, much of this work can stand on its own as Russell's contribution to the philosophy of physics. Although the discussion of mathematical and scientific ideas infuses his new version of Neutral Monism with an immense amount of detail not found in *An Outline of Philosophy*, there are no significant additions to that version taken as a metaphysical doctrine. Percepts remain "the epistemological basis of physics" [*AMa*, 257]. When noticed, they become data. Percepts are in physical space, "nearer to the sense organ than to the physical object, nearer to the nerve than to the sense organ, and nearer to the cerebral end of the nerve..." [*AMa*, 383]. Percepts differ from images by the nature of their causal relations to other events. They are known directly through their qualitative content and "are not known to have any intrinsic character which physical events cannot have..." [*AMa*, 384]. Physical events are otherwise known only abstractly, and everything that we can know of the world's intrinsic character "is derived from the mental side" [*AMa*, 402]. Nevertheless, some features that were left implicit or less developed in *An Outline of Philosophy* receive much greater attention in *The Analysis of Matter*, such as the question of determinism, the concept of substance, and the inferability of percepts (as qualitative contents) from the structure of their causes. Despite considerable overlap, therefore, these two books form a complementary presentation of

Russell's Neutral Monism in its most developed form. It is in fact the version of the doctrine that Russell would summarize many years later in *My Philosophical Development* [*MPD*, 20–27].

Between that final summary and *The Analysis of Matter*, Russell published two volumes in which Neutral Monism, while not expounded by name, exerted considerable influence. *An Inquiry Into Meaning and Truth* (1940) discusses a range of topics in logic and philosophy of language, with the work of some logical positivists (among others) providing Russell a useful contrast for his own views. The book begins by applying the method of behaviourism to some questions not covered in *An Outline of Philosophy*: how logical concepts are learned and what role is played by so-called egocentric (or emphatic) particulars like "this". Wearing the clothing of the behaviourist, Russell at last answers the question he posed in 1913 when he demanded that the early Neutral Monists give an account of selective attention. The *Inquiry* describes the concept of "noticing" and the causal conditions between brain and outside world that account for the use of "this" as a response to a stimulus. The psychological side of Neutral Monism reveals itself, nevertheless, in Russell's allowance for a special use of "this" and a related expression, "I-now", which express the experiential state of the person who uses them. Russell thus draws a fine but significant line between the personal and public uses of "this". A person who says "This is a cat", for instance, may be wrong, if taken to mean that there is a cat within sighting distance, yet justified if all that is meant is "This is a cat-percept". "What we directly know when we say 'this is a cat' is a state of ourselves," he claims, "like being hot" [*IMT*, 114]. Russell's solution to his old challenge amounts to a compromise. The egocentric word "this" can be removed from descriptions of external or public states of affairs, but it retains a private use in connection with percepts. Russell introduces a comparable distinction in the *Inquiry* between what sentences *express* and what they *indicate*. He also updates his earlier views about names and particulars to fit the newer, preferred category of events. A name is now taken to designate a set of compresent qualities, or otherwise a quality which is part of a whole. The orientation to immediate experience is evident throughout the *Inquiry* in Russell's examination of the workings of ordinary language, including how logical concepts are expressed, in the emphasis given to what he calls factual premises, and in his criticisms of the preoccupation shown by positivists such as Neurath with artificial observational languages.

In *Human Knowledge*, the last systematic statement of his philosophy, Russell's commitment to science from the viewpoint of Neutral Monism remains strong. Its approach and range of topics are a fusion of those taken in *An Outline of Philosophy*, *The Analysis of Matter*, and *An Inquiry Into Meaning and Truth*, but it also contains two lengthy and detailed sections on probability theory and the foundations of scientific inference in which Russell discusses and adapts the work of Keynes. *Human Knowledge* is thus more comprehensive than any of the others, and were it not for the fact that Russell does not expressly mention Neutral Monism by name, the work could be taken to constitute his fullest exposition of the doctrine. Allowing for that omission, *Human Knowledge* can nevertheless be so regarded, given the now familiar details it contains about events and their causal ordering, the two perspectives of private space and public space, experienced time versus objective time, the primacy of theoretical physics in our knowledge of the universe beyond the contents of immediate experience (percepts), and the fundamental connection between the structure of matter and its intrinsic qualities which makes empirical knowledge possible. Although Russell announces at an early point in the book that inferences will be defended "as opposed to logical constructions" [*HK*, 12], because the former are necessary to science, he has not in fact abandoned his Occamist principle. The distinction serves a dialectical purpose, since the constructions he alludes to are those proposed by a solipsist, and, hence, by an opponent of the working hypothesis that Russell consistently defends. The monistic character of his Realism, moreover, is unchanged. Sensations and volitions, he writes, when "considered as part of the manifold of events ordered in space-time by causal relations... must be located in the brain". A space-time point, he continues, "is a class of events, and there is no reason why some of these events should not be 'mental'. Our feeling to the contrary is only due to obstinate adherence to the mind-matter dualism" [*HK*, 239].

Russell's preface to the book mentions the injunction of the Prophet that if two passages from the Koran were found inconsistent, the latter text is to be accepted as authoritative. He applies a similar injunction to *Human Knowledge,* and the context makes it clear that he means it to apply to that work alone. Nevertheless, if Russell had known when he wrote the preface, that this was to be his last complete philosophical work, he might have approved extending the Prophet's rule to the whole corpus of his writings on Neutral Monism which, at the time, extended back more than a quarter-century. *Human Knowledge* has never acquired that stature, however.

THE DOCTRINE IN PERSPECTIVE

The volume in which Russell's "Logical Atomism" paper appeared in 1924 also contained an essay by one of his Cambridge contemporaries, C.D. Broad, who praised him with faint damnation. While Broad commends Russell for his "speculative boldness", he comments rather chummily to his readers: "As we all know, Mr. Russell produces a different system of philosophy every few years ..." [*Contemporary British Philosophy* (First Series), ed. J.H. Muirhead, 79]. Unkindness apart, Broad's opinion was not inaccurate when one reviews the successive efforts Russell had made during the preceding decade to get to the bottom of human knowledge. There was the *Theory of Knowledge* project, followed soon after by *Our Knowledge of the External World*, the 1918 lectures on logical atomism, followed again soon after by his half-embrace of Neutral Monism in *The Analysis of Mind* – not to mention the extensive remodeling of Neutral Monism presented in the paper that Broad probably had not yet seen. All the same, these different efforts were not really so different as Broad suggested. They are more like variations on the theme of dualism which Russell had brought to the public starting with *The Problems of Philosophy*.

With the appearance of "Logical Atomism" and the major volumes that followed, however, Russell's perspective decidedly changed, for he began to cultivate a philosophical monism that merged with the framework of theoretical physics, entirely confident that Neutral Monism's contribution was important to the scientific outlook and that his doctrine was secure against the claims of any monistic rival, such as Materialism. Given this new "system of philosophy" that Russell outlined in 1924 and developed in subsequent books, Broad may well have felt absolutely confirmed in his opinion about Russell's chameleon metaphysics. Yet a closer look reveals – just as it does in the case of his dualism – abundant similarities: a new theme with many sophisticated variations. More than that, from a vantage point much more distant than Broad was able to enjoy, we can now see that even the two main periods of Russell's metaphysics, his early dualism followed by the monism officially launched in 1924, have many significant resemblances.

Perhaps the most intriguing feature that survives in Russell's Neutral Monism from the earlier period is the emphasis given to first-person experience. Indeed, it is the primacy of such experience that Russell appeals to in his constant rejection of Materialism. He did not oppose this doctrine because it was committed to the existence of some brute, insensate material substance (as Berkeley thought of it), for Russell knew well enough, as would any modern defender of Materialism, that the matter dealt with in corpuscularian philosophy had long since yielded to the insubstantial 'matter' of events. His objection to Materialism is that its characterization of those events stopped, so to speak, at their threshold and therefore only referred to the structural properties of events. Besides structure, some events have intrinsic features or qualities known directly to the people who have them. Far from being curiosities to science, the events he calls percepts are the basis of our knowledge of everything objective, whose most complete understanding lies within science itself. Thus, even theoretical physics has a 'mental' side, he maintained, which can be traced to the brain but never encountered within physical space. With its talk of qualities and structures, of public space and private worlds, such a view certainly seems dualistic. If the difference between Neutral Monism and Materialism concerns exactly what the latter omits, then Russell's mature doctrine perhaps fails to be monistic. Does it?

In *The Analysis of Matter*, Russell describes his doctrine as "psycho-cerebral parallelism", though not according to the "usual" interpretation [*AMa*, 391]. What that might be, he does not say, but his doctrine resolutely avoided creating two different systems of entities, coordinated somehow but in principle detachable from each other. In Russell's Neutral Monism, qualities are pinned to physical events, for the doctrine requires that percepts be real in every respect; otherwise, there would be phenomena that fall outside the scope of causal explanation. Percepts, however, can be completely explained, at least in the sense that their place within causal sequences can be mapped. Qualities therefore also have a place within physical space: they are where percept-events are – in the brain. Russell's view is better described, accordingly, as a psycho-cerebral identity theory, one that involves only an identity of spatial reference. Even then, according to Russell's linguistic criteria, there is an important distinction to be made. To describe a percept structurally and to identify its quality are complementary operations performed by words which thus do not mean the same. As Russell understands referential language, descriptions presuppose names. The complete identification of a percept would therefore presuppose the name of its quality. Consequently, in metaphysics, at least, nothing is omitted from the complete causal explanation of that percept. That names are the starting point for descriptions is a logical point for Russell, not a scientific discovery, and another principle that survived the long progress of his metaphysics.

Although Russell propounded a monistic doctrine, he nevertheless gave it a characteristically dualistic stamp. Introspection, awareness, attention, sensation, volition, the private and inner world of the individual contrasted with the public and outer world common to observers – all notions quite familiar from Russell's dualistic period – were carried over to the later one and expressed in these very terms, suggesting that he wanted Neutral Monism to convey a truth that, paradoxically, monistic claims by themselves could not. The paradox arises because Neutral Monism deals with empirical truths and, in principle, no empirical truth eludes the network of science; yet the language of science, expressed in terms of structural properties and causal relations, fails to capture those truths fully. Perhaps the incorporation of dualistic language in Russell's Neutral Monism was meant to convey a simple truth about science which is not itself a scientific fact, at least not an ordinary one: that science does not assemble facts alone but pieces of knowledge, since knowing facts makes science itself possible. While a truism for science, Russell took it seriously because, in his philosophy, ontology and epistemology are ultimately inseparable. Far from avoiding metaphysics, Russell was one of its great patrons. Like Spinoza and other predecessors in the tradition, he believed that metaphysics should deliver people, whether scientifically inclined or not, from false or incomplete pictures of the world and should provide them instead with a comprehensive sense of what it is to have knowledge. In Russell's mature philosophy, there is one kind of thing that is ultimately real and the facts which it comprises are potentially all within the grasp of science. This is what makes his doctrine a monism. What essentially makes any fact count as knowledge, however, and what ultimately

requires reference to the intrinsic features of events, can only be adequately formulated with the help of dualistic concepts which put
the fact within the context of being known. Although the mental
relations of acquaintance and judgment have been extruded from
the world of particulars, where they were once defended by Russell
against the early Neutral Monists, they have migrated to his later
metaphysics, transformed. Russell regarded Materialism deficient,
not because this rival doctrine omits any content but because it fails
to engage that content completely. Like his metaphysical forbears,
Russell would never accept that philosophy of science is philosophy
enough. For their part, behaviourists and others among Russell's contemporaries doubtless regarded his metaphysical views, whatever
monistic claims he might make for them, as Cartesian at heart – a
case of dualism unrepentant. In this they were partly right. Russell's
metaphysics in its different incarnations throughout his career does
indeed reveal the sensibility of a dualist. In his Neutral Monism that
sensibility found its most sophisticated expression.

Monistic or dualistic, however, all such systems of metaphysics
suffer from their own grandeur. Using the principles of Neutral
Monism, a scientifically astute observer who has a percept know-
ingly refers to a region, perhaps a very specific location, within that
subject's own brain. The working-hypothesis approach that Russell
adopted works nicely here. As physiological information increases,
descriptions will become more accurate about the structural nature
of the percept as well as about its causal connections, those vast
"causal lines" Russell spoke of in *The Analysis of Matter* that join the
observer's brain to everything outside it. Russell's Neutral Monism
could easily incorporate the transactional models based on computer
theory to portray such connections. In terms of its empirical content,
in other words, his doctrine is quite adaptable, hardly imprisoned in a
time warp of theoretical physics created during the first quarter of the
last century. But in another respect Neutral Monism is a remote doctrine which, from a common sense point of view, produces no deep
conviction but rather a kind of indifference. Simply put, the problem is this. As speakers inhabiting a common world, we cannot talk
about things from the viewpoint of our brains. Even if percepts are
indeed inside our heads, that is not where we place their qualitative
features and, if we did so, it is difficult to understand how we could
then have the concept of a head in the first place. The private
space of experience which Russell regarded as so important to his

epistemology, the world which he wanted to distinguish from the public world of physics, is exactly the world which we believe we inhabit in common. Given that science has indeed correctly tracked experiences to their origin in the brain, the doctrine which Russell expounded was unable to use such facts in a cogent manner to re-construct a world for us that we can recognize.

The reason for this has much to do with Russell's perhaps un-consciously patrician attitude, never deferential to the claims of common-sense when metaphysical questions were at issue. In ac-cordance with his moderate scepticism, Russell took it to be ax-iomatic that science, not metaphysics, undermines common-sense beliefs about the nature of physical objects, and he considered it es-sential therefore that science, in making its own assumptions about the world, should be free of such beliefs. This attitude was present no less when he was a dualist than when a monist. Ordinary material objects are to be constructed from sense-data, or sensations, or some elaborate combination of percepts and other events; yet, with regard to all such items, Russell was never able to show by the method of construction how to make the deep and indispensable connection that might enable common-sense beliefs to be grasped and more or less adequately understood, even if not adequately expressed in state-ments embodying his metaphysical views. He produced little more than sketches of how the construction was to proceed, never a set of working plans. Whereas percepts enjoy some credibility in the physiological order of things, the job remained for Russell's Neutral Monism to characterize them in ways that might plausibly merge with the public uses of language, especially those uses he described in his later writings from the standpoint of behaviourism. The so-cial context of language and reference, which so dominated the later Wittgenstein's own conception of philosophy, was of considerably less interest to Russell than the more pressing issues of scientific metaphysics, and, partly as a result of his failure to show the doc-trine's relevance as a way of doing philosophy, his Neutral Monism remained on the periphery of British philosophy in the decades sur-rounding the Second World War, attracting cool respect but exerting increasingly little influence. Ironically, the visceral resistance of dis-belief, which Russell (like Hume) considered was perhaps philoso-phy's strongest response against extreme forms of scepticism, espe-cially when logical opposition fails, seems also to have been directed where he probably least expected it.

11 The Metaphysics of Logical Atomism

Bertrand Russell made use of logic as an analytical tool from the start of his philosophical career and early on adopted a metaphysics that can be called "atomism" in opposition to "monism". The name "logical atomism" is nevertheless useful for identifying a distinctive combination of metaphysical and logical doctrines characteristic of Russell's work from around 1910 to at least 1925. Russell introduced the name in his series of lectures in 1918 (PLA), so characterising his "philosophical position" and used it again later for the title of a 1924 essay (LA). He describes this philosophy as the combination of a "... logical doctrine which seems to me to result from the philosophy of mathematics..." and "... on the basis of this a certain kind of metaphysic" (PLA, 160). The metaphysics is not simply derivative from his logical theory resulting merely from reading a metaphysical theory off the expressions of a logically perspicuous language. In a passage of the lectures on the notion of complexity Russell describes certain definitions as "... *preliminary* because they start from the complexity of the proposition, which we define psychologically, and proceed to the complexity of the fact, whereas it is quite clear that in an orderly, proper procedure it is the complexity of the fact that you would start from" (PLA, 175). The right way to analyze certain expressions into a logical language would seem to follow from a correct metaphysical analysis of facts rather than leading it. In the lectures the project is described in a very world-oriented way:

I think one might describe philosophical logic, the philosophical portion of logic which is the portion that I am concerned with in these lectures since Christmas, as an inventory, or if you like a more humble word, a "Zoo" containing all the different forms that facts may have. I should prefer to say "forms of facts" rather than "forms of propositions"... In accordance with the sort of realistic bias that I should put into all study of metaphysics, I should always wish to be engaged in the investigation of some actual fact or set of facts, and it seems to me that this is so in logic just as it is in zoology. In logic you are concerned with the forms of facts, different *logical* sorts of facts, that there are in the world. (PLA, 191)

Thus, logical atomism is a metaphysical view inspired by logical analysis but not a simple projection of the features of language into the world. Instead the analysis of propositions is a guide to an analysis of the facts which correspond with them, an analysis, however, that leads to the discovery of logical categories in the world and the logical atoms that make it up. A survey of the metaphysics of logical atomism should therefore look at parallel developments in Russell's logical doctrines and his metaphysical views.

Some of the views described as logical atomism in the works from 1918 to 1925 are found in the Introduction to the first edition of *Principia Mathematica* (PM) in 1910 and recur past the appearance of the second edition in 1925. This essay will take the metaphysical and logical views of Russell bounded by the two editions of PM as the scope of "logical atomism" and will trace the development of some of them. Despite the move to the doctrine of extensionality with the Second Edition there is a great deal of uniformity of views on logical matters over this period and just a few striking changes in ontology such as the move to neutral monism. According to this periodization one of the most distinctive features of logical atomism is its account of truth as a correspondence between propositions or their successors, which are the objects of logic, and facts, which constitute the world. In his 1924 paper Russell suggests that "realism" also characterises the view but is not central to it and, indeed, that term certainly does not single out the particular views of this period. From the early rejection of the monistic metaphysics of Bradley and the idealists, Russell's view was always realist, seeing the world as composed of many distinct individuals standing in external relations to each other. This realism and atomism in Russell's metaphysics go back to the earliest stages of his rejection of idealism by 1900, but the limits of a distinctive view properly called "logical atomism" can be settled by the appearance of facts, as clearly distinguished from true propositions, in his ontology from 1910. The many independent objects in the world have properties, that is, exemplify universals, and stand in external relations to each other as constituents of *facts*, as he calls them, "complexes", which are the real substance of the world.

PROPOSITIONS

One obstacle to interpreting the ontology of logical atomism as based on the correspondence between facts and propositions is that at the same time that facts feature prominently in Russell's thought, propositions have disappeared as "single entities". This period is marked by his ongoing search for an analysis or "construction" of the seeming unity of propositions. The various solutions are described as the "multiple relation" theory of judgement. To use his standard example, when x judges that aRb, there is no binary relation of x to some complex proposition, that aRb, which itself will be true or false depending on whether a bears the relation R to b. Rather the judgement is a complex relation between x and those constituents a, R, and b, taken individually. Believing is a relation B which holds between the subject x and those constituents, which together constitute the complex fact that $B(x, a, R, b)$, which exists whether or not a is related by R to b. Because the number of arguments of B and their logical types can vary as widely as there are objects of belief, this relation R is a multigrade, or "multiple" relation. The suggestion is that all occurrences of propositions will be like those in judgements or beliefs, and so propositions are not single entities at all.

This denial of unity to propositions, however, was not accompanied by any reluctance on Russell's part to use variables for propositions, or to speak of "all propositions" and so to quantify over them, although he does say that such a device will not be necessary for the derivations of *Principia* (*PM*, vol. 1, 185). This has suggested to some that the logic of PM is not in keeping with the metaphysics of logical atomism, at least no with the multiple relation theory, and even that a nominalist account of propositions as just sentences was intended. Influenced as analytic philosophers are by Quine's doctrines, it is easy to see the referential devices, ultimately the bound variables, as the very expression of the ontological commitment of a theory. How can Russell both deny the existence of propositions and then use variables 'p' and 'q' for them? This is especially problematic since symbolic logic is based on the logic of propositions and there should be propositions to be the values of propositional functions, which in turn constitute the range of the higher order quantifiers in the logic. One line of interpretation is to argue that Russell must mean all such variables as schematic or stand-ins for sentences. On this interpretation 'p' and 'q' are not variables that range over propositions as ordinary variables 'x' and 'y' range over objects, but really are schematic letters holding the grammatical places of sentences. Quantification over propositional functions, then, is to be interpreted as saying that there is some predicate or expression which, when substituted into what follows, produces a true sentence. This is the "substitutional interpretation" of the quantifiers, by which one treats a first-order predication, '$(\exists x) f(x)$', which seemingly directly quantifies over objects, as rather actually true just in case there is some name 'a', substitutable for 'x', which yields a true instance 'fa'. A second-order sentence, which seemingly quantifies over functions, will be true if some instance is true in which a predicate is substituted for the second-order variable[1]. On this account, propositions are just sentences, and propositional functions nothing more than predicates. The plausibility of such a nominalist interpretation of Russell's logic is a central interpretive issue for students of logical atomism and the problem of reconciling the multiple relation theory with the formalism of the logic is only one that leads to it. Whatever the larger issues, it does seem clear that Russell took the multiple relation theory to be compatible with the theory of PM.[2] One must conclude, then, that some of the primitive expressions of the language of PM do not stand for ontologically primitive nonlinguistic entities. The correlation of basic expressions in the logic with basic items in the ontology is not exact. Still, however, any logical complexity there is in an expression will represent genuine complexity in the fact or entity that it represents.

Russell's worries about propositions, in the form of puzzles about the logical analysis of belief, are a reflection of the central thread in the developments in logical views that frame this period, the

---

[1] Gödel [1944] suggests this interpretation. See Sainsbury [1980] for details.
[2] The fact that these sections were presented with the rest of the introduction as a single paper "The Theory of Logical Types" (*Papers* 6, 3–40) before the publication of *PM* is contrary to the suggestion by Church ([1984], 513) that they are a late addition to the text.

move from the first edition of *PM* to the second.[3] These developments are almost contemporaneous with Russell's interaction with Ludwig Wittgenstein, which began with Wittgenstein's arrival in Cambridge in 1911 and end with Russell's frequent acknowledgment of Wittgenstein's influence both in the second edition of *PM* and in the philosophical writings PLA and LA.

EXTENSIONALITY

The emergence of the doctrine of extensionality is a second development of the atomism period, accompanying Russell's doubts about propositions as unities. In the second edition of *PM* Russell proposes that functions all be treated extensionally by asserting that coextensive functions (those true of the same individuals) are identical. Thus, from $(x)(fx \equiv gx)$ we may infer $f\hat{x} = g\hat{x}$.[4] Russell does not interpret this consequence in a semantic way as Quine does, who holds that in extensional logic propositional function variables range over sets, or as Frege does, holding that predicates designate concepts, which are extensional in virtue of being functions (from objects to truth values) and that sentences (or rather thoughts) designate truth values. Although Russell mentions Frege's view (*PM*, vol. 1, p. 659) describing it as the view that there are only two propositions "one

---

3 The second edition of *PM* differs, aside from the resetting of the first two volumes, just in the addition of a new introduction and of three appendices. The references to the two editions, then, will ordinarily just be to the respective introductions, with reference to the appendices marked. From various indications from Russell and Whitehead it is clear that the introductions were primarily Russell's work, however much collaboration there was in the technical details of the body of the text. I will therefore refer to *PM* as Russell's work, intending the reference to be taken to the views expressed in the introductions.

4 The formulation of the principle of extensionality for higher order propositional functions is a matter of contention and technical complexity. To begin with it must be decided what theory of types is intended for the Second Edition of *PM*. Hazen and Davoren have pointed out that in Gödel's [1944] there is a passing suggestion that although functions will be distinguished by level, that is, by the use of quantification in their definition, a given function will take arguments of any level. If to be coextensive is to agree on all arguments, it becomes unclear how this principle could even be stated, and how it could be used, as it requires a seemingly illegitimate generalization over all levels. Without a clear grasp of the system of the Second Edition, it is not possible to assess its main technical content, the derivation in Appendix B of the principle of mathematical induction without using the axiom of reducibility. It clearly does not work if one stays with the system of the First Edition. Myhill [1974] gives the technical details.

true and one false", he rejects it on the grounds that sentences cannot be names.[5] Truth values do not appear in the metaphysics of logical atomism as individuals or at any level in the hierarchy of types. Propositions do not appear officially either, of course, but in so far as they do appear, they would be of a different logical type than the objects to which Frege assimilates classes and truth values. Russell continues to speak of propositional functions as the basis of logic throughout this period and the no-class theory that defines classes with propositional functions is still maintained.

If the doctrine of extensionality does not amount to the thesis that functions designate extensions, what ontological content does it have? The key to understanding Russell's interpretation of extensionality comes from recalling that the identity symbol, '$=$', is a defined symbol in *PM*. Russell adopts Leibniz' doctrine of the Identity of Indiscernibles as his definition of identity at *PM* *13.01. Objects x and y are identical just in case any ("predicative") function f which is true of x is also true of y. The same applies to all logical types. To say that $f\hat{x} = g\hat{x}$ is to say that any second-order function true of $f\hat{x}$ will also hold of $g\hat{x}$ and vice versa. But what sort of second-order functions hold of first-order functions? Here we find a role for one of the two slogans that Russell uses frequently to characterize extensionality, the thesis that a function "can only enter into a proposition through its values" (*PM2*, xxix). This would appear to be the claim that a propositional function will only contribute its values, which are propositions, to those contexts in which it occurs. In other words, functions yielding the same values for the same arguments will not differ in their properties. If the values of the functions are finely individuated intensional propositions, however, the logic will still not be extensional. The decisive second characterization of extensionality is that propositions may only appear in truth-functional contexts. Officially the only primitive sentential connective in the language of the Second Edition is to be the Sheffer stroke '$p|q$', the truth functional connective with the same values as 'not both p and q', true if one or both of p and q are false, false otherwise. All functions of propositions must be derived from this one connective. Putting the two slogans together, then, if propositional functions $f\hat{x}$ and $g\hat{x}$ are

---

coextensive and also only contribute the truth values of the propositions that are their values to higher-order contexts, their intensional aspects will make no difference and as indistinguishable they will be considered identical.

Russell did not think that adopting the doctrine of extensionality required him to abandon the notions of propositional function and proposition in favour of extension and truth value. Rather he held that logic of *PM* did not have the resources to distinguish functions that were coextensive, or distinguish propositions with the same truth values. Indeed, Russell takes the consequence that class expressions '$\hat{x}(fx)$' and the expressions for propositional functions, '$f\hat{x}$', have the same "meanings" and so there is "no longer any reason to distinguish between functions and classes" (*PM2*, xxxix). But that does not mean that he adopts an ontology of classes. Rather, he goes on to say that this shows that it is classes that have lost even that "shadowy being that they retain in *20". In other words functions are retained in the logic and talk about classes is successfully eliminated because of the extensional nature of the logic.

NOMINALISM

Several different features of the metaphysics and logic of Logical Atomism conspire to suggest that Russell abandoned an earlier platonism about universals, such as is explicitly described in *Problems of Philosophy* (*POP*), and adopted nominalism, identifying propositional functions and universals with predicates in the language of *PM*. These are distinct from the troubles with the multiple relation theory discussed above and mostly arise after the first edition of *PM*. Both Gödel [1944] and Cocchiarella [1987] describe Russell's later ontology as nominalist in this way and this does fit with Russell's own later description of his view as seeing logic as more linguistic than he originally thought (*MPD*). Yet even that work includes a defence of the existence of universals, as he reminds us of the restauranteur who insists on calling horseflesh "beef" (*MPD*, 162). Something, he says, keeps it horseflesh, whatever it is called. An analysis of these issues will show that the purported move to nominalism is not as obvious as is suggested.

One of these developments that suggests a move toward nominalism is Russell's adoption of Wittgenstein's notion that atomic facts only involve lowest level properties and individuals. In the Introduction to the Second Edition of *PM*, atomic propositions are identified as of the forms:

$$R_1(x), R_2(x, y), R_3(x, y, z), \ldots$$

Russell then says that "terms that occur as the *R*'s occur are called 'universals'. . . " whereas the terms that occur in any of these expressions as the values of the variables *x*, *y*, etc, are "individuals" or "particulars" (*PM2*, xix). There are no atomic sentences where the universals $R_1, R_2, \ldots$ in turn appear as subjects, and so, presumably, all atomic facts are composed only of individuals and (first-order) universals. There will be expressions in the language that include higher-order quantifiers, quantifiers ranging over functions, for some notions are defined by generalising with respect to first-order predicates. How are these higher-order formulas to be interpreted? Russell says that "there is no logical matrix of the form $f(\phi!\hat{z}.)$" (*PM2*, xxxi) and that any such purported matrix will be definable as some stroke function of atomic, first-order sentences. A common assumption is that he intends to treat these defined higher-order matrices as merely linguistic, as simply predicates, and not as symbols for some other entity. Indeed later Russell is at pains to prove that any formulas with higher-order quantifiers will be replaceable with first-order equivalents. He considers a purported example, saying that the seemingly atomic sentence "'before' is a relation" should be analysed as "If I assert that *x* is before *y*, I assert a relation between *x* and *y*" (PLA, 182). Higher-order predications, it would seem, are really "logical constructions", so they are linguistic only if logical constructions must be seen as part of some nominalistic project. What's more, nothing is implied by this paraphrase about whether the first-order predicate 'before' stands for a universal. This evidence is inconclusive, at best showing that Russell became suspicious of primitive higher-order functions.

Because logic seemingly demands no more higher-order entities than can be defined, it is possible to give a linguistic interpretation of the system, treating the higher-order quantifiers as "substitutional". The mere existence of a substitutional interpretation, however, does not show that the *intended* interpretation of the quanitifiers is substitutional. Again, the evidence for a nominalist treatment of functions is not strong.

There are other indications of some move towards seeing logic as linguistic. We find, for example, " A proposition is just a symbol" (PLA, 166) and

To understand 'red', for instance, is to understand what is meant by saying that a thing is red. You have to bring in the form of a proposition. (PLA, 182)

and

The theory of types is really a theory of symbols, not of things. (PLA, 232)

These look like explicit statements of nominalism, but a closer examination is necessary. Symbols for Russell are what we would call interpreted symbols, symbols with their meaning.[6] Russell is happy to identify a sentence as object as some collection of marks on a page or vibrations in the air. It is words with their meanings that become more substantial. Within the theory of types words as mere symbols may be individuals, of the lowest types. Their meanings, however, will produce relations between them and entities of differing types. Thus,

... the relation of the symbol to what it means is different in different types. I am not now talking about this hierarchy of classes and so on, but the relation of a predicate to what it means is different from the relation of a name to what it means. There is not one single concept of 'meaning' as one ordinarily thinks there is, so that you can say in a uniform sense 'all symbols have meaning', but there are infinite numbers of different ways of meaning, ie. different sorts of relation of the symbol to the symbolised, which are absolutely distinct. (PLA, 233)

A nominalist should hold that there is just one kind of entity in the world, concrete particulars, which include both names and the individuals they name. Singular terms and predicates or "general terms" differ only in the relations they bear to individuals; where those relations are of the same logical type, they relate particulars to particulars but may differ in the number of entities they relate. A nominalist should see a general term as one that "names" (as suggested by the etymology of "nominalism") or "applies to" many individuals, while

---

[6] "When I speak of a symbol I simply mean something that 'means' something else, and as to what I mean by 'meaning' I am not prepared to tell you" (PLA, 167). He goes on to say that an account of meaning will involve a strictly infinite number of different things including cognitive relations like knowing. This seems to be an allusion to the multiple relation theory of judgement.

a singular term names only one. This is not Russell's notion of meaning. The theory of logical types may be a theory of symbols, but it
is more importantly a theory of the meanings of those symbols seen
as entities which come in different logical types. There is something
essentially predicative about 'red' but that has to do with its logical
type, a type higher than that of individuals. That is what is required
to understand 'red', not knowing something about the symbol 'red'
as a concrete particular.

FACTS

The logical notion of extensionality manifests itself on the ontological side as a view about the nature of complex facts, in particular,
judgements or beliefs. The issue is over what sort of fact corresponds
with propositions reporting beliefs or judgements. At the time of *PM*
Russell seems to allow facts involving other facts as constituents.
Thus, perception is seen as a case where we are directly related to
a fact. "The complex object 'a-in-the-relation-R-to-b' may be capable of being *perceived*; when perceived, it is perceived as one object"
(*PM*, vol. 1, 43). Belief and judgement, however, are quite different, for
they do not directly relate us to facts. We can make a judgement that
is false or believe a proposition that does not obtain. Russell did not
want to analyse propositions about belief and judgement as relations
to propositions and so had to find some other analysis. His response
was the "multiple relation theory" of judgement mentioned above.
Ontologically, it arises out of Russell's rejection of propositions as
the objects of propositional attitudes such as belief and judgement.
Russell's attention is directed to what sort of facts there might be
that would seem to involve at least two different "verbs", as the
sample belief of x that aRb analysed as $B(x, a, R, b)$ above seems
to involve both B and R. A contemporary discussion of these issues
would probably focus on an attempt to find a suitable construction
of propositions, so as to avoid them in some sense, but keep the analysis of belief and the like as relations between an individual and a
proposition. What seems to logicians now to be an investigation into
non-truthfunctional connectives, Russell always couched in terms
of the nature of facts.

Throughout the period of atomism Russell struggles with the
nature of propositions with "two verbs" wondering how they could
be given spatial representation in notation (in *TK* and PLA, for

instance), or replaced by facts about other things, as in *PM*. Russell seems to have found both the original problems with the theory in Wittgenstein's criticisms of his "multiple relation theory" and the ultimate resolution in Wittgenstein's own picture theory of representation in the *Tractatus Logico-Philosophicus* [1922].[7] In his introduction to the *Tractatus* (and again in the Introduction and Appendix C to *PM2*), Russell presents Wittgenstein's proposal that the occurrence of a belief or other mental representation is itself an atomic fact. Just as a sentence is a string of symbols in a certain order, a belief will be composed of some complex of representing mental items. In the example above, x's thoughts will include a series of mental items, one representing a, another R, and another b, all arranged in a way characteristic of the occurrence of items when x is judging that the second applies to the first and third, in that order. This is a reduction of the intensional relation of belief to individual representation relations for mental names and a mode of combination in a mental representative medium, the "language of thought". Russell himself does not seem to see this as a first step in an analysis or elimination of the whole phenomenon of intensionality, but rather a solution to his problem of the combinations of facts in the world. No fact can be included in another; all facts are "atomic" in the sense of only including a relation and one or more individuals that it "relates".

Although Russell agrees with Wittgenstein on the issue of extensionality and the resulting view that facts do not occur "within" each other but are combined solely by truth functions, he does not seem to have come to agree with Wittgenstein about the need for general facts. (General facts appear in the PLA lectures but are not mentioned again in the 1924 paper.) Russell is concerned that any collection of atomic facts, say that a is F, b is F, c is F, etc., will not imply that everything is F unless it is known that a, b, c, etc., are all the individuals. Thus, there is a fact that corresponds with a general proposition which is not just a conjunction of atomic facts about its instances. In the *Tractatus* Wittgenstein holds that a proper language will "show" that the inference from all instances of the form '$F(t)$'

---

[7] See Griffin [1985] for the history of difficulties for the multiple relation theory, and Wittgenstein's role in it. The difficulties centered around the "order problem", how it is that statements of judgements are only well formed if a well-formed proposition is judged, while the multiple relation account seems to allow almost any sequence of objects of various types to be related by the judging relation. What is to keep us from allowing a judgement that "The table penholders the book" or similar nonsense?

to '(x)Fx' is valid, as the language will show that those are all the names there are and all objects will be named. Russell, however, did not accept Wittgenstein's notion of "showing" versus "saying", suggesting in the Introduction to the *Tractatus* (*Papers* 9, 111) that what Wittgenstein thought could only be shown could, in fact, be said in a language of a higher type.

Negative facts figure prominently in PLA and are a striking addition to the ontology. Russell claims to have almost started a "riot" at Harvard when he discussed them there in 1914. However attention grabbing they may be, negative facts are no more mysterious than general facts. A negative fact is simply a fact that corresponds with a true negated atomic sentence, e.g. ~*Fa*.[8] There will be something in the world that makes that proposition true, just as there are general facts that make universal propositions true. Russell balks at disjunctive and conjunctive facts. A disjunctive fact would be one to make *Fa* v *Gb* true, which is nonetheless distinct from the one (or both) of the facts making true the constituent propositions *Fa* and *Gb*. Wittgenstein also sees such extra facts as not necessary. The truth of a truth functional compound, such as a disjunction or conjunction, is determined by the truth value of the atomic propositions into which it can be analysed. Similarly Wittgenstein holds that the mere failing of the fact of *a* being *F* to obtain is enough to account for the falsity of *Fa*. On this semantic conception negation and conjunction are defined in terms of their effects on the truth values of compound sentences rather than some distinctive correlate in facts. Facts are then only needed to account for the truth or falsity of atomic sentences. Apparently, Russell did not come over to Wittgenstein's view on this issue, as negative facts appear after the PLA lectures in *AMi* from 1921 (*AMi*, 276). This leaves him at the end of this period then with an ontology of atomic, negative and general facts.

ANALYSIS AND ATOMS

Russell describes his philosophical method as "analysis" and of a piece with his rejection of Idealism. He repeatedly denied that analysis leads to "falsification" as the monists claimed. Individuals which

---

[8] Recent discussions of "truth makers", that is, of what "makes" a proposition true, sometimes distinguish between what makes a negative sentence ~*Fa* true and what makes the negated *Fa false*. Russell, however, clearly identifies the falsity of a proposition with the truth of its negation (PLA, 189).

have been isolated by analysis can be known accurately without having to acknowledge all the other objects to which they might bear relations of different sorts. While clearly based on analysis, however, logical atomism makes suprisingly little use of the idea of an "atom". The project of analysis has metaphysical, logical, and epistemological aspects, leading to what W. Lycan has distinguished as three corresponding notions of the end product of analysis, the atom (Lycan [1981]). We may look for a use for "atoms" in each of these three aspects of the philosophy.

Russell's metaphysical alternative to Monism with its single substance, the Absolute, is a world involving many independent and externally related individuals. Analysis will reveal the constituents of facts or complexes that make up that world and if there are ultimate constituents those will be what we may call "ontological atoms" (following Lycan). In PLA Russell suggests that his project does not require that there be any such ultimate constituents. It might be that the analysis would never halt, yet it would be no less correct as a method for that. This notion of an "atom" as an ultimate constituent of a fact contrasts with others in use in metaphysics. Atoms are always "simple" in some way, but proposals as to what dimension of complexity is to be considered varies. Some hold that it is with respect to parts, thus an atom has no spatial parts. Russell seems to rely on the relation of an object to a complex or fact of which it is a constituent. Indeed, he speaks of facts as "complexes" (as in the quote above from *PM*); it would seem not only because they have constituents and so are complex, but also, one might argue, because they are the only sort of complex entities that there are.[9] Russell does not consider complexes to be "mereological sums" or just wholes of which the constituents are parts, as the part–whole relation is not a simple relation between individuals as it was later for mereology, but rather a logical relation like that of predication.[10] Simple substances are also often held to be independent in some sense, not relying for their existence or nature on other objects. Russell is silent about contingent existence and modal issues in general, and concentrates rather on the notion of "nature" for discussions of substance. The doctrine of external relations, which Russell and Moore championed from early on, holds that objects can stand in genuinely external

[9] Thus "I mean by a fact anything complex", from OP (*Papers* 8, 278).
[10] See the discussion in *Principles of Mathematics*, chapt. XVI.

relations, which are not reflected in the natures of their relata. Thus, metaphysical atoms would be things that stand in relations without those relations being part of their natures. Since it is in the nature of a whole to contain its parts, atoms will have to be simple, that is, without parts. Russell does seem clearly to be committed to the notion of atoms in this metaphysical sense, even if it may turn out that there are none, as analysis can continue indefinitely.

Russell sometimes characterises monism in an epistemological rather than metaphysical way. In this form monism becomes the doctrine that one cannot know an object without knowing all of its relata, and to know those adequately in turn will ultimately require knowing about everything. To parallel his metaphysical atomism, Russell would have an epistemological atomism. It is possible to "know" objects adequately without knowing their relations to other objects. Indeed this form of knowledge is not necessarily based on the features of an object at all; it can be known simply by direct "acquaintance", without being known somehow indirectly through its qualities at all. There is no simple notion of "epistemological atom" for this epistemological atomism, to go along with metaphysical atoms. It is not correct to say that objects of acquaintance are atoms, for Russell suggests that it is possible to be acquainted with a complex object, say our total perceptual experience at a moment, without having analysed it into atoms. Thus:

We may be acquainted with a complex without being able to discover, by any introspective effort, that we are acquainted with the objects that are in fact its constituents. (TK, 121)

A complex sense datum, say of a red patch next to a blue patch, would not be an atom, but could, seemingly, be an object of acquaintance. Upon analysis, however, that complex will be seen as a fact, the red patch's standing next to the blue patch, and so be analysed into its constituents, themselves possibly atomic. Sense data in general are not atomic, as they can have duration and seemingly have parts as well.

The notion of atom does not fit clearly into Russell's epistemology of experience any better than its metaphysics. One important epistemological role for analysis does not seem to rely on a notion of atom at all. Russell describes that process of finding axioms for mathematics, and the subsequent derivation of them from logic as a process of analysis. In this process the results of analysis, the axioms, do not have the usual role of epistemic primitives. The consequences of the axioms, say that $1 + 1 = 2$, may be much more certain than the axioms, the principles of classes and the logic on which they are based. Russell proposes that axioms be accepted if they allow us to derive all the consequences that we seek in a simple and systematic fashion. Thus, analysis can result in knowledge of truths having a certain epistemic priority, but that priority is not one of certainty. They are rather prior in the order of justification where justification is a matter of systematic derivation, not a process which passes on some of the certainty of axioms to their consequences. (See Godwyn and Irvine in this volume.)

The notion of a logical atom is the most straightforward of the three. Logical analysis produces atomic propositions as an ultimate product, propositions that correspond directly with atomic facts. Each atomic proposition asserts the holding of a relation among one or more particulars. Logically proper names will stand for objects of acquaintance. Logical atoms then, will be propositions that are atomic with respect to logical analysis. It is, of course, a characteristic thesis of logical atomism as a metaphysical doctrine that the logical analysis and metaphysical analysis coincide, that the atoms for one are the atoms for the other and that the logical analysis of facts constitutes some sort of metaphysical analysis. If there is no end to metaphysical analysis, and thus no metaphysical atoms, nothing we use can be a genuinely atomic proposition. Propositions seemingly applying an atomic predicate to some names will be liable to further logical analysis, either analysis of the predicate or the replacement of some of the names by definite descriptions.

That a proposition is not genuinely or ultimately atomic, however, does mean that its analysis as atomic is not adequate for logical purposes. A sentence may be treated as atomic for logical purposes even though it is subject to further analysis. Consider the case of definite descriptions. It is an important part of Russell's account of descriptions that while descriptions may look like singular terms in the surface or apparent syntax of sentences, they must be distinguished in ultimate logical form. Still, however, a result in logic of the theory of descriptions is that descriptions such as "the F", when proper (when there is exactly one F), and in extensional contexts, in fact, obey the logical principles governing names. This is the purpose of section *14 of *PM* devoted to descriptions. Since functions such as "the successor of *n*" will be defined using relations as "the entity *m* such that *m* is the successor of *n*", it is necessary to prove that function expressions (provided they are well defined) will obey the logic of singular terms. Thus, in fact, the theorems of *14 show that if proper, coreferential descriptions can be substituted for each other, and, in general, are subject to the basic logical laws. As a result a sentence with a description, say "the *F* is *G*", can be treated as analogous to a genuinely atomic sentence "*a* is *G*", provided that the description is proper. There is, thus, no need to determine whether a given sentence is genuinely atomic in order to determine its logical properties as long as the singular terms in it are seen to be well defined, that is, denote a unique object. The application of logic to sentences, thus, does not require that they be completely analysed into logically atomic sentences. Logical atomism and its method of logical analysis does not require the existence of logical atoms!

These unsuccessful searches for atoms suggest that one should regard the "atomism" in "logical atomism" as just expressing a commitment to analysis as a method, and perhaps also as expressing the central role of atomic sentences in logic, rather than as some more substantive view about the end results or products of analysis.[11]

LOGICAL CONSTRUCTION

Many of these issues over various notions of analysis and the products of the process can be resolved by examining the complementary process of logical construction. In LA Russell attributes the method to Whitehead, but from the examples he gives it is clear that it is a thread running through the whole of his own philosophy. In a famous *bon mot* Russell describes construction by contrasting it with the method of hypotheses:

> The method of "postulating" what we want has many advantages; they are the same as the advantages of theft over honest toil. Let us leave them to others and proceed with our honest toil. (*IMP*, 71)

The honest toil is that of logical construction; the method of hypotheses is that of adopting axioms to describe purported entities.

[11] Russell discusses the possibility that analysis does not end in his reply to Urmson in *MPD*, Chapt. XIII.

The best model of construction is Russell's original project of constructing numbers from classes of equinumerous classes. Here the method of postulating would be to rest content with Peano's Axioms, thus making all claims about numbers hypothetical with the axioms as hypothesis. Rather the work is to construct the numbers, in Russell's case to treat numbers as classes of equinumerous classes, in such a way that the theory of numbers including Peano's "Axioms" could in fact be derived as theorems.

In LA Russell lists other examples of the method of construction, starting with the method of "abstraction", of "substituting equivalence classes for a common quality, e.g., a shared magnitude". Another example is the elimination of classes "as single entities" in *PM* *20, the "no-class" theory of classes. Then Russell includes the theory of definite descriptions, and mathematical examples such as the construction of series, ordinal numbers, and real numbers. Finally, there are the examples of the construction of points and instants as sets of events and the construction of matter from events. It is the construction of matter from events of experience, the project that Russell describes as "neutral monism", that is one of the most striking doctrines of the logical atomism period. The construction of matter from sense-data and the theory of definite descriptions are often taken as models of Russell's method, and taken as such suggest the prevailing view of the ontological import of logical construction that can be challenged. That view, defended by M. Sainsbury [1980], is that the project of construction is to replace purported entities with classes of other objects, ultimately of sense-data. Those classes are then eliminated via the "no-class" theory in favour of propositional functions. Functions, in turn, are subject to the nominalist interpretation discussed, and quantification over them disarmed of ontological import by being given a substitutional interpretation. The upshot is that logical construction is the first step in a nominalist ontological program of "elimination" of purported entities in favour of linguistic items and sense-data. This interpretation of the program may be challenged, however.

Russell's discussions of logical constructions do indeed center on the issue of avoiding ontological commitment:

One very important heuristic maxim which Dr. Whitehead and I found, by experience, to be applicable to mathematical logic, and have since applied to various other fields, is a form of Ockham's razor. When some set of supposed entities has neat logical properties, it turns out, in a great many instances, that the supposed entities can be replaced by purely logical structures composed of entities which have not such neat properties. In that case, in interpreting a body of propositions hitherto believed to be about the supposed entities, we can substitute the logical structures without altering any of the detail of the body of propositions in question. This is an economy, because entities with neat logical properties are always inferred, and if the propositions in which they occur can be interpreted without making this inference, the ground for the inference fails, and our body of propositions is secured against the need of a doubtful step. The principle may be stated in the form: "Whenever possible, substitute constructions out of known entities for inferences to unknown entities." (LA, 164)

The ground for adopting a construction does not seem to be ontological parsimony for its own sake. The reduction in ontology has the effect of reducing the number of assumed propositions that are needed in order to derive the "neat" properties of the objects, those features that have a logical character to them. It is a parsimony of theory, allowing what would otherwise have to be assumed as axioms to rather be proved as theorems using the definitions supplied by logical constructions. This is a general feature of all the constructions. Consider, for example, the instance of the theory of descriptions. While specifically aimed at replacing Russell's own prior theory of denoting concepts, and perhaps generally motivated by the desire to avoid Meinong's commitment to the likes of the Golden Mountain, the concrete project of the theory is to allow the derivation in *PM* of a number of theorems using definite descriptions as discussed earlier. Indeed, examination of Russell's objections to Meinong's theory shows that they concentrate on seemingly inconsistent consequences that can be derived from the postulates of object theory, rather than a simple objection to unnecessary entities.[12] Thus, for example, Meinong's use of an unrestricted principle that "the F is F" leads to the proof that "the existent round square exists". Russell's theory of descriptions provides a refined theory. His analogue of this principle is that one must first establish that the description "the F" is proper, essentially proving that there is exactly one F first. The objection to Meinong's theory was more that it lead to the wrong theorems as much as that it postulated unnecessary entities. Likewise, the no-class theory clearly is intended to allow the derivation

---

[12] In "On Denoting" from 1905, and his reviews of Meinong all reprinted in *EA*.

of the features of classes as theorems, rather having to hypothesize them with axioms.

The same even applies to the treatment of matter. Russell describes certain "neat" features of matter, for example, that no two physical objects can be in the same place at the same time, as having a logical flavour to them. If physical objects and spatial relations are "constructed" from sense-data, it will be possible to derive such "neat" features of physical geometry from logic alone. It isn't obvious then that Russell's position should be described as the view that physical objects simply are classes of mental sense-data, thus, as a genuine phenomenalism. That Russell might have ended this period as such a phenomenalist would be an ironic development for the Realist philosopher who began his career criticising idealism with its ontology of ideas rather than matter.[13] At the time of his *POP* Russell saw matter as something inferred as the source of our sensations, known by description as "the cause of such and such sense data". In the passage previously cited, he might seem to say that under Whitehead's influence he has come to replace inferred matter with constructions. Although Russell does talk about matter as constructed of sense-data, this seems to be only relative to certain purposes, in particular the derivation of "neat" features of matter that look too much like logical features to be inductive generalisations. The positive project of finding the definitions ensures the derivation of "neat" features that constitutes the program of logical construction. Attention to these definitions will explain some of the problematic features of analysis mentioned earlier. The goal of analysis is to find the appropriate objects and definitions with which to carry out the program of construction. These may not coincide with what is intuitively certain or simple. Indeed, it is not clear that the resulting construction has any claim to being a "reduction" of ordinary objects and notions. Russell says that a construction will serve all the "scientific purposes that anyone can desire" (PLA, 236). Those scientific purposes, however, do not seem to be those of current scientific realism, which proposes that we take as genuinely real just those entities postulated by our best scientific theories. Rather than trying to give an account of what ordinary objects really are, Russell is proposing a substitute that will allow certain derivations in logic

[13] See Alberto Coffa ([1991], 87, 93) who describes the theory of sense data as "reified psychologism", suggesting that they amount to a relapse into idealism. Russell's "neutral monism", however, makes sense data less clearly in the idealist tradition.

of truths that seem logical in character. Logical construction may not be a construction of our world, but rather of a replacement that serves certain theoretical purposes.

This, indeed, seems to be how Russell's project of construction was perceived by Carnap, whose later *Logical Structure of the World* ([1928]) abandons claims to ontological truth in favour of extensional isomorphism between the world and its construction. The project of construction, so conceived, continued in the project of producing set theoretic "models" of various theories and entities. A set theoretic construction of time or space is not intended as a theory of what those things really are, but rather of a structure which shares structural features with the object studied, those structural features being derivable from the constructing definitions. With the development of logic it became clear that it was trivial to find some set theoretic construction to provide entities for any consistent theory. The issue then became how to find from those various models one that was "intended" or real, one that was a genuine model of the world rather than an artificial construction. Perhaps, for this reason, the project of logical construction withered, despite Carnap's early contribution to it.

Logical atomism played an important role as a foil for succeeding analytic philosophy. Both Wittgenstein's early views in the *Tractatus* and his subsequent turn from those views were directed at Russell. As J.O. Urmson details in his history [1956], the logical positivists and later ordinary language philosophers used criticisms of the language and ontology of atomism as a starting point for their own positions. Logical positivists retained the central role for the symbolic logic but, using the verifiability criterion of meaning, abandoned the sort of metaphysical considerations that are central to atomism. Urmson argues that even before the post World War II flowering of ordinary language philosophy, criticisms of atomism had focused on the commitment to extensionality and associated independence of atomic facts, the picturing account of truth and correspondence, and the phenomenalist reading of the project that came from emphasizing the nature of sense data and phenomena as the basic objects. The characteristic issues of postwar analytic philosophy can be seen as arising from criticisms of atomism, including the criticism of logic as "ideal language", the attack on sense-data and their connection with a foundationalist epistemology based on acquaintance and the very idea of drawing realist ontological conclusions from the use of language. One cannot read classics of later linguistic philosophers such as Wittgenstein (1953), Austin (1962), or Strawson (1959) without keeping Russell's logical atomism clearly in mind.

BIBLIOGRAPHY

Austin, J. L., *Sense and Sensibilia.*, Oxford: Clarendon Press. 1962.

Carnap, Rudolf, *The Logical Structure of the World & Pseudoproblems in Philosophy*, tr. by R.A. George. [2nd ed.], London, Routledge & K. Paul, 1967. Originally published 1928.

Cocchiarella, Nino B. "Russell's Theory of Logical Types and the Atomistic Hierarchy of Sentences", in *Logical Studies in Early Analytic Philosophy*, Columbus, Ohio State University Press, 1987, 193–221.

Coffa, J. Alberto, *The Semantic Tradition from Kant to Carnap: To the Vienna Station*, Linda Wessels, ed., Cambridge, Cambridge University Press, 1991.

Church, Alonzo, "Russell's Theory of the Identity of Propositions", *Philosophia Naturalis* 21, 1984, 513–22.

Gödel Kurt, "Russell's Mathematical Logic" in *The Philosophy of Bertrand Russell*, P.A. Schilpp, ed., *The Library of Living Philosophers*, Evanston, Northwestern University. 1944, 125–53, reprinted with an addendum in *Philosophy of Mathematics: Selected Readings*, 2nd ed., P. Benacerraf and H. Putnam, eds. Cambridge, Cambridge University Press, 1983, 447–69.

Griffin, Nicholas, "Russell's Multiple Relation Theory of Judgement", *Philosophical Studies*, 47, March 1985, 213–48.

Hazen, A.P. and Davoren, J.M., "Russell's 1925 Logic", *Australasian Journal of Philosophy*, 78, 2000, 534–56.

Lycan, William, "Logical Atomism and Ontological Atoms", *Synthese* 46, 1981, 207–29.

Myhill, John, "The Undefinability of the Set of Natural Numbers in the Ramified *Principia*", in G. Nakhnikian, ed., *Bertrand Russell's Philosophy*, New York, Harper and Row, 1974.

Sainsbury, R.M., "Russell on Constructions and Fictions", *Theoria* 46, 1980, 19–36.

Strawson, P.F., *Individuals*, London, Methuen & Co., 1959.

Urmson, J.O., *Philosophical Analysis: Its Development Between the Two World Wars*, Oxford, Clarendon Press, 1956.

Wittgenstein, Ludwig, *Tractaus Logico-Philosophicus*, trans. C.K. Ogden, London, Routledge & Kegan Paul, 1922.

Wittgenstein, Ludwig, *Philosophical Investigations*, London, Macmillan, 1953.

12 Russell's Structuralism and the Absolute Description of the World

There are three major ideas arising from Russell's work in logic and philosophy of mathematics which he believed to be of philosophical importance for the theory of our knowledge of the physical world. The first was his theory of descriptions; the second, the concept of structure; and the third, the notion of a logical construction. The use of logical constructions in theory of knowledge was most prominent during Russell's phenomenalist period, the period which culminated with *Knowledge of the External World*. This phase of Russell's thought falls outside the purview of the present work. Logical constructions play an important – but very different – role in his subsequent realism, where they occur mainly in connection with the "interpretation"[1] of the theory of space–time, and where they subserve both metaphysical and epistemological goals. Although we will have occasion to refer to this application of logical constructions toward the very end of the essay, considerations of space prevent us from exploring their use in any detail. Our focus here will be on the second of these ideas – the concept of structure – and the development of Russell's "structuralism." But before turning to this topic, it will be worthwhile to sketch Russell's application of his theory of descriptions to theory of knowledge; this application and his structuralism are often discussed together with the result that they are not always as sharply distinguished from one another as they should be.

* I wish to thank Darcy Cutler and Timothy Kenyon for reading earlier versions of this paper and providing helpful suggestions regarding its presentation. I am much indebted to Anil Gupta for his comments on the penultimate draft. To Graham Solomon I owe a debt of gratitude for the many conversations we have had on the topics dealt with here and for numerous references to the literature. My research was partially supported by a grant from the Social Sciences and Humanities Research Council of Canada. This paper is dedicated to the memory of Grover Maxwell.

I

The epistemological interest of the theory of descriptions for our knowledge of matter was announced as early as "On Denoting," but its first fully explicit development was given in *The Problems of Philosophy*. There the theory of descriptions is first deployed in support of an exceptionally simple theory of propositional understanding (or theory of meaning).[2] To appreciate the relevant application of the theory of understanding, let us put to one side the issue of vacuous names. Then Russell's theory of meaning tells us that if a sentence contains a name for an individual with whom we are not acquainted, the proposition expressed by the sentence cannot contain the bearer of the name among its constituents. We must instead imagine that the name is short-hand for a description. This description is in turn analyzed – "contextually defined" – after the fashion of the theory of descriptions into expressions for individuals and propositional functions which *are* proper constituents of the proposition expressed. The individuals and propositional functions must be so chosen that the resulting proposition satisfies what Russell calls "the fundamental principle in the analysis of propositions containing descriptions":

Every proposition which we can understand must be composed wholly of constituents with which we are acquainted. (*POP2*, 58)

Now by hypothesis, the bearer of the name exists and is the unique individual satisfying some (possibly complex) propositional function. However, not being known by acquaintance, the bearer of the name is not *itself* a constituent of the proposition expressed. It is nevertheless something to which we are able to refer, so that, as Russell says, the proposition we express manages to make an assertion *about* this individual, even though it is not among the proposition's constituents. It follows that although our understanding of a sentence rests on our acquaintance with the constituents of the proposition it expresses, we are not thereby precluded from having knowledge of things which fall outside the realm of our immediate experience.

The application of this theory of meaning to our knowledge of the material world proceeds from three assumptions: (i) we are not acquainted with matter; but (ii) it is always possible to formulate a description which is uniquely satisfied by the material object to which we take ourselves to refer; and (iii) these descriptions involve only propositional functions and individuals with which we are acquainted. The theory allows Russell to dispense with primitive nonlogical vocabulary items which name or, as Russell sometimes says, "indicate,"anything with which we are not acquainted; at the same time, the theory allows him to maintain that we can have knowledge *about* things which fall outside the realm of our acquaintance. In particular, the application of the theory to our knowledge of matter purports to explain how our ability to formulate propositions which express truths about the material world does not require our acquaintance with that world.

I have been careful to present Russell's elaboration of his theory of propositional understanding in such a way that its connection with a subsequent development by F.P. Ramsey will be transparent. A feature of Russell's theory that I have emphasized is the technique by which it avoids the use of a name – or more generally, of any nonlogical expression – for something which is not an object of acquaintance. It is this consequence of Russell's deployment of his theory of descriptions that was imitated by Ramsey, in his posthumously published "Theories,"[3] when he proposed that the content of a physical theory can be captured by what has come to be called its "Ramsey sentence." It will be recalled that the Ramsey sentence $R(\theta)$ of a theory $\theta = \theta(O_1, \ldots, O_m; T_1, \ldots, T_n)$ with theoretical vocabulary $T_1, \ldots, T_n$ and observational vocabulary $O_1, \ldots, O_m$ is just the result

$$\exists X_1 \ldots \exists X_n \, \theta(O_1, \ldots, O_m; X_1, \ldots, X_n)$$

of existentially quantifying on the theoretical terms and replacing them by variables $X_1, \ldots, X_n$ of the appropriate parity and type (or sort, if the underlying logic of $R(\theta)$ is taken to be first-order). The replacement of θ by $R(\theta)$ preserves the class of derivable consequences involving the observational vocabulary – what Ramsey called "the primary propositions" of θ – although it must necessarily diverge from those consequences involving the theoretical vocabulary (Ramsey's so-called "secondary propositions"). It is in this sense that, for Ramsey, $R(\theta)$ can be said to capture the *content* of θ. Thus, the point of Ramsey's proposal is to explicitly address the role of theoretical terms only in the *deductive structure* of θ, and then, to address their role only in that part of its deductive structure which is relevant to the derivation of the *primary* propositions. Ramsey in effect observed that if θ contains sufficiently explicit deductions of its primary propositions, then these deductions have a representation in $R(\theta)$. But since in $R(\theta)$ the "propositions" which are the transforms of secondary propositions contain variables wherever the original propositions contain theoretical terms, their meaning is exhausted by the contribution of the observational vocabulary they contain. As Ramsey put it, "[w]e can say, therefore, that the incompleteness of the 'propositions' of the secondary system [more exactly, their transforms in $R(\theta)$] affects our *disputes* but not our *reasoning*" ("Theories," 232, italics in the original). And since it is *only our reasoning* we need to reconstruct, this incompleteness is irrelevant to science. The idea of a Ramsey sentence thus depends on nothing more contentious than this elementary observation about the formal character of logical derivation. But of course to grant this is in no way to prejudge the correctness of the view of "secondary propositions" – as mere auxiliaries in the derivation of primary propositions – which it advances.[4]

Russell's structuralism is based on his general characterization of structure in terms of structural similarity and its elaboration in the "relation arithmetic" of *Principia Mathematica*. Clearly, the model on which Russell's definition of a structure was based was the Frege–Russell definition of the cardinal numbers in terms of similarity classes under the relation of one–one correspondence: a structure is just the "relation-number" (isomorphism class) of a relation under a one–one "structure-preserving" mapping of the field of the relation onto the fields of "similar" relations. To return briefly to the notion of a Ramsey sentence, it will be observed that if $\theta = \theta(O_1, \ldots, O_m; T_i)$ yields a suitable characterization[5] of the isomorphism class of a relation T_i, then $R(\theta)$ illustrates *perfectly* Russell's claim that our theoretical knowledge consists in assertions regarding the structure of relations over a given domain. The Ramsey sentence of θ represents it as asserting that *there is* a relation X_i having the structure characterized by θ, while preserving the primary propositional consequences of θ. And this is, in essence, the central contention of structuralism. *Notice, however, that this is an exceptional case.* If, as may well happen, θ does *not* capture the isomorphism class of the relation T_i or fails to state some formal property of T_i, then the connection between structuralism and θ's Ramsey sentence is lost. Indeed, it is easy to devise trivial examples of theories whose Ramsey sentences achieve their intended effect – that of enabling the derivation of primary propositions – without expressing structure in Russell's sense, and, therefore, without illuminating the broader claims of structuralism. (Simply recall that *any* finitely axiomatized theory has a Ramsey sentence. If the theory is not finitely axiomatized but has a recursive set of axioms, the situation is slightly more complex, without, however, affecting the basic soundness of Ramsey's observation that the primary propositions can be captured by a sentence "in the same form as" $R(\theta)$.[6]) So again, Ramsey's suggestion is best seen in light of the theory of descriptions, and its use in connection with the elimination of names for things falling outside our acquaintance, rather than as a development or articulation of structuralism.[7]

It is important to appreciate the sense in which Russell regarded the notion of structural similarity one to which he could lay claim, since the notion was of course present, with varying degrees of explicitness, in the mathematical tradition to which the foundational contributions of *PM* belong. For Russell, the *philosophical* interest of structural similarity derived from his recognition of the fact that it is a notion of pure logic. As Frege perceived in *Grundlagen*, and as Russell was to discover some years later, the notion of one–one correspondence, being definable in wholly logical terms, owes nothing to spatio-temporal intuition. It follows that this must also be true of structural similarity. From very early on, Russell seems to have seen his account of structure as capable of providing a framework within which it would be possible to articulate the nature of the similarity philosophers had supposed to exist between appearance and reality or, to use Kantian terminology, between the phenomenal and the noumenal worlds – a point whose significance was not lost on Russell, nor, I dare-say, was the irony that a concept which owed its genesis to logicism might usefully contribute to the articulation of Kantian doctrine. What had defeated previous attempts was the want of a notion of similarity which was not so great that it would collapse the gulf that was supposed to exist between phenomena and noumena, and was not so slight that it could not be reckoned a significant sense of similarity. Russell believed that with the discovery of the notion of structural similarity, he had solved this metaphysical and epistemological problem, a claim that is explicitly announced in just these terms in an important passage of *Introduction to Mathematical Philosophy:*

There has been a great deal of speculation in traditional philosophy which might have been avoided if the importance of structure, and the difficulty of getting behind it, had been realized. For example, it is often said that space and time are subjective, but they have objective counterparts; or that phenomena are subjective, but are caused by things in themselves, which must have differences *inter se* corresponding with the differences in the phenomena to which they give rise. Where such hypotheses are made, it is generally supposed that we can know very little about the objective counterparts. In actual fact, however, if the hypotheses as stated were correct, the objective counterparts would form a world having the same structure as the phenomenal world, and allowing us to infer from phenomena the truth of all propositions that can be stated in abstract terms and are known to be true of phenomena. If the phenomenal world has three dimensions, so must the world behind phenomena; if the phenomenal world is Euclidean, so must the other be; and so on. In short, every proposition having a communicable significance must be true of both worlds or of neither: the only difference must lie in just that essence of individuality which always eludes words and baffles description, but which, for that very reason is irrelevant to science. Now the only purpose that philosophers have in view in condemning phenomena is in order to persuade themselves and others that the real world is very different from the world of appearance. We can all sympathize with their wish to prove such a very desirable proposition, but we cannot congratulate them on their success. It is true that many of them do not assert objective counterparts to phenomena, and these escape from the above argument. Those who do assert counterparts are, as a rule, very reticent on the subject, probably because they feel instinctively that, if pursued, it will bring about too much of a *rapprochement* between the real and the phenomenal world. If they were to pursue the topic, they could hardly avoid the conclusions which we have been suggesting. In such ways, as well as in many others, the notion of structure . . . is important. (*IMP* 61–2)

Russell's picture of how the application to Kant should go seems to have been something like this: The noumenal world, not being given to us in intuition, cannot, apparently, be required to have properties in common with the phenomenal world. This leaves us with the problem of understanding how to formulate any conception of what the noumenal world is like, and of understanding how it can fail to be unknowable. But because structural similarity has a purely logical characterization, it is independent of intuition. The noumenal world thus emerges as an isomorphic copy of the phenomenal world, one which we may suppose has the requisite similarity with the world of phenomena without thereby committing ourselves to the idea that it shares any of the intuitive properties of the phenomenal world. Had it not proved possible to capture this notion of similarity by purely logical means, we would have been precluded from assuming even this degree of similarity between noumena and phenomena, and might, therefore, have been inclined toward some form of idealism regarding the world behind phenomena. The logical notion of structural similarity preserves us from this tendency toward idealism.

This is an elegant application of a technical idea of mathematical logic to a philosophical problem. It is, however, subject to an important limitation. If we intend the statement that the noumenal world is isomorphic to the phenomenal one to be more than part of its *definition*, if, that is, we intend it to be a significant claim about the noumenal world, then we are implicitly assuming that we have access to the relations holding among things in themselves independently of the isomorphism in terms of which their similarity to phenomenal relations has been characterized. Otherwise, the observation that structural similarity allows us to preserve the comparability of the noumenal and phenomenal worlds becomes a mere tautology, the character of the noumenal world being defined in terms of the isomorphism. Since it owes nothing to intuition, structural similarity may be used to address the objection that there is literally *nothing* that can be said regarding things in themselves. But the conception of the noumenal world to which we are led falls short of a conception of a world which can be said to be similar to the phenomenal world in some significant – i.e., not purely stipulative – sense. The nature of a claim of structural similarity is such that it is a significant claim only when the relations being compared are given independently of the mapping which establishes their similarity. To achieve this result, Russell requires more than an appropriately general notion of similarity; he must, in addition, have independent knowledge of the relations between which the similarity is supposed to hold. Knowledge of the relations among things in themselves cannot be purely structural, since that would make the claim of similarity empty; but, things in themselves being "in themselves," neither can it be intuitive. The noumenal world would seem, therefore, to have retained almost all of its elusive character. As we shall see, a related issue recurs in connection with Russell's own positive view.

II

Russell's structuralism is fully articulated only in his later work, *The Analysis of Matter* – where it receives its fullest exposition – and in subsequent writings up to and including *Human Knowledge: Its Scope and Limits*. But in addition to the anticipation in *IMP*, cited earlier, it can be found as early as *Problems*, where it arises (albeit, not entirely explicitly) in connection with the discussion of what we can know of the world as it is "in itself," as opposed to how it "appears" in perception. In the early chapters of *Problems*, Russell makes heavy use of familiar forms of the argument from the "relativity" of perception, its relativity, that is, to the peculiarities of our "point of view," both in respect of our spatial position relative to the things around us and in respect of our unique perceptual endowment. By the use of such arguments, Russell sought to show that we cannot suppose things are as they appear to us in perception and that if the appearance of things is to be preserved, a plausible way of doing so is by the introduction of what he called "sense data." I will have little to say regarding Russell's use of sense data (or of their analogues in later writings: "percepts" in *AMa* and "sensations" in *HK*) other than to acknowledge, at various stages of the discussion, that Russell was firmly committed to their existence in all of his many discussions of theory of perception. I will focus instead on Russell's attempt to establish the disparity between things as they appear to us and as they are in themselves. The nature of this attempt, and what it does and does not assume, is best brought out by reflecting on an objection that was urged by G. Dawes Hicks shortly after the publication of *Problems*.[8] The objection consists of a simple observation: Relativity arguments typically make use of a premise having the form of a conditional. The premise is not obvious, but neither is it obviously false. However, when we replace it with its contrapositive, it seems clearly unacceptable. It follows that any argument which depends upon such an assumption is in fact unsupported insofar as we are entitled to deny the assumption on which it is based.

In greater detail, according to Dawes Hicks, relativity arguments in general, and Russell's uses of them in particular, assume the following premise:

(C) If something appears to have the property F to some observers and appears not to have the property F to others (or to the same observers under different conditions), then it cannot be said to be intrinsically F; it is not F "in itself."[9]

But the contrapositive (C*) of (C):

(C*) If something is intrinsically F, then it appears the same to all observers (either F or not F)

(or equivalently, if something is F "in itself," then it appears to all observers as F or it appears to all observers as not F), is clearly false, since it is not part of *our* concept of something's being intrinsically F that everyone should perceive it as F. Prescinding for the moment from the well-known phenomenon of color constancy, no one expects a white table to look anything but pink in red light, or blue in blue light. Indeed, we wouldn't say that it was white if it didn't look pink or blue in such circumstances. Ignoring shape constancy, the same holds of shape: what circular table would not look oval from an end view and circular when seen straight on? Each relativity argument can, therefore, be turned on its head: rather than showing that something is *not* F "in itself," the argument shows that it *really is* F. To quote Dawes Hicks:

... It is obvious, I think, that [such an] argument is fallacious, and that the conclusion does not follow from the premises. For, in order to test it, suppose that colour of some kind is inherent in the table, that the table has a specific colour. Then, surely, there would be nothing to conflict with this supposition in the circumstances that such real colour will present a different aspect if another colour be reflected upon it, or if a blue pair of spectacles intervene between it and the eyes of the observer, or if it be enveloped in darkness rather than daylight. The reasoning would only be valid on the assumption that if the table is really coloured, the real colour must appear the same in darkness and in daylight, through a pair of blue spectacles and without them, in artificial light and in the sun's light – an assumption which, on the view I am taking, is at once to be dismissed as untenable. If the colour did appear to be the same in these varying circumstances, then there certainly would be reason, and sufficient reason, for doubting the reliability of visual apprehension. For obviously the conditions mentioned – real, objective conditions, as I take them to be – cannot be without influence upon any real colour the table may be said to possess. (42)

Attention has recently been drawn to this analysis by Myles Burnyeat, for whom it is "the logical refutation neatly laid out, clear and conclusive, just one year after the publication of *Problems*. Why did it make no difference? Why, if straightforward logical refutation is enough, do the arguments from conflicting appearances live on?"[10] Burnyeat suggests that "(C*) is manifestly implausible in some way that (C) is not. That would imply that (C) has been persuasive because it wraps things up a bit, keeps hidden an influence which comes closer to the surface in (C*)."[11] In other words, failing to notice the implausible but logically equivalent contrapositive, we are lulled into a complacent acceptance of the original conditional. But however well Burnyeat's explanation might fit other philosophers' uses of the argument from "conflicting appearances," there are two difficulties with applying it to Russell. First, Russell's discussion (in *POP2*, 9–11) shows him to have anticipated Dawes Hicks's own analysis of the significance of conflicting appearances, according to which the "real" color and shape of the table are the sorts of things we would expect to appear different under different conditions of viewing. And secondly, Russell argues – how convincingly we shall not pause to consider – that such an analysis, however useful for practical life, fails to establish anything that could be called the "real" color and shape of the table.

Interestingly, Russell explicitly accepts the *converse* of the contrapositive (C*) by endorsing the following instance regarding *order:*

... if a regiment of men are marching along a road, the *shape* of the regiment will look different from different points of view, *but the men will appear arranged in the same order from all points of view. Hence we regard the order as true also in physical space*, whereas the shape is only supposed to correspond to the physical space so far as is required for the preservation of the order. (*POP2*, 32–3, long italics added)

Taking the mention of order to be an allusion to structure, this passage is important, not only because it supports the historical contention that *Problems* contains a strong pre-echo of Russell's structuralism, but also because it suggests an interpretation of his use of the notion which I wish to emphasize: the concept of structure was important for Russell because it facilitated what has been called "an absolute form of description," one which is free of any reliance on the specific quality of the perceptual experience which forms its epistemic basis and justification, and one which is, therefore, independent of any reference to its origin in the experience of beings like us, knowing the world as we do, from a particular vantage point and with our peculiar perceptual and physiological endowment.[12] For Russell, what I am calling the "absoluteness" of the descriptions of physics was achieved at the price of its abstractness, and a major goal of *AMa* was to bridge the gulf between physics and perception which the former's move toward abstractness created. Thus, in a chapter titled "The abstractness of physics" Russell puts the difficulty this way: "Physics and perception are like two people on opposite sides of a brook which slowly widens as they walk: at first it is easy to jump across, but imperceptibly it grows more difficult, and at last a vast labour is required to get from one side to the other" (*AMa* 137). Let us try to clarify the assumptions underlying Russell's formulation of the difference between the accounts of physics and perception or common sense.

The passage cited earlier from *Problems* shows that Russell treated a "primary quality" like shape on a par with a "secondary quality" like color. So from the point of view of the traditional Lockean distinction, Russell's arguments for the relativity of perception extend to both primary and secondary qualities – a point on which he is in agreement with Berkeley, despite the overall tendency of *Problems*, *AMa* and *HK* toward a form of representationalism or causal theory of perception in the spirit of Locke. Although, as we have just observed, Russell had a uniform account of the primary and secondary qualities, we will focus on the case of color, where we will distinguish two different, but related, doctrines concerning the status of color and our color vocabulary. A complete account would require correlative formulations for all the traditional primary and secondary qualities.

The first doctrine I will call "the thesis of the subjectivity of color" or "the subjectivist position" or, even more briefly, "subjectivism." This is the doctrine on which I believe Russell eventually settled, and it is this doctrine which, as we shall see, leads to the standard formulation of his structuralism, together with its attendant difficulties. There are numerous superficially similar theses in the philosophical literature which nevertheless differ quite significantly from the one defended by Russell. Rather than attempt any kind of survey, I will simply highlight the main features of Russell's view and make the occasional contrast with views with which it might be conflated.

The second doctrine I will call "the thesis of the relativity of our common sense color *vocabulary*," "the relativist position" or simply, "relativism." Our common sense color vocabulary constitutes a form of description whose "relativity" is the proper contrast with the "absolute" form of description to which our theoretical knowledge aspires. Relativism is less contentious than subjectivism. Even though Russell never fixed upon relativism as a statement of his view (in *Problems* he comes closest to doing so), there are several important features which it shares with many of his explicit pronouncements concerning our theoretical knowledge of the physical world and the emphasis it places on the importance of structure. Thus, while it is reasonably clear and generally well-known that Russell subscribed to some version of subjectivism, it has not, to my knowledge, been sufficiently appreciated that many of the most striking aspects of his metaphysics and theory of knowledge can be expressed and defended within the much less revisionist framework of relativism. Or so at least I shall argue.

III

Let us begin with subjectivism; once we are clear about it, we can turn to the idea that our ordinary forms of description involving color have a "relative" character. One form of subjectivism about color, a form which captures important features of Russell's view, proposes to analyze the use of 'yellow' as a predicate of surfaces of things in terms of our understanding of 'yellow' as a predicate of "percepts" or "sensations." On this view, the meaning of 'yellow' as a predicate of surfaces is to be understood in terms of our acquaintance with the property when we have what we call "perceptions of yellow objects." We are not however, acquainted with the surface of the object, but with the terminal event of a causal chain which constitutes what we naively call "our perception of the object." Our understanding of the ordinary predicate 'yellow' – which we, of course, regard as a predicate true of physical surfaces – is given by our acquaintance with a property, a property which, however, qualifies our subjective experience or percepts.

A key respect in which this is a properly subjectivist position derives from the primacy it gives to our subjective experience in its account of our understanding of color predicates. The contention that, despite its emphasis on subjective experience, such a view might nevertheless provide an adequate explanation of our usual understanding of our color vocabulary, is commonplace. It has, for example, been well expressed by one of the foremost color scientists of our time: "What we know as reality is the experience at the terminal end of [a] computation. Since we all use the same computation mechanism, we share the terminal experiences. We name them, talk about them, train ourselves to relate to them and to handle them."[13] Whether or not subjectivism is entitled to this contention is not a matter I will discuss; at this point I am merely concerned to indicate some of the principal theses which the view regards as its own.

It is important not to exaggerate the subjectivist elements of Russell's position. For one thing, Russell's elaboration of the doctrine is thoroughly compatible with the discovery of an objective, physical basis in the surfaces of things for our perceptions of color; his position is even compatible with (although it does not require) the stronger thesis that this basis might be susceptible of a simple physical characterization.[14] The point to be emphasized, therefore, is that while Russell was a subjectivist in his analysis of our ordinary, common sense, color vocabulary, his subjectivism had nothing to do with an anticipated difficulty in the elaboration of the physical basis of color. In this respect, his view differs from more recent "interest-relative" theories. Such theories tend to be based on the contention that the physical causes of our perception of color are likely to "form an unreasonably broad and heterogeneous class or [to require] a list of excluded cases which may prove vexing to specify satisfactorily."[15] On this view, what we understand by the color of a surface may depend on a wide variety of "subjective" considerations deriving from what interests or purposes are served by our characterization of a surface as one or another color. By contrast, Russell's position in no way depends on the failure of a fully autonomous physical theory of the external stimulus to our perception of the colors of surfaces: it would be unaffected if there were a complete correspondence between our ordinary color predicates and their physical correlates.

At the same time, Russell is clearly opposed to the "objectivity" of our ordinary color vocabulary: for Russell, our common sense beliefs about the colors of surfaces are uniformly *false*, since color predicates, as we commonly understand them, do not correctly characterize the surfaces of things. This position is perhaps best expressed in the Introduction to *Inquiry into Meaning and Truth*:

> ...Physics assures us that the occurrences which we call "perceiving objects," are at the end of a long causal chain which starts from the objects, and are not likely to resemble the objects except in very abstract ways. We all start from "naive realism," i.e., the doctrine that things are what they seem. We think that grass is green, that stones are hard, and that snow is cold. But physics assures us that the greenness of grass, the hardness of stones, and the coldness of snow, are not the greenness, hardness, and coldness that we know in our own experience, but something very different. The observer, when he seems to himself to be observing a stone, is really, if physics is to be believed, observing the effects of the stone upon himself. Thus science seems to be at war with itself: when it most means to be objective, it finds itself plunged into subjectivity against its will. Naive realism leads to physics, and physics, if true, shows that naive realism is false. Therefore naive realism, if true, is false; therefore it is false. (*IMT* 15)

Notice that it is implicit in this presentation that the objective correlates of color will at best support an "abstract resemblance" between things and their perceptual correlates, an idea which shows *IMT* to have retained a significant measure of the structuralism of *Problems* and *AMa*.

A striking feature of this component of Russell's subjectivism emerges when it is juxtaposed with the idea that there is a simple basis for our perception of color. To appreciate the point, it is necessary to put to one side the question of whether or not the hypothesis of the simplicity of the physical basis is correct. If we are to understand Russell's position, the point to hold on to is that he would count as false our common sense judgements regarding the colors of surfaces even under the assumption of a complete extensional equivalence between the color predicates of our ordinary judgements and their physically reconstructed correlates. This is puzzling to pre-analytic intuition since, under these circumstances, it would appear more natural to say that while the senses of our color words are radically altered when we achieve a scientific understanding of color, their reference remains the same. But then it would seem that we could easily avoid the idea that our ordinary judgements about the colors of things are uniformly false. Russell, however, does not take this option, a point to which we shall return.

To sum up, the main components of the subjectivist view I am attributing to Russell include: (i) a theory of the meaning of our ordinary color vocabulary, one that explains our understanding of color predicates in terms of our acquaintance with properties which characterize our subjective experience; (ii) the contention that, despite its subjective elements, the theory supports the existence of a common "language of color"; (iii) the thesis that our ordinary judgments regarding the colors of surfaces are false – the surfaces of objects are either *not* colored *(IMT)* or cannot be *known* to be colored in the sense required by common sense *(Problems* and *AMa)*; (iv) the thesis that the scientific reconstruction of our judgments regarding color involves correlative properties that are at best known to be abstractly similar to those we naively assume to hold of things.

IV

Let us now turn to the relativist position and to the thesis that our commonsense color vocabulary constitutes a form of description whose "relativity" is the proper contrast with the "absolute" form of description to which our theoretical knowledge aspires. I want to indicate how this position is able to preserve Russell's recognition of the abstractness of physics without, at the same time, resorting to the revisionism about our commonsense color judgments which characterizes his subjectivism. Our starting point is the question, "What role do biconditionals such as

(*) x is yellow iff there are specifiable circumstances and states of human perceivers – so-called "normal conditions" – under which x leads to perceptions of yellow

play according to the view that there is, in some interesting sense, a relativity to color?" We note first that this view involves a claim about our understanding of our color vocabulary which it contends is guided by how objects appear to us under "normal" conditions of viewing, conditions of the sort we appeal to when we are pressed to defend an assertion about the color of a surface. For relativism, (*) exemplifies a general principle which underwrites assertions about the colors of surfaces and comprises a criterion of application for the color predicate it mentions.[16] Since this criterion of application makes a direct reference to our perception of color, it acknowledges that our application of color predicates is tied to the peculiarities of our perceptual systems. The relativity of color is first and foremost a thesis concerning our understanding of our ordinary color predicates, which it maintains is expressed in terms of how the surfaces of objects appear to us, under "normal" conditions of viewing. But by allowing that our understanding of such predicates involves criteria of application given in terms of our perceptual capacities, it by no means excludes an understanding which is independent of criteria of this sort. Indeed, on the relativist position, there is the expectation that as we come to refine our understanding of the physical basis of color, we will be confirmed in our belief that our ordinary judgments regarding surface color are largely correct and complete. This means that if, in the development of our theory of color, we come to an account which is expressed independently of how the colors of surfaces might be perceived by beings endowed as we are, then that family of reconstructed predicates will coincide in extension with our ordinary, unreconstructed, color predicates, despite any differences the reconstructed and unreconstructed *senses* of these predicates might bear. If this is in fact how things go, then (*) is susceptible of simple pre- and post-theoretic interpretations. On its *pre*-theoretic interpretation, (*) is, as noted, a criterion of application which controls our common sense use of our color vocabulary. On its *post*-theoretic interpretation, (*) relates a theoretically reconstructed use of a predicate (in our example, 'yellow' on the left) to its unreconstructed use ('yellow' on the right); as such it expresses the contention that when we have a scientific understanding of colors, this will bear out our pre-theoretic judgments. Clearly, for (*) to support the transition from its pre- to its post-theoretic interpretation, it suffices that it should express a simple material truth, or, at least, a reasonable approximation to one.

Under these circumstances, the relativist position permits the very simple resolution of the status of our ordinary color judgements which we saw Russell reject, namely, that while the senses of color words change with our scientific understanding of the physics of color, their reference is preserved. For relativism, there is no need to maintain the strongly revisionist thesis according to which such judgements are uniformly false. This need not stand in the way of accommodating the importance of structure, since it is one measure of our achievement of an absolute form of description that it capture the structural features of the domain under investigation. But of the properties and relations of the damain, we know more than that they satisfy an absolute form of description: as the case of color illustrates, the difference between absolute and relative forms of description is not marked by the fact that one is true, the other false; rather the idea is that one yields a characterization of things whose understanding places minimal demands on our knowledge of its basis in our perceptual capacities. For relativism, absoluteness in this sense is precisely what motivates the drive toward abstraction which Russell sought to explain.

This interpretation of the relation between our pre-theoretic understanding of color and its theoretical explanation is consonant with recent developments in the computational approach to color vision.[17] On the computational approach, the fundamental theoretical problem of color vision is to determine the principles which permit the inference to the spectral reflectances of surfaces when we are given only the *product* of the spectral power distribution of the light source and the spectral reflectance of the surface, and when we are, in addition, restricted to only a small number of photoreceptors of limited bandwidth sensitivity. Under a suitable "coarse graining" of spectral reflectances, surface colors are identified with surface spectral reflectances, and the central phenomenon of color vision requiring explanation is the phenomenon of color constancy: the fact that a surface presents the same color appearance under a wide variety of variations in illumination. The characterization of color vision as a "computational problem" arises naturally as the question, how, given that surface reflectance and illumination are "confounded," does the visual system "discount" illumination to recover the correct reflectance? In this respect, the computational theory of color vision is completely continuous with the computational theory of shape perception, where the celebrated account of Shimon Ullman addresses the homologous problem of recovering the shape of a moving object given only a limited number of "views."[18] To achieve its successes, the computational approach to perception articulates systems of "natural constraints" which guide the perceptual systems in solving their separate computational tasks. Without natural constraints, the problems are unsolvable. In the case of shape from motion, a key constraint is expressed by the assumption of rigidity, the assumption, that is, that the different "views" of the object are orthographic projections of *rigid* motions. In the color-vision case, the natural constraints serve to restrict which illuminants and surface reflectances are likely to occur. A solution is achieved within the so-called "linear models" framework by limiting the weights assignable to the set of basic functions along which spectra are constrained to vary.

V

It is difficult to state clearly why Russell's subjectivism prevented him from pursuing a rapprochement with common sense along the lines just indicated here, but certainly a large part of the difficulty is attributable to his theory of propositional understanding or theory of meaning. Recall that according to that theory, our understanding of a predicate consists in our acquaintance with the property to which it refers. In order, therefore, for the predicate to occur with the same reference, both in our ordinary and our theoretical descriptions of the world, it would have to satisfy demands which appear to be in tension: The predicate must refer to an "intrinsic" property of things, one which holds or fails to hold independently of whether the world contains beings like us, endowed as we are with the perceptual organs we possess. At the same time, the referent of the predicate must be something about which we can derive "complete" knowledge from our perceptual interaction with the world – even though how the world is given to us in perception is a complex function of the character of the stimulus, the nature of the intervening medium and the peculiarities of our perceptual apparatus.[19]

Russell, like Locke before him, sought to resolve this tension by invoking *two* properties, one characteristic of our experience of a color and qualifying our subjective experience, the other, utterly distinct, and known only to co-vary with it. From this perspective, it is difficult to resist the idea that our knowledge of the physical world is restricted to its structural features: of our percepts we may be said to know *both* their quality and their structure, while of the external world we know only that *there are* properties and relations having an assigned structure, but are otherwise ignorant of what those properties and relations are.[20] As natural and inevitable as this view may seem, it is by no means the only way to understand the significance of the abstractness of physics. The relativist will say that our absolute forms of description give expression to our knowledge of structure. Our relative forms express "qualitative" knowledge only in the sense that their criteria of application are given in terms of our perceptual capacities; it is, however, the *same* properties and relations, described "qualitatively" in the second instance, and "structurally" in the first, which are the proper subject of both forms of description.

But not only is Russell's view *not* inevitable, it is also subject to difficulties which are sufficient to show that it cannot be a correct account of the nature of our theoretical knowledge of the physical world. The central observation, which was first made by M.H.A. Newman,[21] may be put as follows: a basic desideratum of any successful account of our theoretical knowledge of the physical world must preserve the idea that it is non-trivially true – which is to say: not true as a matter of logic or set theory. But in the form in which it emerges from Russell's theory of perception, structuralism fails to meet this condition, since it tells us that our knowledge of the physical world is *purely* structural. But any purely structural claim to the effect that for a collection of things (or "events," as Russell says in *AMa* and *HK*) of given cardinality, there is a relation having a particular structure, *is* true as a matter of set theory or higher order logic. It follows that on Russell's view, that part of our knowledge of the physical world that is not a priori is exhausted by claims regarding its cardinality.[22] The difficulty here parallels the limitation which, as we saw at the conclusion of Section I, afflicts Russell's explication of Kant's doctrine of the noumenal world. There the difficulty arose from having overlooked the fact that an assertion of structural similarity is significant only when the relations between which it is claimed to hold are given independently of the mapping which establishes the similarity. This difficulty could, however, be dismissed as "so much the worse for Kant." In the present case, we are concerned with a claim about what passes for the content of *our* theories, and we cannot rest content with such a serious distortion of the nature of our theoretical knowledge. It is simply not true that, modulo the cardinality of the domain, what passes for our knowledge of the physical world is guaranteed to be true as a matter of higher order logic or set theory.[23]

Although Russell conceded Newman's point,[24] his remarks suggest that he believed the difficulty to have resulted from a mere oversight in his formulations. Thus, Russell says that he "had always assumed spatio-temporal continuity with the world of percepts . . . [so that] there might be copunctuality between percepts and non-percepts." This would make copunctuality a relation which might "exist among percepts while at the same time being itself perceptible."[25] To understand these remarks, it will be necessary to look more closely at Russell's notion of copunctuality and his use of "logical constructions." In *AMa* a class of events is said to be *copunctual* when every quintet of events in the class have a "common overlap." When a quintet of events have a common overlap, Russell says they stand in the relation of *copunctuality (AMa* 299). Thus, 'copunctual' refers to a property of *classes* of events, while 'copunctuality' refers to a relation *among* events. The two notions are defined in terms of quintets rather than some other number for technical reasons having to do with the dimensionality of the space whose points (point-instants) are being characterized as logical constructions – set-theoretic structures, as we would today say – out of events. Russell's point-instants are defined as maximal copunctual classes of events, maximal, that is, with respect to class inclusion. Assuming that there are copunctual classes of events, the success of the proof of the existence of space–time points, which occupies Chapter xxviii of *AMa*, falls on showing that every such copunctual class can be extended to a maximally copunctual class. Russell's proof uses Well Ordering, applied to the domain of all events, and his theorem has an evident similarity to the Ultrafilter (or Maximal Dual Ideal) Theorem for Boolean Algebras,[26] with the property of being a copunctual class playing an analogous role to that played by the "finite intersection property" in the context of the representation theory of Boolean algebras.[27]

As I indicated at the very beginning of the paper, the logical construction of point-instants was intended to serve a combination of metaphysical and epistemological goals connected with the issue of "interpretation." Russell explains this notion in the Introduction to *AMa*:

It frequently happens that we have a deductive mathematical system, starting from hypotheses concerning undefined objects, and that we have reason to believe that there are objects fulfilling these hypotheses, although, initially, we are unable to point out any such objects with certainty. Usually, in such cases, although many different sets of objects are abstractly available as fulfilling the hypotheses, there is one such set which is much more important than the others .... The substitution of such a set for the undefined objects is "interpretation." This process is essential in discovering the philosophical import of physics. (*AMa* 4–5)

For Russell, the point-instants of the theory of space–time pose a problem exactly similar to that posed by the numbers in Peano's axiomatization of arithmetic. So far as the Peano axioms are concerned, *any* ω-sequence (what Russell calls a "progression") forms the basis of a suitable model of the axioms. But among ω-sequences, there is one that is distinguished, namely the one which consists of "the" cardinal numbers, since, as Russell says, this fulfills the requirement "that our numbers should have a *definite* meaning, not merely that they should have certain formal properties. This definite meaning is defined by the logical theory of arithmetic" (*IMP* 10).

The Frege–Russell cardinals are perhaps the simplest example of a successful application of the method of logical construction to a problem of "interpretation" in Russell's sense. We would today express this by saying that the set-theoretic construction consisting of the Frege–Russell cardinals form the basis of a *representation* of any model of the Peano axioms. Even "abstractness" has an analogue here: the abstractness of the number-theoretic axioms consists in the fact that they fail to distinguish, among all possible ω-sequences, the one which is associated with their most important application, and which explains their role in counting. Russell's construction of point-instants was intended to accomplish for the theory of space–time what the definition of the Frege–Russell cardinals achieved for number theory. In each case, the axiomatically primitive notions of number and point-instant were to be replaced by something else – maximal copunctual classes of events and equivalence classes of propositional functions, respectively – in order to display the canonical applications of the theories in which these notions occur. In the arithmetical case, as we have seen, the canonical application of the theory was the use of numbers in counting. Under the influence of Eddington,[28] Russell took the canonical application of the theory of space–time to be its role in *measurement*. Since Russell's construction of point-instants in terms of events is compatible with the assumption that events comprise only finite volumes, the representation of point-instants by classes of events could be motivated by the observation that in any actual measurement we are always restricted to finite quantities.

There is, however, an important difference between the numerical and spatio-temporal cases, one which arises from the fact that they involve applications of theories of very different character. In the arithmetical case, the structure which the numbers comprise should exist "as a matter of logical necessity." More precisely, given a domain of *individuals* of the right cardinality, can we recover the structure of the *numbers* as a theorem of *PM*? It is a remarkable and insufficiently appreciated fact that we can.[29] The Axiom of Infinity asserts that the class of individuals or entities of Type 0 is *non-inductive*. On the basis of this assumption, Russell was able to prove (in *PM* Vol. II, *124.57) – without the Axiom of Choice – that the Frege–Russell cardinals, which occur as entities of Type 2 in the simple type hierarchy, comprise a *Dedekind*-infinite class, and thus, form the domain of a model of the Peano axioms.

For Russell the analysis of matter *is* just the extension of the method of logical construction to physics in general, and to the theory of space–time, in particular. Restricting our attention to the space–time case, here the successful execution of Russell's program requires that every abstract model of the theory should have an isomorphic representation by one constructed in terms of maximally copunctual classes of events, where, in analogy with the use of the Axiom of Infinity in the number-theoretic case, events are presumed to comprise a countable collection of concrete individuals (events are the "basic constituents of the material world"). The program of construction requires, quite properly, and again in parallel with the number-theoretic case, that it be provable that the class of events give rise to an isomorphic representation of any model of the theory of space–time. Thus formulated, the program of logical construction is a now familiar part of the nature and methodology of representation theorems, a part which Russell understood very well. But the successful execution of this program lends no support to the central epistemological contention of structuralism: from the fact that the representation is purely structure-preserving, it by no means follows that the knowledge expressed by the original theory – in this case, the theory of space–time – is purely structural. This is the point which Newman perceived when, summarizing his argument, he emphasized the difference between Russell's problem of interpretation and the problem he was urging. For Newman, the problem is to

distinguish between systems of relations that hold among the members of a given aggregate... [so that i]n the present case we should have to compare the importance of relations of which nothing is known save their incidence (the same for all of them) in a certain aggregate. For this comparison there is no possible criterion, so that "importance" would have to be reckoned among the prime unanalyzable qualities of the constituents of the world, which is, I think, absurd. The statement that there is an *important* relation which sets up the structure [of] the unperceived events of the world cannot, then, be accepted as a true interpretation of our beliefs about these events, and it seems necessary to give up the "structure/quality" division of knowledge in its strict form. (147)

Now when Russell says that copunctuality might be assumed to be a relation among percepts, which is itself perceptible, he presumably means that the primitive relation of "overlapping" which we perceive among percepts, as, for example, when we see a train pass while hearing its whistle, is qualitatively the same relation which obtains among events which are *not* percepts. This, however, has at least the appearance of incompatibility with his subjectivism, for which there is always supposed to be a gulf between the properties that qualify *percepts* and their correlates among *non-percepts*. For the view to work, overlapping, and therefore copunctuality, which is understood in terms of it, must constitute an exception to this rule. But it is unclear how, within the framework of *AMa* or of subsequent work – all of which retains the structuralist tenor of *AMa* – Russell might incorporate the assumption that our knowledge of events which are not percepts is not, after all, purely structural, but is knowledge of *spatio-temporal* structure. Insofar as the difficulty emerges from those aspects of his theory of perception and theory of meaning to which we have drawn attention, it is not clear how, compatibly with those theories, it is possible to maintain that we have knowledge of spatio-temporal structure, or more generally, that we have non-structural knowledge of *any* property or relation of those events which are not percepts.

By way of conclusion, let us return to relativism and to the contrast with Russell's subjectivism. The doctrine of the relativity of color, it will be recalled, involved a claim about our understanding of color predicates. According to relativism, it can perfectly well happen that while our understanding of such predicates is given in terms of perceptual criteria for their application, we allow for the possibility that they may come to have a sense in physical theory which makes no reference to the perceptual capacities by which we recognize their correct application, one which is expressed by a vocabulary that is "absolute." The account of color in terms of surface reflectance is a case in point: our understanding of color predicates prior to their theoretical reconstruction is infused with the perceptual criteria we deploy in assigning colors to physical surfaces. Afterwards, it is expressed in a vocabulary that does not, in this way, rely on this perceptual capacity for its correct application. To this extent, our notion of color begins as one that is relative to peculiarities of our way of perceiving the world, dependent as this is upon features of our perceptual systems. Nevertheless, our pre-theoretic understanding of color predicates may be entirely continuous with our post-theoretic understanding, if, as we have been assuming, there is a measure of extensional equivalence in the pre- and post-theoretic applications of these predicates. An absolute form of description differs from a relative one, not by virtue of its being true where the relative description is false, but because it seeks to isolate the characterization of what is true from any dependence on the particular perspective we bring to our knowledge of the world on the basis of our perception of it. For relativism, it is simply not true that of the properties and relations themselves we know only their structure; they also satisfy our relative forms of description. Were we to look for analogues in Russell's view, our absolute descriptions would correspond to Russell's "intrinsic" knowledge and our relative forms of description, to his "qualitative" knowledge. But from the perspective of absolute and relative forms of description, it is obscure just what would satisfy Russell's search for intrinsic knowledge of things in themselves, since it would have to be expressed by a form of description which is at the same time both absolute and relative: absolute because an intrinsic property is one which holds or fails to hold independently of whether the world contains beings like us, endowed as we are, with our peculiar perceptual capacities; and relative because qualitative knowledge of the property is exhausted by our acquaintance with it in perception. Of course, the fact that this simple translation, of Russell's subjectivism into the absolute/relative framework, is problematic does not by itself establish an incoherence in Russell's view. However, it *does* show that the proposal to pursue certain of the aims of structuralism by exploiting the contrast between absolute and relative forms of description is not merely terminological. Relativism can preserve the idea, fundamental to our conception of our theoretical knowledge of the physical world, that our claims regarding its structure are significant, since the same properties and relations are characterized by both relative and absolute forms of description; but it achieves this only by giving up Russell's structure/quality division of our knowledge.

REFERENCES

1. The term 'interpretation' is used in a special sense by Russell. I will return to its discussion in Section V.

2. The theory is discussed in some detail in my paper, "On the Theory of Meaning of 'On Denoting,'" *Noûs* **33** (1999), 439–58.

3. In R.B. Braithwaite (ed.), *The Foundations of Mathematics and Other Logical Essays* (Littlefield and Adams: 1960).

4. My remarks in the text apply only to the notion of a Ramsey sentence; I am not claiming to have exhausted Ramsey's concerns in his essay. Unpublished notes found with the material included in both editions of Ramsey's *Foundations* as the chapter "Theories" shows Ramsey to have had an interest in the notion of a purely auxiliary element which went beyond its relevance to instrumentalism.

5. Here a "suitable characterization" amounts to what is sometimes called an implicit definition in the sense of Hilbert, although Hilbert's use of the idea was from the very first associated with controversy. For a discussion, see my "Frege, Hilbert, and the Conceptual Structure of Model Theory," *History and Philosophy of Logic* **15** (1994), 211–25.

6. The central results go back to the paper of W. Craig and R.L. Vaught, "Finite Axiomatizability Using Additional Predicates," *Journal of Symbolic Logic* **23** (1958) 289–308. For a succinct summary of the relevant definitions and theorems see J.F.A.K. van Bentham, "Ramsey Eliminability," *Studia Logica* **37** (1978), 321–36; cf. especially pp. 327–29, Definition 3.9 through the discussion following Theorem 3.14, which can be read independently of the rest of van Bentham's article.

7. The secondary literature is frequently misleading on this point, often suggesting a closer conceptual link between Russell's structuralism and the notion of a Ramsey sentence than in fact exists. The literature is too vast to survey here. For an informative overview of the role of

the Ramsey sentence in neo-positivist theories of theories, see Stathis Psillos, *Scientific Realism: How Science Tracks the Truth* (London: 1999).

8. Dawes Hicks's criticism of *Problems* forms part of a longer article, "Appearance and Real Existence," *Proceedings of the Aristotelian Society* **14** (1913/14), 1–48. His objection to the argument from the relativity of perception occurs (in a slightly different form) in Thomas Reid's *Essays on the Intellectual Powers of Man*, Essay II, Chapter XIV. (I am indebted to John Koethe for providing me with this reference.)

9. Cf. *POP2*, 29–30.

10. "Conflicting Appearances," *Proceedings of the British Academy* **65** (1979/1980), 69–111, p. 111.

11. Burnyeat, p. 75; I have changed the labeling to conform with my own.

12. In my use of the notion of an absolute (vs relative) form of description, I have followed Michael Dummett, "Common Sense and Physics," (1979) reprinted in *The Seas of Language* (Oxford: 1993). I believe Dummett's first introduction of the idea of an absolute form of description is in his 1960 paper "A Defence of McTaggart's Argument for the Unreality of Time," reprinted in *Truth and Other Enigmas* (Harvard: 1978). What is there called a "complete" description of reality corresponds to what Dummett later terms an "absolute form of description." (Related ideas can also be found in Bernard Williams's *Descartes: The Project of Pure Inquiry* (Harvester: 1978, pp. 237ff) and in Peter Strawson's *Analysis and Metaphysics* (Oxford: 1992, pp. 65f).

13. Edwin Land, quoted by David Hilbert in his *Color and Color Perception* (CSLI: 1987, p. 17); original reference: *Proceedings of the National Academy of Sciences USA* **80** (1983), p. 5164.

14. Indeed, Russell explicitly endorses just such a theory of the physical basis – one according to which color corresponds simply to wavelength – a theory we now regard as having been displaced. (Cf. Hilbert, 48f for a discussion of Russell and related "Newtonian" views. In connection with Russell, Hilbert cites *HK* 278; *AMa* is replete with allusions to the same conception of color's physical basis.) Hilbert's book is such an admirable one that I hesitate to register a disagreement. Nevertheless, contrary to Hilbert, I believe that Russell's "philosophical theory of color" – his account of perceptual qualities – does not depend at all essentially on the deficiencies of this model; in some respects, it is even brought into sharper focus by being placed within the context of the computational framework of Land and others (a framework which Hilbert, himself, very ably defends).

15. C.L. Hardin "Colors, Normal Observers, and Standard Conditions," *The Journal of Philosophy* **80** (1983), p. 813.

16. The difficulty which a precise elaboration of such a criterion presents is invariably underestimated in philosophical discussions of color. See especially Chapter 2 of C.L. Hardin, *Color for Philosophers* (Hackett: 1988), for an overview.

17. See Laurence T. Maloney and Brian A. Wandell, "Color Constancy: A Method for Recovering Surface Spectral Reflectance," *Journal of the Optical Society of America* A **3** (1986), 29–33 and David Brainard et al. "Color Constancy: From Physics to Appearance," *Current Directions in Psychological Science* **2** (1993), 165–70. I am very much indebted to my colleague, Professor Keith Humphrey of the Psychology Department of The University of Western Ontario, for discussions on the topic of this paragraph.

18. Ullman's work is reported in his book, *The Interpretation of Visual Motion* (MIT: 1979).

19. There are numerous passages in *AMa* which give expression to this idea: "Common sense is, in most respects, naively realistic: it believes that, as a rule, our perceptions show us objects as they really are" (149). "... [But while we have] a great deal of knowledge as to the structure of stimuli their intrinsic characters, it is true, must remain unknown" (227).

20. Cp. "... Colours and sounds can be arranged in an order with respect to several characteristics; we have a right to assume that their stimuli can be arranged in an order with respect to corresponding characteristics, but this, by itself, determines only certain logical properties of the stimuli. This applies to all varieties of percepts, and accounts for the fact that our knowledge of physics is mathematical: it is mathematical because no non-mathematical properties of the physical world can be inferred from perception .... Thus it would seem that, wherever we infer from perceptions, it is only structure that we can validly infer; and structure is what can be expressed by mathematical logic, which includes mathematics." (*AMa* 253, 254)

21. "Mr. Russell's 'Causal Theory of Perception,'" *Mind* **37** (1928), 137–48. Newman's article is discussed more fully in my paper with Michael Friedman, "Russell's *Analysis of Matter*: Its Historical Context and Contemporary Interest," *Philosophy of Science* **52** (1985), 621–39; reprinted under the title, "The Concept of Structure in *The Analysis of Matter*," in C. Wade Savage and C. Anthony Anderson (eds.) *Rereading Russell: Critical Essays on Bertrand Russell's Metaphysics and Epistemology* (University of Minnesota Press: 1989) and in A. Irvine (ed.) *Bertrand Russell: Critical Assessments Vol. 3* (Routledge: 1998). Graham Solomon considers applications to Eddington's views in his discussion note, "Addendum to Demopoulos and Friedman," *Philosophy of Science* **56** (1989) 497–501.

22. Newman's criticism has been challenged by Herbert Hochberg ("Causal Connections, Universals, and Russell's Hypothetico-Scientific Realism," *The Monist* 77 (1994) 71–92) on the ground that it depends on an overly extensional notion of relation, one which supports the existence of *sets* with the appropriate structure, but fails to support the existence of *relations* when relations are taken to be appropriately intensional entities. Perhaps there is a notion of relation which will serve this purpose; but if so, it is not Russell's, since on the logical notion of set – to which Russell was surely committed – *every* set is determined by a property or relation. So, if we have the set, we also have a determining property or relation.

23. A comparison between Newman's objection to Russell's structuralism and Hilary Putnam's model theoretic argument was first drawn by myself and Michael Friedman in the paper cited in note 21. For the bearing of Newman's observation on subsequent developments, see my paper, "On the Rational Reconstruction of Our Theoretical Knowledge", *British Journal for the Philosophy of Science* 54 (2003) [in press].

24. See his letter to Newman (of 24 April 1928) in the second volume of his *Autobiography* (Allen & Unwin: 1968, p. 176).

25. Ibid.

26. Proved by M.H. Stone, "The Theory of Representations for Boolean Algebras," *Transactions of the American Mathematical Society* 40 (1936), 37–111.

27. Indeed, the analogy can be developed further to illuminate the difference between Russell's construction and the earlier, but more restricted, construction by Whitehead in terms of "enclosure series." My comments here are merely suggestive and are not intended as a substitute for a close analysis of Chapters xxviii and xxix of *AMa*. C. Anthony Anderson's "Russell on Order in Time" (in the Anderson and Savage volume cited in fn. 18) has set the standard which any such analysis must meet.

28. Russell's understanding of General Relativity seems to have been largely derived from Eddington's *Mathematical Theory of Relativity* (Cambridge: 1924). This is not to say that Russell's reading of Eddington was uncritical; see, e.g., *AMa* 90ff for an assessment of Eddington's operationalism.

29. For an elaboration of the significance of *PM* Vol. II, *124.57, see George Boolos, "The Advantages of Honest Toil over Theft," in Alexander George (ed.), *Mathematics and Mind* (Oxford: 1994).

13 From Knowledge by Acquaintance to Knowledge by Causation

People are not so different from gramophones as they like to believe (*AMi*: 166).

There are many familiar themes in Russell's repertoire, but his later discussions of knowledge include many insights which have received little notice. Indeed, it is often supposed that in the years after 1914, after the heroic foundational phase of analytical philosophy celebrated in countless anthologies, Russell ceased to engage in creative philosophy and turned instead to popular tracts on marriage and morals, idleness and happiness. One thing I want to show here is that during these years Russell was in fact developing a new conception of epistemology, linked to a new philosophy of mind, which was so far ahead of his time that it passed by largely unappreciated. It is only now that our own philosophy of mind has caught up with the 'naturalisation' of the mind that Russell was teaching from 1921 onwards that we can recognise in his later writings the central themes of our current debates – concerning the significance of the causation of belief, the tension between 'externalist' and 'internalist' perspectives concerning knowledge, and the limits of empiricism.

To discuss these later themes properly, however, we have to start from a discussion of the tensions inherent in his earlier epistemology, and the text from which to start is his famous 'shilling-shocker' *The Problems of Philosophy* (1912), in which Russell presents a general survey of the subject grounded in a theory of knowledge.

I

This epistemological bias of Russell's conception of 'the problems of philosophy' is in fact one of the striking features of the book. It shows that in 1912, Russell still philosophised within the familiar tradition that stretches back to Descartes. If in the 1880s Frege had initiated a 'revolution in philosophy' which substituted logic and the philosophy of language for epistemology as the foundational discipline of philosophy,[1] no one had yet told Russell about it even if, retrospectively, the works leading up to *Principia Mathematica* are held to contribute to it.

At an early stage in *POP* (39–40), Russell says that an important function of philosophy is that of arriving at an 'orderly systematic organisation of our knowledge' which minimizes, even though it does not altogether banish, grounds for doubt. Russell's way of organising our knowledge begins from a distinction between knowledge of things and knowledge of truths, and then divides each of these types into two kinds: knowledge of things is divided into knowledge by acquaintance and knowledge by description; and knowledge of truths into intuitive knowledge and derivative knowledge (*POP* 170–1). This suggests that our knowledge has the following structure:

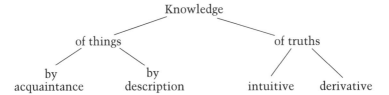

As Russell makes clear, however, this is somewhat misleading. There are also important connections between knowledge of things and knowledge of truths: intuitive knowledge of truths depends upon knowledge by acquaintance of the things involved, and knowledge by description of things depends upon derivative knowledge of truths concerning the things described. So a different way of representing the structure of knowledge would be one which represents this pattern of dependence:

knowledge by description of things
(depends on)
derivative knowledge of truths
(depends on)
intuitive knowledge of truths
(depends on)
knowledge by acquaintance of things

This diagram implies, as Russell puts it (*POP* 75), that knowledge by acquaintance is the 'foundation' of all our knowledge. Thus, one question concerning his early epistemology is whether acquaintance can carry this weight; another is how far Russell qualifies this foundationalist structure in order to accommodate kinds of knowledge that he would otherwise have to repudiate.

Russell connects the distinction between knowledge by acquaintance of things and knowledge of truths with the *connaître/savoir* and *kennen/wissen* distinctions in French and German (*POP* 70) and this provides a way into his conception of knowledge by acquaintance. Ordinary knowledge of things (*connaître* and *kennen*) requires some first-hand experience of a thing (usually a person or place) which gives rise to an ability to provide information about it. Similarly, Russell's conception of knowledge by acquaintance requires a perceptual experience, or something similar, in which an object is 'presented' in such a way that the subject acquires some knowledge about it, that it exists and has the properties it is presented as having. But the comparison also breaks down in an important respect: ordinary knowledge of things admits of degrees – we speak of knowing someone well, or not so well, depending upon the extent of our information about them. Russellian knowledge by acquaintance, by contrast, is always only top quality: it is so 'perfect' and 'complete' (*POP* 73) that it excludes the possibility of doubt (*POP* 74). Russell takes it, of course, that only knowledge of this kind could provide the firm foundation for all other knowledge that knowledge by acquaintance is supposed to be; nonetheless, this is one of the features that make it problematic, as Russell also recognises.

Ordinary knowledge of things includes, but is not exhausted by, knowledge of truths. Similarly, Russell distinguishes knowledge by acquaintance of a thing from the intuitive knowledge of simple truths concerning the thing to which it gives rise. But the fact that acquaintance is supposed to be both a simple act–object relationship and also inherently cognitive (so that there is no distinction between acquaintance and knowledge by acquaintance) gives rise to difficulties. For example Russell holds that we are each acquainted with ourselves (*POP* 80): suppose now that, unknown to myself, I am also the tallest winner of the latest lottery jackpot. Then, since acquaintance is a simple act–object relationship, it follows that I am acquainted with the tallest winner of the latest lottery jackpot. But in a case of this kind, Russell holds that in fact I have 'merely descriptive knowledge' of the tallest winner, since although I know that there is just one tallest winner, I do not know who it is (*POP* 83).

The way to block this inference is to recognise, as Russell allows in connection with our acquaintance with the past (e.g., *POP* 180, *TK* 74), that all acquaintance is 'acquaintance as', so that my acquaintance with myself is with myself *as such* rather than with myself *as the tallest winner*. But this refinement implies that acquaintance is not a simple act–object relationship and is instead implicitly propositional: my acquaintance with myself *as such* just is my intuitive knowledge concerning myself *that I am myself*. Hence, once knowledge by acquaintance is explicated in a way which is adequate to the distinctions Russell draws, it turns out to be intuitive *de re* knowledge of truths. Such a revision cannot be combined with Russell's multiple-relation theory of judgment, since one feature of that theory is that all propositional attitudes are to be construed as relationships between a subject and certain 'objective' terms with which the subject is acquainted. For if acquaintance is itself a propositional attitude, then the theory fails to eliminate them. But since the multiple-relation theory is the weakest strand of Russell's early epistemology, and one which he himself abandoned in 1913, this problem is no great objection to the revised conception of acquaintance. What is more of an objection is the implied account of perception, which is the primary case of acquaintance. For although the implication that all perceiving is perceiving *as* seems correct, it remains plausible to hold that the content of perception itself, as opposed to perceptual knowledge, is nonconceptual. The way to accommodate this point is to distinguish, as Russell does not, between acquaintance itself, which will include perception, and knowledge by acquaintance: only the latter will be intuitive *de re* knowledge of truths. The former can then be some non-conceptual state (whose details are to be settled by a theory of perception) which enables the subject to single out a particular thing or aspect. The relationship between the two will then be that knowledge by acquaintance depends upon acquaintance for its *de re* structure.

So far, I have concentrated upon acquaintance itself. What is crucial for Russell's foundationalist project is the extent of our acquaintance, the kinds of things with which we can become acquainted and thereby acquire knowledge by acquaintance. Because Russell has set the standards for acquaintance so high that it excludes the possibility of error, it turns out that our acquaintance is correspondingly restricted and excludes physical objects (POP 23) and other minds (POP 85–6); instead it is restricted to sense-data, our own thoughts and feelings, our 'self', our own immediate past, and universals. The interesting items here are the last two.

Russell's account of memory is that it involves acquaintance with a past object – it is 'having immediately before the mind an object which is recognised as past' (POP 180). The kind of object is, of course, a sense-datum, such as that involved in seeing a flash of lightning (POP 181); and Russell's claim is that the mind, rather like a flash of lightning, can 'arc' back into the past to generate intuitive knowledge that 'this is past' where this, though now past, is 'an object of present acquaintance' (TK 71). What is hard to accept here is the combination of tenses involved: present acquaintance with what is both past and is immediately recognised as past. Although we do of course have underived beliefs concerning what is past as such, and we have perceptions of past events, e.g., a super-nova explosion, these cases do not accommodate what Russell has in mind. He holds that, in thinking 'This is past', I am not thinking, say, 'the cause of this (present) visual experience is past': I am instead, now, directly identifying something which is not present but past as past. Russell is treating memory as if it includes a quasi-perceptual experiential element which enables us to think directly about past objects.

It is not easy to argue against a hypothesis of this kind, though we can note with some relief that it is abandoned in the light of the new philosophy of mind adopted in The Analysis of Mind (1921). Russell offers two general considerations in its favour: first, that we must have some intuitive knowledge of the past if we are to have any knowledge of it at all, and second, that some such acquaintance with the past is a prerequisite of our ability to be able to understand talk of the past (POP 180). Some version of the first of these points must, I think, be granted: what, however, is not required is that the knowledge in question be de re knowledge concerning something past as such, and it is only this feature which generates the requirement for acquaintance with something past as such that is so difficult to swallow.

The second point invokes a connection between acquaintance and understanding which is enshrined in Russell's 'fundamental principle'

Every proposition we can understand must be composed of constituents with which we are acquainted (POP 91)

This principle draws implicitly on the relatively uncontentious thesis that any sentence we can understand must be composed of words we can understand. For although Russell's conception of a proposition in *POP* is not linguistic, his talk of 'understanding' here introduces implicit reference to the understanding of language, which becomes explicit when he adds, as an argument for his principle, the further thesis that our understanding of words is fundamentally such that 'the meaning we attach to our words must be something with which we are acquainted' (*POP* 91). Russell would of course qualify this second thesis to allow for incomplete symbols such as descriptions which 'are not supposed to have any meaning in isolation' (*PM* vol. 1, 66); but these are, for him, necessarily only exceptions.

This is a principle which reflects the fundamental role of acquaintance in Russell's early philosophy, as setting the limits to understanding as well providing a foundation for knowledge. As the case of our supposed acquaintance with the past as such shows, in *POP* Russell gives a simple-minded interpretation of it for which he offers no argument and which is not easy to accept. We shall see that in his later writings Russell himself abandons the principle thus interpreted. What remains conceivable, however, is that there is a different and much more defensible interpretation of the principle, such as the principle elaborated and defended as 'Russell's principle' by Gareth Evans in *The Varieties of Reference*[2]; but I shall not pursue this matter here.

Returning now to *POP*, Russell takes it that his fundamental principle implies that an account of the meaning of 'substantives, adjectives, prepositions, and verbs' (*POP* 145) requires a specification of the constituents of propositions our acquaintance with which constitutes our grasp of these meanings. These meanings, he claims, are universals, both qualities and relations, and he famously proceeds to endorse a strongly Platonic account (*POP* 145) of them. The commitment partly reflects his strong, Moore-inspired, hostility to psychologism in all forms, and thus to empiricist doctrines of ideas

(*POP* 154–5); but it also reflects his presumption that these meanings should enter into *a priori* truths. For, he thinks, it is by taking it that '*All* a priori *knowledge deals exclusively with the relations of universals*' (*POP* 162) that he can give an account of the way in which *a priori* knowledge seems to give a structure to our experience of the world without drawing upon Kant's transcendental idealism (*POP* 132–3).

This conception of intuitive knowledge of a priori truths is something that Russell abandons soon after *POP*, but there are two points worth making here about it. One concerns the modal concepts – possibility and necessity. Only a little later Russell is suspicious of these concepts; but here he is uncritical in affirming that *a priori* truths are true 'in any possible world' (*POP* 121). Nonetheless he shows no awareness here of the fact that his fundamental principle implies that his understanding of modal concepts is grounded in acquaintance with something inherently modal as such (just as he argued that our understanding of temporal concepts is grounded in acquaintance with the immediate past as past). So far from entertaining at this time the hypothesis of our acquaintance with the merely possible as such, however, Russell rejects the modal realism implied by such a hypothesis:

It may be laid down generally that *possibility* always marks insufficient analysis: when analysis is completed, only the *actual* can be relevant, for the simple reason that there is only the actual, and that the merely possible is nothing (*TK* 27).

The other point to make concerning Russell's account of *a priori* knowledge in *POP* concerns the role of something comparable to perception in our acquaintance with universals and knowledge about them. Russell, of course, acknowledges that acquaintance here is not sense-perception and he calls it '*conceiving*' (*POP* 81); so acquaintance here cannot be the non-conceptual way of identifying an object that I suggested perceptual acquaintance needs to be. Nonetheless, Russell still needs to hold that there is a quasi-perceptual element to '*conceiving*' since at this time he holds that important *a priori* truths, including mathematics and logic, are synthetic, and, therefore, not simply such that an understanding of the propositions suffices by itself for a grasp of their truth. Thus, he regularly writes of us having 'the power of sometimes perceiving such relations between universals and, therefore, of sometimes knowing general *a priori* propositions such as those of arithmetic and logic' (*POP*

164–5). Equally, however, potentially subversive thoughts sometimes slip out – as when he remarks concerning the law of contradiction 'This is evident as soon as it is understood' (*POP* 177).

Acquaintance was supposed to be the foundation for all knowledge, and when Russell first describes *derivative* knowledge as 'everything that we can deduce from self-evident truths by the use of
self-evident principles of deduction' (*POP* 171–2) this description appears to be in accordance with his foundationalist programme. As
Russell discusses the subject, however, complications and qualifica-
tions enter in. The first complication (despite the remarks quoted
just now about the impropriety of invoking possibility) concerns the
fact that the account of derivative knowledge is couched in terms of
what 'we *can* deduce' and not simply what 'we *have* deduced'. For
although a strict foundationalist might limit a person's knowledge
to what they have validly deduced, the resulting account, Russell argues, would be much too restrictive. For example, we take it that people often obtain knowledge by reading newspapers and other authoritative texts, but in most cases the reader 'does not in fact perform any
operation which can be called logical inference' in forming beliefs as
they read (*POP* 208–9). So by the strict test, no knowledge would be
acquired by such readers; yet this, Russell thinks, is 'absurd':

If the newspapers announce the death of the King, we are fairly well justified
in believing that the King is dead, since this is the sort of announcement
which would not be made if it were false. And we are quite amply justified in
believing that the newspaper asserts that the King is dead . . . . <Indeed>
it would be absurd to say that the reader does not *know* that the newspaper
announces the King's death. (*POP* 208–9)

To handle this kind of case, Russell introduces the conception
of 'psychological inference' to characterise the causal connection
between beliefs (*POP* 209), which is exemplified by the way in
which a newspaper reader forms beliefs. He then maintains that
beliefs formed by a process of psychological inference count as
derivative knowledge as long as there is also a valid logical connection between the beliefs of which the believer could have become
aware by reflection. In the case he has described, however, Russell
in fact makes no effort to spell out the logical connection, which is
supposed to be discoverable by the average newspaper reader, and as
soon as one thinks about it, a host of questions arise concerning the
understanding of language and our reasons for believing what we
read in newspapers, which are not at all easily answered within the

framework provided by Russell's official conception of derivative knowledge. So although he maintains a formal commitment to the gold standard of logical justifications for beliefs, he appears in practice content to accept the paper money provided by the causal connections inherent in his conception of psychological inference. It is, then, not going to be a big step to allow that where these causal connections are reliable enough, there is no need for a hypothetically discoverable logical connection as well.

That is not a step Russell takes in *POP*. But he does note that it is an implication of his appeal to these hypothetically discoverable logical connections that the concept of knowledge is not precise, since the issue of what is discoverable on reflection is not precise (*POP* 209). This is a thesis which has been advanced recently in the light of discussions of the famous 'Gettier-cases' and the similarity here should come as no surprise since Russell's discussion of knowledge in *POP* (Chapter XIII) includes an anticipation of Gettier's observations and subsequent debates.[3] Russell constructs 'Gettier-cases' of true beliefs which are not knowledge even though there is some justification for the belief (*POP* 205), identifies the disabling role of false beliefs in the supposedly justifying derivation of such beliefs (*POP* 205–6), and notes the role of reliable causal connections ('psychological inference') in the explanation of many ordinary cases of knowledge. Where Russell differs from many contemporary philosophers who have discussed these matters is in not seeking to construct a definition of knowledge which in some complex way sidesteps all these difficulties; instead he wisely draws the conclusion that the concept of knowledge does not admit of any precise definition because it is incurably vague.

Russell then reinforces this conclusion by arguing that vagueness also infects the conception of self-evidence, which enters into his account of knowledge. And it is in this connection that his departure from a foundationalist strategy is most significant. For, alongside the intuitive knowledge by acquaintance discussed earlier, which is, he now says, self-evident only 'in the first and most absolute sense' (*POP* 212), he introduces the possibility of intuitive (i.e., nonderivative) knowledge which is only self-evident to some degree, in that the underlying belief is one concerning which some degree of doubt is possible. Cases of this second kind include memory (*POP* 183 – apart from memories of the immediate past), fine perceptual discriminations (*POP* 216), complex logical inferences (*POP* 216), ethical judgments (*POP* 184) and inductive inferences (*POP* 184). Since these are all supposed to be cases of intuitive knowledge (*POP* 210), Russell implies that we are not dealing here with beliefs that can be derived from strongly self-evident knowledge by acquaintance; nonetheless, these are beliefs which have a sufficiently high degree of self-evidence, or credibility, for them to count (as long as they are true) as knowledge themselves.

Because self-evidence of this second kind comes in degrees, the difference between knowledge and '*probable opinion*', for which the degree of self-evidence is insufficient (*POP* 217), is inherently vague. In connection with probable opinion Russell allows that considerations of coherence have a legitimate, and indeed important, role: in the case of both scientific and philosophical hypotheses, a significant degree of coherence implies that beliefs which, when considered by themselves, are merely probable opinions 'become pretty nearly certain' (*POP* 218). Thus, for example, it is the test of coherence which assures us that our ordinary waking life is not a dream. The way Russell writes here suggests that he takes it that coherence never supports claims to knowledge; but in fact his own thesis that there is no sharp distinction between knowledge and probable opinion precludes this position. In all cases of knowledge not involving self-evidence of the first absolute kind, he is committed to allowing that these considerations of coherence have a legitimate role in diminishing grounds for doubt.

In truth there is a certain ambivalence in *POP* on this matter. At times Russell writes as a foundationalist, with acquaintance as the sole foundation for knowledge of all kinds. This position would support a firm distinction between knowledge and probable opinion and would exclude coherence, as opposed to derivation from strictly self-evident truths, from a proper place in the legitimation of knowledge. But this position is revisionary, since it implies that most claims to knowledge involving induction and memory cannot be substantiated, and thus that most of what we think we know is only more or less probable opinion. Sometimes Russell seems content to endorse this conclusion. 'Thus, the greater part of what would commonly pass as knowledge is more or less probable opinion' (*POP* 217); but at other places he rejects it:

But as regards what would be commonly accepted as knowledge, our result is in the main positive: we have seldom found reason to reject such knowledge as the result of our criticism, and we have seen no reason to suppose man incapable of the kind of knowledge which he is generally believed to possess. (*POP* 233–4)

It is, then, in connection with this second attitude that he introduces his second kind of intuitive knowledge, which shades off imperceptibly into probable opinion and which is inimical to a strict foundationalist approach.

An area of derivative knowledge to which Russell attaches great importance in *POP* is that involving what he calls 'knowledge by description'. This is knowledge which involves knowing that there is some one thing with certain properties even though we do not know who or what it is, in the sense that we are not acquainted with it. The importance for Russell of this form of knowledge is that he thinks it enables us to extend our knowledge to concern things with which we are not acquainted despite his fundamental principle, which limits our understanding to propositions with whose constituents we are acquainted, and his strict limits on the range of our acquaintance. Whether this really works is disputable, as we shall see in a moment; but Russell thinks that what enables him to obtain what he wants here is our acquaintance with the universals which are 'meant' by the general descriptions we employ, together with our capacity to derive general descriptive hypotheses, concerning the existence of such things as other minds and physical objects, from the fragmentary sense-data with which we are acquainted. Since these inferences typically involve induction, or, indeed, hypothetical speculation, the thought that we can formulate in this way (*knowledge* by description) clearly rests on his less stringent requirements for self-evidence.

Russell, of course, connects this conception of knowledge by description with his theory of descriptions. Indeed, he had ended 'On Denoting' by suggesting that this conception of knowledge by description of things which extends well beyond our acquaintance with them is one of the 'interesting results' of the theory (*Papers* 4, 427) though the intuitive contrast between 'knowing that' and 'knowing what' is readily accommodated within a Fregean conception of descriptions as complex names: Frege's position does not imply that in, say, knowing that $(56)^2$ is an even number, one needs to know what number $(56)^2$ is. Furthermore, although the combination of his own theory of descriptions with his conception of knowledge by description is of course consistent, Russell does not observe that this combination is not consistent with the multiple-relation theory of judgment, which he also affirms in *POP*. Although Russell makes some suggestions in *PM* (vol. i, 45–6) as to how one might apply the multiple relation theory to general judgments by separating out a quantifier (e.g., generality) and a propositional function (e.g., if mon (*x*) then mortal (*x*)), his suggestion does not cover judgments which involve multiple generality, since in such cases it is crucial to retain the information of which quantifier binds which variables. Since his theory of descriptions involves multiple generality, knowledge by description cannot be combined with the multiple relation theory. Although Russell's reasons for abandoning his *Theory of Knowledge* project do not appear to have included a recognition of this point, it is, I think, significant that his notes towards the unwritten part III of the project on 'Molecular Propositional Thought' (*Papers* 7, 201) do not contain any suggestion as to how he was going to handle multiple generality and bound variables.

This last point is no great objection to the conception of knowledge by description, though it is, I think, a decisive objection to the multiple-relation theory. But the combination of knowledge by description with Russell's fundamental principle and his limitations on our acquaintance gives rise to many difficulties. These are well illustrated by his own example of our knowledge concerning Bismarck (*POP* 89). Since it is only Bismarck who is acquainted with himself, our knowledge of him is inevitably knowledge by description, involving such descriptions as 'the first Chancellor of the German Empire'. So our knowledge cannot be knowledge of the proposition that Bismarck was an astute diplomatist; we can only approximate to this by knowing such propositions as that the first Chancellor of the German Empire was an astute diplomatist. But since we cannot know such propositions as that Bismarck was the first Chancellor of the German Empire, we can never know that our descriptive knowledge is knowledge about the 'right' thing. Furthermore, our descriptive knowledge is knowledge of a general proposition whose particular instances we do not, and can not, know. We know the proposition that there is at least and at most one first Chancellor of the German Empire and that he was an astute diplomatist, but we can know (and know that we can know) no proposition of the form '*x* is a first Chancellor of the German Empire and x was an astute diplomatist'. For an appropriate value of '*x*' would have to be a person and the only person we are acquainted with is ourself; but we know that we are not a value for which the proposition is true. Indeed, since the only propositions we can understand are such that we are acquainted with their constituents, we cannot even make sense of any sentence which expresses the proposition that Bismarck was an astute diplomatist, the proposition which is the true instance of the general proposition that we are supposed to know.

Russell shows some awareness of these *prima facie* puzzling features of knowledge by description (*POP* 168–70). He attempts to disarm them by introducing a different case of general knowledge for which no instances can be given: simplifying a little, his case is our knowledge that all the numbers which will never be thought of are greater than 100. Because there is an infinity of numbers we know that most of them will never be thought of, and we also know that all such numbers are greater than 100; but of course we cannot instantiate, since that would involve thinking of the number we pick as our instance. The example is reminiscent of Berkeley's famous 'Master Argument',[4] though it is one that Russell himself cannot deploy with a clear conscience since the way in which he interprets his Vicious Circle Principle when defusing the semantic paradoxes would suggest that the general knowledge in this case implicitly involves a 'totality' of thoughts about numbers to which a subsequent instantiation does not belong because it is of a higher 'order'. Furthermore, since Russell interprets general propositions as conditionals, for him instantiation does in fact yield truths – conditionals with a false antecedent. These points are, perhaps, rather too *ad hominem* to enable one to set aside Russell's case; but, more generally, the case does not, I think, defuse the doubts raised concerning Russell's conception of knowledge by description. Not only does it depend on a form of pragmatic self-reference, which is not a feature of knowledge by description in general, it does not address the puzzle that we cannot even understand the particular proposition on whose truth the truth of our general knowledge depends. In this respect, Russell's position looks remarkably similar to those Kantian doctrines concerning unthinkable things-in-themselves, which he elsewhere likes to poke fun at.

One way to illustrate Russell's difficulty is consider his claim that we are able to communicate with each other concerning Bismarck despite the fact we are not acquainted with him because we all employ descriptions that are in fact descriptions of him. Once the details of each person's knowledge by description are fully spelled out, they will be found to involve reference to particulars, to sense-data, with which that person alone is acquainted, for it is only by starting out from sense-data that derivative knowledge of a matter of fact can be obtained. Hence, each person's knowledge by description concerning Bismarck is knowledge of a proposition which is understandable only to that person; in which case there cannot be a common understanding of the sentences which express these propositions. So knowledge of them cannot after all provide a way in which we can communicate with others. It is not just that we cannot ever know that we are describing the same thing (Bismarck); even more simply, we cannot attach the same meaning to our words as we attempt to describe him.

II

Russell's continuing commitment to epistemology is shown by the fact that his first major project after completing *POP* was his ill-fated work *Theory of Knowledge* (1913); and again by the fact after he had abandoned this, he took as his title for the Lowell lectures, delivered in Harvard in 1914, *Our Knowledge of the External World*. Without attempting to deal in any detail with these works or others from the 'logical atomist' period 1914–19, I shall pick out the points that are important in connection with his epistemology.

In *TK* Russell sees the main task of epistemology as the discovery of 'epistemological premises', which he distinguishes from logical premises in that the former, unlike the latter, must be such that they can be known to be true without being derived from other propositions (*TK* 50). Thus, they are to be a set of self-evident propositions which provide a basis for the derivation of some putative body of knowledge. Russell initially says that the identification of these self-evident premises is a task for 'psychology', and that for this reason the theory of knowledge is dependent upon both psychology and logic, which provides the principles according to which derivations are to be conducted (*TK* 46). But when he returns later to the topic of self-evidence, he takes it to involve metaphysics and logic as well as psychology (*TK* 156), and his own account certainly has implications that extend beyond psychology, for he takes it that self-evidence consists in the fact that the judgments in question involve 'acquaintance with their truth' (*TK* 166).

So far the substance of this position does not differ much from his account of the role of 'intuitive' knowledge in POP, but there is an important difference when he proceeds to deny that self-evidence, or certainty, comes in degrees (TK 174–6). The result is that the position in TK is more straightforwardly foundationalist than that advanced in POP. Equally, it follows that the position is less hospitable to much of what we think we know – e.g., Russell now takes the view that memory judgments which do not involve immediate acquaintance with the past are 'not worthy to be called "knowledge' (TK 174).

TK also includes a discussion of 'logical data' (TK Part I chapter IX) which draws on his 'fundamental principle', but also shows that he has lost his previous confidence about its application in the case of logic:

> Such words as or, not. all, some, plainly involve logical notions; and since we can use such words intelligently, we must be acquainted with the logical objects involved. But the difficulty of isolation is here very great, and I do not know what the logical objects involved really are.
>
> In the present chaotic state of our knowledge concerning the primitive ideas of logic, it is impossible to pursue this topic further. (TK 99)

This passage is a remarkable confession from the author of Principia Mathematica. Perhaps, it is indicative of the uncertainty Russell was beginning to feel in the light of Wittgenstein's criticisms. One year later, in OKEW, Russell seems altogether more confident about the status of logic – so much so that he is prepared to celebrate 'logic as the essence of philosophy' (OKEW lecture II) and to suggest that all general a priori knowledge is provided by logic (OKEW p. 56), in accordance with which he proposes that inductive inference rests upon a fundamental 'logical' principle concerning probability (OKEW pp. 222–3).

Russell does not advance here a clear account of our knowledge of logic, though in other writings of this time he implies that logic is not synthetic ('On Scientific Method in Philosophy' (1914) Papers 8, 70). What he does seek to do is to apply what he now calls his 'logical-analytic method of scientific philosophy' (OKEW 65) to 'the problem of our knowledge of the external world'. Given the distinction he had just drawn in TK between logical and epistemological premises, this is on the face of it a surprising new initiative. In part it turns out to be just an affirmation of the need for logical derivations to replace the merely causal psychological connections between our beliefs if they are to count as knowledge, which is not quite as stringent as it seems at first since Russell is here counting inductive inferences as logical. But it also reflects his confidence, as one who seeks to follow a 'scientific method in philosophy', in his new technique of 'logical construction' which he had just introduced in his paper 'The Relation of Sense-Data to Physics' (1914) in the following terms:

The supreme maxim in scientific philosophizing is this: *Wherever possible, logical constructions are to be substituted for inferred entities.* (*Papers* 8, 11)

The technique of logical 'construction' is best thought of from the opposite perspective (top-down, rather than bottom-up) as one of reduction whereby propositions concerning entities of one kind are held to be reducible, given some background theory, to propositions concerning entities of other kinds. A straightforward case was Peano's reduction of propositions concerning rational numbers to propositions concerning sets of natural numbers, which Russell and Whitehead followed in *Principia Mathematica*. Russell now thought he had discovered a comparable way of reducing propositions concerning persisting physical objects to propositions concerning appearances, or sense-data, which Russell now conceives of as themselves physical ('The Relation of Sense-Data to Physics', *Papers* 8, 8). The details of this treatment involve some complex and questionable assumptions which do not matter here; what is important is that the reduction (or construction) is intended to vindicate knowledge of the physical world and physical science in particular.

In *POP* Russell had taken the familiar indirect realist view that the physical world is something different in kind from sense-data whose existence can only be 'inferred' as providing the simplest, and thus the best, explanation of the structure of our sense-data (*POP* 36–7). As such, its existence is at best a speculative hypothesis and is, therefore, a matter of probable opinion rather than knowledge (insofar as a distinction between the two is to be drawn). By 'substituting' a logical construction of the physical world, which involves reference only to sense-data, Russell now proposes a phenomenalist (though not idealist) reduction, which makes the legitimation of knowledge of the physical world more straightforward. For, on Russell's new position, such knowledge requires only the legitimacy of a straightforward inductive inference, that further similar sense-data would be observed if certain procedures were followed, instead of the indirect realist's speculative hypothesis.

Thus, the 'logical-analytic method of scientific philosophy' Russell employs in *OKEW* has an epistemological purpose. What is not altogether clear is whether Russell thinks that his method of logical construction can in fact fulfil this purpose. The difficulty concerns 'other minds': Russell takes it that his logical construction of the physical world requires reference to the sense-data of other persons, but he does not offer a logical construction of them. Instead, he treats belief in other minds much as the indirect realist treats belief in physical objects, as a speculative hypothesis which merits assent because it systematises the observed facts concerning behaviour (*OKEW* 96); and he recognises that the familiar argument by analogy for this hypothesis is not conclusive (*OKEW* 93). His conclusion is somewhat equivocal: we have 'good reason to use it as a working hypothesis' (*OKEW* 96), which does not seem to be a way of satisfying his own standard for knowledge, and yet once we accept it 'it enables us to extend our knowledge of the sensible world by testimony' (*OKEW* 96), which it can surely only do if it does itself count as knowledge. As in *POP* Russell finds himself torn between a desire to vindicate our unreflective 'common knowledge' and a desire to provide a logically rigorous ('scientific') account of what we know.

His third extended piece of writing from this period is the text of his 1918 lectures on 'The Philosophy of Logical Atomism' (*Papers* 8, 160–244). Again Russell makes it clear right from the start that his main concern is epistemological. As in *TK*, it is to identify the 'epistemological premises' required to vindicate our claims to knowledge (*Papers* 8, 162), and at the end of the lectures he again brings in his method of logical construction to provide an account of the physical world, which enables us to have knowledge of it, though he now admits that this account is in some respects revisionary, in that it implies that 'all the objects of ordinary life are extruded from the world of what there is' (*Papers* 8, 237). As before, too, he takes it that the accomplishment of this project requires a proper grasp of logic, but what he now stresses much more than before is that logical analysis is itself dependent upon epistemology. The reason for this is that the logical 'atoms' with which logical analysis terminates must be things, particulars, and universals, with which we are acquainted:

All analysis . . . . . depends, in the last analysis, upon direct acquaintance with the objects which are the meanings of certain simple symbols. (*Papers* 8, 173)

So the relationship between logic and epistemology is one of mutual interdependence.

One important development in these lectures is Russell's hesitant adoption of what one might call a 'linguistic' theory of the logical *a priori*. He is clear here that his previous view (cf the passage from *TK* quoted above) that our understanding of logic rests upon acquaintance with logical objects is incorrect (*Papers* 8, 175), and he offers a truth-table exposition of the meaning of the truth-functional logical connectives as an alternative account which is intended to show that there is no need to introduce logical complexity into facts themselves (*Papers* 8, 186–7). There are, however, two important exceptions to this principle: negation and generality – Russell famously defends negative facts as required by his correspondence theory of truth (*Papers* 8, 187–90) and argues in the same way for general facts (*Papers* 8, 206–7). The case of general facts is the more interesting.

Russell's tentative view in *TK* and *OKEW* had been that the only epistemologically fundamental general truths are logical, and these general truths threaten to reintroduce a requirement for logical objects as constituents of the corresponding general facts. Russell, however, heads this off by denying that there are any such general facts of logic. Instead, because the generality of the fundamental propositions of logic is expressed through the use of variables, he now suggests that they are 'in some sense or other like a tautology' (*Papers* 8, 211), though he is unable to provide any details:

> Those are propositions of logic. They have a certain peculiar quality which marks them out from other propositions and enables us to know them a priori. But what exactly this characteristic is, I am not able to tell you. (*Papers* 8, 211)

Despite Russell's hesitation here, it is, I think, plausible to read him as moving, under Wittgenstein's influence, towards a conception of logic as analytic, such that the propositions of logic provide implicit definitions of the logical constants involved (he is a bit less hesitant in suggesting this position in his *Introduction to Mathematical Philosophy* (1919) pp. 214–5, where he alludes specifically to Wittgenstein). Although, perhaps, Russell in this way removes any requirement for general logical facts, he himself recognises that this does not eliminate all general facts, such as that all men are mortal. But concerning their analysis he remarks, in an enigmatic way, that

'I am sure that, although the convenient technical treatment is by means of propositional functions, that is not the whole of the right analysis. Beyond that I cannot go' (*Papers* 8, 208).

When discussing *OKEW*, I mentioned Russell's difficulty concerning knowledge of other minds. In his 1918 lectures he proposes a logical construction of persons comparable to his construction of the physical world (*Papers* 8, 239–40), but it is not clear how far this new construction helps with the epistemological issue since others are to be constructed from their own experiences, not from our experiences 'of' them. And there is a different point where the issue of radical privacy arises sharply: namely, where Russell confronts the implication of founding his theory of understanding on each individual's acquaintance. He recognises that a 'logically perfect language' which makes explicit the names for simple objects would be 'very largely private to one speaker' (*Papers* 8, 176), because these objects are themselves private. But he suggests that the infirmity of such a language does not imply that we cannot use our ordinary language for our ordinary purposes of communication, because, unlike the words of a logically perfect language, those of an ordinary language are 'ambiguous', and can therefore be used by different speakers with different meanings while they are still true of the same objects (*Papers* 8, 174). It is obvious that the doctrine of 'knowledge by description' is implicit here, and the objections that I raised earlier to its application in *POP* apply equally here. Communication requires the ability of speakers to understand each other; but such an ability is precluded by Russell's doctrine that understanding is founded upon acquaintance, at least as he then conceives it. So the way in which Russell's philosophy of language in his lectures on 'The Philosophy of Logical Atomism' depends upon his epistemology implies that the resulting conception of language, and thus of thought, is an essentially private one. Russell's epistemology still imprisons the mind within its own private limits.

III

Soon after delivering these lectures in early 1918 Russell was literally imprisoned in Brixton prison for six months on account of his anti-war propaganda. Russell spent these months reading and writing philosophy and emerged with a substantially revised philosophical programme, which he then refined and developed for the rest of his long life. His imprisonment marks his transformation from the familiar author of *Principia Mathematica* to the unfamiliar author of *The Analysis of Mind* and his subsequent writings. The key change is his new determination to bring science into philosophy: metaphysics is to be based upon physics and epistemology upon psychology, and it is in this latter respect that the changes are most far-reaching. So although he retains his commitment to logic ('The business of philosophy, as I conceive it, is essentially that of logical analysis, followed by logical synthesis' – 'Logical Atomism' (1924) *LK* p. 341; *Papers* 9, p. 176), his interest is no longer in logic, but in bringing the rest of philosophy into line with the sciences, with physics and psychology in particular.

My concern here is with Russell's epistemology; so what I shall be primarily discussing is the way in which he radically revises his conception of this subject as he thinks through the implications of adopting a scientific understanding of our cognitive capacities, as he embarks upon the enterprise of 'naturalising epistemology' (as Quine was later to describe his own version of this project). In undertaking this Russell, of course, draws on the psychology of his own time, and he does not altogether free himself from the characteristic assumptions of the epistemology of his earlier writings; furthermore, some aspects of Russell's new epistemology draw on his metaphysics of 'neutral monism' in ways that complicate his position. So in many respects Russell's position differs from that of contemporary 'naturalistic' epistemologists. Nonetheless, I hope to show that Russell sketches out lines of thought that connect directly with contemporary debates and thereby to present the basis for a reevaluation of Russell's later writings, especially *The Analysis of Mind* (1921) and *Human Knowledge: Its Scope and Limits* (1948).

Russell begins *The Analysis of Mind* with a critical discussion of the conception of acquaintance. His critical thoughts on this subject are not altogether new: he had been writing about the matter since 1913 (e.g., in *TK*), having been stimulated by reading William James' posthumous collection *Essays on Radical Empiricism* (1912). In the first two essays (both first published in 1904) 'Does Consciousness Exist?' and 'A World of Pure Experience' James had argued that the traditional metaphysical opposition between mind and matter is a mistake, in that they are really just different conceptualisations of something inherently neutral, which he called 'experience'. Russell took it that because acquaintance typically involves a distinctively mental awareness of something non-mental, it is inconsistent with this 'neutral monism', and he had originally held that this was one reason for rejecting the latter (e.g., *TK* 23). In *AMi*, however, he switches sides and argues that his earlier conception of acquaintance was an illusion; in the following passage he disavows his former self before setting out his new conception of knowledge:

> But I will say . . . that the feeling assumes an ideal of knowing which I believe to be quite mistaken: it assumes, if it is thought out, something like a mystic union of knower and known . . . For my part, I think such theories and feelings wholly mistaken: I believe knowing to be a very external and complicated relation, incapable of exact definition, dependent upon causal laws . . . . (*AMi* 234–5)

Russell's version of neutral monism is founded upon a conception of 'sensations' as supposedly neutral between mind and matter. These sensations are, roughly speaking, the sense-data of his previous doctrines, but now conceived of as capable of forming the basis for logical constructions of both mind and matter. The details and merits of these constructions/reductions do not matter here; what is worth noting in passing is Russell's thesis that his metaphysical monism is consistent with a nomological dualism – in that he holds that the laws of psychology are not reducible to those of physics or vice-versa. In this respect, Russell's position anticipates the kind of non-reductive physicalism propounded by Fodor and others.[5]

What does require attention, however, is the epistemological status of sensations in Russell's new position. For having stated that 'sensations are obviously the source of our knowledge of the world, including our own body' (*AMi* 141), it might seem that his old foundationalist theory is to be reconstructed within a new context. But Russell goes to affirm that his old mistake was precisely to think of sensations as cognitive, whereas in fact 'in itself the pure sensation is not cognitive' (*AMi* 142). So the sense in which sensations are the 'source' of knowledge is to be different from his old conception of knowledge by acquaintance with sense-data, and it would fit with much of Russell's discussion if the interpretation here were merely causal. This fits, for example, the reference to causality in the passage quoted earlier (*AMi* 234–5); and his later account of verification as resting an 'external and causal' relation between the world and our sensations (*AMi* 270). But the matter is not clear, and there are passages in which Russell characterises knowledge as having the kind of inferential structure typical of a foundationalist theory:

> if anything can be known by me outside my biography, it can only be known in one of two ways:
> (1) By inference from things within my biography, or
> (2) By some *a priori* principle independent of experience.
> I do not myself believe that anything approaching certainty is to be attained by either of these methods, and therefore whatever lies outside my personal biography must be regarded, theoretically, as hypothesis. (*AMi* 132; cf. 230)

I think that the best way to fit these points together is to take it that the causal theory applies primarily to knowledge of one's own sensations, to one's 'biography'; and that Russell takes it that once one's beliefs concern other matters (all of which, he holds, are in one way or another reducible to sensations, but not just one's own), knowledge can only be a matter of speculative inference. If this is right, it is disappointing, for Russell's 'external and causal' conception of knowledge could be applied much more widely. But perhaps it is not surprising, in the light of all of Russell's earlier epistemology, that he should retain this traditional indirect account of knowledge of 'the external world'. On one related point, however, Russell does clearly break with the past: whereas knowledge by acquaintance was supposed to provide 'absolute' self-evidence, he now holds that judgments of perception are never absolutely self-evident (*AMi* 265–6); and although he still holds that elementary truths of mathematics and logic are self-evident, their self-evidence has nothing to do with acquaintance, but simply arises from the fact that 'they are concerned with the meanings of symbols' (*AMi* 264).

A further decisive break with the past concerns the treatment of 'propositional attitudes', such as belief. Having abandoned the multiple-relation theory in 1913 in the light of Wittgenstein's criticisms of it, Russell had not subsequently endorsed an alternative position (e.g., in his lectures on the 'Philosophy of Logical Atomism' he contents himself with 'pointing out difficulties rather than laying down quite clear solutions' *Papers* 8, 199). In *AMi*, however, Russell sees that what he needs to do is to break with the relational conception of belief, and replace it with a position derived from Meinong's (actually Twardowski's) tripartite 'act-content-object' conception (*AMi* 16–7). Russell rejects Meinong's 'act' as implying an actor, i.e., a mental subject, and equally argues that the 'object' of belief is extrinsic to it, leaving himself, therefore, with a conception of belief as primarily constituted by a certain 'content'. This content (though ultimately reducible to sensations) is basically constituted by words and images; we can think of it as an indicative sentence, which Russell here calls a 'proposition', whose meaning specifies the object of the belief. The great advantage of this account, as Russell recognises in his 1919 paper 'On Propositions (*Papers* 8, 295–6), is that it provides an easy way of handling false belief without 'objective' falsehoods. The new account requires only a content, e.g., a sentence, which is false.

The context in which Russell first turns to questions of knowledge is that of memory. Although he here introduces the sceptical hypothesis that the world came into existence five minutes ago, complete with all our present 'memories' of earlier times (*AMi* 159), he maintains that it is 'indubitable' that there is knowledge of the past (*AMi* 164). The sceptical hypothesis is, like others, 'logical tenable, but uninteresting' (*AMi* 160). He now explicitly rejects his previous account of this knowledge as acquaintance with the past as such (*AMi* 163), and equally rejects a simple pragmatist account of it in terms of successful practice (*AMi* 165). Instead, he sketches a reliabilist account by comparing memory to a measuring instrument such as a thermometer (*AMi* 181) and then defining the instrument's reliability in terms of an appropriate relationship between a range of stimuli and the responses of the instrument. In the case of memory, the relationship will then be that, over a range of cases, the memory's 'content' should match its cause, and he concludes the discussion by remarking that

These definitions will be found useful, not only in the case of memory, but in almost all questions concerning knowledge. (*AMi* 188)

It is in remarks of this kind that Russell appears to suggest a quite general causal/reliabilist theory of knowledge, despite the residual expression of a more traditional theory quoted earlier. We shall encounter further waverings below.

A reliabilist account of this kind requires some account of what is 'meant' by the sentences which give the content of a belief, and this is the topic to which he next turns. Given his rejection of his old conception of acquaintance, the earlier dependence of understanding and meaning upon acquaintance enshrined in his 'fundamental principle' is no longer appropriate. So although he still alludes to the possibility of a perfect, but private, language in which sensations, the ultimate simples, are named (*AMi* 193), there is now no reason for him to require that all ordinary forms of understanding be grounded in this merely hypothetical language; hence, he is here freed from the theoretical commitment to the privacy of meaning that runs through his earlier writings. In place of his old reliance on acquaintance he now holds that meaning is fixed by use: 'the use of the word comes first, and the meaning is to be distilled out of it by observation and analysis' (*AMi* 197). Further, this 'distillation' is a matter of identifying the causes and effects of the use: so 'The relation of a word to its meaning is of the nature of a causal law governing our use of the word and our actions when we hear it used' (*AMi* 198). Thus, causation straightforwardly replaces acquaintance in Russell's philosophy of language.

All this emphasis on causality raises the question of Russell's general conception of mental states in *AMi*. Russell is engaged throughout the book in a complex debate concerning Watson's behaviourism (as represented by *Behavior*, New York, 1914) which he had been studying alongside James' neutral monism. He is sympathetic to Watson's 'scientific' approach to psychology and to his scepticism concerning 'consciousness'. But he is also critical of Watson's denial of phenomena such as mental imagery (*AMi* 153–4) and his unwillingness to give a substantial role to mental states such as desires and beliefs. By contrast Russell affirms in the opening sentences of *AMi* the importance of beliefs and desires as mental 'occurrences' (*AMi* 9), and offers extended accounts of their potential causal roles in the explanation of behaviour. So it is not, I think, anachronistic to characterise Russell's position as an early 'functionalist' theory of the mind, although his commitment to a theoretical reduction of mental states to sensations sometimes interferes with the functionalist theory. For example, although he is strongly drawn to an account of beliefs which identifies them by their 'causal efficacy'(*AMi* 244), he rejects this position in favour of one which draws on a specific 'belief-feeling' (*AMi* 240).

Russell's final discussion of knowledge is affected by similar waverings. Drawing on his earlier discussion of memory, he makes a strong case for a reliabilist conception of knowledge but then backs off from it because he judges it unable to accommodate the requirement that the judgments of one who knows be 'appropriate' as well as reliable (AMi 260–1). Instead of discussing how this requirement might be met from within his general approach, however, he turns his attention to the hypothesis that there is some 'intrinsic' criterion of knowledge, such as self-evidence. Not surprisingly, this is rejected and Russell indeed raises the 'problem of the criterion' later made famous by Chisholm[6] (AMi 269). So, having rejected both externalist and internalist accounts of knowledge, he ends up rather weakly offering an account of knowledge as the ideal outcome of processes of verification, conceived of as an 'external and causal' relation (AMi 270). Although this conclusion fits with his earlier doubts about the possibility of knowledge of the external world, it is hard not to feel that at this point Russell simply lost confidence in his project, for his objection to the reliabilist account is not strong and the matter is especially puzzling since he goes on to give a pragmatist account of the value of truth and affirm that issues concerning 'appropriateness' and 'purpose' are, indeed, 'a vital part of the theory of knowledge' (AMi 278).

The explanation for Russell's hesitation, I think, is that he regards the reliabilist account of knowledge as behaviourist (AMi 254), and he rejects behaviourism. If this is right, it indicates that at this early stage in his development of a new position, he has not seen that a reliabilist account can be detached from behaviourism, and, indeed, fits better with the non-behaviourist treatment of desire and belief that he offers. Yet, despite his hesitations, the positive account of knowledge that emerges from the book is a reliabilist one, though it was left to Ramsey to unequivocally formulate and affirm a position of this kind in his 1929 note on 'Knowledge'[7] (it is unclear how far Ramsey was aware that he was here making explicit a theme from AMi, to which he does not refer; but in another paper in the same collection he writes 'My pragmatism is derived from Mr. Russell' (p. 155), and this can only be an allusion to AMi).

IV

Russell begins An Outline of Philosophy (1928) by advancing an externalist conception of knowledge rather more confidently: 'we shall do well to begin our philosophical journey by an attempt to

understand knowing as part of the relation of man to his environment' (*OOP* 15); and in a chapter entitled 'Knowledge Behaviouris-
tically Considered' he sets out a reliabilist/pragmatist account of
knowledge similar to that suggested in *AMi* (including again the thermometer analogy – *OOP* 92). That chapter occurs in a part of the book
entitled 'Man From Without'. But this is balanced by another part entitled 'Man From Within', and here Russell reintroduces, along with
his neutral monism, his emphasis on the epistemic priority of our
knowledge derived from our own sensations or 'percepts' as he now
calls them (*OOP* 139, 224–5). As in *AMi* Russell does not manage to
bring these two points of view ('From without'/'From Within') into
harmony. If anything it is the second, internalist, perspective that
is now given priority and taken to provide a corrective to the first,
externalist, one (*OOP* 306).

In his *Inquiry into Meaning and Truth* (1940), a similar tension,
and priority, is apparent. Russell again begins the book by sketching
a reliabilist account of knowledge (*IMT* 12–14), but then remarks:

Within its limitations, theory of knowledge of the above sort is legitimate
and important. But there is another kind of theory of knowledge which goes
deeper and has, I think, much greater importance. (*IMT* 14)

This second kind is induced by sceptical arguments and reflection on
the indirect structure of our perception of the familiar objects of the
external world. This leads us into a 'critical scrutiny of what passes
as knowledge' (*IMT* 15), which takes us back to 'basic propositions':

We thus arrive at the momentary object of perception as the least questionable thing in our experience, and as therefore the criterion and touchstone
of all other certainties and pseudo-certainties. (*IMT* 151)

At this point it is clear that the second type of theory of knowledge
is traditional epistemology with a foundationalist structure and all
the familiar problems to which this gives rise. Despite the interest
of some of Russell's discussions in *IMT*, it is hard not to feel that he
here regresses to a position similar in essence to that of *POP*. The
new ways of thinking about epistemology, including about critical
questions, introduced by *AMi* seem to have been set aside.

In his last major work *Human Knowledge: Its Scope and Limits*
(1948), however, Russell returns to these new ways of thinking in the
course of a long discussion of inductive inference – a topic discussed
in *POP* but only marginally thereafter. The context from which he

starts is provided by the traditional doctrines we have just encountered, to the effect that knowledge has a foundational structure involving certain basic 'matters of fact' and principles of inference (*HK* 171). The basic matters of fact 'of which, independently of inference, we have a right to feel most certain' (*HK* 186) concern, Russell says, sensations and memory, and are all essentially private. So sceptical solipsism is a serious threat, and can only be rejected by arguments which establish principles of inference that enable us to justify our ordinary common sense and scientific beliefs (*HK* 197).

So far Russell is still trapped within his old habits of thought. But as he reflects on these principles of inference and their status he breaks with his past. He recognises that these principles cannot themselves be established by experience and must, therefore, be *a priori*. But the key step he takes in *HK* is to introduce a new type of *a priori* principle alongside the traditional necessary truths of reason: the new type is to be contingent and our belief in it is to be susceptible of a causal explanation but not of a rational justification (I shall call these 'strong' and 'weak' a priori truths, respectively.)

Deductive logic is strongly *a priori*, but it can never licence inference from one matter of fact to another, and it is precisely inferences of this latter type that are at issue. Such inferences are typically inductive, and his position in *POP* had been that these are licensed by a fundamental principle concerning probable inference which, though not deductive, is also strongly *a priori* (though not absolutely self-evident in the manner of the elementary truths of logic). Russell now argues (*HK* 422) that there is no fundamental inductive principle which can count as a 'logical' principle, and since for him logic and mathematics are the only strong *a priori* truths there are, it follows that the principle(s) governing inductive inference must be weakly *a priori*. His reason for denying that induction is a matter of logic is that it is only too easy to construct counterexamples to any proposed general inductive principle by selecting or constructing predicates that are not 'projectible', to use Nelson's Goodman's term (which is appropriate since Russell's discussion of this point is entirely comparable to Goodman's famous 'paradox'[8]). Hence, he concludes,

scientific inferences, if they are in general valid, must be so in virtue of some law or laws of nature, stating a synthetic property of the actual world, or several such properties. The truth of any propositions asserting such properties cannot be made even probable by any argument from experience, since such arguments, when they go beyond hitherto recorded experience, depend for their validity upon the very principles in question.

It remains to inquire what those principles are, and in what sense, if any, we can be said to know them. (*HK* 436)

We need not concern ourselves with the principles which Russell identifies; what concerns us is the sense in which 'we can be said to know them'. Russell's answer to this is now unequivocally causal and reliabilist: habits and expectations which have been produced in such a way that they match causal connections within the world count as knowledge (*HK* 445–6). Thus, he is here content to ascribe such knowledge to animals and to explain their possession of this knowledge in evolutionary terms. Where we humans differ from other animals is in our capacity to reflect on the inferences which enter into our expectations and to formulate explicit principles of inference; this capacity enables us to have explicit, conceptual knowledge, where other animals have only implicit practical knowledge. But it remains the case that our knowledge of these principles, and our knowledge of all matters which draws upon them, is grounded in *the facts* that the practice of inference in accordance with them is a generally reliable method of acquiring true beliefs and that the practice has itself developed because it is a reliable method. Russell sums up his discussion as follows:

Owing to the world being such as it is, certain occurrences are sometimes, in fact, evidence for certain others; and owing to animals being adapted to their environment, occurrences which are, in fact, evidence of others tend to arouse expectations of those others. By reflecting on this process and refining it, we arrive at the canons of inductive inference. These canons are valid if the world has certain characteristics which we all believe it to have . . . .

I think, therefore, that we may be said to "know" what is necessary for scientific inference . . . . (*HK* 514–5)

I shall not attempt to assess the merits of this account of inductive inference, which was of course anticipated by Ramsey.[9] Russell presents it, slightly ironically, as a limit to empiricism because it offers a new, naturalistic, category of the *a priori* (what I have called the 'weak' *a priori*) and the status Russell gives to his 'canons of inductive inference' bears comparison with the status Wittgenstein gives to his 'Moorean propositions' in *On Certainty*.[10] What is most important in the present context, however, is Russell's recognition here that there is a form of knowledge by causation – a form of non-inferential knowledge whose characterisation as such depends not on perception or memory or rational insight, but upon causation. Furthermore, instead of just acknowledging this as a possible way of thinking about the matter when one is thinking about 'Man from without' which will have to be discarded once one embarks upon the serious business of critical epistemology, Russell here grasps that he needs to use this causal conception of knowledge within his critical epistemology. It provides him with an account of the validity of inductive inference, which avoids both the circularity inherent in empiricist accounts and the counter-examples inherent in the rationalist account he had earlier espoused. So, at the end of his last major work of philosophy Russell recognises the merits of the conception of knowledge by causation he had sketched out nearly thirty years earlier in *AMi*.

NOTES

1. cf. M. Dummett *Frege Philosophy of Language* (Duckworth, London 1973) ch. 19.
2. cf. G. Evans *The Varieties of Reference* (Clarendon, Oxford 1982) ch. 4
3. cf. E. Gettier 'Is Justified True Belief Knowledge?' *Analysis* 23 (1963) 121–3.
4. cf. G. Berkeley *Three Dialogues between Hylas and Philonous* ed. R. Woolhouse (Penguin, London 1988) p. 149.
5. e.g. J. Fodor 'Special Sciences' *Synthese* 28 (1974) 298–319.
6. R. Chisholm *Theory of Knowledge* (Prentice-Hall, Englewood Cliffs 1966) ch. 4.
7. Published posthumously in *The Foundations of Mathematics* (Routledge & Kegan Paul, London 1931) 258–9.
8. 'The New Riddle of Induction' in *Fact, Fiction and Forecast* (Bobbs-Merrill, Indianapolis 1955) ch. 3.
9. cf 'Truth and Probability' (1926) published posthumously in *The Foundations of Mathematics* (Routledge & Kegan Paul, London 1931) esp. 196–8.
10. cf. L. Wittgenstein *On Certainty* (Blackwell, Oxford 1969). Of course there are important differences, especially Wittgenstein's hostility to the suggestion that scientific explanations can have any role in philosophy.

14 Russell, Experience, and the Roots of Science

I

Empiricism is the family of theories which in one or another may locate the source or, at very least, the test of contingent knowledge in experience – specifically, in sensory experience. More circumstantially, it is the family of theories which variously require experiential grounds for concepts to have content or applicability, or for expressions in a given language to have sense. In these versions of a formulation, due allowance is made for the thought that the content of perceptual states, suitably construed, are to be considered the occasion or basis for certain kinds of fundamental judgments from which, together with other premises, our less fundamental judgments about the world (or things other than the content of those states of sensitivity themselves) can be inferred.

In a qualified sense of this broadly characterised position, Russell was an empiricist, and his epistemology remained, in that qualified sense, empiricist throughout its development. But he was also critical of certain forms of empiricism, and the focus of his own concerns were such that his aims in formulating epistemological views, and his evolving attempts to realise these aims in detail, are not straightforwardly traditional. The chief reason for this is that his overarching concern was the question of how science is related to subjective experience, beginning (in the work done in 1911–14) with attempts to show how the fundamental concepts of physics can be derived from experience, and ending (in 1948) by shifting attention to the question of the non-empirical features of knowledge-acquisition required for bridging the gap between experience and science.

449

In these aims for epistemology Russell was remarkably consistent throughout the period 1911–48, which is to say, from the time he finished work on the first edition of PM until his last major philosophical book, HK. His concern was not the traditional epistemological one of showing that knowledge is justified by experience, where this task is typically specified by a response to sceptical arguments. Russell was thoroughly Lockean in his attitude to the theory of knowledge, in the sense that he did not think scepticism a serious option, and, therefore, did not waste time attempting to rebut it.

This last point might not, on the face of it, be obvious. In the cluster of texts addressing the question of the experience–science relation in the immediate post-PM period, Russell describes his aim as showing how physics is 'verified' by observation and experiment – by which he meant: having its predictions confirmed by these means. Given that all that can be directly observed are the data of sense, he saw the question as one of explaining the correlation of the contents of the physical world with the data of sensory experience by which they are alone verifiable.[1] But he did not put the point by saying that *claims* about the content of the physical world are verified (still less justified) by sensory experience; and this is neither an accidental nor a merely historically conditioned trick of formulation. It is a feature of robust realism not to construe the point of epistemology as being the justification of knowledge-claims, but as being an explication of the relation between what the claims are about and the nature of experience. 'Justifying science by grounding it in experience' and 'showing how physics succeeds in being an empirical science, based on observation and experiment' are two different aims, and Russell's was the latter.

It is true that in POP, which gives the outlines of Russell's early view in popular form, the project begins by adopting the Cartesian air of a justificatory, scepticism-rebutting enterprise. The same is also true of the discussion in IMT and Russell's replies in Schilpp. This was because Russell saw the principal task of showing how experience and science relate as the obverse of the coin whose reverse is the more familiar form of discussion in which experience is invoked as the ground of knowledge, so that one could get to the main concern by either route – and taking the more familiar route has its conveniences. But because Russell assumed throughout that science is (or at least is on the way to discovering) the truth about the world (and his considered views consistently respected this assumption), he did not see epistemology's primary task to be the defence of science against doubt, but instead the demonstration of how finite human subjectivity acquires knowledge of the objective reality which science describes. In showing this, it also shows that the degree of certainty possible in contingent knowledge is less than absolute. In this sense, Russell was happy to concede something to scepticism without being much troubled by it; after all – so in effect he thought – what else is to be expected from contingent empirical knowledge.

A closely allied point is that in the earlier phases of his endeavour Russell saw the task of technical philosophy (philosophy conceived as logic; in fact, though, this aspect of Russell's endeavour is more accurately described as metaphysics) as principally being one of showing how the fundamental concepts of science (as he then took them to be) – space, time, causality and matter – can be constructed, and in his view this was a more important and more interesting matter than the epistemological question of how one relatively insignificant fragment of reality – humanity – manages more or less successfully to represent the rest of reality to itself. It is easy to overlook the fact that these two of Russell's tasks – the logical construction of the then-conceived fundamental scientific concepts, and the question of how finite subjective experience connects with scientific knowledge – are different, although of course they impinge upon one another at most points. But Russell's attention came rapidly to focus almost exclusively on the epistemological task to which the larger part of his strictly philosophical writings after 1911 were addressed.

What changed over time in Russell's thought after 1911 was not his epistemological aim, but the strategies he successively adopted to try to achieve it. Perhaps, because science itself dramatically altered the question of which concepts are fundamental to it (space and time had become space–time in Einstein's theories, and matter had vanished in the wake both of them and quantum theory), Russell ceased to look for a logical construction of these specific concepts. Indeed, he abandoned the logical constructivist programme long before the likes of Carnap and Goodman attempted them, and before Wisdom had shown that getting the world out of sense-data without residue is impossible.[2]

The continuities and developments in Russell's relation-of-sense-to-science project are well displayed as the similarities and contrasts between his description of the project's aims, and of the methods to be employed in carrying it out, in the 1911–14 writings and HK in 1948. Commentators generally take at face value Russell's own claim, in MPD, that in AMi (1921) he abandoned not just the nomenclature of the sense-datum theory but what it was trying to achieve; and this is taken among other things to mark a more expressly 'neutral monist' turn as the metaphysical basis of his epistemological efforts until, in his very late work, another and final shift of perspective occurs, this time away from efforts to carry out the original project and towards the task of identifying the non-empirical supplements which, by that stage, he saw as the chief interest in discussing the bridge over the experience–science gap. But in fact it can be shown that despite the asseverations of MPD and the apparent elimination of the subject in AMi (courtesy of Russell's by then further developed conception of the 'neutral monist' stance), the underlying theme of specifying the connections between experience and science remained. Of course, from the period of AMi onward Russell changed the terms of the relation at issue dramatically; acquaintance vanished, and was replaced (to begin with) by 'noticing' (experiential salience) and successor conceptions. Acquaintance and the subject seemed to go so intimately together that their departure appeared jointly necessary; but it is no surprise to find the epistemic subject still in view in HK, having been merely in disguise in the interim.

The purpose in what follows is accordingly to illustrate, by way of an account of the development of Russell's project, the remarkable consistency of aim it displays. I do this by tracing the project's history, chiefly to establish an accurate characterisation of it, but also to provide a corrective to the impression that in epistemology Russell merely offered a sequence of ad hoc moves in response to a problem which has since been understood, but even then was already beginning to be recognised, as misconceived, viz. the endeavour to erect a justificatory theory of knowledge on the flawed Cartesian grounds of deriving certainty from the private data of experience. But to repeat: Russell's task was, interestingly and significantly, different from that; he did not see epistemology as a justificatory enterprise aimed at refuting scepticism, but as a descriptive enterprise aimed at explaining the fact (which he did not question) that finite subjects attain scientific knowledge. He was, thus, a naturalist long before Quine or anyone else, despite rightly insisting, as later naturalists did not, that one cannot premise epistemology in science;[3] and he was far more consistent in his aims and principles than most (agreeing with Charles Broad) have allowed.

Certain corollaries attend the picture I offer. One is that Hylton misdescribes Russell's turn to epistemological themes after PM as involving 'considerable concessions to psychologism'.[4] Whatever else the label means, 'psychologism' is at least the view that the objects of acquaintance and judgment (to use period Russellian terms for the purpose) cannot themselves be described independently of features attaching to them as a result of the psychological conditions of their apprehension. This is never Russell's claim, and indeed anything like it was expressly disavowed in his pre-PM flight from idealism.[5] Post-PM Russell was realist to excess, rather than psychologistic, in allowing a wider range of objective targets of acquaintance than a traditional empiricist would allow, embracing as it did both physical particulars and abstract entities of various kinds. So much is familiar. And this is not to deny that Russell's interests lay in connecting the content of psychological states (mental states of the subject-relatum in acquaintance and judgment) with the independent objects such states brought into the subject's ken. After all, it was the 'transition from sense to science' as he still called it at the end of his philosophical life (MPD 153) that was his focus, and this requires addressing the question of what and how much the psychological states of epistemic subjects can be said to give them of objective scientific truth.

A corollary of the consistency thesis which I here argue on Russell's behalf is that the celebrated derailment of Russell's project in TK, ascribed to Wittgenstein as a result of some (characteristically hyperbolic) remarks by Russell in a letter to Lady Ottoline Morrell, might not be quite what it seems; for in a footnote added to the text of 'On Knowledge by Acquaintance and Knowledge by Description' when this 1911 essay was reprinted in ML in 1917, Russell remarks of his multiple relation theory of judgment, 'I have been persuaded by Mr. Wittgenstein that this theory is somewhat unduly simple, but the modification which I believe it to require does not affect [its fundamentals].' The same point occurs more fully in PLA where Russell discusses the difficulties faced by the theory involving subordinate 'verbs'. He subsequently, somewhat without fanfare, abandoned the theory; but it is clear from the fact that he continued to the end with the larger project of clarifying the experience–science connection that he found his multiple relation theory of judgment to be inessential to it; and, therefore, the fact that Russell dismembered TK and left some parts of it unused is not the same as his abandoning the project in whose working out TK was a chapter.

II

A good way to begin is to observe the images Russell employs early and late in preparing readers for the epistemological task as he conceived it. In the Preface to HK, he observes that the terms 'belief', 'truth', 'knowledge', and 'perception' all have imprecise common uses which will require progressive clarification as the enquiry proceeds. 'Our increase of knowledge, assuming that we are successful, is like that of a traveller approaching a mountain through a haze: at first only certain large features are discernible, and even they have indistinct boundaries, but gradually more detail becomes visible and edges become sharper.' Compare this to what Russell says in TK of the ambiguities of the words 'experience', 'mind', 'knowledge', and 'perception': "The meanings of common words are vague, fluctuating, and ambiguous, like the shadow thrown by a flickering street-lamp on a windy night; yet, in the nucleus of this uncertain patch of meaning, we may find some precise concept for which philosophy requires a name' – which, Russell concludes, should best be the common expressions themselves, made suitably definite. Imagery aside, part of the method of both early and late epistemology is thus characterised as the same: clarification of concepts, on one familiar view the central task of analysis characteristic of 'analytic philosophy'. But Russell also took the view that analysis is only the propaedeutical part of the story; more important (so he early believed and hoped) was the constructive task of showing how complexes of various kinds – and not least, knowledge of complexes – can be constructed out of simples – early on, the simples with which we are acquainted. The constructive task is the one which ended in failure, and the changes in Russell's epistemology are a direct function of the difficulties met with in the course of the project, which he increasingly saw as insurmountable. The hope had been to couple analysis and synthesis, the first activity preparing the way for the second, reflecting Russell's early ambition, formed on a walk one day in Berlin in the 1890s, to link abstract and scientific knowledge into a grand synthesis.

The synthetic task failed, but one thing which did not change was the aim subserved by the method developed to carry it out. In TK, Russell plunges straight into the task of analysing acquaintance, which he calls 'the simplest and most pervading aspect of experience', a dyadic relation (an important point, for cognate polyadic relations of higher-order constitute something significantly different, namely, judgments) between a 'mental subject' and what turned out to be the catholically conceived objects of its attitudes. This was to fulfil a promise implicit in the outline of a programme given in March 1911 in three lectures: the Aristotelian Society address 'Knowledge by Acquaintance and Knowledge by Description' (Papers 6, pp. 148–61), and two lectures delivered in Paris, 'Le Realisme Analytique' (Papers 6, pp. 133–46) and "L' importance philosophique de la logistique' (Papers 6, pp. 33–40). In the first of these latter he reasserts his commitment to realism both in epistemology and as regards universals, and outlines the technique of analysis of complex into simples to which he there first applies the name 'logical atomism'. In that and the companion lecture he launches the work characteristic of the 1911–14 period, worked out in most detail in a series of papers – 'On Matter' (1912) (Papers 6, pp. 80–95), 'The Relation of Sense-Data to Physics' (RSDP) and 'On Scientific Method in Philosophy' (1914) (Papers 8, pp. 57–73), and 'The Ultimate Constituents of Matter' (1915) (Papers 8, pp. 75–86) – the three latter are reprinted in ML – whose chief precipitate constitutes OKEW (1914).[6] Notoriously, the project was first planned to result in TK; but the difficulties over the theory of judgment obliged Russell to dismantle the task into what he doubtless hoped would be more manageable components.

The project is sketched in a letter from Russell to Ottoline Morrell in October 1912. 'The sort of thing that interests me now is this: some of our knowledge comes from sense, some comes otherwise; what comes otherwise is called "a priori". Most actual knowledge is a mixture of both. The analysis of a piece of actual knowledge into pure sense and pure a priori is often very difficult, but almost always very important.'[7] Russell had chosen both parts of the task: to trace the transition from sense to science, and to isolate the a priori elements of the latter and to axiomatise them, as a preparation for defining the central concepts (space, time, causality, and matter itself). Arguably, the epistemological task came to seem pressing to Russell for the two reasons that whereas, at the outset, the business of defining the fundamental concepts of physics appeared to be a straightforward parallel to defining the fundamental concepts of arithmetic, it quickly transpired that the relation of sense to science was not easy to carry out and, moreover, that it was a necessary preliminary to completing the task of logically constructing the concepts of physics from whatever primitive concepts could be discovered in the then fundamental areas of physics, electrodynamics, and classical mechanics, together with the relations among them. The reason for the latter is that the empirical content of the primitives requires that they themselves be constructible from sensory experience, as required by the principle that everything we know must be anchored at last in acquaintance.

Russell accordingly deferred the attempt to construct science's central concepts to deal with the epistemological questions first. It is instructive to see how these, in their own right, came to seem to him problematic, given that his first sketch of them (in POP) was an optimistic one, in that it canvassed the traditional questions about the relation of experience to knowledge with a robust acceptance of the fallibility of such knowledge, and the presence in it of assumptions or principles themselves neither independently testable nor matters of logic alone.

III

In POP Russell introduced the label 'sense-data' to designate what is immediately known in sensation: particular instances in perceptual awareness of colours, sounds, tastes, smells, and textures, each class of data corresponding to one of the five sensory modalities. Not only must sense-data be distinguished from acts of sensing them, they must also be distinguished from objects in space outside us with which we suppose them associated. Russell's primary question therefore was: what is the relation of sense-data to these objects?

Russell was not, as noted, concerned to address scepticism. His tack was to say that although sceptical arguments are strictly speaking irrefutable, there is nevertheless 'not the slightest reason' to suppose them true (POP2 p 17). Instead, he assembles persuasive considerations in support of the view that having sense-data provides access to reasonable knowledge of things in space. First, we can take it that our immediate sensory experiences have a 'primitive certainty'. We recognise that when we register sense-data, which we naturally regard as associated with, say, a table, we have not said everything there is to be said about the table. We think, for example, that the table continues to exist when we are not perceiving it, and that the same table is publicly available to more than one perceiver at a time. This makes it clear that a table is something over and above the sense-data that appear to any given subject of experience. But if there were no table existing independently of us in space, we should have to formulate a complicated hypothesis about there being as many different seeming-tables as there are perceivers, and explain why nevertheless all the perceivers talk as if they were perceiving the same object.

But note that on the sceptical view, as Russell points out, we ought not even to think that there are other perceivers either, for if we cannot refute scepticism about objects, we are as badly placed to refute scepticism about other minds.

Russell short-circuits the difficulty by accepting a version of the argument to the best explanation. It is simpler and more powerful, he argues, to adopt the hypothesis that, first, there are physical objects existing independently of our sensory experience, and, secondly, that they cause our perceptions and therefore 'correspond' to them in a reliable way. Following Hume, Russell regards belief in this hypothesis as 'instinctive'.

To this, he argues, we can add another kind of knowledge, namely, *a priori* knowledge of the truths of logic and mathematics. Such knowledge is independent of experience, and depends only on the self-evidence of the truths known. When perceptual knowledge and *a priori* knowledge are conjoined, they enable us to acquire general knowledge of the world beyond immediate experience, for the first kind of knowledge gives us empirical data and the second permits us to draw inferences from it.

These two kinds of knowledge can each be further divided into subkinds, described by Russell as immediate and derivative knowledge, respectively. He gives the name 'acquaintance' to immediate knowledge of things. The objects of acquaintance include particulars, that is, individual sense-data (and perhaps ourselves), and universals. Derivative knowledge of things Russell calls 'knowledge by description', which is general knowledge of facts made possible by combination of and inference from what we are acquainted with.

Immediate knowledge of truths Russell calls 'intuitive knowledge', and he describes the truths so known as *self-evident*. These are propositions which are just 'luminously evident, and not capable of being deduced from anything more evident'. For example, we just *see* that '$1 + 1 = 2$' is true. Among the items of intuitive knowledge are reports of immediate experience; if I simply state what sense-data I am now aware of, I cannot (barring trivial slips of the tongue) be wrong.

Derivative knowledge of truths consists of whatever can be inferred from self-evident truths by self-evident principles of deduction.

Russell concedes that despite the appearance of rigour introduced by the availability of *a priori* knowledge, we have to accept that ordinary general knowledge is only as good as its foundation in the 'best explanation' justification and the instincts which render it plausible. Ordinary knowledge amounts at best, therefore, to 'more or less probable opinion'. But when we note that probable opinions form a coherent and mutually supportive system – the more coherent and stable the system, the greater the probability of the opinions forming it – we see why we are entitled to be confident in them.

An important feature of Russell's theory concerns space, and particularly the distinction between the all-embracing public space assumed by science and the private spaces in which the sense-data of individual perceivers exist. Private space is built out of the various visual, tactual, and other experiences which a perceiver co-ordinates into a framework with himself at the centre. But because we do not have acquaintance with the public space of science, its existence and nature is a matter of inference.

IV

Thus, Russell's first version of a theory of knowledge, and, moreover, because its chief outlines are found in POP, is the one most familiarly associated with his name. But he was by no means content with the expression of it in POP, which after all was a popular book and did not essay a rigorous exposition of its theses. The technical papers TK and OKEW which followed were his considered versions of these same questions, and marked an advancement over this first sketch. One difference between the theories of POP and OKEW is that Russell had come to see that the experiencing subject's basis for knowledge – the sense-data that appear to him alone, and his intuitive knowledge of the laws of logic – is insufficient as a starting point. He accordingly placed greater weight on an experiencer's memories and his grasp of spatial and temporal relations holding among the elements of occurrent experience. The subject is also empowered to compare data, for example as to differences of colour and shape. Ordinary common beliefs, and belief in the existence of other minds, are still excluded.

This appeal to an enriched conception of cognitive capacities required at the foundations of knowledge is almost invariably made by empiricist epistemologists – consider Locke and Ayer also – when the thin beams of sensory experience and inference are found, as they invariably are, to be insufficient to bear the weight of knowledge.

With this enriched basis of what he now called 'hard data' Russell reformulated the question to be answered, thus: 'can the existence of anything other than our own hard data be inferred?' His approach was first to show how we can construct, as a hypothesis, a notion of space into which the facts of experience – both the subject's own and those he learns by others' testimony – can be placed. Then, to see whether we have reason for believing that the spatial world is real, Russell gives an argument for believing that other minds exist, because if one is indeed entitled to believe this, then one can rely on the testimony of others, which, jointly with one's own experience, will underwrite the view that there is a spatial (a real) world.

This strategy is ingenious. In 'The Relation of Sense-Data to Physics' Russell adds an equally ingenious way of thinking about the relation of sense-experience to its objects. In POP he had said that we infer the existence of physical things from sense-data; now he describes them as functions of or 'constructions' out of sense-data. This employs the technique of logic in which a thing of one (more complex) kind can be shown to be analysable into things of another (simpler) kind. Russell was here relying on what he called the 'supreme maxim of scientific philosophising', namely, the principle that 'wherever possible, logical constructions are to be substituted for inferred entities.' Concordantly with this principle, physical objects are to be analysed as constructions out of sense-data – but not out of actual or occurrent sense-data only, but out of possible sense-data too. For actual and possible sense-data Russell coined the term 'sensibilia' by which is meant 'appearances' or, in Russell's phrase, 'how things appear', irrespective of whether they constitute sense-data currently part of any perceiver's experience. This is intended to explain what it is for an object to exist when not being perceived.

An important aspect of this view, Russell now held, is that sensibilia are not private mental entities, but part of the actual subject matter of physics. They are, indeed, 'the ultimate constituents of the physical world', because it is in terms of them that verification of common sense and physics ultimately depends. This is important because we usually think that sense-data are functions of physical objects, that is, exist and have their nature because physical objects cause them; but verification is only possible if matters are the other way round, with physical objects as functions of sense-data. This theory 'constructs' physical objects out of sensibilia; the existence of these latter therefore verifies the existence of the former.

V

Such was the epistemology Russell developed in the period to 1914. Instead of developing this distinctive theory further, Russell abandoned it. In later work, particularly AMa and HK, he reverted to treating physical objects and the space they occupy as inferred from sense-experience. A number of considerations made him do this. One was his acceptance of the standard view offered by physics and physiology that perception is caused by the action of the environment on our sensory surfaces. 'Whoever accepts the causal theory of perception,' he wrote (AMa p 32), 'is compelled to conclude that percepts are in our heads, for they come at the end of a causal chain of physical events leading, spatially, from the object to the brain of the percipient'. In AMi he gave up talk of 'sense-data', and ceased to distinguish between the act of sensing and what is sensed. His reason for this relates to his acceptance – long in coming, for he had repeatedly resisted it in print – of James's 'neutral monism'.

Another reason for Russell's abandonment of the sensibilia theory was the sheer complexity and, as he came to see it, implausibility of the views he tried to formulate about private and public spaces, the relations between them, and the way sensibilia are supposed to occupy them. He makes passing mention of this cluster of problems in MPD, before there reporting, as his main reason for abandoning the attempt to construct 'matter out of experienced data alone,' that it 'is an impossible programme ... physical objects cannot be interpreted as structures composed of elements actually experienced' (MPD p. 79). This last remark is not strictly consistent with Russell's stated view in the original texts that sensibilia are not, and do not have to be, actually sensed; MPD gives a much more phenomenalistic gloss to the theory than it originally possessed. But it touches upon a serious problem with the theory: which is that it is at least problematic to speak of an 'unsensed sense-datum' which does not even require – as its very name seems *per contra* to demand – an intrinsic connection to perception.

In these early endeavours Russell gave only passing attention to other important questions in epistemology which he later, by contrast, came to emphasise. The concern the kind of reasoning traditionally supposed to be the mainstay of science, namely, nondemonstrative inference. It was some years before Russell returned to consider these questions: the main discussion he gives is to be found in HK, but promissory notes are issued in AMa and IMT.

VI

Acceptance of James's 'neutral monism' was an important turning point. Summarily stated, James's theory is that the world ultimately consists neither of mental stuff, as idealists hold, nor material stuff, as materialists hold, nor of both in problematic relation, as dualists hold, but of a neutral stuff from which the appearance of both mind and matter is formed. By Russell's own account, he was converted to this theory soon after finishing PLA. He had written about James's views in 1914, and rejected them; in PLA itself he was more sympathetic, though still undecided; but finally in a paper entitled 'On Propositions' (1919) he embraced the theory, and used it as a basis for AMi.

The question that seemed key to Russell is whether consciousness is the essence of the mental, given that, in line with traditional views, consciousness is itself taken to be essentially intentional. In light of Russell's difficulties with the multiple relation theory of judgement, it is pointful to remember its partial ancestry in Meinong's view that the intentional relation has at least the three elements of act, content, and object. In accepting neutral monism Russell was abandoning the irreducible assumptions of any such view. First, he says, there is no such thing as the 'act'. The occurrence of the content of a thought is the occurrence of the thought, and there is neither empirical evidence nor theoretical need for an 'act' in addition. Russell's diagnosis of why anyone might think otherwise is that we say, '*I* think so-and-so', which suggests that thinking is an act performed by a subject. But he rejects this, for reasons similar to those advanced by Hume, who held that the notion of the self is a fiction, and that we are empirically licensed to say no more, on occasions of specifying them, than that there are bundles of thoughts.

Secondly, Russell criticises the relation of content and object. Meinong and others had taken it that the relation is one of direct reference, but in Russell's view it is more complicated and derivative, consisting largely of beliefs about a variety of more and less indirect connections among contents, between contents and objects, and among objects. Add to this the fact that, in imagination and non-standard experiences like hallucination, one can have thoughts without objects, and one sees that the content–object relation involves many difficulties – not least, Russell says, in giving rise to the dispute between idealists who think that content is more significant than objects, and realists who think objects are more significant than content. (Russell's use of these labels, although standard, is misleading: we should for accuracy substitute the label 'anti-realist' for 'idealist' here. This is because whereas, at bottom, realism and anti-realism are indeed differing theses about the relation of contents to objects and, thus, are *epistemological* theses, idealism is a *metaphysical* thesis about the nature of the world; namely, that it is ultimately mental in character. This point is frequently missed in philosophical debate, so Russell is in good company.[8]) All these difficulties can be avoided, Russell claims, if we adopt a version of neutral monism.

James argued that the single kind of metaphysically ultimate raw material is arranged in different patterns by its interrelations, some of which we call 'mental' and some 'physical'. He attributed his view to dissatisfaction with theories of consciousness, which in his view are merely the wispy inheritors of old-fashioned talk about 'souls'. He agreed that thoughts exist; what he denied is that they are entities. They are, instead, functions: there is 'no aboriginal stuff or quality of being, contrasted with that of which material objects are made, out of which our thoughts of them are made; but there is a function in experience which thoughts perform, and for the performance of which this quality of being is invoked. That function is *knowing*.[9]

In James's view the single kind of 'primal stuff', as he called it, is 'pure experience'. Knowing is a relation into which different portions of primal stuff can enter; the relation itself is as much part of pure experience as its relata.

Russell could not go along with quite all of this. He thought that James's use of the phrase 'pure experience' showed a lingering influence of idealism, and rejected it; he preferred the use made by others of the term 'neutral-stuff', a nomenclatural move of importance because whatever the primal stuff is, it has to be able – when differently arranged – to give rise to what could not appropriately be called 'experience', for example, stars and stones. But even with this modified view Russell only partially agreed. He thought that it is right to reject the idea of consciousness as an entity, and that it is partly but not wholly right to consider both mind and matter as composed of neutral-stuff, which in isolation is neither; especially in regard to sensations – an important point for Russell, with his overriding objective of marrying sense to physics. But he insisted that certain things belong only to the mental world (images and feelings) and others only to the physical world (everything which cannot be described as experience). What distinguishes them is the kind of causality that governs them; there are two different kinds of causal law, one applicable only to psychological phenomena, the other only to physical phenomena. Hume's law of association exemplifies the first kind, the law of gravity the second. Sensation obeys both kinds and is, therefore, truly neutral.

Adopting this version of neutral monism obliged Russell to abandon some of his earlier views. One important change was abandonment of 'sense-data'. He did this because sense-data are objects of mental acts, which he now rejected; therefore, since there can be no question of a relation between nonexistent acts and supposed objects of those acts, there can be no such objects either. And because there is no distinction between sensation and sense-data – that is, because we now understand that the sensation we have in seeing, for example, a colour-patch *just is* the colour-patch itself – we need only one term here, for which Russell adopts the name 'percept'.

Before accepting neutral monism, Russell had objected to it on a number of grounds, one being that it could not properly account for belief. And as noted, even when he adopted the theory it was in a qualified form; mind and matter overlap on common ground, but each has irreducible aspects. Nevertheless, what at last persuaded him was the fact, as it seemed to him, that psychology and physics had come very close: the new physics both of the atom and of relativistic space–time had effectively dematerialised matter, and psychology, especially in the form of behaviourism, had effectively materialised mind. From the internal viewpoint of introspection, mental reality is composed of sensations and images. From the external viewpoint of observation, material things are composed of sensations and sensibilia. A more or less unified theory therefore seems possible by treating the fundamental difference as one of arrangement: a mind is a construction of materials organised in one way, a brain more or less the same materials organised in another.

A striking feature of this view is, surprisingly, how idealist it is. Russell had, as noted, charged James with residual idealism. But here he is arguing something hardly distinguishable: that minds are composed of sensed percepts – viz. sensations and images – and matter is a logical fiction constructed of unsensed percepts. Now Russell had often insisted (using his earlier terminology) that sensibilia are 'physical' entities, in somewhat the sense in which, if one were talking about an item of sensory information in a nervous system, that datum would be present as impulses in a nerve or activity in a brain. But then nerves and brains, as objects of physical theory, are themselves to be understood as a constructions from sensibilia, not as traditionally-understood 'material substance', the concept of which physics has shown to be untenable. At the end of AMi (pp. 305, 308) Russell accordingly says that 'an ultimate scientific account of what goes on in the world, if it were ascertainable, would resemble psychology rather than physics ... [because] psychology is nearer to what exists'. This explains Russell's notorious claim that 'brains consist of thoughts' and that when a physiologist looks at another person's brain, what he 'sees' is a portion of his own brain (RTC, Papers 11, pp. 36–7).

For robuster versions of materialism this aspect of Russell's view is hard to accept. But it is not the only difficulty with his version of neutral monism. Not least among others is the fact that he failed in his main aim, which was to refute the view that consciousness is essential to the distinction between mental and physical phenomena. He had not of course attempted to analyse consciousness quite away; his aim was rather to reduce its importance to the mind–matter question. But images, feelings, and sensations, which play so central a role in his theory, stubbornly remain *conscious* phenomena, whereas the sensibilia (by definition including unsensed sensa) which constitute the greater part of matter are not. Russell accepted this, but tried to specify a criterion of difference, which did not trade on these facts, namely, the criterion of membership of different causal realms. But whereas that difference is open to question – and even if it exists might be too often hard to see – the consciousness difference is clear-cut. Relatedly, the intentionality which characterises consciousness cannot be left out of accounts of knowledge; memory and perception are inexplicable without it. Russell later acknowledged this point and gave it as a reason in MPD for having to return to the question of perception and knowledge in later writings.

He also later came to abandon the idea – anyway deeply unsatisfactory from the point of view of a theory supposed to be both *neutral* and *monist* – that images and feelings are essentially mental, that is, not wholly reducible to neutral-stuff; for in a very late essay he says, 'An event is not rendered either mental or material by any intrinsic quality, but only by its causal relations. It is perfectly possible for an event to have both the causal relations characteristic of physics and those characteristic of psychology. In that case, the event is both mental and material at once'.[10] This, for consistency, is what he should have argued in AMi itself, where only sensations have this character.

But this view in turn generates another problem, which is that it comes into unstable tension with a view to which Russell returned after AMi; namely, that the causes of percepts are inferred from the occurrence of the percepts themselves. As noted earlier, Russell wavered between treating physical things as logical constructions of sensibilia and as entities inferred as the causes of perception; he held this latter view in POP and returned to it after AMi. But on the face of it, one is going to need a delicate connection between one's metaphysics and one's epistemology in order to hold both that minds and things are of one stuff, and that things are the unknown external inferred causes of what happens in minds. So those parts of the legacy of AMi which remain in his later thinking raise considerable difficulties for his views there about matter.

VII

One of the chief reasons for Russell's reversion to a realistic, inferential view about physical things was the difficulty inherent in the notion of unsensed sensa or, in the later terminology, percepts. As noted above, the idea had been to replace inferred entities with logically constructed ones. If physical things can be logically constructed out of sensibilia, then two desiderata have been realised simultaneously: the theory is empirically based and inferred entities have been shaved away by Ockham's Razor. But it is obvious that the idea of unsensed sensa (or unperceived percepts) is, if not indeed contradictory, at least problematic. It makes sense – although, without a careful gloss, it is metaphysically questionable – to talk of the existence of *possibilities* of sensation; but to talk of the existence of *possible sensations* arguably does not (recall Russell's definition of sensibilia as entities having the 'same metaphysical and physical status as sense-data without necessarily being data to any mind'). If the choice lay between inferred material particulars and non-actual perceptions existing unperceived, it would seem best to accept the former. This is just what Russell himself came to think. But he did not return to the cruder form of inferential realism held in POP; he had something more ingenious – though in the end no more successful – up his sleeve.

Another reason for Russell's reversion to realism was his recognition that the notion of causality is problematic for phenomenalism. Things in the world seem to affect one another causally in ways hard to explain on the mere basis of reports of sense-experience. Moreover, a causal theory of perception is a natural and powerful way of explaining how experience itself arises. In Russell's mature philosophy of science contained in AMa and HK, he did not opt for a Lockean view which says that our percepts resemble their causal origins on the ground that we cannot be directly acquainted with things and, therefore, cannot expect to know their qualities and relations. Rather, he now argued, changes in the world and our perceptions are correlated, or co-vary, at least for orders of things in the world that our perceptual apparatus is competent to register (we do not, for example, perceive electrons swarming in the table, so there is no associated covariation of world and perception at that level). The correspondence between percepts and things is one of *structure* at the appropriate level: 'Whatever we infer from perceptions it is only structure that we can validly infer; and structure is what can be expressed by mathematical logic' (AMa 254). And this means that we have to be 'agnostic' about all but the physical world's mathematical properties, which is what physics describes (ibid 270).

Russell had come to think that the best candidate for what is metaphysically most basic in the world is the 'event'. Objects are constructed out of events in the following way: the world is a collection of events, most of which cluster together around a multitude of 'centres' thus constituting individual 'objects'. Each cluster radiates 'chains' of events, which interact with and react upon chains radiating from other centres – among which are perceivers. When a chain interacts with the events constituting the perceptual apparatus of a perceiver, the last link in the chain is a percept. Since everything is ultimately constituted of events, they are in effect the 'neutral-stuff' of which minds and material things are made. Minds are clusters of events connected by 'mental' relations, not least among them memory; otherwise, there is no metaphysical difference between mind and matter. Finally, the interrelations of event-chains is what scientific causal laws describe.

This view enabled Russell to formulate the argument he had long been trying to state satisfactorily, namely, that percepts are parts of things. For on this view it is not the case that there are events which constitute things, and then in addition other events which are perceptions of those things; rather, there are just events constituting the object, some of which are percepts – these being the terminal events of the chains radiating from the object which interact with events constituting the perceiver.

This theory is inferential not in the earlier sense in which the causes of percepts, lying inaccessibly beyond a veil of perception, are guessed from the nature of the percepts themselves. Rather, the inference is from certain terminal events, viz. percepts – which are interactions between (using the term heuristically) 'mental' events and that level of structure in the rest of the event-world with which the 'mental' events are capable of interacting – to the clusters and chains of events constituting the world as a whole.

In AMa the core of the theory is the idea that knowledge of the world is purely structural. We know the qualities and relations as well as the structure of percepts, but we know only the structure of external events, not their qualities. This seems somewhat reminiscent of Locke's distinction between primary and secondary qualities, but it is not; Russell is saying that all we can infer from our percepts is the structure of the qualities and relations of things, not the qualities and relations themselves; and that this is the limit of knowledge.

This theory has a fatal flaw, which was quickly recognised by the mathematician M.H.A. Newman and set out in an article published soon after the appearance of AMa. It is that since our knowledge of the structure of events is not a mere result of our stipulating them, but is manifestly non-trivial, it follows that our inferential knowledge cannot be limited solely to questions of structure. This is because – to put the point by a rough analogy – a number of different worlds could be abstractly definable as having the same structure, and if they were, knowledge of their structure alone could not separate them and in particular could not individuate the 'real' one. If science genuinely consists of discoveries about the world through observation and experiment, the distinction between what we observe and what we infer cannot, therefore, be collapsed into a distinction between pure structure and qualities. (See Demopoulos's paper in this volume.)

Russell accepted Newman's point: 'You make it entirely obvious that my statements to the effect that nothing is known about the physical world except its structure are either false or trivial, and I am somewhat ashamed not to have noticed it myself.'

VIII

As repeatedly noted, the common thread linking Russell's earlier and later views is the aim of securing the move from perception to the objects of physical theory. On his view, this move must either be inferential, in which it takes us from the incorrigible data of sense to something else, or it is analytic, that is, it consists in a process of constructing physical entities out of percepts. On the later view just reported, the inference has a special advantage over more usual inferential theories, in that the inference is not from one kind of thing to another, but from one part of something to its other parts.

In his earlier views, Russell had accorded primary reality to sense-data and built everything else out of them. On the later view, reality belongs to events as the ultimate entities, and an important change of emphasis was introduced: percepts remain immediate and as certain as anything can be, but they are not construed as having accurately to represent the physical world, which, in the picture offered by science as the most powerful way to understand it, is anyway very different from how it appears.

Crucially, however, there remains a familiar and major problem about whether inferences from perception to the world are secure. A large part of Russell's aim in HK was to state grounds for taking them to be so. Throughout his thinking about the relation of perception and science he was convinced, as his above-quoted remark in the October 1912 letter to Ottoline Morrell shows, that something has to be known independently of experience for scientific knowledge to be possible. Earlier, as noted, he thought that purely logical principles provide such knowledge. But he now saw that logic alone is insufficient; we must know something more substantial. His solution was to say that inference from perception to events is justified in the light of certain 'postulates' which nevertheless state contingent facts about the word. So stated, Russell's view immediately reminds one of Kant's thesis that possession of 'synthetic *a priori* knowledge' is a condition of the possibility of knowledge in general, a view which Russell robustly dismissed in the Preface to HK. The difference is explained by the tentative and probabilistic account that Russell, in this last major attempt to state a theory of knowledge, felt it was all that could be hoped for.

Two features of Russell's approach in HK explain this result. One is that he now thought that knowledge should be understood in 'naturalistic' terms, that is, as a feature of our biological circumstances, taken together with the way the world is constituted. The other is that he had come to make a positive virtue of the fact (which he always otherwise accepted) that contingent knowledge is never certain, but at best merely credible to some degree. This second point enters into the detailed working out of the views in HK. The first makes its appearance whenever Russell needs to justify the justifications which HK attempts to provide for scientific knowledge.

When data have a certain credibility independently of their relations to other data, Russell describes them as having a degree of 'intrinsic' credibility. Propositions having some intrinsic credibility lend support to propositions inferred from them. The chief question then becomes: how do propositions with some measure of intrinsic credibility transfer that credibility to the hypotheses of science? Another way of framing the question is to ask how reports of observation and experiment can function as evidence. This is where Russell's postulates come in.

There are five postulates. The first, 'the postulate of quasi-permanence', is intended to replace the ordinary idea of a persisting thing: 'given any event A, it happens very frequently that, at any neighbouring time, there is at some neighbouring place an event very similar to A'. Thus, the 'things' of common sense are analysed into sequences of similar events. The ancestor of this idea is Hume's analysis of the 'identity' of things in terms of our propensity to take a sequence of resembling perceptions to be evidence for a single thing, as when you have perceptions of a rose bush every time you go into the garden and, therefore, take it that there is a single persisting rose bush there even when no perceivers are present.

The second, 'the postulate of separable causal lines', states that 'it is frequently possible to form a series of events such that, from one or two members of the series, something can be inferred as to all the other members'. For example, we can keep track of a billiard ball throughout a game of billiards; common sense thinks of the ball as a single thing changing its position, which according to this postulate is to be explained by treating the ball and its movements as a series of events from some of which you can infer information about the others.

The third is 'the postulate of spatio-temporal continuity', designed to deny 'action at a distance' by requiring that if there is a causal connection between two events that are not contiguous, there must be a chain of intermediate links between them. Many of our inferences to unobserved occurrences depend upon this postulate.

The fourth is 'the structural postulate', which states that 'when a number of structurally similar complexes are ranged about a centre in regions not widely separated, it is usually the case that all belong to causal lines having their origin in an event of the same structure at the centre'. This is intended to make sense of the idea that there exists a world of physical objects common to all perceivers. If six million people all listen to the Prime Minister's broadcast on the wireless, and upon comparing notes find that they heard remarkably similar things, they are entitled to the view that the reason is the common sense one that they all heard the same man speaking over the airwaves.

The fifth and last is 'the postulate of analogy', which states that 'given two classes of events A and B, and given that, whenever both A and B can be observed, there is reason to believe that A causes B, then if, in a given case, A is observed, but there is no way of observing whether B occurs or not, it is probable that B occurs; and similarly if B is observed, but the presence or absence of A cannot be observed'. This postulate speaks for itself (HK 506–12).

The point of the postulates is, Russell says, to justify the first steps towards science. They state what we have to know, in addition to observed facts, if scientific inferences are to be valid. It is not advanced science which is thus justified, but its more elementary parts, themselves based on common sense experience.

But what is the sense of 'know' here? On Russell's view, the knowing involved in 'knowledge of the postulates' is a kind of 'animal knowing', which arises as habitual beliefs from the experience of interaction with the world and experience in general. It is far from being certain knowledge. 'Owing to the world being such as it is,' Russell says, 'certain occurrences are sometimes, in fact, evidence for certain others; and owing to animals being adapted to their environment, occurrences which are, in fact, evidence of others tend to arouse expectation of those others. By reflecting on this process and refining it, we arrive at the canons of inductive inference. These canons are valid if the world has certain characteristics which we all believe it to have' (HK 514–15). These are the common-sense facts that the postulates in effect embody, and it is in this sense that we 'know' them. They are implied in the inferences we make, and our inferences are by and large successful; so the postulates can be regarded as in a sense self-confirming.

Although Russell thinks of the postulates as something we know *a priori*, it is clear that their status is odd. They are in fact empirical in one sense, since they either record or are suggested by experience. What gives them their *a priori* status is that they are *treated as known* independently of empirical confirmation (except indirectly in practice), rather than as generalisations in need of such justification. In effect, Russell selected some general contingent beliefs which are especially useful to have as premises in thinking about the world, and elevated them to the dignity of postulates. Their indirect justification, in turn, is that on the whole they, or the results of their application, work. Allied to the extremely modest ambition Russell has for epistemology in HK, this might be enough. But it has no pretensions to be a theory of knowledge as traditionally conceived, nor a rigorous account of non-demonstrative reasoning.

These last remarks suggest why Russell's arguments in HK received little response, much to his disappointment. He recognised well enough that canons of evidence and scientific reasoning are worth investigating only if we can be confident that, if we got them right, they would reliably deliver science. But the most that Russell's argument establishes is that, so far, the general principles on which our empirical thinking relies have been largely successful. But this looks like exactly the kind of unbuttressed inductive inference Russell was anxious to caution against, citing the example of the chicken who, on being fed day after day, grew increasingly pleased with the world – until the day the butcher came.

In particular, we have no guarantee against the possibility that use of the postulates leads to falsehood, either occasionally or in some systematic way. Now this possibility is in effect allowed by Russell in asking very little of epistemology. The complaint must therefore be that the argument in HK is in fact an admission of failure, when taken in the light of the epistemological tradition. Descartes and his successors in modern philosophy raised questions about the nature of knowledge and how we get it precisely so that they could distinguish between some enterprises – alchemy, astrology, and magic, say – and others – chemistry, astronomy, and medicine, say – which differ not merely in the number of genuinely practical applications they offer, but in telling us something true about the world; and where, moreover, the latter fact explains the former, and opens the way to more of both by the same route. Moreover, our ancient prejudices and animal beliefs might be controverted in the process, as indeed happens: for the world depicted by science is remarkably different from the world of common sense. But Russell in HK says the utility of applications and those same animal habits of belief are the only final justification we can hope for in epistemology. This is very much less than the project of epistemology traditionally aims to achieve, and it is much less than Russell himself hoped to achieve on first launching his epistemological project after PM.

Russell had charged Kant with a 'Ptolemaic counter-revolution' in the Preface to HK, but it is not clear that HK itself escapes a Ptolemaic tinge. The postulates are expressly not transcendentally necessary framework features in any sense comparable to Kant's categorial concepts, or to any other species of foundational principle. They are in effect rules of thumb, 'distilled' as Russell puts it, from the epistemological pragmatics of common sense, and justified – if that is the right thing to expect them to be – by their manifest utility in scientific enquiry and ordinary life.

Nevertheless, they prompt two thoughts. One is that a solid argument can be given in favour of strengthening postulates of the kind envisaged by Russell into structural conditions of inquiry. For what are in effect temperamental reasons it was not open to Russell to consider investigating, by means of transcendental arguments, what is required for the possibility of the kind of knowledge in which science consists. No doubt the precipitate of something like the postulates would result; and that is a suggestive thought. Such an argument would be in fact Russellian, because it would follow his example in his earlier epistemological work of seeking the logical distribution of the problem, so to speak, as when, in the 1911–14 work, he distinguished what was logically primitive from what was derived from it, and how both parts of this classification related to one another in the structure they formed.

It is, of course, no more than a coincidence, but a remarkable one, that at the time Russell was writing HK, Wittgenstein was coming to not dissimilar conclusions in *On Certainty* – as if they had been travelling different routes and arriving at near-points at the end of the journey. Wittgenstein's late interest in problems of scepticism and knowledge is rather striking in being straightforward workaday philosophy of just the kind he earlier dismissed as fly-in-the-bottle. His interest in epistemology, therefore, looks like acceptance that philosophical problems are real ones after all, amenable to investigation – and even *solution*.[11] His contribution is to insist on the internal connection between the concepts of knowing and doubting and equally to insist that epistemic justification is provided by the conceptual scheme within which talk of knowledge and doubt alone gets content. The similarities between the very late Russell and Wittgenstein lie in the thought that (to put the matter neutrally as between them) a given area of discourse requires that we accept certain things in order to be able to get along in it – the 'grammatical' propositions which key a discourse's sense, in Wittgenstein; the postulates required by inquiry, for Russell. Of course the parallel is not direct, but it is suggestive.

NOTES

1. 'The Relations of Sense-Data to Physics', *ML* p. 145 (*Papers* 8, p. 5).
2. See R. Carnap, *The Logical Structure of the World* (1928), translated by Rolf George (Routledge and Kegan Paul, 1967); N. Goodman, *The Structure of Appearance* (Harvard University Press, 1951); J. Wisdom, 'Logical Constructions', *Mind* (1931–3).
3. See *TK*, pp. 50–2. And see also A.C. Grayling, 'Naturalistic Assumptions' in Kotatko and Orenstein (eds.), *Essays on Quine* (Kluwer, 2000).
4. P. Hylton, *Russell, Idealism, and the Emergence of Analytic Philosophy* (Oxford University Press, 1990), p. 330.
5. See for example *ML* p. 101 (*Papers* 8, p. 59).
6. 'On Matter' was unpublished until *The Collected Papers of Bertrand Russell*; its dating was ascertained by Kenneth Blackwell from his study of the Russell-Ottoline Morrell correspondence.
7. The letter is dated 30 October 1912.
8. See A.C. Grayling, 'Understanding Realism' in M. Marsonet (ed.), *Metaphysics and Logic* (Kluwer, forthcoming).
9. W. James, *Essays in Radical Empiricism* (Longmans, Green, 1912), pp. 3–4.
10. 'Mind and Matter', *Portraits from Memory*, p. 152 (*Papers* 11, p. 292).
11. See A.C. Grayling, 'Wittgenstein on Knowledge and Certainty', in H. Glock (ed.), *Wittgenstein: A Critical Reader* (Routledge, 2001).

15 Bertrand Russell: Moral Philosopher or Unphilosophical Moralist?

I. INTRODUCTION

'I do not myself think very well of what I have said on ethics', wrote Russell in extreme old age (*Dear Bertrand Russell*, p. 132). And most subsequent philosophers have agreed with him. Either they do not think very well of what he said or they do not think of it at all. Until very recently, Russell hardly rated a mention in most books and bibliographies on twentieth-century ethics. His most anthologised paper on the subject is 'The Elements of Ethics' (1910) in which he expounds, not his own ideas, but the ideas of his colleague and sometime friend, G.E. Moore. Even dedicated Russell fans such as John Slater (*Bertrand Russell* (1994)) and Anthony Grayling (*Russell* 1996) are a bit lukewarm about his theoretical ethics, whilst R.M. Sainsbury in his 'Arguments of the Philosophers' book *Russell* (1979), is positively dismissive: 'I have left aside his work on moral philosophy, on the grounds that in both its main phases, it is too derivative to justify a discussion of it'. In the first phase, represented by 'The Elements of Ethics' (1910), Sainsbury suggests that Russell's ideas were derived from G.E. Moore, and in the second, represented by *Human Society in Ethics and Politics*, they were 'close to Hume's, with a dash of emotivism' (Sainsbury 1979, p. x).

In my view this is a consensus of error. In the latter part of this essay I contend:

1) that Russell's 'work on moral philosophy' had at least three, and (depending how you look at it) up to six 'main phases';
2) that in some of those phases, it was *not* derivative, but on the contrary, highly original;

3) that Russell was a pioneer of *two* of the chief forms of ethical anti-realism that have dominated debate in the twentieth century, emotivism and the error theory (so that if the theory of *HSEP* was derived from emotivism, it was derived from a family of theories which Russell helped to create);

4) that the revolt against Hegelianism which led to the birth of Analytic Philosophy, had an ethical dimension to it; and

5) that Russell played an important part in the debates that led up to Moore's *Principia Ethica*, the book, which he summarizes in 'The Elements of Ethics'.

Russell, in other words, was not the ethical non-entity he is widely believed to be, but an ethical theorist to be reckoned with.

II. WHEN IS MORAL PHILOSOPHY NOT MORAL PHILOSOPHY?

But before going on I need to forestall an objection. To some readers, what I have just said may seem absurd, bordering on the insane. How can there be a consensus, albeit a consensus of error, that Russell was not much to write home about as a moral philosopher? What about all those books and articles on moral and political themes from *The Principles of Social Reconstruction* (1916) through *Marriage and Morals* to *Has Man a Future* (1962), books which have continued to sell, in some cases, for over eighty years? Some of this stuff is a little lightweight to be sure. 'Should Socialists Smoke Good Cigars?' is a good question to which Russell supplies a sensible answer ('Yes') but it does not really qualify as philosophy (*Mortals and Others* 1, p. 140). But Russell devoted a lot of serious thought to the kinds of topics that have concerned moral philosophers in the past and it seems odd to deny that this counts as moral philosophy. (After all, it is often classified as such, sometimes by Russell himself!) And *if* this stuff counts, and if one measure of the importance of a philosopher is his influence, then Russell must have been an important moral philosopher. For his influence on his numerous readers, though hard to quantify, has been immense. If it is intellectual calibre which makes the difference, then Russell's moral and political writings are certainly no worse, and in my view rather better than the moral and political writings of, say, Sartre, Nietzsche, or Voltaire. And if *their* writings on power, politics, and morality count as philosophy, which they are generally agreed to do, why not Russell's?

To deal with this objection I need to make some distinctions. Moral philosophy can be divided into three sub-disciplines: metaethics, normative ethics, and practical ethics. Practical or applied ethics, as its name suggests, is a practical affair. It deals with the rights and wrongs of real-world issues; of war and peace, of euthanasia and abortion, of sex, love, and marriage; it deals with social justice, and our obligations (if any) to remote people and to future generations. Practical or applied ethics is itself divided into a number of sub-sub-disciplines, such as environmental ethics, business ethics, bioethics, and political philosophy. Practical ethics is distinguished from ethical theory, which itself has two branches: normative ethics and metaethics. Normative ethics supplies (and criticizes) the premises for practical ethics, by providing 'general principles which help to determine the rules of conduct' as Russell himself puts it (*OOP* p. 180). It deals with such questions as what things are good and bad in themselves and what is the good for human beings. It asks what makes right acts right – are they right because of their beneficial consequences or because they are instances of some virtue? Given that consequences are relevant to determining the value of an action, normative ethics asks whether anything *else* is relevant. A normative theory, therefore, is an attempt to answer such questions: it is often (at any rate) a theory of the right and the good. Metaethics is a more theoretical study still. It deals with the nature and justification for moral judgments. It asks what moral judgments mean and what, if anything, makes them true. A metaethical theory will specify the *truthmakers* for moral judgments, the facts, if any, required to make them true, or perhaps it will deny that moral judgments *have* any truthmakers at all, because (for example) they are neither true nor false. Now, this rough and ready way of dividing up the discipline of moral philosophy is a fairly recent invention, but it can be applied without undue strain to the philosophers of the past. That is, it is often possible to say whether some late great of the subject is doing metaethics, practical ethics, normative ethics, or some combination of the three.

Until about 1920 and since about 1970, practical ethics was regarded as a legitimate branch of philosophy. There are now, and there have been in the past, famous philosophers, such as Jeremy

Bentham and Peter Singer, who have devoted themselves to practical ethics. They did not suppose that they thereby ceased to be *philosophers* or that they had given up philosophy for something else. And though Peter Singer has perhaps had to fight to make practical ethics philosophically respectable, most of his contemporaries (like most of Bentham's contemporaries) have considered him to be a philosopher. But in the intervening years Russell helped to create a more austere conception of the subject, which tended to exclude not only practical ethics, but even normative ethics as beyond the pale of philosophy. 'I should like to exclude all value judgments from philosophy, except that this would be too violent a breach with usage. The only matter concerned with ethics that I can regard as properly belonging to philosophy is the argument that ethical propositions should be expressed in the optative mood, not in the indicative' (RTC, *Papers* 11, p. 47). Russell's exclusive conception of moral philosophy caught on, leading to the sort of situation complained of by Dale Jamieson. During the sixties, John Searle's ethics classes at Berkeley were disrupted by students because Searle (in this respect a good Russellian) wanted to talk about metaethical issues such as deriving 'ought' from 'is' whereas the students (Russellians perhaps, but in a rather different sense) wanted to talk about the rights and wrongs of the Vietnam War (Jamieson ed. (1999) p. 3).

Russell had a reason for this austere policy of exclusion derived from his metaethical opinions. For Russell, philosophy was an *inquiry*, that is, an activity aimed at truth. But from 1913 onwards he ceased to believe that there *were* any ethical truths, or at least that there were any truths about what is good and bad in itself. His dominant view (though as we shall see, he shifted about a bit) was that moral judgments such as 'X is good', or 'Y is bad' are in the optative mood and merely express the desires or the feelings of the speaker. The point of such pronouncements is generally to influence others and, thus, to change the world. Thus, 'X is good' means something like 'Would that everybody desired X!' Obviously such an optative pronouncement is not a candidate for truth. Indeed, it is not the kind of thing that can be true *or* false. Hence, judgments about what is good or bad in itself, which (for Russell) constitute the core or normative ethics, fall outside the domain of philosophy. And since normative ethics provides the premises for practical ethics, practical ethics falls outside the domain of philosophy too. But whether or not moral judgments are really in the optative mood is a question with a true answer, and an answer to be determined by conceptual analysis. So although normative ethics and practical ethics would appear to be excluded, metaethics, which deals with such questions, is safely within the sphere of philosophy. We can sum up Russell by paraphrasing Marx. Philosophers hitherto have attempted to interpret the world in various ways. The point of practical ethics, however, is to change it. Hence, practical ethics is not a branch of philosophy.

But this is a bit swift. For even on Russell's own premises, there are parts of practical ethics that are not extruded from philosophy. Though he wobbled occasionally, Russell was some sort of utilitarian for most of his life. That is, he believed that we ought to do that action which seems likely (given the evidence) to produce the maximum of good and the minimum of evil (where good and evil have something to do with human happiness and misery). But if judgments about good and evil are in the optative mood, does this not mean that judgments about what ought to be done are in the optative mood too? Not necessarily. If we index 'ought' to contextually specified standards it can be a plain matter of fact whether a given action ought to be done. For it can be a plain matter of fact whether a given action is likely to maximize what someone *calls* good and minimize what someone *calls* evil. Of course such 'ought-judgments' will be hypothetical in a certain sense – they will state what ought to be done to realize sombody-or-other's ends – but they can be objectively true for all that. Thus, according to Russell, 'the framing of moral rules, so long as the ultimate Good is supposed known, is a matter for science. For example: should capital punishment be inflicted for theft, or only for murder, or not at all? Jeremy Bentham, who considered pleasure to be the Good, devoted himself to working out what criminal code would most promote pleasure, and concluded it ought to be much less severe than that prevailing in his day. All this, except the proposition that pleasure is the Good, comes within the sphere of science' (*RS*, ch. ix, pp. 228–9; *ROE*, pp. 137–8). However, these rules and the associated ought-judgments will not offer any guidance to people who do not subscribe to the relevant ends. At best, they can have a sort of *ersatz* authority if all or most people can be persuaded to agree on good and evil. And since there are no facts to fall back on here, persuasion will be a rhetorical rather than a rational process. 'Persuasion in ethical matters is necessarily different from persuasion in scientific matters. According to me, the person who judges that A is good is wishing others to feel certain desires. He will therefore ... try to rouse those desires in other people ... This is the purpose of preaching, and it was my purpose in the books in which I have expressed ethical opinions.' (*RTC, Papers* 11, p. 51; *ROE*, p. 149). Preaching, as Russell makes plain, is a legitimate activity, but it is not philosophy. However, that is not quite the end of the matter. For on Russell's own showing, a book on practical ethics can in principle be divided into two parts: the part which consists in preaching, in which the writer advocates certain ends, and the factual or 'scientific' part, in which the moralist argues that his policies are calculated to achieve those ends.[1] Thus, a book on education might preach the gospel of a generation raised in fearless freedom (which would be a constituent of the Good) and suggest a set of strategies to achieve this goal, based on experience, common sense, and educational research (*On Education, Education and the Social Order*). Alternatively a book on Bolshevism might concede the goal of a classless society but criticize the Bolshevik strategy for achieving that goal as counterproductive or unduly costly in terms of human suffering (*Practice and Theory of Bolshevism*, especially ch. vi.)[2] Let us grant that the pronouncements of the preacher do not constitute philosophy since they are neither true nor false. Still, the claim that this or that policy either will or will not achieve the preacher's ends is an obvious candidate for truth, and the same goes for the factual reasonings used to support such claims. And since the moralist's reasonings can be true, they are not automatically excluded from the sphere of philosophy by the proviso that philosophy is an inquiry aimed at truth. Hobbes, whose metaethic is a rude ancestor of Russell's ('whatsoever is the

---

[1] This holds even if the ethic in question does *not* have a utilitarian or consequentialist structure. For Robert Nozick 'individuals have rights, and there are things no person or group may do to them (without violating those rights)'. (Nozick, 1974, p. ix). If this claim is construed non-cognitively ('Would that nobody did certain things to individuals!') it could still be a matter of fact whether a given course of action violated an individual's Nozickian rights and hence was wrong-according-to-Nozick.

[2] Russell's critiques of Communism and of Marxism generally are usually of this nature. The underlying theory is false, hence the policies proposed are unlikely to succeed. See *ROE*, ch. 26, *In Praise of Idleness*, ch. 6; *Freedom and Organization*, chs. xvii–xx.

object of any man's appetite or desire that it is which he for his part calleth *good'*,[3]) still thought he could construct a set of 'theorems' pointing the way to civil peace; a goal that rational people could be persuaded to share. Thus, there is more to practical ethics than preaching and we need a fresh argument to show that this 'more' does not constitute philosophy.

Russell's writings suggest two incompatible responses: (1) that his social and political writings do not count as philosophy because they are not intended as contributions to learning; and (2) that they do not constitute philosophy because the factual part falls within the sphere of science. I shall take them in turn.

1) *The Principles of Social Reconstruction*, says Russell, (and this applies 'to some extent to my other popular books') 'was not intended as a contribution to learning but had an entirely practical purpose'. 'I did not write it in my capacity as a "philosopher"; I wrote it as a human being who suffered from the state of the world, wished to find some way of improving it, and was anxious to speak in plain terms to others who had similar feelings.' (*RTC, Papers* 11, pp. 55–6). Russell wrote these passages in response to V.G McGill, who had taken him to task for his sloppy use of the term 'instinct'. Russell's point is that in writing for the general public, it is unreasonable to demand the same standards of verbal precision or even, perhaps, of argument that are required in an academic treatise. Like Russell, I dabble in political journalism, and I well remember the remark of my editor at what he considered an excessively laboured attempt to prove a contentious point: 'You have to have the belt *and* the braces, don't you, Charles?' In popular writing, precision can be pedantry and it is possible and, perhaps, even a good idea, to dispense with the either the belt or the braces (though some support is no doubt necessary to prevent the trousers of your argument from falling about your ankles). Fair enough. But as a response to McGill, this is a little self-serving. For unless there is a reasonably coherent and sensible psychology underlying Russell's loose talk of 'instincts' and 'impulses' then the 'ways of improving the world' that he suggests will not be likely to work. If he is wrong about human beings, then he is probably wrong about the best way to ameliorate the human condition. Moreover, although the arguments can be simplified and sometimes left unstated,

---

[3] Hobbes, *Leviathan*, vi. 7.

the program should be susceptible of a rational defence. (The belt and the brace's do not have to be *on display* but both should be *available* in case the trousers come under attack.) If not, the program would be (ex hypothesi) an irrational one and, hence, unlikely to succeed. In which case, Russell would be duping those sufferers from the state of the world that he was anxious to speak to in plain terms. In other words, the fact that the *PSR* is not intended as a 'contribution to learning' and is addressed to the general public does not entail that it is not philosophy, or that it is not susceptible to philosophical criticism. All it means is that the fair-minded critic must make due allowance for the audience to whom it is addressed, and must be willing to do a little rational reconstruction before getting down to critical business. After all, Russell was not the only philosopher to write books that were not intended as contributions to learning but had a principally practical purpose.

Locke's *Essay Concerning Human Understanding* was certainly intended as a contribution to learning, but the The *Second Treatise* was written to justify an aborted rebellion and published to glorify a successful one,[4] both eminently practical purposes. Mill's *System of Logic* was likewise intended as a contribution to learning, but *The Subjection of Women* and *On Liberty* were written with the practical purposes of liberating women and securing civil liberties, respectively. Yet all three of these practical works count as philosophy in Russell's book. Russell seems to think that Locke's *Second Treatise* is a rather derivative and second-rate piece of philosophy (though beneficial in its consequences) but he regards it as a piece of philosophy nonetheless (*HWP* BK. III, ch. xiv). As for Mill's *On Liberty*, Russell actually prefers it to his *Logic*, which is not 'an important work' (*Papers* 11, pp. 467–520).

---

[4] Scholars agree that *Two Treatises* was drafted to justify a projected rebellion on the part of Shaftsbury and his associates during the period of the Exclusion Crisis, though the exact date is still a matter of dispute. (Russell's ancestor William, Lord Russell was executed as a result of his complicity in these plots.) But the book was published, as the preface proclaims, 'to establish the Throne of Our Great Restorer, Our present King William [and] to make good his title in the Consent of the People'. Locke seems to have drawn an almost Russellian distinction between his contributions to learning, and his more practical productions. He put his name to the former but was secretive to the point of paranoia about his authorship of the latter. But this was probably because 'contributions to learning' do not usually expose a man to any great risks whereas books written for a practical purpose can cost a man his head.

Perhaps what Russell is getting at is this: Philosophy as practised by Russell is a demanding technical discipline: it requires a capacity for abstract thought, a knowledge not only of mathematics but also of mathematical logic, and a broad grounding in the sciences, particularly physics and psychology. Thus, it is only accessible (and only of interest) to a small intellectual elite. But (fortunately for the possibility of democratic debate) you do not need so much in the way of brains and background reading to arrive at reasonable opinions about the problems of morality, politics, and everyday life. In advocating such opinions therefore, Russell was not 'doing philosophy' as he conceived it. As an ethicist, I am not entirely happy about this. I think there is a certain tendency on the part of tough-minded philosophers to think of ethics as something to do on a wet Sunday afternoon. Accordingly, they hold themselves to much lower standards on their ethical Sundays than they do in their week-day work. But however that may be, the fact (if it is a fact) that practical ethics is less demanding and abstruse than the philosophy of mathematics, does not prove that it is not philosophy. It proves, at best, that it is a relatively easy branch of the subject. It is true that philosophy is often difficult, but it does not follow that what is not difficult is not philosophy.

Perhaps, Russell wants to disclaim any special *authority* for his moral and political opinions; to deny that such metaphysical expertise as he may have possessed gave him any special license to pronounce on questions of morals and politics. He was not (as Hegel believed himself to be) an interpreter of the Absolute as it manifested itself in history nor (as Heidegger believed himself to be) a person whose profound philosophic insights enabled him to pick the best political party. (Heidegger picked the Nazis.) *PSR* could in principle have been written by someone who was *not* the co-author of *Principia Mathematica* and the author of 'On Denoting'. It is true, of course, that Russell thought his ideas worth a hearing, but an opinion can be worth hearing even if it is largely devoid of metaphysical support. Russell was 'a human being who suffered from the state of the world' but a well-read and intelligent human being who had devoted some thought to improving it. As such, he could hope for attention, but he could not lay claim to any special deference. His arguments were supposed to stand on their own feet, not to lean on his expertise as a technical philosopher. Again, this is fair enough, maybe even admirable, but again, it does not prove Russell's point.

For it does not distinguish *PSR* from Mill's *On Liberty* or Locke's *Second Treatise*, which both count as philosophy. *On Liberty* could in principle have been written by someone who was not the author of a *System of Logic* and is largely independent of Mill's empiricist epistemology. As for the *Second Treatise*, it is not just independent of Locke's more technical *Essay*, but actually inconsistent with it (as many scholars have noted). So far from trying to bolster his arguments as a Whig pamphleteer with the prestige he was to acquire as the author of the Essay, Locke published the *Second Treatise* anonymously and did not own up to it until he was on the point of death. Both Locke and Mill wrote as 'human beings who suffered from the state of the world' (Locke so much so that he became a revolutionary and was forced into exile); they too 'wished to find some way of improving it', and they too were 'anxious to speak in plain terms to others who had similar feelings'. But this did not entail that what they wrote was not philosophy.

2) In *RS* Russell seems to take the opposite tack. The factual component in practical ethics is excluded from philosophy because it is included in the sphere of science. Penal policy provides a case in point. Whether or not the death penalty deters can, in principle, be settled by statistics. In fact the evidence suggests that it is no more of a deterrent than long-term imprisonment, the usual alternative. But even if we assume (say) utilitarian values, science cannot tell us to drop the death penalty. In a poor country, where even the innocent find it hard to get by, it may be difficult to maintain convicted murderers in humane conditions. Would it not be more cost-effective to execute the killers and to devote the money saved to public health programs? Now it may be that there is a rational response to such a question but it is bound to go beyond the scientifically established facts. In particular, it will depend on delicate economic considerations, and economics is not a science in the strict sense of the word. It will also depend upon an estimate of the joys and sorrows involved, which is so far well beyond the reach of science. So although scientific facts are often crucial to questions of morals and public policy, they are seldom decisive even if a clear set of ends is assumed. Furthermore, science sometimes speaks with a divided voice (*Education and the Social Order*, ch. 3); 'scientifically established facts' can prove to be ideologically constructed fictions, and scientists can be surprisingly unscientific, investing their prejudices with the aura

of scientific authority (*Mortals and Others* 1, pp. 66–7). For all these reasons, the factual side of practical ethics cannot be abandoned to the scientists since philosophical reasoning is often required to sort out how science is relevant (which is not to say that someone trained as a scientist might not be better at it than someone trained as a philosopher). Indeed, I am inclined to think that some knowledge of the philosophy of science (which tends to alert you to the issues raised above) is especially useful for anyone engaged with public policy. At all events, Russell's own writings on practical ethics do not look like science even if we exclude the element of 'preaching'. Though they are scientifically well-informed, the factual component often includes claims which are not (and are not likely to be) scientifically justified, though they may, of course, be true.

But, perhaps, the best reason to suppose that Russell's writings on morals and politics constitute philosophy is that they embody distinctively philosophic ideas and are susceptible to philosophic criticism. Take, for example, Russell's views on world government . . . .

III. A CASE STUDY: RUSSELL, HOBBES, AND WORLD GOVERNMENT

It was Russell's belief that international peace would be impossible in the long term without world government, a thesis he reiterated over and over again from 1914 till 1964 (*Papers* 13, pp. 45–6; *PSR*, pp. 71–4; *Papers* 11, pp. 460–1). This led to some dire predictions. In 1950 he confidently prophesied that 'before the end of this century, unless something quite unforeseeable occurs, one of three possibilities will have been realized:

I. The end of human life, perhaps of all life on our planet
II. A reversion to barbarism after a catastrophic diminution of the population of the globe.
III. A unification of the world under a single government possessing a monopoly of all the major weapons of war. (*Unpopular Essays*, p. 45)

There is an apocalyptic tendency to Russell's thought, a *penchant* for dramatic disjunctions. We are at a fork in the road, and must either choose the rational route to an Earthly Paradise or the highway to a

Nuclear Hell. There was something to be said for this view in 1964 when he roundly declared that 'we have now only the choice between mutual destruction and mutual happiness' (*Papers* 11, p. 461). But the interesting thing is that he voiced much the same sentiments fifty years earlier, long before the advent of nuclear weapons. 'The civilized races of the world are faced with the alternative of cooperation or mutual destruction' (*Papers* 13, p. 270). The idea that things might just jog along without getting much better or much worse is one that never seemed to occur to him.[5] This bias in Russell's thought (which is very marked) was partly a matter of temperament and partly due to his historical experience. After all, twice in his lifetime things had failed to jog along in a truly spectacular fashion and civilization had shuddered into the catastrophe of a World War.

But in the realm of international affairs, Russell had a *reason* for discounting the jog-along disjunct and insisting on the need for world government – he subscribed to Hobbes's thesis that the international state of nature is in fact a state of war (*HWP*, p. 579).[6] Thomas Hobbes (1588–1679) is principally famous as the philosopher of absolutism. Though his preference was for monarchy he was willing to concede that oligarchies might work so long as the power of the government is absolute. But government (and an undivided government with a monopoly of armed force) was, in his view, essential both for civil peace and for civilization. According to Hobbes, men are selfish, acquisitive, foward-looking and fearful and some of them aggressive and vainglorious to boot. They are subject to a 'perpetual and restless desire for power after power [by which Hobbes means 'resource after resource'] that ceaseth only in death' (*Leviathan*, xi. 2). Absent the restraints of government, this 'restless desire' leads to conflict as people compete for scarce resources; a conflict which is exacerbated by two other factors: a) fear or diffidence which leads the fearful to 'anticipate' attacks with preemptive strikes of their own and b) the desire on the part of a significant minority to domineer and exalt over others. 'So that in the nature of man we find three principal causes of quarrel; first, competition; secondly, diffidence; thirdly, glory. The first maketh men invade for gain; the second, for safety; and the third

---

[5] See Ryan (1988) p. 186

[6] That Russell was a closet Hobbist has been remarked on by Alan Ryan (1988) p. 80 and argued at length by Mark Lippincott (1990).

for reputation.' Thus a state of nature in which 'men live without a common power to keep them all in awe' would be a state of war, indeed a war 'of every man against every man' in which the life of man would be 'solitary, poor, nasty, brutish and short' (*Leviathan*, xiii. 6–9).

Hobbes seeks to confirm his account of how individuals *would* behave in an *interpersonal* state of nature by appealing to the way that sovereign states *do* behave in the *international* state of nature. For Hobbes, states are 'artificial men', big robots composed of people, which inherit the psychological quirks of their constituent parts. The sovereign state reduplicates the psychology of the individual or individuals who constitute 'the sovereignty', the 'artificial soul' which gives 'life and motion to the whole body' (*Leviathan*, 'Introduction'). Thus, a ruler like Louis XIV would have had *two* bodies, a natural body of his own and an artificial body composed of the organized force of the French State. It was, therefore, a pardonable exaggeration, but an exaggeration nonetheless, for Louis to declare 'L'etat, c'est moi!'. What he *should* have said is 'L'ame de l'etat, c'est moi!'. Now, since these artificial men live 'without a common power to keep them all in awe', and since they share the psychology of the individuals who direct them, it would follow, if Hobbes were correct, that the international state of nature would be a state of war. And this, Hobbes claims, is born out by the facts: 'kings and persons of sovereign authority, because of their independency, are in continual jealousies and in the state and posture of gladiators, having their weapons pointing and their eyes fixed upon one another . . . which is a posture of war (*Leviathan* xiii. 12). For Hobbes 'war consisteth not in actual fighting , but in the known disposition thereto during all the time there is no assurance to the contrary' (*Leviathan* xiii. 8). So what Hobbes is saying is that the artificial men are in a continuous state of cold war with hot war a constant and simmering possibility.

Hobbes was oddly unfazed by this fact, presumably because he believed that international war was far less destructive than either civil war or the war of all against all. And it is, indeed, true that England sustained no serious damage in all the international conflicts of Hobbes' prolonged lifetime (though *Germany* lost between a third and a half of its population). But with the destructive power of modern weapons we cannot afford to be so sanguine. If war is endemic in the international state of nature then, perhaps, what we need is an international sovereign to put a stop to it. And this is precisely what Russell believed. 'The present system [that of interpersonal government and international anarchy] is irrational since external and internal anarchy must be both right or both wrong' (*PSR*, p. 43). 'There is not a word in *Leviathan* to suggest any relation between [states] except war and conquest, with occasional interludes. This follows on his principles from the absence of an international government, for the relations of states are still in a state nature, which is that of a war of all against all. Every argument that [Hobbes] adduces in favour of government, in so far as it is valid at all, is valid in favour of international government' (*HWP*, p. 579).

This is, perhaps, a bit swift. After all, it might be the case, as Hobbes evidently believed, that international war is far less destructive than domestic conflict, in which case the absence of an international sovereign might be tolerable. Besides, Hobbes' argument that the international state of nature is necessarily a state of war (that is a state of cold war with frequent eruptions of hot violence) is dependent on two premises: 1) that *individuals* are such that an interpersonal state of nature would be a state of war and 2) that the psychology of states reduplicates the psychology of their ruling individuals. The evidence is a bit equivocal, but I do not think Russell subscribed to either of these premises. To begin with Russell was much less of a biological determinist than Hobbes. For Hobbes, human action is dependent on human nature, which manifests itself in much the same way whatever the social circumstances. For Russell, human action is dependent on human desires, which can be extensively modified by education and opportunity. Thus, the question of what people would do in the absence of government does not have an unequivocal answer, since it depends upon the people and the upbringing they have received. Russell's careful refutation of anarchism in *Roads to Freedom*, ch. 5, suggests that though anarchy (that is a state of nature) would be bad – indeed bad enough to warrant a government – it would not be as bad as Hobbes supposes, and certainly not as bad as war of all against all. And though the psychology of artificial men is determined by the psychology of the people that control them, Russell never suggests that the one simply reduplicates the other. And this is fortunate since it is obviously false. For the ruler's relation to his artificial body is very different from his relation to his natural body. No doubt Louis XIV suffered when

Marlborough lopped off one of his armies at the Battle of Blenheim. But he would have suffered a lot more and in a profoundly different way if Marlborough had lopped off one of his arms. Had the pain been the same, his decisions as a ruler might have been rather different.

But if Russell rejects Hobbes' argument that the international state of nature is necessarily a state of war, why does he accept his conclusion? Because, in Russell's view, there are independent reasons to suppose *not* that the psychology of the state reduplicates the psychology of *real* individuals, but that the psychology of the state reduplicates the psychology of *Hobbesian* individuals. Scattered throughout Russell's writings are a series of observations that add up to the Hobbesian claim 'that in the nature of [states] we find three principal causes of quarrel: first, competition; secondly, diffidence; thirdly, glory'. To begin with, states, especially capitalist states, are acquisitive. This is because people, especially capitalists, are acquisitive, with a voracious appetite for markets and investment opportunities, and because capitalists can often call upon the services of the state to foster their acquisitive schemes. 'Whatever may be the psychoanalysis of acquisitiveness, no one can deny that it is one of the great motives – especially among the more powerful, for, as I said before, it is one of the infinite motives' (*HSEP*, p. 161). (The qualification 'especially among the more powerful' is important because the more powerful are precisely the people with the most influence in determining the psychology of states.) Where the states are capitalistic 'the desire for exclusive markets is one of the most potent causes of war' (*Papers* 14, p. 271. See also *Roads to Freedom*, pp. 111–13). Next comes fear. 'War the Offspring of Fear' was the title of one of Russell's first anti-war pamphlets, and he continued to think that the fear of aggression was one of the principle causes of war, tempting diffident states to 'anticipate' their opponents (*Papers* 13, pp. 37–47; *HSEP*, pp. 170 and 230). Finally, glory: Russell, unlike Hobbes, distinguishes between two motives which tend to go together, namely vanity and the love of power. The merely vain demand the trappings of outward admiration whilst pure power-freaks (like the reclusive Baron Holstein) revel in the reality of secret dominion (*HSEP*, pp. 162–5). But both motives can be dangerous if they predominate within the ruling classes, since people tend to identify their personal greatness with the greatness of the state. And unfortunately, the love of power and the disposition to domineer are particularly virulent amongst the ruling classes. 'Pride of dominion, unwillingness to decide disputes otherwise than by force or the threat of force is a habit of mind greatly encouraged by the possession of power' (*PSR*, p. 45. See also *Roads to Freedom* pp. 114–15). Thus, the psychology of states resembles the psychology of Hobbesian individuals, since the rulers, in their capacity *as* rulers, are often actuated by the Hobbesian motives of competition, diffidence, and glory. 'The first maketh [states] invade for gain; the second, for safety; and the third for reputation [or, as Russell would have added, dominion]'.

Thus, one of Russell's key theses, that world government is essential for the sake of long-term peace, depends upon an interesting philosophical argument that ultimately derives from Hobbes. (If not, it is quite gratuitous!) It is also susceptible to philosophic criticism. For the argument only works on two conditions: (1) that Hobbesian individuals in the interpersonal state of nature would indeed be in a state of war; and (2) that the international state of nature is not only analogous, but necessarily analogous, to the interpersonal state of nature envisaged by Hobbes. The first condition is questionable and the second, false. One of the most interesting results of recent Hobbes scholarship is that unless the state of nature is very carefully specified, there is a frightful risk of peace breaking out. (See Hampton (1986), pp. 58–89, and Kavka (1986), pp. 83–174. I mostly follow Kavka.) If Hobbesian individuals were merely selfish, resource-hungry, and diffident (that is death/pain averse), a policy of conditional cooperation might well be more rational (that is, more likely to pay) than a ruthless policy of aggressive anticipation. At least three extra circumstances are required to trip the majority of moderates (who do not desire to dominate) into a program of aggressive action: (a) the policy of anticipation must be a much better bet than simply lying low; (b) there must be a sizeable minority of dominators; and (c) it must be difficult to tell whether a neighbour is a dominator or not. If (a) were false there would be no war of all against all. Rational moderates would not attack each other, since it would pay better to stand on the defensive, and the irrational dominators would edit themselves out by a process of Darwinian selection. If defence, rather than attack, were the best form of defence, attackers would destroy themselves by pursuing such a risky strategy. If (b) were false, then again there would be no war since conditional cooperation would pay better than conflict and there would be no irrational dominators to upset the apple-cart of enlightened self-interest. Finally, if (c) were false, the war might be won by the moderates combining against the dominators. What triggers the war of all against all is the fear on the part of the diffident moderates that unless they act like dominators by mounting preemptive strikes, they will be destroyed either by dominators or by moderates who are likewise forced to act like dominators. But if it is possible to tell dominators from moderates a more nuanced response is available – combine to attack the dominators whilst leaving the other moderates intact. So unless the settings are exactly right, the Hobbesian state of nature need not generate a state of war.

Happily for us and unhappily for Russell's argument, the international state of nature is *not* analogous to Hobbes' interpersonal state of nature. For a crucial premise of Hobbes's argument is that the Hobbesian individuals are functionally equal. For though one man may be 'manifestly stronger in body or quicker in mind' than another, 'the weakest has strength enough to kill the strongest, either by secret machination or by confederacy'. We are the physical equals of the bully because either singly or in a group we can sneak up on him in the middle of the night and slit his throat. 'From this equality ariseth hope' (by which Hobbes means the hope of victory), which leads to the policy of anticipation (*Leviathan*, xiii. 1–4). But small nation states are not in a position to assassinate large nation states nor are minor nuclear powers in a position to assassinate major nuclear powers. France could no doubt do considerable damage if it chose to attack the United States, but it could not hope to finish off its opponent, which means that the two are not functionally equal in Hobbes's sense. Secondly, it is far from obvious that in the international arena anticipation is the best policy. In the wars of the twentieth century, anticipation has often led to defeat. Another disanalogy is that nowadays it is almost always irrational to invade for gain since modern wars are ruinous to victors and vanquished alike.[7] This removes the motive of competition, which, in Hobbes' eyes, is

---

[7] The Iraqi invasion of Kuwait was motivated by the desire for gain and the thirst for glory and if no other powers had intervened it might have been a profitable venture. But the circumstances were unusual since Kuwait is both fabulously rich and militarily defenceless. And by declaring himself publicly to be a dominator Saddam caused the world's other powers both moderate and otherwise to combine against him.

one of the principal causes of conflict. Finally, in the modern world, it is relatively easy for modern states to identify the dominators and to combine against them, as in the Gulf War. There is nothing to trigger aggressive behaviour on the part of moderates without which there would be no war of all against all. Thus, the argument for a world government – at least the Hobbesian argument for a world government, which is the only one that is even hinted at by Russell – collapses completely (See Kavka (1987), ch. 7.)

There is another objection which can be urged against Hobbes which applies with even greater force to Russell. If the inhabitants of Hobbes's state of nature are sufficiently peaceable to get together and sign a social contract setting up an absolute sovereign, then they don't really need him, since they have achieved a measure of cooperation without him. On the other hand, if they need an absolute sovereign to keep them in line, it is hard to see how they could get together to create one by signing the contract. Once Russell abandoned the option of creating a world government by force (which he did when the USSR acquired nuclear weapons), he faced a similar problem. If the Great Powers were sufficiently peaceable and their relations sufficiently friendly to agree to a world government, it is not clear that they would need one, while if they *really* needed a world government to prevent a hot war breaking out, it is hard to see how they would ever agree to set one up. If a world government is possible, it is not necessary, and if it is necessary, it is not possible. This is a much more urgent problem for Russell than Hobbes, because Russell's argument is prospective whereas Hobbes' is retrospective. Hobbes is not trying to persuade people in a state of nature to set up a sovereign. He is trying to persuade people who have already got a sovereign not to pull him down. Thus, the difficulties of setting up a sovereign in the state of nature are not necessarily fatal to his argument. It is otherwise with Russell, since the world government does not yet exist, and we are actually living in an international state of nature (Kavka (1987), p. 130). Now I do not pretend that this is a knock-down drag-out argument. The Great Powers might be just rational enough to see the need for a world government and to act on that perception, but not rational enough to coexist or cooperate in the long term. They might be a bit like the wealthy social democrat who votes for higher taxes every three years, but cannot bring herself to keep giving away the money that she believes the state should subtract... But we can, I think, say this: the more likely world government is, the less there is a need for it, and the more there is a need for it, the less likely it is.

This is not to say that Russell is wrong. Maybe long-term peace *is* impossible without world government. But the argument, as I understand it, is a failure. I do not deny that a better argument might be constructed nor that such an argument might draw on Hobbes. But Hobbes must be modified if he is to prove the need for an international sovereign and if Russell is to convince us, he must provide us with something better.

Now what I have been doing for the last few pages certainly looks like philosophy. Which means that Russell's case for a world government is susceptible to a philosophic critique. To be sure, it is a critique which draws its data from a wide range of disciplines – game theory, psychology, history, and political science – a fact which would have been more apparent if I had spelt out the argument in greater detail. But a discussion does not cease to be philosophical because it takes other disciplines into account. Russell himself would have been the first to pour scorn on such an idea. But a thesis that must be defended or attacked by philosophical argument bids fair to being a philosophical thesis. Such is Russell's claim that we cannot get by without world government. This illustrates the contention that I have been arguing all along – that Russell did not abandon his vocation as a philosopher when he took to practical ethics (which includes political philosophy). When he wrote on these topics he often wrote as a moral philosopher and not – as he sometimes pretended – an unphilosophical moralist. This would have been rather more obvious if I had discussed Russell's repeated critiques of Marxism in general and Communism in particular. Russell argues, for example, that materialism is dubious since matter (as traditionally conceived) tends to evaporate under the critical gaze of modern physicists and that dialectical materialism is absurd since a dialectical development only makes sense on the assumption that mind is the ultimate reality. He argues that the course of human history is detemined by many factors besides the development of the means of production. And he argues that the theory of surplus value is flawed and that Marx's politico-economic predictions have been falsified by the facts. Now when Popper in the *Open Society* argues along similar lines everybody agrees that it is philosophy, whether they like it or not. And when the analytic Marxists try to reconstruct Marxism so as to deal with such criticisms, so far from being regarded as nonphilosophers, they are rewarded with chairs at Oxford and Chicago. Why then are Russell's writings excluded from the canon? But I do not think we should stop with his overtly political philosphy. After all, Hume did not cease to be a philosopher when he wrote on chastity and modesty, and feminist philosophy would be virtually non-existent if feminist philosphers were not allowed to talk about marriage and (sexual) morals. Even the topic of happiness, whose conquest preoccupied Russell, is now well within the fold of respectable philosophy since well-being has become a big philosophical business especially at Oxford. It is time, I think, to stop taking Russell at his word, to rescind his self-denying ordinance, and to admit that his social philosophy really is philosophy. That way we can give it the critical scrutiny that it deserves. For Russell is not just a philosopher but an *interesting* philosopher – even when he is wrong, there is often much to be gained by arguing with him.

IV. THE SIX PHASES OF RUSSELL

I now turn to Russell's ethical theory. This too needs to be vindicated. For Russell has suffered a double injustice. Having created a conception of philosophy which tended to exclude some of his own efforts, he was taken at his word by subsequent philosophers who went on to develop a much less exclusive conception of the subject. This accounts for the neglect of his practical ethics. But his ethical theory has been neglected too and this for a different reason. Much of it went unpublished in Russell's lifetime (and this includes some of his most original contributions) and much of it was dribbled out in a series of asides when he was ostensibly talking about something else. Thus, it was not known until 1988 that Russell had anticipated Mackie's famous error theory (the idea that moral judgments are factual but false) and not fully realized until recently that he was one of the pioneers of emotivism, anticipating both Ayer and Stevenson (its alleged inventors) by something like twenty years. It is only now that Russell is coming into his own as an emotivist with the inclusion of chapter ix of *Religion and Science* (note that this is a book chapter and note the title the book!) in James Rachels' Oxford Readings in Philosophy anthology *Ethical Theory* (1998). This helps to explain

Sainsbury's mistaken belief that Russell's 'work on moral philosophy' had only two main phases, both of them derivative. In fact it
had about six, at least two of them highly original.

Phase 1: 1889–1903. 'We called him "old Sidg" and regarded him
as merely out of date'. So said Russell of the great Victorian moral
philosopher Henry Sidgwick who taught him ethics at Cambridge.
'At the time, I, in common with other young people, did not give
him nearly as much respect as he deserved' (*MPD*, p. 30). Maybe
not, but Sidgwick did influence Russell almost without his noticing
it. Although Russell's principle preoccupation during the 1890s was
the philosophy of mathematics, he devoted some effort to ethics,
wrestling with two problems, both set by Sidgwick's philosophy.

The first problem was the nature and justification of the axioms
of ethics. Since 'ought' could not be derived from 'is' it appeared to
follow that ethics depended on certain self-evident axioms which
had nothing to do with what is, has been or will be (*ROE*, ch. 3).
Russell was clearly unhappy with this and tried to justify the axioms of ethics by defining 'good' in terms of desire. After several
unsuccessful efforts he arrived at the conclusion that 'good' means
what we desire to desire, a view he abandoned under the influence
of G.E. Moore. (See *ROE*, chs. 7, 9, and 10.[8]) But Russell, in turn, appears to have influenced Moore. Not only does Moore single out
Russell's definition for critical attention in his famous *Principia
Ethica*, but also the need to deal with such definitions may have led
him to invent the Open Question Argument, one of his two principal
arguments against naturalism (the view that moral properties can be
identified with natural properties of some kind). The first argument
(which I shall call the Argument from Advocacy) occurs in the early
draft of *Principia Ethica* known as *The Elements of Ethics* and contends that 'good' cannot be synonymous with any naturalistic 'X',
if 'X things are good' is supposed to be a reason for action rather
than a 'barren tautology'. (See *Principia Ethica*, §11; *ROE*, pp. 96 and
100.) The second argument (widely known as the Open Question Argument) only appears in the final version and contends that 'good'
cannot be synonymous with any naturalistic predicate 'X', since
'Are X things good?' is a significant or open question for every 'X'

---

[8] The theory has been resurrected and revamped in a famous paper by David Lewis
(1989) who did not realize that he was reviving Russell.

(*Principia Ethica*, §13). Now the Argument from Advocacy does not refute Russell's 'desire to desire' theory since 'What we desire to desire is good', is not *intended* to be anything but a barren but illuminating tautology: barren, because it does not provide any extra reason for the pursuit or promotion of what we desire to desire, but illuminating, since it is supposed to explain why the goodness of something (i.e., its being what we desire to desire) provides us with a reason to pursue or promote it. But the Open Question Argument, if sound, refutes *all* forms of naturalism, including theories such as Russell's, since it is supposed to be an Open Question whether what we desire to desire is good. It is significant in this connection that Moore refers to Russell's 'desire to desire' theory precisely at the point where he is expounding the Open Question Argument (i.e., *Principia Ethica*, §13). However, he does not credit it to Russell, presumably because Russell propounded it at a meeting of the Apostles whose transactions were supposed to be secret. (Moore was so scrupulous about keeping the doings of the Apostles secret that he worried about discussing them by postcard. See *Selected Letters of Bertrand Russell* I, p. 191.) If this is correct, Russell played a part in the formation of the the Moorean theory that he went on to expound in his second, derivative phase.

The other problem that bothered Russell during the 1890s was also due to Sidgwick – the Dualism of Practical Reason. In Sidgwick's opinion, to say that one ought to do something is to say that it is reasonable to do it. It is reasonable to promote one's private interest and reasonable to promote the public interest. The problem is that the one does not seem any more reasonable than the other. So in the event of a clash, the 'Cosmos of Duty is reduced to a Chaos', since what one ought to do is indeterminate. (See Mackie (1976) and Sidgwick (1907), pp. xviii–xxiii, 162–75, 496–509.) The problem goes back to Thomas Reid, who considered conscience and a regard for one's good on the whole to be distinct but complementary, rational principles. However, in Reid's view, the two could not clash. 'While the world is under a wise and benevolent adminstration, it is impossible that in the issue any man should be a loser by doing his duty'. But Sidgwick did not believe that the world *was* under a wise and benevolent administration, since he had ceased to believe in God. Thus, a clash could not be ruled out. Accordingly, Sidgwick might, in Reid's words, be 'reduced to this miserable dilemma, whether it is

best to be a fool or a knave' (Schneewind (1977), p. 69). Now Russell
was much exercised by this problem, and tried to solve it with the aid
of Hegelian metaphysics. He wanted to show that in the long run –
or failing the long run, in Reality – there could be no clash between
duty and prudence or between altruism and rational self-interest.
His first effort drew on the metaphysics of McTaggart as expressed
in *The Further Determination of the Absolute* (1893).[9] McTaggart
believed – and for a while induced Russell to believe – that 'reality
is exclusively spirit' and that the 'universe and ourselves are implicitly in harmony – a harmony that must one day become explicit'
(McTaggart (1996) pp. 210–11.) Since we are also immortal, we will
one day experience this harmony, which is (or will be) a communion
of spirits in a loving state of mutual awareness. Since this future
harmony will be a state of mutual awareness, I will not be able to
promote my private happiness without promoting that of everybody
else, nor will I be able to harm others without hurting myself. Furthermore, selfish action in the present may retard that happy day
when the harmony will become explicit. Thus, in the long-term,
altruism and enlightened self-interest coincide (*ROE*, 2; *Papers* 1:
31). This solution evaporated once Russell ceased to believe in immortality. Instead he flirted with a Bradleian solution according to
which altruism and self-interest *already* coincide (though 'already'
isn't quite the right word here) since in Reality we are all one – or
rather, we are all united in the Absolute, a sort of timeless cosmic
experience of which our separate selves are delusory aspects. (See
ROE, pp. 59 and 66–67, *Papers* 1, pp. 97–8; Bradley (1930) chs. x, xiii,
xiv, and xxv.) Hence, if I hurt you in pursuit of my private ends, I am
Really hurting myself – or rather the Absolute in which our separate
selves are dissolved. Russell's famous paper 'Seems Madam? Nay It
Is' (*ROE*, ch. 11, *Papers* 1, ch. 16) puts the kybosh on this solution.
Not that Russell mentions the problem directly – rather it is a corollary of his chief argument that any supposed unity of selves cannot
solve Sidgwick's problem unless that unity is *experienced*. Russell
argues that (Hegelian) philosophy can provide no 'comfort in adver-
sity'. It may be that the timeless world of Reality is perfect, but since
what we experience is the world of Appearance, the perfection of the

---

[9] Reprinted in McTaggart, J. McT. Ellis (1996). *Philosophical Studies*, Keeling, S.V.
ed., Bristol, Thoemmes.

Real world affords no consolation. By parity of reasoning, it may be that in Reality we are part of a unity of selves, but since we do not *experience* that unity – since we do not experience other people's joys or sorrows – this gives us no self-interested reason to promote other people's interests. As Russell put it in a letter to Moore, 'for all purposes that are not *purely* intellectual [which presumably includes the purpose of solving Sidgwick's problem], the world of Appearance is the real world' (*Papers* 1, p. 105). Once Russell realized that the Hegelian Absolute served no practical purpose – neither affording consolation nor providing us with a reason to be good – he speedily concluded that it served no intellectual purpose either, and thereupon dismissed it as a myth. *One* reason, I suspect, for the revolt against Hegelianism was that the Absolute could not deliver the goods – neither the emotional good of comfort nor the moral good of a solution to Sidgwick's problem.

Phase 2: 1903–1913. Phase 2 was genuinely derivative since Russell became a convert to the doctrines of Moore's *Principia Ethica*. It was in this phase that Russell wrote 'The Elements of Ethics' as well as two highly laudatory reviews of *Principia Ethica* (*Papers* 4, chs. 27 and 28; *ROE*, ch. 13). Russell was not an uncritical disciple, however. In Moore's view, 'what we ought to do is that action which will produce the best results on the whole; and this [he] regarded as constituting a definition of *ought*. Russell held that 'this is not a definition but significant proposition and, in fact, a false one' (a) because it is an Open Question whether we ought to do what will produce the best results on the whole and (b) because the answer to this Open Question is 'No', since what we ought to do is 'what we have *reason to think* will have the best results' (*ROE*, p. 101, my italics). But Russell agreed with Moore that 'good' is the name of a non-natural property, a property which cannot be reduced to or identified with any other property accessible to either science or metaphysics. This doctrine continued to influence Russell, even after he had abandoned it. He was at least half-inclined to think that *if* there was such a property as goodness, it had to be the kind of property specified by Moore. He just ceased to believe that there was any such property.

Phase 3: 1913–1922. In February 1913 Russell read Santayana's *The Winds of Doctrine* and gave up the Moorean good. If there is no such thing as goodness then it cannot be true that anything is good. But this still leaves two alternatives. Good judgments could be just plain false, or they could lack a truth-value altogether. In 1913, Russell seems to have opted for the second alternative and to have embraced some kind of emotivism. But the 'seems' is quite important here, since Russell is never very explicit about what exactly he believes. Santayana, whose delicate mockeries (they can hardly be called arguments), destroyed Russell's faith in the Moorean good, appears to have been a proto-emotivist. 'But to speak of the truth of a ultimate good would be a false collocation of terms; an ultimate good is chosen, found or aimed at; it is not opined'. Ethical intuitions 'are not opinions that we hazard but preferences we feel' (quoted in *ROE*, p. 105). If Russell took over this opinion, this would make sense of his arguments in 'The Place of Science in a Liberal Education' (1913) and 'On Scientific Method in Philosophy' (1914) (*Papers* 12, p. 396; *Papers* 8, pp. 62–4). In both these pieces he argues that 'ethical notions' should be 'extruded from scientific philosophy'. Why? Partly (I think) because philosophy is an inquiry aimed at truth, and judgments about good and evil lack a truth-value, and partly because 'human ethical notions . . . when used in metaphysics, [involve] an attempt, however veiled, to legislate for the universe on the basis of the present desires of men' – a remark which suggests that moral judgments typically *express* such desires. But Russell's arguments for his view (whatever exactly it was) are not so much arguments *for* proto-emotivism as *against* the Moorean good. They, therefore, favour the error theory as much as any form of emotivism (*ROE*, pp. 16–22 and 105–18). There are two undercurrents in Russell's thinking at this time that are worthy of note: (1) a growing disenchantment with the institution of morality brought on by the War ('the universal outburst of righteousness in all nations since the war began . . . has given me a disgust for all ethical notions which evidently are chiefly useful as an excuse for murder' (*ROE*, p. 107)), and a belief that a 'recognition of the subjectivity of ethics' (whatever that means) would lead to 'less cruelty, persecution, punishment and moral reprobation than exists at present' (*ROE*, p. 117).

Phase 4: 1922. In March 1922, Russell read a two-page paper to the Apostles, entitled 'Is There an Absolute Good?'. Russell refrained from publishing this piece during his lifetime, perhaps because he soon ceased to believe it or, perhaps, because he considered it too dangerous to do so. (It first appeared in *Russell* n.s. 1987, pp. 144–9, with a long introduction by Alan Ryan.) By 1922 Russell was already something of a pariah, widely reviled by both Right and Left, and if he had gone public with his metaethic, it might have alienated many of his remaining admirers. But whatever the reasons for Russell's reticence, he thereby lost an opportunity for fame as the founding father of the error theory, a doctrine subsequently developed by J.L. Mackie ((1946) and (1977)).[10] Russell rejects the proto-emotivism that he seemed to favour during the war years and insists that there is 'no doubt that our ethical judgments claim objectivity'. However, 'this claim, to my mind, makes them all false'. Because 'good' is meaningful, it seems natural to infer that there must be a property which it means. This, however, is 'a fallacy'. 'Good' is rather like 'the present King of France' – it is an 'incomplete symbol' which contributes to the meanings of the sentences in which it occurs without having a meaning (in the sense of a reference) of its own. Thus 'when we define ['good'] as nearly as possible in the usage of absolutists, *all* propositions in which the word "good" has primary occurence are false' (*ROE*, pp. 122–3). The qualification 'when we define ["good"] as nearly as possible in the usage of absolutists' is important. For Russell, unlike Mackie, does not deny the existence of a non-natural property of goodness. In Russell's semantics things which do not exist have to be defined in terms of things which do if the propositions concerned are to be meaningful. Indeed, in order to make sense of a proposition, we must be acquainted with *all* of its ultimate constituents. This entails that 'good', if it is to contribute to the meaning of a sentence (even a false one), must be given a naturalistic analysis, since it must be definable in terms of things which we can sense. Russell's analysis runs thus: To say that 'M is good' is to say that M possesses the property common to A, B, C, ... (which happen to be the things the speaker approves of) but absent in X, Y, Z... (which happen to be the things the speaker disapproves of). It is because there is, in general, no such property that good-judgments are false.

There is much to criticize in this analysis. (It entails, for example that people who approve and disapprove of different things are condemned to talk at cross purposes and cannot genuinely disagree

---

[10] Mackie, with a good war record behind him, was, perhaps, in a better position to publish a 'Refutation of Morals' in 1946. Nevertheless, his metaethical frankness may well have cost him at least one job. He lost out on the Chair of Philosophy at the University of Tasmania to the metaethically acceptable but normatively suspect Sydney Sparkes Orr. See Pybus (1993), p. 206.

about what is good.) But under the influence of the error theory, Russell went on to develop what I call *humanistic amoralism*. In November 1922, he wrote a review in which a devil's advocate argues that morality is not only false but also pernicious, an excuse for cruelty and a prop to predatory elites, and that the human race would be better off if we tried to get by with the aid of friendly feelings and enlightened self-interest (*ROE*, ch. 25, *Papers* 9, ch. 59).

Russell soon abandoned both the error theory and humanistic amoralism, reverting to emotivism on the one hand and the view that 'undoubtedly the world needs a new morality [as opposed to *no* morality] and not merely a revolt against the old one' on the other (*ROE*, p. 189). Why he did so is not entirely clear. In *RTC* (*Papers* 11, p. 48; *ROE*, p. 146) Russell declares that 'no amount of logic even if it were my own' would persuade him to give up feeling and expressing ethical passions; yet, if the error theory were correct, expressing ethical passions would amount to mouthing falsehoods. Perhaps Russell could not bring himself to accept a theory which made moralizing such a disreputable business, especially as moralizing was, by this time, one of his chief sources of income.

As for humanistic amoralism, my conjecture (for what it is worth) is that his experience as a schoolteacher convinced him that friendly feelings cannot always be relied on and that self-interest is not always sufficiently enlightend to secure civilized behaviour; whilst his knowledge of the Bolsheviks convinced him that a belief in the 'subjectivity of ethics' and a contempt for the institution of morality are quite compatible with 'cruelty, persecution, punishment and moral reprobation' (*ROE*, Interlude 1). However, though Russell pulled back from the full-on humanistic amoralism of writers like Richard Garner (1994) and Ian Hinckfuss (1987), he continued to think that there was a dark side to morality. Witness *HSEP*, pp. 173–4 and one of his 'Newly Discovered Maxims of La Rochefoucauld': 'The purpose of morals is to allow people to inflict suffering without compunction' (*Fact and Fiction*, p. 184). Russell does say that he is not 'at all points, ... in agreement with the epigramatic Duke [i.e., La Rochefoucauld]' but I take it that this is a device on the part of the epigramatic Earl to distance himself from sentiments that he only half-believed.

Phase 5: 1923–1945. After some confused subjectivist stumblings which I shall pass over in silence (*ROE*, pp. 125–30), Russell developed a sophisticated variant of emotivism during the thirties which he first publshed in 1935, anticipating Ayer's *Language, Truth and Logic* (1936) by one year, and Stevenson's 'The Emotive Meaning of Ethical Terms' (1937) by two. (Russell may have been aware of W.H.F. Barnes' 'A Suggestion About Value' *Analysis* 1, (1933) but then again, he may not, since at the time he did not regard himself as a professional philosopher and may not have been keeping up with the literature.) Russell's version of emotivism did not excite much comment at the time,[11] perhaps because it is buried towards the back of *Religion and Science*, a book largely devoted to knocking religion in the name of science (*RS* ch. ix, *ROE*, pp. 131–44). (Russell did not enhance his status as an emotivist by burying his second exposition towards the back of *Power: A New Social Analysis* (1938), which, as its title suggests, is largely devoted to the analysis of power.) The theory would appear to be a direct descendant of Russell's 'desire to desire' theory of 1897. According to the 1897 theory, to say that X is good is to *state* that the speaker (or perhaps the community) desires to desire X. According to the 1935 theory, to say that X is good is to *express* (in the optative mood) the desire that everyone should desire X. Thus, 'X is good' is equivalent to 'Would that everyone desired X!'. Not only did Russell anticipate Ayer and Stevenson but also his version of emotivism is distinctly superior to the versions they went on to invent. The early emotivists had trouble making room for moral contradictions – special curlicues had to be added to allow 'X is good' and 'X is bad' to contradict one another. This is not a problem for Russell. Two optatives contradict one another if the desires expressed cannot be jointly realized. For Russell 'X is good', means 'Would that everyone desired X!' and 'X is bad', means 'Would that nobody desired X!' – a pair of optatives which cannot both be fulfilled. Thus, we have moral contradictions without the need of curlicues. More generally, Russell's theory allows for logical relations between moral judgments which the theories of Stevenson and Ayer notoriously do not. We can define a consequence relation for optatives such that optative B is a consequence of the set of optatives A and a (possibly empty) set of propositions C, iff A cannot be realized under circumstances C unless B is realized too.

---

[11] Nor has it excited much comment since. Urmson in his *The Emotive Theory of Ethics* (1968) and Warnock in her *Ethics Since 1900* (1st edn. 1960, 3rd ed. 1978) both seem to be completely unaware of it.

Finally, Russell's theory, unlike the theories of Ayer and Stevenson, is not menaced by a vicious circularity. For Ayer and Stevenson,
to say that X is good is to express approval of X. But to approve of
X is to think or feel that X is good, which begets a vicious circle.
For Russell, there is no such circle, since 'good' and 'bad' are defined in terms of desire rather than the thought-saturated emotions
of approval and disappproval. The theory had another advantage from
Russell's point of view – it allowed him to moralize with a clean intellectual conscience. In *RTC* (*ROE*, ch. 20) Russell considers the charge
that his penchant for 'vehement ethical judgments' is incompatible
with his official metaethic. He replies that according to his own
theory, the function of moral discourse is to express desires as to the
desires of mankind. Since he felt such desires, why not express them?
The moralizing error theorist is, at worst, a hypocrite, and at best, a
dealer in useful fictions. The moralizing emotivist, by contrast, is an
honest man who uses moral language for its express purpose. However, Russell remained unhappy with emotivism. When moralizing
he continued to feel not only that he was expressing his desires, but
also that his desires were somehow *right* (*ROE*, p. 149). His last effort
in metaethics was an attempt to do justice to this feeling.

Phase 6: 1946–1970. The metaethical part of *HSEP* was written in
1946 but not published till 1954. What Russell hoped to do (and what
he half-believed he had achieved) was to inject a little objectivity
into ethics, by conjuring intersubjective truth out of subjective sentiments. His definitions and propositions would, 'if accepted', provide
a 'coherent body of propositions ... true (or false) in the same sense
as [the] propositions of science' (*HSEP*, p. 116, *ROE*, p. 162). Sainsbury is at least right about *HSEP*. The theory is indeed, derivative,
'close to Hume's, with a dash of emotivism', though what Sainsbury
manages to miss is that there is also a substantial dollop of Sidgwick.
I shall not discuss the theory in detail since in my view, and I think
Russell's, it is something of a failure. (See *ROE*, pp. 151–4 and 164–6.)
Russell was ambivalent about it at the time and soon abandoned it,
reverting to a dissatisfied and perplexed emotivism (*ROE*, pp. 164–5).
'I cannot see how to refute the arguments for the subjectivity of
ethical values,' he declared in 1960, 'but I find myself incapable of
believing that all that is wrong with wanton cruelty is that I don't
like it ... when it comes to the philosophy of moral judgments, I am
impelled in two opposite directions and remain perplexed. I have

already expressed this perplexity in print, and I should deeply rejoice if I could find or be shown a way to resolve it, but as yet I remain dissatisfied' (*ROE* pp. 165–6). And on that sad note, Russell ended his career as an ethical theorist.

There is more, much more, to be said about Russell's ethical theory and I try to say some of it in the introduction and notes to *ROE*. The encounters with Moore, the variants of emotivism, the error theory, and the humanistic amoralism – all could do with an extended treatment. But space is limited and time is short. Though Russell did not solve the problems of metaethics to his own satisfaction, I think I have done enough to demonstrate that he was an ethical thinker of interest and distinction. I do not, of course, claim for Russell the same gigantic stature as an ethical theorist that he enjoys as a logician and a philosopher of mathematics. But I do claim that he was a highly inventive ethical thinker whose achievement ranks rather higher than writers such as Stevenson who have nothing but their metaethics to boast of.[12]

---

[12] I would like to thank Ray Perkins for some useful comments on an earlier draft.

BIBLIOGRAPHY

Ayer, A.J. 1946. *Language, Truth and Logic*, 2nd ed. New York: Dover.

Barnes, W.H.F. 1933. 'A suggestion about value', *Analysis*, 1.

Bradley, F.H. 1930. *Appearance and Reality*, 9th impression. Oxford: Oxford University Press.

Garner, Richard. 1994. *Beyond Morality*. Philadelphia: Temple University Press.

Grayling, Anthony. 1996. *Russell*. Oxford: Oxford University Press.

Hampton, Jean. 1986. *Hobbes and the Social Contract Tradition*. Cambridge: Cambridge University Press.

Hinckfuss, Ian. 1987. *The Moral Society: Its Structure and Effects*. Canberra: Department of Philosophy, Australian National University.

Hobbes, Thomas. 1994. *Leviathan*, edited by Edwin Curley. Indianapolis: Hackett.

Hume, David. 1978. *A Treatise of Human Nature*, 2nd ed., edited by Selby-Bigge, L.A. and Nidditch, P.H. Oxford: Oxford University Press.

Jamieson, Dale, ed. 1999. *Singer and His Critics*. Oxford: Oxford University Press.

Kavka, Gregory. 1986. *Hobbesian Moral and Political Theory*. Princeton: Princeton University Press.

Kavka, Gregory. 1987. *The Moral Paradoxes of Nuclear Deterrence*. Cambridge: Cambridge University Press.

Lewis, David. 1989. 'Dispositional Theories of Value', *Aristotelian Society Supp. Vol.* 63.

Lippincott, Mark. 1990. 'Russell's Leviathan'. *Russell*, n.s. Vol. 10, no. 1.

Locke, John. 1988. *Two Treatises of Government*, student edn., edited by Peter Laslett. Cambridge: Cambridge University Press.

Locke, John 1975. *An Essay Concerning Human Understanding*, edited by P.H. Nidditch. Oxford: Oxford University Press.

McGill, V.J. 'Russell's Political and Economic Philosophy' in Schlipp, ed. 1944. *The Philosophy of Bertrand Russell*. Evanston. IL: Northwestern University Press.

Mackie, J.L. 1946. 'The Refutation of Morals', *Australasian Journal of Psychology and Philosophy*, 24: 77–90.

Mackie, J.L. 1976. 'Sidgwick's Pessimism', *Philosophical Quarterly*, 26, 105. (Reprinted in Mackie 1985: 77–90, all references to this reprint.)

Mackie, J.L. 1977. *Ethics: Inventing Right and Wrong*. Harmondsworth: Penguin.

Mackie, J.L. 1985. *Selected Papers vol. 2, Persons and Values*. Oxford: Oxford University Press.

McTaggart, J. McT. Ellis. 1996. *Philosophical Studies*, edited by S.V. Keeling. Bristol: Thoemmes Press.

Marx, Karl. 1845. 'Theses on Feurbach' in Marx, Karl and Engels, Friederich. 1976. *The German Ideology*. Moscow: Progress Publishers.

Mill, J.S. 1843. *A System of Logic, Ratiocinative and Inductive*. London: J.W. Parker.

Mill, J.S. 1989. *On Liberty and Other Writings*, edited by Stefan Collini. Cambridge: Cambridge University Press.

Moore, G.E. 1991. *The Elements of Ethics*, edited by T. Regan. Philadelphia: Temple University Press.

Moore, G.E. 1993. *Principia Ethica*, revised ed., edited by T. Baldwin. Cambridge: Cambridge University Press.

Nozick, Robert. 1974. *Anarchy, State and Utopia*. Oxford: Blackwell.

Popper, Sir K.R. 1966. *The Open Society and its Enemies*, 5th ed., 2 vols., vol. 1, *The Spell of Plato*, vol. 2, *The High Tide of Prophecy: Hegel and Marx*. London, Routledge.

Pybus, Cassandra. 1993. *Gross Moral Turpitude: the Orr Case Reconsidered*. Melbourne: Heinemann.

Rachels, James, ed. 1998. *Ethical Theory*. Oxford: Oxford University Press.

Ryan, Alan. 1988. *Bertrand Russell: A Political Life.* Harmondsworth: Penguin.

Sainsbury, Mark. 1979. *Russell.* London: Routledge.

Santayana, George. 1913. *The Winds of Doctrine: Studies in Contemporary Opinion.* London: J.M. Dent & Sons.

Schlipp, Paul Arthur, ed. 1944. *The Philosophy of Bertrand Russell.* Evanston, IL: Northwestern University Press.

Schneewind, J.B. 1977. *Sidgwick's Ethics and Victorian Moral Philosophy.* Oxford: Oxford University Press.

Sidgwick, Henry. 1907. *The Methods of Ethics*, 7th edn. London: Macmillan.

Slater, John. 1994. *Bertrand Russell.* Bristol: Thoemmes.

Stevenson, C.L. 1937. 'The Emotive Meaning of Ethical Terms'. *Mind*, 46.

Stevenson, C.L. 1944. *Ethics and Language.* New Haven: Yale University Press.

Stevenson, C.L. 1963. *Facts and Values.* New Haven: Yale University Press.

Urmson, J.O. 1968. *The Emotive Theory of Ethics.* London: Hutchinson.

Warnock. Mary. 1978. *Ethics Since 1900*, 3rd ed. Oxford: Oxford University Press.

Works by Russell

'The Elements of Ethics', 1910, *Papers* 6, pp. 217–50.

Roads to Freedom. London: Allen and Unwin, 1918.

The Practice and Theory of Bolshevism. London: Allen and Unwin, 1920.

On Education, especially in Early Childood. London: Allen and Unwin, 1926.

Education and the Social Order. London: Allen and Unwin, 1932.

Freedom and Organisation, 1814–1914. London: Allen and Unwin, 1934.

In Praise of Idleness and Other Essays. London: Allen and Unwin, 1935.

Unpopular Essays. London: Allen and Unwin, 1950.

Fact and Fiction. London: Allen and Unwin, 1961.

Dear Bertrand Russell, edited by Barry Feinberg and Ronald Kasrils. London: Allen and Unwin, 1969.

Mortals and Others, edited by Harry Ruja. London: Allen and Unwin, 1975. vol. 1.

Selected Letters of Bertrand Russell, vol. 1, *The Private Years, 1884–1914*, edited by Nicholas Griffin. London: Penguin.

SELECTIVE BIBLIOGRAPHY

PART I: WORKS BY RUSSELL
THE COLLECTED PAPERS OF BERTRAND RUSSELL

Volume 1: *Cambridge Essays: 1888–99*. Edited by Kenneth Blackwell, Andrew Brink, Nicholas Griffin, Richard A. Rempel, and John G. Slater. London: George Allen and Unwin, 1983.

Volume 2: *Philosophical Papers: 1896–99*. Edited by Nicholas Griffin and Albert C. Lewis. London: Unwin Hyman, 1990.

Volume 3: *Toward the "Principles of Mathematics", 1900–02*. Edited by Gregory H. Moore. London and New York: Routledge, 1993.

Volume 4: *Foundations of Logic, 1903–05*. Edited by Alasdair Urquhart. London and New York: Routledge, 1994.

Volume 6: *Logical and Philosophical Papers, 1909–13*. Edited by John G. Slater. London, Boston, and Sydney: Allen and Unwin, 1992.

Volume 7: *Theory of Knowledge: The 1913 Manuscript*. Edited by Elizabeth Ramsden Eames in collaboration with Kenneth Blackwell. London: George Allen and Unwin, 1984.

Volume 8: *The Philosophy of Logical Atomism and Other Essays: 1914–19*. Edited by John G. Slater. London: George Allen and Unwin, 1986.

Volume 9: *Essays on Language, Mind and Matter, 1919–26*. Edited by John G. Slater. London, Boston, Sydney, Wellington: Unwin Hyman, 1988.

Volume 10: *A Fresh Look at Empiricism, 1927–42*. Edited by John G. Slater. London and New York: Routledge, 1996.

Volume 11: *Last Philosophical Testament, 1943–68*. Edited by John G. Slater. London and New York: Routledge, 1997.

Volume 12: *Contemplation and Action: 1902–14*. Edited by Richard A. Rempel, Andrew Brink, and Margaret Moran. London: George Allen and Unwin, 1985.

Volume 13: *Prophecy and Dissent, 1914–16*. Edited by Richard A. Rempel. London, Boston, and Sydney: Unwin Hyman, 1988.

Volume 14: *Pacifism and Revolution: 1916–18*. Edited by Richard A. Rempel, Louis Greenspan, Beryl Haslam, Albert C. Lewis and Mark Lippincott. London and New York: Routledge, 1995.

Volume 15: *Uncertain Paths to Freedom: Russia and China, 1919–22*. Edited by Richard A. Rempel and Beryl Haslam. London and New York: Routledge, 2000.

Volume 28: *Man's Peril, 1954–55*. Edited by Andrew G. Bone. London: Routledge, 2003.

Other Collections

1910. *Philosophical Essays*. London: Longmans, Green.

1918. *Mysticism and Logic*. London: Longmans, Green.

1927. *Selected Papers of Bertrand Russell*. New York: Modern Library.

1928. *Sceptical Essays*. London: Allen and Unwin.

1935. *In Praise of Idleness and Other Essays*. London: Allen and Unwin.

1941. *Let the People Think*. London: Watts.

1950. *Unpopular Essays*. London: Allen and Unwin.

1953. *Satan in the Suburbs and Other Stories*. London: Bodley Head.

1954. *Nightmares of Eminent Persons*. London: Bodley Head.

1956. *Portraits from Memory and Other Essays*. London: Allen and Unwin.

1956. *Logic and Knowledge*, edited by Robert C. Marsh. London: Allen and Unwin.

1957. *Why I am Not a Christian*, edited by Paul Edwards. London: Allen and Unwin.

1961. *The Basic Writings of Bertrand Russell*, edited by R.E. Egner and L.E. Denonn. London: Allen and Unwin.

1961. *Fact and Fiction*. London: Allen and Unwin.

1967. *War Crimes in Vietnam*. London: Allen and Unwin.

1969. *Dear Bertrand Russell*, edited by Barry Feinberg and Ronald Kasrils. London: Allen and Unwin.

1972. *The Collected Stories of Bertrand Russell*, edited by Barry Feinberg. London: Allen and Unwin.

1972. *The Philosophy of Logical Atomism*, edited by David Pears. London: Collins.

1973–83. *Bertrand Russell's America*, edited by Barry Feinberg and Ronald Kasrils. London: Allen and Unwin; 2 vols.

1973. *Essays in Analysis*, edited by Douglas Lackey. London: Allen and Unwin.

1975. *Mortals and Others*, edited by Harry Ruja. London: Allen and Unwin.

1986. *Bertrand Russell on God and Religion*, edited by Al Seckel. Buffalo: Prometheus.

1987. *Bertrand Russell on Ethics, Sex and Marriage*, edited by Al Seckel. Buffalo: Prometheus.

1992. *The Selected Letters of Bertrand Russell*, vol. 1, *The Private Years, 1884–1914*, edited by Nicholas Griffin. London: Penguin.

1999. *Russell on Religion*, edited by Louis Greenspan and Stefan Andersson. London: Routledge.

1999. *Russell on Ethics*, edited by Charles Pigden. London: Routledge.

2001. *The Selected Letters of Bertrand Russell*, vol. 2, *The Public Years, 1914–70*, edited by Nicholas Griffin, with A.R. Miculan. London: Routledge.

2001. *Correspondance sur la philosophie, la logique et la politique avec Louis Couturat (1897–1913)*, edited by Anne-Françoise Schmid. Paris: Kimé; 2 vols.

2002. *Yours Faithfully, Bertrand Russell*, edited by Ray Perkins Jr. Chicago: Open Court.

Books

1896. *German Social Democracy*. London: Longmans, Green.

1897. *An Essay on the Foundations of Geometry*. Cambridge: Cambridge University Press.

1900. *A Critical Exposition of the Philosophy of Leibniz*. Cambridge: Cambridge University Press.

1903. *The Principles of Mathematics*. Cambridge: Cambridge University Press.

1910–13 *Principia Mathematica*, with A.N. Whitehead. Cambridge: Cambridge University Press. 3 vols. (revised edition, 1925–7).

1912. *The Problems of Philosophy*. London: Williams and Norgate.

1914. *Our Knowledge of the External World as a Field for Scientific Method in Philosophy*. Chicago: Open Court (revised edition, London: Allen and Unwin, 1926).

1916. *Principles of Social Reconstruction*. London: Allen and Unwin.

1917. *Political Ideals*. New York: Century.

1918. *Roads to Freedom*. London: Allen and Unwin.

1919. *Introduction to Mathematical Philosophy*. London: Allen and Unwin.

1920. *The Practice and Theory of Bolshevism*. London: Allen and Unwin.

1921. *The Analysis of Mind*. London: Allen and Unwin.

1922. *The Problem of China*. London: Allen and Unwin.

1923. *The Prospects of Industrial Civilization*, with Dora Russell. London: Allen and Unwin.

1923. *The ABC of Atoms*. London: Kegan Paul.

1924. *Icarus, of the Future of Science*. London: Kegan Paul.

1925. *The ABC of Relativity*. London: Kegan Paul.

1926. *On Education, especially in Early Childhood*. London: Allen and Unwin.

1927. *The Analysis of Matter*. London: Kegan Paul.

1927. *An Outline of Philosophy*. London: Allen and Unwin.

1929. *Marriage and Morals*. London: Allen and Unwin.

1930. *The Conquest of Happiness*. London: Allen and Unwin.

1931. *The Scientific Outlook*. London: Allen and Unwin.

1932. *Education and the Social Order*. London: Allen and Unwin.

1934. *Freedom and Organization, 1814–1914*. London: Allen and Unwin.

1935. *Religion and Science*. London: Thornton Butterworth.

1936. *Which Way to Peace?* London: Michael Joseph.

1938. *Power: A New Social Analysis*. London: Allen and Unwin.

1940. *An Inquiry into Meaning and Truth*. New York: Norton.

1945. *A History of Western Philosophy*. New York: Simon and Schuster.

1948. *Human Knowledge: Its Scope and Limits*. London: Allen and Unwin.

1949. *Authority and the Individual*. London: Allen and Unwin.

1951. *The Impact of Science on Society*. New York: Columbia University Press.

1951. *New Hopes for a Changing World*. London: Allen and Unwin.

1954. *Human Society in Ethics and Politics*. London: Allen and Unwin.

1959. *Common Sense and Nuclear Warfare*. London: Allen and Unwin.

1959. *My Philosophical Development*. London: Allen and Unwin.

1960. *Bertrand Russell Speaks His Mind*. New York: World Publishing.

1961. *Has Man a Future?* London: Allen and Unwin.

1963. *Unarmed Victory*. London: Allen and Unwin.

1967–9. *The Autobiography of Bertrand Russell*. London: Allen and Unwin; 3 vols.

Selected Articles

Since Russell wrote well over 2000 articles, the following list, long as it is, is necessarily highly selective. The bias is towards philosophical articles, though I have construed 'philosophy' widely and also included a number of his more important non–philosophical articles. Usually the place of first publication is cited, unless it is utterly obscure or publication took place long after the piece was written. Where the title appears in italics, the piece was first published as a pamphlet. References to reprintings in *The Collected Papers of Bertrand Russell*, *Logic and Knowledge* (LK), and *Essays in Analysis* (EA) are also given. In addition I indicate if the work was included in one of the following collections of Russell's papers (all of which remain in print): *Philosophical Essays* (PE), *Mysticism and Logic* (ML), *Sceptical Essays* (SE),

In Praise of Idleness (*IPI*), *Unpopular Essays* (*UE*), *Portraits from Memory* (*PFM*), and *Why I Am Not a Christian* (*WNC*). Page references for these last are not given, since different printings of these books have different paginations. English titles are used, even when first published in another language. Full bibliographic details may be found in the bibliography by Blackwell and Ruja cited below.

'The Logic of Geometry' (1896), *Mind*, 5: 1–23; repr. *Papers* 2: 267–86.

'The A Priori in Geometry' (1896), *Proceedings of the Aristotelian Society*, 3: 97–112; repr. *Papers* 1: 291–304.

'On the Relations of Number and Quantity' (1897), *Mind*, 6: 326–41; repr. *Papers* 2: 70–82.

'An Analysis of Mathematical Reasoning' (1898), *Papers* 2: 162–242.

'The Classification of Relations' (1899), *Papers* 2: 138–46.

'Fundamental Ideas and Axioms of Mathematics' (1899), *Papers* 2: 265–305.

'The Axioms of Geometry' (1899), *Revue de métaphysique et de morale*, 7: 684–707; 1st complete publication: *Papers* 2: 394–415.

'The Principles of Mathematics' (draft of 1899–1900), *Papers* 3: 13–180.

'The Notion of Order and Absolute Position in Space and Time' (1901), *Bibliothèque du Congrès Internationale de Philosophie*, 3: 241–77; repr. *Papers* 3: 241–58.

'The Logic of Relations with Some Applications to the Theory of Series' (1901), *Revue de mathématiques*, 7: 115–48; repr. *Papers* 3: 314–49; *LK*, 3–38.

'Recent Italian Work on the Foundations of Mathematics' (1901), *Papers* 3: 352–62.

'Recent Work on the Principles of Mathematics' (1901), *International Monthly*, 4:83–101; repr. *Papers* 3: 366–79; *ML*.

'General Theory of Well-Ordered Series' (1902), *Revue de mathématiques*, 8: 12-43; repr. *Papers* 3: 389–421.

'On Finite and Infinite Cardinal Numbers' (1902), with A.N. Whitehead, *American Journal of Mathematics*, 24: 367–94; Russell's contribution repr. *Papers* 3: 425–30.

'The Free Man's Worship', *The Independent Review*, 1:415–24; repr. *Papers* 12, 66–72; *ML*.

'Recent Work on the Philosophy of Leibniz' (1903), *Mind*, 12: 177–201; repr. *Papers* 3: 537–61.

'Meinong's Theory of Complexes and Assumptions' (1904), *Mind*, 13: 204–19, 336–54, 509–24; repr. *Papers* 3: 432–74; *EA*, 21–76.

'The Axiom of Infinity' (1904), *The Hibbert Journal*, 2: 809–12; repr. *Papers* 3: 476–8; *EA*, 256–9.

'The Existential Import of Propositions' (1905), *Mind*, 14: 398–401; repr. *Papers* 3: 486–9; *EA*, 98–102.

'On Denoting' (1905), *Mind*, 14: 479–93; repr. *Papers* 3: 415–27; *EA*, 103–119; *LK*, 41–56.

'The Nature of Truth' (1905), *Papers* 3: 492–506.

'Necessity and Possibility' (1905). *Papers* 3: 508–20.

'On the Relation of Mathematics to Symbolic Logic' (1905), *Revue de métaphysique et de morale*, 13: 906–16; repr. *Papers* 3: 524–32; *EA*, 260–71.

Review of Meinong *et. al.*, *Untersuchungen zur Gegenstandstheorie und Psychologie*, *Mind*, 14: 530–8; repr. *Papers* 3: 596–604; *EA*, 77–88.

'On Substitution' (1905); forthcoming in *Papers* 5.

'On Some Difficulties in the Theory of Transfinite Numbers and Order Types' (1906), *Proceedings of the London Mathematical Society*, 4: 29–53; repr. *EA*, 135–64.

'On "Insolubilia" and their Solution by Symbolic Logic' (1906), *Revue de métaphysique et de morale*, 14: 627–50; *EA*, 190–214.

'On the Substitutional Theory of Classes and Relations' (1906), *EA*, 165–89.

'On Substitution' (1906), forthcoming in *Papers* 5.

'The Theory of Implication' (1906), *American Journal of Mathematics*, 28: 159–202.

'The Paradox of the Liar' (1906), forthcoming in *Papers* 5.

'On the Nature of Truth' (1907), *Proceedings of the Aristotelian Society*, 7: 28–49.

'The Regressive Method of Discovering the Premises of Mathematics' (1907), *EA*, 272–83.

'Transatlantic "Truth"' (1908), *The Albany Review*, 2: 393–410; repr. *PE*.

'Mathematical Logic as Based on the Theory of Types' (1908), *American Journal of Mathematics*, 30: 222–62; repr. *LK*, 59–102.

'Pragmatism' (1909), *The Edinburgh Review*, 209: 363–88; repr. *Papers* 6: 260–84; *PE*.

'The Elements of Ethics' (1910), *Philosophical Essays*; repr. *Papers* 6, 217–50.

'The Theory of Logical Types' (1910), *Revue de métaphysique et de morale*, 18: 263–301; repr. *Papers* 6: 4–31; *EA*, 215–52.

'On the Nature of Truth and Falsehood' (1910), *Philosophical Essays*; repr. *Papers* 6: 116–24.

Anti-Suffragist Anxieties (1910), repr. *Papers* 12: 306–16.

'The Philosophical Importance of Mathematical Logic' (1911), *Revue de métaphysique et de morale*, 19: 282–91; repr. *Papers* 6: 33–40, *EA*, 284–294.

'On the Axioms of the Infinite and of the Transfinite' (1911), *Société mathématique de France, Comptes rendus des séances*, 2: 22–35; repr. *Papers* 6, 43–53.

'Analytic Realism' (1911), *Bulletin de la société française de philosophie*, 11: 282–91; repr. *Papers* 6, 133–146.

'Knowledge by Acquaintance and Knowledge by Description' (1911), *Proceedings of the Aristotelian Society*, 11: 108–28; repr. *Papers* 6, 148–161; *ML*.

'On the Relations of Universals and Particulars' (1912), *Proceedings of the Aristotelian Society*, 12: 1–24; repr. *Papers* 6: 167–82; *LK*, 105–124.

'The Philosophy of Bergson' (1912), *The Monist*, 22: 321–47; repr. *Papers* 6: 320–37.

'The Essence of Religion' (1912), *The Hibbert Journal*, 11: 46–62; repr. *Papers* 12: 112–22.

'On Matter' (1912), *Papers* 6: 80–95.

'On the Notion of Cause' (1913), *Proceedings of the Aristotelian Society*, 13: 1–26; repr. *Papers* 6: 193–210; *ML*.

'The Relation of Sense-Data to Physics' (1914), *Scientia*, 16: 1–27; repr. *Papers* 8: 5–26; *ML*.

'Mysticism and Logic' (1914), *The Hibbert Journal*, 12: 780–803; repr. *Papers* 8: 30–49; *ML*.

'The Ultimate Constituents of Matter' (1915), *The Monist*, 25: 399–417; *Papers* 8: 75–86; *ML*.

'The Ethics of War' (1915), *The International Journal of Ethics*, 25: 127–42; repr. *Papers*, 13: 63–73.

The Policy of the Entente, 1904–14 (1915), repr. *Papers* 13: 214–280.

'The Philosophy of Logical Atomism' (1918), *The Monist*, 28: 495–27, 29: 32–63, 190–222, 345–80; repr. *Papers* 8: 160–244; *LK*, 178–281.

Review of Dewey's *Essays in Experimental Logic* (1919), *The Journal of Philosophy, Psychology, and Scientific Methods*, 16: 5–26; repr. *Papers* 8: 134–54.

'On Propositions: What They Are and How They Mean' (1919), *Aristotelian Supplementary Volume* 2: 1–43; repr. *Papers* 8: 278–306; *LK*, 285–320.

Introduction to Wittgenstein's *Tractatus Logico-Philosophicus* (1922), repr. *Papers* 9: 101–12.

'Is There an Absolute Good?' (1922), *Papers* 9: 345–6.

Free Thought and Official Propaganda (1922), repr. *Papers* 15: 348–61; *SE*.

'Vagueness' (1923), *Australasian Journal of Psychology and Philosophy*, 1: 84–92; repr. *Papers* 9: 147–54.

'Logical Atomism' (1924), *Contemporary British Philosophy*, ed. by J.H. Muirhead, pp. 357–83; repr. *Papers* 9: 162–79; *LK*, 323–43.

'Philosophy in the Twentieth Century' (1924), *The Dial*, 77: 271–90; repr. *Papers* 9: 451–66; *SE*.

Why I Am Not a Christian (1927), repr. *Papers* 10: 181–93; *WNC*.

'The Danger of Creed Wars' (1927), *The Socialist Register*, 16: 7–19; *SE*.

Review of Ramsey, *The Foundations of Mathematics* (1931), *Mind*, 40: 476–82; repr. *Papers* 10: 107–14.

'The Philosophy of Communism' (1934), *Papers* 10: 412–21.

'The Ancestry of Fascism' (1935), *The Political Quarterly*, 6: 1–19; repr. *Papers* 10: 423–35; *IPI*.

'Determinism and Physics' (1936), *Proceedings of the University of Durham Philosophical Society*, 9: 228–45; repr. *Papers* 10: 68–80.

'Auto-obituary', *The Listener* 16: 289; *UE*.

'The Limits of Empiricism' (1936), *Proceedings of the Aristotelian Society*, 36: 131–50; repr. *Papers* 10: 314–28.

'Philosophy's Ulterior Motives' (1937), *Atlantic Monthly*, 159: 149–55; repr. *Papers* 10: 336–43; *UE*.

'The Superior Virtue of the Oppressed' (1937), *The Nation*, 144: 731–2; *UE*.

'On Verification' (1938), *Proceedings of the Aristotelian Society*, 38: 1–20; repr. *Papers* 10: 345–59.

'The Relevance of Psychology to Logic' (1938), *Aristotelian Society Supplementary Volume*, 17: 42–53; repr. *Papers* 10: 362–70.

'On Order in Time' (1938), *Proceedings of the Cambridge Philosophical Society*, 32: 216–28; repr. *Papers* 10: 124–37; *LK*, 347–63.

'Dewey's New *Logic*' (1939), *The Philosophy of John Dewey*, ed. by P.A. Schilpp, pp. 137–56; repr. *Papers* 10: 145–60.

'The Role of the Intellectual in the Modern World' (1939), *American Journal of Sociology*, 44: 491–8.

'The Philosophy of Santayana' (1940), *The Philosophy of George Santayana*, ed. by P.A. Schilpp, pp. 453–74; repr. *Papers* 10: 472–90.

'My Mental Development' (1944), *The Philosophy of Bertrand Russell*, ed. by P.A. Schilpp; repr. *Papers* 11: 5–18.

'Reply to Criticisms' (1944), *The Philosophy of Bertrand Russell*, ed. by P.A. Schilpp; repr. *Papers* 11: 18–64.

'Logical Positivism' (1945), *Polemic*, 1: 6–13; repr. *Papers* 11: 148–55.

'My Own Philosophy' (1946), *Papers* 11: 69–82.

'The Problem of Universals' (1946), *Polemic*, 2: 21–35; repr. *Papers* 11: 258–73.

'Philosophy for Laymen' (1946), *Universities Quarterly*, 1: 38–49; repr. *Papers* 11: 376–83; *UE*.

'The Atomic Bomb and the Prevention of War' (1946), *Polemic*, 4: 15–22.

'The Faith of a Rationalist' (1947), *The Listener*, 37: 826, 836; repr. *Papers* 11: 85–88.

Philosophy and Politics (1947), repr. *Papers* 11: 391–404; *UE*.

'The Outlook for Mankind' (1948), *Horizon*, 17: 238–46.

Debate with Copleston on the existence of God (1948), *Humanitas*, 2: 2–17; rep. *Papers* 11: 524–41; *WNC*.

'Le Philosophe en temps de crise' (1950), *Papers* 11: 409–16.

'Is Mathematics Purely Linguistic?' (1950), *EA*, 295–306; repr. *Papers* 11: 353–62.

'Logical Positivism' (1950), *Revue internationale de philosophie*, 4: 3–19; repr. *Papers* 11: 155–67; *LK*, 367–82.

'Mind and Matter' (1950), *Portraits from Memory*; repr. *Papers* 11: 280–92.

'The Principle of Individuation' (1950), *Revue de métaphysique et de morale*, 55: 1–15; repr. *Papers* 11: 294–303.

'Reflections on my Eightieth Birthday'. *The Listener*, 47: 823–4; *PFM*.

'A Philosophy for Our Time' (1953), *London Calling*, 737: 8, 18; repr. *Papers* 11: 443–9; *PFM*.

'The Cult of "Common Usage"' (1953), *British Journal for the Philosophy of Science*, 3: 303–7; repr. *Papers* 11: 610–14; *PFM*.

'Man's Peril from the Hydrogen Bomb' (1954), *The Listener*, 52: 1135–6; repr. *Papers* 28; *PFM*.

'John Stuart Mill' (1955), *Proceedings of the British Academy*, 55: 43–59; repr. *Papers* 11: 497–511; *PFM*.

Russell-Einstein Manifesto (1955), *New York Times*, 10 July; repr. *Papers* 28.

'Philosophical Analysis' (1956), *The Hibbert Journal*, 54: 320–9; repr. *Papers* 11: 614–25.

'Perception' (1957), *Papers* 11: 305–7.

'Logic and Ontology' (1957), *Journal of Philosophy*, 54: 225–30; repr. *Papers* 11: 625–30.

'Mr Strawson on Referring' (1957), *Mind*, 66: 385–9; repr. *Papers* 11: 630–5.

'What is Mind?' (1958), *Journal of Philosophy*, 55: 5–12; repr. *Papers* 11: 635–42.

'The Case for British Nuclear Disarmament' (1962), *Bulletin of the Atomic Scientists*, 18: 6–10.

'The Duty of a Philosopher in this Age' (1964), *Essays in Honor of Paul Arthur Schilpp*, ed. by E. Freeman; repr. *Papers* 11: 457–63.

SECONDARY SOURCES – BOOKS

Bibliographies

Blackwell, Kenneth and Ruja, Harry (1994), *A Bibliography of Bertrand Russell*, London: Routledge (3 vols.).

Blackwell, Kenneth and Spadoni, Carl (1992), *A Detailed Catalogue of the Second Archives of Bertrand Russell*, Bristol: Thoemmes.

Feinberg, Barry (1967), *A Detailed Catalogue of the Archives of Bertrand Russell*, London: Continuum 1.

Biographies

Clark, Ronald William (1975), *The Life of Bertrand Russell*, London: J. Cape.

Monk, Ray (1996), *Bertrand Russell: The Spirit of Solitude*, London: J. Cape.

Monk, Ray (2000) *Bertrand Russell 1921–1970: The Ghost of Madness*, London: J. Cape.

Moorehead, Caroline (1992) *Bertrand Russell*, New York: Viking.

Wood, Alan (1957) *Bertrand Russell: The Passionate Sceptic*, London: Allen and Unwin.

Philosophical Monographs

Aiken, Lillian W. (1963) *Bertrand Russell's Philosophy of Morals*, New York: Humanities Press.

Ayer, Alfred Jules (1972) *Russell*, London: Fontana-Collins.

Blackwell, Kenneth (1985) *The Spinozistic Ethics of Bertrand Russell*, London: George Allen and Unwin.

Darbon, André (1949) *La philosophie des mathématiques; études sur la logistique de Russell*, Paris: PUF.

de Almeida, Claudio (1998) *Russell on the Foundations of Logic*, Porto Alegre: PUCRS.

Dejnožka, Jan (1999) *Bertrand Russell on Modality and Logical Relevance*. Aldershot: Ashgate.

Eames, Elizabeth R. (1969) *Bertrand Russell's Theory of Knowledge*, London: George Allen and Unwin.

Eames, Elizabeth R., (1989) *Bertrand Russell's Dialogue with his Contemporaries*, Southern Illinois University Press.

Fritz, Charles Andrew, Jr (1952) *Bertrand Russell's Construction of the External World*, London: Routledge and Kegan Paul.

Garciadiego (Dantan), Alejandro Ricardo (1992), *Bertrand Russell and the Origins of the Set-Theoretic "Paradoxes"*, Basle: Birkhauser Verlag.

Gotlind, Erik (1952) *Bertrand Russell's Theories of Causation*, Uppsala: Almquist and Wiksell.

Grattan-Guinness, Ivor (1977) *Dear Russell, Dear Jourdain: A Commentary on Russell's Logic, Based on His Correspondence with Philip Jourdain*, New York: Columbia University Press.

Grayling, A.C. (1996) *Bertrand Russell*, London: Oxford University Press.

Griffin, Nicholas (1991) *Russell's Idealist Apprenticeship*, Oxford: Clarendon.

Hager, Paul J., (1994) *Continuity and Change in the Development of Russell's Philosophy*, Dordrecht: Kluwer.

Hylton, Peter W. (1990) *Russell, Idealism, and the Emergence of Analytical Philosophy*, Oxford: Clarendon.

Jager, Ronald (1972) *The Development of Bertrand Russell's Philosophy*, London: George Allen and Unwin.

Jourdain, Philip E.B. (1918) *The Philosophy of Mr B*rtr*nd R*ss*ll*, London: George Allen and Unwin.

Kilmister, Clive William (1984) *Russell*, Brighton: Harvester.

Linsky, Bernard (1999) *Russell's Metaphysical Logic*, Stanford: CSLI.

Miah, Sajahan (1998) *Russell's Theory of Perception (1905–1919)*, Dhaka: Dhaka University.

Pears, David F. (1967) *Bertrand Russell and the British Tradition in Philosophy*, London: Collins.

Rodrigues-Consuegra, Francisco A. (1991), *The Mathematical Philosophy of Bertrand Russell: Origins and Development*, Basle: Birkhäuser.

Sainsbury, Richard Mark (1979) *Russell*, London: Routledge and Kegan Paul.

Slater, John G. (1994) *Bertrand Russell*, Bristol: Thoemmes.

Thalheimer, Ross (1931) *A Critical Examination of the Epistemological and Psycho-physical Doctrines of Bertrand Russell*, Baltimore: Johns Hopkins Press.

Vuillemin, Jules (1968) *Leçons sur la première philosophie de Russell*, Paris: Colin.

Watling, John (1970) *Bertrand Russell*, Edinburgh: Oliver and Boyd.

Other Monographs

Greenspan, Louis (1978), *The Incompatible Prophecies: An Essay on Science and Liberty in the Political Writings of Bertrand Russell*, Oakville, Ont.: Mosaic.

Denton, Peter (2001) *The ABC of Armageddon: Bertrand Russell on science, religion, and the next war, 1919–1938*, Albany: State University of New York Press.

Hardy, G.H. (1970) *Bertrand Russell and Trinity*, Cambridge: Cambridge University Press.

Ironside, Philip (1996), *The Social and Political Thought of Bertrand Russell*, London: Cambridge University Press.

Park, Joe (1963) *Bertrand Russell on Education*, Columbus: Ohio State University Press.

Ryan, Alan (1988) *Bertrand Russell: A Political Life*, New York: Hill and Wang.

Vellacott, Jo (1980) *Bertrand Russell and the Pacifists in the First World War*, New York: St Martins.

Other Books in which Russell's Work Figures Prominently

Ayer, A.J., et al., (1956) *The Revolution in Philosophy*, London: Macmillan.

Ayer, Alfred Jules (1971) *Russell and Moore: The Analytical Heritage*, Cambridge, Mass.: Harvard University Press.

Baillie, James (1997) *Contemporary Analytic Philosophy*, Upper Saddle River, N.J.: Prentice Hall.

Cocchiarella, Nino B. (1987) *Logical Studies in Early Analytical Philosophy*, Columbus: Ohio State University Press.

Coffa, J. Alberto (1991) *The Semantic Tradition from Kant to Carnap. To the Vienna Station*, Cambridge: Cambridge University Press.

Copi, Irving M. (1971) *The Theory of Logical Types*, London: Routledge.

Copleston, Frederick (1966) *A History of Philosophy*, vol. 8, *Modern Philosophy: Bentham to Russell*. London: The Newman Press.

Dejnožka, Jan (1996) *The Ontology of the Analytic Tradition and its Origins: Realism and Identity in Frege, Russell, Wittgenstein and Quine*, Lanham, MD: Littlefield Adams.

Evans, Gareth (1982) *The Varieties of Reference*, New York: Oxford University Press.

Everdell, William (1997) *The First Moderns*, Chicago: University of Chicago Press.

Grayling, A.C. (ed.) (1998) *Philosophy 2: Further Through the Subject*, New York: Oxford University Press.

Hartshorne, Charles (1983) *Insights and Oversights of Great Thinkers*, New York: State University of New York Press.

Heijenoort, Jean van (ed.) *From Frege to Gödel. A Source Book in Mathematical Logic, 1879–1931*, Cambridge, Mass.: Harvard University Press.

Hochberg, Herbert (1978) *Thought, Fact, and Reference. The Origins and Ontology of Logical Atomism*, Minneapolis: University of Minnesota Press.

Lewis, C.I. (1918) *A Survey of Symbolic Logic*, New York: Dover, 1960.

Linsky, Leonard (1967) *Referring*, London: Routledge and Kegan Paul.

Magee, Bryan, (1971) *Modern British Philosophy*, London: Secker and Warburg.

Makin, Gideon (2000) *The Metaphysicians of Meaning. Russell and Frege on Sense and Denotation*, London: Routledge.

Neale, Stephen (1990) *Descriptions*, Cambridge, Mass.: MIT Press.

Oaklander, L. Nathan (1984) *Temporal Relations and Temporal Becoming: A Defense of a Russellian Theory of Time*, Lanham, M.D.: University Press of America.

Ostertag, Gary (ed.) (1998) *Definite Descriptions: A Reader*, Cambridge, Mass.: MIT Press.

Passmore, John Arthur (1957) *A Hundred Years of Philosophy*, New York: Macmillan.

Potter, Michael (2000) *Reason's Nearest Kin, Philosophies of Arithmetic from Kant to Carnap*, Oxford: Oxford University Press.

Urmson, J.O. (1956) *Philosophical Analysis: Its Development Between the Two World Wars*, Oxford: Oxford University Press.

Wang, Hao (1974) *From Mathematics to Philosophy*, London: Routledge and Kegan Paul.

Wang, Hao (1986) *Beyond Analytic Philosophy*, Cambridge, Mass.: MIT Press.

Journal

(Note: Individual papers published in *Russell* are not separately listed.)

Russell: The Journal of Bertrand Russell Studies, The Bertrand Russell Research Centre, McMaster University, Hamilton, Ontario.

Collections of Papers

Irvine, A.D., and G.A. Wedeking (eds) (1993) *Russell and Analytic Philosophy*, Toronto: University of Toronto Press.

Klemke, E.D. (ed.) (1970) *Essays on Bertrand Russell*, Urbana: University of Illinois Press.

Monk, Ray, and Anthony Palmer (eds) (1996) *Bertrand Russell and the Origins of Analytical Philosophy*, Bristol: Theommes Press.

Moran, Margaret, and Carl Spadoni (eds) (1984) *Intellect and Social Conscience: Essays on Bertrand Russell's Early Work*, Hamilton: McMaster University Library Press. Preprinted in *Russell*, n.s. 4 (1984), 1–238.

Nakhnikian, George (ed.) (1974) *Bertrand Russell's Philosophy*, London: Duckworth.

Pears, David F. (ed.) (1972) *Bertrand Russell: A Collection of Critical Essays*, New York: Doubleday.

Roberts, George W. (ed.). (1979) *Bertrand Russell Memorial Volume*, London: Allen and Unwin.

Savage, C. Wade, and C. Anthony Anderson (eds) (1989) *Rereading Russell: Essays on Bertrand Russell's Metaphysics and Epistemology*, Minneapolis: University of Minnesota Press.

Schilpp, Paul Arthur (ed.) (1944) *The Philosophy of Bertrand Russell*, Chicago: Northwestern University; 3rd edn, New York: Harper and Row, 1963.

Schoenman, Ralph (ed.) (1967) *Bertrand Russell: Philosopher of the Century*, London: Allen and Unwin.

Thomas, J.E., and Kenneth Blackwell (eds) (1976) *Russell in Review*, Toronto: Samuel Stevens, Hakkert and Co.

Winchester, Ian, and Kenneth Blackwell (eds) (1988) *Antinomies and Paradoxes: Studies in Russell's Early Philosophy*, Hamilton: McMaster University Library Press. Preprinted in *Russell*, n.s. 8 (1988), 1–248.

Special Issues of Journals

(Note: Individual papers in these collections are not separately listed.)

Hermes vol. 7 (1990).
Inquiry. Critical Thinking Across the Disciplines vol. 20 (2001).
Philosophy vol. 35 (1960).
Philosophy of the Social Sciences vol. 26 (1996).
Revue Internationale de Philosophie, no. 102 (1972).
Synthese vols. 45 and 46 (1980–1981).

Secondary Sources – Articles
General Surveys

Blanshard, Brand (1969) "Bertrand Russell in Retrospect", *Dialogue*, 7, 584–607.

Braithwaite, R.B. (1970) "Bertrand Russell as Philosopher of Science", *British Journal for the Philosophy of Science*, 21, 129–32.

Broad, C.D. (1973) "Bertrand Russell, as Philosopher", *Bulletin of the London Mathematical Society*, 5, 328–41.

Gandy, R.O. (1973) "Bertrand Russell, as Mathematician", *Bulletin of the London Mathematical Society*, 5, 342–48.

Grattan-Guinness, Ivor (1990) "Bertrand Russell (1872–1970) After Twenty Years", *Notes and Records of the Royal Society London*, 44, 280–306.

Kreisel, George (1973) "Bertrand Arthur William Russell, Earl Russell: 1872–1970", *Biographical Memoirs of Fellows of the Royal Society*, 19, 583–620.

Monk, Ray (1999) "Russell", *Philosophy*, 74, 105–17.

Quinton, Anthony (1960) "Russell's Philosophical Development", *Philosophy*, 35, 1–13. Repr. in Quinton, Anthony, *Thoughts and Thinkers*, New York: Holmes and Meier, 1982, 277–87.

Wang, Hao (1965) "Russell and His Logic", *Ratio*, 7, 1–34.

Wang, Hao (1966) "Russell and Philosophy", *Journal of Philosophy*, 63, 670–2.

Wisdom, John (1953) "Bertrand Russell and Modern Philosophy", in Wisdom, John, *Philosophy and Psychoanalysis*, Oxford: Blackwell, 195–209.

Philosophical Papers

Almog, Joseph (1999) "Nothing, Something, Infinity", *Journal of Philosophy*, 96, 462–78.

Anderson, C. Anthony (1986) "Some Difficulties Concerning Russellian Intensional Logic", *Nous*, 20, 35–43.

Anderson, C. Anthony (1989) "Russellian Intensional Logic", in Almog, Joseph, John Perry, and Howard Wettstein (eds), *Themes from Kaplan*, New York: Oxford University Press, 67–103.

Austin, James W. (1978) "Russell's Cryptic Response to Strawson", *Philosophy and Phenomenological Research*, 38, 531–37.

Avey, Albert E. (1942) "Russell's Quest for Objectivity", *Philosophy and Phenomenological Research*, 2, 376–93.

Ayer, Alfred Jules (1938) "On the Scope of Empirical Knowledge", *Erkenntnis*, 7, 267–74.

Ayer, Alfred Jules (1941) "Bertrand Russell on Meaning and Truth", *Nature*, 148, 206–7.

Bach, Kent (1994) "Ramachandran versus Russell", *Analysis*, 54, 183–6.

Bacon, John (1965) "An Alternative Contextual Definition for Descriptions", *Philosophical Studies*, 16, 75–6.

Bar-Elli, Gilead (1980) "Constituents and Denotation in Russell", *Theoria*, 46, 37–51.

Beck, Lewis W. (1950) "Constructions and Inferred Entities", *Philosophy of Science*, 17, 74–86.

Bell, David (1999) "The Revolution of Moore and Russell: A Very British Coup?", in O'Hear, Anthony (ed.), *German Philosophy Since Kant*, New York: Cambridge University Press.

Bell, John L., and William Demopoulos (1996) "Elementary Propositions and Independence", *Notre Dame Journal of Formal Logic*, 37, 112–24.

Ben Yami, Hanoch (1997) "Against Characterizing Mental States as Propositional Attitudes", *Philosophical Quarterly*, 47, 84–9.

Bergmann, Gustav (1947) "Russell on Particulars", *Philosophical Review*, 56, 59–72. Repr. in Bergmann, Gustav, *The Metaphysics of Logical Positivism*, Madison: University of Wisconsin Press, 1954, 197–209.

Bergmann, Gustav (1957, 1958), "The Revolt Against Logical Atomism", *Philosophical Quarterly*, 7, 323–39, and 8, 1–13. Repr. in Bergmann, Gustav, *Meaning and Existence*, Madison: University of Wisconsin Press, 1969, 39–72.

Berka, K., (1970) "Russell's Theory of Quantity and Magnitude", *Teorie a Metoda*, 2, 35–51.

Beyer, Christian (1998) "Russell's Principle Considered from Both a Neo-Fregean and a Husserlian Viewpoint", *Acta Analytica*, 103–29.

Blackburn, Simon, and Alan Code (1978) "Reply to Geach's 'Russell on Denoting'", *Analysis*, 38, 206–7.

Blackman, Larry Lee (1983) "Russell on the Relations of Universals and Particulars", *Philosophy Research Archives*, 9, 265–78.

Blackwell, Kenneth (1981) "The Early Wittgenstein and the Middle Russell", in Block, Irving Leonard (ed.), *Perspectives on the Philosophy of Wittgenstein*, Oxford: Blackwell, 1–30.

Boër, Steven E. (1973) "Russell on Classes as Logical Fictions", *Analysis*, 33, 206–8.

Boolos, George (1993) "The Advantages of Honest Toil Over Theft", in George Alexander (ed.), *Mathematics and Mind*, Oxford University Press, 27–44. Repr. in Boolos, George, *Logic, Logic, and Logic*, Cambridge, Mass.: Harvard University Press, 1998, 255–74.

Bradie, Michael P. (1977) "The Development of Russell's Structural Postulates", *Philosophy of Science*, 44, 441–63.

Bradley, Michael C. (1986) "Russell and the Identity of Indiscernibles", *History of Philosophy Quarterly*, 3. 325–33.

Braun, David M. (1998) "Understanding Belief Reports", *Philosophical Review*, 107, 555–95.

Brinton, Alan (1977) "Uses of Definite Descriptions and Russell's Theory", *Philosophical Studies*, 31, 261–7.

Broad, C.D. (1919) "Is There 'Knowledge by Acquaintance'?", *Aristotelian Society*, Supplementary Vol. 2, 206–20.

Burge, Tyler (1983) "Russell's Problem and Intentional Identity", in Tomberlin, James E. (ed.), *Agent, Language, and the Structure of the World*, Indianapolis: Hackett, 79–110.

Burke, Tom (1998) "Dewey and Russell on the Possibility of Immediate Knowledge", *Studies in Philosophy and-Education*, 17, 149–53.

Butchvarov, Panayot (1985/1986) "Our Robust Sense of Reality", *Grazer Philosophische Studien*, 25–26, 403–421.

Butchvarov, Panayot (1988) "Russell's Views on Reality", *Grazer Philosophische Studien*, 32, 165–7.

Butler, Ronald J. (1954) "The Scaffolding of Russell's Theory of Descriptions", *Philosophical Review*, 63, 350–64.

Cargile, James (1998) "The Problem of Induction", *Philosophy*, 73, 247–75.

Carney, James D. (1980) "Russell's 'Proof', Again", *Canadian Journal of Philosophy*, 10, 587–92.

Carney, James D., and G.W. Fitch (1979), "Can Russell avoid Frege's Sense?", *Mind*, 88, 384–93.

Carruthers, Peter (1987) "Russellian Thoughts", *Mind*, 96, 18–35.

Cartwright, Richard (1987) "On the Origins of Russell's Theory of Descriptions", in Cartwright, Richard, *Philosophical Essays*, Cambridge, Mass.: MIT Press, 95–133.

Cassin, Chrystine E. (1971) "Existential Quantification in Russell's Analysis of Definite Descriptions", *Mind*, 10, 553–7.

Castaneda, Hector-Neri (1976) "Ontology and Grammar: I. Russell's Paradox and the General Theory of Properties in Natural Language", *Theoria*, 42, 44–92.

Casullo, Albert (1981) "Russell on the Reduction of Particulars", *Analysis*, 41, 199–205.

Casullo, Albert (1982) "Particulars, Substrata, and the Identity of Indiscernibles", *Philosophy of Science*, 49, 591–41.

Casullo, Albert (1984) "The Contingent Identity of Particulars and Universals", *Mind*, 93, 527–41.

Caton, C.E. (1959) "Strawson on Referring", *Mind*, 68, 539–44.

Chihara, Charles S. (1973) "Russell's Solution to the Paradoxes", in Chihara, Charles S., *Ontology and the Vicious-Circle Principle*, Ithaca, N.Y.: Cornell University Press, 1–59.

Chihara, Charles S. (1980) "Ramsey's Theory of Types: Suggestions for a Return to Fregean Sources", in Mellor, D.H. (ed.), *Prospects for Pragmatism*, Cambridge: Cambridge University Press, 21–47.

Church, Alonzo (1940) "A Formulation of the Simple Theory of Types", *Journal of Symbolic Logic*, 5, 56–68.

Church, Alonzo (1960) "Mathematics and Logic", in Nagel, Ernest, Patrick Suppes, and Alfred Tarski (eds), *Logic, Methodology, and Philosophy of Science, Proceedings of the 1960 International Congress*, Stanford: Stanford University Press, 181–6.

Church, Alonzo (1974) "Russellian Simple Type Theory", *Proceedings and Addresses of the American Philosophical Association*, 47, 21–33.

Church, Alonzo (1976) "A Comparison of Russell's Resolution of the Semantical Antinomies with that of Tarski", *Journal of Symbolic Logic*, 41, 747–60.

Church, Alonzo (1984) "Comparison of Russell's Resolution of the Semantical Antinomies with That of Tarski", in Martin, Robert L. (ed.), *Recent Essays on Truth and the Liar Paradox*, Oxford: Clarendon, 289–306.

Church, Alonzo (1984) "Russell's Theory of Identity of Propositions", *Philosophia Naturalis*, 21, 513–22.

Chwistek, Leon (1921) "Antynomje Logiki Formalnej", *Przeglad Filozoficzny*, 24, 164–71. Repr. as "Antinomies of Formal Logic" in McCall, Storrs (ed.), *Polish Logic*, Oxford: Clarendon, 1967, 338–45.

Chwistek, Leon (1924, 1925) "The Theory of Constructive Types", *Annales de la Société Polonaise de Mathématique*, 2, 9–48; 3, 92–141.

Clement, William C. (1953) "Russell's Structuralist Thesis", *Philosophical Review*, 62, 266–75.

Cocchiarella, Nino B. (1982) "Meinong Reconstructed Versus Early Russell Reconstructed", *Journal of Philosophical Logic*, 11, 183–214.

Cometti, Jean-Pierre (1999) "Remarques sur le pragmatisme, la politique et la culture", *Revue Internationale de Philosophie*, 53, 101–17.

Copi, Irving M. (1950) "The Inconsistency or Redundancy of *Principia Mathematica*", *Philosophy and Phenomenological Research*, 11, 190–99.

Corazza, Eros (1997) "Reference directe et psychologisme", *Revue Philosophique de la France et de l'Etranger*, 2, 195–204.

Crittenden, Charles (1970) "Ontology and the Theory of Descriptions", *Philosophy and Phenomenological Research*, 31, 85–96.

Croddy, W. Stephen (1976) "Russell on the Meaning of Descriptions", *Notre Dame Journal of Formal Logic*, 17, 424–28.

Croddy, W. Stephen (1979) "Do Descriptions Have Meaning?", *Logique et Analyse*, 22, 23–30.

Cross, Charles Byron (1979) "Time and the Russell Definition of Number", *Southwestern Journal of Philosophy*, 10, 177–80.

Da Costa, Newton C.A. and Steven French (1991) "On Russell's Principle of Induction", *Synthese*, 86, 285–95.

Dau, Paulo (1985) "The Complex Matter of Denoting", *Analysis*, 45, 190–7.

Dau, Paulo (1986) "Russell's First Theory of Denoting and Quantification", *Notre Dame Journal of Formal Logic*, 27, 133–66.

Davant, James B. (1975) "Wittgenstein on Russell's Theory of Types", *Notre Dame Journal of Formal Logic*, 16, 102–8.

D'Cruz, Mark (2000) "A Theory of Ordinary Proper Names", *Mind*, 109, 721–53.

Degen, J. (1993) "Two Formal Vindications of Logicism", in Czermak, Johannes (ed.), *Philosophy of Mathematics*, Vienna: Verlag Holder-Pichler-Tempsky, 243–50.

Dejnožka, Jan (1988) "A Reply to Butchvarov's 'Russell's Views on Reality'", *Grazer Philosophische Studien*, 32, 181–4.

Dejnožka, Jan (1988) "Russell's Robust Sense of Reality: A Reply to Butchvarov", *Grazer Philosophische Studien*, 32, 155–64.

Dejnožka, Jan (1990) "The Ontological Foundations of Russell's Theory of Modality", *Erkenntnis*, 32, 383–419.

Demopoulos, William (1999) "On the Theory of Meaning of 'On Denoting'", *Nous*, 33, 439–58.

De Rouilhan, Philippe (1992) "Russell and the Vicious Circle Principle", *Philosophical Studies*, 65, 169–82.

Donagan, Alan (1952) "Recent Criticisms of Russell's Analysis of Existence", *Analysis*, 12, 132–7.

Donnellan, Keith S. (1966) "Reference and Definite Descriptions", *Philosophical Review*, 75, 281–304.

Donnellan, Keith S. (1966) "Substitution and Reference", *Journal of Philosophy*, 63, 685–7.

Donnellan, Keith S. (1990) "Genuine Names and Knowledge by Acquaintance", *Dialectica*, 44, 99–112.

Dukelow, Owen W. (1976) "The Problem of Negative Facts in Russell's Logical Atomism", *Southwestern Journal of Philosophy*, 7, 7–13.

Dukran, Jane (1987) "Russell on Names", *Philosophy Research Archives*, 13, 463–70.

Eames, Elizabeth R. (1967) "The Consistency of Russell's Realism", *Philosophy and Phenomenological Research*, 27, 502–11.

Eames, Elizabeth R. (1972) "Russell on 'What There Is'", *Revue Internationale de Philosophie*, 26, 483–98.

Eames, Elizabeth R. (1976) "Bertrand Russell's Philosophical Method", *Midwestern Journal of Philosophy*, 4, 3–13.

Eames, Elizabeth R. (1986) "Russell and the Experience of Time", *Philosophy and Phenomenological Research*, 46, 681–2.

Edgell, Beatrice (1919) "Is There 'Knowledge by Acquaintance'?", *Aristotelian Society*, Supplementary Vol. 2, 194–205.

Edwards, Paul (1949) "Bertrand Russell's Doubts about Induction", *Mind*, 58, 141–163. Repr. in Flew, Antony G.N. (ed.), *Essays on Logic and Language*, New York: Philosophical Library, 55–79.

Elugardo, Reinaldo (1997) "Descriptions, Indexicals, and Speaker Meaning", *Protosociology*, 10, 155–89.

Falkenburg, Brigitte and Schnepf, Robert (1998) "Kausalität in Metaphysik und Physik", *Dialektik*, 2, 27–48.

Feser, Edward (1998) "Can Phenomenal Qualities Exist Unperceived?", *Journal of Consciousness Studies*, 5, 405–14.

Findlay, J.N. (1949) "Is There Knowledge by Acquaintance?", *Aristotelian Society*, Supplementary Vol. 23, 111–28.

Fitch, Frederic (1938) "The Consistency of the Ramified *Principia*", *Journal of Symbolic Logic*, 3, 140–50.

Fitch, Frederic (1971) "Propositions as the Only Realities", *American Philosophical Quarterly*, 8, 99–103.

Fleischhacker, L.E. (1979) "Is Russell's Vicious Circle Principle False or Meaningless?", *Dialectica*, 33, 23–30.

Fogelin, Robert J. (1974) "Negative Elementary Propositions", *Philosophical Studies*, 25, 189–97.

Fortier, Evelyn (1996) "Was the Dispute Between Russell and Bradley About Internal Relations?", in Mander, W.J. (ed.), *Perspectives on the Logic and Metaphysics of F.H. Bradley*, Bristol: Thoemmes, 25–37.

Ganeri, Jonardon (1995) "Contextually Incomplete Descriptions – A New Counterexample to Russell?", *Analysis*, 55, 287–90.

Garciadiego, Alejandro R. (1995) "*The Principles of Mathematics* of Bertrand Russell", in Ramirez, Santiago, and Robert S. Cohen (eds), *Mexican Studies in the History and Philosophy of Science*, Dordrecht: Kluwer, 213–34.

Gaskin, Richard (1997) "Fregean Sense and Russellian Propositions", *Philosophical Studies*, 86, 131–54.

Gastwirth, Paul (1932) "ϕa, ϕx, and $\phi\hat{x}$", *Monist*, 42, 313–15.

Gastwirth, Paul (1932) "The Hypothesis of Reducibility", *Monist*, 42, 384–7.

Geach, P.T. (1950) "Russell's Theory of Descriptions", *Analysis*, 10, 84–8. Repr. in Macdonald, Margaret (ed.), *Philosophy and Analysis*, New York: Barnes and Noble, 1954, 32–6.

Geach, P.T. (1970) "Two Paradoxes of Russell's", *Journal of Philosophy*, 67, 89–97.

Geach, P.T. (1978) "Russell on Denoting", *Analysis*, 38, 204–5.

Geirsson, Heimir (1998) "True Belief Reports and Sharing of Beliefs", *Journal of Philosophical Research*, 23, 331–42.

Gerrard, Steve (1997) "Desire and Desirability: Bradley, Russell and Moore versus Mill", in Tait, William W. (ed.), *Early Analytic Philosophy: Frege, Russell, Wittgenstein*, Chicago: Open Court, 37–74.

Giaretta, Pierdaniele (1997) "Analysis and Logical Form in Russell: The 1913 Paradigm", *Dialectica*, 51, 273–93.

Goldfarb, Warren D. (1987) "Poincaré Against the Logicists", in Aspray, William, and Philip Kitcher (eds), *Essays in the History of Mathematics*, Minneapolis: University of Minnesota Press, 61–81.

Goldstein, Laurence (2000) "A Unified Solution to Some Paradoxes", *Proceedings of the Aristotelian Society*, 100, 53–74.

Gorman, Jonathan (1999) "On Hedgehogs and Foxes", *Philosophical Inquiry*, 21, 61–86.

Graff, Delia (2001) "Descriptions As Predicates", *Philosophical Studies*, 102, 1–42.

Graham, George (1986) "Russell's Deceptive Desires", *Philosophical Quarterly*, 36, 223–29.

Grandy, Richard E. (1981) "Forms of Belief", *Synthese*, 46, 271–84.

Grattan-Guinness, Ivor (1972) "Bertrand Russell on His Paradox and the Multiplicative Axiom", *Journal of Philosophical Logic*, 1, 103–110.

Grattan-Guinness, Ivor (1978) "How Bertrand Russell Discovered His Paradox", *Historia Mathematica*, 5, 127–37.

Grattan-Guinness, Ivor (1980) "Georg Cantor's Influence of Bertrand Russell", *History and Philosophy of Logic*, 1, 61–93.

Grattan-Guinness, Ivor (1981) "On the Development of Logics Between the Two World Wars", *American Mathematical Monthly*, 88, 495–509.

Grattan-Guinness, Ivor (1984) "Notes on the Fate of Logicism from *Principia Mathematica* to Gödel's Incompletability Theorem", *History and Philosophy of Logic*, 5, 67–78.

Grelling, Kurt (1929) "Realism and Logic: An Investigation of Russell's Metaphysics", *Monist*, 39, 501–20.

Griffin, Nicholas (1985) "Russell's Critique of Meinong's Theory of Objects", *Grazer Philosophische Studien*, 25–6, 375–401.

Griffin, Nicholas (1985) "Russell's Multiple Relation Theory of Judgment", *Philosophical Studies*, 47, 213–48.

Griffin, Nicholas (1989) "Why did Russell Think 'E!a' was Meaningless?", in Donald Stewart (ed.) *Entities and Individuation. Studies in Ontology and Language in Honour of Neil Wilson*, (Queenston: Edwin Mellen), 107–23.

Griffin, Nicholas (1998) "Did Russell's Criticisms of Bradley's Theory of Relations Miss their Mark?" in Guy Stock (ed.), *Appearance versus Reality. New Essays on Bradley's Metaphysics*, Oxford: Clarendon Press, 153–62.

Griffin, Nicholas, and Gad Zak (1982) "Russell on Specific and Universal Relations", *History and Philosophy of Logic*, 3, 55–67.

Griffiths, D.A. (1976) "Russell on Existence and Descriptions", *Philosophical Quarterly*, 26, 157–62.

Griffiths, D.A. (1981) "A Reconsideration of Russell's Early Ontological Development", *Philosophical Quarterly*, 31, 145–52.

Grossmann, Reinhardt (1972) "Russell's Paradox and Complete Properties", *Nous*, 6, 153–64.

Grossmann, Reinhardt (1975) "Definite Descriptions", *Philosophical Studies*, 27, 127–44.

Gyekye, Kwame (1973) "An Examination of the Bundle-Theory of Substance", *Philosophy and Phenomenological Research*, 34, 51–61.

Hailperin, Theodore, and Hughes Leblanc (1959) "Nondesignating Singular Terms", *Philosophical Review*, 68, 239–43.

Halbasch, Keith (1971) "A Critical Examination of Russell's View of Facts", *Nous*, 5, 395–409.

Hambourger, Robert (1977) "A Difficulty with the Frege-Russell Definition of Number", *Journal of Philosophy*, 74, 409–14.

Hampshire, Stuart N. (1972) "Russell, Radicalism, and Reason", in Held, Virginia, Kai Nielsen, and Charles Parson (eds), *Philosophy and Political Action*, New York: Oxford University Press, 258–74.

Haque, Nayeema (2000) "Russell's Argument against Fregean Sense", *Journal of Indian Council of Philosophical Research*, 17, 63–85.

Hare, William (2001) "Bertrand Russell on Critical Thinking", *Journal of Thought*, 36, 7–16.

Hark, Michael Ter (1994) "Cognitive Science, Propositional Attitudes, and the Debate Between Russell and Wittgenstein", in Meggle, Georg, and Ulla Wessels (eds), *Analyomen 1: Proceedings of the First Conference: Perspectives in Analytical Philosophy*, Berlin: Walter de Gruyter, 612–17.

Hart, H.L.A. (1949) "Is There Knowledge by Acquaintance?", *Aristotelian Society*, Supplementary Vol. 23, 69–90.

Hart, W.D. (1983) "Russell and Ramsey", *Pacific Philosophical Quarterly*, 64, 193–210.

Hartshorne, Charles (1968) "Russell on Causality", in Hartshorne, Charles, *Beyond Humanism*, Lincoln: University of Nebraska Press, 211–24.

Hausman, David B. (1974) "Russell on Negative Facts", *Southwestern Journal of Philosophy*, 12, 49–53.

Hawkins, Benjamin (1997) "Peirce and Russell: The History of a Neglected 'Controversy'", in Houser, Nathan, Don D. Roberts, and James Van Evra (eds), *Studies in the Logic of Charles Sanders Peirce*, Bloomington, IN.: Indiana University Press, 111–46.

Hawkins, Denis John Bernard (1962) "Moore, Russell and Sense-Data", in Hawkins, Denis John Bernard, *Crucial Problems of Modern Philosophy*, Notre Dame: University of Notre Dame Press, 55–65.

Hay, William H. (1950) "Bertrand Russell on the Justification of Induction", *Philosophy of Science*, 17, 266–77.

Hayner, Paul (1969) "Knowledge by Acquaintance", *Philosophy and Phenomenological Research*, 29, 423–31.

Hazen, A.P. and Davoren, J.M. (2000) "Russell's 1925 Logic", *Australasian Journal of Philosophy*, 78, 534–56.

Heath, A.E. (1920) "Logical Atomism and the Law of Parsimony", *Monist*, 30, 309–10.

Hellman, Geoffrey (1981) "How to Gödel a Frege-Russell: Gödel's Incompleteness Theorems and Logicism", *Nous*, 15, 451–68.

Hempel, Carl G. (1966) "On Russell's Phenomenological Construction", *Journal of Philosophy*, 63, 668–69.

Henkin, Leon (1949) "Completeness in the Theory of Types", *Journal of Symbolic Logic*, 14, 159–66.

Henkin, Leon (1962) "Are Mathematics and Logic Identical?", *Science*, 138 (no. 3542, 16 November), 788–94.

Hicks, G. Dawes (1919) "Is There 'Knowledge by Acquaintance'?", *Aristotelian Society*, Supplementary Vol. 2, 159–78.

Hintikka, Jaakko (1959) "Existential Presuppositions and Existential Commitment", *Journal of Philosophy*, 63, 125–37.

Hintikka, Jaakko (1981) "On Denoting What?", *Synthese*, 46, 167–83.

Hintikka, Jaakko and Jack Kulas (1982) "Russell Vindicated: Towards a General Theory of Definite Descriptions", *Journal of Semantics*, 1, 387–97.

Hiz, H. (1977) "Descriptions in Russell's Theory and in Ontology", *Studia Logica*, 36, 271–83.

Hochberg, Herbert (1976) "Russell's Attack on Frege's Theory of Meaning", *Philosophica*, 18, 9–34.

Hochberg, Herbert (1980) "Russell's Proof of Realism Reproved", *Philosophical Studies*, 37, 37–44.

Hochberg, Herbert (1987) "Russell, Ramsey, and Wittgenstein on Ramification and Quantification", *Erkenntnis*, 27, 257–81.

Hochberg, Herbert (1994) "Causal Connections, Universals, and Russell's Hypothetico-Scientific Realism", *Monist*, 77, 71–92.

Hochberg, Herbert (1995) "Abstracts, Functions, Existence and Relations in the Russell-Meinong Dispute, the Bradley Paradox and the Realism-

Nominalism Controversy", *Grazer Philosophische Studien*, 50, 273–91.

Hochberg, Herbert (1995) "Particulars as Universals: Russell's Ontological Essay of Particularity and Phenomenological Space-Time", *Journal of Philosophical Research*, 20, 83–111.

Hochberg, Herbert (1996) "Particulars, Universals, and Russell's Late Ontology", *Journal of Philosophical Research*, 21, 129–37.

Hochberg, Herbert (2000) "Propositions, Truth and Belief: The Wittgenstein-Russell Dispute", *Theoria*, 66, 3–40.

Hoensbroech, F. Graf (1939) "On Russell's Paradox", *Mind*, 48, 365–8.

Hoernlé, Reinhold F.A. (1916) "The Religious Aspect of Bertrand Russell's Philosophy", *Harvard Theological Review*, 9, 157–89.

Holley, David M. (1997) "Self-Transforming Experiences", *Personalist Forum*, 13, 174–94.

Honderich, Ted (1969) "On the Theory of Descriptions", *Proceedings of the Aristotelian Society*, 69, 87–100.

Hooker, C.A. (1972) "Definite Descriptions", *Philosophical Studies*, 23, 365–75.

Hope, V. (1969) "The Picture Theory of Meaning in the *Tractatus* as a Development of Moore's and Russell's Theories of Judgement", *Philosophy*, 44, 140–8.

Hughes, George E. (1949) "Is There Knowledge by Acquaintance?", *Aristotelian Society*, Supplementary Vol. 23, 91–110.

Hurley, Patrick J. (1979) "Russell, Poincaré, and Whitehead's 'Relational Theory of Space'", *Process Studies*, 9, 14–21.

Hylton, Peter W. (1984) "The Nature of the Proposition and the Revolt Against Idealism", in Rorty, Richard, J.B. Schneewind, and Quentin Skinner (eds), *Philosophy in History*, Cambridge: Cambridge University Press, 375–97.

Iglesias, M. Teresa (1981) "Russell and Wittgenstein: Two Views of Ordinary Language", *Philosophical Studies* (Ireland), 28, 149–63.

Iglesias, M. Teresa (1984) "Russell's *Theory of Knowledge* and Wittgenstein's Earliest Writings", *Synthese*, 60, 285–32.

Irvine, A.D. (1989) "Epistemic Logicism and Russell's Regressive Method", *Philosophical Studies*, 55, 303–27.

Irvine, William B. (1984) "Russell's Construction of Space from Perspectives", *Synthese*, 60, 333–48.

Iseminger, Gary (1986) "Russell's Much-Admired Argument Against Naive Realism", *Journal of Indian Council of Philosophical Research*, 4, 173–6.

Jadacki, Jacek Juliusz (1986) "Leon Chwistek-Bertrand Russell's Scientific Correspondence", *Dialectics and Humanism*, 13, 239–63.

Jeffreys, Harold (1950) "Bertrand Russell on Probability", *Mind*, 59, 313–19.

Jourdain, Philip E.B. (1912) "Mr Bertrand Russell's First Work on the Principles of Mathematics", *Monist*, 22, 149–58.

Judson, Lindsay (1987) "Russell on Memory", *Proceedings of the Aristotelian Society*, 88, 65–82.

Jung, Darryl (1999) "Russell, Presupposition, and the Vicious-Circle Principle", *Notre Dame Journal of Formal Logic*, 40, 55–80.

Kaplan, David (1975) "How to Russell a Frege-Church", *Journal of Philosophy*, 72, 716–29.

Kaplan, David (1979) "The Logic of Demonstratives", in French, Peter A., Theodore E. Uehling, Jr, and Howard K. Wettstein (eds) *Contemporary Perspectives in the Philosophy of Language*, Minneapolis: University of Minnosota Press, 401–10.

Keane, E.F. (1961) "Bertrand Russell and the Emotive Theory", *Indian Journal of Philosophy*, 3, 26–36.

Kemp, Gary (1998) "Propositions and Reasoning in Russell and Frege", *Pacific Philosophical Quarterly*, 79, 218–35.

Kennedy, H.C. (1973) "What Russell Learned from Peano", *Notre Dame Journal of Formal Logic*, 14, 367–71.

Kennedy, H.C. (1975) "Nine Letters from Guiseppe Peano to Bertrand Russell", *Journal of the History of Philosophy*, 13, 205–20.

Kenyon, Timothy A. (1991) "Russell on Pastness", *Dialogue*, 33, 57–9.

Kleinknecht, Reinhard (2001) "Zeitordnung und Zeitpunkte", *Erkenntnis*, 54, 55–75.

Kline, A. David (1985) "Humean Causation and the Necessity of Temporal Discontinuity", *Mind*, 94, 550–56.

Kneale, William C. (1934) "The Objects of Acquaintance", *Proceeding of the Aristotelian Society*, 34, 187–210.

Kneale, William C. (1936) "Is Existence a Predicate?", *Aristotelian Society*, Supplementary Vol. 15, 154–74.

Kneale, William C. (1968) "Methods of Designation", *Proceedings of the Aristotelian Society*, 68, 249–70.

Knight, Gordon (2001) "Idealism, Intentionality, and Nonexistent Objects", *Journal of Philosophical Research*, 26, 43–52.

Koehler, Conrad J. (1972) "Studies in Bertrand Russell's Theory of Knowledge", *Revue Internationale de Philosophie*, 26, 499–512.

Kohl, Marvin (1969) "Bertrand Russell on Vagueness", *Australasian Journal of Philosophy*, 47, 31–41.

Kremer, Michael (1994) "The Argument of 'On Denoting'", *Philosophical Review*, 103, 249–97.

Kripke, Saul A. (1972) "Naming and Necessity", in Davidson, Donald, and Gilbert Harman (eds), *Semantics of Natural Language*, Dordrecht: Reidel, 253–355, 763–9.

Kultgen, J.H. (1956) "Operations and Events in Russell's Empiricism", *Journal of Philosophy*, 53, 157–67.

Kumar Sen, Amit (2000) "Strawson on Presupposition", *Indian Philosophical Quarterly*, 27, 151–66.

Labson, Sam (1997) "Bertrand Russell and the Scientific Spirit", *Philosophy in Science*, (Tucson), 7, 37–51.

Lackey, Douglas P. (1963) "Russell's Unknown Theory of Classes: The Substitutional System of 1906", *Journal of the History of Philosophy*, 14, 69–78.

Lackey, Douglas P. (1981) "Russell's 1913 Map of the Mind", *Midwest Studies in Philosophy*, 6, 125–42.

Lambert, Karel (1984) "What is Russell's Theory of Descriptions? An Addendum", *Pacific Philosophical Quarterly*, 65, 140–8.

Lambert, Karel (1990) "Russell's Theory of Definite Descriptions", *Dialectica*, 44, 137–52.

Lambert, Karel (1992) "Russell's Version of the Theory of Definite Descriptions", *Philosophical Studies*, 65, 153–67.

Lambert, Karel (2000) "Set Theory and Definite Descriptions 'Four Solutions in Search of a Common Problem'", *Grazer Philosophische Studien*, 60, 1–11.

Landini, Gregory (1987) "Russell's Substitutional Theory of Classes and Relations", *History and Philosophy of Logic*, 8, 171–200.

Landini, Gregory (1990) "How to Russell Another Meinongian: A Russellian Theory of Fictional Objects versus Zalta's Theory of Abstract Objects", *Grazer Philosophische Studien*, 37, 93–122.

Landini, Gregory (1991) "A New Interpretation of Russell's Multiple-Relation Theory of Judgment", *History and Philosophy of Logic*, 12, 37–69.

Landini, Gregory (1996) "The 'Definability' of the Set of Natural Numbers in the 1925 *Principia Mathematica*", *Journal of Philosophical Logic*, 25, 597–615.

Landini, Gregory (1996) "Logic in Russell's *Principles of Mathematics*", *Notre Dame Journal of Formal Logic*, 37, 554–84.

Landini, Gregory (1998) "Russell's Intensional Logic of Propositions: A Resurrection of Logicism?" in Orilia, F. and Rapaport, W.J. (eds.), *Thought, Language and Ontology*, The Hague: Kluwer, 61–93.

Landini, Gregory (2000) "Quantification Theory in *9 of *Principia Mathematica*", *History and Philosophy of Logic*, 21, 57–78.

Lejewski, Czeslaw (1960) "A Re-Examination of the Russellian Theory of Descriptions", *Philosophy*, 35, 14–29.

Leonard, Henry (1956) "The Logic of Existence", *Philosophical Studies*, 7, 49–64.

Levine, James (1998) "Acquaintance, Denoting Concepts, and Sense", *Philosophical Review*, 107, 415–45.

Levine, James (1998) "From Absolute Idealism to 'The Principles of Mathematics'", *International Journal of Philosophical Studies*, 6, 87–127.

Lewis, C.I. (1917) "The Issues Concerning Material Implication", *Journal of Philosophy, Psychology, and Scientific Methods*, 14, 350–56.

Lindberg, Jordan J. (1990) "From Russell to Quine: Basic Statements, Foundationalism, Truth, and Other Myths", *Dialogue*, 33, 27–31.

Linsky, Bernard (1988) "Propositional Functions and Universals in *Principia Mathematica*", *Australasian Journal of Philosophy*, 66, 447–60.

Linsky, Bernard (1995) "Russell's Logical Constructions", *Studies in Dialectics of Nature* (Beijing), Supplementary Vol. 11, 129–48.

Linsky, Leonard (1987) "Russell's 'No-Classes' Theory of Classes", in Thomson, Judith Jarvis (ed.), *On Being and Saying*, Cambridge: MIT Press, 21–39.

Linsky, Leonard (1988) "Terms and Propositions in Russell's *Principles of Mathematics*", *Journal of the History of Philosophy*, 26, 621–42.

Linsky, Leonard (1992) "The Unity of the Proposition", *Journal of the History of Philosophy*, 30, 243–73.

Lipkind, Donald (1979) "Russell on the Notion of Cause", *Canadian Journal of Philosophy*, 9, 701–20.

Livingston, Paul M. (2001) "Russellian and Wittgensteinian Atomism", *Philosophical Investigations*, 24, 30–54.

Lockwood, Michael (1981) "What *Was* Russell's Neutral Monism?", *Midwest Studies in Philosophy*, 6, 143–58.

Lovejoy, Arthur O. (1929) "Mr Bertrand Russell and the Unification of Mind and Matter", in Lovejoy, Arthur O., *The Revolt Against Dualism*, Chicago: Open Court, 190–256.

Lucas, George R. (1989) "Whitehead and Russell", in Lucas, George R., *The Rehabilitation of Whitehead*, New York: State University of New York Press, 109–25.

Ludlow, Peter (1991) "Indefinite Descriptions: In Defence of Russell", *Linguistics and Philosophy*, 14, 171–202.

Lycan, William G. (1970) "Transformational Grammar and the Russell-Strawson Dispute", *Metaphilosophy*, 1, 335–7.

McCawley, J.D. (1988) "Actions and Events Despite Bertrand Russell", in LePore, Ernest, and Brian P. McLaughlin (eds), *Actions and Events*, Oxford: Blackwell, 177–92.

McDermott, Michael (1988) "A Russellian Account of Belief Sentences", *Philosophical Quarterly*, 38, 141–57.

McGrew, Timothy and McGrew, Lydia (1998) "Internalism and the Collapse of the Gettier Problem", *Journal of Philosophical Research*, 23, 239–56.

McGuinness, Brian (1972) "Bertrand Russell's and Ludwig Wittgenstein's 'Notes on Logic'", *Revue Internationale de Philosophie*, 26, 444–60.

McKenney, John L. (1958) "Concerning Russell's Analysis of Value Judgements", *Journal of Philosophy*, 55, 382–9.

McKeon, Matthew (1999) "Bertrand Russell and Logical Truth", *Philosophia*, 27, 541–53.

McKinsey, Michael (1999) "The Semantics of Belief Ascriptions", *Nous*, 33, 519–57.

McLendon, Hiram J. (1952) "Has Russell Answered Hume?", *Journal of Philosophy*, 49, 145–59.

McLendon, Hiram J. (1957) "Has Russell Proved Naive Realism Self-Contradictory?", *Journal of Philosophy*, 53, 289–302.

McMahon, M. Brian (1976) "Russell's Denoting Relation", *The Personalist*, 57, 345–50.

Magnell, Thomas (1991) "The Extent of Russell's Modal Views", *Erkenntnis*, 34, 171–85.

Makin, Gideon (1995) "Making Sense of 'On Denoting'", *Synthese*, 102, 383–412.

Makin, Gideon (1996) "Why the Theory of Descriptions?", *Philosophical Quarterly*, 46, 158–67.

Marcus, Ruth Barcan (1993) "On Some Post-1920's Views of Russell on Particularity, Identity, and Individualism", in Marcus, Ruth Barcan, *Modalities*, Oxford: Oxford University Press, 177–88.

Martin, Richard M. (1952) "On the Berkeley-Russell Theory of Proper Names", *Philosophy and Phenomenological Research*, 13, 221–31.

Martin, Richard M. (1964) "The Philosophic Import of Virtual Classes", *Journal of Philosophy*, 61, 377–86.

Martinich, Aloysius P. (1975) "Russell, Frege and the Puzzle of Denoting", *International Studies in Philosophy*, 7, 145–54.

Martinich, Aloysius P. (1976) "Russell's Theory of Meaning and Descriptions", *Journal of the History of Philosophy*, 14, 183–201.

Martinich, Aloysius P. (1983) "Sense, Reference, and Russell's Theory of Descriptions", *Journal of the History of Philosophy*, 21, 85–92.

Masciarelli, Pasqualino (2000) "On a Notion of Extra-Essential Identity: Critical Notes on an Objection of Russell's to Hegel", *Topoi*, 19, 179–99.

Mates, Benson (1973) "Descriptions and Reference", *Foundations of Language*, 10, 409–18.

Maxwell, Grover (1975) "Russell on Perception and Mind-Body: A Study in Philosophical Method", in Cheng, Chung-Ying (ed.), *Philosophical Aspects of the Mind-Body Problem*, Honolulu: University of Hawaii Press, 131–53.

Meyers, Robert G. (1970) "Knowledge by Acquaintance: A Reply to Hayner", *Philosophy and Phenomenological Research*, 31, 293–6.

Miah, Sajahan (1997) "Constructionism: Russell's Resolution of Realism-Empiricism Dilemma", *Indian Philosophical Quarterly*, 24, 481–96.

Michell, Joel (1993) "The Origins of the Representational Theory of Measurement: Helmholtz, Hölder, and Russell", *Studies in History and Philosophy of Science*, 24, 185–206.

Michell, Joel (1997) "Bertrand Russell's 1897 Critique of the Traditional Theory of Measurement", *Synthese*, 110, 257–76.

Mijuskovic, Ben (1976) "The Simplicity Argument in Wittgenstein and Russell", *Critica*, 8, 85–103.

Milkov, Nikolay (2000) "Lotze and the Early Cambridge Analytic Philosophy", *Prima Philosophia*, 13, 133–53.

Moorcroft, Francis (1993) "Why Russell's Paradox Won't Go Away", *Philosophy*, 68, 99–104.

Moore, G.E. (1919) "Is There 'Knowledge by Acquaintance'?", *Aristotelian Society*, Supplementary Vol. 2, 179–93.

Moore, G.E. (1936) "Is Existence a Predicate?", *Aristotelian Society*, Supplementary Vol. 15, 175–88.

Morris, William Edward (1979) "Moore and Russell on Philosophy and Science", *Metaphilosophy*, 10, 111–38.

Moss, J.M.B. (1972) "Some B. Russell's Sprouts (1903–1908)", in Hodges, Wilfrid (ed.), *Conference in Mathematical Logic – London '70* (Lecture Notes in Mathematics, 255), Berlin: Springer Verlag, 211–50.

Moulder, James (1974) "Is Russell's Paradox Genuine?", *Philosophy*, 49, 295–302.

Moulines, C. Ulises (2001) "Die Mathematisierung der Erfahrung: Vorganger zu Carnaps 'Aufbau'", *Erkenntnis*, 54, 105–20.

Muehlmann, Robert (1969) "Russell and Wittgenstein on Identity", *Philosophical Quarterly*, 19, 221–30.

Mulligan, Kevin (1998) "Relations–Through Thick and Thin", *Erkenntnis*, 48, 325–53.

Musgrave, Alan (1977) "Logicism Revisited", *British Journal for the Philosophy of Science*, 28, 99–127.

Myhill, John (1951) "Report of Some Investigations Concerning the Consistency of the Axiom of Reducibility", *Journal of Symbolic Logic*, 16, 35–42.

Nagel, Ernest (1954) "Basis of Human Knowledge", in Nagel, Ernest, *Sovereign Reason*, New York: Free Press, 211–15.

Nelson, John O. (1964) "On Sommers' Reinstatement of Russell's Ontological Program", *Philosophical Review*, 73, 517–21.

Nelson, Mark T. (1998) "Bertrand Russell's Defence of the Cosmological Argument", *American Philosophical Quarterly*, 35, 87–100.

Newman, M.H.A. (1928) "Mr Russell's 'Causal Theory of Perception'", *Mind*, 37, 137–48.

Nielson, Kai (1958) "Bertrand Russell's New Ethic", *Methodos*, 10, 151–82.

Oaklander, L. Nathan (1982) "Does the Russellian Theory of Time Entail Fatalism?", *The Modern Schoolman*, 59, 206–12.

Oaklander, L. Nathan (1983) "The Russellian Theory of Time", *Philosophia*, 12, 363–92.

Oaklander, L. Nathan, and Silvano Miracchi (1980) "Russell, Negative Facts, and Ontology", *Philosophy of Science*, 47, 434–55.

Over, D.E. (1987) "Russell's Hierarchy of Acquaintance", *Philosophical Papers*, 16, 107–124.

Pakaluk, Michael (1992) "The Doctrine of Relations in Bertrand Russell's *Principles of Mathematics*", *Topicos*, 2, 153–82.

Pape, Helmut (1992) "Peirce and Russell on Proper Names", *Transactions of the Charles S. Peirce Society*, 18, 339–48.

Parker, DeWitt H. (1945) "Knowledge by Acquaintance", *Philosophical Review*, 54, 1–18.

Parker, DeWitt H. (1945) "Knowledge by Description", *Philosophical Review*, 54, 458–88.

Parris, Henry (1965) "The Political Thought of Bertrand Russell", *Durham University Journal*, 58, 86–94.

Parsons, Terence D. (1988) "Russell's Early Views on Denoting", in Austin, David F. (ed.), *Philosophical Analysis*, Dordrecht: Kluwer, 17–44.

Patzold, Detlev (1998) "Wandlungen des Kausalitatsbegriffs", *Dialektik*, 2, 9–26.

Pears, David F. (1977) "The Relation Between Wittgenstein's Picture Theory and Russell's Theories of Judgement", *Philosophical Review*, 86, 177–96.

Pears, David F. (1979) "A Comparison between Ayer's Views about the Privileges of Sense-Datum Statements and the Views of Russell and Austin", in Macdonald, G.F. (ed.), *Perception and Identity*, New York: Cornell University Press, 61–83.

Pelham, Judy (1999) "Russell, Frege, and the Nature of Implication", *Topoi*, 18, 175–84.

Peregrin, Jaroslav (2000) "'Fregean' Logic and 'Russellian' Logic", *Australasian Journal of Philosophy*, 78, 557–74.

Peressini, Anthony (1997) "Cumulative Versus Noncumulative Ramified Types", *Notre Dame Journal of Formal Logic*, 38, 385–97.

Perkins, Ray, Jr (1973) "Russell on Memory", *Mind*, 82, 600–1.

Perkins, Ray, Jr (1976) "Russell's Realist Theory of Remote Memory", *Journal of the History of Philosophy*, 14, 358–60.

Perkins, Ray, Jr (1992) "Russell, Frege, and the Meaning of the Theory of Descriptions (or): Did Russell Know his Frege?", *Journal of the History of Philosophy*, 20, 407–24.

Pineau, Lois (1990) "Russell on Ordinary Names and Synonymy", *History of Philosophy Quarterly*, 7, 93–108.

Pitt, Jack (1975) "Russell on Religion", *International Journal for Philosophy of Religion*, 6 40–53.

Popper, Karl R., and F. Hansdorff (1949) "Scientific Inference According to Bertrand Russell", *Hibbert Journal*, 47, 375–81.

Prasad, B. Sambsiva (2000) "Sajahan Miah on Russell's Constructionism", *Indian Philosophical Quarterly*, 27, 181–6.

Pratt, Scott L. (1998) "Inquiry and Analysis: Dewey and Russell on Philosophy", *Studies in Philosophy and Education*, 17, 101–22.

Predelli, Stefano (2000) "The Teetotaler and His Martini", *Mind and Language*, 15, 511–27.

Prior, A.N. (1965) "Existence in Lesniewski and in Russell", in Crossley, John N., and Michael A.E. Dummett (eds), *Formal Systems and Recursive Functions*, Amsterdam: North-Holland, 149–55.

Psillos, Stathis (2000) "Carnap, the Ramsey-Sentence and Realistic Empiricism", *Erkenntnis*, 52, 253–79.

Pulkkinen, Jarmo (2001) "Russell and the Neo-Kantians", *Studies in History and Philosophy of Science*, 32A, 99–117.

Quine, Willard Van Orman (1937) "New Foundations for Mathematical Logic", *American Mathematical Monthly*, 44, 70–80.

Quine, Willard Van Orman (1938) "On the Theory of Types", *Journal of Symbolic Logic*, 3, 125–39.

Quine, Willard Van Orman (1939) "Designation and Existence", *Journal of Philosophy*, 36, 701–9.

Quine, Willard Van Orman (1948) "On What There Is", *Review of Metaphysics*, 2, 21–38.

Radford, Colin (1995) "MacColl, Russell, the Existential Import of Propositions, and the Null-Class", *Philosophical Quarterly*, 45, 316–31.

Ramachandran, Murali (1993) "A Strawsonian Objection to Russell's Theory of Descriptions", *Analysis*, 53, 209–12.

Ramachandran, Murali (1995) "Bach on Behalf of Russell", *Analysis*, 55, 283–7.

Ramachandran, Murali and Rosental, Nadja (2000) "The Ambiguity Thesis vs. Kripke's Defence of Russell: Further Developments", *Philosophical Writings*, 14, 49–57.

Ramsey, Frank Plumpton (1925) "The Foundations of Mathematics", *Proceedings of the London Mathematical Society*, series 2, 25, 338–84. Repr. in Ramsey, Frank Plumpton, *The Foundations of Mathematics and other Logical Essays*, London: Routledge, 1931, 1–61.

Richards, John (1980) "Propositional Functions and Russell's Philosophy of Language, 1903–1914", *Philosophical Forum*, 11, 315–39.

Richardson, Alan (1990) "How Not to Russell Carnap's *Aufbau*", *Proceedings of the Biennial Meetings of the Philosophy of Science Association*, 1, 3–14.

Rieber, Steven (1998) "Could Demonstratives Be Descriptions?", *Philosophia*, 26, 65–77.

Riska, Augustin (1980) "Knowledge by Acquaintance Reconsidered", *Grazer Philosophische Studien*, 11, 129–40.

Riverso, Emanuele (1992) "Ayer's Treatment of Russell", in Hahn, Lewis Edwin (ed.), *The Philosophy of A.J. Ayer*, La Salle, Ill.: Open Court, 517–41.

Roberts, Lawrence (1984) "Russell on the Semantics and Pragmatics of Indexicals", *Philosophia*, 14, 111–28.

Rodrigues-Consuegra, Francisco A. (1987) "Russell's Logistic Definitions of Numbers, 1898–1913: Chronology and Significance", *History and Philosophy of Logic*, 8, 141–69.

Rodrigues-Consuegra, Francisco A. (1989) "Russell's Theory of Types, 1901–1910: Its Complex Origins in the Unpublished Manuscripts", *History and Philosophy of Logic*, 10, 131–64.

Rodrigues-Consuegra, Francisco A. (1993) "Russell, Gödel and Logicism", in Czermak, Johannes (ed.), *Philosophy of Mathematics*, Vienna: Hölder-Pichler-Tempsky, 233–42.

Rodrigues-Consuegra, Francisco A. (1995) "Bertrand Russell and Bradley's Ghost (I)", in Hintikka, J., and K. Puhl (eds), *The British Tradition in Twentieth Century Philosophy*, Vienna: Hölder-Pichler-Tempsky, 353–66.

Rolf, Bertil (1982) "Russell's Theses on Vagueness", *History and Philosophy of Logic*, 3, 69–83.

Rolston, John (1973) "Bradley on Russell and Relations", *Philosophical Forum*, 4, 513–30.

Rosenberg, Alexander (1989) "Russell Versus Steiner on Physics and Causality", *Philosophy of Science*, 56, 341–47.

Rosenberg, Jay F. (1972) "Russell on Negative Facts", *Nous*, 6, 27–40.

Ruffino, Marco Antonio (1994) "The Context Principle and Wittgenstein's Criticism of Russell's Theory of Types", *Synthese*, 93, 401–14.

Saarinen, Esa (1982) "How to Frege a Russell-Kaplan", *Nous*, 16, 257–76.

Sainsbury, Richard Mark (1980) "Russell on Constructions and Fictions", *Theoria*, 46, 19–36.

Sainsbury, Richard Mark (1986) "Russell on Acquaintance", in Vesey, Godfrey (ed.), *Philosophers Ancient and Modern*, Cambridge: Cambridge University Press, 219–44.

Salmon, Nathan (1998) "Nonexistence", *Nous*, 32, 277–319.

Schock, Rolf (1962) "Some Remarks on Russell's Treatment of Definite Descriptions", *Logique et Analyse*, 5, 77–80.

Schultz, Bart (1992) "Bertrand Russell in Ethics and Politics", *Ethics*, 102, 594–634.

Schutte, Karl (1960) "Syntactical and Semantical Properties of Simple Type Theory", *Journal of Symbolic Logic*, 25, 305–26.

Schwerin, Alan (1999) "Some Remarks on Russell's Account of Vagueness", *Contemporary Philosophy*, 21, 51–7.

Searle, John R. (1958) "Russell's Objections to Frege's Theory of Sense and Reference", *Analysis*, 18, 137–43.

Sellars, Wilfrid (1949) "Acquaintance and Description Again", *Journal of Philosophy*, 46, 496–504.

Sellars, Wilfrid (1963) "Classes as Abstract Entities and the Russell Paradox", *Review of Metaphysics*, 17, 67–90.

Shanker, Stuart (1993) "Wittgenstein versus James and Russell on the Nature of Willing", in Canfield, John V., and Stuart Shanker (eds), *Wittgenstein's Intentions*, New York: Garland, 195–243.

Sharvy, Richard (1980) "A More General Theory of Definite Descriptions", *Philosophical Review*, 89, 607–24.

Shearn, Martin (1950) "Whitehead and Russell's Theory of Types – A Reply to J.J.C. Smart's 'Whitehead and Russell's Theory of Types'", *Analysis*, 11, 45–8.

Shearn, Martin (1951) "Russell's Analysis of Existence", *Analysis*, 11, 124–31.

Siitonen, Arto (1993) "Logical Atomism Reconsidered", in Puhl, Klaus (ed.) *Wittgenstein's Philosophy of Mathematics*, Vienna: Verlag Hölder-Pichler-Tempsky, 201–6.

Simons, Peter, (1992) "On What There Isn't: The Meinong-Russell Dispute", in Simons, Peter, *Philosophy and Logic in Central Europe From Bolzano to Tarski*, Dordrecht: Kluwer, 159–91.

Skyrms, Brian (1993) "Logical Atoms and Combinatorial Possibility", *Journal of Philosophy*, 90, 219–32.

Sluga, Hans (1998) "Truth Before Tarski", *Vienna Circle Institute Yearbook*, 6, 27–41.

Smart, J.J.C. (1950) "Whitehead and Russell's Theory of Types", *Analysis*, 10, 93–6.

Smith, Janet Farrell (1985) "The Russell-Meinong Debate", *Philosophy and Phenomenological Research*, 45, 305–50.

Smith, Quentin (1999) "Marcus' 1961 Article as a Termination of Russellian Dominance in Analytic Philosophy", *Dialectica*, 53, 179–210.

Smullyan, Arthur F. (1948) "Modality and Description", *Journal of Symbolic Logic*, 13, 31–7.

Smullyan, Arthur F. (1958) "Incomplete Symbols", *Philosophical Review*, 67, 237–42.

Solomon, Graham (1989) "An Addendum to Demopoulos and Friedman (1985)", *Philosophy of Science*, 56, 497–501.

Sosa, David (2001) "Rigidity in the Scope of Russell's Theory", *Nous*, 35, 1–38.

Stock, G. (1972) "Russell's Theory of Judgment in Logical Atomism", *Revista Portuguesa de Filosophia*, 28, 458–89.

Stock, G. (1974) "Wittgenstein on Russell's Theory of Judgment", in Royal Institute of Philosophy, *Understanding Wittgenstein*, New York: St Martin's Press, 62–75.

Stroll, Avrum (1978) "Four Comments on Russell's Theory of Descriptions", *Canadian Journal of Philosophy*, 8, 147–55.

Szabo, Zoltan Gendler (2000) "Descriptions and Uniqueness", *Philosophical Studies*, 101, 29–57.

Tatievskaia, Elena (1999) "On Logical Form" in Falguera, Jose L. (ed.), *La Filosofia Analitica en el Cambio de Milenio*, S.I.E.U.: Santiago de Compostela.

Taylor, Gladys G. (1981) "The Analytic and Synthetic in Russell's Philosophy of Mathematics", *Philosophical Studies*, 39, 51–9.

Taylor, Gladys G. (1984) "The *Double Entente* of Russell's Thesis that Mathematics is Logic", *International Logic Review*, 15, 105–17.

Taylor, Kenneth A. (1997) "Francois Recanati's 'Direct Reference: From Language to Thought'", *Nous*, 31, 538–56.

Tibbetts, Paul (1972) "Phenomenological and Empirical Inadequacies of Russell's Theory of Perception", *Philosophical Studies (Ireland.)*, 20, 98–108.

Urmson, J.O. (1969) "Russell on Acquaintance with the Past", *Philosophical Review*, 78, 510–15.

Urmson, J.O. (1973) "Russell's Incomplete Symbols", *Analysis*, 33, 111–12.

Urmson, J.O. (1986) "Russell on Universals", in Vesey, Godfrey (ed.), *Philosophers Ancient and Modern*, Cambridge: Cambridge University Press, 245–58.

van Patten, James (1965) "Some Reflections on Bertrand Russell's Philosophy", *Educational Theory*, 15, 58–65.

Vardy, P. (1979) "Some Remarks on the Relationship Between Russell's Vicious-Circle Principle and Russell's Paradox", *Dialectica*, 33, 3–19.

Vernant, Denis (1997) "Le statut de la verité dans le calcul implicationnel de Russell en 1903", *Revue Internationale de Philosophie*, 51, 221–9.

Wahl, Russell (1986) "Bertrand Russell's Theory of Judgement", *Synthese*, 68, 383–407.

Wahl, Russell (1993) "Russell's Theory of Meaning and Denotation and 'On Denoting'", *Journal of the History of Philosophy*, 31, 71–94.

Weiss, Bernard (1994) "On Russell's Argument for Restricting Modes of Specification and Domains of Quantification", *History and Philosophy of Logic*, 15, 173–88.

Welding, S.O. (1971) "Frege's Conception of Sense and Reference Related to Russell's Theory of Definite Descriptions", *Revue Internationale de Philosophie*, 25, 389–402.

Welding, S.O. (1972) "Russell's Theory of Definite Description as Opposed to Quine's Singular Terms", *Revue Internationale de Philosophie*, 26, 513–33.

Wettstein, Howard D. (1990) "Frege-Russell Semantics?", *Dialectica*, 44, 113–35.

Wettstein, Howard K. (1981) "Demonstrative Reference and Definite Descriptions", *Philosophical Studies*, 40, 241–58.

Wetzel, Thomas (1998) "Possible States of Affairs", *Philosophical Studies*, 91, 43–60.

White, Alan R. (1981) "Knowledge, Acquaintance, and Awareness", *Midwest Studies in Philosophy*, 6, 159–72.

Wilson, W. Kent (1980) "Incomplete Symbols and Russell's Proof.", *Canadian Journal of Philosophy*, 10, 233–50.

Woodger, J.H. (1930) "Russell's Theory of Perception", *Monist*, 40, 621–36.

Yagisawa, Takashi (1997) "A Somewhat Russellian Theory of Intensional Contexts", in Tomberlin, James E. (ed.), *Philosophical Perspectives*, 11, *Mind, Causation, and World*, Boston: Blackwell.

Yourgrau, Palle (1985) "Russell and Kaplan on Denoting", *Philosophy and Phenomenological Research*, 46, 315–21.

Zimmerman, David (1999) "Born Yesterday: Personal Autonomy for Agents without a Past", *Midwest Studies in Philosophy*, 23, 236–66.

INDEX

ABC of Atoms, The (Russell), 9
ABC of Relativity, The (Russell), 9
Abel, Niels, 184
acquaintance, 33, 347, 350–2, 423–4,
    439–40, 441
  and imagination, 347
  and inference, 342, 422
  and introspection, 347, 422–3
  and knowledge, 342, 344–5, 352, 355,
    384, 421–4, 426–9, 442, 457
  and linguistic meaning, 345
  and memory, 347, 424, 434, 442
  and perception, 422–4
  and reasoning, 342
  and sensation, 347, 422
  as mental relations, 341, 342, 344,
    345, 350, 356, 384, 422
  dismissal of, 351–2, 356
  objects of, 342, 422, 423–4
  principle of, 22, 26, 29, 226–7, 239n,
    341–2, 434
  with universals, 426–7
analysis, 20, 25, 26, 105, 113–14, 125,
    153–5, 160n, 163, 167–8, 223,
    310–30, 383, 386n, 436, 439
  See also logical atomism, logical
    construction
"Analysis of Mathematical Reasoning,
    An" (Russell), 103, 104, 134
  contradiction of relativity, 98, 101–2
Analysis of Matter, The (Russell), 9, 317,
    365, 406, 411–2, 418n, 461
  copunctuality, 411, 414
  events, 32
  neutral monism, 332, 356, 367–8,
    460

percepts, 362–3, 367–8, 399, 414,
    418n, 460, 466–8
physics, 362–3, 402, 460
scepticism, 33
structuralism, 399, 414, 466–8
structural realism, 34
Analysis of Mind, The (Russell), 317,
    362, 420, 424, 448, 464
  acquaintance, 439, 441, 442–3, 452
  behaviourism, 443–4
  beliefs, 354, 356, 441, 443
  causality, 442–3
  empiricism, 35
  foundationalism, 441
  functionalism, 443
  images, 354, 356, 360, 443
  introspection, 354, 360
  knowledge, 440–4
  language, 35, 442–3
  matter, 357
  memory, 442
  negative facts, 382
  neutral monism, 332, 353–7, 366,
    440–4, 452, 460
  reliabilism, 442–4, 445
  scepticism (five-minute hypothesis),
    33
  sensations ("neutral stuff"), 32, 336,
    354–5, 356, 357, 360, 440, 465
analytic philosophy, 128, 153–68, 329
"Analytic Realism" (Russell), 44
anarchism, 488
antinomies in Russell's idealism,
  of free mobility, 96–7
  of the point, 96, 97, 103
  of quantity, 98

Austin, J.L., 391
Authority and the Individual (Russell), 15
Autobiography (Russell), 57, 74, 79, 130–1, 135n, 181n, 283
axioms,
  of choice (multiplicative), 63–4, 71, 184, 193, 413
  of infinity, 64, 70, 184–5, 192–3, 297–8, 305, 413
  of internal relations, 123
  of reducibility, 70, 184–5, 193, 200, 297–305
Ayer, A.J., 1, 40, 459, 494, 502

Barnes, Albert, 13, 14
Barnes, W.H.F., 502
behaviourism, 41, 340, 354, 356, 360–1, 362, 369, 443–4, 464
  changing human nature, 10n
  linguistic meaning, 35, 36, 345–6
  methodology, 32, 336, 350, 361, 364, 443
Behmann, Heinrich, 78
Bentham, Jeremy, 156, 477–8, 479
Bergson, Henri, 41
Berkeley, George, 333, 432
Berry, G.G., 63
Black, Dora, 8–9, 11, 12
Bloomsbury group, 8
Bohr, Niels, 29
bolshevism, 8, 9, 10, 501
Bolzano, Bernard, 184
Boole, George, 56, 175
Boolos, George, 305, 419n
Bradley, F.H., 86–8, 95, 100, 102, 103, 108, 155, 163, 236n, 497
Broad, Charlie, D. 18, 89, 366, 453
Brouwer, L.E.J., 76
Burali-Forti, Cesare, 55, 57, 62, 181
  Burali-Forti paradox, 62
Burkamp, Wilhelm, 76
Burnyeat, Myles, 401

Cantor, Georg, 51, 58, 59, 62, 63, 71, 96, 184, 190, 248, 286
  set theory, 53, 54
  theory of derived classes, 54, 72
  theory of the principal order-types, 56, 72

  theory of transfinite numbers, 54, 70, 248
  topology of classes of points, 53, 54
capitalism, 11, 489
Carnap, Rudolf, 1, 31, 51n, 78, 157, 168, 390, 451
Carroll, Lewis, 75
Cassirer, Ernst, 76
Cauchy, A.L., 51, 53, 58, 59, 64, 184
causality, 442–3
Chisholm, Roderick, 44
Church, Alonzo, 76, 249, 262n, 289, 297
Chwistek, Leon, 76, 77
Cocchiarella, Nino B., 245, 272n, 278
communism, 8, 11, 16, 17, 493
consciousness, 461–5
contradiction of relativity, 98, 101–2
Couturat, Louis, 56, 57, 64, 96
Critical Exposition of the Philosophy of Leibniz, A (Russell), 7, 25, 173, 174
Cuban missile crisis, 16, 17

Dawes Hicks, G., 30, 399–401, 417n
Dedekind, Richard, 53, 54, 58, 85, 184, 243, 248
  definition of number, 179
  theory of numbers, 72, 178–80
denoting concepts, 120, 135, 155, 212, 214–22, 225, 227, 237n
descriptions, theory of, 23–6, 29, 59, 65, 66, 125, 135, 151, 153, 187–8, 202–35, 239n, 246, 247, 283, 290, 388, 392, 393, 430–1
  See also "On Denoting"
desire-to-desire theory, 495, 502
Descartes, René, 155, 333, 472
Determinism, 363
Donnellan, Keith, 231–2
Dubislav, Walter, 78
Dummett, Michael, 37, 158, 161, 417n

Education and the Social Order (Russell), 480, 484
Edwards, Paul, 42
Einstein, Albert, 16, 29
"Elements of Ethics, The" (Russell), 475, 498
emotivism, 476, 478, 494, 499, 501, 502–3
empiricism, 35, 38–41, 55, 333, 449–50

error theory, 476, 494, 499–501
Essay on the Foundations of Geometry, An (Russell), 4, 55, 88, 89, 90, 103
extensionality, principle of, 375–7

fallibilism, 325
feminism, 5, 12n
Finch, Edith, 14n
Firth, Roderick, 30–1
Fodor, Jerry, 440
Fraenkel, W., 51n
free logic, 206
Freedom and Organization (Russell), 11
Frege, Gottlob, 1, 60–1, 102, 128–68, 185, 243, 288, 313, 375–6, 396, 421, 430
    analysis of number, 72, 139–45, 152–3, 176–8
    analytic philosophy, 153–68
    ancestral relation, 71, 137
    arithmetic, 21, 60, 131–2, 152, 176–7, 194, 241–2
    definite descriptions, 23, 166–8
    definition by abstraction, 143
    empty names, 166–8
    equinumerosity, 142–3, 144
    foundations of mathematics, 128, 176–7
    hereditary properties, 136–7
    Hume's principle, 143, 147, 150, 176
    logicism, 21, 60, 132, 137, 144–5, 153, 175, 184, 194
    mathematical logic, 19, 60
    quantification theory, 23, 24, 132–3, 175–80
    relational propositions, 132, 133, 135
    Russell paradox, 60, 146–52, 180–2, 243, 287, 289–90
    sense/reference distinction, 210, 214, 236n, 238n
    symbolization, 131–2
    unity of proposition, 162–5
"The Fundamental Ideas and Axioms of Mathematics" (Russell), 20–1, 104–6

Genocchi, Angelo, 54
geometry, 69, 73
    general metrical, 90–3
German Social Democracy (Russell), 5, 17

Gödel, Kurt, 78, 79, 186, 293, 303, 304, 305–6
Goodman, Nelson, 42, 446, 451
Grassmann, Hermann G., 54, 56, 184
Greg, W.W., 77
Grelling, Kurt, 69
Grice, Paul, 230–232

Haack, Susan, 194
Hahn, Hans, 78
Hallett, Garth, 35
Hamilton, William, 184
Hardy, G.H., 62
Has Man a Future? (Russell), 476
Hausdorff, Felix, 71
Hawtrey, Ralph, 66
Hegel, G.W.F., 88–9, 108, 483
Heidegger, Martin, 483
Hilbert, David, 76
History of Western Philosophy (Russell), 14, 88, 129, 153, 312, 315n, 482, 486, 488
Hobbes, Thomas, 480–1, 486–92
Hölder, Otto, 76
Human Knowledge: Its Scope and Limits (Russell), 14, 312, 317, 323, 328n, 452, 454, 460
    defeasible reasoning, 42
    Goodman's riddle, 42, 446–7
    inference, 41–42, 318–319, 445–7, 461, 469–73
    neutral monism, 332, 356, 365–6
    postulates of non-demonstrative inference, 42–3, 318, 319–20, 326, 470–3
    probability, 319, 365
    reliabilism, 447–8, 471–2
    representationalism, 402
    scientific knowledge, 318, 319, 324, 365, 446, 466–7, 469
    sensations, 399
    solipsism, 446
Human Society in Ethics and Politics (Russell), 475, 476, 489, 501, 503
humanistic amoralism, 501
Hume, David, 39, 155, 338–9, 462, 475, 503
    Hume's principle, 143, 147, 150, 176
Husserl, Edmund, 102, 105, 326

Icarus (Russell), 10
idealism, 85–104, 153, 213–4, 327,
    462–3, 497–8
  antimony of free mobility, 96–7
  antimony of the point, 96, 97
  antimony of quantity, 98
  arithmetic, 97–8
  Bradley, F.H., 86–7, 88, 100, 103, 108,
    236n, 497
  conceptual structures, 207–8
  contradiction of relativity, 99–102
  general metrical geometry, 90–3
  Hegel, G.W.F., 89, 108, 236n
  immortality, 497
  Kant, Immanuel, 89–90, 91, 102–3,
    108, 236n
  McTaggart, J.M.E., 87, 88, 89, 108–9,
    497
  Moore, G.E., 103–4, 108
  pluralism, 87–8, 109
  psychologism, 19–20, 103, 207–8
  relations, 88
  science, 88–90, 93–6, 98–100
Inquiry into Meaning and Truth, An
    (Russell), 41, 317, 328n, 404–5, 406,
    461
  behaviourism, 36, 364
  empiricism, 38
  foundationalism, 445
  hierarchy of languages, 36
  knowledge, 364, 445
  law of excluded middle, 36–8
  logical positivism, 364–5
  logical truth, 38
  neutral monism, 332, 364
  ordinary language, 364
  realism versus anti-realism, 37–8
  reference, 35–6
  reliabilism, 445
  scepticism, 445, 450
  structuralism, 405
*Introduction to Mathematical
    Philosophy* (Russell), 131, 138, 313,
    412, 437
  analysis, 153n, 154n, 163n
  axioms, 192–3
  classes, 145–6, 189
  definition of number, 314
  logicism, 79n
  logical constructions, 192, 386

  logical synthesis, 312
  realism, 188
  structuralism, 396–7, 399
"Is Mathematics Purely Linguistic?"
    (Russell), 192n
"Is There an Absolute Good?" (Russell),
    499

James, William, 335, 339, 343–4, 356,
    439, 443, 460, 461, 462–3
Johnsen, B., 42
Johnson, W.E., 326
Jourdain, Philip, 62

Kant, Immanuel, 89–90, 91, 102–3, 108,
    122, 241–2, 333, 397–8, 410, 469
Keynes, John Maynard, 77
Keyser, Cassius J., 64
Khrushchev, Nikita, 15–16, 17
knowledge, 33–4, 420–48, 450–73
  by acquaintance, 421, 422, 424, 426–7,
    428, 442, 457
  by causation, 447–8
  derivative, 421, 427, 430, 457, 458
  by description, 421, 430–3, 438, 457
  intuitive, 421, 422, 424, 428–30, 434,
    458
  mathematical, 200–1
  scientific, 18, 318, 319, 324, 365, 446,
    466–7, 469
"Knowledge by Acquaintance and
    Knowledge by Description"
    (Russell), 22n, 44, 237n, 240n, 342,
    455
  multiple relation theory of judgment,
    28n, 453–4
  principle of acquaintance, 239n, 342
  theory of descriptions, 29, 239n
Kripke, Saul, 232–5

labour party, 8, 9, 10, 14
Leibniz, Gottfried, 7, 18, 173–6, 241,
    242, 333
Lesniewski, Stanislav, 76
Lewis, C.I., 74
limitation of size, 183, 245
"Limits of Empiricism, The" (Russell),
    41
"L'importance philosophique de la
    logistique" (Russell), 455

Lindenbaum, Adolf, 304
Locke, John, 155, 459, 482, 484
logical atomism, 44, 346, 371–91, 433, 455
"Logical Atomism" (Russell), 363, 371
logical analysis, 311, 312, 314, 439
logical construction, 386–8
logical synthesis, 311, 439
mathematical knowledge, 200–1
neutral monism, 358, 366
logical construction, 44–5, 186, 189–92, 378, 386–9, 392, 436
logical positivism, 19, 364–5
"Logic of Relations, The" (Russell), 21, 135
logicism, 21, 22, 43, 51, 79n, 105, 132, 150, 153, 171–201, 241–7, 255–6, 283–4, 304
See also under Frege, Principia Mathematica, Principles of Mathematics
Lukasiewicz, Jan, 76, 304

MacColl, Hugh, 75n
Mach, Ernst, 335, 339, 343, 356
Mach, James, 39
Mackie, J.L., 494, 496, 500
Malleson, Lady Constance, 8, 9, 14
"Man's Peril" (Russell), 16
Marsh, Robert C., 44
Marriage and Morals (Russell), 476
marxism, 5, 493, 494
mathematical knowledge, 198–9
materialism, 335–7, 354, 366, 367, 369, 464–5, 493
"Mathematical Logic as Based on the Theory of Types" (Russell), 44, 45, 66, 183, 280, 281, 282, 291
"Mathematics and Metaphysicians" (Russell), 181n
McGill, V.G., 481
McKinney, J.P., 320–326
McTaggart, J.M.E., 4, 39, 87–8, 89, 108, 497
Meinong, Alexius, 24, 39, 108, 158, 211, 238, 326, 343, 347, 348, 388, 461, 462
"Meinong's Theory of Complexes and Assumptions" (Russell), 108–9, 111, 118, 126n, 251, 253

Meyerson, Emile, 76
metaethics, 477–9, 494
Mill, John Stuart, 3, 85, 482, 484
Monk, Ray, 327–30
Moore, E.H., 62, 76
Moore, G.E., 1, 62, 66, 105n, 108–25, 153n, 235n
analytic philosophy, 128
argument from advocacy 495–6
denoting, 120
ethics, 475, 476, 495–6, 498
idealism, 20, 56, 103–4, 108, 207, 326
open question argument, 495–6
realism, 20, 56, 74, 103–4, 108–9, 121–3, 125, 186, 208–9
relations, 121–3
truth, 109–12
Morley, Frank, 62
Morrell, Lady Ottoline, 8, 453, 455
Mortals and Others (Russell), 476, 485
multiple relation theory of judgment, 27–9, 348–9, 353, 374, 381, 423, 430–1, 453–4, 461
Myhill, John, 298, 304
My Philosophical Development (Russell), 4, 14, 40, 187n, 192n, 316, 453, 460, 461, 465
analysis, 153n, 160n, 163n, 312, 320–3, 325, 386n
ancestral relations, 130n
behaviourism, 360
Bergson, 41
Frege, 130n, 131
general theory of relativity, 94n
Gödel, 79
idealism, 85, 100, 108
Moore, G.E., 104, 108
neutral monism, 364, 452
nominalism, 377
Peano, 57
pluralism, 100, 157
realism, 20, 104, 108
scientific knowledge, 18
Sidgwick, 495
theory of descriptions, 218
Whitehead, 357
Wittgenstein, 79, 160n

nazism, 10, 12
"Necessity and Possibility" (Russell),
    127
Newman, Max, 34, 77, 410–1, 413–4,
    419n, 468
new realists, 335, 343–4, 348, 356
"Newly Discovered Maxims of La
    Rochefoucauld" (Russell), 501
neutral monism, 32, 332–70, 384,
    439–44, 452, 460, 461–6
Nicod, Jean, 74
Nietzsche, Friedrich, 3, 476
no-classes theory, 183, 246, 247
no conscription fellowship, 7, 8
nominalism, 377–80
normative ethics, 477–9
number, analyses of, 72, 139–46, 152–3,
    176–80, 184, 189, 304, 314

"Observations on Space and Geometry"
    (Russell), 95
Ogden, C.K., 77
"On the Constituents of Space"
    (Russell), 105n
"On Denoting" (Russell), 24–6, 44, 64,
    127n, 158, 167, 202, 219, 223–7,
    254, 341–2, 388n, 393, 430
    Gray's Elegy argument, 45
    principle of acquaintance, 226–7,
    341–2
On Education (Russell), 10, 480
"On the Existential Import of
    Propositions" (Russell), 217, 218,
    238n
"On Fundamentals" (Russell), 237n, 256
"On 'Insolubilia' and Their Solution by
    Symbolic Logic" (Russell), 273–4,
    277–8, 280, 291
"On Matter" (Russell), 455
"On Meaning and Denotation"
    (Russell), 119
"On the Nature of Truth" (Russell), 113,
    122, 125, 283
"On the Notion of Cause" (Russell), 39
"On Propositions" (Russell), 22n, 31–3,
    35, 351–2, 353, 383, 442, 461
"On the Relations of Universals and
    Particulars" (Russell), 39, 41
"On Scientific Method in Philosophy"
    (Russell), 434, 436, 499

"On Some Difficulties in the Theory of
    Transfinite Numbers and Order
    Types" (Russell), 247
"On Substitution" (Russell), 256, 258,
    266n, 272n
"On the Substitutional Theory of
    Classes and Relations" (Russell),
    247
open question argument, 495–6, 498
ordinary language, 1, 334–5, 341
Our Knowledge of the External World
    (Russell), 45n, 74, 75, 76, 163n, 366,
    433, 455, 458–9
    acquaintance, 31, 350
    definition of number, 189
    existential hypothesis, 193
    logical-analytic method of scientific
    philosophy, 325, 434, 436
    logical atomism, 433
    logical constructions, 44–5, 392
    Occam's razor, 188
    phenomenalism, 392
    regressive analysis, 154–5
Outline of Philosophy, An (Russell), 365
    behaviourism, 360–1, 445
    determinism, 363
    neutral monism, 332, 356, 361–2
    normative ethics, 477
    percepts, 361, 362, 363, 445
    physics, 361, 362
    psychology, 360–3
    reliabilism, 444–5

pacifism, 6, 12, 14
Padoa, Alessandro, 55, 57
Peano, Guiseppe, 1, 39n, 57, 80, 130,
    131, 135, 153, 286
    algebra, 54
    arithmetic, 54, 58
    axioms, 154
    geometry, 54
    logicism, 51n
    mathematical logic, 54–5, 64–5, 106,
    130, 134
    method of axiomatization, 54
    natural numbers, 184, 304
    symbolic logic, 21
Pears, D.F., 38–40
Pearsall Smith, Alys, 4, 5, 6–7, 8, 12
Philosophical Essays (Russell), 344

"Philosophical Importance of
    Mathematical Logic, The" (Russell),
    44
"Philosophy of Logical Atomism, The"
    (Russell), 31, 44, 224, 359, 376n,
    441–2
    analysis, 153n, 163, 167–8, 313, 315,
        321, 327, 383, 436
    classes, 189, 351
    knowledge, 436–8
    logical atomism, 346, 371–2, 378–83
    logical constructions, 378, 389, 436
    multiple relation theory of judgment,
        453
    negative facts, 382
    neutral monism, 332, 346, 351, 461
    particulars, 351
    science, 313–4
    simples, 316, 321
    theory of descriptions, 227–8
    theory of types, 379–80
physics, 9, 18, 29, 333–4, 336–7, 340,
    355–6, 359, 361–2, 363, 366, 439,
    440, 449, 450
Pieri, Mario, 55, 57
"Place of Science in a Liberal Education,
    The" (Russell), 499
Poincaré, Henri, 56, 64, 69, 91, 183, 195,
    291
"Points about Denoting" (Russell), 127
Popper, Karl, 325, 493
Power: A New Social Analysis (Russell),
    11, 502
practical ethics, 477–85, 493, 494
Practice and Theory of Bolshevism, The
    (Russell), 8, 14, 17, 480
pragmatism, 344
preaching, 479–480
Principia Mathematica (Russell), 5, 6,
    29, 43, 44, 67–8, 78, 79, 152, 274n,
    306n, 453
    analysis, 20, 311, 314
    ancestral relation, 71, 72
    arithmetic, 68, 70, 71, 413
    axiom of choice, 71, 413
    axiom of infinity, 70, 184–5, 413
    axiom of reducibility, 70, 184–5, 200,
        298, 300, 302, 303–4
    cardinals, 68, 70, 71, 413
    classes, 27, 69, 71, 146, 244

cyclic families, 72
derived classes, 72
descriptions, theory of 66, 283, 431
facts, 380–1
finite and transfinite numbers, 66, 70,
    184
geometry, 69, 73
identity of indiscernibles, 376
incomplete symbols, 222
integers, 72
irrational numbers, 72
logical atomism, 372, 373
logical constructions, 186, 388
logicism, 32n, 68–9, 70, 101n, 105,
    183–6, 199–200
mathematical logic, 68, 185
multiple relation theory of judgments,
    28, 283, 373, 374, 381, 431
negative numbers, 72
neutral monism, 372
order, 101n
ordinals, 68, 71
paradoxes, 69, 70, 185
propositional functions, 27, 66, 69, 70,
    185, 186, 189n, 293, 294–5, 302,
    375, 376, 431
propositions, 32, 66, 69, 373, 378
ramified theory of types, 22, 69–70,
    184, 185, 186, 270–1, 280, 281–2,
    293–7
real numbers, 72
relations, 69, 71, 72, 73, 138, 294,
    295
set theory, 66, 184
structuralism, 395
substitutional theory, 282–283
synthesis, 312
types, theory of, 22, 69–70, 184, 185,
    186, 270–1, 280, 281–2, 293–7
unrestricted variable, 282–3
vicious circle principle, 69
Principles of Mathematics (Russell),
    21n, 45, 61, 62, 74, 79, 98n, 104,
    127, 129, 158, 290
    analysis, 25, 26, 105, 113–4, 125,
        153n, 155, 163, 223, 311
    classes, 59, 71, 144–6, 291
    definite descriptions, 23–5, 59,
        207
    definition by abstraction, 143

Principles of Mathematics (*Cont.*)
  denoting, 23–24, 59, 120, 135, 155,
    215–8, 220, 252–3, 254
  equinumerosity, 144
  function-argument analysis, 134
  language, 224
  logicism, 58–60, 68–9, 105, 181,
    241–2, 246–7
  meaning, 114
  Moore, G.E., 109
  ontology, 186, 254–5
  pluralism, 88
  principle of acquaintance, 22, 227
  propositions, 20, 22–4, 27, 59, 105,
    114–8, 124–5, 161, 164, 186, 223,
    252–3, 254–5
  quantification, 59
  realism, 20, 24, 208–9, 211–4
  relations, 59, 71, 88, 138, 383n
  Russell paradox, 22, 59, 60, 286–7
  set theory, 58, 59
  substitutional theory, 283
  synthesis, 311
  types, theory of, 22, 183, 286–9
Principles of Social Reconstruction
  (Russell), 476, 481, 482, 484, 488,
  490
problem of empty names, 166–8
Problems of Philosophy, The (Russell),
  30, 44, 76, 240n, 417n, 445
  descriptions, theory of, 29, 393
  dualism, 359, 366
  empiricism, 40
  Hume, David, 39n
  induction, 39n
  inference, 446
  knowledge, 41, 420–9, 432, 456,
    458–9
  matter, 389
  multiple relation theory of judgment,
    28n
  perception, 399, 402, 465
  principle of acquaintance, 342
  realism, 435
  representationalism, 402
  scepticism, 450, 456
  sense-data, 456, 459
  structuralism, 399, 401
  subjectivity, 403, 406
  universals, 377

propositions, 20, 22–4, 27, 32, 59, 66, 69,
    105, 114–8, 124–5, 156, 160n, 161,
    164, 186, 223, 252–3, 350, 373, 378
psychologism, 19, 103, 104, 453
psychological egoism, 486–7
psychology, 10, 18, 19, 334, 336, 337,
    339, 340, 355, 356, 362–3, 433, 439,
    440, 464, 481, 488–90

quantum theory, 29
Quine, W.V. 1, 22, 24, 76–7, 117, 157n,
    168, 185, 193, 202, 229–30, 239n,
    240n, 245, 249, 256–7, 280, 304–5,
    373, 452

Ramsey, Frank P., 77, 153, 235n, 279,
    290, 302–4, 394–6, 416n, 444, 447
realism, 20, 33, 109–11, 136, 209–14,
    220, 222, 335
"Le Realisme Analytique" (Russell), 455
"Recent Work on the Principles of
    Mathematics" (Russell), 180–1
regressive method, 197–201
"Regressive Method of Discovering the
    Premises of Mathematics, The"
    (Russell), 93, 154, 195, 196, 197,
    198, 199, 201
Reid, Thomas, 496–7
"Relation of Sense-Data to Physics,
    The" (Russell), 31n, 188, 189, 346,
    352, 356, 435, 455, 459
relativity theory, 29, 336, 357, 363, 419n
reliabilism, 442–3, 444, 445, 447
Religion and Science (Russell), 479, 484,
    494, 502
"Reply to Criticisms" (Russell), 315,
    317, 450, 464, 478, 480, 481, 503
Richard, Jules, 63
Roads to Freedom (Russell), 488, 489,
    490
Royce, Josiah, 74, 76
Russell, Frank, 3, 12n
Russell paradox, 21–2, 60, 63, 146–52,
    180–2, 190, 243–4, 286–7, 288–90,
    303
Russia, 8, 9, 10, 14, 15, 17
Ryle, Gilbert 157n

Salmon, Wesley, 42
Santayana, 3, 498–9

Sartre, Jean-Paul, 476
Scheffer, Henry Maurice, 74
Schlick, Moritz, 78
Schmidt, Erhard, 63
Schroder, Ernst, 57, 73, 130
Scientific Outlook, The (Russell), 10
Searle, John, 478
"Seems, Madam? Nay It Is!" (Russell), 108, 497
"Should Socialists Smoke Good Cigars?" (Russell), 476
Sidgwick, Henry, 495, 498, 503
    dualism of practical reason, 496–7
Singer, Peter, 478
Smith, Kemp, 39
solipsism, 38, 362, 446
Spaier, Albert, 76
Spence, Patricia, 12, 13, 14n
Spinoza, Baruch, 18, 333, 368
stalinism, 10, 14
Stammler, Gerhard, 76
Stebbing, Susan, 77–8
Steiner, Mark, 194
Stevenson, C.L., 494, 502, 504
Stout, G.F., 87n, 99n
Strawson, P.F., 42, 202, 228, 240n, 391
structuralism, 392–416
substitutional theory, 27, 45, 65, 66, 241–84, 290
suffrage, 2, 6

Tarski, Alfred, 36, 78n, 303, 304
"Theory of Implication, The" (Russell), 251n, 258
Theory of Knowledge (Russell), 28, 44, 349, 355–6, 366, 431, 436–7, 453–4
    acquaintance, 346, 347, 350, 384, 426, 439–40, 455
    analysis, 155, 163n
    argument from illusion, 30
    atomic propositions, 29
    emphatic particulars, 344–5
    foundationalism, 434
    James, William, 343–4
    logical data, 434
    multiple relation theory of atomic judgments, 29
    neutral monism, 343–6, 347, 384, 440

new realists, 343
physics, 29
possibility and necessity, 426
pragmatism, 344
principle of acquaintance, 29, 434
propositions, 347–8, 350, 380
realism, 343
self-evidence, 433–4
Wittgenstein, 31, 453
"Theory of Logical Types, The" (Russell), 187, 374n
truth and truths, 18, 19, 172–5, 333, 478–9, 499, 500
truth-table method, 74, 302
types, theory of, 28, 69–70, 150, 152, 182–3, 185, 190, 281, 283, 286–306
    ramified, 22, 28, 183, 270–1, 272, 293–9, 301, 302, 305
    simple, 22, 182–3, 266–70, 271, 286–9, 302, 305

"Ultimate Constituents of Matter, The" (Russell), 455
Unpopular Essays (Russell), 485
Urmson, J.O., 320–6, 329, 390, 502n
utilitarianism, 479

verificationism, 19, 37, 103
vicious circle principle, 69, 183, 291–3, 302, 432
Voltaire, 476

"War the Offspring of Fear" (Russell), 489
Ward, James, 39, 89, 99, 130
Watson, John, 443
Weierstrass, Karl, 53, 54, 85, 184, 248
Weyl, Hermann, 303, 305
Whitehead, Alfred North, 6, 20, 56, 57, 62, 63, 65, 66, 70, 72, 73, 74, 183–5, 271, 357, 363
Wiener, Norbert, 73–74
Wisdom, John, 156, 451
Wittgenstein, Ludwig, 77, 152, 238–9n, 320, 390, 474
    analytic philosophy, 128, 157n, 329
    atomic facts, 377–8, 381–2
    five-minute hypothesis, 33n
    hierarchy of languages, 36

Wittgenstein, Ludwig (*Cont.*)
  influence, by Russell, 1, 33n, 35n,
    155n
  influence, on Russell, 30n, 31, 32n,
    35, 36, 74, 155n, 303, 349–50, 375,
    377, 437, 453
  language, 1, 79
  logical atomism, 44n
  logicism, 195
  monism, 78–9
  Moorean propositions, 447–8
  multiple relation theory of judgment,
    28, 381, 453
  paradox of analysis, 168
  propositions, 156, 160n, 350
  science, 19
  showing versus saying, 382
  truth-table method, 74, 302
Woodger, J.H., 78n
world government, 485–93
world war one, 7, 8, 9, 12, 14, 31, 75
Wrinch, Dorothy, 76, 77
Wundt, Wilhelm, 51n

Zermelo, Ernst, 63, 243, 245, 305
zigzag theory, 183, 245, 290